INTRODUCTION TO

Management

IN THE

Hospitality Industry

NINTH EDITION

Clayton W. Barrows

Professor
Department of Hospitality Management
University of New Hampshire

Tom Powers

Professor Emeritus
School of Hospitality and Tourism
  Management
University of Guelph

WILEY

John Wiley & Sons, Inc.

Copyright © 2009 by John Wiley & Sons, Inc. All rights reserved

Published by John Wiley & Sons, Inc., Hoboken, New Jersey.

Published simultaneously in Canada.

For general information on our other products and services, or technical support, please contact our Customer Care Department within the United States at 800-762-2974, outside the United States at 317-572-3993 or fax 317-572-4002.

Wiley also publishes its books in a variety of electronic formats. Some content that appears in print may not be available in electronic books.

For more information about Wiley products, visit our Web site at http://*www.wiley.com*.

Library of Congress Cataloging-in-Publication Data:
Barrows, Clayton W.
    Introduction to management in the hospitality industry / Clayton W. Barrows, Tom Powers. – 9th ed.
        p. cm.
    In earlier ed. of work, Tom Powers name was listed first on t.p.
        Includes index.
        ISBN 978-0-471-78277-3 (cloth)
    1. Hospitality industry–Management. I. Powers, Thomas F. II. Powers,
    Thomas F. Introduction to management in the hospitality industry. III. Title.
        TX911.3.M27P68 2008
        647.94068–dc22

                                                                                2007021306

Printed in the United States of America

10 9 8 7 6 5 4 3

CONTENTS

Tom and I, like others who both teach and study the hospitality industry, believe that we are associated with one of the most interesting, dynamic, and exciting industries in the world. It is an industry that generates passion among those who work in it. In addition to passion, however, knowledge is also required if one is to be successful in their chosen field. Having the necessary knowledge, however, is an ongoing challenge, even during the best of times, but particularly now with so many changes taking place so quickly. For this reason, we continue to strive to monitor and report on the ever-changing hospitality and tourism industries. In this latest edition, we have introduced content on new and emerging companies, new technologies, and new ways of doing business. Indeed, the challenges as well as the opportunites for graduating students are greater than ever. This is an exciting time to be studying hospitality management and we try to convey that in this edition of the textbook.

Content–Benefits for Students

In our efforts to present the industry in an organized and responsible manner, we have divided *Introduction to Management in the Hospitality Industry, Ninth Edition*, into six primary sections encompassing everything from students' concerns about their role in the industry and operational issues to the function of management. Students should appreciate the organization of the chapters which will help them to understand the relationships between the various topics. Brief descriptions of each of the major sections are as follows.

Part One: Perspectives on Careers in Hospitality begins by developing an industry perspective with a general discussion of hospitality careers. Industry trends, changing demographics, and supply and demand are all important topics covered in these chapters.

Part Two: Food Service takes an in-depth look at food service and its various subsegments. Restaurant operations, organization, environment, competition, on-site food service, and food-service-related topics are covered. The final chapter of the section looks at issues facing the industry.

Part Three: Lodging focuses on the lodging industry and its various segments, products, and brands. These chapters chronicle recent developments, including new modes of financing hotel expansion and new financial trends affecting this sector. Factors relating to the competitive environment of the lodging industry are the subject of the final chapter in Part Three.

Part Four: Travel and Tourism comprises two chapters that focus on tourism. Tourism growth, economic and social impacts, travel trends, career opportunities, and the role that tourism plays in society are all discussed in Chapter 13. Chapter 14 looks at tourism destinations, including the growing area of gaming, theme parks, and natural environments.

Part Five: Management in the Hospitality Industry provides a concise introduction to the tools that managers use to help them achieve their goals. Using theories, examples, and case histories, these six chapters portray the management function as an active force for solving problems that hospitality organizations face.

Part Six: Hospitality as a Service Industry examines service as process and considers the work of rendering service as a personal experience.

In the end, students will have gained a strong overview of the industry, where it fits into the broader world, the major career paths, as well as the important issues and challenges that managers face.

Content—Benefits for Instructors

Instructors will benefit from the flow of *Introduction to Management in the Hospitality Industry, Ninth Edition*, the numerous examples provided, topic headings which can be used to generate class discussion, and numerous supplementary materials including the newly revised *Instructor's Manual* (ISBN 978-0-470-25726-5, discussed later in this preface). In addition, several sections of the book have been revised and/or expanded based upon instructor feedback. These include the following:

- Discussion of demographics and changes with specific generations
- More culinary examples including international culinary programs and a profile of the Research Chefs Association
- A greatly expanded section on franchising
- More examples of the use of technology in the industry including a profile of a leading company and the latest technology usage statistics
- Revised discussions of tourism impacts with a greater emphasis upon international travel

- Discussion of volunteer tourism as a travel trend

- Revised and expanded discussions of prominent gaming destinations such as Atlantic City, Mississippi Gulf Coast, and Macau

- New focus on electronic resources in the management section, including on-line recruiting

- Additional information about spas

- The addition of a profile of the European lodging industry

- An overview of trends in lodging with a focus on electronic distribution channels

Features of the Book for Students and Instructors

Several pedagogical features have been newly developed and/or carried over from previous editions of *Introduction to Management in the Hospitality Industry* in order to help students understand the material more easily and to help bring the world of hospitality alive.

- Additional *international examples* of hospitality and tourism operations have been included throughout the text.

- *The Purpose of this Chapter* section introduces the chapter to students and discusses the significance to the hospitality industry of the topics covered.

- The *This Chapter Should Help You* section lists specific learning objectives at the beginning of each chapter to help students focus their efforts and alert them to the important concepts discussed.

- *Industry Practice Notes* appear in almost every chapter. These boxes take a closer look at specific trends or practices in the hospitality industry, from an interview with a recruiter from a major food service company (Chapter 1) to the relationship between working in the service industry and stress (Chapter 21).

- *Case Histories* support the chapter discussions by highlighting examples from today's hospitality organizations and associations.

- *Global Hospitality Notes* continue to appear to give students more of an international perspective on their studies. The boxes cover topics as diverse as career opportunities overseas (Chapter 1) and a discussion of volunteer tourism (Chapter 14).

CAREERS IN HOSPITALITY

- The *Careers in Hospitality* icon appears throughout the book in the margin of the text to alert students to specific discussions of career opportunities in the hospitality industry.

- The *Summary* provides a concise synopsis of the topics presented in the chapter.

- A list of *Key Words and Concepts* appears at the end of each chapter. Further, key words and concepts are identified in bold type when they first appear in chapters.

- The *Review Questions* test students' recall and understanding of the key points in each chapter. Answers are provided in the Instructor's Manual.

- *Internet Exercises,* which are mini research exercises and projects, were developed to familiarize students with the different ways in which the hospitality industry is using the Internet. They have been updated and revised. Answers are included in the **Instructor's Manual**.

Supplementary Materials

An *Instructor's Manual* (ISBN 978-0-470-25726-5) with test questions accompanies this textbook. The manual includes sample syllabi, chapter overviews and outlines, teaching suggestions, answers to the review questions, and Internet exercises, as well as test questions and answers. A companion Web site, at www.wiley.com/college/barrows, is also available with this text, which includes the *Instructor's Manual* and PowerPoint slides of selected tables and illustrations from the text.

Web CT and **Blackboard** online courses are available for this book. Visit www.wiley.com/barrows and click on the "Technology Solutions" button at the top of the page for more information, or contact your Wiley representative.

A **Study Guide**, which has been created for this edition (ISBN 978-0-470-28546-6), includes chapter objectives, detailed chapter outlines, review questions, and activities to help students reinforce and test their understanding of the key concepts and features within the text.

Acknowledgments

First of all, we would like to acknowledge those individuals who provided direct assistance in the revision of the chapters. Our thanks go out to Dr. Debra Cannon, director of the Cecil B. Day School of Hospitality Management at Georgia State University, who revised the lodging chapters. Second, we would like to acknowledge the help of Rong Lin, a graduate from the University of Guelph's Hospitality and Tourism MBA program, who revised the Instructor's Manual. Dr. Richard Patterson, of Western Kentucky University, drew upon his extensive knowledge of the Web to develop the

Internet Exercises at the end of each chapter. He also provided Internet addresses for the organizations and associations discussed in the case histories. His commitment and enthusiasm have been invaluable. Finally, special thanks go out to Novie Johan of the University of Surrey who assisted with research, writing, and editing.

We would also like to acknowledge many people who have helped in shaping this book, even at the risk of inadvertently overlooking some of the friends and colleagues who have helped us. Tom's wife, Jo Marie Powers, has been the source of many ideas found in this text—not all, we're afraid, properly acknowledged. Her advice and critical reactions have been vital to developing the text over the course of earlier editions. She also has made major contributions to the test bank developed for this edition and has served as editor and co-author on earlier editions of the Instructor's Manual.

Many faculty from hospitality management programs around the world have provided helpful information and feedback in the preparation of the manuscript. Many of our colleagues were quick to answer questions for us or to guide us to proper sources in their particular areas of expertise. Colleagues from the Department of Hospitality Management at the University of New Hampshire have provided us with numerous insights that have shaped this text in important ways. We are also grateful to the professors who reviewed the previous editions and early drafts of this edition. Their comments and suggestions have helped us immensely in the preparation of this revision.

Anthony Agbeh, Northampton Community College, PA

Patricia Agnew, Johnson & Wales University, RI

James Bardi, Penn State University, Berks Campus, PA

James Bennett, Indiana University, Purdue

John Courtney, Johnson County Community College, KA

Linsley T. DeVeau, Lynn University, FL

John Dunn, Santa Barbara City College, CA

Susan Gregory, Colorado State University

Choon-Chiang Leong, Nanyang Technological University, Singapore

Marcia Hajduk, Harrisburg Area Community College, PA

Kathryn Hashimoto, University of New Orleans, LA

Jim Hogan, Scottsdale Community College, AZ

Lynn Huffman, Texas Tech University

Wayne A. Johnson, The Ohio State University

Soo K. Kang, Colorado State University

William Kent, Auburn University, AL

Frank Lattuca, University of Massachusetts, Amherst

Melih Madanoglu, Virginia Polytechnic Institute and State University

Brian Miller, University of Massachusetts, Amherst

Paul Myer, Northwestern Business College, IL

Daryl Nosek, Westchester Community College, NY

Kathleen M. O'Brien, Buffalo State College, NY

Esra Onat, Virginia Polytechnic Institute and State University

James W. Paul, Art Institute of Atlanta, GA

Howard Reichbart, Northern Virginia Community College

Denney Rutherford, Washington State University

Randy Sahajdack, Grand Rapids Community College, MI

Andrew Schwarz, Sullivan County Community College, NY

David L. Tucker, Widener University, DE

Many industry professionals assisted in the preparation of the text by providing helpful input on particular sections or by providing us with supporting materials (including photos). Again, we will mention a few here who helped us, at the risk of not mentioning all who helped. As always, the research published by the National Restaurant Association (NRA) forms an important part of the food service chapters of this book and, indeed, has influenced other portions of the text in important ways as well. We are especially indebted to the Information Specialists Group at the NRA, which has helped us time and again when information or a citation went astray. Further assistance was provided by the American Hotel & Lodging Association, Technomic, Inc., Smith Travel Research, and Hospitality Valuation Services International. Other individuals and organizations that provided information and support are identified in citations throughout the text.

As always, Wiley's editors have been most helpful, most notably Rachel Livsey and Julie Kerr. Jacqueline Beach and Kim Nir are the production editors responsible for shepherding an unwieldy typescript, rough illustrations, and a lot of pictures into the book you hold in your hands and have done so with the utmost professionalism.

Clayton Barrows   Tom Powers
Durham, New Hampshire   *Moon River, Ontario*

PART ONE

Perspectives on Careers in Hospitality

The Hospitality Industry

(Courtesy of Four Seasons Hotel, Mexico, D.F.)

CHAPTER ONE

The Hospitality Industry and You

The Purpose of this Chapter

Your own career choice is probably the most important management decision that you will ever make—at least from your point of view. This chapter has been designed, therefore, to help you analyze a career in the hospitality industry and correlate that analysis with your personal, professional, and educational experiences. It will also help prepare you for the first career decision you make just before or after you graduate. This chapter discusses the career decisions that are ahead of you over the next three to five years.

THIS CHAPTER SHOULD HELP YOU

1. List examples of the kinds of businesses that make up the hospitality industry.
2. Identify the reasons people study hospitality management—and list the advantages these academic programs offer.
3. Identify two key components of the job-benefit mix that allow one to profit from work experience.
4. Name three general career goals frequently cited by graduates seeking employment.
5. Identify key trends driving change in employment opportunities in the hospitality industry.
6. Describe your career plan in terms of a life's work and not just as an economic means of survival.

What Is Hospitality Management?

When most people think of the hospitality industry, they usually think of hotels and restaurants. However, the true meaning of **hospitality** is much broader in scope. According to the *Oxford English Dictionary*, hospitality means "the reception and entertainment of guests, visitors or strangers with liberality and good will." The word hospitality is derived from hospice, the term for a medieval house of rest for travelers and pilgrims. Hospice—a word that is clearly related to hospital—also referred to an early form of what we now call a nursing home.

Hospitality, then, not only includes hotels and restaurants but also refers to other kinds of institutions that offer shelter, food, or both to people away from their homes. We can also expand this definition, as many people have, to include those institutions that provide other types of services to people away from home. This might include private clubs, casinos, resorts, attractions, and so on. This wide variety of services will be discussed in later chapters.

These different kinds of operations also have more than a common historical heritage. They share the management problems of providing food and shelter—problems that include erecting a building; providing heat, light, and power; cleaning and maintaining the premises; overseeing employees; and preparing and serving food in a way that pleases the guests. We expect all of this to be done "with liberality and good will" when we stay in a hotel or dine in a restaurant, but we can also rightfully expect the same treatment from the dietary department in a health care facility or while enjoying ourselves at an amusement park.

Turning our attention now from the facilities and services associated with the hospitality industry to the people who staff and manage them, let us consider the profession of the hospitality provider. The hospitality professions are among the oldest of the humane professions, and they involve making a guest, client, member, or resident (whichever is the appropriate term) feel welcome and comfortable. There is a more important reason, however, that people interested in a career in these fields should think of hospitality as an industry. Today, managers and supervisors, as well as skilled employees, find that opportunities for advancement often mean moving from one part of the hospitality industry to another. For example, a hospitality graduate may begin as a management trainee with a restaurant company, complete the necessary training, and shortly thereafter take a job as an assistant manager in a hotel. The next job offer could come from a hospitality conglomerate, such as ARAMARK. ARAMARK provides food service operations not only to businesses but also in such varied areas as recreation centers, sports stadiums, college and university campuses, health care facilities, convention centers, and gourmet restaurants. Similarly, Holiday Inns is in the

Entertainment and attractions, such as the Freemont Street Experience in Las Vegas, play an important part of the hospitality industry. (Courtesy of Las Vegas Convention and Visitors Authority.)

hotel business, but it is also one of the largest food service companies in the United States.

The point is that the hospitality industry is tied together as a clearly recognizable unit by more than just a common heritage and a commitment to "liberality and good will." Careers in the industry are such that your big break may come in a part of the industry that is very different from the one you expected (see Case History 1.1 for a personal example). Hospitality management is one of the few remaining places in our increasingly specialized world of work that calls for a broadly gauged generalist. The student who understands this principle increases his or her opportunity for a rewarding career in one or more segments that make up the hospitality industry.

The Manager's Role in the Hospitality Industry

As a successful manager in the hospitality industry, you must exhibit many skills and command much specialized knowledge, all directed at achieving a variety of management objectives. The **manager's role** is wide and varied. Let's now discuss three general kinds of hospitality objectives with which management must be concerned:

1. A manager wants to make the guest feel welcome. This requires both a friendly manner on your part toward the guest and an atmosphere of "liberality and good will" among the people who work with you in serving the guest. That almost always translates to an organization in which workers get along well with one another.

5

A Former Student's Unexpected Change

When one of the authors was an undergraduate student studying hospitality management at a large state university, he heard repeatedly from his professors how important it was that he become active with the student organizations on campus. There were quite a few student chapters of professional hospitality organizations to choose from, including the Hospitality Sales and Marketing Association International, the Travel and Tourism Research Association, and various food service organizations, among others. Partially to satisfy his professors, and partially out of curiosity, he joined the student chapter of the Club Managers Association of America, which had a strong presence on campus. When he joined, he was quite confident that he would never have occasion to work in a private club, but he had to admit that it sounded like an interesting segment of the industry. He spent two years with the association and even took an elective course on club management to learn a little bit more about the field. He then promptly began his management career with a food service management company. Much to his surprise, he was offered a job at a private club a few short years after graduating. His membership in the student chapter, and the connections that he made while a member, went a long way in helping him secure the club position. He has since enjoyed a long association with the Club Managers Association of America as well as the private club industry. In fact, he was also the faculty advisor to a student chapter of CMAA for ten years. Our own students now share similar stories with us. This just goes to further illustrate how careers can take strange twists and turns and how hospitality graduates can find themselves moving from one sector to another in short order.

2. A manager wants to make things work for the guest. Food has to be savory, hot or cold according to design, and on time. Beds must be made and rooms cleaned. Gaming facilities must be service oriented. A hospitality system requires a lot of work, and the manager must see that it is done.

3. A manager wants to make sure that the operation will continue to provide service while also making a **profit**. When we speak of "liberality and good will," we don't mean giving the whole place away! In a restaurant or hotel operated for profit, portion sizes are related to cost, and so menu and room prices must consider building and operating costs. This enables the establishment to recover the cost of its operation and to make enough additional income to pay back any money borrowed as well as to provide a return to the owner (or investor), who risked a good deal of money—and time—to make the establishment a reality. (The unique challenges associated with the operation of subsidized or noncommercial facilities will be discussed later.) The key lies in achieving a controlled profit, loss, or break-even operation. A good term to describe this management concern is "conformance to budget."

Simply stated, these objectives suggest that managers must be able to relate successfully to employees and guests, direct the work of their operation, and achieve operating goals within a budget—that is, to run a productive operation within certain constraints.

Why Study in a Hospitality Management Program?

One way to learn the hospitality business is to take the direct route: go to work in it and acquire the necessary skills to operate the business (as has been the traditional route). The trouble with this approach, however, is that the skills that accompany the various line-level workstations (cook, server, etc.) are not the same as those needed by hospitality managers. In earlier times of small operations in a slowly changing society, hospitality education was basically skill-centered. Most hospitality managers learned their work through apprenticeships. The old crafts built on apprenticeships assumed that knowledge—and work—was unchanging. However, this assumption no longer holds true. As Peter Drucker, a noted management consultant whose management observations are virtually timeless, pointed out, "Today the center [of our society's productivity] is the **knowledge worker**, the man or woman who applies to productive work ideas, concepts, and information."[1] In other words, knowledge is crucial to success, and studying is a necessary part of your overall preparation for a career as a supervisor or manager.

Many people argue that a liberal-arts education provides an excellent preparation not only for work but also for life. They're quite right. What we've found, however, is that many students just aren't interested in the liberal-arts subject matter. Because they are not interested, they are not eager to learn. On the other hand, these same people become hardworking students in a career-oriented program that interests them, whether that is in the hospitality industry or some other profession. There is no real reason for educational preparation for work to be separate from preparation for life. We spend at least half our waking hours at work. As we will learn shortly, work lies at the heart of a person's life and can lead directly to self-discovery.

Business administration offers one logical route to management preparation. Indeed, many hospitality managers have prepared for their careers in this field. Business administration, however, is principally concerned with the manufacturing and marketing of a physical product in national (and increasingly international) markets. By contrast, the **hospitality industry** is a service industry, and the management of a service institution is vastly different. Food may be the primary product of a restaurant, but most of the "manufacturing" is done right in the same place that offers the service.

High-volume food service depends on a highly skilled team made up of both front-of-the-house and back-of-the-house associates. (Courtesy of ARAMARK.)

The market is often local, and the emphasis is on face-to-face contact with the guest. Hospitality operations also tend to be smaller (with some obvious exceptions), so the problems of a large bureaucracy are not as significant as the problems of face-to-face relationships with employees and guests. Moreover, the hospitality industry has a number of unique characteristics. People work weekends and odd hours. We are expected by both guests and fellow workers to be friendly and cheerful. Furthermore, we are expected to care what happens to the guest. Our product, we will argue in a later chapter, is really the guest's experience. Additionally, the industry has its own unique culture. An important task of both schooling and work experience, then, is that of acculturating people to the work and life of hospitality industry professionals.

Our point is not that there is something wrong with a liberal-arts or business administration education. Rather, the point is that programs that are specifically focused on hospitality management are usually made up of students who are interested in the industry that they are studying. There is a clear difference between the hospitality service system and the typical manufacturing company—between the hospitality product and the manufacturer's product. For these reasons, hospitality management programs provide a distinct advantage for such students.

Why do people want to study in a hospitality management program? Perhaps the best answer can be found in the reasons why students before you have chosen this particular course of study. Their reasons fall into three categories: their experience, their interests, and their ambitions. Figure 1.1 lists the various reasons that students cite, in order of frequency. Many students become interested in the industry because a job

they once had proved particularly capti-
vating. Others learn of the industry
through family or friends working in the
field. Others learn about it through their
experiences as customers.

One final consideration for many
students is that they like and are genuinely interested in people. Working
well with people is a crucial part of a
manager's job in our industry. Many students, too, have a natural interest in
food, and some are attracted by the
glamour of the hospitality industry.

EMPLOYMENT OPPORTUNITIES

**CAREERS IN
HOSPITALITY**

Another important consideration when
choosing a profession is what the future
holds for the industry. In the case of hospitality, the employment outlook is solid
in most segments, particularly for managers. This should encourage those stu-

EXPERIENCE

Personal work experience

Family background in the industry

Contact with other students and faculty
in hospitality management programs

INTERESTS

Enjoy working with people

Enjoy working with food

Enjoy dining out, travel, variety

AMBITION

Opportunity for employment and
advancement

Desire to operate own business

Desire to travel

Desire to be independent

Figure 1.1
The reasons students select hospitality management programs.

dents who are attracted to a field in which they can be reasonably sure they will secure
employment. Others feel that in a job market with more opportunities than applicants,
they will enjoy a good measure of independence, whether in their own businesses or
as company employees. Many students are drawn to the hospitality industry because
they want to get into their own business. Others, with good reason, suspect that there
are opportunities for innovation off the beaten track of the traditional or franchise organizations. There have been many successful examples of the latter throughout the
history of the hospitality industry.

One segment in particular that seems to offer tremendous opportunities is the catering industry. Many young entrepreneurs have chosen catering as a low-investment field
that offers opportunities to people with a flair for foods and the ability to provide cus-
tomized service. Catering is a fast-growing segment of food service and is also a business that students sometimes try while in school, either through student organizations
or as a group of students setting up a small catering operation.

There are ample opportunities in the lodging area as well. One of the areas that
provides opportunities for entrepreneurs is the bed-and-breakfast/inn segment. Operators are typically able to enter these segments with lower capital requirements than
would be necessary in other lodging segments.

LODGING

Sales Managers

Front Office Managers

Guest Services Managers

FOOD SERVICE

Restaurant Managers

Banquet Managers

Food Service Managers

CULINARY

Chef Supervisor

Banquet Cook

Station Cook

TRAVEL AND TOURISM

Meeting and Convention Planner

Festival Manager

Market Researcher

Figure 1.2

Starting positions for hospitality and tourism management graduates.

Whichever the segment, the hospitality industry has always attracted its share of entrepreneurs for the simple reason that it offers everything that small-business owners are looking for. One characteristic that very much appeals to independent-minded individuals is being able to be your own boss.

There are many other opportunities as well. For instance, people with chef's training may open their own business, especially if they feel that they have a sufficient management background. In the health care area, home care organizations are expanding in response to the needs of our growing senior-citizen population and offer a wide range of opportunities to entrepreneurs.

Whether you're studying hospitality management because you want to start a business of your own or because you found your past work experience in the business especially interesting—or perhaps just because the need for managers in the area makes the job prospects attractive—management studies are an important preparation for budding entrepreneurs. Hospitality management students tend to be highly motivated, lively people who take pride in their future in a career of service. Starting positions that hospitality, tourism and culinary students typically accept upon graduation are presented in Figure 1.2.

Planning a Career

THE MEANING OF WORK

We all have several motives for going to work. We work to live—to provide food, clothing, and shelter. Psychologists and sociologists tell us, however, that our work also provides a sense of who we are and binds us to the community in which we live. The ancient Greeks, who had slaves to perform menial tasks, saw work as a curse. Their Hebrew contemporaries saw it as punishment. Early Christians, too, saw work for profit as offensive. By the time of the Middle Ages, however, people began to accept **work as a vocation**, that is, as a calling from God. Gradually, as working conditions improved and work became something that all social classes did, it became a necessary part of maturation and self-fulfillment in our society.

Today, workers at all levels demand more than just a job. Indeed, work has been defined as "an activity that produces something of value for other people."[2] This definition puts work into a social context. That is, it implies that there is a social purpose to work, as well as the crude purpose of survival. It is an important achievement in human history that the majority of North Americans can define their own approach to a life of work as something more than mere survival.

Work contributes to our self-esteem in two ways. First, by doing our work well, we prove our own competence to ourselves. Psychologists tell us that this is essential to a healthy life, as this information gives us a sense of control over both our environment and ourselves. Second, by working, we contribute to others—others come to depend on us. Human beings, as social animals, need this sense of participation. For these reasons, what happens at work becomes a large part of our sense of self-worth.

Education, too, is clearly important. Indeed, education has become essential in most walks of life. There is, moreover, a clear connection between education, work, and income. Studies have shown that workers with a post secondary education earn much more annually than workers with just a high-school education. This difference is expected to grow as the demand for "knowledge workers" continues to increase. The evidence, then, is that your commitment to education will pay off.

The next section explores career planning in regard to employment decisions that you must make while you are still in school. We will also discuss selecting your first employer when you leave school. If you've chosen the hospitality industry as your career, this section will help you map out your job plans. If you are still undecided, the section should help you think about this field in a more concrete way and give you some ideas about exploring your career through part-time employment. A large number of those reading this text already have significant **work experience**, many in hospitality fields. Because not everyone has such experience in his or her background, however, this is a subject that does need to be covered. Perhaps those with more experience will find this a useful opportunity to review plans they've already made. Taking a fresh look at your commitments is always worthwhile.

It's hard to overstate the importance of career planning.

Employment as an Important Part of Your Education

Profit in a business is treated in two ways. Some is paid out to the owner or shareholders as dividends (return on their investment). Some of the profit, however, is retained by the business to provide funds for future growth. This portion of profit that is not paid out is called retained earnings. We need the concept of retained earnings to consider the real place of work experience in career development.

PROFITING FROM WORK EXPERIENCE

The most obvious profit you earn from work is the income paid to you by an employer. In the early years of your career, however, there are other kinds of benefits that are at least as important as income. The key to understanding this statement is the idea of a lifetime income. You'll obviously need income over your entire life span, but giving up some income now may gain you income (and, we ought to note, enjoyment, a sense of satisfaction, and independence) just a few years later. There is, then, a **job benefit mix** made up of both money and knowledge to be gained from any job. Knowledge gained today can be traded with an employer for income tomorrow: a better salary for a more qualified person. The decision to take a job that will add to your knowledge is thus a decision for retained earnings and for acquiring knowledge that you can use later. Many graduates choose their first job on the basis of salary without concern for the potential long-term advantages that one job may offer over another.

Every job, therefore, has to be weighed according to its benefit mix, not just in terms of the dollar income it provides. A part-time job at a retail store might seem attractive because it pays more than a job busing dishes does. However, if you think about the learning portion of the benefit mix and your total income, including what you learn, your decision may—and probably should—be for the job that will add to your professional education.

There is another important point to consider about retained earnings and the benefit mix. Often the only part-time jobs in the industry available to students are unskilled

Hospitality takes many forms including fast growing areas such as takeout and delivery. (Courtesy of Domino's Pizza, Inc.)

ones. Many people find these jobs dull, and they often pay poorly. If you think about these jobs in terms of their total income, however, you may change your perspective. Although the work of a busperson or a dishwasher may not be very challenging, you can improve your total profits from such a job by resolving to learn all you can about the operation. In this way, you can build your retained earnings—the bank of skills and knowledge that nobody can ever take away from you.

LEARNING STRATEGIES FOR WORK EXPERIENCE

When you go to work, regardless of the position you take, you can learn a good deal through careful observation. Look first at how the operation is organized. More specifically, look at both its **managerial organization** and its physical organization.

Managerial Organization. Who is the boss? Who reports to (or works directly with) him or her? Is the work divided into definite departments or sections? Is one person responsible for each department? To whom do the department staff members report? If you can answer these questions, you will have figured out the formal managerial organization of the operation. Indeed, most large companies will have an organization chart that you can look at. If your employer doesn't have such a chart, ask him or her to explain the organization to you. You'll be surprised at how helpful to hospitality management students most employers and supervisors are.

While you're thinking about organization, it is also important to notice the **informal organization**, also known as the social organization, of the group with which you are working. Which of the workers are influential? Who seem to be the informal leaders? Why? Most work groups are made up of cliques with informal leaders. After you identify this informal structure, ask yourself how management deals with it. Remember that someday the management of these informal organizations will be your challenge; in time, you will be helping to manage the organization, and you will need their cooperation. In the meantime, this firsthand experience will help you both in your studies and in sizing up the real world of work.

The Physical Plant. You can learn a great deal about a **physical plant** by making a simple drawing of your workplace, such as the one shown in Figure 1.3. On this drawing, identify the main work areas and major pieces of equipment. Then begin to note on it where you see problems resulting from cross traffic or bottlenecks. For example, if you're working in the back of the house, you can chart the flow of products from the back door (receiver) to storage and from there to preparation. You should also trace the flow of dishes. Dirty dishes come to the dish room window and go to the clean-supply area after washing. How are they transported to the line or to the

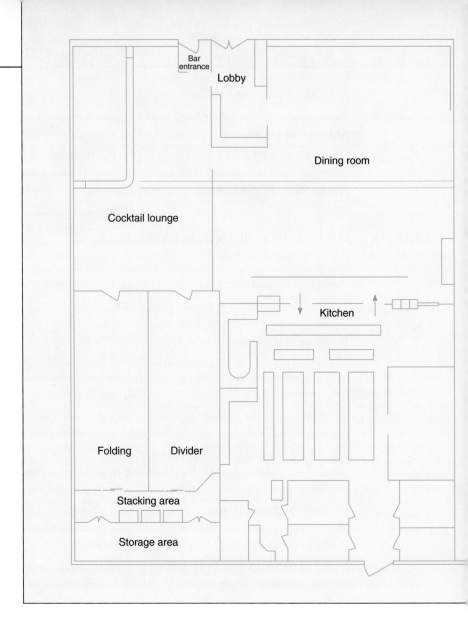

Bar entrance

Lobby

Dining room

Cocktail lounge

Kitchen

Folding   Divider

Stacking area

Storage area

Figure 1.3
A sample layout.

pantry people for use in service? If you are working in the back of the house, you will be looking mostly at the flow of kitchen workers and dishes from the viewpoint of the kitchen, dish room, or pantry. A similar flow analysis of guests and servers (and plates) can also be made from the front of the house (i.e., the dining room).

A study of guest flow in a hotel lobby can also be educational. Trace the flow of room guests, restaurant guests, banquet department guests, and service employees arriving through the lobby. Where do you observe congestion?

These simple charting activities will give you some practical experience that will be useful for later courses in layout and design and in food service operations and analysis and, more important, for decisions that you will make while on the job later in your career. Sometimes simple observations can lead to improvements in workflow patterns.

Learning from the Back of the House. Things to look for in the **back of the house** include how quality is ensured in food preparation, menu planning, recipes, cooking methods, supervision, and food holding. (How is lunch prepared in advance? How is it kept hot or cold? How long can food be held?) How are food costs controlled? (Are food portions standardized? Are they measured? How? How is access to storerooms controlled?) These all are points you'll consider a great deal in later courses. From the very beginning, however, you can collect information that is invaluable to your studies and your career.

Learning from the Front of the House. If you are busing dishes or working as a waiter, a waitress, or a server on a cafeteria line, you can learn a great deal about the operation from observing the guests or clients in the **front of the house.** Who are the customers, and what do they value? Peter Drucker called these the two central questions in determining what a business is and what it should be doing.[3] Are the guests or clients satisfied? What, in particular, seems to please them?

In any job you take, your future work lies in managing others and serving people. Wherever you work and whatever you do, you can observe critically the management and guest or client relations of others. Ask yourself, "How would I have handled that problem? Is this an effective management style? In what other ways have I seen this problem handled?" Your development as a manager also means the development of a management style that suits you, and that is a job that will depend, in large part, on your personal experience.

Getting a Job

CAREERS IN HOSPITALITY

Hospitality jobs can be obtained from several sources. For example, your college may maintain a placement office. Many hospitality management programs receive direct requests for part-time help. Some programs maintain a job bulletin board or file, and some even work with industry to provide internships. There are numerous Web sites devoted to matching employers and job seekers, such as www.hcareers.com. The help-wanted pages of your newspaper also may offer leads, as may your local employment service office. Sometimes, personal contacts established through your fellow students, your instructor, or your family or neighborhood will pay off. Networking is as effective as always, and some would suggest it is still the most important tool.

The New York, New York Casino in Las Vegas captures the feel of the original. (Courtesy of Las Vegas Convention and Visitors Authority.)

Networking occurs both formally and informally—often at industry functions, chapter meetings, and the like. Or you may find it necessary to "pound the pavement," making personal appearances in places where you would like to work.

Some employers may arrange for hospitality management students to rotate through more than one position and even to assume some supervisory responsibility to help them gain broader experience.

GETTING IN THE DOOR

It is not enough just to ask for a job. Careful attention to your appearance is important, too. For an interview, this probably means a coat and tie for men, a conservative dress or suit for women. Neatness and cleanliness are the absolute minimum. (Neatness and cleanliness are, after all, major aspects of the hospitality product.) When you apply for or have an interview for a job, if you can, find out who the manager is; then, if the operation is not a large one, ask for him or her by name. In a larger organization, however, you'll deal with a human-resources manager. The same basic rules of appearance apply, regardless of the organization's size.

Don't be afraid to check up on the status of your application. Here's an old but worthwhile adage from personal selling: It takes three calls to make a sale. The number three isn't magic, but a certain persistence—letting an employer know that you are interested—often will land you a job. Be sure to identify yourself as a hospitality management student, because this tells an employer that you will be interested in your work. Industry Practice Note 1.1 gives you a recruiter's-eye view of the job placement process.

LEARNING ON THE JOB

Many hospitality managers report that they gained the most useful knowledge on the job, earlier in their careers, on their own time. Let's assume you're working as a dishwasher in the summer and your operation has a person assigned to prep work. You may be allowed to observe and then perhaps help out—as long as you do it on your own time. Your "profit" in such a situation is in the "retained earnings" of increased knowledge. Many job skills can be learned through observation and some unpaid practice: bartending (by a waitress or waiter), clerking on a front desk (by a bellperson), and even some cooking (by a dishwasher or cook's helper). With this kind of experience behind you, it may be possible to win the skilled job part time during the year or for the following summer.

One of the best student jobs, from a learning standpoint, is a relief job. Relief jobs are defined as those that require people to fill in on occasion (such as during a regular employee's day off, sickness, or vacation). The training for this fill-in work can teach you a good deal about every skill in your operation. Although these skills differ from the skills a manager uses, they are important for a manager to know, because the structure of the hospitality industry keeps most managers close to the operating level. Knowledge of necessary skills gives managers credibility among their employees, facilitates communication, and equips them to deal confidently with skilled employees. In fact, a good manager ought to be able to pitch in when employees get stuck.[4] For these reasons, one phrase that should never pass your lips is "That's not my job."

OTHER WAYS OF PROFITING FROM A JOB

In addition to income and knowledge, after-school part-time employment has other advantages. For example, your employer might have a full-time job for you upon graduation. This is particularly likely if your employer happens to be a fairly large firm or if you want to remain close to the area of your schooling.

You may choose to take a term or two off from school to pursue a particular interest or just to clarify your longer-term job goals. This does have the advantage of giving you more than "just a summer job" on your résumé—but be sure you don't let the work experience get in the way of acquiring the basic educational requirements for progress into management.

Wherever and for however long you work, remember that through your employment, you may make contacts that will help you after graduation. People with whom you have worked may be able to tell you of interesting opportunities or recommend you for a job.

Global Hospitality Note 1.1 offers some information you may find helpful if you think you might like to work overseas.

An Employer's View of Job Placement—Hyatt

What do you look for in a potential management recruit?

We look for someone who is really thinking about a "long term" career versus getting a good offer. We take pride in the number of managers who have been rewarded with career growth and opportunities. Another characteristic we evaluate is one's energy level and service skills. We look that they have the desire and are able to align with the company service strategy.

What is your favorite question, the one you ask to get the best "read" on a person?

"Tell me what you have learned from past experiences and what you can offer Hyatt." This is a very open question that allows us to hear more about one's experiences. They have to be able to give specific points and apply them to a new career with Hyatt.

How much does Hyatt depend on formal testing and how much on personal interviews?

The personal interview will always outweigh the testing. However, we are experimenting with pre-employment assessments to ensure certain service characteristics are visible. We feel this is a great way to prescreen applicants and create a more focused interview.

What is the quickest way for an interviewee to take him- or herself out of the running?

Indecisiveness. We really want someone to have thought about a future career and have a general direction or goal. In addition, they must be flexible with relocation. A good hotelier is backed by a variety of experiences.

What skills do today's recruits have that those ten years ago didn't?

Hospitality today means much more than it did ten years ago. Today, recruits are introduced to other avenues such as Revenue Management, Retirement Communities, Casino Operations, Recreation, and

Employment at Graduation

Graduation probably seems a long way off right now, but you should already be considering strategies for finding a job when you finish your formal education. Clear goals formed now will direct your work experience plans and, to a lesser degree, the courses you take and the topics you emphasize within those courses. If you have not yet decided on a specific goal, this question deserves prompt but careful consideration

Development. Due to technology, recruits know how to get information about companies and opportunities (blogs, message boards, etc.).

What are some of the current opportunities for graduates of hospitality management programs in the lodging sector?

Lodging will always offer the traditional opportunities in Operations, Culinary, Facilities, Catering, Sales, Accounting, and Human Resources. The lodging sector offers much more today including Revenue Management, Spa Operations, and Development.

To what extent does your company employ the Internet in recruiting?

There is no other way to apply for a Hyatt job other than online. We deploy our training program and all career opportunities on Hyatt career sites. However, we do leverage job openings on other Internet sites, but we are selective. We prefer to post on a few large and some niche sites rather than posting on as many as possible. Everyone uses the Internet to find their next position.

Is there anything else that might be helpful for a hospitality management graduate to know before applying for a job with Hyatt?

Before applying to Hyatt, we ask that a graduate be open to movement [relocation]. We are focused on growth and differentiating our brands. Our current processes allow our associates movement among all Hyatt entities. There is opportunity for experience across all sectors of the industry including Classic Residence, Hyatt Place, and Summerfield Suites by Hyatt. This proves beneficial in building one's experiences.

Randy Goldberg, Executive Director Recruiting
Kristy Seidel, Manager of Staffing
Hyatt Hotels Corporation, February 7, 2006

as you continue your education. You still have plenty of time. Further, you will never know when or where a job opportunity may arise. For this reason alone, you should always keep your résumé up-to-date.

The rest of this section offers a kind of dry-run postgraduation placement procedure. From this distance, you can view the process objectively. When you come closer to graduation, you may find the subject a tense one: People worry about placement as graduation nears, even if they're quite sure of finding a job.

Career Opportunities Overseas

Companies hire North Americans to work in hospitality positions abroad for several reasons. Some countries do not have a large enough pool of trained managers. Moreover, particularly in responsible positions, a good fit with the rest of the firm's executive staff is important—and often easier for an American firm to achieve with someone from North America. The relevant operating experience may not be available to people living outside the United States and Canada. Many factors are considered, however, including familiarity with other cultures and the ability to speak multiple languages.

North American employees, however, are more expensive to hire for most companies than are local nationals because their salaries are usually supplemented by substantial expatriate benefits. But cost is not the only reason for hiring people from the host country. Local people have an understanding of the culture of the employees in a particular country, to say nothing of fluency in the language. Local managers, moreover, do not arouse the resentment that is directed at a foreign manager. For many of the same reasons, foreign-owned firms operating in the United States seek U.S. managers and supervisors in their U.S. operations.

A final point to consider is that many North American firms are using franchising as the vehicle for their overseas expansion. In this case, the franchisee is most often a local national whose local knowledge and contacts are invaluable to the franchisor. Not surprisingly, however, the franchisee is most likely to prefer people from his or her own culture if that is possible.

Although most positions in operations outside the United States are filled with people from those countries, many American companies offer significant opportunities for overseas employment. One of the first obstacles to immediate employment overseas is the immigration restrictions of other countries (similar to the restrictions enforced in the United States). Employment of foreign nationals is usually permitted only if the employer is able to show that the prospective employee has special skills that are not otherwise available in the country. It is not surprising, therefore, that many employees who do receive overseas assignments have been employed by the company for a few years and, thus, have significant operating experience.

Another major problem facing Americans who want to work overseas is a lack of language skills. In fact, many hospitality programs are now encouraging students to select the study of at least one foreign

Goals and Objectives: The Strategy of Job Placement

Most hospitality management students have three concerns. They all speak to the decision that is known as the **strategy of job placement**. First, many students are interested in such income issues as starting salary and the possibility of raises and bonuses.

Second, students are concerned with personal satisfaction. They wonder about opportunities for self-expression, creativity, initiative, and independence. This applies particularly to students coming from culinary schools who want to be able to

language as part of their curriculum. The ability to adapt to a different culture is also important, and probably the only way to get it is to have some experience of living abroad.

Summer or short-term work or study abroad not only gives students experience in living in another culture but also may offer them the opportunity to build up contacts that will help them in securing employment abroad upon graduation. Opportunities to study abroad are plentiful in summer programs offered by many hospitality programs. Some institutions also maintain exchange programs with institutions in foreign countries.

Obtaining work abroad is more difficult because work permits are required for a worker to be legally employed in a foreign country and these are usually not easy to come by. Some colleges and universities have begun to arrange for exchange programs for summer employment, but, unfortunately, many do not yet have such a program.

As a student seeking overseas work, you should begin with your own institution's placement office and international center. The consulate or embassy of the country you seek to work in may be aware of exchange programs or other means to obtain a work permit. Probably the best source of information is other students who have worked abroad. Talk with students at your own institution or those you meet at regional or national restaurant or hotel shows. They know the ropes and can give practical advice on getting jobs and what to expect in the way of pay and working conditions. Whether you are interested in overseas work as a career or not, work, travel, and study abroad can all be unique educational experiences that broaden your understanding of other cultures, increase your sophistication, and enhance your résumé.

Don't underestimate a recommendation. Even if your summer employer doesn't have a career opportunity for you, a favorable recommendation can give your career a big boost when you graduate. In addition, many employers may have contacts they will make available to you—perhaps friends of theirs who can offer interesting opportunities. The lesson here is that the record you make on the job now can help shape your career later.

immediately apply what they have learned. Although few starting jobs offer a great deal of independence, some types of work (e.g., employment with a franchising company) can lead quite rapidly to independent ownership. Students also want to know about the number of hours they'll be investing in their work. Many companies expect long hours, especially from junior management. Other sectors, especially on-site operations, make more modest demands (but may offer more modest prospects for advancement).

Third, many students, particularly in health care food service, want to achieve such professional goals as competence as a registered dietician or a dietetic technician. Professional goals in the commercial sector are clearly associated with developing a topflight reputation as an operator.

These three sets of interests are obviously related; for example, most personal goals include the elements of income, satisfaction, and professional status. Although it may be too early to set definite goals, it is not too early to begin evaluating these elements. From the three concerns we've just discussed, the following are five elements of the strategy of job placement for your consideration:

1. **Income.** The place to begin your analysis is with the issue of survival. How much will you require to meet your financial needs? If your income needs are modest, you may decide to forgo luxuries to take a lower-paying job that offers superior training. Thus, you would make an investment in retained earnings—the knowledge you hope someday to trade for more income, security, and job satisfaction.

2. **Professional status.** Whether your goal is professional certification (as a registered dietitian, for example) or a reputation as a topflight hotelier or restaurateur, you should consider the job benefit mix. In this case, you may choose to accept a lower income (but one on which you can live and in line with what such jobs pay in your region). Although you shouldn't be indifferent to income, you'll want to focus principally on what the job can teach you.

3. **Evaluating an employer.** Students who make snap judgments about a company and act aggressively during an interview often offend potential employers, who, after all, see the interview as an occasion to evaluate a graduating class. Nevertheless, in a quiet way, you should learn about the company's commitment to its employees, often evident through its employee turnover rates and its focus on training. For instance, you might want to explore whether it has a formal training program. If not, how does it translate its entry-level jobs into learning experiences? (Inquiries directed to your acquaintances and the younger management people can help you determine how the company really scores in these areas. Recent graduates from the same hospitality program as yours are good sources of information.) Because training beyond the entry-level basics requires responsibility and access to promotion, you will want to know about the opportunities for advancement. Finally, you need to evaluate the company's operations. Are they quality operations? Can you be proud to work there? If the quality of the facility, the food or the service is consistently poor, can you help improve things? Or will you be misled into learning the wrong way to do things? A final note with regard to evaluating employers who may be independent operators: Sometimes it can be more difficult to research a small business. In this case, it might be worth asking around the local business community to find out what kind of reputation the prospective employer has.

4. **Determining potential job satisfaction.** Some students study hospitality management only to discover that their real love is food preparation. Such students may decide, late in their student careers, to seek a job that provides skill training

in food preparation. Other students may decide they need a high income immediately (to pay off debts or to do some traveling, for example). These students may
decide to trade the skills they have acquired in their work experiences to gain a
high income for a year or two as a server in a topflight operation. Such a goal is
highly personal but perfectly reasonable. The key is to form a goal and keep moving toward it. The student who wants eventually to own an operation will probably have to postpone his or her goal while developing the management skills and
reputation necessary to attract the needed financial backing.

5. **Accepting skilled jobs.** Students sometimes accept skilled jobs rather than management jobs because that is all they can find. This happens quite often, especially
during a period of recession. Younger students, too, are prone to suffer from this
problem for a year or two, as are students who choose to live and work in small
communities. The concept of retained earnings provides the key to riding out these
periods. Learn as much as you can and don't abandon your goals.

A final word is in order on goals, priorities, and opportunities. Hospitality
students' preferences for work upon graduation are summarized in Table 1.1. Hotels
are clearly the favored sector of the hospitality industry, and luxury operations are
preferred over midmarket or midscale operations among this sample of students.
Interestingly, QSR and contract and noncommercial food service are at the bottom of the list. There is an old saying, De gustibus non disputandem est (In tastes, there is no disputing), and that certainly should apply to job preferences. Still, the researchers speak of "how fulfilling and rewarding careers in the QSR industry can be" and suggest
that "perhaps more than any other [this segment] provides an opportunity for hospitality students to fast-track to the
top." On the other hand, later in this text, we will point out that although work in on-site management is not any
easier, its hours are more regular and its pace more predictable. In short, there are many excellent career opportunities
in the food service industry in general, and it is even better in some specific segments.

TABLE 1.1
Hospitality Graduates' Career Preferences Ranked in Order of Preference

RANK	INDUSTRY SEGMENT
1	Luxury hotels
2	Clubs
3	Fine dining/upscale restaurants
4	Midmarket hotels
5	Contract/noncommercial food service
6	Midscale/family restaurants
7	Economy hotels
8	Quick-service restaurants

Source: Robert H. Woods, Seonghee Cho, and Michael P. Sciarini, unpublished manuscript, Michigan State University, 2003.

Luxury hotels, private clubs and fine-dining restaurants are undoubtedly more glamorous than many other operations—or at least seem so—and it does appear that they are attracting the greatest interest from graduates as applicants. In the supply-demand equation, they have a plentiful supply of applicants, and yet they are relatively smaller sectors of hospitality employment. That is to say, they have less demand for employees than many other sectors. In economics, you may recall, a large supply met by a modest demand is generally expected to yield a lower price. Of course, there are no dollar signs on job satisfaction, and these are highly personal choices. Still, the truth is that no job offers everything. You have to decide what your highest priorities are and then choose the opportunity that suits you best. If career advancement, achieving a substantial income, and gaining responsibility—or perhaps just having a manageable work life—are priorities for you, you may want to consider at least interviewing with some of the companies that are on the bottom of everybody else's list.

The Outlook for Hospitality

Over the past two generations, the hospitality industry has evolved to accommodate explosive growth, radically changing consumer demand, and a substantially different social and economic environment. We will examine some of the basic forces driving these changes in Chapter 2. The following brief summary points will alert you to some of the key trends discussed in the balance of this text. We can begin with trends closest to the industry and move outward to broader societal developments. Also, no hospitality text can ignore the short-term and long-term effects of September 11, 2001.

THE EFFECTS OF SEPTEMBER 11, 2001

The effects of the terrorist attacks in the United States on September 11, 2001, on all aspects of life have been examined extensively. Certain high-profile hospitality programs,

The outlook for the hospitality industry includes the continued growth of the casual dining segment. (Courtesy of Mimi's Café.)

including those at Johnson and Wales University and Cornell University, have hosted panel discussions and/or conducted studies on the impact that the day had on the industry. Certainly, there have been significant effects, both short-term and long-term, on the hospitality and tourism industries. These effects have ranged from the initial reaction during which many people in North America (and elsewhere) stopped traveling anywhere for any reason to traveling sporadically and finally to travel patterns reaching some level of normalcy. The airlines were perhaps the most affected industry of all (this is discussed much further in Chapter 13). The effects are sure to be felt for a long time to come, but travel, accommodation, and food service have all reached activity levels equal to those prior to September 11. Discussions of the impact of that day will be found throughout the chapters that follow. The text also discusses effects that other terrorist attacks have had (such as in Madrid, London, and Bali) as well as recent natural disasters in Asia.

POLARIZATION IN HOSPITALITY SERVICE ORGANIZATIONS

Hospitality companies are grouping themselves, to a very large extent, either as limited-service organizations or as service-intensive operations. In lodging, although there are price point divisions—budget, economy, midscale, upscale, and upper upscale—the most basic division is between limited-service and full-service properties. In later chapters, we will be concerned with the possibility of overbuilding and future excess capacity in all but the luxury and extended-stay segments of lodging.

In food service, simpler operations specializing in off-premise service to guests—take-out, drive-through, and delivery—have contributed greatly to the growth in restaurant sales in recent years. Quick-service, too, continues its healthy growth trend. Table service restaurant growth in the more economical family restaurant segment has flattened, but within the table service group a more service-intensive format—casual restaurants—has shown healthy growth.

Restaurants and hotels, then, are tailoring themselves to specialized markets, a practice often referred to as target marketing.

ACCELERATING COMPETITION

One of the major reasons that hotels, restaurants, and other hospitality organizations are increasingly targeting specific market segments is that in most markets, there is more than enough capacity to go around. Competition is likely to be even tougher in the years ahead. In food service, operators are adapting their operations by opening new restaurants and bringing them closer to the customer, that is, making them more convenient. They are also creating smaller prototypes. Lodging capacity, as we have already noted, offers a highly competitive outlook for all but the luxury sector (and even this is changing). The growth in competition makes tightly controlled operations especially important to survival. Competition also exists in the battle for customers in the convention,

Service is becoming the differentiating factor in all segments of hospitality and tourism. (Courtesy of Southwest Airlines.)

resort, and tourist destinations. Competition is no longer just limited to domestic competition, either. International competition has become a concern in some markets. We will consider those issues for restaurants in Chapter 6 and for hotels in Chapter 12.

SERVICE IS THE DIFFERENCE

As competing firms expand their menus and amenities and dress up their operations, all operations at a given price level tend to become more like one another. The crucial differentiation becomes service—usually in the form of personal service. Understanding service and how to manage it is so vitally important that the last chapter of this book is devoted to it. In the world of today and tomorrow, service will be the difference between barely surviving (or worse) and achieving success.

VALUE CONSCIOUSNESS

An educated, sophisticated customer base is placing increasing emphasis on the value of goods or services received in relation to the price paid in the marketplace. This trend probably originates in the baby boom generation and has continued with subsequent generations. The best-educated generation in history, arguably the baby boomers, has become a generation of careful shoppers. With an intensely competitive industry vying to serve them, consumers are in a position to demand good value for their money. Any discussion of value should also include mention of time and how personal time is valued (as it becomes more precious). For this reason, consumers often strive to balance the price they are willing to pay with a trade-off such as time saved. For example, this helps to partially explain the increasing popularity of the "new" fast-casual dining segment.

TECHNOLOGY

Another driving force the industry has wrestled with for some years is the explosion of technology. Technology has already changed the way work is done in operations through increased automation and computerization. Even more fundamental, however, are the changes in marketing and management made possible by technological advances. Lodging marketing, already shaped by a global computerized reservation network, has been reinvented, so to speak, as the Internet continues to expand the communication capacity of operators, their competitors, and the guest. Restaurants, too, are maintaining Web sites, many of which are interactive rather than simply informational. With greatly improved communication and computerized financial and operational reporting, the hierarchy of organizations is collapsing and a flatter organization structure is emerging.

EMPOWERMENT

As a direct result of the reduced number of middle managers, employees and managers at all levels are being asked to assume more responsibility. For example, they are being empowered to solve many of the guest's service problems on the spot. This is an outgrowth not only of improved communication but of a more educated generation of employees. Bright, well-educated people want to do their own problem solving— and generally are able to do so effectively.

DIVERSITY

The face of North America is changing. Whereas the white male has always been the dominant force in the labor market, the majority of people entering the workforce for the foreseeable future will be women and minorities such as African Americans, Hispanics, and Asians. Managers will need a broad background and an openness to many kinds of people and cultures to prosper in the time ahead.

CONCERN WITH SECURITY

The results of September 11 and other more recent terrorist attacks have only served to underscore the value that travelers put on their personal safety and security. As the perceived incidence of violence increases, people worry about their personal security—and so we see a proliferation of private security forces in hotels and restaurants, marshals on airplanes and other public places, as well as high-tech security measures such as keyless electronic locks in hotel rooms. Security has become a commodity that some people are willing to pay for—and that hospitality establishments must provide. In some places in the world (such as Israel), security is everywhere, even in the local supermarkets.

CONCERN WITH FOOD SAFETY AND SANITATION

The incidence of food-borne illness has increased as the food service system has become more complex and the number of operations has expanded. One case of food poisoning can seriously injure a restaurant's reputation. More than one can endanger an operation's survival. The level of food safety demanded by consumers and regulatory agencies alike has escalated in the light of recent cases of food poisoning. That escalation will continue in the years ahead.

GLOBALIZATION

In a sense, this has already become old news. With the falling of trade barriers such as that brought on by the North American Free Trade Agreement and the European Community, borders have become less important. The ease of financial transactions and information flow means that some of the largest "U.S. firms" are owned abroad—and that U.S. firms are major players overseas as well. Holiday Inn, for example, is owned by a British company, and Motel 6 by a French firm. On the other hand, McDonald's is the largest restaurant chain in Europe and has restaurants in more countries than any other food service company in the world (currently at 121 and counting). Forecasters are expecting tremendous growth opportunities in both China and India, which are positioned to greatly influence global commerce in the coming years. With all of the dynamism that the hospitality industry offers, an exciting future beckons as you begin this study of the industry and what makes it tick.

Summary

As we have seen, the hospitality industry includes hotels and restaurants, as well as many other types of institutions that offer shelter and/or food (and entertainment, etc.) to people away from home. A manager in the hospitality industry, therefore, must keep in mind the following three objectives: (1) making the guest welcome personally, (2) making things work for the guest, and (3) making sure that the operation will continue to provide service and meet its budget.

We mentioned the many reasons for studying in a hospitality management or culinary management program, including past experiences working in the field, interests in the field, and ambitions in the field.

We also discussed the meaning of work and how to get the most from a job, including weighing both retained earnings and the job benefit mix. We pointed out that in the hospitality industry, you can learn a lot from studying the physical plant and from how the front and the back of the house are managed.

We then turned to ways to get a job—including always having a résumé ready and preparing for an interview—and how to gain the most from whatever job you do find. We also talked about what you should consider in regard to a more permanent job: income, professional status, your employer, potential job satisfaction, and accepting an interim less-skilled job. We noted as well that supply and demand work in the hospitality job market as they do elsewhere, suggesting that what is most popular in terms of employment may not necessarily translate into the best opportunity.

Finally, we began our continuing discussion of the outlook for the hospitality industry, which we found to be bright but full of change and competition.

Key Words and Concepts

Hospitality	Job benefit mix
Manager's role	Managerial organization
Profit	Informal organization
Knowledge worker	Physical plant
Hospitality industry	Back of the house
Work as a vocation	Front of the house
Work experience	Strategy of job placement

Review Questions

1. What kinds of institutions or establishments does the hospitality industry include besides hotels and restaurants?

2. What is the role of a manager in the hospitality industry?

3. Why did you choose to study in a hospitality management program? What alternatives were available to you?

4. What are some of the reasons that people work?

5. What does the concept of retained earnings mean as it relates to a career?

6. Describe the concept of the job benefit mix. Give examples from your experience or from that of your classmates.

7. What are some things to observe in both the front of the house and the back of the house in the early stages of your career?

8. What kinds of things can you learn from a part-time (or summer) job that are not strictly part of the job?

9. What are three principal concerns in regard to a job after graduation?

10. What are the five elements of the strategy of job placement?

Internet Exercises

1. **Site name:** Résumés and Cover Letters

URL: www.wku.edu/~hrtm/resumes.htm

Background information: This site provides a listing of Internet resources for writing résumés and cover letters.

Exercises:

a. Surf the résumé and cover letter Web sites for information on writing résumés and cover letters. Write a simple résumé and cover letter for an entry-level hotel, restaurant or tourism position for which you are interested and qualified. Use only experience that you have already acquired.

b. After writing the résumé and cover letter, describe the experiences you will need to acquire in the future to obtain an entry-level management position in the hospitality industry.

2. **Site name:** Hotel, Restaurant and Tourism Management Career Opportunities

URL: www.wku.edu/~hrtm/hrtmjobs.htm

Background information: This site is a launch pad for hospitality management career Web sites. The site provides links to generic hospitality Web sites such as HCareers.com, HospitalityLink.com, and HospitalityJobOnline.com as well as Web sites that specialize in hotels, food service/restaurants, casinos, and travel.

Exercises:

a. Explore at least two of the Web sites indicated above. Look through the job opportunities in your area of interest.

  i. What job opportunities are available for entry-level management positions (recent graduates of a hospitality management program)?

  ii. Are there abundant job opportunities in a location where you would like to be after graduation?

b. Which support/career services does the Web site provide candidates to assist them with their job search (for example: résumé, cover letter, electronic résumé help, etc.)?

c. Explore the "Career Services" Web site at the college or university you are currently attending.

    i. What types of services does your career services office offer to students (résumé and cover letters, job search assistance, etc.)?

    ii. Is there a person in your career services office who has been specifically designated to assist hospitality management students? If so, what is the name of this person?

    iii. Does the career services office hold job/career fairs for students on your campus? If so, when are these job fairs typically held and do they include potential hospitality employers as exhibitors?

    iv. Does your career services office maintain a database of current job opportunities for students? If so, how do they make this information available to students?

3. **Site name:** Council on International Educational Exchange
URL: http://www.ciee.org/
Background information: Study abroad or work abroad opportunities—CIEE provides quality programs and services.
Site name: Hospitality Internships Abroad
URL: www.internabroad.com/listings.cfm/interntypeID/110
Background information: GoAbroad.com was launched to fill an information void in the area of international student travel. GoAbroad.com was conceptualized to provide a one-stop information center for students wishing to travel internationally. The site was created to link prospective travelers with organizations providing international opportunities.
Site name: Idealist.org
URL: www.idealist.org/
Background information: Search for worldwide internship opportunities by location, dates, and required skills.
Exercises:

a. Browse through all three Web sites and describe the countries that are represented and the hospitality job opportunities available on each Web site.

b. Choose an international internship Web site and select an internship that you might be interested in pursuing. Describe the benefits and drawbacks of pursuing an international internship.

Notes

1. Peter F. Drucker, *The Age of Discontinuity* (New York: Harper & Row, 1968), p. 264.
2. *Work in America* (Cambridge, MA: MIT Press, 1973), p. 3.
3. Peter F. Drucker, *Management: Tasks, Responsibilities, Practices* (New York: Harper & Row, 1974), pp. 80–86.
4. If they get stuck too often, of course, management must find out why and correct the problem. If a manager has to pitch in frequently, it can be a sign of an inefficient organization.

The Hospitality Industry

(Courtesy of National Park Service.)

CHAPTER TWO

Forces Affecting Growth and Change in the Hospitality Industry

---

The Purpose of this Chapter

The hospitality industry, as it is today and will be tomorrow, is the result of the interaction of basic market forces. In this chapter, we will look at two of the most basic of these forces. The first is the demand for hospitality services from consumers. The second is the supply of those things required to provide service, such as land and its produce, food, and labor. We begin by considering demand; it is the most fundamental factor that gives rise to business activity. We will then consider the supply of the factors of production used by hospitality service companies.

THIS CHAPTER SHOULD HELP YOU

1. Explain how the changing demographics of the North American population impact the demand for hospitality services, and give examples of demographics that affect both food service and lodging operations.

2. Describe the current and expected future impact of baby boomers on the demand for hospitality services.

3. Give examples of the opportunities and challenges inherent in the North American population's increasing diversity.

4. Explain how changes in the female workforce and alterations in family structure affect consumer behavior and the markets for hospitality services.

5. Identify and describe the key supply factors that are important to hospitality organizations.

6. Identify and describe the trends that are changing the relative cost of supplies.

7. Give examples of ways in which hospitality service companies are responding to changes in the labor force.

Managing Change

A t the outset of this chapter, it is important to place the topic of forces (market, environmental, societal, etc.) into its proper context. Managers in any line of business must understand the external forces that are at work if they are going to be effective managers. This is especially true of managers in the hospitality industry. There are forces that impact hospitality businesses on a daily basis, or on some other cyclical basis, and there are singular events that have an immediate and ongoing effect. Some forces may invoke gradual changes; others may come suddenly. Such factors as demographic changes, fluctuating food costs, resource scarcity, and workforce diversity are ever present and are all important to understand as a manager. We have continued to discuss these topics in this as well as in previous editions of this book, because of their ongoing importance. And then there are "one-time" events, such as the September 11 attacks that occurred in the United States. Following the attacks, it was oft repeated that the industry most affected was the hospitality and tourism industry. Since that time the industry has also coped with recession, war, mad cow disease, terrorism attacks in Europe and Asia, natural disasters (such as Hurricane Katrina and the Asian Tsunami), and Severe Acute Respiratory Syndrome (SARS). SARS, for instance, threw entire segments of the industry (primarily in North America and Asia) into a tailspin during the latter part of 2003. Managers must now be more aware than ever—indeed, it has been said that there may never be a return to "normalcy." This chapter sheds light on some of the changes that continue to shape the industry and the ways in which managers behave and react to events. We will begin with the effects of demand.

Demand

U ltimately, **demand** translates into customers. We will look at customers from three different perspectives. First, we need to understand what the population's changing age patterns are; second, we will explore how they affect the demand for hospitality products. Finally, we will look at other patterns of change, such as the continued increase in the number of working women, the transformation of family structure, and changes in income and spending patterns. Finally, we will consider the effect that the September 11 and other events had on demand.

One way to better understand these changes is by looking at changes in demographics. **Demographics** is the study of objectively measurable characteristics of our population such as age and income. As we review demographic data, however, it is important to keep in mind the human face behind the numbers. To do that, we will

Life events such as marriage, birth, and death affect demographic changes. (Courtesy of Treasure Island, Mirage Resorts.)

want to consider what the facts mean in terms of our customer base. The material in this section is vital to understanding the most basic force driving the hospitality industry's development, which is demand—that is, customers.

THE CHANGING AGE COMPOSITION OF OUR POPULATION

It should be clear to students of the industry that the population of North America is changing in many ways. This, in turn, is setting off an entire chain reaction of events and associated challenges. To understand the scope of the changing population, one must first understand one of the driving forces behind this change—the baby boom generation. "Baby boomer" is the term applied to a person born between 1946 and 1964. To properly understand the boomer phenomenon, a little history is in order.

Beginning with the Great Depression, the birthrate fell dramatically and remained low throughout the 1930s (a "baby bust"). Then came World War II, which also produced a low birthrate. After the war, however, servicemen came home and began to get married in very large numbers. Not surprisingly, between 1946 and 1964 the number of births rose as well. The boom in births was far out of proportion to anything North America had experienced before. As one could imagine, the resulting **baby boomers** have, as a generation, had an unprecedented impact on all facets of North American life, ranging from economics to politics to social change.

In 2006 there were just over 78 million baby boomers ranging in age from 42 to 60, constituting more than one-fourth of the U.S. population. Although the number of native-born baby boomers was at its highest in 1964 at the end of the baby boom, immigration has increased the size of the boomer cohort by significantly more than deaths have decreased it since that time. The year 2006 was significant because the oldest of the baby boomers turned 60.

By the mid-1960s, most of the boomers' parents had passed the age when people have children. Furthermore, just at that point, the smaller generation born during the Depression and war years reached the age of marrying—and childbearing. Because there were fewer people in their childbearing years, fewer children were born. The result was the "birth dearth" generation, those born between 1965 and 1975 (although some demographers include additional years).

Labeled **Generation X** (or GenXers), this group ranged in age from 31 to 41 and numbered about 42 million in 2006 (note that despite all of the attention this group gets in the press, they are still far outnumbered by the baby boomers). This generation was born into a difficult period in the 1970s and began to come of age as the growth of the 1980s flattened into the recession of the early 1990s. The GenXers ". . . reveal the sensibilities of a generation shaped by economic uncertainty."[1] Not surprisingly, they are quite different from their boomer counterparts in a variety of ways. Among other things, they have a reputation for being worldly wise, independent, pragmatic, and intelligent consumers. Further, they tend to be technologically savvy, having grown up during the computer age (which earlier generations, believe it or not, didn't). Factors with a direct bearing on the hospitality industry are that they spend a large proportion of their income eating out, have a predisposition to fast food, and look for value in their purchases. Finally, they too are becoming parents and passing along many of these same characteristics to their children.

As we saw in our brief view of GenXers, food service makes a perfect case history for assessing the impact of generational change on the hospitality industry. Quick-service restaurants (QSRs) grew up along with the boomers when they were children and when their parents, still young, had limited incomes and needed to economize. Then, starting in the late 1950s, the boomers, as young people, began to have money to spend of their own. McDonald's, Burger King, and other quick-service operations suited their tastes and their pocketbooks. In the late 1960s and

Demographics in Practice

"Gourmet" hamburger companies such as Fuddruckers are aggressively targeting baby boomers and their offspring. As part of the relatively new restaurant classification known as "fast-casual," Fuddruckers, and other companies within the segment, attempt to offer an alternative to quick service to the aging baby boomers. Fuddruckers, which was started in 1980 in San Antonio and now has 200 stores across the United States, seems to be in the right place at the right time. The company represents many of the changes that are taking place in the restaurant industry and particularly in this growing segment. They offer a product that has the feel of a cross between quick service and casual, thus the fast-casual moniker. Fast-casual restaurants, as a group, are tending to put a lot of emphasis on food quality, in an effort to attract the baby boomers and the like. With an emphasis on food, there is also a spillover effect that helps to bring in other demographic groups.

Fuddruckers prides itself on its food quality—the freshness of its product, their toppings bar, big servings, and the ability to appeal to a variety of demographic groups in addition to baby boomers. They are able to identify and target the different groups by a variety of methods. First, they have created three different types of restaurant facilities (prototypes) for use in three different types of locations (freestanding, urban, and mall). Second, they offer a variety of foods and flavors for different palates—including items such as ostrich burgers for the more adventurous. Finally, their hours and their average check (about $8.00) make their restaurants very accessible. They feel that they have found the right mix in their strategy to target a range of customers through different menu offerings and locations. The company plans to continue to open approximately 12 restaurants per year for the foreseeable future, maintaining the majority as company owned and operated.

early 1970s, however, the boomers were becoming young adults—and Wendy's, among others, developed more upscale fast-food operations to meet their moderately higher incomes and more sophisticated tastes. Similarly, in the early 1980s, as a significant number of boomers passed the age of 30, the "gourmet hamburger" restaurant appeared (such as the Fuddruckers and the Red Robin chains), which accommodated boomers' increasing incomes and aspirations. Industry Practice Note 2.1 gives another example of how changing demographics are influencing operations and company marketing strategies.

The baby boomers have also had a significant impact on lodging. Kemmons Wilson's first Holiday Inn was built when the oldest boomers were six years old. Holiday Inns began as a roadside chain serving business travelers, but the big profits came in the summer days of 100 percent occupancy, with the surge in family travel that accompanied the growing up of the boomers. Later in the 1980s, about the time boomers began to move into their middle years, all-suite properties began to multiply to meet

Children will continue to drive the popularity and success of attractions such as the Serengeti Plain at Busch Gardens. (Courtesy of Busch Gardens Tampa Bay; © 2004 Busch Entertainment.)

a surging demand for more spacious accommodations. Boomers on a short holiday make up a significant portion of the all-suite weekend occupancy, and much of the all-suite weekday trade is boomers on business. Moreover, it seems reasonable to assume that the growth of midscale limited-service properties is related, at least to some degree, to the boomers' taste for informality and their desire for value.

In the mid-1970s, we saw the boomers themselves come into the family formation age. The increase in the number of children born beginning in the late 1970s has been referred to as the "echo" of the baby boom (resulting in the **echo boomers, or Generation Y**). As the huge generation of boomers entered their childbearing years, births rose simply because there were more potential parents. The echo boom, however, was somewhat smaller because the boomers chose to have smaller families than their parents had had.

Getting back to the baby boomers, the baby boom is a tide that is bound to recede as boomers age and death takes its toll. In fact, 1997 was the first year in which the number of boomers—including immigrants—actually declined. By 2010, the U.S. Census Bureau projects, the size of the baby boom will have fallen to about 75 million, and by 2020 to below 70 million.[2] Boomers will continue to be important not only because they are numerous but because they are in their middle years, a time normally associated with high average earnings. Older boomers outspend other demographic groups in several areas, including food away from home, transportation, and entertainment.[3] Over the next few years, much of their budgets are expected to be diverted toward health and health care.

Significantly, the total amount of the food budget spent on food away from home rises as household income rises, as does the propensity to travel. Households headed by people age 45 to 54 spend more total dollars on dining out than younger patrons.[4] Because of their higher average incomes, though, they spend a lower proportion of their income on restaurant purchases.

Even while the boomers occupy center stage, we have noted that another generation has begun to edge toward the limelight. Generation Y, born between 1976 and 1994, were age 12 to 30 in 2006. By 2010, this generation will have overtaken the boomer generation in size, numbering over 77 million compared to the boomers' reduced numbers (see Table 2.1).

Table 2.1 highlights the relative change of each age group resulting from births, deaths, and immigration for 2010 and 2020. There will be a modest growth in the number of children, supporting a continuing emphasis on services aimed at families with young children such as special rates, accommodations, and services for families in lodging and child-friendly services such as playgrounds, games, and children's menus in restaurants. One food service chain that puts real emphasis on targeting children is Denny's. Its children's menu won *Restaurant Hospitality* magazine's 2005 award for

TABLE 2.1

U.S. Population 2010 to 2020[a]

	2010	% OF POP.[b]	2020	% OF POP.[b]	% CHANGE 2010–2020
All ages	299,862		324,927		8.4%
Under age 5	20,099	6.7%	21,951	6.8%	9.2%
5 to 9	19,438	6.5%	21,403	6.6%	10.1%
10 to 14	19,908	6.6%	21,146	6.5%	6.2%
15 to 19	21,668	7.2%	21,224	6.5%	(2.0)%
20 to 29	41,000	13.7%	42,404	13.1%	(3.4)%
30 to 39	38,041	12.7%	42,348	13.0%	11.3%
40 to 49	42,631	14.2%	38,807	11.9%	(9.0)%
50 to 59	41,111	13.7%	41,216	12.7%	0.3%
60 to 64	16,252	5.4%	20,696	6.4%	27.3%
65 to 84	33,929	11.3%	46,970	14.5%	38.4%
85 and older	5,786	1.9%	6,764	2.1%	16.9%

[a]Projected U.S. population by age, 2010, 2020 and percentage change, 2010–2020, number in thousands.
[b]Totals do not add to 100 percent due to rounding.
Source: U.S. Census Bureau.

children's menus in the Family Restaurant category. Other companies that have received recognition for their children's menus in recent years have been California Café, Skipjack's, Which Wich?, and Taco Bell.

The number of young adults will be expanding over the period to 2010, which is good news for the purveyors of inexpensive, no-frills food service such as QSRs and certain casual dining concepts. There is mixed news when it comes to the teenage group—the number of those between 10 and 14 is expected to decrease, while there is expected to be a significant increase in the 15-to-19 age group. Teenagers spend an average of $104 a week, amounting to a staggering $172 billion a year as a group.[5] Their impact, however, is even greater than this because of the substantial influence they have over family buying decisions—including where to dine, where to go on vacations, and what lodging to use on family trips.

The number of people age 30 to 49 in North America will decline between now and 2010. This has implications for labor supply, which are discussed in a later section. The baby boomers' move into their middle years marks a major shift in the population, as those in the 50-to-59 age group increase significantly over the next decade, as will those of preretirement age. As we have noted, these age groups are normally associated with relatively high incomes (peak earning years). Growth of this population segment is likely to support a continuing increase in demand for upscale food service and other hospitality products such as lodging and travel.

The slow but steady growth in the over-65 age group will be a preview of the trend toward growing demand for services of all kinds for retirees, which will explode after 2010 as the baby boomers move into retirement (the first boomers begin to turn 65 in 2011). To summarize, the age composition of the U.S. population continues to shift, having significant implications for the hospitality services. The changes that are taking place in North America, though, do not accurately reflect the changes that are taking place elsewhere in the world. Global Hospitality Note 2.1 discusses demographic changes in other areas of the world.

DIVERSITY AND CULTURAL CHANGE

We need to consider four other basic structural changes that will shape the demand for hospitality services in the twenty-first century: an increasingly diverse population, the proportion of women working, changing family composition, and a changing income distribution.

A moment's reflection suggests what the relationship of these factors to the hospitality industry might be. One of the factors accounting for the success of ethnic restaurants, for instance, is America's already great **diversity** (the number and scope of ethnic dining options has increased dramatically in recent years, especially in smaller

As North America Ages, Some Parts of the World Are Getting Younger

It should be clear from our discussion so far that the population of North America is rapidly aging. We can take this one step further and say that, in general, the population worldwide is aging and, more specifically, the population of the developed world is aging faster than the rest of the world. Europe, for instance, is experiencing much the same effects as the United States—Germany perhaps to the greatest extent. According to *The Economist*, by 2030, almost one-half of the population in Germany will be over 65.[1] Other European countries, such as Italy and France, are experiencing similar shifts. In Asia, Japan is also getting older. The aging of the Japanese population is exacerbated by the country's strict immigration policies. Japan has the oldest population in the world with a median age of just over 41 (compare this to the median age of the United States, which is just over 35, and to Iraq's, which is 17).[2]

Perhaps the greatest changes taking place in the world are in the Middle East. *American Demographics* magazine reports that there are nearly 380 million residents living in 20 Middle Eastern countries and that the demographic makeup of the region is changing drastically. A number of factors, including lower infant mortality rates, immigration, and an increase in the size of families, have all contributed to the region's population growth rate being the highest anywhere. The region is experiencing a baby boom similar to what occurred in the United States in the 1960s. The total population in the 20 Middle Eastern countries has almost quadrupled since 1950. The median ages in many of the countries, including Iraq, are much lower than most of the world's. These trends are expected to increase throughout the next two decades. In Saudi Arabia, the number of persons under 25 is expected to double between 2000 and 2025.[3] Such changes in the average age will result in shifting demand for jobs, consumer goods, education, and hospitality services, just as it has in the United States. Together, it is important to understand that demographic changes affect different parts of the world in different ways and at different rates.

1. *The Economist*, "A Tale of Two Bellies," August 24, 2002.
2. United Nations Department of Economic and Social Affairs (unstats.un.org/unsd/).
3. *American Demographics*, "The Middle East Baby Boom," September 2002.

markets). In addition to ethnic diversity, the composition of the workforce is also changing. For instance, during the recent past, women have moved from being competitors of the restaurant business to being its customers. A family with two working partners simply approaches life differently. For instance, such families usually find it easier to schedule shorter, more frequent vacations. Further, more children (or fewer, for that matter) means a difference in the kind of hospitality service concepts that will succeed—and much the same can be said for more (or less) income. These issues are discussed further in the following sections.

Diversity of the U.S. Population. According to U.S. Census Bureau projections, African Americans, Asians, Native Americans, and Hispanics together will constitute a majority of the U.S. population shortly after 2050. In less than one life span, non-Hispanic whites will go from being the dominant majority to a minority. This shift in the balance of North America's ethnic makeup has already taken place in entire states such as New Mexico and Hawaii, and in many large cities across the United States. Major states such as California and Texas are expected to reach the point where minorities achieve a collective majority within the first decade of the twenty-first century.

The U.S. population of Hispanics and African Americans is about equal, with both groups representing just less than 13 percent of the population, respectively. The Hispanic population is expected to triple in size between the years 2000 and 2050.[6] The Hispanic population is increasing rapidly because of a higher birthrate and also because of immigration, both legal and illegal.

The term *Hispanics,* we should note, is convenient, but it masks substantial differences that exist among subgroups. Most U.S. Hispanics are of Mexican origin (almost 60 percent), but two-thirds of these were born in the United States. The Census Bureau says that approximately 10 percent of Hispanics are of Puerto Rican origin. Most Puerto Ricans on the U.S. mainland were born in the United States. All Puerto Ricans are U.S. citizens. Less than 5 percent of Hispanics are of Cuban origin. Hispanic Americans also include a significant number of people from other Latin American countries.[7]

During the years from 2010 to 2020, the U.S. population of African American extraction is projected to increase from 40 million to 45 million. African Americans continue to represent the largest minority group in the U.S, but just barely. As a group, they have experienced increases in education and income. Finally, the majority of African Americans live in the South.[8]

Asian Americans will number 14.2 million in 2010, up almost 100 percent from the 1990 level of 7.3 million. Their median household income, at $54,488 in 2002, was substantially higher than the non-Hispanic white household average of $47,041 for the overall population.[9]

We will be discussing the topic of diversity again in a later section on the hospitality workforce. At this point, we can note that the shift toward the popularity of ethnic foods almost certainly reflects a change in demand resulting from the increase in America's present diversity (most polls reflect that Americans' favorite cuisines are Chinese, Italian, and Mexican, in no particular order). Another example of diversity's present impact is the number of convention and visitor bureaus all over North America that are targeting African-American groups. Note the increase in African-American–sponsored events (The music festival in New Orleans sponsored by *Essence* magazine is one such example). This trend is likely to continue as our population

Women are playing an increasingly prominent role in the hospitality industry. (Courtesy of Las Vegas Convention and Visitors Authority.)

continues to diversify, and firms will have a heightened need to adapt their products and services to the tastes of different groups.

We have been discussing ethnic diversity, but this is by no means the only way in which the population mix is changing or diversity is expressed in the general population. The gradual aging of the boomers means that our population will soon have a much larger senior population. Students of demographics speak of a "dependency ratio" to express the relationship between people in certain age groups who are, for the most part, working and people in other age groups who have not yet begun to work or have retired. In short, it is expected that as the age of the general population increases, so too will the age of the workforce.

Another form of diversity has developed in the last two generations as women's presence and roles in the workforce have changed, a topic to which we now turn.

Working Women. The changes in our views of women and the family have had an enormous impact on the hospitality industry over the last 100 years. Figure 2.1 shows the change in women's employment over the past 50 years (along with projections for the next 50). In the early part of this century, women working outside the home were the exception. Until the start of World War II, less than a quarter of women were in the workforce—that is, they either had a job or were looking for one. World War II saw that rate increase to nearly one-third of women. Over the next five years, the rate

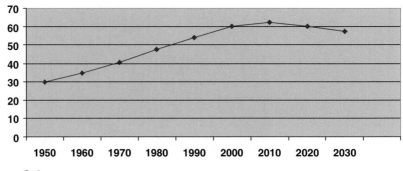

Figure 2.1
Female Workforce Participation, 1950–2030. (Source: Bureau of Labor Statistics, Workforce Participation, 2006.)

rose until, in 1980, over 50 percent of women were at work away from home, resulting in a large percentage of **two-income families**. The participation rate of women in the workforce is expected to continue to increase in the short term and long term. Further, the share of women in the workforce continues to increase as well.

This is a change of major proportions in a relatively short period of time. It has resulted in significant changes in many aspects of our society—including, of course, the hospitality industry. Moreover, we have moved from a time when it was unusual for mothers to work outside the home to a world in which the unusual mother is the one who is not also a wage earner. More women are moving into the managerial ranks as well. Women represent 50 percent of management and professional workers in the workforce. Women represented 41 percent of all managers in food service and 51 percent of managers in the lodging segment in 2004.[10] Estimates indicate that the percentage of women in management roles will also continue to increase.

It seems likely that the statistics we have cited actually understate women's work roles. Women enter and exit the workforce more frequently than men to accommodate life changes such as marriage and childbirth. Counted as nonparticipants are many women who are not working at the moment but who expect to return to work shortly.

While the roles of women are changing and improving, they continue to experience challenges in some areas of the hospitality industry, as illustrated in Industry Practice Note 2.2.

Family Composition. Family composition is also rapidly changing. Just a few short years ago, the largest segment of households in the United States were those with children under age 18. Now, however, out of 109 million housholds in the United States, there are 36 million households with just two people (the largest category) followed by 29 million households with just one person. The U.S. Census Bureau indicates that the number of family households, as a percentage of total households, has decreased dramatically since 1970. Also, family households are simply getting smaller. Married couples with children under 18 are expected to continue to decrease as the baby boomers' children continue to grow up and leave home.[11] One significant aspect of these population changes is that couples without children to support—**empty nesters** and those who chose not to have children—spend more than any other household. They spend more on take-out food, for instance, than they do on groceries. They are also avid travelers.

Another change in family structure is illustrated by the growth in **single-person** (or nonfamily) **households**. People are putting off marriage until much later in life—single-family households have increased as a percentage of total households from 17.1 percent in 1970 to 26.3 percent in 2002. This group of households is expected to continue growing through the year 2010.[12]

Such changes are affecting major life decisions as well as spending habits. Male singles are younger, whereas women living alone tend to be older widows, reflecting the tendency for wives to outlive their husbands. Males have higher incomes, and their per capita spending is larger than women's. Men spend twice as much of their annual food budgets on food away from home, as do women. Although they exhibit different trends, both types of single-person household are good potential customers, and as women's incomes continue to rise, the two types of household are likely to resemble one another more.

Single parents, on the other hand, are a group who have relatively lower incomes. They eat out less often than the average North American, for instance. They are less likely to be hotel customers because their budgets do not permit them to travel as freely as other groups.

Changing Income Distribution. In the 1980s, the **middle class** decreased in size, with more people leaving it than entering it. In general, the "winners" were university-educated people, retirees with investment income, and women with full-time jobs. Women's average income, adjusted for inflation, has increased (but is still just 77 percent of that of men's, and some estimates indicate that it is even lower than this). This has resulted in a changing **income distribution**.

Couples without children are a growing segment of the population. (Courtesy of Las Vegas Convention and Visitors Authority.)

Advocacy for the Advancement of Women in Food Service[1]

The advancement and empowerment of women in the corporate world is still a major concern today. Working women face a variety of labor market challenges and opportunities. One of the signs that things are changing is the formation of many support groups and research/educational centers. The Institute for Women and Work (IWW) at Cornell University, for example, is "an applied research and educational resource center, which provides a forum for examining and evaluating the forces that affect women and work".[1] It offers "expert training, hosts seminars, and creates connections among workers, advocates, employers, students, academics, and others who share a concern about women's role in the workplace."[2] With offices in New York City, Ithaca, and Washington, D.C. and through its roundtable sessions and research conferences, IWW has the opportunity to influence public policy.

In the hospitality industry, similar groups have been formed to support the well-being and advancement of women in industry. One such group, the Women's Foodservice Forum (WFF), was created in 1989 to "promote leadership development and career advancement of executive women for the benefit of the food service industry."[3] Since its inception, WFF's membership has grown to more than 2,200 members. This membership reflects all segments of the industry: restaurant operations, manufacturing, distribution, publishing, and consulting. Such highly visible companies as Darden, Luby's, McDonald's, and Pizza Hut are represented on the WFF board of directors. The group helps to build leadership abilities in women through a variety of activities. Among other things, the WFF sponsors a mentor program, hosts an annual leadership conference, hosts keynote speakers and regional networking events, publishes a newsletter, provides scholarships, and commissions research studies on issues affecting women.

WFF has also conducted longitudinal research since late 2001 with the Top 100 Foodservice Operators, the Top 100 Foodservice Manufacturers, and the Top 50 Distributors in the U.S. Foodservice Market. These

In the 1990s, the middle class took a further jolt from restructuring. White-collar workers and middle managers were hardest hit by the efforts to increase efficiency in many large firms. Most reports indicate that there is a widening gap between the rich and the poor, with the rich getting richer, although this has been tempered somewhat in recent years. Industry Practice Note 2.3 discusses the issue of the size of the middle class further.

Figure 2.2 shows that the higher a household's income, the more frequently its members dine out. But because a significant proportion of guests who eat out do so out of necessity, many who have moved down the economic ladder have not been lost entirely to food service. In lodging and travel, however, this is much less true, because these are almost entirely discretionary expenditures. Although the large numerical growth in lower-income families discussed in Industry Practice Note 2.3 probably studies have been conducted to record the progress of female executives in the food service industry. Among the key findings are that women only occupy 10 percent of Board of Director positions and 12 percent of C-Level positions (e.g., C.E.O.) in the companies surveyed. The research also suggests that it is two to three times more likely for a woman to hold an Executive Staff position such as Marketing, Finance, or HR than it is for a woman to hold an Executive Line position in operations.

Based on the results of this research, as well as other anecdotal evidence, the hospitality industry can be a challenging environment for women intending to move up the career ladder. Nevertheless, the findings also proposed what may seem to be an opportunity for best practice in the industry: The companies with better than average profiles of gender equity have two commonalities in their best practices: (1) their CEO is on the public record in support of gender equity and the development of women in the executive career path and (2) the company integrates support of gender diversity into other training. Accordingly, encouraging these practices in the industry is likely to assist the empowerment and advancement of women.

The research has indicated that there is much room for improvement in order for women to completely advance to the highest job titles in the hospitality industry, as well as in many other industries. The continuous role of these advocacy groups is to persevere toward eliminating the barriers to women's advancement.

Information for this Industry Practice Note was gathered from the Web sites of: The Institute for Women and Work, Cornell University, and the Women's Foodservice Forum.
1. The Institute for Women and Work, Cornell University (www.ilr.cornell.edu/extension/iww/default.html)
2. Ibid.
3. The Women's Foodservice Forum (www.womensfoodserviceforum.com).

indicates a growing number of customers for lower-check-average restaurants, it almost certainly denotes a group that is effectively less able to participate in the high-end travel market. It is important to recognize that not all factors affecting demand can be as numerically specific as the demographic data that we have been reviewing. People's different patterns of **activities**, **interests**, **and opinions**, sometimes called **psychographics**, also affect the demand for food service.

Also remember that households in the upper-income groups frequently represent dual-income families where both spouses are working. These families experience great time pressure, which undoubtedly explains the rapid growth in sales in both take-out and the upscale casual category, a haven offering a quick moment of fun and relaxation to these busy people.

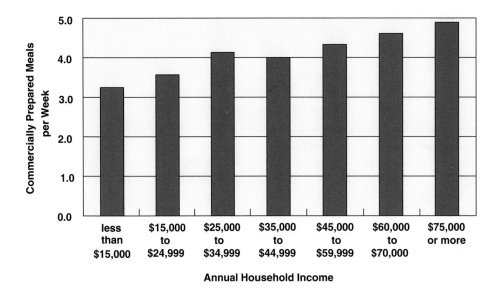

Figure 2.2
Higher income equals more dining–out occasions, 2000. (Source: Meal Consumption Behavior, National Restaurant Association.)

 **Supply**

    The key factors of supply that concern us are land and its produce, food, and labor. Capital is a third factor of production, but we will reserve discussion of it until the lodging chapters. The patterns of access to public markets discussed there can, however, be applied to the hospitality industry in general.

LAND AND ITS PRODUCE

Land and the things that come from the land are classically one of the major factors of production in economics. In hospitality, we are concerned with land itself, as well as with a major product of the land, food.

Land. Because hospitality firms need land for their locations, certain kinds of land are critical to the industry. Good locations, such as high-traffic areas, locations near major destinations, or locations associated with scenic beauty, fall into this category.[13] Furthermore, they are becoming scarcer with every passing day for at least two reasons: the existence of established operations and **environmental pressures**.

Is the Middle Class Shrinking?

Most North Americans think of themselves as middle class, whatever their actual income is. In the short term, people's incomes are growing and will continue to grow. After years of salary stagnation in the early 1990s, the typical U.S. household's income rose by 3.5 percent to $38,885 in 1998. Over a longer time period, from 1990 to 1998, the average household's income increased 4.1 percent. These averages, however, conceal certain trends. In 1998, the average income of the poorest fifth increased by only 2.4 percent, about the same amount that the top fifth increased. These changes are not as drastic as they have been in previous years, where increases in the upper quintile were much higher.

Defining Middle Class

American Demographics (www.demographics.com/Publications/AD) proposes three definitions of middle class: (1) those with incomes ranging around the national average ($25,000 to $50,000), (2) a broader group with incomes of $15,000 to $75,000, and (3) households with incomes between 75 percent and 125 percent of the median. Although the numbers that emerge from these three categories differ, they all point to a similar conclusion: The proportion of the population that is middle class is decreasing, but with a growing total population, the absolute number of middle-class households is increasing.

The following table shows changes in the number of U.S. households with incomes in the middle range of $25,000 to $75,000 throughout the last three decades. The size of the middle class, in relative terms, decreased from the 1970s into the 1980s but has since shown moderate decreases. The real dynamics seem to be in the two far right-hand columns. Here, we see the number of households increasing significantly during the same period and the proportion tripling. This suggests a growing number of people are stretching the definition of "middle class" by becoming wealthier. To balance that view, however, it is worth remembering that the number in the lower-income category (far left-hand column) increased by 8.1 million people just since 1994,

To deal with the first of these, the simple fact is that most of the best high-traffic locations are already occupied. What creates good locations are changes in the transportation system and changes in population concentrations. The building of new highways has slowed greatly compared to the time when the interstate highway system was under construction. As a result, fewer new locations are being created in this way.

In recent years, we have seen restaurant chains acquired by other restaurant chains principally in order to obtain their locations for expansion. One of the factors that led QSR chains to seek locations in malls some years ago was the very shortage of free-standing locations we are discussing.

A second reason for the growing scarcity of locations is environmental pressure. Location scarcity is especially severe in locations such as seashores or wetlands, which are often zoned to prevent building—especially commercial building—in scenic or environmentally sensitive locations. Environmental pressures do, however, go beyond scenic locations. Restaurants, particularly QSRs, are meeting more resistance because of the

while at the same time the proportion has decreased somewhat. Finally, the poverty rate in the United States did decline somewhat between 1997 and 1998, from 13.3 percent of the population to 12.7 percent.

The Middle Class is Changing[1]

INCOME YEAR	LESS THAN $25,000		$25,000 TO $74,999		$75,000 OR MORE	
	NO. (000,000)	%	NO. (000,000)	%	NO. (000,000)	%
1980	32.5	39.4	42.1	51.1	7.8	9.5
1985	34.4	38.9	43.9	49.6	10.2	11.5
1990	35.3	37.4	46.5	49.3	12.5	13.3
1992	37.2	35.9	50.3	48.5	16.3	15.7
1994	39.0	39.4	46.5	47.0	13.5	13.6
1996	35.0	34.6	48.2	47.7	17.9	17.7
1998	33.4	32.1	49.7	47.8	20.9	20.1
2000	31.3	29.4	49.9	46.9	25.3	23.8
2001	31.5	28.8	50.3	46.0	27.7	25.3
2002	32.6	29.3	50.9	45.7	27.9	25.1

1. Household income in constant 2000 dollars.
Source: U.S. Census Bureau, "Money Income in the United States," 2003.

As land and resources become scarcer, companies such as Checkers are making greater use of the space available. (Courtesy of Checkers Drive-In Restaurants, Inc.)

noise, traffic, odor, roadside litter, and crowding that can accompany such operations. Restaurants have been "zoned out" of many communities or parts of communities.

On balance, the greater pressure comes from the impact of present locations being occupied, but, for both reasons discussed previously, land in the form of good locations is a scarce commodity.

Food. Although the cost of food may vary from season to season, for the most part these variations affect all food service competitors in roughly the same way. Food service price changes would have to reflect any change in raw food cost. **Food supply** conditions do not suggest any major price changes in North America in the foreseeable future, although weather conditions or temporary shortages of certain foods can always drive up some prices in the short term. We should note, however, that major climatic changes, such as those that could be brought on by the greenhouse effect and the Earth's warming, do pose a longer-term threat to world food supplies.

LABOR

The Bureau of Labor Statistics (BLS) has developed a long-term forecast of the demand for labor extending over a ten-year period.[14] For the years 2000 through 2010, the forecast predicts a growth in the U.S. workforce of 15.2 percent overall. This represents a slight decrease (down from 17.1 percent) from the previous ten-year forecast (1990 to 2000). The same study predicts that the greatest growth will be in jobs requiring advanced education, which bodes well for new college and university graduates. Management jobs, across occupations, will grow by 12 percent over the period, a little less than the overall growth. People interested in careers in food service management, though, can take encouragement from the fact that demand for managers is expected to be about equal to the average for all occupations through 2014 (growth is expected to range from 9 percent to 17 percent). The BLS predicts that new management positions in lodging will grow by the same amount; new chef and head cook positions will increase within the same range as well.

Employment prospects appear to be about average (or a little less) for some of the primary hospitality management occupations. What makes that outlook somewhat more difficult, however, is the relatively high turnover in the industry, highlighted in Table 2.2. High turnover magnifies the demand for labor because it takes a relatively larger number of people to keep positions filled, as indicated in Table 2.3.

Cooking and food preparation jobs will increase—again, a little less than the overall average—by 12.3 percent. Food and beverage server positions, on the other hand, will grow by over 20 percent (22.7 percent). Gaming service workers represent another growth area.[15]

It is more difficult for us to make projections for the lodging workforce, because in the BLS categories, lodging workers are often merged into other, larger categories—as,

TABLE 2.2

Employee Turnover in Food Service

RESTAURANT TYPE	ALL EMPLOYEES	SALARIED EMPLOYEES	HOURLY EMPLOYEES
Full service			
Average check under $15	64%	33%	67%
Full service			
Average check $15 to $24.99	56%	33%	60%
Limited service			
Fast food	73%	50%	82%

Source: National Restaurant Association, "Restaurant Industry Operations Report," 2004.

for instance, with "baggage porters and bellhops," where bell staff are considered along with a number of other, somewhat similar jobs in transportation. Similarly, people working in housekeeping are included in the category of "janitors and cleaners, including maids and housekeeping cleaners."[16]

Two categories related to the travel industry are travel agents, slated to grow 3.2 percent (a direct result of changes taking place in the travel industry), and flight attendants, a group projected to increase by 18.4 percent.[17]

The growth that is expected to occur in these various segments of the hospitality industry means that there will be continued opportunities for hospitality graduates. However, this takes on a different meaning when one adopts a management perspective. Wherever you observe a growth figure higher than the average of 15 percent for the workforce as a whole, you may wonder how the industry will go about attracting more than its proportionate share of workforce growth to that category of worker. Of course, it is the managers who will have the job of finding people to fill these fast-growing needs. This is of particular concern during periods of low unemployment. Moreover, competitive industries, such as retailing and health care, are growing right along with the hospitality industry. For instance, retail sales positions will continue to grow at about the same rate as the total workforce, and health care support

TABLE 2.3

Top Seven Reasons for Industry Exit by Former Food Service Employees

1	More money
2	Better work schedule
3	More enjoyable work
4	Pursue current occupation
5	Advancement opportunity
6	Better employee benefits
7	To go to school

Source: Restaurants and Institutions, May 1, 1997, p. 108, based on the Industry of Choice study of the NRA Educational Foundation.

occupations (those that are most directly competitive with hourly hospitality jobs) will grow at over twice the average rate, at 33.4 percent.[18] As an industry, then, we can expect to face stiff competition for workers.

What means is the industry likely to use to fill these positions? Already in many markets, starting food service workers are receiving well above minimum wage. In some markets, employers are offering increased benefits, bonuses, transportation, and an assortment of offerings designed to encourage hourly employees to stay with their company.

Further, companies are target-marketing segments of potential employees such as seniors and other groups. Some operations, for instance, have held free breakfasts for seniors to get them interested in jobs. Marriott aggressively targets potential female employees. A Marriott representative stated that "One of the most difficult challenges in the 21st century is the scarcity of talent. . . . That makes female leadership a do or die business . . . you need to recruit and retain female talent as though your future depends on it—because it does."[19] Many other companies have also realized that it is prudent to take more of a marketing-oriented approach to attracting employees.

Another source of labor will be **immigrants**, both legal and illegal. The non-Hispanic white labor force will grow by 12 percent between 2000 and 2010, but the number of Hispanic workers will increase about three times as fast, at 36.3 percent. The number of Asian workers will grow 44.1 percent in the same period.[20]

Illegal immigration is like floodwater around a dike—always there and always seeking entry through any hole in the structure. Repeated crackdowns, like temporary repairs to a dike, stanch the flow for a time. However, as long as the employment outlook in the United States is better and wages several times higher than in Latin America, it is likely that immigrants will continue to be an important source of labor in certain parts of North America.

Finally, **part-time workers**, who have always played a major role in food service, will continue to be important. Interestingly, approximately one-half of all food service employees work part-time. This is a far higher percentage of the working population than in the workforce, overall, which is 20 percent.[21] The part-time labor pool is made of many people who have other claims on their time and need to supplement their income. This can make them an attractive source of labor.

Table 2.4 provides a visual description of the net impact that employment fluctuations can have on staffing requirements.

Workforce Diversity

The components of diversity include ethnic background and place of birth, education and skill level, income level, gender, age, differing abilities, and sexual orientation. Organizations have generally tolerated diversity and tried to regulate it. With growing

TABLE 2.4

Staffing Requirements–Chain Restaurants
Chain Restaurant Staffing Requirements

	NO. OF UNITS BEGINNING OF YEAR	UNITS ADDED	PERCENT CHANGE	NEW MANAGERS NEEDED[1]	HOURLY EMPLOYEES PROMOTED TO ASST. MANAGERS	DEPARTING TRAINEES	MAN-AGERS HIRED FROM OUTSIDE	EXISTING MANAGERS MOVED TO NEW UNITS[2]
Year 1	20	8	40%	60	20	8	48	20
Year 2	28	11	40	83	28	11	66	28
Year 3	39	16	40	119	39	16	96	39
Year 4	55	22	40	165	55	22	132	55
Year 5	77	31	40	233	77	31	187	77
Year 6	108	43	40	323	108	43	258	108

1. Assumes 1 general manager and 4 associate managers per unit, and assumes 20 percent annual turnover at existing units.
2. Assumes one per existing unit.
Source: Thomas Weisel Partners, San Francisco.

diversity, however, students of organizational dynamics call for an approach that goes beyond tolerating diversity to valuing it, seeing people for the contribution they can make rather than their surface differences. Increased organizational diversity necessarily benefits organizations by expanding its ability to meet the new challenges of the market.

Why is this important? Historically, the main component of the workforce has been the white male. Even with the increasing female workforce participation rate, in 1991 almost 50 percent of those entering the workforce were white males. African Americans in the labor force, however, are increasing nearly twice as fast as the white male workforce, and the Hispanic workforce is growing four times as fast. Because female employment is also growing faster than male employment, we can forecast a dramatic change in the type of people entering the workforce. Compared with 50 percent in the early 1990s, white males now account for less than 10 percent of new entrants to the workforce.[22] **Workforce diversity** has become a permanent fact of life in North America. Because a large part of the growth will occur among minorities, who historically have had lower incomes than average, an even larger component of workers will probably come from disadvantaged backgrounds with poorer educational preparation.

The Impact of Labor Scarcity

The evidence we have suggests it is food service that will experience the tightest pressure in the hospitality industry from trying to keep up with the demand for workers because of the projected growth for new jobs. It is important, however, to keep in mind that a significant number of U.S. hotels are full-service operations and so have a commitment to food service, with some of them—resorts, luxury operations, and convention hotels—having a very extensive commitment. Accordingly, the hotel industry will not escape unscathed by a shortage of labor.

Both segments face high levels of employee turnover and increasing competition from other industries. The interaction of those forces in good times, when competition

Labor shortages have made it even more critical for operators to retain qualified workers. (Courtesy of Mimi's Café.)

from other employers is sharp, almost certainly spells higher prices. Even in slower times, it suggests that hiring and retaining workers, especially in the skilled and supervisory categories, will be difficult. The food service and lodging industries have recognized the labor crisis for some time, however. In addition to raising wages, many operators have enhanced benefit programs and instituted support services such as generous family leave policies. On-the-job efforts to recognize supervisor performance and to provide career ladders for successful people are becoming a more conscious and purposive force. Attracting good people and keeping them once they are in place is simply cost-effective management of human resources.

Summary

Demand, ultimately, means customers. We looked at how one customer group, the baby boomers, has changed the hospitality industry. Our customers' average age is increasing as the boomers move into their middle years. We also looked at two other cohorts, the GenXers and the echo boomers. Family travel continues to create demand for child-friendly hospitality. The slow but steady growth in the over-65 population foreshadows the explosion in that age group in 2010, when boomers start to turn 65. We discussed four other demographic changes: diversity, working women, changing families, and changing incomes.

Working women are an established workforce fact. Seventy-five percent of women in their childbearing years work, and as many as 90 percent work sometime during the year. Two-income families mean more demand for food service and for travel but more pressure on time, making shorter vacations popular.

Families without children—empty nesters and those who chose not to have children—have higher disposable incomes and make up a fast-growing group. The growth in single-person households is partly the result of a later marriage age because of longer times spent in education. Another single-person household group is widows, as wives tend to outlive husbands.

In the changing income trends, we find the winners are college-educated people, affluent retirees, and women in full-time work. The number of middle-class households is increasing, but their proportion is declining as upper- and lower-income groups increase more rapidly.

The factors of production we considered are land and its produce and labor. Available locations are a category of land that is important to all segments of hospitality, as they continue to become scarcer. Environmental pressures add to the difficulty of finding new locations. Although food supply is expected to be adequate, short-term weather problems or a major change in the climate could lead to scarcity and higher-cost food.

The other factor of production we considered, labor, offers good news and bad news. There will be plenty of jobs for people who seek hospitality management careers—but they will face a difficult challenge of keeping the operation staffed. The industry's growth and high turnover continue to require a greater share of a slow-growing workforce. Moreover, there will be stiff competition from other industries for the workers we seek.

To fill the demand for workers, wages are rising at many hospitality firms, as are fringe benefits and bonuses. Sources of labor supply are being targeted, such as "restless retirees." Immigrants and part-timers will continue to be an important part of the hospitality workforce.

Key Words and Concepts

Demand	Single-person households
Demographics	Middle class
Baby boomers	Income distribution
Generation X	Activities, interests, opinions
Echo boomers	Psychographics
Generation Y	Environmental pressures
Diversity	Food supply
Two-income families	Immigrants
Family composition	Part-time workers
Empty nesters	Workforce diversity

Review Questions

1. How would you define demand? What critical changes in demand do you foresee in the future? Why?

2. Why are the baby boomers so important? What impact do you see them having on the hospitality industry in the next few years? In the longer-term future?

3. Besides the baby boomers, what other significant age groups were discussed in the chapter?

4. Trace the impact of the boomers on the hospitality industry. What impact do you think your age group will have on food service? On lodging?

5. What are the main elements of diversity discussed in this chapter? What are the major trends related to diversity? What are their likely effects?

6. Discuss the growth in the proportion of women working. What changes have working women caused as they relate to the hospitality industry? What does the future appear to hold regarding women in the workforce?

7. What is the largest household type? What are some rapidly growing household types? What kind of customer for hospitality is each of these groups?

8. Is the middle class shrinking? Which income groups are growing in absolute numbers? In proportionate share of population?

9. What categories of land as a factor of production are important to the hospitality industry? What is likely to affect the cost and availability of those factors?

10. The food service workforce is expected to grow at about the pace of the total workforce. In spite of this, what factors make the need for food service workers problematic? How does this affect the hotel business? What are some sources of supply that can be tapped?

Internet Exercises

1. **Site name:** Look Smart–Find Articles (American Demographics)
   URL: findarticles.com/p/articles/mi_m4021
   Background information: FindArticles has articles from thousands of resources, with archives dating back to 1984. This search engine allows you to search for exactly what you need, from millions of articles not found on any other search engine.
   Site name: Ethnic Majority
   URL: www.ethnicmajority.com/demographics_home.htm
   Background information: While race relations in the U.S. have continued to improve since the Civil Rights movement of the 1960s, we are still a long way from being a "color-blind" society. EthnicMajority.com was launched in 2002 to educate, assist, and empower African, Hispanic, and Asian Americans to achieve advancement in politics, business, at work, and society in general.
   Site name: About.com
   URL: marketing.about.com/od/demographics/a/generationmktg.htm
   Background information: Provides information on a wide variety of topics and includes links to other resources.
   Exercises:
   a. Identify the generation in which you belong (Baby boomer, Generation X, Generation Y, Millennials). Research the characteristics of your generation using the Web sites listed here or through a Google search. If you were to start your

own restaurant, how would you market your restaurant to others in your generational group? What types of foods would you have on the menu that would appeal to your generational group?

b. Using the Web sites listed here and/or a Google search, identify the differences among the following generational groups: Baby boomers, Generation X, Generation Y, and Millennials. What techniques would you use to market to each generational group?

c. Using a Google search on "managing different generations," identify the different managerial styles needed to manage the workers from different generational groups (Baby boomers, Generation X, Generation Y, and Millennials). What motivates each group and how do they differ?

2. **Site name:** U.S. Department of Labor, Bureau of Labor Statistics

   URL: www.bls.gov

   Background information: The Bureau of Labor Statistics (BLS) is the principal fact-finding agency for the federal government in the broad field of labor economics and statistics.

   Exercises:

   a. Describe the information that can be obtained from the BLS Web site and how this information could be helpful to a hospitality management student.

   b. Under "Wages, Earnings, & Benefits," determine the average annual salary for both Food Service Managers and Lodging Managers. How does the state you live in compare to the national average for these occupations?

   c. Click on the "Occupational Outlook Handbook" link. Search for either lodging managers or food service managers. Describe the information that is available from BLS regarding these two occupations. What is the employment outlook for these two occupations?

3. **Site name:** Site name: U.S. Census Bureau

   URL: www.census.gov

   Background information: The U.S. Census Bureau is the federal government's leading source of data about the United States' people and its economy.

   Exercises: Search the latest "Data Profiles–ACS" for a state/region/city selected by the instructor or choose your own. Scan both the "Tabular Profile" and "Narrative Profile" for the state/region/city that was selected.

   a. Describe the type of demographic data that is available from the U.S. Census Bureau for the state/region/city you selected.

   b. How diverse is the geographical area you selected in terms of ethnic makeup? Which ethnic groups are the largest and which are the smallest?

  c. What is the mean household income for the area selected?

  d. What percentage of the population has an associate degree or higher?

  e. What percentage of the population works in the leisure and hospitality industry? How does it compare with other occupations in the same area?

  f. Discuss why you think demographic data might be useful to a manager in the hospitality industry.

Notes

1. Pamela Paul, "Meet the Parents," *American Demographics*, vol. 24, Issue , 2002, pp. 42–47.

2. U.S. Census Bureau, "Projections of the Population by Age, Sex, Race and Hispanic Origin: 1999–2100" (January 23, 2006).

3. Consumer Expenditure survey, 2003 (U.S. Bureau of Labor Statistics).

4. "The New Consumer Paradigm," *American Demographics*, April 1999 (www.american-demographics.com), p. 11.

5. Teenage Research Unlimited (www.teenresearch.com/Preview), July 11, 2002.

6. U.S. Census Bureau, "Projections of the Resident Population by Age, Sex, Race and Hispanic Origin: 2000–2050" (January 22, 2006).

7. Joan Raymond, "The Multicultural Report," *American Demographics*, November, 2001, pp. S3–S6.

8. Ibid.

9. U.S. Census Bureau, "Income in the United States, 2002" (January 22, 2006).

10. U.S. Census Bureau, "Women in the Labor Force, 2004" (January 25, 2006).

11. U.S. Census Bureau, "America's Families and Living Arrangements, 2002." (January 25, 2006).

12. *American Demographics*, "U.S. Households, 1980–2010" (www.americandemographics.com), July 12, 2002.

13. For a fuller discussion of the importance of locations in the hospitality industry, see Cathy Hsu and Tom Powers, *Marketing Hospitality,* 3rd ed. (New York: John Wiley & Sons, 2001), especially Chapter 10.

14. Daniel Hecker, "Occupational Employment Projections to 2010," *Bureau of Labor Statistics Monthly Labor Review,* November 2001.

15. Ibid.

16. Ibid.

17. Ibid.

18. Ibid.

19. Robyn Taylor Parets, "Woman Talk," *Lodging News,* May 2001.

20. "Civilian Labor Force by Sex, Age, Race, and Hispanic Origin1990, 2000, and Projected 2010," Bureau of Labor Statistics, July 18, 2002 (www.bls.gov/news.release/ecopro.t05.htm).

21. "Employed and Unemployed Full- and Part-Time Workers by Age, Sex, and Race," Bureau of Labor Statistics, July 19, 2002 (www.bls.gov/cps/cpsaat8.pdf).

22. "Employment Projections," Bureau of Labor Statistics, July 19, 2002 (www.bls.gov/emp/home.htm).

PART TWO

Food Service

The Hospitality Industry

(Courtesy of Four Seasons Hotel, London.)

CHAPTER THREE

The Restaurant Business

The Purpose of this Chapter

This chapter first presents an overview of the restaurant business. It then focuses on two basic markets served by restaurants: the dining market and the eating market. Under dining, we are primarily concerned with the "casualization" of fine dining and the growth of the casual and up-scale casual food service segments.

A still growing part of the eating market is in off-premise operations, such as home meal replacement (HMR). We will also look at the contemporary popular-priced restaurants that are the largest segments of the existing restaurant industry: quick-service and midscale operations such as family restaurants. This discussion of the major components of the restaurant industry closes with a look at restaurants in retail settings such as malls.

THIS CHAPTER SHOULD HELP YOU

1. List by size the major components of the food service industry, and describe the economic impact that the food service industry has on the economy.
2. Define the terms *dining market* and *eating market*, and describe and contrast the major kinds of restaurant operations in each.
3. Identify the food service segments that are currently growing or declining, and explain the reasons for these trends.
4. Name three principal categories of casual restaurants, and describe their special characteristics and appeals.
5. Describe the relationship that exists between shopping and dining and how healthy this particular segment is.

The Varied Field of Food Service

The word restaurant covers a broad range of food service operations. The term comes from the French word restaurant, meaning "restorer of energy." The term was used as early as the mid-1700s to describe public places that offered soup and bread. Today, any public place that specializes in the sale of prepared food for consumption on- or off-premise can be described as a restaurant. Food service is generally used to represent the broader term, which encompasses all sorts of public and private locations that provide food for sale.

Food service is a basic part of the North American way of life and a growing part of life in other parts of the world. Americans are expected to spend 53 percent of their food budget (or **food dollar**) on **food away from home** by 2010 (they currently spend just less than 50 percent).[1] Most of that amount was spent in commercial restaurants, as described above. Virtually everyone in North America has eaten in a restaurant, and on average, roughly half the population eats in a restaurant at least once in any given month. In fact, in a survey conducted by *Restaurants & Institutions* magazine, it was found that 98 percent of households surveyed ate out in the prior month.[2]

Food service plays an important role in all environments including tourism destinations. (Courtesy of LEGOLAND® CALIFORNIA.)

Food away from home may be purchased in a variety of locations. This speaks to the size and scope of the food service industry that includes employee cafeterias, convenience stores, traditional restaurants, hotel facilities, casinos, and taverns, among others. Most of these segments are experiencing positive growth—a trend that has been sustained for over a decade (the industry even experienced positive growth in 2001, a year that brought a whole host of challenges). In 2006, **full-service restaurants** increased by 5.2 percent and **quick-service restaurants** by almost 5 percent.[3] In fact, all major commercial segments experienced positive growth.

The other major food service sector, on-site food service (sometimes referred to as institutional or noncommercial food service), represents a smaller but equally important part of the greater food service industry. (Chapter 7 discusses the on-site sector of the industry in depth.) This part of the industry is composed of contractors and caterers (who serve food in places such as manufacturing plants and office buildings, health care facilities, and schools and colleges) and those institutions that own and operate their own food service (self-ops). Managed services (the contract side) account for 6.5 percent of total food service industry sales, while those that provide their own generate 8.2 percent of sales. An additional 3.6 percent of sales are made through vending machines. Approximately 14 percent of food-away-from-home expenditures are accounted for by the on-site market. These estimates are summarized in Table 3.1.

TABLE 3.1

The Major Areas of Food Service, 2006

FOOD AND DRINK SALES (2006)[a]

	SALES ($ BILLIONS)	PERCENTAGE OF TOTAL
Eating places	345.2	67.6
Bars and taverns	15.7	3.1
Food service in lodging	25.0	4.9
Managed services	34.0	6.7
Other commercial	47.7	9.3
Institutions operating own food service	41.6	8.1
Military	1.8	0.3
TOTAL	511.0	100.0

[a]Dollar amounts and percentages shown are based on estimates for 2006 made by the National Restaurant Association.
Source: National Restaurant Association, *2006 Restaurant Industry Forecast,* December 2006, p. 10.

The relative shares of the market held by the segments identified in Table 3.1 tend to be rather stable from year to year. Such seeming stability, however, hides important evolutionary processes that are going on within each category. In fact, the industry is in the throes of change.

Although food service sales overall grew 5.1 percent between 2005 and 2006, some areas have actually decreased. Within the employee restaurant services segment (employee cafeterias and dining rooms) there was a significant decrease (mostly a result of businesses outsourcing their food service to managed-services companies) as well as decreases in self-operated secondary schools and colleges and universities food service operations.

For some years, the biggest growth in food service has been in operations such as **takeout**, **drive-through**, and **delivery**, which we will call collectively **off-premise** sales. In fact, off-premise food service has accounted for the lion's share of the growth in total restaurant sales since the late 1980s. Even though on-premise (i.e., in-restaurant) sales have increased each year since 1992, off-premise sales have done even better in recent years. Off-premise options are no longer limited to quick-service restaurants (QSR), either. One of the growth areas is in full-service restaurants with higher-than-average check averages, although fast food and pizza still command a large share of this market. (The average check represents the amount that the "average" customer spends and is calculated by dividing the total food and beverage sales for the period by the total number of customers for the period). Bennigan's, a **casual dining** chain, has recently added separate entrances (and service systems) for their takeout customers. The trend in many segments of the restaurant industry is toward a higher proportion of takeout, delivery, and drive-through.

During the 1960s and 1970s, quick service altered dramatically the meaning of what a restaurant was. The trend toward off-premise consumption suggests that another fundamental change in the business definition of restaurants may be evolving.

Another set of changes involves **fine dining**, for years the mainstay of the upscale restaurant segment. By and large, fine dining, with its trappings of formality, has been declining in relative importance, whereas casual dining has been growing very rapidly. To some degree, fine dining's decline appears to be a result of consumers' apparent interest in value in food service and a sensitivity to the relatively high prices fine dining must charge. Today's consumers also are more predisposed to a casual dining experience. Food tastes are changing as well. All of these changes have resulted in a change in the way that the fine dining experience is perceived. Some suggest that the decline is just part of a cycle, though, and that fine dining will someday achieve its previous stature.

Many of the changes in food service result from changes in the age composition of North America's population, as discussed in earlier chapters. Members of the huge generation born in the 20 years following World War II, the baby boomers, have entered middle age. As they do so, their lifestyles have changed. They were raised with fast food and prefer an informal ambience. Now, as parents, they find a casual atmosphere more comfortable for the whole family. More will be said about the importance of casual dining later in the chapter.

Quick-service restaurant (QSR) sales continue to rise also, by 2.3 percent in 2006 over 2005. Furthermore, as we noted, sales in casual-dining restaurants are rising rapidly, too. Finally, we should note that on-site sales have also shown healthy growth, with contractors and caterers (private companies providing food service to institutions) continuing to capture market share from self-operated units even in segments that have traditionally been self-operated, such as public schools.

THE OUTLOOK FOR FOOD SERVICE

One authoritative study suggested that "by the year 2005, many Americans will have never cooked a meal from basic ingredients."[4] Now that we can view this statement from a historical perspecive, we can determine that it was made with a great deal of accuracy. Considering the trends, this statement has proven to be very true. People are apparently less willing to spend the time to cook their own food, which suggests growing business for those of us in the business of providing food to people away from home.

Gains in restaurant traffic are outpacing population gains by a significant factor. Customers are also generally pleased with the value they receive at restaurants. According to the National Restaurant Association, 81 percent of customers of moderately priced full-service restaurants indicated that their expectations regarding value were met or exceeded, while seventy-five percent of quick-service restaurant customers said that their expectations were met or exceeded.[5]

Finally, the study cited earlier concludes that changes in demographics and lifestyles will combine to produce "the greatest decade of growth the food service industry has ever known."[6]

The Restaurant Business

Describing the restaurant business is like trying to hit a moving target: The restaurant market is constantly changing. One could go so far as to say that it is constantly reinventing itself. There are so many types of restaurants that it is difficult to devise a model to fit them all. Nevertheless, we need some basic terminology to describe the field, even if in general terms.

More customers are looking for restaurants that offer comfort and value. (Courtesy of Mimi's Café.)

First, we need to consider the basic distinction between the dining market and the eating market. We will look at dining operations such as fine dining and casual dining restaurants, and at the other extreme, we will discuss the rapidly growing off-premise operations, such as takeout and delivery (much of which is now being referred to as **home meal replacement**), that are accounting for major growth in the eating market. In the next major section of this chapter, we will consider contemporary popular-priced restaurants that represent the largest segments of the restaurant business today. These include the quick-service restaurants and midscale operations such as **family restaurants**. The chapter will conclude with a consideration of restaurants as part of larger establishments.

The Dining Market and the Eating Market

One of the twentieth century's most innovative restaurateurs, Joe Baum (former president of Restaurant Associates), suggested that a primary role of a restaurant is to transform the act of eating into something greater and more civilized. This is one of the great challenges of the restaurant operator today.

Building upon this, we can say that restaurants serve both our social needs and our biological needs. We can divide restaurants into those serving predominantly our social needs (the **dining market**) and those serving our biological needs (the **eating market**). Nearly all meals eaten in the company of others have a social dimension, just as the most formal state dinner has its biological aspect. The main purpose, however, is usually clear.

DINING WELL

People dine out for a variety of reasons, including to escape from boredom, to socialize, to avoid drudgery, to be waited on, to have foods different from those served at home, and for convenience.

Because dining (as opposed to eating) is predominantly a social event, service is important. Servers are expected to be friendly, as signified by a warm smile, and accurate. The role of the server is, therefore, much more than a mechanical one. In the relatively expensive restaurants serving the dining market, the operation that falls short on service is likely to lose customers quickly. (Service is discussed in more detail in the final chapter of the book.)

The demographics of such customers, as always, are important. The guest who dines in a fine restaurant usually is older, is more highly educated, has a higher-than-average income, and is well accustomed to dining out and traveling. We will now try to break the dining market into further subsegments.

Fine-Dining Restaurants. Most full-service, fine-dining establishments are small, independent operations, some seating fewer than 100 guests, which is quite small by today's standards. Despite their modest capacities, these restaurants succeed (or don't) because of their quality. Many are staffed by trained professional chefs who have brought with them a craft tradition that dates back to the Middle Ages.

Excellence is the absolute prerequisite in fine dining because the prices charged are necessarily high. An operator may do everything possible to make the restaurant efficient, but the guests still expect careful, personal service: food prepared to order by highly skilled chefs and delivered by expert servers. Because this service is, quite literally, manual labor, only marginal improvements in productivity are possible. For example, a cook, server, or bartender can move only so much faster before she or he reaches the limits of human performance. Thus, only moderate savings are possible through improved efficiency, which makes an escalation of prices inevitable. (It is an axiom of economics that as prices rise, consumers become more discriminating.) Thus, the clientele of the fine-dining restaurant expects, demands, and is willing to pay for excellence.

These distinguished operations generally require the right combination of three elements: a large market, skilled workers, and devoted management. First, because of the high prices they must charge, most are located in or near large population centers

Fine dining offers the experience of luxury and enhances the importance of special occasions. (City Club of San Francisco; Courtesy of ClubCorp.)

or in major tourism areas where there is a sufficiently large number of people with high incomes to ensure a satisfactory sales volume. Fine dining accounts for only about 2 percent of total food service sales each year, but the majority of its customers are repeat customers. Getting and keeping customers is critical in most segments but is particularly important in fine dining.

A second requirement of these restaurants is having qualified personnel: chefs, servers, and the like with highly polished skills. It was, for a time, difficult to find this kind of staff, but the growth in culinary education and training programs has reduced the shortage somewhat. People with these skills are most likely to be found in large metropolitan areas, although there are some obvious exceptions to this generalization.

A third and most important requirement for successful fine-dining restaurants is a special devotion from the key operating personnel, especially the owners and/or managers. The hours tend to be long, and the owners, although they may be amply compensated, generally devote their lives to their work.

As we have already noted, fine-dining sales have been falling for the last two decades due to a growing preference for all things casual. According to a study by *Restaurants & Institutions* magazine, 40 percent of respondents reported that they had dined less in fine dining restaurants than in the previous year.[7] Although some part of this decline may be due to price sensitivity, the recession, and health concerns about rich foods, there seems to have been a basic shift in consumer service preferences as well. Older patrons have been accustomed to the kind of service rituals that characterize these operations. As younger customers advance in income and age to the point where they might be customers for fine dining, they may be put off by overly formal dining. In many instances, they prefer an upscale experience that is more casual. While fine dining has declined in popularity in recent years, it is certainly here to stay: Consumers are simply viewing the fine dining experience in a slightly different light. For a large segment of the population, casual upscale dining offers an attractive alternative.

Casual Upscale Dining. The question that arises, then, is what has taken the place of the fine-dining segment? One of the fastest-growing segments of food service is what is referred to as "casual dining." Casual dining appeals to consumers on many levels. In fact, the casual segment can be further segmented by price and service level. Casual upscale dining represents those restaurants that are at the top end of the casual segment. They may even be referred to as "casual fine dining." Some examples, on a national level, include Houston's, which has a very devoted clientele, Mimi's Café, the Cheesecake Factory, P. F. Chang's, and the Chart House (recently purchased by Landry's). Casual upscale dining, in particular, seems to have filled part of the void left by fine dining.

The movement of the baby boomers into their peak earning years partially explains the growth of casual upscale dining. As consumers age and more restaurant options are available to them, taste preferences become more sophisticated. Excellence in food is one of the appeals of these restaurants. The menus in casual upscale dining restaurants, and in casual dining in general, have become increasingly sophisticated and interesting in recent years. Another is the topflight service that is offered by many such restaurants. Although meals here are less time-consuming and elaborate than in more formal and higher-priced restaurants, successful casual upscale restaurants deliver professional and attentive service at a significantly lower price than in fine-dining restaurants.

Most casual upscale restaurants have a unifying theme that is pervasive in the design of their menu, interior decor, and often the exterior of the building. Menu specialties are increasingly highly varied and wine lists are ample. Part of the reason for

Houston's, a leading casual upscale dining chain, pays great attention to detail in the decor of their restaurants. (Courtesy of Houston's Restaurants.)

the more significant role that this segment is playing is due to the increasing role played by the large chain operators. Multiple-concept chains such as The Hillstone Restaurant Group (formerly Houston's) play a critical role in defining the casual-dining landscape. The Hillstone Restaurant Group operates several concepts in addition to their flagship brand, including Bandera, Gulfstream, Cherry Creek Grill, Rutherford Grill, Palm Beach Grill, Los Altos Grill, and Café R&D.

Concepts for a new chain operation (whether casual upscale or otherwise) are developed through extensive market research, tested in one or more pilot operations, and, once proven, rolled out to the regional or national market. Sometimes, rather than developing a concept themselves, multiple-concept chains purchase a promising independent operation, fine-tune the concept for a wider market, and then roll it out to regional and national markets. Either of these strategies can prove to be a risky proposition—most successful operators have a respectable portfolio of brands that have failed or that did not meet sales expectations and were discontinued.

In contrast to the QSR and midpriced segments with their breakfast/lunch focus, casual upscale restaurants cater to a higher-check-average clientele for the lunch and dinner day parts. Naturally, this results in a higher dollar amount of sales. Some, such as Outback Steakhouse, go so far as to limit their operations to a single meal period (dinner). Casual upscale unit sales are also helped by the addition of alcoholic beverages, which usually add greater profit potential.

Noting the success of the casual upscale segment, many fine-dining operators have made changes. Because of the competitive market, many fine-dining restaurants have made the decision to move to meet the market demand for a more relaxed atmosphere and more reasonable prices. Other operators made the decision to balance their fine-dining outlet with a more casual option for their customers—Emeril Lagasse in New Orleans with his namesake restaurant, Emeril's, and the more casual NOLA is one example. (Lagasse also operates a second fine-dining restaurant, Delmonico, in the same city.)

Some operators closed their fine-dining outlets outright. Kevin Taylor, the operator of the Zenith American Grill in Denver, closed a very successful four-diamond restaurant and opened more casual restaurants, including jou jou and Nicois.

THE EATING MARKET AND ITS DYNAMICS

The eating market consists of those segments that cater primarily to the biological needs as opposed to primarily social needs. Quick-service restaurants, which we will look at in more detail in a moment, constitute a sizable segment of the eating market—one that is patronized by nearly every household. A survey by *Restaurants & Institutions* magazine revealed some interesting insights into dining-out behavior. Forty-four percent of respondents reported eating in a quick-service restaurant at least once a week. This compared with 35 percent of respondents who reported eating out at least once a week in casual-dining outlets. Two-thirds of households patronize quick-service restaurants frequently; that is, some member of those households buys fast food three or four times a week.[8] In other words, these quick-service and midscale restaurant customers are the heart of the eating markets. The quick-service sector, as we noted earlier, is continuing its growth at a compound annual rate of 5 percent from 2005 to 2006. Off-premise dining is another segment of the restaurant business that continues to grow.

As discussed earlier, the three main components of off-premise dining are takeout, drive-through, and delivery. Home meal replacement, still a relatively new term, can include any or all of these components. HMR (or the even more current term "meal solutions") is usually meant to encompass a good portion of this market, specifically those prepared food products that are purchased away from the home but consumed at home. Each of these has maintained roughly the same share of off-premise sales for some years. Together they account for over 50 percent of the entire food service market. The largest part of off-premise sales is takeout, with nearly two-thirds of the traffic (visits) and volume. Drive-through is the second most frequent. Either way one views it, off-premise dining represents an important part of food service industry sales. While it all began with fast food, it has spread across other segments to the point where there are now establishments designed strictly for customers to pick up fully prepared food to be brought home. Such examples include Foodies Kitchen (New Orleans), Tasteez (Denver), and Eatzi's (Texas). Such operations are best described as a hybrid of restaurant and upscale supermarket. Each of the three primary areas identified above are discussed in turn.

Takeout. Takeout is an old, established part of food service, but its continued growth has increased its prominence. Consumers have indicated their interest in takeout with their growing patronage. Not surprisingly, operators have responded to this consumer interest. Nearly all quick-service operations offer take-out meals, and quick-service operations account for the lion's share of takeout sales. The vast majority of midscale table service restaurants also offer takeout, as do many upscale operations (which is only increasing). Thus, increased sales of takeout food are fueled not only by consumer preference but by the wide availability of takeout food service. *Restaurants & Institutions* magazine reports that restaurants such as Golden Corral and Piccadilly Cafeterias represent a new breed of restaurants that are trying to capture a piece of the growing takeout business.[9] Both companies have found that they were able to operationalize the process and that it represents a significant part of their overall business.

Drive-Through. Initially, drive-through service was introduced as a part of an existing quick-service restaurant, and that is still an important use of the drive-through. Since its introduction, though, it has become an integral part of the QSR service strategy. Further, it should be mentioned, that it is no longer limited to the burger chains but has also been adopted by such chains as Starbucks and is also being tested by 7-Eleven.

The drive-through came into its own, however, with the introduction of the double drive-through. These operations enjoyed the advantage of low capital costs because of the small building and relatively small size lot on which they could be fitted. Highly simplified menus gave them an operating cost advantage, too, and fast delivery times appealed to many customers.

It quickly became apparent to QSR operators that the double drive-through was a serious competitive threat, and the competitive response was not long in coming. Existing QSRs improved their drive-through facilities and used their powerful brands in a promotional push. Many QSRs that lacked drive-through facilities added them. In the shakeout that followed, a number of double drive-through chains, which had been growing rapidly, went out of business. Some survived, but these now serve a specialty niche, and the dominant force in the drive-through market is the branded QSRs, such as McDonald's and Burger King. Certain companies, such as Checkers and Rally's, are defined by the double drive-through concept.

Delivery. Delivery is a slightly different segment of the industry. Delivery operations do not fit well in the same unit with table service operations for a variety of reasons. Not only does demand peak just when the dining room is busiest (as is also true with takeout), but the parking lot is jammed with customers' cars just when delivery vehicle traffic in and out is at its peak. Moreover, the skills of the service staff are different. A person who is very effective as a server in face-to-face service will not automatically

Checkers is a major company in the drive-through segment. (Courtesy of © Checkers Drive-In Restaurants, Inc.)

be effective in the telephone contact that is the typical start of a delivery transaction, at least not without specific training and an operating system designed to handle delivery. For these reasons, many companies have found it best to limit delivery operations to separate delivery units. This can result in cost advantages, too, in that they can be located on less expensive real estate.

For the reasons identified above, many of the chains that offer delivery specialize in it. In this way, their entire operation may be based upon this single premise. For instance, many delivery chains use a single telephone number for all units. At the central answering facility, employees take calls at computer terminals. When a customer places an order, the operator asks for his or her phone number and address. Using this information, the order is passed to the nearest unit for dispatch. At the same time, the customer's name and order go into the computerized guest history system. Then on subsequent calls, the operator is able to bring up the customer's record using his or her phone number. Thus, when John Doe calls, the operator can say, "Good to hear from you again, Mr. Doe. Would you like to have your usual pepperoni and mushroom? Shall we deliver it to the side door again?" The single-number system is spreading and is being used not only for pizza but also for a wide variety of other food service delivery products.

Contemporary Popular-Priced Restaurants

We have already discussed casual upscale restaurants and off-premise dining. In this section, we will discuss the on-premise business of the two largest segments of today's popular-priced restaurant business: QSR and midscale operations (such as family restaurants and commercial cafeterias).

To compare two of the more traditional restaurant formats (full-service and quick-service operations), quick-service restaurants account for slightly less than half of all restaurant sales (compared to 28 percent in 1970) and nearly three-quarters of customer traffic. Full-service restaurants, including both midscale and upscale, with a much lower share of traffic still achieve just over one-half of restaurant dollar sales because of their higher check average.

The QSR segment has experienced healthy growth, but the results for full-service operations have shown wide variation—generally lagging behind the QSR segment in the early 1990s and exceeding their growth in the latter part of the decade. The two segments cannot escape comparison, since one's loss is often the other's gain and vice versa.

In Figure 3.1, the various types of restaurants are compared in terms of their price level and the meal experience that is provided. The meal experience includes the services and amenities provided, as well as such factors as the time available, the importance of convenience (as in location), the degree to which the meal is utilitarian (i.e., a biological event), and the degree to which it is tied to other activities. Utilitarian meals (a hurried lunch during the working day) where convenience and speed are essential would be at one end of the dining experience scale. A special occasion, perhaps a wedding anniversary celebration, where a couple might drive 50 miles to visit a unique restaurant and spend two or three hours dining, would be at the other end.

The full-service segment includes an important subsegment: midscale restaurants. These operations have somewhat higher prices (about $7.00 to $10.00, compared to $5.00 to $7.00 for QSRs).

With this overview in mind, let us now turn our attention to a more detailed consideration of the basic restaurant groups identified.

QUICK-SERVICE RESTAURANTS

One managerial concern that helps to distinguish between the various segments is their individual levels of productivity. Table 3.2 reflects productivity levels across several food service segments. An understanding of productivity is important from a management

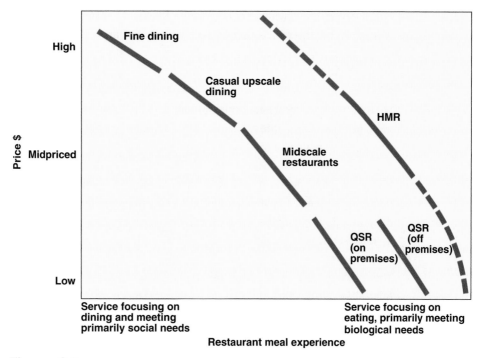

High

Fine dining

Casual upscale
dining

HMR

Price $

Midpriced

Midscale
restaurants

QSR
(on
premises)

QSR
(off
premises)

Low

Service focusing on
dining and meeting
primarily social needs

Service focusing on
eating, primarily meeting
biological needs

Restaurant meal experience

Figure 3.1

Factors bearing on meal experience include time available, importance of convenience, utilitarian as opposed to social event, and degree of subordination to other activities.

perspective. For instance, note that QSR operations lead the way in productivity—such operations tend to simplify their production processes and use self-service. The result is a drastic reduction in labor in both the front and back of the house. Because QSRs require less labor, they can pass on their savings to the customer in the form of lower prices. Furthermore, these operations, even with their lower prices, have historically earned profits substantially higher than those of other operations.

The Quick-Service Concept. Some people do not realize how long quick-service (formerly fast food) has been with us—quick-service restaurants are the product of a long evolution dating back to the 1940s (for instance,

TABLE 3.2

Productivity in Food Service Establishments

FOOD SERVICE TYPE	DIRECT LABOR HOURS PER 100 GUESTS
Quick-Service	10.5
Cafeterias	18.3
Family restaurants	20.7
Luxury restaurants	72.3

Carl Karcher began with a hot dog cart in 1941 and In-N-Out, a California institution, began in 1948). Other companies also got their start around this same time. Despite the array of quick-service choices, any discussion of fast food must begin and end with McDonald's. McDonald's began as a drive-in, selling inexpensive hamburgers, french fries, and milk shakes to be consumed in the car or taken away. The original menu was very limited. It is still very fresh in one author's mind the day that McDonald's decided to expand its menu to include apple pie. The company has obviously made other, and more significant, changes in the last 25 years.

From a small production unit, McDonald's expanded the food pickup area in the front of the store slightly to provide a limited amount of seating. This worked well enough that a larger seating area was added to one side—and then to both sides—of the production unit. These units were still originally quite simple, with plain white walls for ease in housekeeping. The early units had a utilitarian air about them. Gradually, however, decoration was added to the seating area, very simply at first and then more extensively. Today, McDonald's restaurants are generally attractively decorated, and some units are quite elaborate. In 2002, McDonald's announced that it would reinvest a significant amount of capital into its older restaurants, focusing on physical improvements and, in some cases, total remodeling. McDonald's is but one example of some well-established quick-service companies that are undergoing remodeling/renovation plans to their restaurants. Other companies following a similar strategy include Burger King, Sonic, and Taco Bell.

The decor and physical plant were certainly not the only things that evolved. The early, very simple menu was gradually expanded. To attract people who wanted something other than a variety of hamburgers, chicken and fish were added. To attract an increasingly health-conscious public, salad and decaffeinated coffee were added. To meet demand for service earlier in the day, breakfast was added. Although the menu still remains quite simple, the hamburger-only menu of the early days has been replaced by much wider variety.

McDonald's has periodically faced difficult internal and external challenges, including crowded markets, well-heeled competitors set on taking away its customers, and disgruntled franchisees. For a short time, their stock prices suffered as a result of these challenges, there was a change of CEOs, and the company closed some restaurant locations. They have since refocused, upgraded some restaurants, and slowed their growth rates. They began to turn things around in 2003 and 2004, which was evidenced by an increase in same-store sales, a measure of performance. Now with over $50 billion in annual worldwide sales, McDonald's is the best-selling food service brand in the world, with over three times the sales of the next largest brand.[10] We can, therefore, safely proclaim the original concept and subsequent evolution of McDonald's to be a resounding success.

This evolution of the QSR concept at McDonald's was matched in a general way by other quick-service giants. Over time, quick-service menus came to offer a wider selection, until they were offering enough choice to make them a serious threat to family restaurants because of their lower prices.

The key to the success of quick service, nevertheless, is its simplicity. A key simplification remains quick service's limited menu. Each item on the menu has been engineered to simplify and standardize its purchasing, production, and service. Simplification of the production process permits the use of unskilled labor. The quick-service operation is, in many ways, more like a manufacturing enterprise than a traditional restaurant. Even a cursory tour of the back of the house of any quick-service restaurant will support this statement.

Unique Characteristics. The presence of quick-service operations in every market of any size is a key characteristic of quick service and one of the main factors supporting its growth over the past 50 years. Because of their many locations, they make eating out convenient. That convenience reinforces patronage. Further, quick-service food seems to cut effectively across a variety of demographic groups. It has truly become an integral part of living in North America and, increasingly, in other parts of the world.

We have already noted that simplified menus and operations that use unskilled labor result in a price that is very attractive to the consumer. This simple operating format results in fast service and has earned quick service its name. Self-service is built into the operating format, reinforcing both speed of service and lower cost, especially in the absence of any tipping.

The quick-service segment is dominated by chains, which introduces an interesting note of complexity into what appears to be a fairly simple operation. Although the operation of any single QSR unit is relatively straightforward compared with other, more service-intensive restaurants, the operation of the restaurant chain as a whole—that is, as a system of interactive parts—is highly complex. With over 30,000 systemwide restaurants (over one-half are outside of the United States), McDonald's requires a huge management structure to make all the parts of the system function together in a consistent fashion that the consumer can depend on.

An interesting illustration of this complexity can be found in the area of purchasing. When the corner restaurant adds baked potatoes or chicken to the menu, the whole process can be accomplished by instructing the cook, ordering the necessary ingredients, and changing the day's menu. In a complex system, however, much more is involved. When Wendy's first added baked potatoes to its menu, for instance, the entire U.S. potato market was disrupted by the huge increase in demand. Similarly, when Burger King introduced the bacon cheeseburger, those three strips of bacon (multiplied by millions of customers) so increased the demand for bacon that it disrupted the national commodities market in hog bellies.

Although we have asserted that a fast-food unit is a relatively simple operation, it is not true that managing one is in any way a simple task. Managing the very tight quality and cost controls on which QSR operations depend is, indeed, demanding. Very high sales volumes and extreme peaks and valleys of demand throughout the day require managers to hire numerous part-time employees whose schedules vary from day to day and week to week. Keeping this crew properly trained and motivated is a major task, particularly in this age of low unemployment. Given the costs associated with turnover, such as lost training time as well as the management time required to hire and train new employees, maintaining staff morale is also a major factor in controlling payroll costs. That means real leadership skills are needed.

Quick service, as you will have noticed, is dominated by chain organizations (many of which are franchises). This is probably true because there are real economies of scale available to operations that are—within a given chain—virtually clones of one another. These economies are achieved not only in purchasing raw product but also in advertising and marketing and in the development of operating skills. A person new to the business must necessarily follow a learning curve in which he or she begins with ignorance of food service and only gradually develops sufficient know-how to operate successfully. The concept of the learning curve is simply that over time, with acquisition of knowledge and experience, a person develops greater abilities. A management trainee or franchisee of a successful chain can use the systems developed by the organization to begin well ahead on the management learning curve and to move more quickly along that curve.

Another reason for chain dominance is the highly standardized product. How much difference is there, really, between one hamburger and another, or between fried chicken products? With such a simple and narrow product line, it is difficult for an independent in this segment to achieve a viable basis for product differentiation. Whatever differentiation the independent may achieve, it must then withstand the blast of advertising deployed by its chain competitors. For all these difficulties, smaller regional chains, however, can and do compete successfully against the market leaders—in their own regional markets.

As we have suggested, quick service is a vital North American social institution and one that has been adopted by many countries around the globe. In Table 3.3, we summarize its most significant distinguishing characteristics.

TABLE 3.3

What Makes Quick-Service Food Different?

Location strategy (they are everywhere)
Relatively limited menus
Sales volume (very high and highly variable)
Fast service (high degree of self-service)
Numerous part-time employees with various schedules
Use of unskilled labor and highly skilled management
Key role for unit managers
Highly competitive prices
Chain domination
Simple unit, complex system

Quick Service's Continuing Evolution. We noted at the beginning of this section that the quick-service industry of today is the product of over 50 years of evolution, and this process continues. Profit-oriented companies sometimes make mistakes, but they quickly correct them if they want to survive.

One of the positive aspects of quick service's evolution was the upgraded unit's physical plant and decor. Because of the high capital costs (such as depreciation and interest on borrowed capital), however, the cost of building a unit has a major impact on its cost structure. As investment costs began to mount in the 1980s, they drove costs out of line. New, smaller prototype units, however, have now been developed that reduce this investment.

New product development has also been a vital force in rejuvenating quick-service concepts. Whenever a Wendy's concept has become dated in consumers' minds—and sales have begun to fall—the company has redefined its business with new products. Beginning with salad bars and baked potatoes, food bars, the Fresh Stuffed Pita, and, more recently, the Garden Sensations, the company has regained its earlier popularity— and done so repeatedly.

The quick service business is concentrated in the breakfast and lunch day parts and, to a lesser degree, in snack periods. All of these day parts have in common a relatively smaller check average than dinner, and most firms are continually seeking to enter the higher-check-average dinner day part.

Distribution: Expanding Points of Distribution. Distribution refers to the marketing problem of gaining a presence in many markets. Quick-service chains and other food service operators began several years ago to expand the number of markets they could serve by developing not just downsized units but special limited versions of their concepts. These newer prototypes were developed to be able to offer some of the company's product line in locations such as colleges and universities, shopping malls, retail outlets, hospitals, and the like. These smaller **points of distribution** (or **PODs**) can be located almost anyplace where there is consumer traffic. The large unit in which a POD is located is called a host. Hosts provide venues for PODs. Venues are analogous to a restaurant location, but they denote not only a place but also a particular category of guests that the host's premises provide: students at colleges, shoppers in a department store, workers in an office complex. Hosts and food service operators benefit each other. Food service enhances the host's operation by providing additional service to its customers, another revenue stream in the form of rent, and, ideally, keeping employees, shoppers, or visitors on site longer than they might have been otherwise. The host's venue provides a profitable location to the food service company. The theory behind PODs has been dubbed "intercept marketing," in that the idea is to offer product wherever the consumer is, intercepting them in work or play. The other side of a firm's successful distribution is consumer convenience.[11] Points of distribution are proving to be a major vehicle for the continuing growth of fast food and will be discussed further in Chapter 6.

The Future of Quick Service. Perhaps the most difficult challenge that QSRs collectively face is the shift in the composition of the population, that is, the aging of the baby boomers. (Individually, the greatest challenge is more likely the ever-increasing competition.) Baby boomers played a major role in creating demand for fast food when they were children and for its gradual upscaling as they entered their teens and 20s in the years just before and after 1970. As they leave their youth behind and enter middle age (and beyond), baby boomers' tastes are naturally changing. They are able to afford a more expensive restaurant and prefer a more upscale environment and more extensive service. This translates into increased demand for full-service restaurants and "newer" segments such as the fast-casual segment. The fast-casual segment is a natural extension of the traditional quick-service segment. It has been described as offering "full service quality food in a quick-service format."[12] Hudson Riehle of the National Restaurant Association states that it is " . . . a hybrid concept that offers the convenience of a typical quick-service establishment while combining food offerings and ingredients historically associated with more 'casual' table service operations."[13] Examples would include Panera Bread (Missouri), Baja Fresh (California), Wingstop (Texas), Au Bon Pain (Massachusetts), and Qdoba Mexican Grill (Colorado). Some of the more "mainstream" quick-service companies are also investing in this new segment, including McDonald's (with 3'n1) and Wendy's (with Café Express). According to Restaurant Research, this "new" segment accounts for $3.6 billion.[14]

Although quick service operators have made every effort to adapt to changing tastes, the traditional QSR footprint may no longer fit their needs as well as it did when they were younger. For this reason alone, newer niche segments such as fast casual seem to be an appropriate response.

On the other hand, there is a large group of younger customers who have come along—and will continue to do so—to replace the boomers. Moreover, quick service, as we noted earlier, is a part of the harried American lifestyle. Whatever age they may be, when speed or cost is especially important, fast food is the easiest choice. As a result, quick-service management opportunities continue to be promising.

CAREERS IN
HOSPITALITY

Indeed, with so many units in operation and with healthy growth, there is a need for large numbers of new managers to replace those who are promoted or leave the business. There is, moreover, a persistent shortage of qualified managers. Quick-service restaurants are likely to continue to offer attractive opportunities. They give significant responsibility to new managers and generous compensation to those who can deliver results. Their many units mean numerous opportunities for advancement.

MIDSCALE RESTAURANTS

Although midscale restaurants may not look like quick-service operations, the heart of all their operating systems closely resembles the QSR format. Their production systems have been simplified through the development of specialized menus that serve to reduce the skill level required of employees. This, in turn, holds down wage costs and increases speed of service. Midscale restaurants might, therefore, be called "moderately fast food." Although the customers in these operations are prepared to wait a bit longer for their food, they will not have to wait that much longer than in a QSR. We will discuss three of the more common restaurant types within this category: family restaurants, cafeterias and buffets, and pizza operations. Home meal replacement will also be discussed further in this section.

Family Restaurants: A Step Up. Family restaurants, such as Denny's, Shoney's, or Cracker Barrel, are table service restaurants that compete principally with QSR operations and have more in common with these lower-priced operations than with units that are more upscale. Although they provide table service, they typically offer self-service in the form of salad bars, breakfast bars, and dessert bars. Another distinguishing feature is that family restaurants usually offer breakfast, lunch, and dinner.

Family restaurants such as Piccadilly offer a different alternative to fast food. (Courtesy of Piccadilly Cafeterias, Inc.)

Menus at family restaurants offer a wider selection, and in this they resemble their upscale cousins more than QSRs. This resemblance to full service is, however, deceiving. First, the production staff is limited to one or more short-order cooks. Almost everything is prepared to order, sometimes from scratch (as with the sandwiches and breakfast items that give the menu much of its variety) and sometimes from frozen or chilled prepared foods that are reheated to order. The production process is really almost as straightforward as the quick-service process.

Furthermore, the service the customers receive is anything but elaborate. Place settings usually consist of paper place mats and a minimum of china and flatware. Most meals consist of a choice of soup or salad, an entrée with rolls and butter, and perhaps a dessert. This reduction in courses simplifies service. Platters, sandwiches, and salads are the mainstay of the menu, all attractively but simply served. Breakfast is the largest meal for some operators and a significant one for most others. Snacks and coffee breaks are also an important source of business, particularly for family restaurants that combine a bakery with their unit. Table 3.4 shows the ten leading family chains. In this segment, chains dominate, with over three-quarters of the market.

The relatively straightforward operating format of family restaurants helps keep the cost of training new service employees manageable. In addition, the flexible menu permits operations to drop menu items when their food costs advance too rapidly, substituting less costly items.

The guests who visit a family restaurant want to be waited on, and in choosing a family restaurant, they are opting for an informal, simple, relatively inexpensive style of service. These operations generally offer a pleasant, modern restaurant located near high pedestrian or vehicular traffic and convenient to shoppers and suburban family diners.

TABLE 3.4

Ten Largest Family Restaurant Chains

Denny's	www.dennys.com
IHOP (International House of Pancakes)	www.ihop.com
Cracker Barrel	www.crackerbarrelocs.com
Bob Evans Farms	www.bobevans.com
Perkins Family Restaurants	www.perkinsrestaurants.com
Waffle House	www.wafflehouse.com
Friendly's Restaurants	www.friendlys.com
Steak 'n Shake	www.steaknshake.com
Marie Callender's	www.mcpies.com
Village Inn	www.villageinnrestaurants.com

Family restaurants, with their more varied menus, table service, and modest price level, offer considerable appeal to the aging baby boomer. For families, children's menus are available that often cost less than feeding the same child at a QSR. In addition, many chains offer kids' programs that may include a free meal on a particular night of the week. Another strong market for family restaurants is 55-to-64-year-olds, a segment of the population that has been in a growth phase since 1995. Many family restaurants offer budget menus or special selections for seniors. To appeal to all these market segments, family restaurants are offering expanded menus featuring selections that are lighter and healthier.

On the downside, the food service "pie" is only so big. That is to say, customers are willing to spend only a certain amount of their disposable income on food outside of the home. Family restaurants have been losing market share to their competitors: primarily casual restaurants and QSR operations. On one hand, customers can choose a QSR that offers less menu choice and service but lower prices and an ambience that is frequently equal to that offered by a family restaurant. At the other extreme, family restaurants face competition from casual, full-service restaurants, some of which offer prices that are not much higher. Like any operation in the middle, family restaurants have to watch out for price competition from those below and value competition from those on the next rung up. In the past, customers have shown substantially greater satisfaction with the value received in moderately priced restaurants than with QSRs or higher-priced restaurants. This suggests that customers recognize the quality of the mid-priced operations, but perhaps their real preference is for something more upscale—or else they are pressed financially and must choose the lower-cost alternative. They recognize value in the midpriced segment, but the greater growth goes to that segment's up- and downscale competitors. Whatever is going on in the guests' minds, family restaurants seem to be caught in a competitive middle ground.

Commercial Cafeterias and Buffets. These segments are primarily limited to certain regions of the United States, but between them, they represent a sizable portion of the restaurant industry. There are some slight but rather important differences between cafeterias and buffet restaurants and the category of family-oriented restaurants that we just discussed. Cafeterias are popular in the southern United States, while buffet-style restaurants seem to be most popular in the American Midwest, Northeast, and Mid-Atlantic regions. Both styles of restaurants cater to consumer markets similar to those for restaurants in the family category—that is, young families and seniors.

Cafeterias became known for serving value-laden home-style meals throughout the southern states. Customers are able to choose from a wide variety of food as they proceed down the cafeteria line. Piccadilly Cafeterias, for instance, offers customers over 130 items daily, with different core items offered each day. Other large cafeteria companies include Luby's and Furr's. Most of the activity that has occurred in this segment of late has been the result of mergers and acquisitions as opposed to expansion.

Cafeterias offer value, selection, a comfortable atmosphere, and a family environment—characteristics that appeal to several different demographic groups. The segment faces many of the same challenges that we discussed with respect to family restaurants, however.

A segment that is closer to cafeterias than it is to family restaurants is buffet-style restaurants. Buffet restaurants are similar to commercial cafeterias operationally but differ from the customers' perspective. Their main differentiating quality is the scatter buffet concept, where restaurant guests go to different "stations" in the dining room to retrieve their food. Each station offers different types of foods. The scatter system, among other things, eliminates some of the bottlenecks that can occur as a result of customer lineups along traditional cafeteria lines. Some of the larger buffet companies include Golden Corral, Ryan's Grill, and Shoney's. One of the largest operators of this style of restaurants is Buffets, Inc., which operates the Old Country Buffet, Hometown Buffet, and Country Buffet brands, among other concepts. According to Glenn Drasher, the executive vice president of marketing for Buffets, Inc., the company's different concepts tend to attract a broad customer base that includes families with kids, baby boomers, and seniors. Many of their special programs are developed with this in mind. For instance, they offer special pricing for kids based upon how old they are (50 cents per year for lunch). They also change their menu at 3:30 in the afternoon for those who are interested in eating an early dinner.[15]

Cafeterias and buffets, together, account for approximately $7 billion in sales each year.

Other Midscale Restaurants. There are numerous other types of restaurants that we could include in the midscale category, for instance, pizza, seafood, Mexican food, and Asian food. They generally fit the pattern already described: limited menus, highly efficient productivity, limited service, and a product characterized by a relatively low food cost. Pizza restaurants will be described here briefly.

Pizza Restaurants. Pizza is big business. Among the major chain concepts studied by *Restaurants & Institutions* in its annual chain restaurant study, "The Top 400 Restaurant Concepts," several are pizza chains—in fact, four pizza companies are billion-dollar-a-year companies.[16]

Pizza restaurants once depended almost exclusively on a single item. In recent years, however, pizza restaurants have extended their product line to appeal to more customers. New items include deep-dish, Chicago-style pizza; pizza with thick or thin crust; specialty two-crusted pizza; and, at lunch, individual-sized pizzas. All have added variety and choice to the pizza menu. Newer items that have appeared on the menus of national pizza chains in recent years include breads, salads, chicken wings, pastas, and sandwiches. Some chains, such as California Pizza Kitchen, have totally reconceptualized the traditional pizza offerings with toppings such as barbeque chicken, Peking duck, and goat cheese. Despite all their menu and service expansion, however, these operations are still principally pizza restaurants. The cost of their food product itself is relatively low, and these operations also have low labor costs, making them attractive investment opportunities.

Home Meal Replacement. The final category of food service that we will discuss in the midscale category is home meal replacement (HMR), which has been mentioned earlier. Unlike the previous examples discussed, HMR is not a restaurant type but rather a delivery method. The reason it is included in this section is that much of HMR occurs in the midscale segment. Pizza is perhaps the original North American HMR product. However, several nonpizza chains, as discussed below, have capitalized on the popularity of HMR.

Operations such as Kenny Rogers Roasters and Boston Market have helped to pioneer a new kind of takeout/eat-in operation, featuring a kind of food different from the burger, sandwich, and pizza that have dominated the take-out market for years. HMR features (but is not limited to) American "comfort foods" such as chicken, turkey, and ham prepared in a way that consumers might use themselves at home. HMR food not only tastes good but also fits the image of family food and is often referred to as "home cooked." (The concept of "truth in menu" suggests it should be called "home-style cooking," and in some jurisdictions advertising "home cooking" in a restaurant could lead to criminal charges under the laws covering fraud.)

At one time, Boston Market was a real growth phenomenon, expanding from a single unit to 1,200 units in six years. The most recent development with this chain was its purchase by McDonald's. McDonald's now owns and manages some 650 Boston Market restaurants in the United States, Canada, and Australia. The menu continues to emphasize such "comfort" foods as chicken, turkey, ham, meatloaf, and pot pies.

Grocery store and delicatessen chains have long featured variants of the HMR concept, and they, too, are expanding their take-out offerings aggressively. We should recognize as well that take-out operations of all kinds are competitors with HMR operators. A number of new HMR concepts have entered the field, some featuring colocation with an existing brand.

Casual Restaurants

Casual restaurants have been an important component of the restaurant industry in recent years. Casual restaurants provide a relaxed atmosphere and reasonably priced menus that appeal to baby boomers and multiple other demographic segments. The types of restaurants, and affiliated chains, that are a part of this segment are becoming almost as recognizable as certain quick-service chains; Chili's, Red Lobster, Applebee's, T.G.I. Friday's, and California Pizza Kitchen have all become a familiar part of the dining landscape. Several of these companies have active franchising programs that allow the companies to continue to expand domestically and internationally. Some are part of companies that operate multiple concepts such as Brinker (Romano's Macaroni Grill, On the Border Mexican Grill and Cantina, and Chili's Grill and Bar) and Darden Restaurants (Red Lobster, Bahama Breeze, Olive Garden, Smokey Bones).

Specialty Restaurants. **Specialty restaurants** featuring a specific kind of food constitute a significant component of the casual restaurant segment. Most of these offer a theme related to the food specialty, such as steaks, seafood, or pasta. With a slightly more relaxed view of diet than the one that prevailed just a few years ago, customers are flocking to steakhouses, for instance. To give an indication of just how popular steak restaurants have become, some of the *Restaurants & Institutions Top 400* (hereafter *R&I 400*) top concepts are steakhouse chains (Outback Steakhouse, Lone Star Steakhouse and Saloon, and Longhorn Steakhouse, just to name a few). Many steakhouses feature a Western decor that adds a themed element to the dining experience.

Seafood restaurants represent a popular specialty segment. (Courtesy of Las Vegas Convention and Visitors Authority.)

Seafood restaurants are another specialty segment that is demanding of attention (witness the popularity of Red Lobster). Seafood restaurants provide a combination of a healthy, low-fat image with a popular food product. The sea offers plenty of nautical themes for an ambience to enhance the diners' experience. Diners have become much more knowledgeable about seafood in recent years, and seafood-oriented restaurants such as Landry's (based in Houston) have been able to capitalize upon this. It should also be noted that the seafood segment continues to include many independent restaurant operators, some of which are among the busiest independent restaurants in the United States, including Joe's Stone Crab (Miami), Bob Chinn's Crab House (Wheeling, Illinois), Atlanta Fish Market (Atlanta), and Anthony's Pier 4 (Boston).

Pasta is also proving its continuing popularity, offering not only a healthy, low-fat product but also one that has a relatively low cost. Pasta restaurants, which are not necessarily Italian, have begun to spring up around North America. One such example is Semolina's, a chain of pasta-themed restaurants clustered in the southern United States whose menu focuses on international pasta dishes.

Another type of restaurant that we can include in the specialty category are brewpubs, which feature a combination of food and beer made in the operation's own facility. Beer continues to be a popular beverage and accounts for much of the alcoholic beverages that accompany meals. According to the Association of Brewers, the number of brewpubs almost reached 1,000 (979) in the United States in 2005. There are now even several brewpub chains including Rock Bottom (Louisville, Colorado), Gordon Biersch Brewery Restaurant (Chattanooga, Tennessee), and Hops Grill and Bar (Tampa, Florida). The segment is still dominated by smaller independently owned operations, though, such as Goose Island in Chicago, Crescent City Brewhouse in New Orleans, and Copper Tank Brewing Company in Austin, Texas.

Ethnic Restaurants. Ethnic restaurants offer a cuisine and theme that combine to provide a "getaway" experience. Ethnic restaurants are a mainstay in the U.S. restaurant industry, and Americans continue to explore new types of foods from around the world. While the most popular ethnic cuisines continue to be Italian, Chinese, and Mexican, some of the ethnic restaurants that have been gaining ground in recent years include Thai, Ethiopian, and Indian. Ethnic restaurants have long been dominated by independents but are now seeing the proliferation of chains as well.

"Eatertainment." For the specialty restaurants discussed earlier, the focus of the guests' experience is the food, often enhanced by a related ambience. Ethnic restaurants, too, feature a specialized food, with a matching ambience playing a somewhat larger role. There are, however, "**eatertainment**," or theme, restaurants, in which the diner's experience is centered in the entertainment provided by the restaurants'

A restaurant's theme serves to augment diners' surroundings and creates an exciting experience. (Courtesy of Rainforest Cafe.)

Food, service, theme, and entertainment all contribute to the overall experience of the guest. (Courtesy of Rainforest Cafe.)

Quark's Restaurant Serves Earthlings, Too

To walk into the *Star Trek*-themed restaurant at the Las Vegas Hilton is to be transported to another time and dimension. The theme is different than that of many other themed restaurants: It is based exclusively on the *Star Trek* television series (and movies). The restaurant is one part of a larger complex within the hotel that also features a museum, a simulated ride, and an extensive gift shop. In this way it is different than many "stand-alone" theme restaurants.

The restaurant entrance is located off of the Promenade on Deep Space Nine (a *Star Trek* space station); features futuristic tables, lighting, and ambience; and offers menu items named after intergalactic specialties such as "The Wrap of Khan" and "Glop on a Stick." Specialty drinks include "Romulan Ale" and "Klingon Warnog Ale," both named after famous *Star Trek* villainous alien races. As with many theme restaurants, the menu plays an integral part of the dining experience.

Diners are greeted by *Star Trek* characters who roam the dining room, including Klingons and Ferengi. The characters freely interact with diners, and humorously insult the guests. This feature alone distinguishes the restaurant from theme restaurant chains.

In short, the restaurant provides the total experience for *Star Trek* fans. Like other theme restaurants, it is also unique in another way: Fans must go to Las Vegas to enjoy it, since it is the only restaurant (and attraction) of its kind. The restaurant is part of a $70 million complex operated by Paramount Parks.

stage-set-like decor. Here, the food is an important but secondary consideration. One of the best known of these operations is the Hard Rock Cafe, which in 1971 first introduced this concept. The Hard Rock Cafe, and its competitors in this segment, offer a combination of the typical restaurant experience with the addition of the atmosphere and ambience (which may include entertainment, props, etc.) appropriate for the theme that is being conveyed. These operations offer movie-quality special effects, professional actors, and audio-animatronic creatures to create their atmosphere. And the atmosphere, or theme, ranges from undersea submarines (DIVE!) to race cars (NASCAR) to movies and television shows (*Star Trek*). For additional information about Quark's Restaurant at Star Trek: The Experience, see Case History 3.1.

The economics of theme restaurants call for big investors. The operators of Dave and Buster's typically spend $10 million on each unit, which includes not only multiple food and beverage operations but also computer and virtual-reality games. In addition to food sales, these units offer alcoholic beverages and sometimes charge an entrance fee. Sales of branded merchandise such as T-shirts, caps, and sweaters are also a major source of revenue for most theme operations. Some chains derive as much as 60 percent of their revenues from merchandise. Rainforest Cafe's president notes that a large staff as well as heavy investment combine to make a 200-seat restaurant the minimum size feasible. Many are much larger.

The experience offered by the restaurant is the center of the concept. At Rainforest Cafe, thunderstorms regularly pass through the restaurant, but operators agree that the "wow" factor is good for only the first visit—or perhaps one or two more. After that, the quality of food and service becomes critical. The danger of obsolescence is a real problem for these high-investment operations unless food and service are excellent—and perhaps even if they are. Accordingly, these operations are located in high-population areas and near major tourist attractions, where there is a high audience turnover. Not every concept will make it, but the idea of a popular restaurant featuring entertainment and food—as well as liquor—has been validated by Hard Rock Cafe's 35 years of successful growth. It should be noted that at the time of this writing, several chains within this category are experiencing financial difficulties and the segment, as a whole, is reevaluating how it is viewed by customers.

HIGH-CHECK-AVERAGE RESTAURANTS

Now, let's go back to the other end of the dining spectrum and revisit high-check-average operations. As we indicated earlier, fine dining, if it is defined as an elaborate ritual of service combined with a European-style kitchen, appears to be in decline. If, however, it is defined simply as restaurants with a check average over $30, fine dining in a new "casualized" version is still very much with us. These high-check-average restaurants, however, account for only a small percentage of restaurant sales.

High-check-average operations are primarily found in large U.S. cities such as New York, Chicago, or Los Angeles (and others large cities worldwide). These operations are also associated with areas that have a high per capita income. Certain cities, such as West Palm Beach and Boca Raton, Florida, for instance, are relatively small markets but may in fact have more high-end restaurants than such large cities as Chicago. A third factor that supports demand for this kind of operation is tourism. In tourism centers, visitors can create a demand local people might not be able to sustain. For example, New Orleans, a tourism center, had almost 70 restaurants (prior to Hurricane Katrina) with a check average over $30, despite Louisiana's relatively low per capita income. Las Vegas is another example of a tourism-dependent city that has successfully added several new high-check-average restaurants in recent years. Several high-profile chefs, such as Emeril Lagasse, Wolfgang Puck, Todd English, and Mark Miller, have all opened restaurants in Las Vegas. Others are sure to follow.

One substantial reason for the growth in high-check-average restaurants—but one that doesn't show up in the statistics—is the great expansion in programs preparing skilled culinarians. Programs such as these are supplying a native-born cadre to an industry that a generation ago relied mostly on Europe for skilled cooks. Now North America is able to prepare its fair share of professional culinarians. (See Global Hospitality Note 3.1.)

Culinary Preparation

As reported in *Restaurants & Institutions* magazine, there are more than 500 culinary schools internationally, many of which are in North America. Some of the better known ones hardly need mentioning: the Culinary Institute of America, the California Culinary Academy, and Johnson & Wales. Numerous programs exist outside of North America as well. Le Cordon Bleu, which began in Europe, operates campuses around the world, including in Australia. Le Cordon Bleu actually has two campuses in Australia—in Adelaide and at Ryde TAFE in Sydney. Other culinary programs in Australia include the Academy Sofitel in Melbourne and The Inter-Continental Hotel School in Sydney. Institut Paul Bocuse, located in Lyon, France, offers a diploma in culinary arts and a bachelor's degree in culinary arts and restaurant management. The Institut is housed in a nineteenth-century chateau on the outskirts of Lyon, has state-of the-art facilities which includes Saisons, a teaching restaurant. Famed Chef Paul Bocuse is the Founder and Honorary President of the Institut.

Aside from stand-alone programs, there are also many others located at community colleges and technical colleges—far too many to mention here. Many are regional or local in scope serving the surrounding areas, while others draw internationally. The growth in culinary programs is a result of the (renewed) interest in careers as a chef. Many students quickly reach the conclusion that attending culinary school is an effective way to accelerate a career. Also, more and more employers are recognizing the importance of some sort of formalized education.

Perhaps the most recent trend in culinary education is the movement toward layering management education on top of the culinary component, since the management side is becoming ever more important at every culinary level from supervisor on up. Mike Zema, coordinator of the Culinary Management Program at Elgin Community College, puts it succinctly when he says: "The Chef's role has dramatically changed in the last 20 years. . . . Most executive chefs in large hotels don't cook anymore. Their focus is on managing food costs, labor costs and other operational expenses."[1]

Aside from providing students with applicable skills, culinary programs are also able to offer the opportunity for networking, on-the-job work experience, and placement opportunities. Further, the jobs seem to be there for students upon graduation, at least for the foreseeable future. The Bureau of Labor Statistics is predicting double-digit growth in back-of-the-house positions through the decade. This bodes well for culinarians and culinary programs alike.

Source: The information in this note was gathered from: Allison Perlik, Restaurants & Institutions, October 1, 2001 (rimag.com).
1. Northwood University Advantage, Winter 2003, page 2.

Restaurants as Part of a Larger Business

Thus far, this chapter has examined primarily freestanding restaurants—separate and distinct operations. A substantial part of the food service industry, however, is made up of operations that are the food service units of larger centers. A major area that we should consider briefly are restaurants in retailing. Some of these are located in department stores and shopping malls. It is interesting to see how trends in these catering establishments match those in the restaurant business elsewhere.

RESTAURANTS IN RETAIL STORES

Restaurants in retail stores (usually department stores and drugstores) were originally built as a service to shoppers. After all, a shopper who had to leave the store for lunch might resume shopping in some other store. The restaurants, therefore, helped keep the shoppers in the store and often helped attract them there in the first place. Over time, some stores either downsized their food service operations, contracted the restaurants to food service companies, or eliminated them entirely, instead choosing to focus on their core business. It seems that restaurants in retail stores have come full cycle again—more companies are rethinking their role in the retail shopping experience. Increasingly, in-store restaurants are themselves becoming worthwhile businesses in that they often generate higher profit margins than do the store's other retail sales. In fact, if properly merchandised, restaurants can bring shoppers into the store, not just keep them there. To give some examples of retail restaurant operations, first consider those retail stores that provide space to large restaurant companies, as with Wal-Mart and McDonald's. A similar example is the partnership that exists between Starbucks and Barnes and Noble. IKEA, Old Navy, and Golfsmith are other examples of chains that entice shoppers with dining options.

Restaurants exist in other types of stores as well, including upscale department stores. Two such examples include RL, the restaurant at Ralph Lauren in Chicago, and Café Bistro, the restaurant at Nordstrom's. RL is currently the only restaurant of its kind at a Ralph Lauren location. Located just off of the "Magnificent Mile" in Chicago, RL serves lunch, dinner, and Sunday brunch in an upscale environment. Nordstrom is another retail company that offers its customers a dining option. It currently has two dining concepts: Marketplace (currently located in 17 stores) and Café Bistro (a smaller prototype) with six locations. According to John Clem, vice president of restaurants, the restaurants have been designed to be a "part of Nordstrom's commitment to style and service." It appears that "upscale" dining in these types of shopping environments is experiencing a renewal as shopping becomes an increasingly important part of the

American lifestyle. Research indicates that Americans spend $4 trillion each year on goods and services. In short, the future looks promising for retail dining operations as long as consumers keep spending.

RESTAURANTS IN SHOPPING MALLS

A generation ago, Americans did 5 percent of their shopping in malls. Today, malls account for well over half of nonautomotive retail sales. Malls have become a place to relax as well as shop. Insulated from the weather, with excellent security, they are a clean and comfortable place to stroll. Malls have been thought of as "places to buy," but they are also "places to be." Consumers visit malls, in large part, to browse. And as food service retailers know, when people browse, they also eat. As a result, one of the major attractions of the larger malls is their food service establishments. The food court idea, first developed in malls, offers the consumer significant choice yet gives each operator a chance to specialize and achieve high productivity because of the large volume of customers provided. In fact, the food court concept has been adopted in a number of other settings, such as hotels, casinos, hospitals, and expressway food service.

The composition of mall food service is quite similar to the restaurant industry as a whole, where quick-service restaurants account for the majority of customer traffic and midscale restaurants for a lesser amount. The balance is accounted for by the more upscale table service concepts (which are recognizing the business opportunities in malls). Mall locations have been growing faster than the rest of food service for several years. Less traditional units and ethnic units have fared the best in malls. Chains such as A&W have targeted malls as their primary growth vehicle. This is probably because the mall provides a basic volume of visitors, and the smaller operator does not have to support major advertising expenditures. There is also the added benefit of being able to service mall employees, who can account for a large amount of the volume. Based on the success that some chains have had with their mall locations, other restaurant chains are following suit. Ruby Tuesday's, California Pizza Kitchen, and Cheesecake Factory have targeted malls for new-restaurant development.

Summary

Food service is an integral and vital part of the North American way of life. Table 3.1 summarizes the major components of the food service business. Gains in restaurant traffic have outpaced population growth in recent years, and experts are forecasting continuing growth. Food service can be divided into the dining market and the eating market. Fine-dining restaurants require a large market, skilled workers, and devoted management. Fine-dining restaurant sales have been falling since the late 1980s, probably as a result of some combination of changing tastes, price sensitivity, and health concerns about rich foods. Casual upscale restaurants, on the other hand, have become very popular.

The most dynamic part of the eating market is the off-premise segment, made up of takeout, drive-through, and delivery. Other contemporary popular-priced restaurants are quick-service restaurants (QSRs) and midscale restaurants such as family restaurants, cafeterias, and buffets. Quick-service restaurants are characterized by wide distribution, limited menus, and the use of unskilled labor. Other characteristics are summarized in Table 3.3. Even wider distribution is made possible by the development of PODs, downsized units that can provide food service in a host's venue, following a strategy of intercept marketing and a philosophy of maximum convenience for the customer. Midscale restaurants use a simplified menu and production system that resembles fast food, but these operations offer table service. (Cafeterias and buffets fill a similar niche but differ in their operations.) Family restaurants are in a difficult competitive position, caught in the middle between quick-service and casual restaurants.

Fine dining, which has redefined itself to fit contemporary customers' preferences for casual restaurants, takes a variety of forms. "Eatertainment" operations, which combine food with various kinds of entertainment, are relatively new on the scene, and their long-term viability is questionable.

Some restaurants are part of a larger enterprise, such as a department store or a mall. Their success is usually dependent on the success of the larger unit.

Key Words and Concepts

Food dollar	Home meal replacement (HMR)
Food away from home	Family restaurants
Full-service restaurants	Dining market
Quick-service restaurant (QSR)	Eating market
	Distribution
Takeout	Points of distribution (PODs)
Drive-through	Specialty restaurants
Delivery	Ethnic restaurants
Off-premise	"Eatertainment"
Casual dining	Restaurants in retail stores
Fine dining	

Review Questions

1. How do the dining market and the eating market differ?

2. What kinds of restaurants are included in the dining market and the eating market?

3. What are the growth concepts in the dining market and the eating market?

4. Do you agree or disagree that fast food is a part of the American lifestyle?

5. What is the outlook for the QSR?

6. How are midscale restaurants different from QSRs? How are they similar?

7. What are the risks inherent in "eatertainment"?

8. What are the prospects for fine dining?

9. What larger businesses do restaurants serve?

Internet Exercises

1. **Site name:** Mimi's Cafe

URL: www.mimiscafe.com

Background information: Mimi's Cafe serves classic American dishes, made from scratch, in a colorful, French New Orleans-inspired atmosphere with locations in ten states.

Site name: Houston's Restaurant

URL: www.houstons.com

Background information: Houston's is a private restaurant organization operating in various cities throughout the United States. While they are a nationwide organization, they do not consider themselves a "chain" in the traditional sense—rather, it is a collection of restaurants. Their restaurants have one of the highest per-unit sales averages of any restaurant company in America. Houston's menu is straightforward and made from scratch.

Site name: P. F. Chang's China Bistro

URL: www.pfchangs.com

Background information: P. F. Chang's serves fresh, contemporary Chinese cuisine. Founded in 1993, the P. F. Chang's experience is a unique combination of Chinese cuisine, attentive service, wine, and tempting desserts all served in a stylish, high-energy bistro.

Exercises:

a. Most casual restaurants have a unifying theme that is pervasive in the design of their menu, decor, and Web site. Identify the theme for each of the restaurants listed above. How do the menu, interior decor, and building exterior support their theme?

b. Which of the above companies provides a means for applying for jobs via their Web site?

c. Which of the above companies provides information regarding their menus and plans for new menu items?

d. After viewing all three Web sites, choose the site that has the most useful information and discuss why you chose that Web site.

2. **Site name:** Fuddruckers

URL: www.fuddruckers.com

Background information: Fuddruckers operates and franchises restaurants that specialize in upscale hamburgers cooked to order. They encourage guests to garnish their own entrées by providing an array of fresh produce and condiments. Some restaurants have a butcher shop where beef is ground fresh every day, and some have on-premise bakeries where bread and dessert items are baked fresh daily. Fuddruckers operates more than 200 restaurants throughout the United States and around the world.

Site name: Wendy's

URL: www.wendys.com

Background information: When Dave Thomas opened the first "Wendy's Old Fashioned Hamburgers" restaurant, he had created something new and different in the restaurant industry. He offered high-quality food made with the freshest ingredients and served the way the customer wanted it. Wendy's is a quick-service restaurant that has over 5,000 stores.

Site name: McDonald's

URL: www.mcdonalds.com

Background information: McDonald's is the world's leading food service retailer, with more than 30,000 restaurants in 119 countries serving 47 million customers each day. It is one of the world's most well-known brands and holds a leading share in the globally branded quick-service restaurant segment of the informal eating-out market in virtually every country in which it does business.

Exercise: All three of the above restaurants are "burger joints," but they differ in many ways. Discuss how each restaurant tries to differentiate itself from the other two, especially with respect to target market, menu, interior/exterior decor, and corporate goals.

Notes

1. National Restaurant Association (www.restaurant.org), May 12, 2006.
2. Jacqueline Dulen, "Changing Tastes," *Restaurants & Institutions,* February 1, 1998 (www.rimag.com).
3. National Restaurant Association, "2006 Restaurant Industry Forecast," p. 10.

4. McKinsey and Company, "Foodservice 2005." Presentation made at the annual conference of the International Food and Agribusiness Management Association, Chicago, 2000.
5. National Restaurant Association, "2006 Restaurant Industry Forecast," p. 7.
6. McKinsey and Company, "Foodservice 2005."
7. Allison Perlik, "Staying the Course," *Restaurants & Institutions,* February 15, 2002 (www.rimag.com).
8. Dulen, "Changing Tastes."
9. Margaret Sheridan, "Buffets Help Themselves," *Restaurants & Institutions,* August 15, 2001 (www.rimag.com).
10. *Restaurants & Institutions,* "Top 400 Restaurant Chains," July 1, 2005.
11. This is a somewhat simplified statement of the problem of distribution. For a more extended discussion, see Cathy Hsu and Tom Powers, *Marketing Hospitality,* 3rd ed. (New York: John Wiley & Sons, 2001), especially Chapter 9.
12. Sarah Smith Hamaker and Beth Panitz, "In Vogue: What's Hot in the Restaurant Industry." *Restaurants USA,* May 2002 (www.restaurant.org).
13. Ibid.
14. Restaurant Research, LLC, *Restaurant Research Journal,* February 2003. (www.restaurantresearch.info).
15. Interview with Glenn Drasher, executive vice president of marketing, Buffets, Inc., February 25, 2003.
16. *Restaurants & Institutions,* "Top 400," July 1, 2006.

The Hospitality Industry

(Courtesy of Sodexho.)

CHAPTER FOUR

Restaurant Operations

The Purpose of this Chapter

The best opportunities for advancement in food service are in operations. Staff specialists, such as marketers, accountants, and human-resources people, all play an important role in the food service industry, but most restaurant chains and on-site operations have operations people in the top jobs. An independent restaurant operator is, first and foremost, an operations executive who often does most of the staff specialist work as well. Indeed, many senior executives boast of having started at the bottom in food service operations; for instance, this is a common trait among McDonald's executives. Although their time spent washing dishes or performing other unskilled jobs may have been only a few months—perhaps during a summer vacation—many executives feel that that kind of operational experience helped them understand the work of the employees they lead.

In this chapter, we develop an overview of the all-important topic of restaurant operations. The opening section reviews the key responsibilities in major operational areas and describes a typical day in the life of food service. This should help you to start thinking about the paths to advancement that best suit you.

The chapter concludes with a section on profitability in food service operations and a summary of the elements of financial statements. These statements are used to track operating results, that is, income, expenses, and profit.

THIS CHAPTER SHOULD HELP YOU

1. Identify the three main divisions of activity found in restaurant operations, and summarize their respective roles.
2. Explain the best way to become familiar with operations in a restaurant or other food service organization.
3. Describe the main responsibilities and jobs associated with each of the following: front of the house, back of the house, and office.
4. Identify the two basic approaches to increasing profits and the primary tools used to measure financial results in food service operations.

Restaurant Operations

CAREERS IN
HOSPITALITY

The best way to become familiar with operations in a restaurant or other food service organization is to work in one. The following discussion, however, should give you useful background and a framework for thinking about your experiences. We will focus on three areas of the restaurant: the **front of the house**, the **back of the house**, and the "office." Within each section, we will look at the principal responsibilities of each area, the tasks that are performed there, and the kinds of roles played in the food service drama by employees working in that area. Finally, we will look at the general supervisory and managerial positions typical of that area.

Because our concern is with the whole range of restaurants, from QSR to fine dining, the amount of detail we can deal with will be limited. In general, we'll take as our model a medium-priced, casual table service restaurant. Where there are substantial variations in quick service or fine dining, we'll note those, however.

THE FRONT OF THE HOUSE

This is the part of the operation with which everyone is familiar because they can see it. It is more complex, however, than it appears at first. The front of the house is at once an operating system, a business place, and a social stage setting. As an operating system, it is laid out to provide maximum efficiency to workers and ease of movement to guests. As a business, it is a marketplace that provides an exchange of service for money, which requires appropriate controls. Finally, it is a social place where people not only enjoy their meals but enjoy one another's company, good service, and a pleasing atmosphere.

Responsibilities. The key responsibility of the front of the house is **guest satisfaction**, with particular emphasis on personal service. The chapter "The Role of Service in the Hospitality Industry" discusses service in more detail, but here we will note that service goes beyond the mechanical delivery of the food to include the way the guest is served by the people in the restaurant.

The kind of service that should be delivered has a great deal to do with what the guest wants and expects. In a quick-service restaurant, for example, guests expect economy and speedy service at the counter and self-service—even to the point of discarding their own used disposables after they are finished eating. Although there is emphasis on speed and economy, the guest is still entitled to expect a friendly greeting, accuracy in order filling, and a cheerful willingness to handle any problems that occur. In midscale restaurants, the table service provided raises the level of interaction with the guest. Although speed of service is still usually expected, the success of the guest's experience is more dependent on the server's personal style. A grouchy server can ruin a good meal, while a pleasant disposition can help immensely when things do go wrong.

In casual, casual upscale, and fine dining, guest satisfaction and service requirements have a considerably different frame of reference. As a rule, casual dining implies a leisurely meal, and that is even more true for fine dining. Accordingly, speed is not always as important as the timely arrival of courses, that is, when the guest is ready. The higher price the guest pays raises the level of service he or she expects. A server in a coffee shop may serve from the improper side or ask "who gets which sandwich" without arousing a strong reaction. Errors should not happen there, either, but when the price is modest, guests' expectations are usually modest. On the other hand, when people are paying more for a meal, they expect professional service and a high degree of expertise on the part of the staff.

Although service provision is the most obvious job of the front of the house, those who work there share in the responsibility for a quality food product as well. This means that orders should be relayed accurately to the kitchen. This also means food shouldn't be left to get cold (or baked dry under heat lamps) at a kitchen pickup station. If there is an error in the way food is prepared, the front of the house is where it is likely to show up in a guest complaint. People in the front of the house, therefore, need to be prepared to deal with complaints. This requires at least two things. First, there must be a willingness to listen sympathetically to a guest's complaint. Second, a system must be in place that permits the server or a supervisor to correct any error promptly and cheerfully. In other words, employees must be empowered to satisfy guests' needs. (Empowerment, which is discussed in the final chapter of the book, refers to an approach to managing people that gives employees discretion over as many decisions as possible affecting the quality of the guest's experience.) Because customers represent potential future sales and powerful word-of-mouth advertising, an unhappy guest is much more expensive than a lost meal.

The front of the house is also the place where the exchange of goods and services takes place. As a result, a lot of money changes hands. Thus, the "control" aspects of the operation, such as **check control**, **credit card control**, and **cash control**, are very important. Guest check control—being sure that every order is recorded—prevents servers from "going into business for themselves." An unscrupulous server might take orders, serve the food, and pocket some or all of the money. Today, point-of-sale systems make this kind of scam much more difficult, but there are still ways around even the most scientific system. Because money is the most valuable commodity, ounce for ounce, that a person can steal, extreme vigilance is called for in controlling cash. Further, servers must take responsibility for securing payment for meals served, on behalf of the restaurant. Everything that is ordered by customers must be bought and paid for, or at least accounted for.

Tasks. From the preceding description of responsibilities, you can see the kinds of tasks performed in the front of the house:

- Greeting the guest
- Taking the order
- Serving the food
- Removing used tableware
- Accepting payment and accounting for sales, charge as well as cash
- Thanking the guest and inviting comments and return business

Roles. The tasks are performed quite differently in different levels of restaurants. The hostess or host (in more upscale operations, the headwaiter or waitress or maître d'hôtel) greets the guests, shows them to their table, and, often, supervises the service. Some large, very busy restaurants separate greeting and seating, with hostesses or hosts from several dining rooms (seaters) taking guests to their table after the guests have been directed to them by the person at the main entrance, sometimes called the greeter. At the opposite end of the scale, in QSRs, the counter person is the greeter/order-taker and change-maker, thus making the smile and personal greeting there more important than casual observation might suggest.

The cashier's main duty is taking money or charge slips from guests and giving change when the check is paid. In some smaller operations, however, the cashier doubles as a host or hostess. The cashier is also sometimes responsible for taking reservations and making a record of them. Having a separate cashier to perform this function is one of the original "controls" evident in the restaurant industry. By separating the cash function, accountability is placed solely on one person.

In table service operations, the food server takes the order and looks after the guest's needs for the balance of the meal. The server is the person who spends more time with the guest than any other employee. What the guest expects regarding service is based on the type of operation. More elaborate service, potentially longer interactions with the server, and highly considerate behavior on the part of the server are all expected in more expensive operations. In family restaurants and quick-service operations, although the length and intensity of interaction are much lower, the guest is entitled to certain minimum—and reasonable—expectations: a genuine interest in the customers on the part of the server, a friendly and cheerful manner, and competence in serving the right food promptly. At all levels of restaurant service, excellent service is crucial to success in an increasingly competitive market.

Servers are generally assigned to a specific group of tables, called a station. In some restaurants, servers work in teams to cover a larger station, often with the understanding that only one of them will be in the kitchen at a time so that at least one of them will be in the dining room and available to the guests at all times. In European dining rooms and those in North America patterned after them, a chef de rang and commis de rang—effectively, the chief of station and his or her assistant—work together in a team. In less formal operations, food servers are supported by a busperson who clears and sets tables but provides no service directly to the guest, except perhaps to pour water or coffee. The busperson's job is basically to heighten the productivity of the service staff and to speed table turnover and service to the guest. Their personal appearance and manner, however, are a part of the guest's experience. (Many operations fall somewhere in between the two extremes and use different types of service teams.)

Supervision. Front-of-the-house supervision is ideally exercised by the senior manager on duty. The importance of having a **management presence** cannot be overstated. It is important from the view of employees and customers, and it also provides greater confidence to the customers. Most managers should be expected to devote the majority of their time to the front of the house during meal hours to ensure that guests are served well (although adequate attention must also be paid to the back of the house). This enables the manager to greet and speak with guests. In this sense, the manager is expected to be a public figure whose recognition is important to the guest—"I know the manager here." At the same time, she or he can deal with complaints, follow up on employee training, and generally assess the quality of the operation. In some cases, of course, the manager finds it necessary to spend more time in the back of the house.

In larger operations, a dining room manager is delegated responsibility from the general manager to manage service in a specific area or in the

Cash control is a critical function in front-of-the-house operations. (Courtesy of NCR Corporation.)

whole front of the house. In many operations, the job of host or hostess includes supervisory responsibility for the service in the room or rooms for which he or she is responsible.

In addition to supervising service, managers in the front of the house have responsibility for supervising cleaning staff and cashiers, and for **opening and closing procedures** in the restaurant. Opening and closing duties are sometimes discharged by a lead employee.

THE BACK OF THE HOUSE

In many ways, the back of the house is like a factory, of which there may be two varieties. Some factories are virtually assembly plants. Others manufacture goods from raw materials. A similar distinction can be made regarding restaurants. Some are really an assembly operation, where food is simply finished and plated by kitchen staff. This is true of operations that use a lot of prepared foods such as portioned steaks or a sandwich operation such as a QSR. In others, the product is actually manufactured on the premises or, as we more commonly say, cooked from scratch.

Responsibilities. The principal responsibility of the back of the house is the quality of the food the guest is served. This is a matter not only of food taste; **food safety**, **sanitation**, food cost control, management of supplies, and so on are also significant responsibilities of the back of the house. Because prompt, timely service is dependent on being able to get the food out of the kitchen on time, the kitchen also has a major responsibility with regard to service.

Tasks. Food production stands out as the predominant work done in the back of the house. Controlling quality and cost are usually parallel activities. In other words, standardized recipes and carefully thought-out procedures, used consistently, will produce food that has the correct ingredients, thus ensuring both quality and cost.

An important dimension of cost control is portion control. Say a sandwich that calls for 2 ounces of ham has 2 ½ ounces. Although the portion may be "only" ½ ounce overweight, that is 25 percent additional meat and probably represents an increase of 20 percent in cost. Portion control has a quality dimension as well. Assume two guests order fish and the planned portion is 8 ounces. One receives a 7-ounce portion and the other 9 ounces. Although the average is the same and so cost won't be affected, the guests are likely to notice the discrepancy. Portions should be the same for a guest at every visit—and they should be the same for every guest. Needless to say, controlling costs has a direct impact on the profitability of a restaurant.

Quality control is important in all types of food service operations. (Courtesy of Domino's Pizza, Inc.)

Dishwashing and pot washing are not skilled jobs, but they are certainly important work. Anyone who has been in a restaurant that ran out of clean dishes in the middle of the meal or pots during a heavy preparation period can testify to this. These are activities that use a significant amount of labor in any operation that serves food on permanent ware and has a varied menu (i.e., most operations outside of quick service). Labor cost control is, therefore, an important element in planning ware washing. Because detergent is a commodity that restaurants use in large quantity, the cost of supplies is a significant concern. Quality work, which relates not only to the workers' performance but also to adequate water temperatures and soap solutions, is absolutely essential.

Cleanup work is important in both the front and back of the house, but because it is more clearly related to sanitation, back-of-the-house cleanup is especially significant. Although in most operations workers clean up as they go during the day, the heavy cleanup is usually done at night, when the restaurant is closed.

Roles. Cooks and chefs come not only in all sizes and shapes but also with varying skill levels. In fine dining, cooking is generally done by people with professional chef's credentials, received only after serving a lengthy apprenticeship or a combination of formal education and on-the-job experience. The much-talked-about "hamburger flippers" of quick-service operations are at the other end of the scale. It is not surprising that the work that this group performs can be learned quickly, because the operation has been deliberately designed to reduce the skill requirements. In between these extremes lie the short-order cook, the grill person, the salad preparation person, and many others who have a significant amount of skill but in a narrow range of specialized activities. Whatever the skill level, it is crucial to the success of the operation that this work is done well.

Dishwashers are often people who have taken the job on a short-term—and often part-time—basis. Because the job is repetitive, monotonous, and messy, it is not surprising that it has a high turnover. We ought to note, however, that an inquisitive, observant person working in the dish room—or on the pot sink—is in a position to learn a lot about what makes a restaurant run. Many successful restaurant operators (and college and university professors) got their start in this position.

Some operations employ people with disabilities in dish and pot work as well as in salad and vegetable preparation. Mentally handicapped employees often find the routine, repetitive nature of the work suited to their abilities. Not surprisingly, they find that their dignity as individuals is enhanced by their success in doing an important job well. As a result, employers such as Marriott, which has developed successful programs for disabled workers, have experienced a significantly lower turnover among this group of workers.

An important role we haven't touched on yet is that of the person (or persons) responsible for receiving the shipments of food at the back door as they are delivered. It is the receiver's responsibility to accept shipments to the restaurant and to check them for accuracy in weight or count as well as quality.

In large operations such as hotels, resorts, and casinos, the receiver may report directly to the accounting department because the work relates to control. The receiver needs a good working relationship with the kitchen staff, whatever the formal reporting procedure. In most operations, the receiver has duties closely involved with kitchen operations, such as storing food and keeping storage and receiving areas clean and sanitary. Some restaurants distribute the tasks of the receiver among two or more people. In a hotel one of the authors ran, for instance, counting and weighing of goods received was done by the pot washer, whereas verifying quality was the responsibility of the restaurant manager on duty. Responsibilities vary greatly from operation to operation.

Food production is generally headed by a person carrying the title of chef, executive chef, or food production manager. In smaller, simpler operations, the title may be head cook or just cook. In these latter operations, the general manager and her or his assistants usually exercise some supervision over cooks, so it is important that they have cooking experience in their own backgrounds. In fact, one of the trends in casual dining has been to eliminate the position of chef and replace it with several cooks and a kitchen manager who is responsible for back-of-the-house administrative duties.

The role of chef continues to evolve. One association for a certain type of chef, a culinologist, is profiled in Industry Practice Note 4.1.

Closing (cleaning up, shutting down, and locking up) responsibility is very much related to these activities but deserves separate discussion because of its importance in relation to sanitation and security. The closing kitchen manager is responsible for the major cleanup of the food production areas each day (and probably has the same responsibility in the front of the house). This person also oversees putting valuable food and beverage products into secure storage at the end of the day and locking up the restaurant itself when all employees have left. The job is not a very glamorous one, but it is clearly important. In this day and age of security concerns, the position takes on added importance and responsibility.

THE "OFFICE"

We have put "office" in quotation marks because it has many organizational designations, from "manager's office" to "accounting office." The functions relate to the administrative coordination and accounting in the operation.

Responsibilities and Tasks. The office has as its first task administrative assistance to the general manager and his or her staff. The office staff handles correspondence, phone calls, and other office procedures. These activities, although routine, are essential to maintaining the image of the restaurant in the eyes of its public. Ideally, managers should not be bogged down in this time-consuming work. It is essential to have office staff to free managers to manage.

A second major area of responsibility is keeping the books. Often, the actual books of account are kept in some other place (a chain's home office or an accountant's office for an independent), but the preliminary processing of cashier's deposits, preparation of payrolls, and approval of bills to be paid are all included in this function. Prompt payment of bills is very important to a restaurant's good name in the community; so whether this is done in-house, at a home office, or by a local bookkeeping service, it deserves careful and prompt attention. Either on the premises or off, regular cost control reports must be prepared, usually including the statement of income and expenses (which is discussed later in this chapter).

Roles. The manager's administrative assistant often functions as office manager. Independent operators commonly employ a bookkeeper or accountant full- or part-time or use an outside service. On the other hand, chains handle most accounting centrally. Often, the secretary or office manager is responsible for filling out forms that serve as the basis for the more formal reports.

Research Chefs Association

The Research Chefs Association (RCA) is an organization for professionals who are involved with food product development and have a specific interest in the future of food. Its mission is focused on the concept of Culinology®, which is "the blending of the culinary arts and food science." The association was formed in 1996 by a group of food professionals interested in food, culinary arts, new product development, and food science. The association attempts to bring all of these dimensions together for practitioners, educators, and students. There are now approximately 2,000 members spread across the United States among various regions. The approximate breakdown of members by type is 42 percent chefs; 31 percent affiliates (food scientists and affiliated fields); 14 percent associates (sales fields); and 13 percent students. Many of the students are studying Culinology at one of the seven academic institutions offering academic programs in this area.

One of the ways that the RCA is able to accomplish its objectives is through education and professional development (and certification). RCA-approved Culinology degree programs are housed in such universities as Cal Poly Pomona, Clemson University, and the University of Massachusetts. The University of Massachusetts, which has a particularly renowned food science program, provides extensive information about Culinology as an academic area and offers it as a degree program. An excerpt from their Web site states:

> Today, when consumers enter the grocery store they not only expect foods to be inexpensive and safe but also to have a wide variety of flavors and textures that are often inspired by ethnic food traditions and unique innovations. In addition, books such as *On Food and Cooking: The Science and Lore of the Kitchen* by Harold McGee and television shows like *Good Eats* starring Alton Brown, have been instrumental in expanding cooking beyond the traditional Culinary Arts into the world of Food Science. These developments have made Culinary Science one of the hottest areas of the Food and Food Service Industries. The Department of Food Science has developed a unique concentration in Culinology that has been recognized by the Research Chefs Association. This program combines culinary Arts and Food Science by accepting students with a 2-year culinary arts degree and providing them with a science-oriented framework that enables them to obtain a B.S. in Food Science from the University of Massachusetts in three years.

> The great benefit of Culinary Science training is that it outweighs all the competition because it's the best of both worlds. As a culinologist, one not only has the scientific understanding of food processing but also the much-valued understanding of culinary arts. Combined together, this opens a spectacular opportunity to work in the food industry. The passion of food shared by culinarians allows them, through their research and development, to impact the food culture: a great example is Chef Boyardee who started his career as a chef and with the help of technology brought canned pasta and sauce to where it is today.

The food science world is a unique industry offering a great working experience in its many kitchen-laboratories. Included in this environment are all the benefits of corporate America with endless opportunity for individual career advancement, and most of all, the satisfaction of a food lover's passion of working in the kitchen.[1]

Besides formal education through their links with academic institutions, the RCA also does a lot of work in the area of professional development of its members. Certification programs that the association provides include Certified Research Chef (CRC) and Certified Culinary Scientist (CCS) credentials. Both certifications require that certain qualification standards be met before a candidate can sit for the exam. The standards include formal education and professional experience in both food service and product research and development. Dr. Jerald Chesser (a professor of hospitality management at Cal Poly Pomona) is the Chair of the Certification Commission for the RCA, which oversees the certification program and its standards.

The RCA is fulfilling its mission in several other ways as well, including quarterly newsletters, outreach, sponsoring student scholarships, hosting regional meetings, and hosting an annual conference and tradeshow.

Culinology is an expanding field as a result of the growing interest in food in today's society, as well as the continued professionalization of the industry. Interest in food, food development, and Culinology cuts across industry segments to include suppliers, quick-service, casual dining, and others. Food companies, for instance, are allocating more money to research and development than ever before as commercialization within the industry grows. Some of the latest trends and developments in food-related products (all of which were covered at a recent RCA conference) include umami flavors, packaging technologies, astronaut food, sustainable agriculture, baking science, and hospital haute cuisine.

For students who are interested in combining their interests in food, culinary arts, and food science, a degree (or a career) in Culinology allows them to put these skills to work. Potential employers include food service companies, manufacturers, distributors and suppliers, research companies, and academic institutions.

1. University of Massachusetts Department of Food Science, Culinary Science program (http://www.umass.edu/foodsci/culinaryscience.html).
Sources: Correspondence with the Research Chefs' Association (www.culinology.org); University of Massachusetts Department of Food Science (http://www.umass.edu/foodsci/).

Supervision. As noted previously, the person who supervises on-premise clerical work usually reports to the general manager, as does any in-house accountant. We should note, however, that there are many smaller operations whose low sales volume will not support clerical staff. In these cases, the clerical and accounting routines are usually handled by the managers themselves. In chains, particularly QSR chains, reporting systems have become highly automated. Here, most reports are prepared from routine entries made in the point-of-sale register and transmitted directly to the central accounting office automatically.

General Management

We should now add one additional category to our framework for observing a restaurant—the general managers and their assistants. It is essential that there be someone in charge whenever an operation is open. One possible schedule is as follows (for a full-service casual restaurant that is open for the lunch and dinner periods): An assistant manager comes in before the restaurant opens and oversees all the opening routines. These include turning on equipment, unlocking storage areas, and seeing to it that all of the crew has shown up and that all the necessary stations are covered. The general manager arrives in midmorning and stays at least through the evening meal rush. The closing manager arrives sometime in the afternoon and is usually the last person to leave, locking up for the night. Effective managers, and restaurant companies, often use checklists as reminders, which are a good way to document tasks. An operation with different hours of operation would have a different schedule in some of the details, but the essential functions identified here would all have to be covered in some way. The key point is that someone in the unit is in charge at all times.

In talking about management, we have really been describing management presence. We may not always see the title "manager" used, however. Many of the duties of management are carried out by supervisors. In quick-service (as well as smaller) restaurants, managers and their assistants are often supplemented by crew chiefs and lead employees. Whatever the title, the responsibility of managing these various tasks must be taken care of.

We have used the title "general manager" in this section but should note that this is a title used principally in larger operations. The function of overall direction, however, is the same even if the title used is "unit manager" or "store manager" or simply "manager." Because the general manager can't be present every hour of the day, her or his assistants, whatever their titles, stand in for the manager when she or he cannot be physically present. A key point is that managers act as a team to give direction to the unit, to maintain standards (quality and cost), and to secure the best possible experience for their guests.

The work of managers in food service puts a high priority on communication. (Courtesy of Sodexho.)

Daily Routine. As we have already mentioned, opening and closing a restaurant require specialized work. The highest levels of activity, of course, occur during the meal periods. Between the rush hours, a lot of routine work is accomplished. The following is a look at the major divisions of a restaurant's day.

Opening. Somebody has to unlock the door. In a small operation, it may be a lead employee; in a large operation, it will probably be an assistant manager. As other employees arrive for work, storage areas and walk-ins must be unlocked. If a junior-level supervisor was in charge of closing the night before, it is especially important that the first manager on duty inspect the restaurant and especially the back of the house for cleanliness and sanitation. One additional note that must be added here: It seems that restaurants have recently become targets of robberies, particularly in large U.S. cities. As a result, many restaurant companies are and have been reevaluating their opening and closing procedures. One strategy used to increase safety in restaurants is changing opening and closing procedures to ensure the safety of restaurant employees; for instance, some restaurants are requiring that restaurants be opened and closed by pairs of managers instead of individuals. Other safety measures include installing cameras at entry points (including the loading dock).

In larger restaurants, a considerable amount of equipment has to be turned on. Sometimes this process is automated, but in other operations, equipment is turned on by hand, following a carefully planned schedule. One element of a utility's charge relates to the amount of power used, but another relates to the peak demand level. If someone throws all the electrical panel switches, turning on air conditioners, lights, exhaust fans, ovens, and so forth all at once, this will create a costly, artificially high demand peak. Schedules to phase in electrical equipment over a longer period may be followed by the person who opens up to avoid this problem.

As noted earlier, it is important to be sure that all stations are covered, that is, that everybody is coming to work. If an employee calls in at 6:30 A.M. to say he or she can't make it, or if somebody just doesn't show up, appropriate steps must be taken to cover that position. This could mean calling the appropriate supervisor at home to let that person know of the problem. Alternatively, the opening manager might also handle it more directly by calling in someone who can cover the position (having an "on-call" person each day helps to alleviate this problem).

Before and after the rush. Much of the work done outside the meal period is routine. Probably the most important is "making your setup," that is, preparing the food that will be needed during the next meal period. In a full-menu operation, this will likely involve roasting and baking meats, chopping lettuce and other salad ingredients, and performing other food preparation tasks. In more specialized operations, it may involve slicing prepared meats or simply transferring an appropriate amount of ready-to-use food from the walk-in to a working refrigerator. It is essential that safe food-handling procedures always be followed to prevent food contamination. In some QSRs, a key portion of the setup actually occurs just as the meal period is about to begin, when product is prepared and stored in the bin, ready for the rush that is about to commence. The key element in making the setup is to do as much as possible before the meal to be ready to serve customers promptly.

Sidework is another important activity done by servers on a regular schedule. Sidework includes such tasks as cleaning and filling salt and pepper shakers, cleaning the side stands, and, in many restaurants, some cleaning of the dining room itself. This is work that can't be done during the rush of the meal hour. The front of the house has a sidework setup for every meal period, too. Side stands must be stocked with flatware, napkins, butter, sugar packets, or whatever guest and food supplies might be needed during the coming rush.

Other routine work, such as calling in orders, preparing cash deposits and reports on the previous day's business, and preparing and posting work schedules, is tended to by management staff or under their supervision. It is important that this routine work be done during off-peak hours so that managers on duty can be available during rush hours to greet guests, supervise service, and help out if a worker gets stuck. When you see a manager moving through the dining room pouring coffee, that manager is (or should be) using that opportunity as a way of greeting guests, observing operations, and helping busy servers rather than covering a shortage in the service staff.

The meal periods. Not every meal is a rush in terms of the restaurant's seating capacity. Employees are scheduled, however, to meet the levels of business, so there should be no extra help around. Accordingly, those who are there will probably experience most meal periods as a rush. Each meal has its own characteristics—probably somewhat different in different operations—and the service offered needs to be adapted to that style. In a hotel one of the authors ran, breakfast guests came from the hotel. They were slightly distracted, thinking about the day ahead, and were more interested in their newspaper or breakfast companion than in visiting with dining room staff. Lunch was mostly local businesspeople on a business lunch with clients or in a party of co-workers. The emphasis at both breakfast and lunch was on speed and efficiency. Most guests had to go somewhere else on a fairly tight schedule.

In contrast, dinner was a more relaxed meal. The day was over and people were not in as much of a hurry. There were more single diners, and many were quite happy to visit for a few minutes with staff.

Closing. We have already discussed the importance of the housekeeping, sanitation, and security duties involved in closing activities. We might just note, in addition, that there is guest contact work, that is, easing the last few people out of the restaurant without offending them or waiting until they're ready to leave, depending on house policy. Special care must be employed, in operations serving alcohol, with guests who may be intoxicated, to avoid liability to the operation for any harm they might do to themselves or others. There should be written house policies covering this contingency.

Making a Profit in Food Service Operations

Restaurants have three basic stakeholders. One is the customers. Another is the employees, who seek a good place to work and a decent living. At bottom, though, the purpose that underlies the logic of any business is to make a profit. Without profit, funds to renew the business—to remodel, to launch new products or services, to expand to serve a changing market—and keep employees on the payroll are just not available. Moreover, the third stakeholder is the owners, who, like all of us, need some reward for their effort and risk. Profit, then, serves a vital role in any business.

There are two basic approaches to increasing profit. One is to increase sales; the other is to reduce costs. Most commonly, operators try to do both to the limits of what will make sense for the other stakeholders.

INCREASING SALES

The two basic approaches to **increasing sales** are to sell to more people or to sell more to your present customers—or to do both (the term revenue management is preferred by some). Increasing the customer base is usually thought of as the job of marketing (and specifically, advertising and promotion). A superior operation that achieves a good reputation may build its customer base through word-of-mouth referrals. For instance, Houston's Restaurants do not do any mass-media advertising but have a very loyal following.

Another approach is to increase sales to the customers you now have, that is, to increase the check average. One obvious way to do this is simply to raise prices. Unless the price level of the competition is also going up, however, this will most probably result in a loss of customers (the result of something called price resistance). Some effective approaches to increasing the average check are menu redesign, "**bundling**" of food items, and suggestive selling.

Menu redesign can be accomplished through the actual redesign of the menu, repositioning the menu items to draw attention to high-profit items or changing (or removing) menu items. Each of these strategies can contribute to encouraging the customer to spend more and to purchase higher-profit items.

Bundling is another strategy that can result in the same thing. One of the most common bundling strategies is the combination meal. Several items that are sold separately—for instance, a hamburger, french fries, a soft drink, and dessert in the quick-service arena—are sold together for a price that is less than the price of each sold separately. If this is a good value to the customer, it is likely to persuade a certain percentage to buy more than they might otherwise have done. In a table service restaurant, this kind of combination is referred to as a complete dinner (or lunch) or table d'hôte. The higher check average results in an increase in sales. Another result is likely to be a slightly higher food cost percentage because the selling price is reduced but the food cost remains the same. On the other hand, because total dollar sales have increased and, almost certainly, no additional labor has been scheduled, the labor cost percentage will be lower. The intent is that the higher food cost will be more than offset by the reduced labor cost percentage.

Suggestive selling is another potentially effective technique for increasing sales. Common targets for increased sales are appetizers, side dishes, wine, desserts, or after-dinner drinks, although main courses should not be overlooked. The service staff is crucial to this effort: "May I suggest something from our wine cellar? A bottle of Pommard would complement the roast beef perfectly." These techniques can be applied to most every menu category. For instance, with certain segments of the population reducing their alcohol intake, suggestive selling of bottled water is a simple way of increasing sales. Operators often offer prizes or bonuses for the server most effective in selling.

REDUCING COSTS

Just as raising prices faster than the competition will drive off customers, so will cheapening quality through the use of inferior ingredients or smaller portions. Customers

COST GROUP	TECHNIQUE	EXAMPLE OF MEASUREMENT
Food	Yielding	Dollar cost or weight per portion served
Labor	Productivity standards	Number of guests served per server hour
China, glass, and silver	Breakage/loss counts	Guests served per broken/missing piece
Supplies	Usage monitoring	Gallons/pounds of soap used per 100 guests

Figure 4.1
Some common cost-control techniques.

inevitably notice such changes. Thus, **reducing costs** must result from improved efficiency, which is a fit subject for not one but several books. We will content our-selves here with noting that some of the most common techniques for reducing costs in food service involve more careful scheduling of employees, improved portion con-trol, and more careful monitoring of the issue and use of supplies such as soap, paper goods, and other disposables. Generally, the key to reducing costs is a careful review of the operation to find places where waste can be reduced without loss of quality. Following such a review, realistic standards are set and performance is monitored against those standards. Figure 4.1 shows some common techniques for monitoring cost performance with examples of the kind of measurement used.

Provided that the reductions in costs come from improved efficiency rather than cheapening quality, it will have a greater impact on profit. A dollar saved in cost, af-ter all, is a dollar more profit. An increase in sales, however, will be accompanied by some increased cost—the variable cost, such as food cost, for instance—and so will not produce as much profit.

Keeping the Score in Operations: Accounting Statements and Operating Ratios

A discussion of operations is not complete without a brief review of the common scorekeeping methods used in the field. Elsewhere in your hospitality curriculum, you will undoubtedly study the subject of control at more length. As part of your in-troduction to the hospitality field, however, this section will discuss briefly some key food service control terms, accounting statements, and operating statistics.

Cost of Sales

The **cost of sales** refers to the cost of products consumed by the guest in the process of operations. The principal product costs include:

- *Food cost*—The cost of food prepared for and consumed by guests
- *Beverage or bar cost*—The cost of alcoholic beverages and other ingredients, such as juices, carbonated water, or fruit, used to make drinks for guests

Note that these (and all other) costs are customarily stated both in dollar amounts and as a percentage of sales. For example, if your food cost is $25,000 and your food sales are $75,000, then the food cost percentage will be $25,000/$75,000, or 33.3 percent. Although dollar costs are essential to the accounting system, the percentage of the cost (i.e., its size relative to the sales level) is more useful to managers because the percentages for one month (or for some other period) can readily be compared with those of other months, with a budget, and with industry averages.

Controllable Expenses

Controllable expenses are costs that may be expected to vary to some degree and over which operating management can exercise direct control. Controllable expenses include:

- *Payroll costs.* Payroll costs are the wages and salaries paid to employees.
- *Employee benefits.* Employee benefits include social security taxes, workers' compensation insurance, and pension payments.
- *Other variable costs.* Other costs that generally vary with sales are laundry, linen, uniforms, china, glass and silver, guest supplies, cleaning supplies, and menus. Some costs in the category of controllable expenses have both a fixed and a variable component (utilities cost), but others are fixed by management decision, which is subject to change (advertising and promotion, utilities, administrative and general, and repairs and maintenance).

Capital Costs

This group of costs varies with the value of the fixed assets, usually land, building, furniture and fixtures, and equipment. The higher the value, for instance, the higher the property taxes or insurance. The same is true of depreciation, which is a bookkeeping entry to write off the cost of a capital asset. Interest varies, of course, with the size of the debt and the interest rate.

By categorizing cost information in this way, we focus attention on the operation's key variables. The cost percentages also reflect the efficiency of various segments of an operation. Food costs reflect management pricing and the kitchen crew's efficiency. Labor costs reflect efficiency in employee scheduling and the adequacy of sales volume in proportion to the operation's crew size. Results can be improved by either reducing employee hours or increasing sales.

Two key operating statistics are **covers** and **check averages**. The number of covers refers to the number of guests. ("Guest count" is an alternative term.) The check average can be what it sounds like, the average dollar amount of a check. Because parties (a group of guests seated together) vary in size, however, the check average is usually quoted as the average sale per guest. This figure is found by dividing the total dollar sales by the number of guests served during the period and is sometimes referred to as the average cover.

Figure 4.2 shows an example of a restaurant statement of income and expenses (also called an operating statement or a profit-and-loss statement). This statement shows the relationship of the costs we have just discussed and also how the check averages are computed.

As a final way to compare and contrast differing restaurants, Table 4.1 presents selected average operating ratios for the kinds of restaurants we described in the previous chapter.

Life in the Restaurant Business

The decision of whether or not to work in the restaurant business is really a decision about the kind of life you want to lead. Weekend and holiday work is common, and workweeks of 50 and 60 hours are, too, especially while you are working your way up in management. The work is often physically demanding because you are on your feet, under pressure, and in a hurry for most of the working day.

On the other hand, it is an exciting business. It involves working with people—both employees and guests—in a way that is very rewarding. Every day—every meal—is a new challenge, and there are literally hundreds of opportunities to make people feel good. Few things are as pleasant as the end of a meal when a restaurant crew can take satisfaction in the success of its joint efforts.

STATEMENT OF INCOME AND EXPENSES

Suburban Restaurant

Year Ending December 31, 20XX

SALES		
Food	$962,400	80.2%
Beverage	237,600	19.8
Total sales	1,200,000	100.0
COST OF SALES		
Food	$348,400	36.2%
Beverage	66,100	27.8
Total cost of sales	414,500	34.5
GROSS PROFIT	785,500	65.5
CONTROLLABLE EXPENSES		
Payroll	$338,400	28.2%
Employee benefits	62,400	5.2
Direct operating expenses	64,800	5.4
Music and entertainment	3,600	0.3
Advertising and promotion	22,800	1.9
Utilities	38,400	3.2
Administrative and general	46,800	3.9
Repairs and maintenance	21,600	1.8
Total controllable expenses	598,800	49.9
INCOME BEFORE CAPITAL COSTS	$186,700	15.6%
CAPITAL COSTS		
Rent, property taxes, and insurance	$84,000	7.0%
Interest and depreciation	46,800	3.9
Total capital costs	130,800	10.9
NET PROFIT BEFORE INCOME TAXES	$56,400	4.7%
Number of covers served	74,918	
Food check average	$12.85	
Beverage check average	$3.17	
Total check average	$16.02	

Figure 4.2

Restaurant statement of income and expenses.

TABLE 4.1

Comparison of U.S. Restaurant Operating Statistics

	LIMITED SERVICE	FULL-SERVICE (UNDER $15)	FULL-SERVICE ($15 TO $24.99)
Food cost[a]	31.3%	32.6%	36.4%
Beverage cost[b]	30.0%	30.0%	28.4%
Product cost[c]	30.8%	32.0%	34.1%
Payroll and related costs[d]	30.8%	34.0%	34.0%
Prime cost[e]	61.6%	66.0%	68.1%
Occupancy and capital costs[f]	9.4%	8.0%	8.9%
Profit before income taxes	7.3%	5.4%	4.0%

[a]Food cost as percentage of food sales.
[b]Beverage cost as percentage of beverage sales.
[c]Total food and beverage cost as percentage of total food and beverage sales.
[d]Includes employee benefits.
[e]Total of product cost and labor cost.
[f]Includes occupancy costs, depreciation, and interest expense.
Source: National Restaurant Association, "Restaurant Industry Operations Report—2004."

SALARY LEVELS

According to the Bureau of Labor Statistics, the median salary for food service managers in 2004 was just under $40,000. Keep in mind that the salary level is obviously dependent upon geographic location, the restaurant company, length of service, sales volume, and so forth. Some segments are known to pay more than others, for instance, managers in the casual/theme segment are among the highest paid. On the other hand, the average salary for unit managers of family restaurants tends to be on the lower side.

Bonuses can also add an additional $2,000 to $10,000 at the unit level, again depending upon the segment and individual company policies.[1] Restaurant companies tend to compensate their general managers significantly better than they do managers at the assistant level. After all, it is the general manager who is ultimately responsible for the performance of the unit. Employers tend to view the assistant manager's position as an entry-level management position. The same compensation survey by the NRA indicated that the median salary for assistant managers was $28,000. The typical experience requirement for this position is between one and three years. The time that it takes to achieve the level of general manager has gotten progressively shorter over time but is between three and six years for most chains. On the lower end of the spectrum are management trainees, earning $25,000, and at the upper end, regional managers (of chains), earning $62,500. Chefs' earnings ranged from $30,000 for pastry chefs to $48,000 for executive chefs (including, on average, a bonus of $5,000).[2]

Another salary survey by Hospitality Valuation Services looked at the compensation of higher level managers. The median salary for Directors ranged from $76,000 to $97,000; median salaries for Vice Presidents ranged from $133,000 to $165,000, and median salaries for CEOs was $400,999.[3]

As we are dealing with averages, there are many people earning both more and less than these amounts. There is a considerable range in earnings because pay depends on the size of the operation, profit levels, and the responsibilities involved. Nevertheless, the figures give benchmarks that you may find useful.

Summary

A good way to structure your observation of food service is around the major divisions of the front of the house, the back of the house, and the office or the administrative function, which is the way we have organized this chapter. Guest satisfaction, personal service, and accounting for sales are the major responsibilities of the front of the house. Food quality as well as food safety, sanitation, and food cost control are crucial in the back of the house. The office staff provides administrative assistance to managers and handles routine accounting and cost control functions. It is vital to ensure that there is some kind of management presence whenever an operation's employees are at work. The food service day revolves around opening and closing routines and rush periods at meals. We covered a variety of issues relating to revenues and costs. Food service operations can be made profitable by increasing revenues or decreasing costs. Sales can be increased by selling more to existing customers or by broadening the customer base. Costs must be reduced through greater efficiency, rather than by cheapening the product and service. In operations, the effectiveness of results is measured with financial statements, particularly the statement of income and expense, and in operating statistics and ratios.

Key Words and Concepts

Front of the house	Management presence
Back of the house	Opening and closing
Guest satisfaction	Food safety
Check control	Sanitation
Credit card control	Increasing sales
Cash control	Bundling

Reducing costs   **Covers**

Cost of sales   **Check average**

Controllable expenses

Review Questions

1. What are the most important elements of quality in food service? How are they attained?

2. What is meant by management presence? Why is it important? Have you seen it provided in operations in which you have worked? What are some of the consequences of a lack of management presence?

3. What characteristics do you think are important in a person who chooses to work in food service operations?

4. What pitfalls can you see in the attempts to increase sales? To reduce costs?

5. What are the major approaches to increasing profit? Which is the best way? Why? What are its dangers?

6. What are the main controllable costs? Why are they called controllable?

Internet Exercises

1. **Site name:** All Food Business
   URL: www.allfoodbusiness.com/job_descriptions.php
   Background information: Provides food service industry information and resources free of charge.
   Site name: Famous Dave's
   URL: www.famousdaves.com/careers/Docs/Restaurant%20Manager%20Job%20Description.pdf
   Background information: Famous Dave's is a chain of barbeque restaurants headquartered in Minnetonka, MN.
   Site name: Zoe's Kitchen
   URL: www.zoeskitchen.com/MANAGER_OPERATOR.pdf
   Background information: Zoe's is a small chain of restaurants headquartered in Birmingham, AL.
   Site name: Red Lobster
   URL: www.redlobster.com/jobs/management_positions.asp

Background information: Red Lobster is a chain seafood restaurant and is part of Darden Restaurants, Inc. It was built on the promise of offering great-tasting seafood at a value price.

Exercises:

a. Review the management job descriptions for each of the restaurants above. Describe the differences and similarities among the restaurant groups and compare them with those indicated in the textbook.

b. What training is provided by the restaurants to prepare entry-level managers for positions in their organization? Which restaurant company seems to provide the best training?

c. Based on the job descriptions indicated on the Web sites above, describe what you need to do to prepare yourself for a restaurant manager position between now and graduation.

2. **Site name:** PayScale.com

   URL: www.payscale.com/research/US/Job=Restaurant_Manager/Salary/show_all

   Background information: PayScale is an online salary and benefit information source, providing reliable and accurate compensation data for both employees and employers.

   Site name: Bureau of Labor Statistics

   URL: http://www.bls.gov/oes/current/oes119051.htm

   Background information: The Bureau of Labor Statistics is the principal fact-finding agency for the Federal Government in the broad field of labor economics and statistics.

   Site name: StarChefs.com

   URL: http://www.starchefs.com/features/editors_dish/salary_survey/index.shtml

   Background information: *StarChefs*™ is an award-winning online magazine, serving the food service industry and food aficionados since 1995.

   Exercises:

   a. Using the Web sites above, compare the salary levels for food service managers. Describe any differences and why you believe there is a difference.

   b. Describe the difference that location in the United States makes for basically the same job. Other than cost of living, what would account for differences in salaries in various locations?

3. **Site name:** Key Operating Ratios for Restaurants

   URL: http://www.wku.edu/~hrtm/wiley/foodratio

   Background information: Comparisons of these indicators with earlier operating results and with the budget provide important clues to an operation's problems or success.

Exercises: Based on the Key Operating Ratio formulas in Chapter 4 of the textbook and the sample data on the above Web page, calculate:

a. Average sale per guest

b. Average check

c. Average number of guests per check

d. Food cost percentage

e. Beverage cost percentage

Notes

1. National Restaurant Association, "2001 Compensation for Salaried Personnel in Restaurants." Page 2.
2. Ibid.
3. *Hospitality Compensation Exchange*, HVS International, 2005.

The Hospitality Industry

(Courtesy of Rainforest Cafe.)

CHAPTER FIVE

Restaurant Industry Organization: Chain, Independent, or Franchise?

The Purpose of This Chapter

This chapter is concerned with the relationship between the form of ownership of the restaurant and the likelihood of success. Chains have many advantages, but so do independents. The advantage—or disadvantage—often depends on the situation; factors such as location, type of operation, and the operation's relationship to the community all have a bearing.

Somewhere between private ownership and chain ownership is the franchised operation. Franchisees have some of the independence of ownership but agree to give up much of it for the right to be a part of a successful concept. Because franchises play such an important role in food service, it is essential for you to assess this means of organizing ownership, too.

We sometimes hear that the days of the independent restaurant are past. Although this is certainly not true, the role of the independent restaurant in the industry is changing. Chains have advantages in some industry segments, but independents have strengths that are hard to match in others. It is useful, therefore, to discuss the competitive advantages of both independents and chains. Most restaurant chains include company-owned units as well as franchised units. Franchised units have some aspects in common with chain operations and others in common with independents. For that reason, the chapter concludes with a discussion of franchised restaurant systems.

THIS CHAPTER SHOULD HELP YOU

1. List the relative advantages and disadvantages of chains and independents in the following key areas: marketing and brand recognition; site selection; access to capital; purchasing economies; control and information systems; new product development; and human resources.

2. Identify the independent's imperative for success; provide an example of this imperative; and identify the independent's unique market advantage.

3. Explain the difference between product franchising and business format franchising, and identify which is most commonly used in the hospitality industry.

4. List the services the franchisor offers the new franchisee and those offered the established franchisee.

5. List the advantages and disadvantages of franchising to both the franchisor and the franchisee.

Chain Restaurant Systems

Chains are playing a growing role in food service in North America and elsewhere in the world. Moreover, they are prominent among the pool of companies that recruit graduates of hospitality programs and culinary programs. Both factors make them of interest to us.

Chains have strengths in seven different areas: (1) **marketing** and **brand recognition**, (2) **site selection** expertise, (3) **access to capital**, (4) **purchasing economies**, (5) centrally administered **control and information systems**, (6) new product development, and (7) human-resource development. All of these strengths represent economies of scale: The savings come, in one way or another, from spreading a centralized activity over a large number of units so that each absorbs only a small portion of the cost but all have the benefit of specialized expertise or buying power when they need it.

MARKETING AND BRAND RECOGNITION

More young children in America recognize Santa Claus than any other public figure. Ronald McDonald comes second. Because McDonald's and its franchisees spend well over $2 billion on marketing and advertising, it's no wonder more children recognize Ronald than, say, Mickey Mouse, Donald Duck, or the Easter Bunny. Indeed, McDonald's has created a generic item—the Big Mac. The company has done for the hamburger what Coke did for cola, Avon for cosmetics, and Kodak for film. The reasons for this success are threefold: simplicity of message, enormous spending on marketing, and the additive effect. Ideally, for a company, the spending results in brand recognition.

The message of modern advertising is affected by the form in which it is offered: 10-, 30-, or 60-second television commercials, for instance. Even in the print media, the

Many chains are synonymous with well-known brand names. (Courtesy of Darden Restaurants.)

message must be kept simple, because an advertisement in a newspaper or magazine has to compete with other ads and news or feature stories for the consumer's casual attention. The message of the specialty restaurant resembles its menu. It boils down to a simple statement or a catchphrase. In fact, marketing people generally try to design a "tag line" that summarizes the benefits they want an advertising campaign to tell the consumer. Some years ago, Wendy's used the slogan "Ain't no reason to go anyplace else." Although this slogan set off a letter-writing campaign complaining about the grammar (apparently organized by high-school English teachers), Wendy's officials judged it effective in "breaking through the clutter." Of the many other advertising messages that assail the consumer, you will remember classic tag lines of the past that are still revived from time to time:

"We do it all for you."

"You deserve a break today."

"Finger lickin' good."

A standard exterior appearance gives franchise operators and company-owned brands a high recognition value. (Courtesy of Carlson Restaurants Worldwide.)

And, more recently:

"It's that good."

"Pizza, Pizza."

"Burger King, you got it."

Television advertising, even at the local level, is very expensive. To advertise regularly on national or even regional television is so expensive that it is limited to the very largest companies. Chains can pool the advertising dollars of their many units to make television affordable. Few independents, however, can afford to use television.

Independent restaurants, generally, spend less than chains on marketing as a percentage of sales (of all kinds, including television advertising). Chains have a need to establish and maintain a brand name in multiple markets and to maintain a presence in the regional and national media. Further, restaurants that generate a higher level of sales tend to spend a higher percentage of their revenues on marketing. Table 5.1 reflects spending on marketing, expressed as a percentage of sales, and categorized by check average. In Table 5.1, it is noticeable that the median level of marketing spending for restaurants with check averages of $15 to $24.99 is greater than other categories. Also, full-service restaurants spend more than limited service restaurants. This can be explained by economies of scale. Quick-service company-owned and franchised chain units are fairly close to one another in spending on marketing.[1]

TABLE 5.1

Marketing Expenditures in Food Service

	LOWER QUARTILE (%)	MEDIAN (%)	UPPER QUARTILE (%)
LEVEL OF MARKETING EXPENSE[a]			
RESTAURANT TYPE			
Full service–check average under $15			
Under $500,000 in annual sales	0.6	1.1	2.3
Between $500,000 and $999,000	0.8	1.8	3.6
Between $1,000,000 and $1,999,000	1.2	2.4	4.1
$2,000,000 and over	0.9	2.4	3.3
Table service–check average $15 to $24.99			
Under $500,000 in annual sales	0.9	1.5	3.3
Between $500,000 and $999,000	1.0	1.7	2.4
Between $1,000,000 and $1,999,000	0.7	1.8	2.6
$2,000,000 and over	1.2	1.9	3.0
Limited service restaurants			
Under $500,000 in annual sales	1.0	1.4	3.4
Between $500,000 and $999,000	0.6	1.1	3.7
Between $1,000,000 and $1,999,000	0.6	1.7	4.0
$2,000,000 and over	n/a	n/a	n/a

[a]Ratio to total sales.
Source: National Restaurant Association, "Restaurant Industry Operations Report—2004."

All this advertising will be effective only if consumers get exactly what they expect. Therefore, chains also concentrate on ensuring consistency of quality and service in operations. Customers know what to expect in each of the units, and in an increasingly mobile society, that is important. For those on the go such as tourists, shoppers, or businesspeople, what is more natural than to stop at a familiar sign? If that experience is pleasant, it will reinforce the desire to return to that sign in the local market or wherever else it might appear.

SITE SELECTION EXPERTISE

The success of most restaurants is also enhanced by a location near the heart of major traffic patterns. The technique for analyzing location potential requires a special kind of knowledge, and chains can afford to staff real-estate departments with people that possess this expertise. Numerous examples abound about independent restaurants not "doing their homework" when choosing a site. While there is no exact formula that will guarantee the absolute best site, and success, chains have both experience and expertise backing them. Site selection, most experts would agree, is only getting more complex, and successful companies are becoming more sophisticated in their approach to it. To quote one industry observer: "Restaurant site selection is increasingly complicated business these days. Demographic studies, focus groups, consumer surveys, consultants and endless number crunching are all part of the formula. No restaurateur—single shingle, multiconcept operator, or large chain—can afford to open an eatery today without spending time and money on some or all of the above."[2] Sophisticated software is now available to assist operators in their decision making. Papa John's, Krispy Kreme, AFC, and of course, McDonald's are all companies that are recognized for doing an admirable job of site selection.

ACCESS TO CAPITAL

Most bankers and other lenders have traditionally treated restaurants as risky businesses, therefore making access to capital (at least from this source) problematic. Because of this, an independent operator who wants to open a restaurant (or even remodel or expand an existing operation) may find it difficult to raise the needed capital. However, the banker's willingness to lend increases with the size of the company: If one unit should falter, the banker knows that the company will want to protect its credit record. To do so, it can divert funds from successful operations to carry one in trouble until the problems can be worked out. Although franchisees are not likely to be supported financially by the franchisor, franchise companies regard a failure of one unit as a threat to the reputation of their whole franchise system and often buy up failing units rather than let them go under. In any case, failure is much less common among franchised restaurants than among independent operations. Not surprisingly, banks not only make capital available to units of larger companies and to franchised units but also offer lower interest rates on these loans.

Publicly traded companies, whose stocks are bought and sold on markets such as the New York Stock Exchange, can tap capital from sources such as individual investors buying for their own account, as well as mutual funds, insurance companies, and pension funds that invest people's savings for them. Hospitality companies with well-known brand names and well-established operating track records enjoy a wide following among investors, and their activity is important enough to the industry that *Nation's Restaurant News* carries a weekly section, "Finance," featuring a summary of approximately 100 publicly traded restaurant stocks. In addition to funds raised through stock sales, companies can sell bonds through public markets, raising larger sums than are typically available through bank loans. Among others, Norman Brinker (Jack-in-the-Box, Steak n' Ale, and Chili's) developed a reputation for successfully taking his restaurant companies public and thus achieving his growth objectives.[3]

It should be noted here that the evidence suggests restaurant failure rates tend to be greatly exaggerated. Without publishing the commonly touted failure rates, we can say that recent research indicates that the failure rate is relatively similar to other types of businesses—somewhat lower than 60 percent over a three-year period according to one study.[4]

PURCHASING ECONOMIES

Chains can centralize their purchasing, thereby creating purchasing economies. This is accomplished either by buying centrally in their own commissary or by negotiating centrally with suppliers who then deliver the products, made according to rigid specifications, from their own warehouses and processing plants. Chains purchase in great quantity, and they can use this bargaining leverage to negotiate the best possible prices and terms. Indeed, the leverage of a large purchaser goes beyond price. McDonald's, for instance, has persuaded competing suppliers to work together on the development of new technology or to share their proprietary technology to benefit McDonald's. In addition, chains can afford their own research and development laboratories for testing products and developing new equipment.

CONTROL AND INFORMATION SYSTEMS

Economies of scale are important when it comes to control and information systems as well. Chains can spend large sums on developing procedures for collecting and analyzing accounting and marketing information. They can devise costly computer programs and purchase or lease expensive computer equipment, again spreading the cost over a large number of operations. Daily reports often go from the unit's computerized point-of-sale (POS) system to the central-office computer. There they are analyzed, problems are highlighted, and reports are sent to area supervisors as well as to the unit. This means follow-up on operating results can be handled quickly. Moreover, centrally managed inspection and quality control staff review units' efficiency and quality regularly.

New Product Development

The quest to create newer, better, and more interesting food products continues as competition in the restaurant industry only intensifies. Chains have the luxury of being able to staff (and finance) research and development departments that champion the development of new menu items. With adequate financial support and expertise, companies are able to test and launch new products such as McDonald's new Toasted Deli Sandwiches, Burger King's Chicken Fries and Chicken Whopper, or Papa John's Cheesesticker. The development of new products for restaurant companies is a combination of culinary expertise and food science expertise. Many of the chefs that head culinary development departments for restaurants are enthusiastic members of the Research Chefs Association. The association currently has over 1,000 members and is devoted to "providing the

Houston's Restaurants, a privately owned company, is well known for its development programs. (Courtesy of Houston's Restaurants.)

research chef with a forum for professional and educational development." Many chain organizations have membership in the association including such companies such as Starbucks and Brinker International. The ability to add new products to the menu mix is an important quality; new products can create positive press, increases in sales and profits, and increased **market share**.

HUMAN-RESOURCE PROGRAM DEVELOPMENT

Some restaurant chains have established sophisticated **training programs** for hourly employees, using computer-based, and increasingly, Internet-based techniques to demonstrate the proper ways of performing food service tasks and jobs. Special training exercises are also now available to subscribing companies through closed-circuit television. The standardized procedures emphasized in company training programs, in turn, lower the cost of training and improve its effectiveness. This saving is especially advantageous in semiskilled and unskilled jobs, which traditionally experience high turnover rates and, therefore, consume considerable training time. Companies that are leading the way in computer-based training include Captain D's, Sonic, and Damon's Grill. According to a report on training by *Restaurants & Institutions*, Damon's Grill employees can access the company's computerized training program through their POS system.[5]

Management training is also important, and large food service organizations can usually afford the cost of thorough entry-level management training programs. One food service company, for instance, estimates the costs for training a management trainee fresh out of college to be about $20,000 over a 12- to 18-month period. This includes the trainee's salary while in training, fringe benefits, travel and classroom costs, and the cost of the manager's time to provide on-the-job training. In effect, this company spends as much as or more than a year of college costs on its trainees, a truly valuable education for the person who receives it.

Because of their multiple operations, moreover, chains can instill in beginning managers an incentive to work hard by offering transfers, which involve gradual increases in responsibility and compensation. In addition, a district and regional management organization monitors each manager's progress. Early in a manager's career, he or she begins to receive performance bonuses tied to the unit's operating results. These bonuses and the success they represent are powerful motivators.

CHAINS' MARKET SHARE

As Figure 5.1 suggests, chains have dramatically increased their market share (share of sales) over the last three decades. The top chains generate over half the restaurant

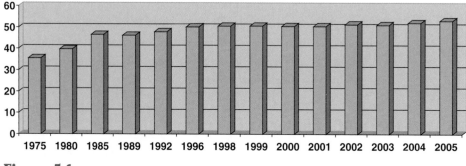

Figure 5.1

Market share of 100 largest U.S. restaurant chains. (Source: Data from Technomic Inc., Chicago.)

sales in the United States, up from less than 33 percent in the early 1970s.[6] What is particularly interesting, though, is that the chains' market share growth seems to be slowing, increasing less than 1 percent in the most recent year reported.

Because successful chains usually have deep pockets (i.e., adequate financial reserves), they are able to ride out recessions. Indeed, some larger chains look on a recession as a time when they can purchase smaller or less successful chains having trouble weathering the economic storm. Although most experts agree that the concentration of chains will continue, fierce competition from regional chains (note the numerous examples used throughout this book), shifting consumer preferences, and competitive patterns will ensure that few, if any, players will establish anything resembling market dominance except on a local or temporary basis.

Independent Restaurants

Although chains undeniably have advantages in the competitive battle for the consumer's dollar, **independent restaurants** also enjoy advantages that will ensure them a continuing place in the market—a place different from that of the chains, perhaps, but significant nevertheless. It is also important to remember that many of the successful independent restaurants of today represent the chains of tomorrow.

OPERATING ADVANTAGES

We can use the same method to analyze the strengths of the independents that we used to examine the chain specialty restaurants. The advantages of the chains derive basically from the large size of their organization. The advantages of the independent derive from a somewhat different common core but in many ways also claim size as their advantage. The independent's flexibility, the motivation of its owner, and the owner's presence in the operation affect its success.

In large organizations, a bureaucracy must grow up to guide decision making. Although this is a necessary—and in some ways healthy—development, it does result in a slower and more impersonal approach to problem solving in larger organizations.

In contrast, to survive and prosper, the independent must achieve differentiation: The operation must have unique characteristics in its marketplace that earn consumers' repeat patronage. Flexibility and a highly focused operation, then, are the independent's edge. Differentiation is the independent's imperative.

Although the following analysis does not deal directly with the issue, we should note that economies of scale are important in the independent restaurant also. The small operation, the mom-and-pop restaurant, finds itself increasingly pressed by rising costs. We cannot specify a minimum volume requirement for success, but National Restaurant Association (NRA) figures show that in each size grouping, the restaurants with higher total sales achieve not only a higher dollar profit but a higher percentage of sales as profit.

MARKETING AND BRAND RECOGNITION

Ronald McDonald may be a popular figure, but he is not a real person (even though he has been named Chief Happiness Officer). The successful restaurant proprietor, however, is real. In fact, successful restaurateurs often become well known, are involved in community affairs, and establish strong ties of friendship with many of their customers. You can probably think of a local restaurant operator that fits this very profile. In a sense, they take on celebrity status. This local "celebrity" can be especially effective in differentiating the operation in the community, generally being visible, greeting guests by name as they arrive, moving through the dining room recognizing friends and acquaintances, dealing graciously with complaints, and expressing gratitude for praise. "Thanks and come back again" has an especially pleasant ring when it comes from the boss—the owner whose status in the town isn't subject to corporate whim or sudden transfer.

Although the chain may have advantages among transients, the operator of a high-quality restaurant enjoys an almost unique advantage in the local market. Moreover, word-of-mouth advertising may spread his or her reputation to an even larger area. The key to recognition for the independent is more than just personality; it is, first and foremost, quality.

Chains clearly have the advantage when it comes to advertising because of their national or regional advertising. This can create brand recognition. In contrast to chains, however, many independents spend relatively little on paid advertising, relying instead on personal relationships, their reputation, and word of mouth. Moreover, independents begin with an advantage that chain units must work very hard to achieve: local identity.

SITE SELECTION

The chain operation continually faces the problem of selecting the right site as it seeks new locations for expansion. It may seem that site selection would not be a problem for an independent operation because that operation is already in place. On the other hand, successful independents sometimes expand by moving to a newer and larger location or by adding locations. These may be full-scale operations or, quite commonly in recent years, scaled-down versions such as the PODs discussed in Chapter 3. Another occasion when independents need to make location decisions is when evolving urban patterns and real-estate values change a location's attractiveness. In some cases, a neighborhood goes into decline, bringing a threatening environment that is unattractive to guests. Alternatively, a restaurant may have a lease (rather than outright ownership) in an area that has become too attractive—at least in terms of rising rents. When the lease comes up for renewal, the owner may decide to move.

When the topic of relocation or adding a location arises, however, the independent operator begins with her or his own knowledge of the area and can add to that by hiring one of the consulting firms that specialize in location analysis. This can be an expensive service, but such services are generally available and the added expense will probably be worthwhile.

ACCESS TO CAPITAL

In most cases, chains will have the readiest access to capital. Sources of capital, however, are also available to small businesses. As noted earlier, banks are often hesitant to lend to restaurants because they are viewed as high-risk enterprises (although their willingness tends to move in cycles just like everything else). On the other hand, if an operator has a well-established banking relationship and a carefully worked-out business plan covering a proposed expansion, the local bank may be happy to make the loan.

The bank, however, is more likely to become involved if the operator can gain support from the U.S. **Small Business Administration (SBA)**. Participation by the SBA does not eliminate risk for the bank, but it reduces it by guaranteeing a percentage of the loan against loss. An SBA loan is likely to be for a longer period, thus lowering the monthly payments required from the borrower. Industry Practice Note 5.1 discusses how operators can gain SBA participation.

Working with the SBA

The key to securing an SBA loan is being prepared and finding the right lender, knowing your needs, and being able to explain how you arrived at the amount you are requesting.

A successful loan application package will provide a financial history of the restaurant. It will also include a narrative background on the operation, the principal participants, and goals for the restaurant. Personal financial statements and tax returns for the owners will be required. Most important are monthly cash flow projections. However, the SBA counsels that if you can obtain a conventional loan, that's what you should do. The SBA is authorized to back loans only where credit is not available on the same terms without a guarantee and only up to 85 percent. According to the National Restaurant Association, about 5,000 U.S. lenders grant SBA loans. SBA loans can take a variety of forms including the 7(a) loan. According to the SBA, "7(a) loans are the most basic and most used type loan of SBA's business loan programs. Its name comes from section 7(a) of the Small Business Act, which authorizes the Agency to provide business loans to American small businesses."[1]

There are certain things about the loan process you can control; the amount of preparation and how you approach a bank are two of them. The SBA recommends contacting your bank and asking what elements it requires in a loan request package. Once you have pulled together all the necessary materials, deliver the package to your banker a few days in advance of your meeting, so that there will be adequate time for him or her to review your request. That way, the banker is ready to respond to your request. The following are four common criteria used to determine the viability of a loan request: previous management experience, net worth, collateral, and cash flow projections.

Whatever you, as a borrower, can bring to the table to calm the fears of the lender and show that you are well prepared to run your own business helps. That includes training, education, and experience. Knowing the business is not all it takes to be successful; you also need to have management and financial skills.

One successful borrower contacted four banks in his hunt for financing and spent nearly two years preparing his business plan. The plan included recipes, sample menus, equipment prices, and sources of supplies.

If your banker doesn't handle SBA-guaranteed loans, call the SBA district office in your area to locate banks in your state that are approved SBA lending sources. To find the district office's telephone number, consult the Small Business Administration listings under "United States Government" in the telephone book, or call the SBA at (800) 8ASK-SBA or consult their Web site (www.sba.gov).

1. Small Business Administration (www.sba.gov).

SBA loans vary widely, from $5,000 to $2 million, according to the NRA. During the ten-year period between 1990 and 2000, the SBA guaranteed to restaurants approximately 26,000 loans worth an estimated $4.8 billion. In fiscal year 2002, an additional 5,450 loans were made worth over $910 million.[7]

Why Go Public?

The decision to take a restaurant company public can be a tough one for many operators. "There are really only two strong reasons for restaurant companies to go public," says Barry M. Stouffer, a restaurant analyst for J. C. Bradford of Nashville, Tennessee. "You go public to raise capital or you go public for liquidity reasons, [meaning] you go from private to public ownership so that investors can get better valuation and can readily sell some of their interest."

Initial public offerings did generate excitement early in the 1990s, including those of the Lone Star Steakhouse and Outback Steakhouse. While restaurants are still going public in the current decade, getting backing from a private equity firm seems to be a more attractive option than ever before. According to Scott Pressly, a partner with Roark Capital Group, "You're seeing larger companies go public but not seeing smaller concepts with 10 units going public. You're seeing liquidity being provided by private equity firms. In the 1990s, restaurants went public with 10 or 20 units. You're not seeing that today."[1]

Although the decision to go public is usually predicated on the need to raise capital or to provide an exit strategy for private investors (i.e., a way to convert their ownership in a private corporation into stock that can be sold for cash if they wish to leave the business), public offerings do provide other competitive advantages for companies. Customers often feel more comfortable doing business with a public company, banks are more likely to make loans to interested franchisees, and management can add stock option plans to its arsenal of employee incentives. On the other hand, with the additional capital come increased expectations. Some suggest that restaurants and the stock market are not good partners. In fact, some food service companies have gone public but decided to go private again—Rock Bottom Restaurant and ARAMARK, among others.

Sources: 1. Jamie Popp, Interface with Scott Pressly, *Restaurants and Institutions*, July 1, 2006.

Attracting outside equity capital involves giving up a share of ownership in the business by selling stock. Although such sales are generally limited to small chains, an independent with a concept that can form the basis of a viable chain may be a candidate for equity investment through a **venture capital** group. Industry Practice Note 5.2 discusses reasons for obtaining additional equity (i.e., ownership) capital.

Venture capital groups are made up of wealthy individuals who pool their funds under the direction of a manager with financial experience and expertise. A venture capital group will expect to have a considerable voice in the running of the business and may take a significant share of ownership in the company without necessarily increasing the value of the owner's equity in the way that a stock offering normally does. **Initial public offerings (IPOs)** involve the sale of stock through an underwriting firm of stockbrokers. An IPO would be very difficult for any but the largest independent. This method does, however, apply to successful independents that have expanded to the point where they are now small chains. Well-known restaurant companies that achieved their early expansion through IPOs include Buca di Beppo, P.F. Chang's, and California Pizza Kitchen. In recent years, the number of IPOs has decreased a bit with private equity firms becoming more involved in the financing of restaurant chains. In 2005, there were only three restaurant IPOs—Ruth's Chris Steak House, Caribou Coffee, and Kona Grill—although this figure is expected to increase again over the next several years.[8]

PURCHASING ECONOMIES

The chain enjoys substantial advantages in its purchasing economies. The independent's problem, however, may differ somewhat from the chain's. Because of the importance of quality in the independent operation, the price advantages in centralized purchasing may not be as important as an ability to find top-quality products consistently. Thus, long-standing personal friendships with local purveyors can be an advantage for the independent.

CONTROL AND INFORMATION SYSTEMS

Chains can use centralized cost control systems. These systems also yield a wealth of marketing information. This practice is, in fact, essential to companies operating many units in a national market. Independents are able to purchase POS systems that have standardized but highly complex software, which will generate management reports that are on a par with those available in chains. Moreover, the complex menu of the single, independent, full-service restaurant lends itself to the operator's subjective interpretation, impressions, and hunches about the changing preferences of the guests. In the end, the one difference may be in the effectiveness with which a restaurant utilizes the information provided in the reports.

Cost control procedures may be more stringent in the chain operation, but if an owner keeps an eye on everything from preparation to portion sizes to the garbage can (the amount of food left on a plate is often a good clue to overportioning), effective cost control can be achieved even when a POS system to fit the operator's needs is not available or when the cost of such a system is prohibitive. By using the Uniform System of Accounts and professional advice available from restaurant accounting specialists, independents can readily develop control systems adequate to their needs.

This description of the independent operator suggests what has become a food service axiom: Anyone who cannot operate successfully without the corporate brass looking over his or her shoulder will probably be out of business as an independent in a short time.

HUMAN RESOURCES

The independent proprietor can, and usually does, develop close personal ties with the employees, a practice that can help reduce turnover. Even though "old hand" employees can act as trainers, the cost of training new workers tends to be higher for the independent because of the complex operation and because he or she lacks the economies of a centralized training program.

Although advancement incentives are not as abundant in independent operations as in the chains, some successful independents hire young people, train them over a period of several years to become effective supervisors, and then help them move on to a larger operation. Often, too, the independent finds key employees whose life goals are satisfied by their positions as chef, host or hostess, or head bartender. These employees may receive bonus plans similar to those offered by the chains.

Independents have a special attraction for employees who are tied by family obligations or a strong personal preference to their home community. The problem of being transferred is unlikely to arise with independents. With chains, however, the probability is that advancement is dependent on a willingness to relocate.

THE INDEPENDENT'S EXTRA: FLEXIBILITY

Perhaps the key that independents can boast of is the flexibility inherent in having only one boss or a small partnership. Fast decision making permits the independent to adapt to changing market conditions. In addition, because there is no need to maintain a standard chain image, an independent is free to develop menus that take advantage of local tastes. Finally, there are many one-of-a-kind niches in the marketplace, special situations that don't repeat themselves often enough to make them interesting to chains. Yet these situations may be ideally suited to the strengths of independents.

THE INDEPENDENT'S IMPERATIVE: DIFFERENTIATION

One element of the independent's differentiation, as we have seen, is the personal identity of its owner, and another is its reputation as a local firm. Strategically, it is important to choose a concept—that is, a menu, service style, ambience, and atmosphere—that is fundamentally different from what everybody else is doing. Ninety percent of hamburger sandwich sales are made by the major chains. Logically, then, the quick-service hamburger market (or fried chicken, etc.) is not one for an independent operator unless it has a unique advantage. There is a good chance that KFC's brand appeal will be more powerful than any product differentiation an independent can achieve in a fried chicken take-out unit. Instead, independents must present a menu and dining experience that is uniquely their own. Independents rely on the differentiation

Mimi's Café was privately owned and grew to the point of being acquired by Bob Evans. (Courtesy of Mimi's Café.)

provided by unique foods, outstanding service, pleasing ambience, and personal identity to achieve clear differentiation and consumer preference.

BETWEEN INDEPENDENT AND CHAIN*

Between the independent and the chain lie at least two other possibilities. First, some independent operations are so successful that they open additional units—without, however, becoming so large as to lose the hands-on management of the owner/ operator. *Nation's Restaurant News* refers to these as "independent group operators." They are not exactly chains, but because of their success, they are no longer single-unit operators. Some examples include Richard Melman's Chicago-based "Lettuce Entertain You," Drew Nieporent's NY-based Myriad Group, Danny Meyer's NY-based Union Square Hospitality Group, and Wolfgang Puck's restaurants. All of these concepts started as a single neighborhood restaurant. Some, such as Lettuce Entertain You, operate many different concepts but each is few in number. This has been a successful business format for these operators.

The other possibility, and one that is pursued by thousands of businesspeople, is a franchised operation, which is discussed next.

*The authors would like to acknowledge the assistance and guidance of Udo Schlentrich in the development of this section. Professor Schlentrich is Associate Professor in the Department of Hospitality Management at the University of New Hampshire and director of the William Rosenberg Center of International Franchising.

Franchised Restaurants

Franchising has become a common business format. According to a study by the Educational Foundation of the International Franchise Association (*Economic Impact of Franchised Businesses,* 2004), it is estimated that franchises generate over 45 percent of all retail revenues in the United States.[9] Franchising also generates over 18.1 million jobs in the United States, which represents 13.7 percent of direct and indirect private sector employment. Franchises also earn $1.53 trillion annually, representing 9.5 percent of America's total private sector output. As a point of reference, franchised businesses generate about the same number of jobs in the United States as did the manufacturers of durable goods. In addition, franchised establishments represent the greatest percentage of all line-of-business establishments in quick-service restaurants, lodging, and retail food.

A conversation with a franchisee is likely to yield this contradiction: The franchisee clearly thinks of him- or herself as an independent businessperson but is likely to refer to the franchisor in the course of the conversation as "the parent company." To some, franchises offer the best of both worlds. As William Rosenberg, founder of Dunkin' Donuts, said, franchising allows one to be "in business for yourself, but not by yourself."[10]

Many people automatically think "restaurant" when they hear the word franchising. This is not surprising, since roughly one-half of restaurant sales in the United States are made by franchised units. Quick-service restaurants featuring hamburgers make up the largest category of franchised units. Pizza, steak, full-menu operations, and restaurants featuring chicken also constitute a large number of franchised operations.

There are two basic kinds of franchising: product or trade name franchising and **business format franchising**. Trade name franchising such as a soft drink or automobile dealership franchises confer the right to use a brand name and to sell a particular product.

The type of franchising found in the hospitality industry, however, is called business format franchising. Business format franchising includes use of the product (and service) along with access to, and use of, all other systems and standards associated with the business.

The franchisee has a substantial investment (ownership of the franchise and very possibly of land, building, furniture, and fixtures or a lease on them). Beyond that, he or she has full day-to-day operating control and responsibility. For instance, franchisees are responsible for hiring employees, supervising the daily operation (or managing those who do that supervision), and generally representing themselves in the community as independent businesspeople. The degree of franchisee control over key issues varies from one franchise group to another, but many franchisees share considerable freedom of advertising, choice of some suppliers, and the ability to add to and renovate the physical plant. Although some aspects of the unit's budget are governed by the **franchise agreement**, the franchisee retains significant budgetary discretion under most agreements and in practice exercises even more.

On the other hand, the essence of almost all franchises in the hospitality industry is an agreement by the franchisee to follow the form of the franchisor's business system in order to gain the advantages of that business format. The franchisee has, indeed, relinquished a great deal of discretion in the management of the enterprise and is a part of a system that largely defines its operation. The restaurant franchisee's relationship is neither that of an employee nor that of an independent customer of the franchisor.

The most common characteristics of a franchise agreement include:

Use of trademarks

Location of the franchise

Term of the franchise

Franchisee's fees and other payments

Obligations and duties of the franchisor

Obligations and duties of the franchisee

Restrictions on goods and services offered

Renewal, termination, and transfer of franchise agreement[11]

Additional topics that may be included would be operating procedures and advertising and promotion. Other services that may be provided by the franchisor on a fee basis (such as training or accounting services) would also be included.

THE NEW FRANCHISEE

The franchisor offers to an investor, who often has no previous experience, a proven way of doing business, including established products, an operating system, and a complete marketing program.

A well-developed franchise minimizes risk, but this may not be true of a new, unproven franchise concept. Moreover, a franchise cannot guarantee a profit commensurate with the investment made—nor even guarantee any profit at all. Small Business Administration studies indicate that somewhere between one-fourth and one-third of all businesses fail during their first year, and 65 percent fail within their first five years. The International Franchise Association estimates failure rates among franchised quick-service restaurants at 19 percent and just over 11 percent for other types of restaurants.[12]

In addition to an overall concept, the franchisor provides a number of specific services to the newcomer. Next we will discuss the most common of these.

Screening. Being screened to see whether you are an acceptable franchisee may not seem like a service. A moment's reflection, however, will show that careful franchisee selection is in the best interest not only of the company and other, existing franchisees but of the prospective franchisee as well.

Financing. Because franchising minimizes the risk of business failure, potential franchisees are generally able to obtain financing for established franchise concepts more readily than entrepreneurs who want to launch an independent business concept. This applies especially to the financing of hotels and restaurants, which are particularly high-risk ventures. In addition, some franchisors offer direct financial assistance through formal financing programs.

Site Selection and Planning. Franchisors maintain a real-estate department staffed with site selection experts. The franchise company also has its pooled experience to guide it. Given the importance of location to most hospitality operations, the availability of expert advice is important. The physical layout of the operation, from the site plan to the building, equipment, and furnishings, and even a list of small wares and opening inventory, will be spelled out in detail.

Preopening Training. Virtually all franchise organizations have some means of training the franchisee and his or her key personnel. This service ranges from McDonald's Hamburger University to simpler programs based on experience in an existing store.

Operations Manuals. The backbone of the operating system is typically a set of comprehensive operations manuals and a complete set of recipes that cover all products on the menu. The operations manual sets forth operating procedures from opening to closing and nearly everything in between. All major equipment operations and routine maintenance are described in the operations manual or in a separate equipment manual. Industry Practice Note 5.3 outlines questions a prospective franchisee should keep in mind when assessing a franchisor.

CONTINUING FRANCHISE SERVICES

Once a unit is open and running, the first year or two of advice and assistance are the most crucial. Even once a franchisee is sufficiently experienced to manage his or her unit without close assistance, the advantages of a franchise are still impressive. These services relate to operations and control and to marketing.

Operating and Control Procedures. The franchisor strives to present operating methods that have control procedures designed into them. For instance,

McDonald's not only specifies the portion sizes of its french fries but also has designed packages and serving devices to ensure that the portion sizes will be accurately maintained. Similarly, Long John Silver's specifies a procedure for portioning fish to minimize waste.

The essential ingredient in a successful franchisor's proven way of doing business is not just a great idea but an operational concept. The concept works and is accepted by customers, and its results can be tracked so that its continuing success can be measured and assessed. We should note here, too, that the product and service that underlie the franchise must be continually redeveloped to remain current in the marketplace. Franchisor services in several specialized areas related to operations and control are discussed next.

Information Management. Accounting systems furnished by franchisors normally integrate the individual sales transactions from the POS terminal with both daily management reports and the franchisee's books of account. This makes current management and marketing information available in a timely way and helps hold down the cost of accounting services. This system also provides the franchisor with reliable figures on which to compute the franchisee's royalty payments and other charges such as the advertising assessment.

Quality Control. Inspection systems help keep units on their toes and provide the franchisee with an expert—if sometimes annoying—outsider's view of the operation. Quality control staff use detailed inspection forms that ensure systemwide standards. Inspectors are trained by the franchisor, and their work is generally backed up by detailed written guidelines.

Training. In addition to the opening training effort, franchisors prepare training materials such as videotapes and CD-ROMs that cover standardized ways of accomplishing common tasks in a unit. The franchisor's training department also prepares training manuals and other training aids.

Field Support. There is general agreement on the importance of field support and how it can ultimately determine the quality of the company. Further, the backbone of field support is an experienced franchise district manager. One of the most serious problems with unsuccessful franchise systems is a lack of field staff or field staff lacking in expertise.

Purchasing. Most franchised restaurant companies have purchasing cooperatives. The co-op offers one-stop shopping for virtually all products required in the operation:

Interested in Becoming a Franchisee?

Here are seven basic questions for a prospective franchisee:

1. Is the company itself reasonably secure financially, or is it selling franchises to get cash to cover on-going expenses?

- Is the company selective in choosing franchisees?
- Is it in too big a hurry to get your money? Is this deal too good to be true? Today, sweetheart deals are few and far between.

2. Does the company have a solid base of company-owned units? If it does:

- Is the company in the same business as its franchisees?
- Does the company concentrate on improving marketing and operating systems?

If your primary business is operations and the company's is selling franchises, the system is headed for trouble.

3. Is the system successful on a per-unit basis? To find out, look at several numbers:

- Comparable average sales of stores that have been open longer than one year (sometimes first-year sales are very high and then drop off).
- Unit-level trends: What is really needed are sales data adjusted for inflation or, better yet, customer counts at the unit level.

A business is really only growing when it's serving more people.

4. Is the franchisor innovative across all parts of its business?

- The company should be working on operating and equipment refinements.
- Ask what it is doing in purchasing, recruiting, training, and labor scheduling. Is anyone working to make uniforms more attractive, durable, and comfortable, for instance?

The best companies are consistently trying to upgrade every component of their business.

food, packaging, and equipment, and often, insurance programs. In addition, the co-op periodically publishes a price list that the units can use in negotiating prices with local distributors. The co-op may also publish a newsletter containing information on pricing and trends in equipment, food products, and supply.

Although attractive price and the convenience of one-stop shopping are important franchisee purchasing benefits, particularly with the co-ops, perhaps the most important advantage in the purchasing area is quality maintenance. The lengthy product

5. Does the company share sufficient support services with its franchisees?

- In general, the company should provide guidance and strategic direction on marketing and excellent operations training. In addition, every franchisee should have contact with a company employee whose primary responsibility is a small group of franchised restaurants.
- There are some services that a company can't provide, such as setting prices. In addition, others are risky, such as getting involved in franchisee manager selection.

Support services must be shared in such a way that they respect the franchisee's independence.

6. Does the company respect its franchisees?

- In addition to formal publications, there should be regular informal forums or councils in which selected franchisees meet face-to-face with top management to discuss both problems and opportunities.
- Corporate staff should collect ideas, test them, and if they look good, involve franchisees in expanded testing.

Franchisees should actually participate in the development of any change that will affect their units.

7. Does the franchisor provide long-term leadership for the entire system?

- Franchisee participation is no excuse for the franchisor's abdication of its leadership responsibilities. Somebody has to make the formal decisions, and that must be the franchisor.
- A primary function of the franchisor is to protect the value of each franchise by actively and aggressively monitoring operations, demanding that each unit live up to system standards.

Perhaps a necessary long-term decision is not popular. Making tough decisions and following through may be the best real test of leadership.

Source: Adapted from Don N. Smith, Burtenshaw Lecture, Washington State University.

development process includes careful attention to each product ingredient and the development of detailed product specifications. Often, the franchisor will work with the research department of a supplier's company to develop a product to meet these specifications and to anticipate market fluctuations. Moreover, it is common for franchisors to maintain quality control staff in a supplier's plants and institute rigorous inspection systems that monitor the product from the fabrication plant to regional storage centers and then to the individual operating unit.

Marketing. Second only in importance to providing franchisees with a unique way of doing business is provision of a well-established brand and the ongoing development and execution of the system's marketing plan. Although franchisees usually are consulted about the marketing program, the executive responsibility for developing and implementing the system's marketing program lies with the franchisor's top management and marketing staff.

Advertising. In addition to developing and executing a national or (for smaller chains) regional advertising program, most franchisors assist in operating advertising co-ops that are funded with franchisees' advertising contributions. National advertising co-ops typically provide copies of the company's television and radio commercials to franchisee members for a nominal price as well as mats for both black-and-white and color newspaper ads. Co-ops also develop point-of-purchase promotional materials such as window banners and counter cards. Regional and local co-ops devote their efforts to media buying and to executing the advertising program in their area. The pooling of media buys at the local level yields substantial savings, makes advertising dollars go further, and secures a frequency of advertising that heightens effectiveness. Local and regional co-ops also often coordinate local promotional programs such as those using coupons, games, or premium merchandise.

New Products. The marketplace changes constantly, and it is the franchisor's responsibility to monitor and respond to those changes. The company's marketing department carries out a program of continuing market research. When a new product emerges, from research or from suggestions from franchisees, the company develops the new product in its test kitchens and tests it for consumer acceptance with taste panels and for fit with the operating system in a pilot store or stores. If test marketing in selected units is successful, the product will be rolled out systemwide with standard procedures for operation and extensive promotional support.

New Concepts. Some franchisors have developed or acquired entirely new concepts. Sometimes this effort is undertaken to offer existing franchisees opportunities for new store growth without moving outside the franchisor's system. Increasingly, however, new concepts are used to build volume in an existing store much the same way as adding a new product to the menu. These major changes in the franchisor and franchisee's product line are achieved through co-location of two or more concepts (known as **co-branding** or dual branding). Wendy's, for instance, acquired a coffee and doughnut chain, Tim Horton's, clearly a noncompetitive product line for Wendy's main brand (at the time of this writing, Wendy's is in the process of selling it off as a separate public company).

The Tim Horton's menu draws many customers in the morning, when the Wendy's menu isn't even offered. The concepts work synergistically. By each occupying half the space, Wendy's and Tim Horton's save about 25 percent on building and site costs at each shared site. In some locations, Tim Horton's products are offered at a kiosk adjacent to the Wendy's operation. Although the saving on site costs is important, the greatest benefit is incremental sales. These are achieved, first of all, through the new concept. Equally important, however, is the exposure, in the preceding example, of Tim Horton's breakfast customers to a Wendy's as a possible lunch site and, of course, letting Wendy's lunch and dinner customers know where they can get a quick breakfast. The dual branding of Miami Subs and Baskin-Robbins represents a similarly beneficial arrangement. The concept of dual branding has recently taken another step forward with some companies offering multiple brands in one location. The grouping of Dunkin' Donuts, Baskin-Robbins, and Togo's is an example. The grouping of multiple concepts creates more choice for customers as well as greater profit potential for the company.

Dual branding is not the only strategy that companies use to boost revenues. Some restaurant companies, such as CKE (Carl's Jr. and Hardee's) and Yum! Brands (KFC, Taco Bell, Pizza Hut, Long John Silver's, and A&W) offer food products from other companies (or from other restaurants within the same group).

THE FRANCHISEE'S VIEW

Expansion is an important activity for franchise companies. (Courtesy of Domino's Pizza, Inc.)

Some of the more obvious drawbacks of obtaining a franchise have been implicit in our discussion: loss of independence and payment of substantial advertising assessments and franchise fees. If the franchisee has picked a weak franchising organization, field support and other management services may be inadequate and could result in underperformance or failure of the franchise unit. There are numerous factors to consider, as outlined in the sections that follow.

Advantages to Franchisees. The primary advantages of franchising from the perspective of the franchisee are the provision of a recognizable brand, attested and refined product and service concepts, technical assistance in the areas of site selection, construction, interior design, training, marketing, and ongoing operational support. In addition, franchisors often assist franchise applicants in obtaining financing and/or lease agreements.

The U.S. Trade Commission has issued extensive regulations in order to protect potential franchisees from misrepresentation by franchisors. These regulations are contained in a document called the Uniform Franchise Offering Circular (UFOC). UFOCs include 23 important disclosure statements, such as details about a franchisor's business experience, its key employees, its litigation history, fees and investment requirements, franchisee and franchisor obligations, territorial rights, trademark regulations, and renewal and termination terms. Inaccuracies or misrepresentations by franchisors in their UFOC can result in civil or criminal penalties.

Franchising Is Not Risk-Free: Disadvantages to Franchisees. The franchisee is generally completely dependent on the franchisor not only for marketing but often for purchasing and other operations-oriented assistance. If a franchise concept is not kept up-to-date—as many argue was the case some years ago for Howard Johnson's restaurants, for instance—or loses its focus, it is difficult for the franchisee to do much about it.

What happens when things really go wrong is illustrated by the case of Arthur Treacher's Fish and Chips. A successful and growing franchise in the mid-1970s, Treacher's then had serious difficulties that ended in bankruptcy. Its national marketing efforts virtually ceased. Its product quality control system broke down, yet the franchisees were contractually obligated to purchase only from approved suppliers. The franchisees also were required to pay both advertising fees and royalties but claimed they received few or no services in return. Many franchisees withheld payment of fees and royalties and then became involved in lengthy lawsuits that were expensive in both executive time and attorney's fees. Although some Treacher's franchisees weathered the series of setbacks, virtually all suffered serious losses, and many left the field. Although the Treacher's franchise system has begun to grow again, the turnaround took a number of years.

Franchisors normally charge franchisees a one-time initial fee when a contract is signed. For quick-service franchises, the initial fee normally ranges from $10,000 to $75,000, with a median fee of $25,000. In addition, franchisors charge an ongoing advertising fee and a royalty fee (which covers the use of the brand trademark, the operational systems, and marketing support). Advertising and royalty fees are based on a percentage of gross sales, with the percentage varying from system to system. For quick-service franchises, the average royalty fee is about 5 percent and the average advertising fee is about 2 percent.[13]

THE FRANCHISOR'S VIEW

Advantages to Franchisors. The franchisee makes most—often, all—of the investment in a new unit. As a result, franchising gives the franchisor the means to expand rapidly without extensive use of its own capital. By expanding rapidly, the franchising organization achieves a presence in the marketplace that is, in itself, an advantage. Moreover, the more units a company has in a market, the more advertising media it can afford to buy. In addition, the better the geographic coverage, the easier it will be for people to visit often; the restaurants are simply closer and more convenient. Finally, continuous exposure of all kinds—seeing television commercials, driving past the sign and building, as well as actually visiting the restaurant—contribute to "top-of-mind awareness," that is, being the first place that comes into people's minds when they think of a restaurant. Being in place in a market is a crucial advantage and one more readily secured quickly through franchising.

The franchising organization also gains highly motivated owners/managers who require less field supervision than company-owned units do. A district manager supervising owned units is usually responsible for four to eight units. A supervisor (or franchise consultant, as they are sometimes called) overseeing franchised units is likely to cover somewhere between 15 and 30 units. (This number has been increasing gradually over the last several years as companies have reorganized and tried to improve communications between the field and the home office.) This permits a large company such as McDonald's to operate with a much smaller organization than would be possible if it had to provide close supervision to all of its thousands of units.

Franchising companies also draw on franchisees as a source of know-how. Numerous examples exist where franchisees have come up with a better way for the company to do things or have come up with new products that made sense for the company to offer systemwide. Some of these examples include the Egg McMuffin (McDonald's) and the gun that Taco Bell uses to dispense sour cream.

Disadvantages to Franchisors. The bargain struck with franchisees has its costs to franchisors. Although their experience varies, many franchise companies find that their owned stores yield higher sales and profit margins. In addition, if the company owned all its units—if it could overcome the organizational difficulties of a much larger, more complex organization—the profits earned from the same stores would be higher than the royalties received from a franchised store.

From time to time, franchising companies are struck by the amount of profit they are giving up. In the late 1980s and early 1990s, PepsiCo embarked on an ambitious repurchase program in its restaurant divisions, then made up of KFC, Taco Bell, and Pizza Hut. The effect, however, was to tie up a lot of capital without improving returns enough to justify the investment. PepsiCo and then Yum! Brands (the company that now owns KFC, Taco Bell, and Pizza Hut) and others have more recently followed an aggressive program of refranchising the units they purchased earlier.

Rosenberg International Center of Franchising

The Rosenberg International Center of Franchising (RICF) was created according to the vision of William Rosenberg, a franchising pioneer and the founder of Dunkin' Donuts. Mr. Rosenberg saw the need for a specialized center that would advance the field of franchising through relevant research and innovative teaching. Educational and research guidance is provided by a top level Advisory Board representing the various segments of the franchise community.

The mission of RICF is:

- To produce a broad range of franchise-related research that addresses issues of present and potential future interest
- To educate students and entrepreneurs about franchising and business issues relevant to the franchise community
- To stage periodic international symposia allowing for the interaction of academic and business leaders in the field of franchising

The Center's research focuses on the analysis of the financial performance of franchise companies, both in the United States and internationally. The Center publishes a quarterly Franchise 50 Index that tracks the performance of the top 50 publicly listed U.S.-based franchise companies against that of the Standard & Poor's (S&P) 500. In addition, the Center publishes articles that highlight current issues of interest to the academic, franchise, and financial communities. Key topics include international expansion strategies, risk and opportunity assessment, and valuation of franchise companies. In addition, the Center maintains the world's most extensive Web-based Franchise Bibliography & Database in cooperation with EBSCO.

The Center teaches a franchise course at the Whittemore School of Business and Economics and hosts franchise-specific seminars to senior executives from the hospitality industry. In addition, guest lectures are offered at select universities in the United States and abroad. Franchise case studies are written by the Center's faculty in order to bring the complexity of real business world issues into the classroom.

RICF maintains a close relationship with the International Franchise Association, the largest representative body of franchisors and franchisees in the world, and its Educational Foundation. The Center is also actively involved in advising individuals who are interested in acquiring a franchise or starting their own franchise system.

We should note that not all franchise royalty income is profit. Usually, 2 percent of sales is needed to service a franchise system. Because of start-up costs for a new franchised unit for the franchisor, it may be three years before the royalties begin to contribute to the franchisor's profit. In addition, the franchisor will already have made a considerable investment in legal and accounting costs, as well as executives' time.

FRANCHISOR—FRANCHISEE RELATIONS

We have said that franchisees are independent in some ways and yet subordinate in other ways. It is hardly surprising that this somewhat contradictory relationship sometimes leads to problems. To secure better communication between the parties, most franchisors have a franchisee council—KFC, for example, calls it a Service Council—made up of representatives elected by the franchisees. This council meets with the franchisor's top management to discuss major marketing and operational issues.

FRANCHISING: A MIDDLE WAY

The franchisee is not fully independent, but neither is he or she as much at risk as the independent. Taking part in a larger organization that provides vital services while still allowing a considerable measure of financial and managerial independence has much to say for it. A person who is unable to work within a tightly prescribed system would be uncomfortable as a franchisee. Those who can live within such a framework, however, can reap significant rewards with less risk than they would have in their own business.

Franchising is receiving more attention both from industry and academia. Industry Practice Note 5.4 describes the work of the William Rosenberg Center of International Franchising at the University of New Hampshire and the various services it provides to the franchising community.

Summary

Restaurants are organized into groups in chains or franchise organizations or stand alone as independents. Chains and independents can be compared on the basis of brand recognition, site selection, access to capital, purchasing economies, information and control systems, and human resource programs. Chains' strengths come largely from economies of scale. The independent's advantages lie in flexibility and the closeness of the owner/manager to the operation. To be successful, however, independents must differentiate their operation so that they stand out from the crowd.

Franchising offers operators a degree of independence but requires a willingness to work within a defined operation. Franchisees must give up some control over the operation, but in return their risks are lowered dramatically. Franchisees generally pay a development fee, a royalty fee, and an advertising assessment. The franchisor provides a proven system of operation and expert field staff as well as a marketing program.

Services that are especially helpful to new franchisees include screening, site selection and planning, preopening training, and complete documentation of the operating concept in an operations manual. The chapter identifies ten areas of support to continuing franchisees: operating and control procedures, information management, quality control, training, field support, purchasing, marketing, advertising, new products, and new concepts.

There are positive and negative aspects of franchising for both partners in the arrangement. Franchisees gain a proven format and the assistance described previously but give up much of their independence and are required to pay substantial fees. Moreover, the franchisee is completely dependent on the franchisor. The franchisor can expand rapidly, largely on the franchisee's investment and organization, and has in the franchisee a highly motivated manager and a rich source of innovative ideas. On the other hand, company stores often yield higher sales and better profits, which the franchisor must give up along with a significant degree of operational control. Given the close and somewhat ambiguous nature of their relationship—neither that of employee and employer nor that of independent partners—there is often conflict within the franchise community, which franchisors are moving to contain with franchisee councils.

Key Words and Concepts

Marketing	**Training programs**
Brand recognition	**Independent restaurants**
Site selection	**Small Business Administration**
Access to capital	** (SBA)**
Purchasing economies	**Venture capital**
Control and information	**Initial public offering (IPO)**
** system**	**Business format franchising**
Publicly traded companies	**Franchise agreement**
Market share	**Co-branding**

Review Questions

1. How do you rate the advantages of the chain (and independent) on the seven factors cited in the text? Are there other factors that should be considered?

2. What is the trend in chains' market share in food service? Can you explain this trend?

3. What are the major services provided by the franchisor to the new franchisee? Contrast them with the continuing services provided to established franchisees.

4. How do you assess your prospects as a franchisee? What characteristics do you think would be important to being a successful franchisee?

5. What does the franchisor gain from franchising? What advantages does the franchisor give up by franchising instead of owning units?

Internet Exercises

1. **Site name:** William Rosenberg Center of International Franchising

URL: http://wsbe.unh.edu/centers_wrcif/home.cfm

Background information: The William Rosenberg International Center of Franchising was created according to the vision of William Rosenberg, a franchising pioneer and founder of Dunkin' Donuts. Mr. Rosenberg saw the need for a specialized center that would advance the field of franchising through relevant research and innovative teaching. His generous grant to the University of New Hampshire along with his vision and drive provided the foundation upon which the Center was launched in the Fall of 2002.

Exercises:

a. Analyze the entire Web site and describe the resources available to a potential franchisee.

b. Examine several stock market quarters listed on the Franchise 50 Index page. Which hospitality companies are identified as gaining or losing for the quarter being reviewed?

c. What might account for the increase or decrease of the stock of a publicly traded restaurant chain in any given three-month period?

2. **Site name:** International Franchise Association

URL: www.franchise.org/

Background information: The International Franchise Association (IFA), founded in 1960, is a membership organization of franchisors, franchisees, and suppliers. Their Web site is dedicated to providing members and guests with a one-stop shopping experience for franchise information.

Exercises:

a. Analyze the entire Web site and list and describe the resources available to assist the potential franchisee. Include both information that is free to the general public and courses that are available through the IFA-University for a fee.

b. On the Web site, choose a food-related franchise that is available in your state. Identify the following for that franchise: when the business was first established, when they began franchising, the number of units that are currently franchised, the number of company owned units, estimated start-up costs, total investment needed, training provided, and the qualifications of the potential franchisee.

3. **Site name:** Small Business Administration

URL: www.sba.gov

Background information: The U.S. Small Business Administration (SBA) was created by Congress in 1953 to help America's entrepreneurs form successful small enterprises. Today, SBA's program offices in every state offer financing, training, and advocacy for small firms. These programs are delivered by SBA offices in every state, the District of Columbia, the Virgin Islands, and Puerto Rico. In addition, the SBA works with thousands of lending, educational, and training institutions nationwide.

Exercises:

a. Surf the SBA Web site and identify the programs provided by the SBA for entrepreneurs who wish to start their own business.

b. Describe in detail three SBA programs that may be helpful to you, if you were starting your own business.

c. You want to start your own restaurant but need financing in order to start. Describe in detail what the SBA can do to help you obtain financing.

d. The SBA provides over 65 online training courses for the aspiring entrepreneur. Lead a class discussion on the categories of training provided by the SBA, and discuss some of the courses you think would be most beneficial.

e. The SBA hosts seminars nationwide that would assist an individual who wishes to start his or her own business. Click on your state and identify the workshops that are being offered in your area.

f. Identify the elements of a model business plan, and write a sentence or two describing the information required for each element.

g. The SBA provides information on managing your new enterprise. Describe the leadership traits they consider important for an entrepreneur to be effective.

h. Discuss how the SBA supports women and minorities.

i. Describe the information the SBA provides on franchising.

j. Review an example of a restaurant, food service, bar, or nightclub business plan. Lead a class discussion on how effectively the author addressed all of the elements of a model business plan.

4. **Site name:** Cornell University Links to Independent Restaurants
URL: www.hotelschool.cornell.edu/links/hslinks.html?scid=255&name=Foodservice+Industry&scname=Independent+Restaurants&id=5
Background information: Cornell University's School of Hotel Administration provides a variety of Web resources for the hospitality Industry
Site name: Cornell University Links to Chain Restaurants
URL: www.hotelschool.cornell.edu/links/hslinks.html?scid=284&name=Foodservice+Industry&scname=Restaurant+Chain+Companies&id=5

Exercises:

a. Explore three independent restaurant sites and three chain restaurant sites. Describe the differences and similarities among the independent and the chain groups.

b. After reviewing their Web sites, is there a significant difference between the "look and feel" of the chain Web sites and the independent operator's Web sites?

5. **Site name:** *Restaurants & Institutions magazine*

URL: www.rimag.com

Background information: *Restaurants & Institutions* magazine is a leading trade journal for the restaurant and food service industry. Each year, the April 1 issue of *Restaurants & Institutions* magazine has a major article that features independent restaurants. Click on Archives to find articles from the last three years.

Exercises:

a. Read the article on independent restaurants for two different years. Based on the articles, what are independents striving to do well to maintain a competitive advantage with chain restaurants?

b. Based on the two articles you have read, what do you consider to be the strengths of independent restaurants as compared to chains? What are their weaknesses?

c. Review the list of the top 100 independent restaurants for any year. What are the themes (concepts) for these restaurants? What is their gross income and how does it compare to chain restaurants?

Notes

1. 2004 Restaurant Industry Operations Report (Washington, D.C: National Restaurant Association, 2004).
2. Deborah Silver, "Site Seeing." *Restaurants & Institutions,* January 15, 2000.
3. Clayton Barrows, "A Profile of Norman Brinker." *Journal of Hospitality and Tourism Education*, 17(3): 7–11.
4. H. G. Parsa, Tiffany King, and David Njite, "Why Restaurants Fail," paper presented at the CHRIE conference, August, 2003.
5. Allison Perlik, "Log On Learn," *Restaurants & Institutions,* December 15, 2002.
6. 2003 Technomic Top 100 (Chicago: Technomic, Inc., 2003).
7. The information in this section is based on correspondence with Shawn McKeehan, Freedom of Information Act officer with the SBA, August 26, 2003.
8. Susan Spielberg. "More operators expected to charge into IPOs." *Nation's Restaurant News.* January 23, 2006.
9. Educational Foundation of the International Franchise Association, 2004, Economic Impact of Franchised Businesses.
10. William Rosenberg, 2001, *Time to Make the Donuts*, Lebhar-Friedman Books, NYC.
11. "Introduction to Franchising," International Franchise Association, August 26, 2003 (www.franchise.org).
12. "The Profile of Franchising," International Franchise Association, February 2000.
13. IFA Special Report, "The Profile of Franchising 2006: Series II - Initial Investment, Series III—Royalty and Advertising Fees."

The Hospitality Industry

(Pizza Hut and the Pizza Hut logo are registered trademarks of Pizza Hut, Inc. and are used with permission.)

CHAPTER SIX

Competitive Forces in Food Service

The Purpose of this Chapter

In this chapter, we will look at the all-important subject of competition from three points of view. We will be concerned first with how competitive conditions in food service have evolved over the recent past, as consumer tastes and industry conditions changed. Then, using the marketing mix of product, price, place, and promotion as a framework, we will examine current competitive practices. Finally, we will look at competitors outside the industry such as convenience stores, supermarkets, and the home, which also compete for the food service customer.

THIS CHAPTER SHOULD HELP YOU

1. Describe current competitive conditions in the food service industry.
2. Describe the four Ps that make up the food service marketing mix.
3. Define the food service product, and describe the role of new products in food service competition.
4. List the advantages and disadvantages of competing on price, and describe the conditions under which it is most appropriate.
5. Define PODs and describe how the concept of distribution led to their development.
6. Identify and describe the two major forms of paid marketing communication in the food service industry.
7. Identify the most common media used by the food service industry for advertising communication.
8. Define the term sales promotion, and describe three common sales promotion concepts.
9. Identify the two industries with which food service companies compete, and list their strengths and weaknesses.

Competitive Conditions in Food Service

Competition in food service has always been intense. There are many buyers and many sellers, a condition that makes it hard for any company to achieve control over the market—that is, over prices and other competitive practices. The nature of the competition, however, has changed from the heady days of the growth of new chain concepts in a rapidly expanding market—roughly from the mid 1950s to the early 1980s—to a time today when established food service giants struggle with each other over a much more slowly growing market.

During the period in question, the industry grew rapidly. As more women went to work, more families could afford to eat out—and were pressed by time to do so. In spite of intense competition, firms had lots of opportunities in an expanding market.

Moreover, the competition between new chain concepts was largely to fill unmet demand. The challenge was to grow rapidly enough to snap up the available locations in existing territories and expand into new territories ahead of the competition.

Although there was competition between new concepts for both customers and locations, newer operations were competing, to a large extent, principally against outmoded, independent operations for customers' attention and patronage. It was relatively easy for new, well-advertised, low-priced operations to take business from old, tired units that had high labor costs and usually indifferent, expensive service.

In the 1980s, however, conditions began to change for the chains that had been enjoying success. During the 1970s, it had already become harder to find good locations. Moreover, the marketplace changed from one that was anxious to try a new concept to one already saturated with restaurants constructed during the prior 10 to 15 years. Competition now was more and more between established operations with sophisticated marketing and a proven, accepted operating format. In the hamburger

Many chains are synonymous with well-known brand names. (Courtesy of Tim Horton's.)

Domino's is a well-known brand within the pizza segment. (Courtesy of Domino's Pizza, Inc.)

segment, for instance, competition had gone from Joe's Diner versus McDonald's to McDonald's versus Burger King versus Wendy's versus Hardee's—all struggling aggressively for market share. Nevertheless, the industry continued to expand in numbers of units. Between 1985 and 1987, an incredible 40,000 new restaurants opened.

Since those turbulent times, much has changed. Now, one could argue, most of the prime (traditional) locations have indeed been claimed, at least for the quick-service sector. As a result, much of the expansion is targeting international locations and/or "nontraditional" locations—a concept that will be discussed later. Because of these changing conditions, some companies have left the field, become lesser players, or changed their strategies. Marriott, for instance, sold off most of its restaurants and quick-service divisions. Interestingly, at one time Marriott was known exclusively as a food service company. Basically, the reason for these decisions appears to have been limited food service profits in a crowded industry and competitive pressures that were likely only to get worse. The established players had a dominance that even a company as large and accomplished as Marriott could not challenge. Other companies that have come and gone include Howard Johnson's, which was once a major player in food service with 1,000-odd restaurants. Their last few remaining restaurants in North America have just been closed. The general consensus is that the company was unable to keep up with the times. Further, consider the number of takeovers, mergers, and acquisitions that have occurred over the last ten years and one can quickly see that the food service landscape has changed dramatically.

Although our discussion above (and throughout this chapter) has focused on chain operations, we should note, too, that many independent operations have withdrawn from the market and many of the remaining independents are either very large operations or operators that dominate a small or very specialized market. The independents' role in food service remains a vital one, but their share of the market has fallen steadily for some years. Success appears to come mainly to those who have a very distinct way of differentiating themselves from their competitors. As well, in the end, many of these same successful independents become successful chain operations.

Heightened competition—and food service firms' reactions to it—have created a situation sufficiently different that fundamentally new competitive strategies are emerging or have emerged that are changing the face of food service. This leads us to our discussion of something known as marketing. Marketing is not just advertising. Marketing is defined as "communicating to and giving . . . customers what they want, when they want it, where they want it, at a price they are willing to pay."[1] One of the ways that restaurants accomplish this is by a variety of activities known as the **marketing mix**.

The Marketing Mix

A good frame of reference for examining these strategic changes is to review what is happening in food service marketing. Marketing is a mix of activities that deals with the four Ps: the **product** itself, the product's **price**, the **place** (or places) in which it is offered, and **promotion** of the product.[2] The four Ps are referred to as the marketing mix, and among them, they cover the major areas of competitive activity. The marketing mix is a fundamental tool of analysis, widely used in the hospitality industry. It is important to realize that marketing is a mix of activities. Marketing activities, in the examples that follow, may emphasize one element of the mix, but two or three others are usually involved, either explicitly or implicitly. Case History 6.1 illustrates how one company combines different elements of the marketing mix.

PRODUCT

A useful way of looking at the hospitality product is that it is actually the guest's experience. In a restaurant, this involves not only the food served but the way the server and guest interact and the atmosphere of the place. This is not to argue that the physical product (food) is unimportant, but it needs to be seen in the context of the overall concept of the operation that determines the guest's total experience. Our discussion of product will, therefore, cover food products and restaurant concepts.

The importance of good food hardly needs to be discussed. Guests simply assume the food is acceptable. What is acceptable, of course, varies from operation to operation. Wendy's creates a different product expectation in guests than does the Waldorf-Astoria or the Four Seasons. Product acceptability requires that guest expectation be met or exceeded. It is clear that all elements of this service product are essential. A grouchy server or a dirty dining room can spoil the best experience.

Finding the Proper Marketing Mix—Shakey's Pizza

Many restaurant goers who grew in the 1960s and 1970s fondly remember Shakey's Pizza. Traditional pizza, old time movies, and live music kept many young kids and their families entertained and made for a nice family outing. While Shakey's is no longer represented on the East Coast of the United States, the company is refocusing on the southern California market. They currently have approximately 65 restaurants, primarily in southern California and mostly in greater Los Angeles.

Still firmly entrenched in the pizza/family dining segment of the industry, the company finds itself competing with a different type of competitor than it had earlier in the history of the company. Newer competitors include Chuck E. Cheese and Peter Piper Pizza as well as other family dining restaurants all competing for the same food service dollar. Indications are that they also compete with QSRs for some meal occasions. While the Shakey's menu has not undergone many changes over the last 25 years, it does contain more than just pizza. Shakey's continues to offer a family-oriented menu focusing on pizza but also promoting their Mojos®, deep fried breaded potato slices.

In an effort to target families, Shakey's employs several strategies including targeted advertising (both radio and television), attractive prices, coupons, and direct mail. Their in-store strategies include offering a relaxed dining environment, separate game rooms for children, and a buffet at lunch. Future plans include giving their Web site a facelift and continuing to offer deals over the Internet. They also encourage local store marketing efforts. They are also working on developing new products and ultimately repositioning the brand. The company was founded in Sacramento, California in 1954.

1. The information in this note is based on an interview conducted with Suzi Carragher, Marketing Manager for Shakey's, on January 2, 2003.

New Products. **New products** are often a key part of a campaign to revitalize sales in a well-established chain. New products add a note of excitement for customers. Menu enhancement can be a very important tool available to restaurateurs. It shouldn't come as any surprise that menu analysis and development is taught regularly in hospitality management programs.

New products are also used to target new market segments. Some years ago, for instance, Wendy's noted that it had a mainly male customer base. To target women, Wendy's introduced the baked potato as a main meal dish and installed salad bars. Both products—salads and baked potatoes—had the effect of increasing Wendy's market share among women. Interestingly, Taco Bell later introduced its large-portion tacos and burritos to increase its market share among men. Similarly, larger-portion hamburgers have been introduced by numerous chains in recent years (most recently, Carl's Jr. in the United States and Harvey's in Canada). McDonald's began offering a Happy

Meal for adults not too long ago, which combines several healthy choice items. Salads and fruit have also become big sellers.

The evidence suggests that a majority of QSR guests are very interested in new products, and this is even truer of guests selecting a full-service restaurant. Although not all products need to be new, it is clear that to achieve and maintain good menu variety, the excitement of new products is required from time to time—and on a regular basis.

The term "new product" can mean a product that is a genuine innovation—that is, a product that has not been served before commercially. These are sometimes referred to as "new-to-world." Examples are the Egg McMuffin and Chicken McNuggets, products that set off major sales growth for McDonald's when they were introduced. Other new products, often introduced defensively, are referred to as "new-to-chain" and are essentially an imitation of a successful new product offered by another operator. KFC's chicken nugget product is an example of this category. KFC introduced it as a defensive measure when McNuggets had made McDonald's the biggest "chicken chain" in North America.

Many successful new products appear to follow a **life cycle** similar to that for products in fashion-dominated industries. Figure 6.1 (which depicts the product life cycle) shows new-product sales increasing rapidly during the introduction and growth stages. At the peak of the cycle, total sales of the product are at their highest, largely because everybody is competing to sell it. Many new products can't maintain consumers' interest when everybody else is offering the same or similar products. Consumers tire of them as the novelty wears off.

Figure 6.2 also suggests that maturity doesn't necessarily mean the death of a concept. In fact, most products we all use are at the mature stage of the life cycle, but marketers have learned to spice up an existing product with changes in its marketing

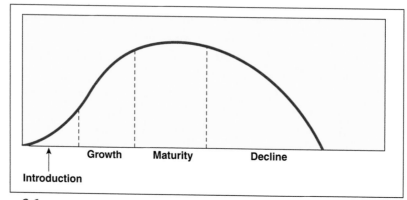

Figure 6.1
The product life cycle.

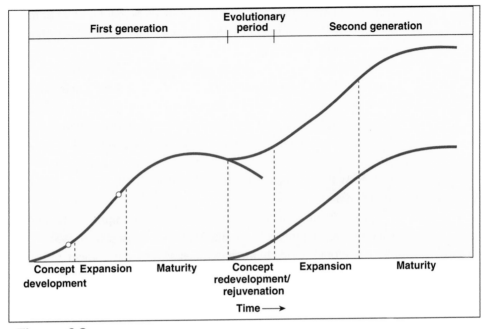

First generation | Evolutionary period | Second generation

Concept development | Expansion | Maturity | Concept redevelopment/ rejuvenation | Expansion | Maturity

Time ⟶

Figure 6.2
Restaurant concept life cycle. (Source: Adapted from Technomic Consultants.)

mix. This is true not just of individual products but also of entire concepts. Products can be reinvented, repackaged or their appearance otherwise changed.

When a concept goes unchanged too long, it does become dated. The Howard Johnson's chain was mentioned earlier in the chapter. The Chi Chi's chain presents another study. Chi Chi's was one of the first chains to offer casual dining as the heart of its concept. That concept, however, remained essentially unchanged for 21 years. As a result, Chi Chi's had several years of declining sales, but in 1997, the chain began working to bring restaurant decor and menu design up-to-date—and supported these product changes with a new advertising campaign. Eventually, Chi Chi's went on to win awards for its food quality and menu variety, including *Restaurant and Institution's* Choice in Chains for the Mexican category. In short, they were able to make the necessary changes to turn the company around. The chain has since closed, its units having been purchased by Outback in 2004—the closing being caused by an outbreak of foodborne illness in one of their restaurants which led to subsequent bankruptcy. Another casual chain, Chili's, responded to decreasing sales by changing 60 percent of its menu items and adding 24 new products to its menu. By the end of 1997, Chili's sales had gone from a decline to nearly a 6 percent increase. By 1998, the same chain was experiencing double-digit growth. Although much of the improvement came from stronger pricing, customer traffic increased 1.5 percent in spite of higher prices. More recently, Brinker International (the parent company of Chili's) has grown revenues every year since 2000.

Addition of services and changes in decor can also be crucial in the competitive struggle. Drive-through restaurants found themselves trapped in price-oriented, 99-cent "sandwich wars." Two of the leaders in that segment decided to sidestep this no-win strategic trap by changing the concept (i.e., product) and adding indoor seating. Although conversion costs were as high as $200,000 per store, increased traffic counts, sales, and profits justified this move. Others have focused on improving drive-through services. With some basic changes in delivery, McDonald's recently reduced the drive-through time for customers by 40 seconds.[3]

Typically, new menu items are introduced to improve sales and/or help to differentiate the restaurant and its menu. Two West Coast chains, Jack in the Box and Carl's Jr., saw an opportunity to increase sales where both of them had a weak day part, at breakfast. Jack in the Box introduced "combo meals," which bundled several products in an attractively priced package. Jack in the Box has since reformulated some of their burger items and also reintroduced some Mexican items as well. Carl's Jr. introduced a proven breakfast menu from Hardee's, a chain owned by CKE, Carl's Jr.'s parent. In each of the preceding cases, the company sought to rejuvenate its concept to achieve the rebound depicted in Figure 6.2. Wendy's recent introduction of a new salad line was immediately successful and contributed greatly to increased profitability in the year they were introduced.

Extension of Concept. In some ways, food service companies are changing the nature of their product by seeking to serve entirely new markets through **concept extension**. This may ultimately change the way the public perceives them, but thus far, it has resulted in increased sales. Quick-service food products, for instance, are increasingly turning up in in-flight meals. Quick-service chains are partnering with gasoline companies, offering food service along the highway in gas stations. Cafeteria chains, such as Piccadilly, are partnering with supermarkets. In addition, many food service companies are packaging their product for distribution through retail stores. Taco Bell, for instance, has sold the rights to its brand name and entered into partnership with food manufacturers that will handle development of the manufactured product and its distribution. Growing customer demand for Chef Paul Prudhomme's spices finally led him to develop a line of packaged seasonings, which are now available nationally. Other famous food service names associated with retail products are as varied as White Castle, Wolfgang Puck, UNO Chicago Grill, and Starbucks.

A development that is in the forefront of concept extension is the introduction of downsized units with limited versions of a franchise brand's menu. These seem to be

White Castle offers their hamburgers for sale in retail outlets. (Courtesy of (© White Castle System, Inc. All rights reserved.)

popping up everywhere, in carts or other portable units. We will return to this topic when we discuss place later in this chapter.

Branding. **Branding** is considered a product characteristic because the brand is used to heighten awareness of the product in the consumer's mind. The uses of branding in food service are on the increase today, and industry practice is highly varied. It can involve branding of individual menu items, as with the Big Mac, to give them greater prominence, or it can involve using a manufacturer's name on an operation's menu, such as Coke in a QSR. In short, it can occur in a variety of ways but with the ultimate objective of promoting the product by leveraging the brand name.

Sometimes it is not just one product but an entire concept that is adopted in a joint location. Miami Subs needed a way to strengthen its weak day parts. Rather than invent and promote a new product of its own, the company added Baskin-Robbins ice cream and frozen yogurt, which sold well in the otherwise slow late-afternoon and late-evening day parts. Other companies have reached similar arrangements, including Baskin-Robbins and Subway, and Wendy's and Tim Horton's (owned by the same company).

A brand name helps to heighten the guest's awareness of the product. (Courtesy of Rainforest Café.)

Finally, product improvements can center around more tightly controlled operations. Quick-service leader McDonald's sought to fight falling sales volume with improvements to existing products, resolving to stop microwaving sandwiches and reintroduced toasted buns for its sandwiches. It continues to add new products and revamp existing ones. New products were also being planned to liven McDonald's familiar menu. At the same time, another familiar name, Pizza Hut, continues to roll out new items including pasta dishes and different types of pizzas such as Chicago-style deep dish.

PRICE

The restaurant industry was reminded of the power of price competition by Taco Bell in the mid-1980s when experiments with lower prices proved so successful that they were adopted as a major strategy of the company. **Value pricing**, as it came to be called, drove sales increases of 60 percent over a three-year period. Some of the hazards of leading with price came home to roost roughly ten years later. John Martin, widely recognized as one of the most talented restaurant executives of a generation, after a ten-year run of value pricing, was replaced as president of Taco Bell. Not long thereafter, Taco Bell was reported to be shifting away from low prices and upgrading to higher quality with higher prices in a move code-named "Project Gold."

The problem with value pricing proved to be that eventually competitors adopted new pricing strategies to counter it. Then what was left was a lower profit margin for everyone.

One way of effectively reducing prices temporarily is by offering coupons that entitle the bearer to a special discount, a practice called **couponing**. Although this does affect price, it is generally treated as a promotional tactic, and so we will treat it under that topic later in the chapter. We should note here, however, that couponing and other price-cutting tactics are sometimes likened to an addiction. It is easy, even pleasant, to start. Sales go up; customers are happy with a bargain; with rising sales, things look brighter for the operation. At the end of a prolonged period of discounting, however, the favorable impact on sales is usually eroded. Moreover, profit margins decrease immediately unless the increase in customer traffic offsets the price reduction. Direct, noticeable competition on price in food service occurs, but it is the exception rather than the rule just because its result is generally to depress everyone's margins. Price competition is most common in the off months (usually January through March), when market leaders seek to maintain volume at or above break-even levels at the expense of their smaller competitors.

There is a risk in price reductions, namely, that the lower price will denote a cheapened product to the customer. On the other hand, in the late 1980s and early 1990s, many fine-dining establishments rewrote their menus when customers rebelled against upscale operations with very high menu prices. The new menus featured foods that had a lower food cost and, hence, could be offered at an attractive price. This led to a turnaround for many of these operations. As with virtually all marketing activities, the key is to keep prices in line with customer expectations and to offer products that are perceived to be a good value to the customer.

Pricing: Strategic Implications. Pressure on prices, we should note, has implications for other elements of the marketing mix. A period of rising prices can mean a favorable climate for competition through innovation. The cost of upgraded decor, new product development, more extensive preparation equipment, and more preparation labor all could be passed on to the consumer in higher prices. In the future, however, the test for innovation may be stiffer. Changes will have to create savings or major increases in sales volume. If innovations don't pass these stricter tests, they may have to be dropped, because their cost cannot be passed on in ever-higher prices.

PLACE—AND PLACES

In marketing, place refers to the **location**, the place where the good or service is offered. The great hotelier Ellsworth Statler said of hotels that the three most important

A good location is an important element of marketing. (Courtesy of Domino's Pizza, Inc.)

factors in success are "location, location, and location." This has often been repeated regarding many other retailers and is certainly true of food service.

Food service chains are now concerned, however, not just with place but with places. They are seeking to achieve wide **distribution** of their product and so are developing tactics to multiply the number of places in which their product—or some version of it—can be offered.

Indeed, one of the most dramatic changes since the introduction of quick service is now under way as multiunit companies continue to change their strategy regarding location. Companies now try to "capture" customers wherever they might be.

Today's customers live harried and hurried lives. Whether members of a two-working-spouse family or a single-parent family, adults (and, increasingly, children) today see themselves as being constantly rushed. The tendency is to fit meals in wherever they happen to be, to "grab a bite," as the phrase has it, "on the run." Effective distribution, then, is achieved by locating an outlet wherever consumers might go in any numbers.

Restaurant companies have developed downsized units for places where a traditional unit won't fit. These units often take the form of a kiosk or mobile cart requiring minimal investment. The name given these new units is **points of distribution (PODs)**.

As an example, the Little Caesars pizza chain, in its partnership with Kmart, has downsized Pizza Express units in many Kmart stores. Other companies that have adopted similar strategies include Piccadilly Cafeterias, with their Piccadilly Express lines. Even companies such as Cheesecake Factory, Applebee's and California Pizza Kitchen have developed smaller prototypes for purposes of meeting space restrictions in mall settings and the like.[4]

In the language marketers have developed to talk about PODs, a host is any establishment, such as Kmart, where high traffic is likely to offer potential high-volume sales. Examples include retail operations, malls, colleges, airports, manufacturing plants, or theme parks. The host offers a food service operator access to the host's traffic. The advantage to the host is that its establishment is enhanced by the additional service; the food service company, on the other hand, gets increased access to customers and sales. Host locations are referred to as venues. A venue includes not only a place but assurance of a particular kind of traffic associated with the location, such as shoppers, students, or office workers. A&W has capitalized on locating units in shopping malls and has been quite successful in doing so.

The expansion of food service chains via PODs has stirred considerable controversy. Other franchisees are concerned that the downsized units will dilute brand image, threaten quality, and create competition for existing franchisees. Some franchisees are against it, believing that sales from POD operations cannibalize sales from existing, full-size stores. Other companies have ventured into introducing express units at the behest of its franchisees, such as with Tony Roma's. This is one of the issues that franchisors and franchisees continue to communicate about.

The expansion of downsized units is not just limited to QSRs. Casual restaurants, including independents, have jumped on the bandwagon of multiplying the places where their food service is offered, often in downsized units with restricted menus. What PODs of all kinds offer the consumer is an advantage highly valued in this fast-paced, hurried age: the convenience of a handy location.

Contract companies have become franchisees of restaurant companies and have also developed their own proprietary brands, such as ARAMARK's Itza Pizza. Restaurant companies now find that they face competition from contract companies that have begun to operate units in retail stores and malls. Contract companies, on the other hand, face competition from restaurant companies in the on-site market. Restaurant companies are franchising "hosts" to operate units as part of their own food service operation. For instance, Subway Express units are springing up on campuses; Baskin-Robbins kiosks and carts are found not only on campuses but also in hospitals, factories, airports, and tollway plazas. Pizza Hut, too, delivers its product for resale in institutions such as hospitals and schools.

PROMOTION

Two major forms of paid promotional activities (or marketing communication, as it is often called) are advertising and sales promotion.[5] We will discuss each briefly. Full-service restaurants (with check averages of $15 to $24.99) spend 1.8 percent of sales on marketing, whereas QSRs spend 0.6 percent.[6]

Advertising. Advertising is used as part of a long-term communications strategy and is often intended to create or burnish an image. The food service industry is one of the largest advertisers in the United States; McDonald's alone spent over $1.6 billion on total advertising spending in 2005.[7] The entire industry spends just over $5 billion annually. Advertising campaigns are generally made up of many different ads and commercials tied together by some common theme. In late 2003, McDonald's announced a campaign whose platform for new ads uses the slogan "I'm lovin' it.™" The campaign is designed to send a single message to consumers of all ages and geographic locations—it is being aired in 12 different languages. All the commercials in this campaign follow a theme depicting different life styles and cultures.[8]

As media become more crowded, themes come and go and are adapted depending on consumer reaction. However, one thing that stands out clearly is the very generous spending on advertising by the larger companies. For instance, in introducing a new dual-patty product, the Big King, Burger King budgeted $30 million. It is important to remember that advertising takes many forms—not just televison advertising. In fact, many successful restaurant chains do no television advertising at all—including Mimi's and Houston's. Advertising may also be conducted through radio, billboards, newspapers, magazines, and the like.

Responding to a Diverse Market. To reach a diverse market, specialized advertising directed at particular ethnic markets is becoming common practice. Both advertising agencies and specialized media have evolved to reach Hispanic and African American consumers, who had $581 billion and $646 billion, respectively, in discretionary income in 2002.[9] Consumer markets can also be segmented by income and wealth. Industry Practice Note 6.1 discusses some characteristics of the weathiest consumers.

The most common media for mass communication in food service are the electronic and print media, billboards, and direct mail. Figure 6.3 shows the breakdown of the major components of each and characteristics frequently associated with each.

The Internet in Food Service Promotion. A newer medium for restaurant advertising is the Internet. Although the use of the Internet in food service marketing is still in its infancy, there are plenty of examples available to illustrate the direction in which the industry is moving. Home pages on the World Wide Web are used primarily as sources of information and to provide links to e-mail addresses. Online service providers such as America Online (AOL) and CompuServe feature information about and for food service professionals. The use of the Internet as a marketing tool is growing by leaps and bounds as this is being written but seems to still be underutilized. A recent study by the National Restaurant Association indicates that just one-half of the

The Wealthiest Consumers

The term "wealthy" can be defined in many different ways—by annual income, by amount of discretionary income, or by highest net worth (total wealth). In a report by *American Demographics* magazine, this group is defined by those households that have a total net worth of $2 million or more. This group represents just 2 percent of all U.S. households. Either way that wealth is defined, this group behaves differently, engages in different recreational activities, and makes different purchases than the rest of the country. They also attract the attention of the media and other groups that track their spending habits. Among other things, *American Demographics* concludes that:

- The highest percentage of wealthy households are in the Northeastern United States and the West Coast.
- Almost three-fourths have a university degree or higher.
- Most heads of these households are still working.
- Many consumers within this group shy away from media based advertising.[1]

The number of companies and organizations that target this group is growing. The *American Affluence Research Center* tracks America's wealthiest 10 percent in "provide[ing] reliable marketing and economic information about the values, lifestyles, attitudes, and purchasing behavior of America's most affluent consumers." Mendelsohn Media Research produces an annual survey of demographic information and spending of households earning $75,000 or more. And The Rich Register publishes an annual directory of the wealthy. It includes information on almost 5,000 of the richest Americans (with a net worth of $25 million or more).

According to the U.S. Census Bureau's Consumer Expenditure survey, the wealthiest consumers spend 50 percent more on food away from home than the next category of consumers (categorized by annual income).[2] For this reason and others, marketers segment and target this select group of consumers. As a result of recent difficulties in the stock market, research indicates that affluent Americans, as a group, report that they expect to spend less in both casual and upscale restaurants in the near term.[3]

Sources:
1. Bureau of Labor Statistics, Consumer Expenditure Survey (2001).
2. Alison Stein Wellner and John Fetto, *American Demographics,* "Worth a Closer Look." June, 2003.
3. American Express, Briefing, September/October 2003.

restaurant operators surveyed indicated that they had a Web site. On the other hand, as the average check increases, the likelihood that the restaurant has a Web site also increases. The most common type of information provided on Web sites is menu listings, general restaurant information, and restaurant locations.[10] It should be noted that the industry, as a whole, has not been as progressive in its use of the Internet as some

MEDIUM	THE MARKETING MIX
BROADCAST MEDIA:	**CHARACTERISTICS**
Television	Large audience, low cost per viewer but high total cost.
	Combines sight, motion, and sound.
Radio	Highly targetable, lower cost than TV.
Cable TV	Highly targetable, fragmented market.
PRINT MEDIA	
Newspapers	Limited targeting possible. Printed word is regarded as credible by many.
Magazines	Targetable, generally prestigious, high-quality reproduction of photos.
ROADSIDE	Excellent for directions. Message limited to about eight words.
DIRECT MEDIA	Excellent targeting but costly per prospect reached. Good coupon distribution vehicle.

Figure 6.3
Advertising media and their characteristics.

would like. The magazine *Hospitality Technology* tracks Internet usage in the industry. According to its editor, Reid Paul, "While nearly every industry in the United States has recognized the power and importance of the Internet and developed online strategies, restaurants lag well behind, largely because there were few recognized opportunities for e-commerce."[11] The magazine supports an annual study of Internet usage in the industry, led by University of Delaware professor, Cihan Cobanoglu. The study evaluates restaurant Web sites on a variety of criteria including technical specifications, technology used, ease of navigation, ease of contact, marketing effectiveness, e-commerce solutions, and legal compliance. The 2006 study found many restaurant Web sites to be lacking although some, including those of Bahama Breeze, Subway, and Legal Sea Foods, scored at the top of the study. Cobanoglu suggests that restaurants make a greater effort to reduce errors in the content, update Web sites more regularly and, most importantly, improve ease of navigation.[12]

Sales Promotion. **Sales promotion** consists of activities other than advertising that are directed at gaining immediate patronage. The most common forms of sales promotion are "deals," which include coupons, games, and promotional merchandise. Deals are intended to enhance the value of the product offered—and to stimulate immediate purchase. Deals have become an increasingly common inducement to customers. The use of deals by customers peaked in the late 1990s and has been fluctuating since then, representing as much as one-fourth of all meal occasions in some years. A study by Adjoined Consulting found that over 40 percent of survey respondents said that coupons influence their choice on where to dine. However, *Restaurants and Institutions* magazine contends that there is little relationship between coupons and loyalty.[13]

Coupons. Coupons are often offered in connection with very-low-product-cost fountain drinks (a product cost as low as 2 or 3 percent). As a result of their low cost, couponing these items has a limited impact on the operation's profit margin. During the off season, however, coupons discounting main meal items are more common.

Games. Games cost considerably less than couponing main meal items. They enhance value by offering a little excitement—the possibility of an all-expenses-paid vacation in some exotic locale, for instance. Moreover, lots of small prizes (french fries, coffee, or the like) make the possibility of winning fairly likely—and winning anything is usually a pleasant experience.

Promotional merchandise. Promotional merchandise such as toys or glassware is often called a "self-liquidator" because the merchandise is usually sold at cost, limiting the impact of the deal on the promotional budget. Typically, merchandise comes in sets of three or four to encourage repeat patronage: "Collect all four!" Such items may also be distributed as part of a meal package for children.

In more upscale operations, special events are a common form of promotion. Special ethnic menus or celebrations of holiday events such as Valentine's Day or Mother's Day fit this category.

An increasingly common form of highly targeted sales promotion involves frequent-guest programs. These programs offer rewards to good customers and encourage repeat patronage. Frequent-guest programs increase guest loyalty and yield valuable information on customers, which can be used in future marketing programs.

Competition with Other Industries

It is an axiom of economics that people's wants will expand indefinitely but that their resources are limited. Most people would like a new car and a vacation in Europe or the Caribbean as well as the latest in DVD, stereo, and computer equipment. They would also like to dine in the finest restaurants. The problem is, however, most must choose, as few can afford all of that. Give up dining out in the best the local restaurant scene has to offer for the next year or so and you may have the cost of that vacation. Forgo lunch at your favorite restaurant and brown-bag it for six weeks and you can probably save the price of a new DVD and two or three rentals. Thus, food service is, in a very real way, in generic **competition with all other industries**, especially those providing leisure services and conveniences.

Some industries, however, challenge food service on its own turf, offering directly competitive products. We will concentrate our attention on these retailers here. Convenience stores offer their own variety of quick service from locations that are so numerous that they seem to be just around the corner from wherever you may be. Supermarkets are not as numerous as convenience stores, but they are conveniently located, and virtually everyone visits them in the course of a week. Both are formidable competitors for food service.

CONVENIENCE STORES

Although their most frequent customers are males under age 35, C-stores, as they are often called, are visited once or twice a month by most of the adult population. A significant part of C-store sales are directly competitive with food service sales, especially beverages (fountain drinks and coffee) and sandwiches. Because nearly all C-stores have microwave equipment and offer prepared foods, these retail units can compete for more than the snack market. Many offer a service deli and a variety of QSR foods. Some C-stores have a point of distribution from one of the major QSR chains located in the store. Although food service is relatively more labor-intensive than other C-store products, it offers a higher contribution to overhead and profits—roughly 60 percent as compared with 30 percent for other products. According to the National Association of Convenience Stores:

■ Over 50 percent of convenience stores offer some kind of prepared food.

■ Average sales for food service in convenience stores in 2005 exceeded $128,000.

■ Industry food service sales exceeded $17.9 billion in 2005.

■ Food service sales represent 13.3 percent of in-store sales for convenience stores.[14]

Food service now accounts for the third largest category of convenience store sales, after cigarettes and packaged beverages.

The Alimentation Couche-Tard and 7-Eleven companies are the largest of those which are solely in the business of convenience stores. Many of the other large convenience store operators are oil companies including ExxonMobil and BP North America although some oil companies are leaving the retail business and focusing on sales and distribution of gasoline instead. Oil companies that continue to operate convenience stores have four

Convenience stores continue to compete with quick-service restaurants. (Courtesy of Irving Oil Corporation.)

distinct advantages over many other C-store operators. First, because of their large gasoline sales, they can afford prime corner locations. Second, they have the backing of cash-rich corporations. Third, they are able to sell gas at lower prices. Finally, consumers can use their gasoline credit card to make their purchase, which is a major convenience.

SUPERMARKETS

Restaurateurs and retailers selling food for consumption at home have always been in competition. For some years, restaurants' share of that market has been increasing. That struggle is intensifying as a result of sharpened competitive practices in the grocery business and changing patterns in leisure-time usage. We will discuss the grocery business in this section and look briefly at the changing patterns in leisure in the next section. Clearly, the two developments are interrelated.

Supermarkets have customers from 100 percent of households over a 52-week period—in effect, everybody. With this kind of exposure and market share, they are formidable competitors for the food dollar. A state-of-the-art store today emphasizes food service, and many grocery stores are adding food courts and full-scale restaurants, including ethnic-themed operations as well as brand-name QSRs. McDonald's, Burger King, Pizza Hut, and Taco Bell all operate units in supermarkets, and contract companies such as ARAMARK have developed branded programs for supermarkets. We discussed the proliferation of PODs earlier, and here we can see it as a part of the blurring of concepts. When is a restaurant "sort of not exactly" a restaurant? When it's part of a grocery store offering food service. Or perhaps we should just say that grocery stores are a very significant part of the ever-increasing competition for the consumer's food dollar.

Supermarkets are endangering restaurants' home meal replacement market share. According to the Food Marketing Institute, a grocery trade industry organization, the percentage of supermarkets with take out food sections rose by over 50 percent in a ten-year period to 94 percent in 2006. Further, a study by the same association found that younger consumers were equally likely to buy takeout food in supermarkets as in quick-service restaurants.[15] Supermarket takeout food is generally less costly to the consumer than restaurant takeout food, and grocery stores offer wider variety. The convenience of being able to get a few staples—milk or bread for breakfast—while picking up dinner is undeniable. According to the Food Marketing Institute, dinner is by far the most popular meal for takeout and one-person households are most likely to purchase prepared meals from supermarkets.

Restaurants, however, have the advantage of a service culture and higher-quality food. Supermarket managers are often rooted in a retail mind-set (although there is evidence that this is changing). This being said, some supermarkets that do offer prepared foods to go take it to a near art form. Stew Leonard's (in Connecticut and New

Grocery stores are increasing their share of the food service market. (Courtesy of Publix Supermarkets.)

York) offers a variety of foods prepared to go including marinated turkey, chicken prepared various ways, and filet mignon. The store has been described as one part amusement park because of the mix of exceptional service, special activities, and quality products. Whole Foods is another "nontraditional" type of supermarket that offers a strong selection of prepared foods, fried rice, rotisserie items, and wood-fired pizza. Partnering with food service operators—or hiring managers and chefs away from restaurants—supermarkets are making efforts to improve their performance. The competition between food service and supermarkets promises to continue to be stiff especially as supermarkets continue to try harder for this piece of the business.

THE HOME AS COMPETITION

As the baby boomers move into their middle years and greater family responsibilities, the attractions of staying at home increase. Baby boomers continually indicate that home life is of the utmost importance to them. Thus, in a way, the home can be considered a form of competition.

The number of meals purchased at restaurants is growing, according to a leading market researcher, but an increasing proportion of these meals are takeout. Indeed, the home is emerging as an entertainment center. Television watching and Internet surfing are two of the top leisure activities. A substantial majority of people own a DVD and make significant use of them while the number of computer owners continues to increase. Americans spend a good portion of their free time watching television (30 percent by one account), and television options have exploded, as anyone with cable, satellite, or digital capabilities can attest. This has only contributed to the ease with which Americans can spend their free time in their homes.

The home computer's capabilities are being expanded by manufacturers. Online computer services such as Prodigy and CompuServe offer functional services such as stock market news and the ability to book your own travel reservations. These services also provide a variety of chat rooms and other entertainment options.

The home is, increasingly, becoming a control point for consumers—it is an environment that maximizes consumers' control over factors that impact their lives. It is their territory. The pattern of activity that emerges suits itself well to staying home with somebody's take-out meal. It is not surprising that plenty of competitors exist for that business. The growth in takeout and delivery is clearly the restaurant business's response to this freezer case competition.

The future probably offers only more encouragement for "cocooning," the term coined by Faith Popcorn to describe the practice of staying at home, as computers continue to play an even more important role in our lives than they did a mere few years ago.

Summary

It should be clear at this point that the food service landscape is changing and that the competitive environment is as well. In competitive terms, food service chains are operating in a mature market characterized by established operations with sophisticated marketing and proven operating formats. Successful independents compete by differentiation or by dominating small specialized markets. In spite of increasing chain market share, the food service market remains a highly competitive one characterized by many buyers and many sellers.

We used the marketing mix to characterize competitive activity in food service. As product is essentially the guest's experience, all the elements of the operation are important. Food quality is absolutely essential, and new food products are a major way of stimulating guest interest and renewing an operation. The product life cycle concept means not that established products or concepts die out but rather that concepts need to be reinvigorated.

Price has been used as a lead variable in the marketing mix, but competitive prices develop eventually. Consequently, long-term competition is usually focused on non-price variables. Temporary price cutting, as with coupons, can be effective in the short run, particularly in the off season. Although price reductions risk cheapening the product in the guests' eyes, sometimes market conditions dictate a long-term reduction in price levels, as in the case of fine dining at the end of the 1980s, when guests' perceptions of value changed.

Place denotes two somewhat different ideas. Place as location involves factors such as traffic, population density, and proximity to major attractions. On the other hand, the notion of places refers to distribution and intercept marketing. This involves having operations, sometimes downscaled PODs, available wherever customers choose to go in large numbers.

Promotion is a critical element in the food service marketing mix. Food service is one of the largest advertisers in North America, and advertising is often built around themes that are used in several ads or commercials. We discussed the increasing role that the Internet is playing. Sales promotion is used to stimulate immediate purchase. Some of its principal tools, usually called deals, are coupons, games, and promotional merchandise. In upscale operations, sales promotion often takes the form of special events. A highly targeted form of sales promotion is aimed at a company's present customers in frequent-guest programs.

Food service must compete with all other consumer products and services but faces particular competitive challenges from C-stores, supermarkets, and the comforts and conveniences of home.

Key Words and Concepts

Marketing mix	**New Products**
Product	**Life cycle**
Price	**Concept extension**
Place	**Branding**
Promotion	**Value pricing**

Couponing	**Advertising**
Location	**Sales promotion**
Distribution	**Competition with all**
Points of distribution	**other industries**
(PODs)	

Review Questions

1. How has the competitive climate in which the food service industry operates changed over the 20 years?

2. What is the role of new products in a competitive strategy?

3. What are the stages of the restaurant life cycle?

4. What are the benefits and risks of value pricing?

5. How is the concept of distribution being used in food service competition?

6. How is the Internet being used in food service competition? What new developments do you anticipate in the use of the Internet in food service competition?

7. When is sales promotion used? What are its principal elements?

8. Discuss the significance of each element of the marketing mix in food service competition in your city. What recent developments strike you as significant in the local competitive scene?

9. What competitive practices have grocery chains in your area engaged in that will affect food service? How do you rate local C-store competition against quick-service restaurants?

Internet Exercises

1. **Site name:** Buca di Beppo
    URL: www.bucadibeppo.com
    Background information: Buca di Beppo is a neighborhood restaurant where guests feast on family platters of real, immigrant, Southern Italian specialties in a boisterous, celebratory environment that recalls the Italian-American supper clubs of the 1940s and 1950s. In immigrant fashion, they serve their food family-style, in portions meant for sharing.
    Site name: Chili's
    URL: www.chilis.com

Background information: Chili's offers a distinct, fresh, healthy mix of grilled American favorites prepared in a way that keeps guests coming back. Chili's is part of a family of restaurants operated by Brinker International.

Site name: Smokey Bones

URL: www.smokeybones.com

Background information: Smokey Bones BBQ is a casual dining restaurant that combines great-tasting, authentic American barbecue with a rustic, mountain lodge decor. Smokey Bones is part of a family of restaurants operated by Darden Restaurants.

Site name: Outback Steakhouse

URL: www.outback.com

Background information: Outback offers high-quality food and service, generous portions at moderate prices, and a casual atmosphere suggestive of the Australian Outback. Although beef and steak items make up a portion of the menu, Outback also offers a variety of chicken, ribs, seafood, and pasta dishes.

Exercises:

a. What characterizes a good restaurant Web site from a marketing standpoint? What elements should be present on a Web site to make it an effective marketing tool?

b. Which of the above Web sites do you believe presents the best marketing effort? Why?

c. Which of the above restaurants advertises promotional merchandise on their Web site? How effective do you believe promotional merchandise is in attracting customers?

d. Overall, discuss how effective you believe Internet Web sites are in marketing a restaurant concept. Why?

2. **Site name:** Convenience Store Decisions

   URL: www.csdecisions.com/

   Background information: Convenience Store Decisions is the in-print "Idea Factory" for the convenience store industry. Written for and read by the industry's decision-makers, the monthly magazine has a qualified circulation of more than 40,000 subscribers and offers award-winning, compelling editorials and consistent coverage of current issues of real concern to convenience store operators.

   Site name: The National Association of Convenience Stores

   URL: www.nacsonline.com/

   Background information: The National Association of Convenience Stores (NACS) is an international trade association representing more than 2,200 retail and 1,800

supplier company members. NACS member companies do business in nearly 40 countries around the world.

Site name: Convenience Store News —Food Service Section

URL: www.csnews.com/csn/foodservice/index.jsp

Background information: *Convenience Store News'* mission is to deliver the insight, analysis, market research, and business intelligence that helps C-store retailers stay ahead of what's next. –The e-publication provides critical information to grow sales and profits.

Exercises:

a. Review the above Web sites to determine the food service products and services provided by convenience stores. What type of food service products are typically sold in convenience stores? What are the emerging products that convenience stores are migrating toward in the future?

b. Who is the target market for convenience-store food services?

c. Which restaurant sectors do the convenience stores compete against and what strategies should that restaurant sector utilize to maintain their customer base?

d. What potential job opportunities might be available for hospitality management students in the convenience store industry?

Notes

1. Robert Lewis and Richard Chambers (2000). *Marketing Leadership in Hospitality*, Hoboken, NJ: John Wiley & Sons.
2. The marketing mix is a convenient frame of reference for discussing current competitive practices. Some would argue, however, for other, different definitions, and in fact, the definition we employ evolves from a simple four-Ps approach to something a bit more complicated.
3. Deborah Silver, "Life in the Fast Lane," *Restaurants and Institutions*, February 15, 2001.
4. Deborah Silver, "Small Change," *Restaurants and Institutions*, August 15, 2000.
5. Another form of marketing communication, which is not discussed here, is public relations. This is particularly important to upscale operations.
6. 2004 Restaurant Industry Operations Report (Washington, D.C.: National Restaurant Association, 2005).
7. Standard and Poor's Net Advantage, 2006.
8. McDonald's Press Release, September 2, 2003, Munich Germany.
9. Rebecca Gardyn and John Fetto, "Race, Ethnicity and the Way We Shop." *American Demographics*, February, 2003.
10. "Restaurant Operator Technology Survey," National Restaurant Association, 2001.
11. Reid Paul, "The Online Experience," *Hospitality Technology*, July/August 2006.

12. Cihan Cobanoglu, "The New Service Frontier: The State of the Online Restaurant Industry," *Hospitality Technology*, July/August 2006.

13. R&I Insider, *Restaurants and Institutions*, April 1, 2005.

14. Correspondence with National Association of Convenience Stores, (www.NACSonline.com), November 14, 2006.

15. Steve Adams, "A Market Heats Up," *The Patriot Ledger*, June 30, 2006.

The Hospitality Industry

(Courtesy of Sodexho.)

CHAPTER SEVEN

On-Site Food Service

The Purpose of this Chapter

This chapter discusses the important and significant segments of the food service industry that make up the on-site segment. Some of the characteristics of this component of the hospitality industry are unique. Yet the increasing emphasis on marketing and use of brand names in the on-site sector would suggest that the lines between on-site food service and so-called commercial segments are becoming increasingly blurred. The on-site segment (including both contracted and self-operated units) offers excellent compensation, good opportunities for advancement, and often more stable working hours. Because many companies operate in both the commercial hospitality industry and the on-site sector, it is an area that you may come into contact with even if your plans now are to work in hotels or restaurants. It is, in short, an area of the industry that deserves careful examination and more attention than it normally receives.

THIS CHAPTER SHOULD HELP YOU

1. Describe the four major segments of on-site food service operations and the employment opportunities each offers.
2. List the differences between self-operated food service facilities and those operated by managed-services companies.
3. Explain the distinction between client and guest in the on-site food service environment.
4. Describe the four basic models under which many retirement housing communities operate.
5. Describe the recreation and transportation segments of the on-site market.
6. Identify the role that private clubs play in the industry, and identify the types of career opportunities they provide.
7. List the advantages that vending offers in meeting guest and client needs.
8. Identify elements common to the different lines of business in the on-site sector.

Comparing On-Site and Commercial Food Services

Any discussion of the **on-site** sector, to those more familiar with traditional restaurants, requires that one expand his or her preconceptions of what the food service industry encompasses. Even the terminology used to describe this segment tends to be different. For instance, there are several terms used to describe this segment—on-site being one of the more current terms in use (although one still hears the terms *institutional* and *noncommercial*, too). Also, the sector is so broad and encompasses so many different types of operations that to attempt to group all of these different businesses under one umbrella does the sector a bit of an injustice. This will become clear as the different subsegments are discussed.

Another reason that discussions of this segment require looking beyond the traditional restaurant model is because of the different types of companies that operate within the segment. For instance, an important distinction within on-site food service is between managed-services companies that manage a food service facility for a third party and organizations that operate their own food service (hereafter, **self-ops**).

Finally, dividing the larger food service industry into commercial and on-site segments is somewhat artificial and misleading, as some of the same firms that profit from providing institutions with food service also operate in other areas of the hospitality industry. ARAMARK, for instance, also operates hotels in national parks and has a line of business that supplies uniforms. Sodexho USA is a member of the Sodexho Alliance.

On-site food service operators can plan the number of meals to serve with more certainty than can commercial restaurants. (Courtesy of Sodexho.)

Sodexho operates ships providing river and harbor cruises throughout North America and Europe. Compass Group, until recently, owned several hotel chains and is also involved with facilities management in the health care sector. As one quickly discovers, there are numerous companies that operate in sometimes completely different hospitality environments simultaneously, as evidenced by the preceding examples.

Returning our focus specifically to the on-site food service sector, we should first attempt to define it. Simply, it consists of all locations where food is served outside of the home but where food service is not the primary business, such as universities or sports arenas. This definition obviously includes a significant number of locations, and indeed, the sector is quite large and varied. This will become clear as we delve further into on-site food service. One way to articulate what this segment is all about is to make comparisons with the more visible restaurant industry.

There are significant differences that exist between restaurants and on-site food service, and students should be aware of these. One important difference is that whereas on-site food service once represented a "captive market," restaurant customers have always had a range of choices, including choices of facilities and menus. This distinction still exists, but to a much lesser extent. On-site food service providers, both self-operated and managed, have found that, with certain exceptions, guests do have a choice in the long run. As a result, food service operators have found that a marketing approach that views patients, company employees, and students as guests and focuses on their preferences is an approach that tends to win more friends than the old eat-it-and-like-it institutional attitude.

Success is also measured a bit differently, by the **participation rate** of the guests. University students who don't like the food withdraw or cut back on board plans; patients who have a choice of hospitals often choose the institution with superior food service; and even prison inmates find ways to assert their food preferences. In an age of consumerism, moreover, even guests who can't "vote with their feet" and go someplace else don't hesitate to complain. Therefore, competition among the various food service **contractors** is often decided on the basis of marketing techniques as well as management skills.

Another major difference between traditional restaurants and on-site services relates to their primary functions. Even though many companies provide both restaurant and on-site food services and use similar marketing and managerial techniques in both areas, the major difference between the two markets is that the food service in institutions is a small part of a larger operation with a greater purpose of overriding importance— health care (hospitals, nursing homes, etc.), education (K-12 and universities), or businesses (services and manufacturing), for instance. In a commercial restaurant, the challenge is to please the guest. In the on-site environment, it is necessary to meet the needs of both the guests and the client (i.e., the institution itself).

The distinction between client and guest is important. The client is the institution (bank, university, etc.) along with its managers and policy makers. These are the people who ultimately award the contract or, when the institution operates its own food service, hire and fire the food service director. Pleasing the guest (i.e., the individual diner, patient, student, or resident) is important, but the client must be pleased as well. The evidence suggests that the food service operator must do what is necessary to keep the client happy. Sometimes this isn't so easy. There may be a substantial difference in an institutional setting between the needs and wants of the guests and those of the client. In school food service, for instance, the client's (i.e., the school's) goal is to provide not only adequate meals but also nutrition education by showing the students what a nutritionally balanced meal is like. The goals of a young schoolchild may obviously be quite a bit different.

If the food service is operated by a managed services company, the two parties must agree upon the type of contract to be followed as well as negotiate the terms of that particular contract. Contracts can take a variety of forms. Contracts sometimes call for the institution to essentially allow the contractor to operate on a break-even basis and to pay the contractor a fee every period for the management of the operation. Other contracts allow the contractor to operate solely on a profit-and-loss basis, where the contractor covers its own expenses and manages the revenues, taking sole responsibility for the profit (or loss) at the end of each period. Other contracts might be a hybrid of these two, depending on the scope of the operation. However, in most segments, the movement seems to be more toward profit-and-loss-type contracts. Whether the operation is subsidized, break-even, or for-profit, however, there is always some budgeted performance target that must be met regardless of who operates the service. Even for self-operated institutions, the trend is for them to become more self-sufficient, with a greater degree of fiscal responsibility.

Finally, the two segments (commercial and on-site) have very different operating challenges. For example, the number of meals and portion sizes are much easier to predict in on-site operations. Because of this greater predictability, these food service operations often operate in a less hurried atmosphere than that in restaurants, in which customer volume and menu popularity often fluctuate (it should be noted that this is not as true as it once was, though, as many operations move more towards a retail model).

Moreover, although managers tend to work long hours in commercial food service, the working hours in on-site food service are usually shorter, or at least more predictable. This is particularly true in environments that have discrete operating periods such as colleges and universities, and most businesses.

On the other hand, although a guest may visit a restaurant frequently, few of them eat as regularly in their favorite restaurant as do the guests in on-site operations. Thus,

International Perspectives

Although the discussion of on-site food service in this chapter is primarily limited to examples in the United States, this should in no way imply that such operations are limited to this country. Companies, hospitals, colleges, and so on in every part of the world have provided food service to their associates/ students/customers for a very long time. One look at the top food service management companies in this sector in North America indicates just how truly international this market is. Current leaders, are ARA-MARK, Sodexho, and Compass Group. Sodexho (www.sodexho.com) is a French-based company that has had a presence in the United States since the mid-1980s. The Compass Group, (www.compass-usa.com), which operates several subsidiaries including Canteen and Chartwells, is based in England and operates in over 45 countries worldwide. Finally, perhaps the best example of ARAMARK's (www.aramark.com) international expertise is its long involvement with providing food service for the Olympics. The company most recently provided the food service for the 2004 Summer Olympics in Athens. ARAMARK also manages a variety of services around the globe—in 18 different countries, to be exact.

varying the menu for a guest who must eat in the same place for weeks, months, or even years at a time can be a demanding task.

There are many other differences that exist between the two segments as discussed throughout this chapter. One major distinction that students should keep in mind is the international reach of some of the major companies in this sector, as discussed in Global Hospitality Note 7.1. Further distinctions are discussed next as we examine the two primary types of operations.

Self-Operated Facilities

Many institutions see no reason to pay to a contract company the overhead and profits that they could potentially garner. This attitude is perhaps most prevalent in primary/secondary school feeding and in health care, where many institutions still operate their own food service facilities. Operating on the assumption that their own employees can manage as efficiently as a contract company can, these institutions choose to keep the overhead and profit they otherwise would have to pay to an outside company. As a result, these institutions can more directly control their operations, and to some extent, they can limit the staff turnover traditionally associated with managed-services companies, which frequently promote or transfer their employees. "If we like a person," said one university official, "we might lose him to a contract company. In our own operation, if we treat him right, we have a good chance of keeping him—of maintaining staff stability." There are some very unique characteristics of self-operated units, not the least of which are related to human resources. The number of self-operators is decreasing, however, as institutions begin to focus more on their core functions and as managed-services companies continue to gain market share.

Managed-Services Companies

Managed-services companies (or contract management companies), on the other hand, feel that their method of operation offers advantages to institutions of all sizes. True, unit managers may be, and are, transferred. We should note, however, that a contract company provides the client with two kinds of managers: the unit manager and the regional and district managers who train, evaluate, and supervise the unit manager's work and ensure management continuity. That continuity is an important offset to the possibility of transfer. Perhaps even more important, the transfer is part of a process of career progression. People who want to advance are drawn to that kind of opportunity. Thus, a contract company is likely to attract aggressive managers. Managers who choose to stay with institutional operators are likely to have less opportunity for advancement, although they will have other advantages, such as stability in where they live.

Another area in which managed-services companies offer advantages is that of purchasing. Selection of the best, most cost-effective purveyor offers major potential for savings. So does knowledgeable negotiation on the client's behalf by national buyers with broad experience. Contract companies conduct audits of cost-plus suppliers' books to ensure accurate billing, an expenditure of effort and money that might not be practical for an individual client. Finally, because contract companies buy on a regional or national scale, they can consolidate purchasing for several clients, thus achieving significant economies. In recent years, however, institutional operators have made moves that can offset this advantage by forming cooperative buying groups and passing the volume discount advantages on to the member institutions.

Managed-services companies also offer to their clients, at cost, extensive facilities planning services. These services include operational design (equipment), interior design, procurement, supervision of construction, and equipment installation. Specialized accounting and market planning services may also be offered to clients.

Finally, contract companies offer the collective experience of management and marketing in many markets. Marketing programs can be tailored to individual clients,

TABLE 7.1

Ten Largest Managed-Service Companies

Compass Group–North America	www.compass-group.com
Sodexho	www.sodexho.com
ARAMARK	www.aramark.com
Delaware North Companies	www.delawarenorth.com
Centerplate	www.centerplate.com
AVI Food Systems, Inc.	www.avifoodsystems.com
Guest Services, Inc.	www.guestservices.com
Guckenheimer Enterprises	www.guckenheimer.com
Xanterra Parks and Resorts	www.xanterra-coporate.com
Thompson Hospitality Services	www.thompsonhospitality.com

for instance, yet also draw on national marketing programs developed by the contractor. This has proved especially helpful in areas such as nutritionally oriented marketing programs. The top ten managed-services companies are identified in Table 7.1.

PROS AND CONS OF MANAGED SERVICES

To all of this, the large institutional operator will likely respond that a sizable institution (medical center, university, or school district) is big enough to achieve most or all of these advantages on its own. A smaller institution might add that voluntary buying co-ops and judicious use of consultants can also achieve a good part of these effects. Both would emphasize that the institution is able to retain full control over the operation, which reports directly to the institution's top management.

No doubt, contract companies would make responses to each of these points. Our purpose is not to settle the issue in any final way or to suggest that one approach is "better" than the other. There really is no one answer to the debate. What we want is to suggest the outlines of the competition between institutional operator and managed-services company for consideration by the reader.

The contract companies' share is substantial and growing in most segments. Although exact figures are difficult to determine, Table 7.2 shows that contract food service companies currently manage a significant number of on-site food services. **Health care** is one area in which contract companies have relatively low market penetration, but even this area is increasing as a result of health care facilities wishing to outsource their food service, and other support services, in an effort to focus

TABLE 7.2

The On-Site Food Service Market

	ESTIMATED SIZE OF TOTAL MARKET (NUMBER OF ACCOUNTS)[a]	DEGREE OF PENETRATION BY CONTRACT COMPANIES[b]
Business and industry	36,367	80–85%
Colleges and universities	3,541	60–65%
Hospitals	6,806	45–50%
Primary and secondary schools	84,422	20–25%
Total	131,136	

[a] International Foodservice Manufacturers Association.
[b] Dennis Reynolds, *On-site Foodservice*, John Wiley & Sons, 2003.

on their core function—care for patients. Contract companies have also had success with public schools in recent years. The two areas in which the contract companies are well established are colleges and universities and business and industry. Each of the four major divisions within on-site food services has unique characteristics. Moreover, the factors that affect the outlook for each vary. We will consider each of them briefly.

Business and Industry Food Service

Business and industry (B&I) food service provides food for the convenience of both the guests (the company associates) and the client (the employer). The client wants inexpensive food with enough variety and quality to satisfy the associates, as the client knows that food can directly affect morale. Quick service is also important, because the time for coffee breaks and lunch is limited. Finally, it is in the best interest of most companies to keep their employees on the premises during food service breaks.

Two of the underlying forces that drive the B&I market are the size of the workforce and the level of employment. The size of the workforce affects the long-term outlook. When it was growing, during the years when the baby boomers were leaving school and entering employment, the workforce was a strong positive force. Now that the surge is over, however, the Bureau of Labor Statistics estimates that the workforce will increase at a more modest rate. To put this into perspective, there are approximately 145 million employed workers in the United States, and this figure has slowly risen since 2002 (from

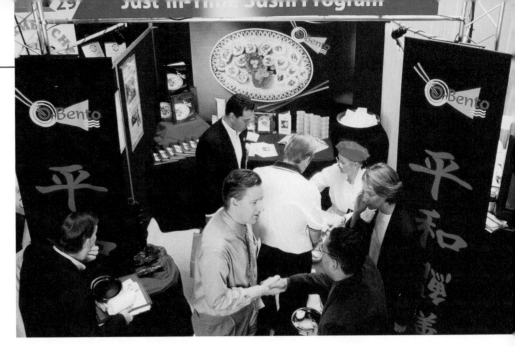

The business and industry food service segment continues to experience growth partially due to innovative new services and concepts. (Courtesy of Sodexho.)

135 million). Within the workforce, the trend is toward an economy increasingly dominated by service industries that employ more office and white-collar employees. The volume of food service in commercial and office buildings is growing at a significantly faster pace than it is in manufacturing plants. In periods of relatively low unemployment (about 5 percent), such as is the case currently, B&I volume may rise. On the other hand, B&I is especially sensitive to downturns in employment.

In recent years, the telecommunications, computer and automotive industries have all lost many thousands of jobs and this has affected the food service operations servicing these industries. Recent downsizings have caused companies to take a close look at their food service operations and to take the necessary measures to streamline them and, increasingly, outsource them. The National Restaurant Association indicates that business and industry sales (managed by contract companies) experienced slow but positive growth between 2004 and 2005, while independent operators experienced negative growth during that same period.[1] Cuts at banks (including the Federal Reserve Bank of New York) have resulted in having to reduce food service staff and rethink service strategies.

Business and Industry food service is also increasingly feeling the effects of outside competition from restaurants. Even with the limited time available, employees may choose to go off-site for their meals. When one considers that the majority of businesses are located near malls, industrial centers, city centers, and the like, one realizes the number of dining options that are available to employees.

All is not doom and gloom for this segment, however. Difficult times have resulted in opportunities for both managed-service companies as well as self-ops and, as a result, they are becoming much more creative in their approaches. Each of the four major on-site segments is combating these competitive forces in its own way, but the B&I segment has been one of the most aggressive. One very effective strategy that managed-services companies, in particular, have adopted has been to develop food service concepts or **brands** of their own or to use established commercial franchise brands. ARAMARK's strategy has been to develop its own brands, such as Gretel's Bake Shop, Itza Pizza, El Pollo Grande, and Leghorn. Likewise, Compass Group, North American Division, offers Ritazza Coffee, Not Just Donuts, and Upper Crust (sandwiches) of its own. Brand-name units are themed much like any other chain operation, and the brand is promoted within the client's establishment. ARAMARK finds a high level of consumer acceptance for their brands, as evidenced by large increases in sales in units where they are established. The other advantage is that no franchise royalties are paid. This results in savings that can be passed on to both guest and client. ARAMARK also makes extensive use, however, of major national franchise brands, as does Sodexho, which has partnered with franchise brands such as Pizza Hut and Nathan's Famous. Other brands that have partnered with managed-services companies include Wendy's, Little Caesars, Dunkin' Donuts, I Can't Believe It's Yogurt, Chick-fil-A, and Starbucks, among many others.

The advantages of the brand-name specialty restaurant format, whether the brand is proprietary or franchised, are startlingly similar to the advantages that food service has in the commercial restaurant business.

- The operation has an identity that helps secure patronage from an increasingly brand-conscious food service customer.
- The facility is simpler to build than is a full-menu concept, and the investment required can be significantly less.
- Operating costs are lower, too, because of the simpler menu and because customers are accustomed to self-busing in fast food.
- Fast food is fast—in-plant feeding at General Motors plants takes only 3 minutes, compared with 12 minutes under earlier formats.

One of the most important considerations when introducing a branded concept is the expected increase in the participation (or capture) rate. Other techniques for increasing the participation rate are described in Industry Practice Note 7.1.

The purpose of employee food service operations changes, however, with different employee levels. Many companies maintain executive dining rooms boasting fancy menus and elegant service. Such dining rooms are often used to entertain important

Measuring Guest Participation

In the commercial food service sector, most activity is driven by sales and vice versa. In on-site food service, whether self-operated or overseen by a management company, the critical factor is the participation (or capture) rate. If company associates, college students, and so forth choose not to participate in the on-site food service, neither the client nor the food service operator will be satisfied. This holds true whether the facility is located in a hospital, ballpark, university, or industrial park.

Food service operators go about managing the participation rate in a variety of ways. One thing is for certain, however—more and more, the strategies that managers are employing closely resemble those used by managers of commercial operations. New services, positioning, branding, quality, attractive pricing, providing innovative menus, offering variety, and merchandising are but a few of the ways that managers attempt to influence the participation rate of guests.

Not too long ago, it would have been hard to imagine being able to order upscale Chinese food in the company cafeteria, find a food court in a hospital, or order a microbrewed beer at the ballpark. Yet with operators focusing ever more attention on customizing their products and services to meet the desires of customers, the battle over participation rate will rage on.

business guests—customers, prospective employees, the press, and politicians. Executive dining room privileges can also be an important status symbol among managerial employees. Further, even though tax law changes have generally lowered the rate at which business meals may be deducted (to 50 percent), meals served to employees at their place of work remain 100 percent deductible under certain conditions. Clearly, there are several legitimate reasons that speak to providing meals to line employees as well as executives.

Some companies (self-ops), such as SAS, Corning, and MCI just to name a few, take their employee food service programs very seriously. SAS attributes its employee loyalty, at least in part, to its food service program. Food service at the company headquarters includes three cafeterias, day care feeding, break centers, and extensive catering. In 2003, the company earned $1 million in revenues (partially subsidized by SAS).[2]

Many of the changes that are occurring in this segment are driven by host companys' increasing emphasis on the bottom line. As a result of this, more and more companies are **outsourcing** the management of their food service operations to management companies. Recall from Table 7.2 that penetration in this segment is the highest of any of the four primary segments (over 80 percent). This has boded well particularly for the big-three contract management companies (ARAMARK, Compass, and

Sodexho), which dominate and hold almost one-third of the market. Bur smaller companies also have respectable market share (among contracted accounts) in this segment. One such company is Guckenheimer Enterprises, Inc. This company is the largest independently owned company specializing on the B&I market. Based in California, Guckenheimer started as a regional company but is now across the United States. This company has approximately 350 corporate (B&I) accounts including John Hancock, Sun Microsystems, and McGraw Hill. The company has established its reputation on service and creativity, resulting in over 35 years of growth. They are an example of one company that believes that it pays to specialize in a particular segment. Others that specialize in B&I include All Seasons Services, CulinArt, and Southern Foodservice Management.

In summary, changes continue to occur in the B&I segment. Aggressive marketing, streamlined operations, more options, better value, increasing usage of branded concepts, innovative menus, increasing employer subsidies (again), and packaged food that is ready to eat (grab and go) are driving this sector. Penetration by contract companies continues to increase as well.

College and University Food Service

The **college and university food service** segment is very different from B&I. To understand college food service, one must first understand the **board plan**. Students eating in residence halls may be required to contract for a minimum number of meals over a term or semester. The food service operator benefits from this arrangement in two ways. First, the absentee factor ensures that some students will miss some meals they contracted for, which permits the food service operation to price the total package below what all the meals would cost if every student ate every meal there. This makes the package price attractive.

Second, and more important, the board plan provides a predictable volume of sales over a fairly long period—a term, a semester, or a year. At the start of that period, the operator can closely estimate what the sales volume will be. Because attendance ratios and the popularity of various menu items are fairly predictable, the operator can also estimate how much food to prepare for each meal.

Full board plans were once the rule rather than the exception, particularly on purely residential campuses. Although some colleges and universities still offer only a full board plan (three meals a day, seven days a week while school is in session), flexible board plans have become more and more popular. A recent article in *Food Management* highlights the food service operations of Notre Dame, where the board plan is still mandatory for all students in residence: Notre Dame offers 14-meal and 21-meal

The introduction of branded concepts has successfully increased sales in college and university food service operations. (Courtesy of Sodexho.)

options (per week) for students. Such restrictions are becoming more uncommon though. Some plans at other colleges and universities exclude breakfast, whereas others drop the weekend meals. With a flexible plan that invites students to contract for only the meals they expect to eat, the absentee rate goes down and the average price charged per meal goes up, because of the lower absentee rates. Nevertheless, in plans that drop a significant number of meals, the total price of the meal contract also drops. In any case, both the full board plan and the flexible plan generally charge students on the basis of the average number of meals they consume.

Some schools, such as New Mexico State University (where the food service is operated by ARAMARK), don't have a mandatory board plan and instead allow students to use their campus identification card (the Money$Card) to purchase food anywhere on campus. The use of such cards is becoming more common. With most card programs, students contract for some minimum dollar value of food service and receive a cash card with the amount they have paid credited to the card. As they use the card, the card is scanned and the amount of each item (or full meal) is electronically deducted from the balance. Students usually receive the food purchased through their card at some discount from what competitive commercial operations charge, and so it is still a bargain. The contracts, on the other hand, give the operator a basis for projecting the demand for the school year for scheduling, purchasing, and general budgeting, and they also guarantee some minimum level of sales volume. Some schools are even allowing students to use these same cards at selected off-campus locations.

As in the B&I segment, colleges and universities are also trying to market their services more. Flexible board plans and the use of cash cards represent just a small part of a total marketing approach, which adapts the services available to the guests' needs and preferences. Only about one-fifth of college and university students, however, live on campus. Roughly half live off campus, and the remaining students live at home with their parents. The need to attract off-campus students as customers heightens the competitive nature of college food service.

Both self-operated and managed operations have recently recognized how brand-conscious students tend to be. As a result, the use of brand names and franchised concepts has taken hold in college and university food service. The acceptance of students' preferences for quick-service outlets and the use of familiar branded concepts has achieved major improvements in sales. At San Diego State University, for instance, while enrollment fell nearly 25 percent, food sales actually rose from $4.3 million to $4.8 million when ten branded concepts were introduced. One-third of colleges and universities now offer branded options, and brand franchisors are becoming more flexible in reducing menus, adapting hours of operation, and reducing the amount of space required as they seek to get their brand in place in institutions. Evidence continues to suggest that brands increase awareness and purchases.

The use of brand names is by no means limited to contract companies, however. Self-ops have had success with that tactic, too. In fact, the National Association of College and University Food Service (NACUFS) has been instrumental in assisting self-operated institutions to capitalize on the branding trend. NACUFS has developed a series of brands for use by its members. Institutional operators can and do have national franchise brands as a part of their operation as well.

The management companies have been very effective with branding in colleges and universities. ARAMARK initially introduced their Pan Geos concept on 44 university campuses. Pan Geos is based on a cluster design offering various contemporary, international cuisines. In the short time that the concept has been in place, various units have experienced higher customer counts, increased check averages, and lower food costs. With the success of Pan Geos and similar concepts, it can be anticipated that more management companies (and self-ops) will develop similar offerings.

One final note with regard to branding—where the national brands were once limited to larger campuses, they are starting to appear at smaller institutions, some having as few as 400 students.

COLLEGE STUDENTS AS CUSTOMERS

College students are generally pleasant to deal with, but at times they can be very demanding. They need to be consulted in planning, and patient attention to complaints is important, too. An unhappy group of college students—with a natural bent for boisterousness—can be a difficult group to deal with. College food service operators stress the need for a strong communication program between the food service staff and the students. All agree that, in addition to good food and tight cost controls, a successful college food service operation must have "people skills," that is, be able to deal effectively with the guests. An example of this occurs at Glendon College in Toronto (Glendon is the French-speaking campus of York University). Stephanie Fontaine, the Food Service Director for Chartwells there, holds monthly meetings with students as a way of maintaining open communication.

The 16- to 24-year-old portion of the population declined between 1990 and 1995 but is now increasing again. As a result, college and university enrollments are expected to increase between 2005 and 2010 and beyond.[3] The average age of the college population continues to climb as well. Adult participation in higher education is expected to continue to increase—perhaps, in part, because of increased competition in the job market. According to a report by the U.S. Department of Education, almost three-fourths of college and university students are considered "nontraditional" in one way or another and almost 40 percent are aged 25 years or older.[4] Older students are more likely to live off campus, which means that retaining their business on campus is a more competitive proposition. The trend in this segment has been for colleges and universities to outsource their food service to food service management companies. In fact, the National Restaurant Association reports the growth rate for management companies in this area was over 7 percent in 2006.[5] Interestingly, however, many of the largest state universities remain self-operated, including Pennsylvania State University, Michigan State University, Purdue University, and the University of Massachusetts (all of which have hospitality management programs). The ten largest self-operated university campuses are listed in Table 7.3.

In summary, the college and university segment appears to be a healthy one, although students continue to

TABLE 7.3

Ten Largest Self-Operated Universities*

UNIVERSITY	ENROLLMENT
Brigham Young University	33,000
Pennsylvania State University	42,000
Michigan State University	43,000
University of Notre Dame	10,000
University of California, LA	38,000
Harvard University	20,000
University of Maryland	35,000
Boston College	15,000
Purdue University	39,000
Rutgers University	36,000

*Based on total food and beverage purchases.
Source: Information compiled from "All the Right Moves," *Restaurants and Institutions*, September 15, 2003.

become more demanding and sophisticated, suggesting greater challenges ahead for food service operators. As a result of increased participation rates and a growing population group, however, college and university food service seems likely to be a growth segment for nearly a generation to come. In addition, nontraditional opportunities are beginning to surface for food service operators. These opportunities might include extending food service responsibilities (such as to arenas, research parks, or catering services), opening "supermarkets," and/or taking on a wider range of responsibilities across college campuses, including the management of mail services, campus bookstores, and facilities management. In short, just like the other segments, the entire food service environment is changing on college campuses.

Health Care Food Service

As changes are occurring in both B&I and colleges and universities, changes are occurring at perhaps an even greater rate in the health care environment. This section will discuss some of these changes as well as provide a general overview of this unique food service segment.

Health care facilities can be divided into three general categories: large hospitals (over 300 beds), small to medium hospitals, and nursing homes. In all three of these settings, health care professionals—dietitians, along with such paraprofessionals as dietetic managers and **dietetic technicians**—play important roles. Some of the key positions in hospital food service operations are described next.

THE DIETETIC PROFESSIONAL

According to the International Committee of Dietetic Associations, a dietitian is "a person with a legally recognized qualification (in Nutrition and Dietetics), who applies the science of nutrition to the feeding and education of groups of people and individuals in health and disease."[6] In the health care food service setting, there are different types of dietitians. The largest group within the profession is made up of **clinical dietitians**, concerned principally with the problems of special diets and with educating patients who have health problems that require temporary or permanent diet changes. Administrative dietitians are concerned principally with the management of food service systems, for the most part in health care. (Dietitians also work in education and non-health-care food services, and their commitment to community nutrition is growing rapidly as well.)

Dietitians who complete a bachelor's degree program and a supervised practice program (either in an internship program or in a coordinated program that combines

Employees in health care food service operations play an important role in meeting the dietary needs of patients. (Courtesy of Sodexho.)

both academic class work and supervised practice) and who pass a national registration examination are considered **registered dietitians (RDs)** by the Commission on Dietetic Registration (CDR), which is the credentialing agency for the American Dietetic Association (ADA). Registered dietitians are required by hospital accreditation standards and government regulations to supervise health care food services either on a full-time basis or as consultants.

Large hospitals generally employ a number of *clinical dietitians* whose primary responsibility is the provision of medical nutrition therapy (MNT) for inpatients as well as outpatients. Medical nutrition therapy is the nutrition therapy component within the medical treatment and management of disease. An important part of the dietitian's work is planning and implementing the nutrition therapy so that the patient and family are able to continue the treatment after discharge.

In a smaller hospital or in a nursing home, the food service manager is somewhat less likely to be a *registered dietitian*. In such cases, however, a consulting registered dietitian will provide professional guidance.

THE DIETETIC TECHNICIAN

A somewhat newer role in health care is that of the dietetic technician. Qualification for this designation requires completion of an appropriate associate degree program. Technicians occupy key roles in medium and large hospitals, working under the direction of registered dietitians. Dietetic technicians screen and interview patients to determine their dietary needs or problems and, in large hospitals, often have supervisory responsibilities. In smaller hospitals, technicians may run dietary departments under the periodic supervision of consulting registered dietitians. One of the most important areas of opportunity for dietetic technicians is in life care facilities, such as nursing homes, where technicians serve as food service managers under the supervision of a consulting registered dietitian. Technicians must take a registration exam, and fully qualified technicians are registered as DTRs, that is, dietetic technicians—registered.

THE DIETARY MANAGER

The **dietary manager** also has an important role in health care food service. Dietary managers must have had a considerable amount of on-the-job experience and must also have completed a course of instruction covering subjects such as food service management, supervision, and basic nutrition. A separate organization, the Dietary Managers Association, provides for their education and certification as certified dietary managers (CDMs). Certified dietary managers are not credentialed by the CDR and are not members of the ADA. Dietary managers are employed principally in nursing homes. Some dietary managers have completed the dietetic technician's more extensive two-year course of instruction and may use either title.

DIETARY DEPARTMENT ORGANIZATION

The organization of the dietary department should be considered in the context of the overall health care facility organization. However, presenting an organization chart of a "typical" hospital would be self-defeating, because hospitals vary greatly in size, are organized differently, and are currently in the midst of wholesale restructuring. Readers should be aware of two trends, however, in the organization of hospitals: (1) organizations are generally becoming flatter and (2) more and more support services are being outsourced. With this being said, the food service department must fit in with what tends to be a large and complex organization. Other functions and professional services in a hospital would include nursing, laboratories, X-ray services, ambulance services, environmental services, fiscal services, administrative services, and pharmacies, among others. The dietary department would probably be found in the general services division along with other support services such as plant engineering and housekeeping. The fiscal services division includes functions such as accounting, receiving, and storage. Thus, in some hospitals, receiving and storage may be carried out for food service by another support unit. Administrative services include the personnel and purchasing functions. Here again, note that another division may assume these functions for the dietary department. This already complex organization is further complicated by the medical and surgical staffs—the professionals on whose services the entire institution is centered.

Patients have many more menu choices than ever before. (Courtesy of Sodexho.)

Work in hospital food service is fast-paced, and many employees find the medical atmosphere exciting. The organizational complexity and need for nutrition care (the provision of special therapeutic diets) as a separate concern makes health care food service one of the most complex and demanding of the food service careers.

The organization of the dietary department will vary in its assignment and reporting relationships according to the size and function of the hospital. The main functions appear in Figure 7.1.

The same kitchen usually prepares the food for all the employees, house diet patients, and visitors, although this can vary. Some hospitals maintain a separate diet kitchen; others allow the same crew to prepare the special diets following appropriate recipes. Some hospitals even utilize decentralized pantries to assemble patient meals.

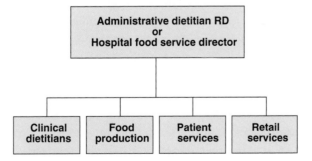

Figure 7.1

Functional organization of the dietary department.

In the traditional model, however, patient food service personnel deliver the food to the floors and return dishes and other equipment to the kitchen after the meals. One trend that is occurring in patient feeding is perhaps best illustrated by what ARAMARK is doing in some of its health care accounts. In an effort to develop a more efficient system, ARAMARK has modified its patient meal plan by moving more toward the airline feeding model. It has all but eliminated written menus and instead offers patients a choice of two items, which are brought up to the floors and held in warming boxes. Patients then indicate their choice and the meal is brought into the room immediately. Although last-minute modifications can still be made and special diets accommodated, the average patient is fed in a much more efficient manner, resulting in fewer late trays and higher levels of patient satisfaction.

In addition to patient feeding, hospitals may have a variety of other food service outlets: Cafeterias serve the staff, visitors, and, in some cases, ambulatory patients. There may also be special dining areas limited for use by the doctors and/or senior staff. Additionally, many hospitals provide catering for in-house events. Others are even branching out and doing off-premise catering for non-hospital-related events. A recent report by *Restaurants and Institutions* reports that ". . . hospital food service departments have blossomed into hospitality businesses where 68% of meals are served to staff, visitors, and guests in stylish serveries. . ."[7]

Nursing homes, smaller hospitals, and extended-care facilities (discussed in a later section) perform these similar functions on a smaller scale. Thus, such an institution may employ only a consulting dietitian and may combine food production and patient food service. Or the cafeterias in some nursing homes may be expanded to serve all ambulatory patients, often in traditional dining rooms.

TRENDS IN HEALTH CARE FOOD SERVICE

In the past, health care was a recession-proof food service segment with strong growth potential. Although health care is still less sensitive to economic conditions than are many other food service segments, regulation by government agencies, which reimburse hospitals for many health care expenditures, complicates administration. Regulators have capped costs by limiting the length of stay that is covered. Private health insurance plans have established similar limits. As a result, hospital occupancy and revenue were limited, too. Hospitals are reacting in several ways, including developing networks, affiliations with other hospitals, and their own health maintenance organizations (HMOs). Health care, in general, has had to learn to live with less. This has had a dramatic impact on dietary departments.

So far, lower hospital occupancy levels have led to greater competition for patients, and the dietary department often plays a key role in this competition by offering special services and frills. Hospitals have also found ways to reduce costs and boost revenue. These often include taking a marketing-oriented approach and building sales. It should be noted, though, at the time of this writing, the number of hospital beds increased over last year—the first time in over 20 years. If this trend continues, it will obviously have a long-term impact on food service operations.

Lowering Costs. With skyrocketing daily charges for hospital rooms and pressure from government and insurance companies for shorter hospital stays, hospitals have developed alternative arrangements for those patients needing less-intensive care. Hospitals have converted facilities to hotel-type accommodations or developed arrangements with nearby hotels to house discharged patients who still need to remain near the hospital. These alternative accommodations are more affordable for the patient, and where in-house space is used, they provide revenue to the hospital.

Another strategy for cost reduction involves consolidation of food production facilities. One large unit takes on responsibility for basic production for several nearby facilities. This centralized location may then employ a cook-chill food production system. An example of this is the Carilion Health System in Virginia. They consolidated the production of their food for their health care system (including eight hospitals) into one central processing kitchen (CPK). Carilion was able to outsource the CPK while retaining operation of the eight food service facilities. The facility now serves 1.5 million meals each year and has achieved a significant cost savings.[8]

Most hospitals that operate their own food service also purchase supplies, including food service products, through cooperative purchasing organizations or **group purchasing organizations (GPOs)**. Pooled purchasing volumes, often in the hundreds of millions of dollars, secure lower unit costs. In addition, hospital food service, like all other food service organizations, has carefully examined its employee scheduling practices and product use to ensure maximum efficiency.

One hospital specializing in short-stay elective surgery, for instance, converted completely to frozen prepared foods, eliminating its production kitchen entirely. The production activity is limited entirely to reconstituting frozen foods and portioning prepared salad greens for distribution to the floors.

Enhancing Revenue. Most hospitals serve more nonpatient than patient meals; the current estimates indicate that less than one-third (32 percent) of meals served in the health care environment are patient meals. Not surprisingly, therefore, the nonpatient side of hospital food service has offered major opportunities for increasing sales. Hospitals have upgraded their public dining facilities to attract more business from staff and visitors in the hospital. Like colleges and universities, some hospitals are adding national brands to their offerings, although not to the same extent.

These not only offer greater market appeal to customers but also lower operating costs.

In addition, hospitals have broadened their food service activities to target customers outside the hospital. Some hospitals have begun offering off-site food delivery programs. Others, as mentioned above, are offering national brands that have helped broaden their customer base. Methodist Hospital in Dallas has added Sonic Drive-in to its product mix and has dramatically increased revenues and dropped operating costs as a result.[9] Still other programs and services currently being offered by hospitals include Meals on Wheels and providing meals to day-care centers.

Additionally, some hospitals offer what is, in effect, commercial catering—handling weddings and other functions both on and off the premises. This is a growing trend: A study conducted by *FoodService Director* magazine found that 73 percent of hospitals offer some kind of catering services and that almost half of these expect to grow their catering services in the near future.[10] Other services offered by hospitals include baking services, theater cooking, and home meal replacement. Hospital bakeries offer freshly baked breads and pastries, including wedding cakes, to the public. The Medical Center at Ohio State University offers special cooking events for patients. Others offer regular takeout meals, delicatessens, even on-premise convenience stores. In general, hospitals are becoming very creative in adding revenue-enhancing services. One New Orleans area hospital, East Jefferson General Hospital, has added meeting and conference space to its facility in an effort to capitalize upon a perceived need in the local market.

In summary, health care institutions have been subject to cost pressures that result from both government regulation and from competitive pressures. Health care institutions have responded with efforts to contain costs and to enhance revenues with a better mix of services aimed at a broader spectrum of customers, that is, with an improved marketing program. Much of the burden has fallen on the food service directors of these facilities, who are taking on more and more responsibilities through expanded roles and increased services. We should end this section by noting, in addition, that health care is expected to be one of the fastest-growing areas in the economy well into the twenty-first century.

School and Community Food Service

The fourth major segment of the on-site sector is **school and community food service**. This segment is quite different from the previously discussed segments in several ways, including the high degree of self-operators and the goals and objectives of the segment. The segment is also facing some of the same challenges as the others' in the way of tight budgetary constraints). There are also differences in terms of scale. While there are obvious challenges associated with food service in every environment, consider the challenges of handling over 1 million customers each day, as New York City schools must do. But first, a little history of the segment is in order.

The earliest government food service programs began around 1900 in Europe.[11] Programs in the United States date from the Great Depression, when the need to use surplus agricultural commodities was joined to concern for feeding the children of poor families. During and after World War II, the explosion in the number of working women fueled the need for a broader program. What was once a function of the family—providing lunch—was, in effect, shifted to the school food service system. The National School Lunch Program is the result of these efforts. The program is designed to provide federally assisted meals to children of school age. From the end of World War II to the early 1980s, funding for school food service expanded steadily. Today it helps to feed children in almost 100,000 schools (and residential child care) across the United States. Its first function is to provide a nutritious lunch to all students; the second is to provide nutritious food at both breakfast and lunch to underprivileged children. If anything, the role of school food service as a replacement for what was once a family function has been expanded.

The U.S. Department of Agriculture (USDA) regulations have, for many years, required that school lunches conform to a basic pattern. As of 1996, schools that receive federal subsidies must establish their meal plans based on the calorie, nutrient, and fat content of foods instead of on food groups, as was the previous practice. These changes are based on the new dietary guidelines developed by the USDA, which in turn are based upon the Dietary Guidelines for Americans (by law, these guidelines must be reviewed every five years).

A significant portion of the cost of school food service is met by subsidies in cash and kind provided by federal and state governments and the local school board. Children who qualify according to a means test receive a free lunch and breakfast. The majority of children participating in the school breakfast program qualify as disadvantaged. Schools are reimbursed on the basis of the number of meals that they serve. Reimbursement costs were $2.19 for each free meal in 2003 to 2004. Other reimbursement rates apply to reduced price lunches, breakfasts, and snacks.

Funding restrictions, however, have presented difficulties for school food service programs. The most obvious response to reduced government funding is to raise prices, but this often results in reduced participation rates. In conversations with school food service managers, as well as the American School Food Service Association, it would appear that the operating premise that many managers abide by is that for every cent that student costs increase, participation drops by 1 percent. School districts have reacted to reduced funding in much the same way that other institutions have, by increased marketing activity and, to a lesser degree, by diversification of activities to gain more revenues.

An additional challenge facing school food service programs has been the requirement of nutritious selections. The most successful response to this has been to develop menu offerings that closely resemble fast-food menus yet meet the USDA guidelines. Pizza, Mexican foods, chicken nuggets, and popular sandwiches such as hamburgers and hot dogs play a major role in such menus. In effect, these menus give the consumers what they want. They are often criticized, however, for not doing the educational job of teaching students what they should eat. Nevertheless, given pressure to sell food at higher prices to maintain their economic viability, schools have had to embrace a marketing approach to survive.

School food service districts have also expanded their operations to outside customers. Efforts to build sales volume include catering and selling take-out items, including freshly baked goods, as well as selling prepared foods to other institutional customers in the community.

Marketing efforts are not limited to menu and format alterations. To meet the need to communicate with customers, student advisory councils are formed in schools. School lunch dining areas are upgraded and remodeled to make them more attractive. Self-service speeds service while reducing cost and giving the customer the sense of having a choice. Food bars, buffets, and scramble systems are seeing greater utilization in schools. An example of how one school combined marketing with service to increase participation is exemplified in the Albuquerque, New Mexico, school system, which is piloting a program in which breakfasts are delivered directly to classrooms. A similar program is in operation in a Texas system, where they were able to increase participation rates threefold.[12]

THE SCHOOL FOOD SERVICE MODEL

The accumulated experience of school food service suggests a model for public-sector food service programs, known as the **school food service model**. The first element in that model is that it meets clearly defined social needs that attract broad public support. School food service provides nutritious meals to needy children who might otherwise go hungry, and it helps make well-balanced meals available to all students.

The second element in the school food service model is that it pools subsidies. The federal subsidy usually requires matching state or local funds. Because the subsidies from the various levels of government are pooled, the result constitutes a bargain. The student's lunch, even if he or she paid the full price, is less expensive than it would be if purchased anywhere else—even if it were brought from home.

The attractiveness of this bargain encourages participation, and participation ensures the third element of the model, a high volume. This high volume makes the

Nutrition is one of the elements on which school food service focuses. (Courtesy of Sodexho.)

meal program more efficient, and it results in further economies. In short, it improves the bargain.

The pattern of administration is the fourth and final element. There is general monitoring of the fairly broad guidelines at the national and state levels, but most operational decisions are made entirely at the local level. Technical advice is always available. Thus, the model encourages adaptation to local tastes and conditions.

The bargain that the program offers to young consumers and their families has never been completely dependent on federal subsidies. Both state and local governments (and, in some communities, charitable organizations) have contributed to the cost of school lunches in direct subsidies of varying amounts.

Increasingly, the school is being seen not just as an educational institution but as a social agency in the community that can use its physical plant—buildings, kitchens, dining areas—and its other resources, such as experienced administration, skilled cooks, and backup custodial staff, to serve a variety of population groups. Schools around the country are now getting involved with the feeding of seniors, food service at day care centers, off-site feeding such as at public parks during the summer, and various other community support services.

CONTRACT COMPANIES IN SCHOOL FOOD SERVICE

A relatively new market for contract companies is the school market. The lowest penetration of contract companies among the four segments is in school food service, and many of the largest school systems in the United States are still self-operated. Many school boards, however, facing tighter budgetary restrictions, are finding it advantageous to bring in a company with specialized food service expertise to take on what is, for them, an activity only indirectly related to education, which is the school system's principal mission and expertise. Because such a high percentage of the market is self-operated, there is a huge market for contract companies to pursue. Although its profit margin is not as high as for some other institutional sectors, school food service is a logical addition to a contract company's operations. Contract companies do not just take over one or two schools when they receive an account. Rather, the numbers can run into the hundreds, as is the case in Chicago, where school lunch programs are available at over 650 different locations. The food service program is overseen by the Department of Food Services for the Chicago public school system, but individual units are managed by three different contract companies.[13] In addition, in many cases, the contract company finds it can serve a school board not only with food service but also in other areas, such as grounds maintenance and custodial services.

In an interview in which she discussed career opportunities with contract companies in the school food service area, Beth Tarter, human-resources manager for Sodexho, pointed out that there are a number of advantages to this area. Because it is growing, there are numerous opportunities for advancement. The excitement of a very large account—$5 million or $6 million—is more likely to come at an earlier stage than in other areas of food service. School food service also has quality-of-life advantages. This is an area that offers a professional career in food service with a five-day week. Night and weekend work occurs occasionally, usually in connection with a special event at a school, but such an event is the exception. Moreover, many people in school food service have ten-and-a-half-month contracts that give them summers off. One manager whose main joy in life is sailing pointed out that he could find no better job to match his professional expertise and his leisure interest. He spends his summers on a sailboat. Clearly, there are some advantages for students who might choose this segment of the industry.

TRENDS IN SCHOOL FOOD SERVICE

Growth in school enrollment is expected to fall off over the next few years, resulting in stabilization of the food services in this area. Growth is expected, however, in the relatively new breakfast program. Perhaps the biggest issue that is facing food service in schools, though, is the concern surrounding child obesity. This is likely to affect the choices offered to students as well as the vending options, as has already happened in some jurisdictions. New York City has banned candy and soda from vending machines in schools. Finally, as identified in a recent report by *Restaurants and Institutions,* many school districts are trying harder to educate students (and parents) on the importance of good nutrition.[14]

Centralized preparation of food in many school systems permits significant economies of scale. (Courtesy of Sodexho.)

SERVICE PROGRAMS FOR THE AGING

One of the fastest-growing segments of our population for the foreseeable future will be people over the age of 65. Although many people in this age bracket are healthy and active, not all of them are. Similarly, many but not all of the people over the age of 65 are comfortable financially. Although retirement incomes for most are not as high as for working people, neither are financial needs. Many live in homes already paid for and have significant savings to draw on. On the other hand, not all elderly are affluent. Many must live on their social security checks and limited savings. People over 75 are more likely to fall into this category. They are more likely to be financially needy and to require assistance to survive. The rapid growth of this group is one reason for the increasing demand for government supportive services for the elderly.

People over 65 commonly have disabilities related to their age. By age 65, for instance, over two-thirds of individuals have at least one chronic condition. Fourteen percent of individuals age 65 and over have difficulty performing at least one of six "activities of daily living" (ADLs).[15] Once they reach the age of 85, almost one-half experience some difficulty with daily activities such as bathing or dressing. Disabilities such as these tend to be concentrated among those in the latter age group and are even greater among institutionalized individuals.

The Census Bureau predicts continuing growth for those in both the 65-and-older age group and the 85-and-older age group. Their predictions suggest that by 2050, the elderly population will increase more than twofold. Those age 65 and older will constitute 20 percent of the population.[16] Certainly, this is a population group that will be growing for the foreseeable future and one that has a set of unique needs. We will look

The population continues to age, which is creating opportunities for new service programs for the aged. (Courtesy of Sodexho.)

briefly at programs to meet the needs for food service in this section. We will also examine the growing life care institutional segment, in which hotel companies such as Hyatt figure prominently.

COMMUNITY-BASED SERVICES

The ideal arrangement for the elderly is to live independently in their own homes. As their physical, cognitive, and mental abilities deteriorate, however, they begin to require assistance. Many Americans provide help to elderly friends or family members without pay, but this does not occur without complications and difficulties. As a result, community agencies have come into being to provide help to people living independently and to families who are helping an elderly relative or friend.

The Older Americans Act (OAA) (Title III-C) provides funding for elderly meal services, much of it through the Meals on Wheels program. Funding provides the ability of thousands of volunteers in every state to serve meals to seniors through congregate meal sites and in their own homes. Over 3 million seniors will benefit from these services this year according to the Administration on Aging (AOA).[17]

The national nutrition program for the elderly is designed to provide older Americans, particularly those with low incomes, with low-cost, nutritionally sound meals. Emphasis is given to providing these meals in group settings. The nutritional projects provide at least one hot meal a day (meeting one-third of the daily nutritional requirements) five days a week to older citizens (60 and over) and their spouses of any age.

Although participants would be given an opportunity to pay for their meals, "no means test will be made and no one will be turned away on the basis of their inability to pay for a meal." **Congregate meals** are funded by the AOA and by state and local agencies and supported by volunteers and private donations.

Meals on Wheels and similar programs also receive direct and indirect support from all levels of government and from local private agencies as well. The programs deliver meals to people living in their homes who have difficulty getting out. In addition to funding from governmental and private agencies, these programs often rely on local volunteers to assist in fulfilling their mission.

SENIOR LIVING CENTERS AND COMMUNITIES

A number of firms, including hotel companies such as Hyatt, have become active in providing housing, and in some cases a mix of additional services, to more affluent senior citizens. Some seniors want to live in a community that can provide the independence of apartment living along with the security of having health care and professional services available without needing to move to another facility. Others desire to live in an environment that provides them with a higher level of assistance with daily activities. Such facilities obviously provide much more than just food service and, in fact, incorporate many components of various hospitality services discussed in this and other chapters.

Different levels of accommodations and services are provided in senior living communities. These are often categorized as follows:

- *Independent living.* Private apartment living allows residents to enjoy an independent lifestyle with the security of knowing that whatever services or professional assistance they may need are readily available.

- *Assisted living.* Private apartment living is also available for residents who can maintain an independent lifestyle but need limited assistance with day-to-day activities such as dressing, grooming, bathing, or monitoring of medication.

- *Personal care.* Personal care takes assisted living a step further by providing a greater level of hands-on assistance in performing daily activities, while allowing residents to maintain as much independence as possible.

- *Licensed nursing facility.* Private and semiprivate rooms are available for residents who need long-term or short-term intermediate and/or skilled nursing care and supervision.

These describe the four basic models under which many senior living communities may operate, although an individual operation may fall anywhere along this

Many retirement residences closely resemble the surroundings that residents were familiar with in their own homes. (Courtesy of The RiverWoods Company at Exeter.)

Retirement residences are now available with many different levels of service and care. (Courtesy of The RiverWoods Company at Exeter.)

continuum. Most facilities at this time are of the assisted-living variety (40 percent of all facilities).[18] There is currently a movement in the industry toward developing **continuing-care retirement communities (CCRCs)**. Companies providing this level of services offer a wide range of life care services, all under one roof. Seniors typically pay one price and are guaranteed different levels of life care as they age and as required.

Hyatt Corporation operated (or are in the process of developing) 21 high-end retirement communities in 2007 under the Classic Residence banner, the senior living affiliate of Hyatt Hotels. Hyatt facilities offer a range of services and in some cases are CCRCs. They are located in selected markets in the United States, predominantly in the Northeast and the South. The company was founded in 1987 and currently houses almost 5,000 residents. Most of their units are classified as independent living. They also have assisted living, memory support/Alzheimer's care, and skilled nursing units.

Aside from receiving the hospitality expertise that Hyatt is known for, residents receive special privileges at Hyatt Hotels.

Other hotel companies have ties to senior living operations including Marriott, which operated 150 Senior Living Services facilities until early 1993. They have since sold off the ownership and management of the facilities. When Sunrise Senior Living purchased Marriott's senior living division, it became the largest provider of assisted living facilities. Another hotel company also divested of its senior living division: Choice Hotels was associated with Manor Care, Inc. until 1997 when the companies separated. Manor Care is a leading owner and operator of long-term care facilities. It remains to be seen if and when additional lodging companies will expand into the senior living market.

The largest single operator of senior living centers is Sunrise Senior Living, which operates over 400 communities in North America and Europe. The company was started by Paul and Terry Klaassen (and now a public company). They offer the full range of services from short-term stays for those with temporary needs to care for Alzheimer's patients.

There are many other service companies that operate in this unique segment, including Alterra Healthcare Corp., Emeritus Assisted Living, and Atria Retirement and Assisted Living. The top ten companies in the industry own or manage over one-half of all available units. However, in addition to the major management companies, there are also many smaller regional, independently operated retirement communities. One such facility is Heritage Pointe, a retirement facility located in Mission Viejo, California. The mission of Heritage Pointe is "To provide residential services for the elderly incorporating Jewish tradition and lifestyle; to offer a continuum of service, and to provide financial assistance to those in need, to the extent provided by the community." They admitted their first resident in 1990 and have since developed a waiting list for their 178 units. They are a unique operation, according to Rina Loveless, the head administrator. For one thing, they are the only Jewish facility in Orange County and only one of two nonprofit facilities in the area. The other is a Presbyterian based facility (the total number of religious based facilities is very small). Jewish traditions drive the mission at Heritage Pointe—food service is Kosher, Friday night and Saturday morning religious services are held, all Jewish holidays are observed, and classes are offered to residents in Jewish culture, among other topics. Most of the residents do not need assistance with ADLs, but do receive housekeeping and food service. Assisted living services are provided to those who need it. Finally, scholarships are provided to applicants who qualify—about 25 percent of residents are on scholarship. Heritage Pointe is strongly supported by the local Jewish community.

In the early 1990s, this sector of hospitality was characterized by high business failure rates. Some of the problems experienced by operators included lack of operating know-how suited to the specific market, poor location choices, overly rapid expansion, a nursing shortage, and increasing regulation. Since that time, new companies have entered the market and failed projects have been absorbed. As a result, industry analysts view this segment very favorably leading into the next decade. The only question that remains is whether supply can continue to meet the ever-increasing demand. One last point must also be made—depending on the type of facility, some residents may move in at the relatively "young" age of 55. For instance, that is the minimum age requirement at Hyatt's Classic Residence. As a result, people can age a good deal after moving in to a senior living environment. For this reason, the trend is to be able to accommodate people's need and to recognize the desire for some to "age in place." This is accomplished by offering more of a mix and match choice of services—assuming the need for additional services increases as one ages. This is causing the industry to take a hard look at the services provided, the facilities, and the fees charged.

Other Segments

In addition to the four institutional segments already discussed, there are a variety of other segments that are sometimes less visible than their higher-profile counterparts yet are still deserving of attention. Unfortunately, it is beyond the scope of this chapter to cover all of the different types of businesses that could conceivably fall into this category, but some very important types of services are discussed next. As evidenced by the large size of the organizations in these sectors, each of them is an important element in the food service sector and related industries.

RECREATION

Recreational food service is one of the widest-reaching of all the segments discussed thus far. This segment can include food service in such diverse facilities as stadiums and arenas, convention centers, zoos and aquariums, and even fairs and expositions, among others. As with other segments, facilities may be managed or self-operated.

One managed-services company, ARAMARK, has its own division devoted to this segment. ARAMARK's Sports and Entertainment Services division presents a profile of a company with involvement in a variety of recreational activities. In 2003, ARAMARK operated food service at over 120 convention centers, 70 stadiums (including 13 Major League Baseball teams), arenas, and racetracks; and a variety of state and national parks. In addition, ARAMARK has been responsible for the food service at virtually all Olympic and Pan American Games since 1968. Other companies that specialize in recreation feeding include Sportservice, a division of Delaware North, Wood

Dining Services (which recently joined Sodexho Alliance), and CulinArt. The latter company recently took over food service operations at the Philadelphia Zoo. More and more, companies seem to be recognizing this segment for its dynamic operating environment as well as for the opportunities it affords. Recreation feeding plays the enviable role of complementing some of life's pleasures, such as a day at the state fair, the zoo, or the ballpark. In fact, it seems that entertainment is nearly as important to stadium operators as a winning team, so we see more and more of a Disneyland kind of format that emphasizes enjoying the experience of coming to a ball game as much as the sport itself. Hospitality services, particularly food service, have an important role to play in delivering the experience.

As in other institutions, brand names are becoming increasingly important. National names such as McDonald's are prominent in stadiums, but often local or regional brands are represented as well. Although hot dogs, soft drinks, and beer are still the most popular items, ballparks and other recreation sites are expanding their menus to include more upscale foods (the tiramisu at the FleetCenter in Boston is rumored to be very good). As the entertainment and recreation sector continues to thrive, so, too, should the food services associated with it.

PRIVATE CLUBS

A segment not totally unrelated to the recreation segment is that segment consisting of private clubs. Private clubs are just that—recreational, social, and/or dining facilities available for the exclusive use of their members. Clubs are characterized by their independence, exclusivity, and unique qualities. In fact, it has been said many times that no two clubs are exactly alike. This segment includes city clubs (which tend to focus on dining services), yacht clubs, swimming clubs, tennis clubs, golf clubs, and country clubs (which tend to be full service), among others. In reality, there may be a club devoted to just about any activity that you may think of, but more often than not, food service constitutes a large part of what they offer to their members. Clubs provide a home away from home for their members, and as a result, they are often characterized by a high level of personal service.

Clubs may be owned by their members (in which case the club usually hires a professional manager). These types of clubs tend to be run on a not-for-profit basis. Clubs may also be owned independently or by a corporation, in which case they would be operated on a for-profit basis. Finally, as with other segments within the larger institutional sector, there are companies that specialize in the management of clubs (such as ClubCorp and others). ClubCorp runs such famous clubs (and resorts) as Pinehurst in North Carolina, the Firestone Country Club in Ohio, and Indian Wells Country Club in California. In total, they own and/or operate almost 200 facilities.

Private clubs such as Pinehurst have a great deal of distinction. (Courtesy of ClubCorp.)

Although the majority of successful club managers have extensive food and beverage experience, students should be aware that, in order to be successful, a manager must be a jack-of-all-trades. Managing a large club usually means overseeing many different types of departments requiring a unique level of expertise. Clubs truly combine all of the best things that the hospitality industry has to offer, all under one roof. In recent years, more and more managers of private clubs have begun to come out of hospitality management programs.

TRANSPORTATION

In the United States, transportation food service is usually synonymous with airline (or **in-flight**) food service. Of course, there is food service associated with other forms of transportation, including rail and ferry, but the industry is dominated by food service geared to air passengers. As with other segments, there are companies that operate their own food service, as well as companies that specialize in in-flight feeding (Dobbs International Services, a part of Gategourmet). Many of these companies are quite large and regularly appear on lists of the largest food service companies.

The airline food service business is fast-paced and requires people who work well under pressure. The uncertain number of passengers on an outbound flight, sudden cancellations or additions to the airlines' flight schedules, and the various equipment configurations used in different aircraft make in-flight food service a challenging field. Add to this the fact that the production area is often located some distance away from the airport and one can imagine some of the challenges associated with this type of food service.

As with every other segment, however, airline food service is changing. There seems to be no clear trend indicating how the different companies are implementing these changes and, more specifically, modifying their services. Some are cutting back their services and some are eliminating their food service entirely, while others are putting a greater emphasis on their food service. Some are beginning to charge for their food service. All are doing so in an effort to balance service with profitability. Those companies that are putting a greater emphasis on food are hiring high-profile chefs as consultants and partnering with other companies (e.g., United Airlines with Starbucks and Au Bon Pain). What is clear is that one decision that every airline must make involves food.

Perhaps one of the biggest changes taking place in transportation food service is happening on the ground. Specifically, food service in airports is becoming big business. Airports around the country now offer a selection of products and services once unimaginable. T.G.I. Friday's, Samuel Adams Brewpubs, Au Bon Pain, Cafe du Monde, Starbucks, and a variety of other recognizable food service providers have begun targeting airline terminals. Even theme restaurants can be found in airports. One recent example is The Encounter, a restaurant with a space theme, located at Los Angeles International Airport. The Encounter has become a popular spot for travelers and non-travelers alike.

Although different companies may sometimes manage in-flight food service and airport food service, the two are irrefutably linked. As more passengers travel by air, they will expect to be able to have the same choices that are available to them elsewhere. Research is also indicating that travelers are now expecting something more than the usual quick-service outlets. The evidence suggests that some of the more dynamic changes in the industry are occurring in this segment.

Vending

Vending is not really a segment of on-site food service but a method of delivering food service that is used across segments. It is an effective means of making food and beverage (and other products) available to customers. Even the casual observer will have noticed vending machines dispensing a variety of products in schools, businesses, attractions, malls, and on the street. Vending is believed to have originated

Many vending operations have incorporated smart card technology. (Courtesy of Sodexho.)

in the late 1800s in the United States and to have caught on with the public in the early 1900s. It has since evolved to the point where industry leaders believe that there are tremendous opportunities for this segment. In fact, because of the recent advances in technologies, sophistication of machines, variety of products offered, and improvements in merchandising, this "channel of distribution" is now commonly referred to as V-Commerce.

To provide some background, over 50 percent of all vending operations are located in manufacturing facilities or office environments. Others are found in schools, lodging, restaurants, hospitals, military bases, and so forth. As the majority of machines (and profits) are found in work settings, the health of the industry fluctuates directly with the level of unemployment in the United States. The industry suffered during early 2000 when jobs were being lost across industries. It has since rebounded though, as the U.S. economy added new jobs between 2003 and 2006 and the unemployment rate dropped to lower levels.

The variety of products that vendors sell is growing and improving. About half of the companies offering vended food services have their own commissaries, and their vending outlets usually are equipped with microwave ovens.

Vending is clearly a part of the eating market, as defined in Chapter 3, rather than the dining market. Vending companies have found that if they offer manual vending (i.e., a cafeteria staffed by "real, live" people) during some of their hours of service, all of their products are more likely to be accepted. One vendor speculated that this is true because the personal touch allows the guests to associate the vended food with the people who provide food services in the more traditional cafeterias.

Vending offers the hospitality industry a means of extending food service hours to meet the convenience of guests and to provide acceptable service where it would be economically impossible to provide full manual food service.

Perhaps the most significant change that is taking place in vending is not with the food products at all but with the management of the machines. New "smart" machines are now available. These new machines allow customers to use cards for payment and help operators track inventory and collect meaningful data on sales trends. The potential for these machines seems limitless.

In the on-site sector, vending is most common in the college and university segment and the business and industry segment; it is least common in schools (where there are increasing restrictions on what can be sold). At over $10 billion, vending is a major factor in food service, accounting for over 2 percent of the 2006 national total.[19] Beyond vending's aggregate size, we need to consider vending here briefly to understand its function for clients and the advantages (and disadvantages) it presents to guests.

Since vending operates under a different business model than many other businesses, it is often "contracted out" to vending specialists, although some food service companies (such as ARAMARK) have vending divisions. Many vending companies are smaller and regional in scope (generating $1 million or less each year). Vending operations require a complete support system that includes route drivers, office support, technicians, sales staff, warehouses to store products, currency management systems, and general management. As a result of the support needed, it is generally not economically feasible for a vending operation to operate in an environment where there are fewer than 100 potential customers.

Most vended food falls in the snack and beverage categories. A significant portion, however, constitutes main meal service, particularly breakfast and, to a lesser degree, lunch. Technological advantages are improving the variety and quality of product offered through vending. The number and types of products that vending has been able to offer has increased in recent years. Food products (aside from snacks and beverages) generally break down into frozen or fresh. At least one of the name brands of popular frozen foods will look familiar from earlier chapters: White Castle hamburgers. Other popular frozen food products (which are developed to be reheated in microwave ovens) include products by Nestle and Pierre Foods. Fresh food products (which represent a smaller but growing segment) include soups, salads, desserts, fruit and veggie cups, and sandwiches. In addition, the snacks and beverages are commonly used to supplement main meals brought from home.

In many sites, and particularly on college and university campuses, vending is seen as a complementary service to offer to customers (students). Since dining halls are rarely open 24 hours a day or available on all parts of campus, vending offers options at different "access points" across campus as well as at all hours of the day and night.

Further, the options to students (and others) continue to increase to include healthier eating options. Students can also purchase work supplies for studying purposes. Vending, therefore, plays an important role in the overall food service business.

Finally, there have been new developments in the way of merchandising (glass front machines), eating options (healthier foods), and quality (coffee). Guests are rarely enthusiastic about vending but the impersonal nature of the machines can be reduced by attended vending and by the environment. In some cases, vending attendants can provide change, give refunds, and handle complaints. Still, vending remains primarily a mechanical, self-service process. Further, vending is convenient, can solve economic and operational problems for building and plant managers, and can increase food service variety.

Summary

It should be clear at this point that the on-site sector is a wide-reaching and incredibly varied segment with many unique qualities. Although the host units may have a greater hold on their market because of convenience, restaurants provide a lively alternative and plenty of competition for most. In addition, on-site food service must serve the needs of both the client and the individual guest. Managed service companies have the largest market share in business and industry food service and college and university food service. On-site operators have the dominant role in health care and school food service, although contract companies' share of those markets has been increasing. Brand-name concepts and aggressive marketing are important in all sectors of on-site food service.

We discussed major segments and found that the largest food service program is school food service. Its long experience in serving young people and their families suggests a model for other public-sector activities. That model is based on acknowledged social need, pooling of subsidies, concentration of activity to achieve high volume, and flexible administration that permits local initiatives.

Retirement housing communities provide affluent older people with as much independence as they can manage but also afford them support, such as health care, without requiring them to move to another place. Other areas discussed were recreation, transportation (mainly airline), and a somewhat unique segment—private clubs.

Vending is an important method of delivering food service, particularly in places that are not large enough to support a full food service operation or where the investment in facilities and operating support needed by food service cannot be made.

The principal arguments regarding the choice between an institutional operation and a contract company involve questions of scale, control of operations, and management expertise.

Key Words and Concepts

On-site
Self-ops
Participation rate
Contractors
Managed-services
  companies
Health care
Business and industry
  (B&I) food service
Brands
Outsourcing
College and university
  food service
Board plan

Dietetic technicians
Clinical dietitians
Registered dietitians (RDs)
Dietary manager
Group purchasing organizations
  (GPOs)
School and community food
  service
School food service model
Congregate meals
Continuing care retirement
  communities (CRCCs)
In-flight
Vending

Review Questions

1. What do on-site and commercial food services have in common? How are they different?

2. How do guest and client interests differ? What interests do they have in common?

3. Who operates the food service in your institution? Do you think an institutional operator or a managed-services company will do the best job of providing for the needs of the guest? Of the client? Why?

4. What characteristics are important to each of the four major divisions of on-site food service?

5. What opportunities do you see for extending hospitality services to the elderly? What facilities are available in your community for independent living for the aging?

6. What do you think might be some of the challenges associated with the management of a member-owned club?

7. What are the advantages and drawbacks of vending for the client? For the guest?

Internet Exercises

1. **Site name:** ARAMARK

   URL: www.aramark.com/

   Background information: ARAMARK is a global leader in professional services. They provide food, hospitality, facility management services, and high-quality uniforms and work apparel.

Site name: Compass Group

URL: www.cgnad.com/

Background information: Compass Group is one of the world's leading food service companies. They specialize in providing food, vending, and related services on their clients' premises in over 90 countries. They pride themselves on developing and delivering original food and service solutions whether in the workplace, schools and colleges, hospitals, at leisure, on the move, or in remote environments.

Site name: Sodexho

URL: www.sodexho.com/

Background information: Sodexho is a leading food and facilities management services company worldwide. Every day, Sodexho employees work to improve the quality of daily life for their clients and customers around the world. They offer a full range of outsourcing solutions to the corporate, health care, education, government, and defense markets.

Exercises: Review all three of the above corporate Web sites and compare each organization based on the following characteristics:

a. What markets do they serve?

b. What hospitality services do they provide?

c. What job opportunities are available to hospitality management graduates with these companies?

d. How many different countries do they serve worldwide?

e. In which country is each company headquartered?

2. **Site name:** The National Association of College & University Food Services

   URL: www.nacufs.org

   Background information: The National Association of College & University Food Services (NACUFS) is the trade association for food service professionals at more than 600 institutions of higher education in the United States, Canada, Mexico, and abroad.

   Site name: National Automatic Merchandising Association (NAMA)

   URL: www.vending.org

   Background information: NAMA is the national trade association of the food and refreshment vending, coffee service, and food service management industries including on-site, commissary, catering, and mobile establishments.

   Site name: International Flight Services Association

   URL: www.ifsanet.com

   Background information: Headquartered in Atlanta, Georgia, the International Flight Services Association is a global professional association created to serve the needs and interests of airline and railway personnel, in-flight and rail caterers, and suppliers responsible for providing passenger food service on regularly scheduled travel routes.

Exercises:

a. Who are the primary members of these associations?

b. What are the benefits of membership in these associations?

c. What educational opportunities do they provide for members?

d. What other services do they provide for members?

e. What are the goals/mission of the association?

f. Do they list job opportunities on their Web sites? If so, what types of jobs are listed?

3. **Site name:** *Restaurants & Institutions* Magazine

   URL: www.rimag.com

   Background information: *Restaurants & Institutions (R&I)* is the leading source of vital information for the entire food service industry, covering chains, independent restaurants, hotels, and institutions. Published 24 times per year, *R&I* reaches over 154,000 subscribers, including executives who operate independent and chain restaurants, hospitals, colleges, schools, airline food service, and hotels/resorts, as well as dealers/distributors and consultants in the food service supplies industry.

   Exercises: Click on the "Archives" link and select the most current year when a September 15 issue is available. Read the article regarding R&I's annual report on on-site (noncommercial) food service business segments.

   a. What are the current trends in on-site food service that are identified in the article?

   b. What are the issues facing this segment of the food service industry and how are they similar/different from the restaurant industry?

   c. Discuss what you consider to be the future direction of on-site food service in each of the four primary segments.

4. **Site name:** Look Smart Find Articles

   URL: www.findarticles.com/

   Background information: FindArticles has articles from thousands of resources, with archives dating back to 1984. That means you get to search for exactly what you need, from millions of articles not found on any other search engine.

   Exercises: Choose either health care, food service, school food service, or food service in retirement communities and use the Look Smart search engine to locate articles. Review the list of articles and choose an article to read and lead a class discussion regarding the following criteria:

   a. What impact does this article have on your chosen sector of the food service industry?

   b. In what ways would this article benefit managers who work in your chosen sector of the food service industry?

    c. If you were a manager, would your behavior change as a result of reading this article?

    d. What other changes, if any, do you believe will occur as a result of this article?

5. **Site name:** Meals on Wheels Association of America

    URL: www.mowaa.org

    Background information: The Meals On Wheels Association of America represents those who provide congregate and home-delivered meal services to people in need. Their mission is to provide visionary leadership and professional training, and to develop partnerships that will ensure the provision of quality nutrition services.

    Exercises:

    a. What factors contribute to hunger among the elderly?

    b. What is being done about hunger among the elderly?

    c. What is the importance of nutrition programs for the elderly?

    d. What are the benefits of belonging to this association?

Notes

1. National Restaurant Association (www.restaurant.org). Foodservice Forecast 2005.
2. Mike Buzalka, "Great Dining at a Great Workplace." *Food Management,* October 2002.
3. "Chronicle of Higher Education Almanac, 2003–2004" (www.chronicle.com).
4. U.S. Department of Education. "Report on the Condition of Education," 2002.
5. National Restaurant Association (www.restaurant.org). Foodservice Forecast 2006.
6. International Committee of Dietetic Associations (www.dietitians.ca/icda), November 10, 2003.
7. Scott Hume, "HealthCare." *Restaurants and Institutions,* September 15, 2003.
8. Mike Buzalka, "Outsourced Production." *Food Management,* August 2002.
9. *FoodService Director,* August 15, 2000, p. 44.
10. Ibid., p. 60.
11. For an authoritative, extended treatment of the school food service program, see Gordon W. Gunderson, "The National School Lunch Program: Background and Development" (www.fns.usda.gov/cnd/includes/content/NSLPBackgroundandDevelopment.htm).
12. *FoodService Director,* August 15, 2000, p. 55.
13. Chicago Public Schools (www.cps.edu), November 19, 2003.
14. Alison Perlik, "Schools." *Restaurants and Institutions,* September 15, 2003.
15. National Center for Health Statistics, "Health, United States, 2003," (http://www.cdc.gov/nchs/data/hus/hus03.pdf), November 20, 2003.
16. Ibid.
17. Administration on Aging (www.aoa.dhhs.gov/oaa).
18. Joan Raymond, "Senior Living," *American Demographics,* November 2000.
19. National Restaurant Association (www.restaurant.org), November 20, 2003. (Note: The figure given is for vending and non-store retailers.)

The Hospitality Industry

(Courtesy of NCR Corporation.)

CHAPTER EIGHT

Issues Facing Food Service

The Purpose of this Chapter

This chapter continues our discussion of the factors shaping the food service business. We will consider food service's reaction to a number of pressing issues. Once again, we will begin with the consumer and consumer concerns, such as nutrition, and with the closely related consumerist movement. We will then turn to the impact on food service of rising consumer concern—as well as growing government action—related to the environment. Akin to the environment in many ways is the topic of energy scarcity and energy management. Finally, we will look at the challenges posed by technology and the technological responses to cost and quality problems with which food service now has to contend.

THIS CHAPTER SHOULD HELP YOU

1. List three common consumer concerns about health and nutrition that have an impact on planning food service operations.
2. Describe the consumerism movement and identify the four hospitality issues it has raised.
3. List the six techniques available to deal with the waste stream.
4. Describe the food service industry's evolving use of technology in the following areas: guest ordering and payment; food production and refrigeration; marketing; managing banquet and catering departments; and management control and communication.

Consumer Concerns

When reading, watching, or listening to the the news these days, consumers will find no shortage of things to concern themselves with: war, Severe Acute Respiratory Syndrome (SARS), Mad Cow Disease, West Nile Virus, Bird Flu, terrorist attacks—the list goes on and on. Some of these affect where, when, and how customers eat when they dine in restaurants. For instance, when fears about SARS were at their highest in Canada, Singapore, Hong Kong, and Taiwan, consumers were reticent to eat in restaurants where they feared carriers of the disease might be working (it affected their travel too, which will be discussed in a later chapter). One Canadian restaurant chain took out a series of full-page ads in the national newspaper trying to assuage customer fears as part of their public relations campaign. Eventually, SARS went away and everything returned to normal.

Other threats and concerns (real or perceived) have much longer life cycles. For instance, during the 1980s, health, diet, nutrition, and exercise were prime topics of concern for food service customers. These concerns leveled off a bit in the 1990s but now seem to be back in full force in the 2000s (one very good barometer of peoples' regard for health issues is by the rate of the addition of healthier items to restaurant menus). Participation in exercise and strenuous activity, for instance, seems to be increasing on all fronts. One good indication of fitness trends is the rise and fall of membership in health clubs. According to the International Health, Racquet and Sportsclub Association (IHRSA), membership in health clubs has increased every year since 1995 before leveling off in 2005 at 41.3 million members.[1] Much of this growth occurred with the over-35 age group, and to an even greater extent, with the 55-and-older set.

Whenever the topics of diet, health, exercise, and nutrition are discussed, the American public sends mixed signals. Fortunately, there are numerous studies that are conducted to monitor the public's behavior. The American Dietetic Association conducts a study periodically to determine nutritional trends in the United States and to measure the public's awareness of certain issues. One of their recent studies looked at behaviors with relation to diet, nutrition, and fitness but also focused on awareness levels surrounding obesity, genetically modified foods, irridation of foods, and dietary supplements—all of which have become relatively recent concerns. Of these four issues, respondents expressed the greatest concern over obesity. Obesity issues have been in the news lately and programs are being implemented to try to prevent obesity, particulary at young ages. The same study by the ADA indicated that more people are making adjustments in their diets and that fewer people were categorized in the "Don't Bother Me" category—those who show little concern for diet, nutrition, and fitness. At the same time, the percentage of people categorized as "Already Doing It" (those who have taken action in the way of diet, nutrition, and exercise) increased significantly between 1999 and 2002, the most recent period studied. The survey also reported that the vast majority of respondents indicated that diet and nutrition (85 percent) and physical exercise (82 percent) are important to them.[2] The results of other surveys, however, indicate that taste is still important (sometimes to the detriment of health and well-being) to Americans and often influences their behaviors, at least as much as these other factors. A "fat replacement technology" has been developed for some foods, substituting ingredients that simulate the taste of fat in products such as ice cream, potato chips, and meat products. Initial consumer reaction to this product suggested the market is much more interested in "real" taste. McDonald's low-fat hamburger, McLean Deluxe, was kept alive only by corporate policy. Sales were so poor that it was dubbed "McFlop"; in 1993, it accounted for only 2 percent of sales. McDonald's kept the McLean around until 1996, but similar products were dropped by competitors a year or two after their introduction because of a lack of demand. Currently, the focus is on trans fats in restaurant foods. For example, New York City has planned to severely restrict the amount of trans fats in restaurant foods (to one-half gram). Certain restaurant companies are taking it upon themselves to eliminate or reduce trans fats in their foods. The public is concerned because trans fats reduce good cholesterol and increase bad cholesterol. Regardless of collective views, however, nutrition continues to be an important issue for consumers and operators alike. This topic is explored more fully in the following section.

HEALTH AND WELLNESS

Americans are often given to extremes, and their attitudes and behaviors toward health and wellness is no exception. Exercise and nutrition have once again made it to the forefront of the North Americans' consciousness. According to the International Health, Racquet and Sportsclub Association, there are over 29,000 health clubs in the United States, with over 41 million members.[3] Clearly, Americans take their exercise seriously. Research in this area indicates that a majority of Americans believe that people who exercise regularly live longer and are happier than nonexercisers.

Oddly, whatever the state of Americans' minds may be, Americans are more overweight (and obese) than ever before. The World Health Organization (WHO) has issued a fact sheet on obesity and excess weight, indicating that it is now a worldwide problem—not one that is limited to affluent countries such as the United States. In North America, obesity is in the news and debates center around to what extent diet (and specifically, prepared foods) affect obesity and what role government should play. To a great extent, restaurants and, specifically, quick-service restaurants, have been demonized. Somewhere between both sides of the argument, good sense and research support the fact that nutrition and exercise play a great role in one's health. Health advocates continue to stress the need for a balanced diet and regular exercise. Among its recommendations for fighting obesity, the WHO recommends that in order to attain optimal health, individuals should:

- Achieve energy balance and a healthy weight.
- Limit energy intake from total fats and shift fat consumption away from saturated fats to unsaturated fats.
- Increase consumption of fruit and vegetables, as well as legumes, whole grains, and nuts.
- Limit the intake of sugars.
- Increase physical activity—at least 30 minutes of regular, moderate-intensity activity on most days. More activity may be required for weight control.[4]

Many of their recommendations focus on **healthy eating** and Americans' eating habits are slowly changing. Beef consumption is falling, and the number of Americans who report never eating red meat stands at around 6 percent of the population. Further, the consumption of chicken—a lower-fat alternative—has increased steadily since the early 1990s to its current level of 84 pounds per capita per year.[5] The number of vegetarians continues to increase as well.

So, the evidence seems to suggest that Americans are more concerned with health and nutrition, are eating healthier (or at least eating lower fat foods) but are still struggling with obesity. This would appear to be yet another American paradox. *American Demographics* magazine explains this by suggesting that as the collective age of Americans increases, peoples' tendency is to become more conscious of health and nutrition issues but to gain weight as well. Again, the baby boomers are at the center of this conundrum and experts expect those patterns will continue for at least the next ten years.

Getting back to obesity (research indicates that the number of **overweight** children has doubled since 1980[6]) some part of the overweight problem relates to the way in which our society is developing. The way we live is physically less demanding than it was a generation or two ago. From automobiles to TV remotes to computers and electronic toys, we expend fewer calories in our everyday living. There are fewer physically demanding jobs and more jobs that involve sitting in front of a computer screen or at a desk. In addition, more and more of our foods are refined and require less energy to digest (Americans eat, on average, three times as much sugar as they should each day). The biggest villain, though, is fat. Americans eat more french fries than they do fresh potatoes. Moreover, as we noted at the beginning of this section, there hasn't been enough of an increase in recreational exercise to make up for a more sedentary

true. The charge may say more about American food habits than about the nutritional adequacy of the food itself.

A typical meal at McDonald's—a hamburger, french fries, and milk shake—provides nearly one-third of the recommended dietary allowance (RDA) for most nutrients, or the equivalent of what a standard school lunch provides, with, however, a deficiency in vitamins A and C. The deficiency in these two vitamins can be remedied somewhat if the customer switches from a hamburger to a Big Mac, which contains the necessary lettuce and tomato slices. If the customer chooses to have a salad, the dietary deficiency is no longer a problem.

Two problems here go beyond the junk-food issue. These critics believe they know what is good for people (which, in a medical sense, they may), and they resent the fact that people choose to disregard their expert advice. The main criticism, however, is really of Americans' poor eating habits, notably "the quick pace inherent in our society." In defense of the purveyors of fast food, it is the consumers who choose to eat what they eat, how much, and how often. This is essentially what the judge ruled in throwing out the obesity case that was brought against McDonald's in 2002. Other obesity lawsuits continue to arise, however.

Whatever else is true, the duty of the American restaurant business in a market economy is to serve consumers, not to reform them. It is difficult, however, for the hospitality industry to deal with this kind of criticism, in which the industry becomes a scapegoat for the annoyance that some feel. In the end, the food service product (s) that are within the reach of most pocketbooks uses food service systems that are not (and cannot be) labor-intensive. They use preparation methods that are quick and unskilled, hence inexpensive. Quick-service food is quick because, all in all, that is what many consumers want.

The second problem raised is that of the effect of advertising on consumer behavior. This issue reflects an old and complex debate in the general field of marketing. It is clear that restaurants are interested in offering only what the guests want, not in forcing something on them. For example, notice that the decor and atmosphere in specialty restaurants have been growing warmer and friendlier to meet earlier criticisms of coldness and austerity. In addition, salad bars and packaged salads were added because that is what consumers wanted. That is, the weight of consumer opinion is usually felt in the marketplace. Change in business institutions comes, of course, more slowly than consumerists would like; particularly in competitive industries such as food service, change comes only when it is clear that the consumer wants it. To some degree, the consumerists' demands for quick change reflect an antibusiness bias, which some consumerists seem to have. Many seem to prefer a command economy (with their preferences ruling) to a market economy where, in the long run, consumers' preferences rule.

The junk-food criticism will not just go away, however. Field studies suggest that many restaurant guests do not follow the Big Mac–fries–milk shake meal profile referred to earlier. For instance, to save money or suit their tastes, many customers replace the milk shake with a soft drink, and the result is a meal with less than one-third the recommended dietary allowance of essential nutrients. In addition, although they appeal to a minority of customers, salads are clearly not the number-one seller in the quick-service sector. Moreover, a number of chains are under fire from consumerists for continuing to use beef fat (which is rich in saturated fat) for some products, especially french fries. We should note, however, that, in response to consumers' concerns, most chains have shifted to vegetable shortening for most frying.

NUTRITIONAL LABELING

The **Nutrition Labeling and Education Act (NLEA)** was passed in 1990, but the restaurant industry was largely exempted from it by the **Food and Drug Administration (FDA)**. In 1996, however, the Center for Science in the Public Interest (CSPI), along with Public Citizen, was successful in a suit in federal court against the FDA. Consequently, as of May 1997, restaurants became covered by the NLEA. The NLEA applies only to menu listings that make nutrient or health claims.

Nutrient claims make a statement about a specific nutrient of a menu item or meal. A nutrient claim typically includes such terms as "reduced," "free" or "low," "low in fat," or "cholesterol free."

Table 8.1 shows a listing of words that might be part of a nutrient claim. Significantly, use of symbols such as a heart or an apple to signify healthful menu items are also considered health claims and are covered by the regulation. Additional information regarding the dos and don'ts of nutritional labeling can be found at the FDA Web site (www.fda.gov).

A **health claim** ties the food or meal with health status or disease prevention. A health claim usually relates to and mentions a specific disease. The government has approved eleven health claims (described in Industry Practice Note 8.1) that the FDA has determined to be scientifically documented.

Notice that one way a restaurant can avoid this regulation is simply to avoid nutrient or health claims on its menu.

TABLE 8.1

Language of Nutrient Claims

Free
Low
Healthy
Reduced
Light/lite
Provides/contains/good source of
High/excellent source of/rich in
Lean/extra-lean

You need to have documentation if your menu uses any of the following words or symbols representing these words:

Defining Health Claims

The following food and health/disease connections are the only ones for which the government allows health claims to be made. In order to make health claims on menus, restaurateurs must follow specific guidelines as to wording.

- Fiber-containing fruits, vegetables, and grains in relation to cancer-prevention claims
- Fruits and vegetables in relation to cancer-prevention claims
- Fiber-containing fruits, vegetables, and grains in relation to heart-disease-prevention claims
- Fat in relation to cancer
- Saturated fat and cholesterol in relation to heart disease
- Sodium in relation to high blood pressure (hypertension)
- Calcium in relation to osteoporosis
- Folate and neural-tube defects
- Dietary sugar alcohol and dental caries
- Soluble fiber from certain foods
- Coronary heart disease and soy protein

Source: Correspondence with CSPI, November 30, 2000.

Moreover, if a claim is made (according to federal guidelines), the restaurant need not publish the information on the menu. It must, however, be able to provide reference material for staff members. Finally, the only thing that must be documented is the claim on the menu. Thus, if a claim is made as to the number of calories, that claim must be documented, but there is no need to document other aspects of the menu item such as the number of grams of fat or the amount of salt. (Note: individual states may have more stringent labeling bills which restaurants must conform to.)

The restaurant is required to have a "reasonable basis" for its belief that the claim made is true. Restaurants can use computer databases, U.S. Department of Agriculture (USDA) handbooks, cookbooks, or other "reasonable sources" to determine nutrient levels.

Although the Center for Science in the Public Interest views the restaurant regulations of the NLEA as a good first step, a spokesperson for the center notes what CSPI regards as several weaknesses in the present regulations.[8] In manufactured food products, all labels must contain the standard ingredient and nutrient information, but in a restaurant, the customer must ask for documentation. Otherwise, the restaurant need not provide it. As a practical matter, however, most restaurants make this information continually available in a pamphlet and have for some years. The requirement did, however, place a new burden on independent restaurants.

A second problem the CSPI cites is the narrowness of the regulation. As noted earlier, the information made available need relate only to claims made rather than provide a complete nutrient profile for the item. This can result in "weak and misleading" information. Moreover, the "reasonable standard" is very loose in the CSPI's view. Simply adding up the ingredients in a recipe—which may or may not be followed closely—is not enough in their view.

Finally, the FDA has made it clear that it will not be involved in enforcement of the NLEA in restaurants. It will leave enforcement to state and local authorities. Given the huge number of restaurants and the FDA's limited resources, this is hardly a surprising decision, but it does suggest the strong possibility of somewhat uneven enforcement. The CSPI position is that restaurant customers deserve to have nutritional information readily available. As CSPI's Dr. Margo Wootan says, "Americans are increasingly relying on restaurants to feed themselves and their families. However, without nutrition information, it's difficult to compare options and make informed decisions. Few people would guess that a small chocolate shake at McDonald's has more calories than a Big Mac." In addition, she states that "Customers don't order meals without knowing the prices, and we can't expect them to make healthy decisions without knowing the nutritional price as well."[9]

Almost certainly, however, the industry has not heard the last of this issue. Should the composition of Congress or the climate of official opinion change, the CSPI will undoubtedly be pressing once again for stricter disclosure standards for restaurants.

FOOD SAFETY AND SANITATION

The issue of food safety, and the overall safety of the food chain, is much on peoples' minds. As with so many consumer issues, **food safety** and **sanitation** involve government regulations—in this case, as embodied in policy makers, public health officers, and inspectors. Sanitation is one aspect of food safety. In the United States, the Food and Drug Administration oversees food safety. Their mission is to protect public health by assuring the safety of the food supply (although the USDA regulates some food categories). In addition to regulating food, the FDA also regulates cosmetics, drugs, medical devices, and other products. Their Web site states that:

Ensuring safe food remains an important public health priority for our nation. An estimated 76 million illnesses, 325,000 hospitalizations, and 5,000 deaths are attributable to foodborne illness in the United States each year. For some consumers, foodborne illness results only in mild, temporary discomfort or lost time from work or other daily activity. For others, especially pre-school age children, older adults, and those with impaired immune systems, foodborne illness may have serious or long-term consequences, and most seriously, may be life threatening. The risk of foodborne illness is of increasing concern due to changes in the global market, aging of our population, increasing numbers of immunocompromised and immunosuppressed individuals, changes in consumer eating habits, and changes in food production practices.[10]

With the increasing use of foods prepared off-premise, the incidence of food poisoning in public accommodations has been rising steeply. The kinds of sanitary precautions associated with food service systems that prepare food, freeze or chill it, and then transport it elsewhere are not universal. First, the risks of thawing and spoilage are high. Second, the food is handled by more people. Some operators resist the increased emphasis on sanitation, but most have accepted—many enthusiastically—the need to upgrade sanitation practices and to establish and enforce high sanitation standards. The Educational Foundation of the National Restaurant Association has pioneered the development of sanitation-related educational materials and programs and has trained several million workers and certified over a million managers.

A strong food safety program should encompass personnel practices, food handling practices, pest control, training, and physical facilities. Even such things as the clothes worn by food service workers may compromise the safety of the food. All of the above should be monitored in all food service establishments.

It is quite clear that, for the most part, the industry and those calling for the highest standards of food safety and sanitation are in the same camp. This is not surprising, because it is common knowledge that a single incident of food poisoning, broadcast to the world via the media, can mean the end of a restaurant. Sizzler restaurants and the Jack-in-the-Box chain received publicity for such incidents in the 1990s. In the case of Sizzler, the resulting bad publicity led to a loss in sales of 30 percent and, ultimately, the closing of 40 restaurants. Less-publicized incidents have occurred in less well-known operations. To be sure, restaurants have a real survival stake in food safety.

Hazard Analysis and Critical Control Points. The best comprehensive approach to food safety and sanitation programs reflects a shift in thinking about sanitation from an inspection system that is largely reactive to one that takes a systematic approach to the prevention of food safety problems. In one sense, **hazard analysis and critical control points (HACCP)** is just the application of good common sense to the production of safe food. HACCP is designed to prevent, reduce, or eliminate potential biological, chemical, and physical food safety hazards.

The elements of an HACCP program are (as established by the FDA and originally developed by NASA): analyze hazards; identify critical control points; establish preventive measures; establish procedures to monitor the critical control points; establish corrective action to be taken; establish procedures to verify that the system is working properly; and establish effective record keeping to document the HACCP system.

The HACCP approach is at the heart of both "ServSafe," the sanitation training program developed by the Educational Foundation of the National Restaurant Association (mentioned earlier), and the inspection system for food products developed by the Food and Drug Administration. Consumers rely on food safety in restaurants as a basic article of faith. It takes hard and continuing effort to fulfill that trust.[11]

ALCOHOL AND DINING

The many fatal accidents that have been attributed to driving under the influence of alcohol have given the hospitality industry a wide-ranging set of problems. In many jurisdictions, restaurants and bars that sell drinks to people who are later involved in accidents are now being held legally responsible for damages. The result has been, among other things, a great rise in liability insurance rates. Laws have been proposed—and in many jurisdictions passed—making illegal "happy hours" and other advertised price reductions on the sale of drinks. In addition, in a less strictly legal sense, operators have been concerned about the image of their operations and the industry in general. Finally, many states and municipalities have passed legislation that requires managers and servers to receive training in responsible beverage service.

The industry's response has generally been swift and positive. One idea is "designated driver" programs. Designated drivers agree not to drink and to drive for the whole group they are with. Many operators recognize designated drivers with a badge and reward them with free soft drinks—and a certificate good for a free drink at their next visit. Alcohol awareness training—teaching bartenders and servers how to tell when people have had too much to drink and how to deal with them—is also becoming more common (and is a requirement in certain jurisdictions). If you work in an operation that serves alcohol, be sure to find out what the establishment's policy is regarding service to intoxicated guests or those who might be intoxicated. You should do this not only because you will want to follow the house policy but because it will help you to understand better the industry's response to a complicated problem.

Consumers are drinking less, and this has posed problems for many operators. Because sales of alcoholic beverages usually carry a much higher profit than food sales, reduction in alcohol consumption has seriously affected profitability. The marketing

Restaurants have become much more sensitive to alcohol-related issues as evidenced by their responsible service programs. (Courtesy of Las Vegas Hilton and Paramount Pictures; Copyright 2001 Paramount Pictures. All rights reserved.)

response that has helped many operators is the development of a whole line of colorful and tasty "mocktails," which are made without alcohol. Featuring "lite" beers and wines also caters to the guest's desire to hold down caloric and alcohol intake and helps maintain sales. The biggest growth area has been in bottled water—bottled water not only replaces alcoholic beverages but is often drunk instead of other nonalcoholic beverages. There has been a tenfold increase in per capita consumption of bottled water since the 1970s, when bottled water was thought of as something to drink in a foreign country, and consumption has tripled just since 1985. In 2005, consumers drank an estimated 26 gallons per capita. Bottled water is actually beginning to rival beer and coffee in consumer consumption.[12]

Food Service and the Environment

Preserving the natural environment generates a great deal of concern and enthusiasm—and rightly so. Our purpose here, however, is to narrow this view somewhat in looking at the impact of the environmental movement on food service. The view we will adopt, not surprisingly, is that of the business community, which looks at environmental proposals in terms of costs and benefits.

It can be difficult to discuss the environment because it is a sensitive issue for many and quickly becomes politicized. The concept can also be so broadly defined—for some, it includes water conservation, scaling back development, avoidance of animal testing by manufacturers of guest amenities, use of foods that have been naturally fertilized and have not been grown using pesticides, planting trees, and saving the rain forests. Problematically, such a broad and multifaceted notion of the environment makes it difficult to focus on the problems where food service can make a really strong contribution to the struggle to save the environment. We certainly cannot afford to be indifferent to the problems of the environment as it is more globally defined. In this chapter, however, we want to examine and understand problems that are a threat and need to be dealt with at the unit level.

Restaurants and food service in general are basically a clean industry rather than a polluting one, at least when compared with the heavy manufacturing industries. In some settings restaurants are faulted for creating traffic or noise problems. A few neighborhoods have objected to cooking odors coming from kitchen exhausts. These, however, are exceptional rather than everyday concerns. There are areas, however, in which food service faces, at the unit level, a serious environmental problem. Along with other businesses and every household in America, **solid-waste disposal**—otherwise called garbage—is a problem whose time has come. Garbage is not only an environmental problem but an operational problem as well. The cost of conventional waste disposal is rising and, because of the scarcity of landfills, is more than likely to continue to increase.

THINKING ABOUT GARBAGE FROM DUMP TO WASTE STREAM

Not very long ago, garbage was taken to the dump, and nobody thought much about the management issues involved. As the pressure of population, an ever richer economy, and a "throwaway society" interacted, however, problems of groundwater contamination, rodent infestation, toxic substances, and smell, to name a few, gave rise to a concern over the safety of what we now call a sanitary landfill. A first-class dump—that is, a **sanitary landfill**—costs something over $500,000 an acre to build. Specialized facilities designed to handle toxic substances, such as ash from incinerators, cost even more. To prevent groundwater contamination, a sanitary landfill is lined with clay or a synthetic liner and is equipped with a groundwater monitoring system. Because rotting garbage produces an explosive gas, landfills have methane collection systems. To keep down the smell as well as the insects and rodents, the day's garbage is covered with a layer of dirt each night.

Sanitary landfills are expensive to build and maintain. More important, it is now hard to find new dump sites, because communities really don't want them in their own backyards. In fact, the number of landfill sites has dropped dramatically in recent years.

Americans generate over 4 pounds of garbage per person every day (from 50 to 100 percent more than other countries with similar standards of living). That is over 100 pounds a week for a family of four, over 3 tons per year. To put this in perspective, the United States generated 245 million tons of solid waste in 2005. The pressure not only from businesses but from households puts an increasing load on a declining number of landfills. The "tipping cost" (the cost to tip the contents of a garbage truck into a landfill) has doubled in a number of cities. The range is quite wide but fees are highest in the northeast ($90 per ton is not unusual). The management of solid waste is a $43 billion industry in the United States.

Just at the point where the demand for landfill space is rising and the supply of such space is declining, another complication arises—public attitudes. The American public views environmental issues as one of the key issues of the day. Environmentally concerned citizens are also food service customers, and their strong views need to be taken into account. In fact, opinion surveys show that environmentally concerned people make up about half the population—and they are both the highest in income and the best educated. Restaurants' interest in the solid-waste problem, then, is driven by a concern to be responsible corporate citizens, by the concerns of their best customers, and by exploding waste-removal costs. As a result, we have replaced the concept of the dump, where things are dropped and forgotten, with that of a **waste stream**, which needs to be managed.

MANAGING THE WASTE STREAM

A study conducted at the University of Wisconsin—Stout gives us a good idea of the composition of the food service waste stream. On-site food service and table service restaurants generate about 1 pound of waste per meal served, whereas quick-service establishments generate roughly 1⅓ pounds per meal.[13] Table 8.2 shows the types and proportions of waste generated by the major categories of food service.[14]

As we set out to consider how the waste stream is to be managed, a word of caution is in order. The public perception of environmentally effective action is not necessarily consistent from year to year. In some cases, popular environmental views don't always make physical sense. McDonald's switched hamburger wrappings in 1976 (from paper to polystyrene) and received positive press for its perceived interest in saving trees. When McDonald's switched back to paper 15 years later, it was again hailed as an environmental victory. Both public perception and scientific fact (as well as timing) need to be taken into consideration when making such decisions. Figure 8.1

TABLE 8.2

Contents of the Food Service Waste Stream by Food Service Type

PROPORTION OF WASTE STREAM

TYPE OF WASTE	INSTITUTIONAL	TABLE SERVICE	QUICK SERVICE
Paper	40%	44%	65%
Plastic	23	16	17
Food	23	21	5
Glass	5	12	4
Tin	8	3	6
Aluminum	1	4	3

Source: Data adapted from Peter A. D'Souza and Leland L. Nicholls, "Waste Management: The Priority for the 1990's," Technical Paper, University of Wisconsin—Stout, n.d.

reflects some of the changes that the McDonald's corporation has made in an effort to reduce its waste stream.

The techniques available to deal with the waste stream can be summarized in three words: **reduce**, **reuse**, **and recycle**. These are the ideal solutions, but the facts of life require our list to be expanded to include **composting**, **incineration**, and the use of landfills.

1990:	Reduced thickness of sundae cups
1991:	Reduced size of napkins by one inch
1992:	Reduced basis weight of Happy Meal bag
1993:	Reduced back flap of fry carton
1994:	Reduced thickness of trash can liners
1995:	Replaced hash brown cartons with bags
1996:	Changed to thinner carry-out bags
1997:	Decreased weight of in-store trays
1998:	Converted to sandwich wraps for fish sandwich
1999:	Introduced insulated wraps for Quarter Pounder sandwich
2002–2004:	Continue to decrease the weight of paper napkins and cardboard packaging and to use a higher percentage of recycled materials in napkins.

Figure 8.1

Changes made to McDonald's packaging materials, 1990–2004 (Source: mcdonalds.com with permission from McDonald's Corporation.)

Reduce. Increasingly, the public is glad to be offered the possibility of receiving a product without wrapping or a bag, and some quick-service companies are offering customers sandwiches without their customary paper wrapping. Often, it is possible to switch to a less bulky form of packaging—from cardboard to paper, for instance. Companies are also insisting that suppliers provide product in packaging that minimizes waste.

McDonald's switch back to paper reduced the volume of packaging waste by 90 percent. We need to note, however, that the plastic-laminated paper it now uses is likely to decay only very, very slowly, if at all, in a landfill.

Thus, although a reduction in bulk was realized by McDonald's decision, it is questionable whether the overall environmental impact has been positive or not. They have made numerous other changes, however, and the combination has undoubtedly had a significant impact.

Reuse. Another seemingly appealing strategy for many operations is a switch from disposables to permanent ware (reusable china or plastic dinnerware). This would reduce dramatically paper and plastic waste. The problems this "solution" creates, however, suggest once again how important it is not to oversimplify. Restaurants built to rely on disposables have no space to locate a dish room or china storage. If they remodeled to put it in, the cost would be exorbitant, and space would probably have to come from customer seating—with reduced sales as the result. A heavy expenditure resulting in reduced sales would bankrupt many restaurants. Even if we assume, implausibly, that such a development could take place, the result of all the additional water discharged would cause the city sewage system, quite literally, to explode. A dishwasher, after all, requires from 70 to 500 gallons of water per hour to operate. Such an increase in dishwashing would also result in thermal pollution of rivers from the hot water and chemical pollution from the very strong soaps used in dishwashing.

Other forms of reuse are more practical. Products can be bought in containers that can be returned to the manufacturers for reuse or reused in the operation.

Instead of discarding skids in a warehouse or commissary, most are now being built to stand up to reuse.

The major opportunities available from a strategy of reducing and reusing appear to lie with changes in the way products are purchased. Minimizing unnecessary packaging, eliminating the use of toxic dyes or other substances that make packaging hard to recycle, and using recycled products or recycling containers all contribute to a reduction in the total waste stream. One enterprising restaurant owner purchases extra flatware at garage sales to "loan" to customers when they purchase takeout meals from his restaurant. He only asks that they return it to the restaurant after using it. He finds that the cost is minimal and outweighs the cost of buying and supplying disposable flatware.

Recycle. A substantial amount of recycling is already going on across food service segments. Metal, paper, cardboard, and glass are already established as recyclables. We should note, however, that, in recycling, all metals are not equal. Steel cans can be and are usefully recycled, but the advantages are nowhere near as great as they are for aluminum cans. In fact, it's now cheaper to recycle aluminum than it is to mine bauxite, the ore from which aluminum is extracted.

The key factor in recycling is its economics. True, the materials in the waste stream have some value, but the basic driving force is the rise in landfill costs. Although some communities still have adequate landfill space, the evidence suggests that waste trucked in from distant cities will, in time, fill these. Overall, landfill costs, as we noted earlier, are rising, and for large metropolitan areas, landfill availability is disappearing.

Recycling, however, requires considerable effort. Think about the case of quick-service food waste. If we want to recycle, it will be necessary to sort the waste into recyclable categories. Some operators, particularly institutions, are using consumer sorting. Consumers may be asked to use different bins for glass, paper, plastic, and food waste. Let us assume that we decide to persuade our customers to sort paper, plastic, and food waste into separate containers. New bins—taking up additional floor space—must be installed and a suitable "training program" set up for our guests. This educational effort would almost certainly include special signage showing the guest what was expected, and tray liners and posters explaining why we're undertaking this effort. At least during the start-up period, some personal assistance to explain the process—and solicit people's support—would probably be required. The trash will then very likely have to be re-sorted either by an employee, by the waste hauler, or by the recycler. Thus, sorting itself requires considerable time and effort. Plastics, moreover, will need to be further sorted according to resin type, using the codes shown in Figure 8.2.

The storage we presently have is probably a dumpster, with perhaps a second container for corrugated boxes. Under the new regimen, however, we will need separate containers for several categories of waste. They certainly won't fit into the present back of the house, so they will almost certainly have to be crowded into the loading dock area, which may require some redesign to make everything fit and still have room for delivery trucks.

This is not the end of the complications. We probably at present have only one hauler, a company that does everything for us with one type of truck. Under the new arrangements, different haulers might be required: one for paper, another for metal, and so forth. Even assuming one company does all of the work, the truck that does the hauling will have to have multiple compartments, or possibly the hauler will have to use more than one truck, each designed for different parts of the waste stream.

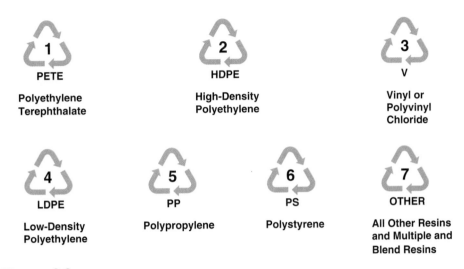

Figure 8.2
Society of the Plastics Industry (SPI) coding system. (Source: plasticindustry.org, 2004.)

Because the technology of sorting garbage is changing rapidly, it may be that much more of the sorting will be done at recycling centers in future years. This could significantly reduce the restaurant's labor cost in sorting and make recycling more attractive.

As we have noted, the advantage to the restaurant of recycling is financial—the hauling fees for recycling are less than the tipping fees at the landfill. A further major advantage is that of public relations. Customers are concerned about the environment and are likely to react favorably to firms that are leaders or solid performers in the environmental arena.

Compost. Composting refers to the collection and processing of food trimmings, scraps, and leftovers. Small-scale composting has been going on in rural areas (and backyards) for centuries. However, as a large-scale movement affecting all of society, it is still in its infancy.

Because of the wet, dense nature of food waste, it must be combined for composting with a bulking agent such as leaves, wood chips, or shredded paper to allow for air circulation. The material is placed in rows and, in most present-day applications, a front-end loader is used to turn the material periodically to maintain exposure to the air. More mechanized plants to manage the composting process will undoubtedly become common in the future. Finished compost can be used as potting soil or to enrich a garden or the soil around trees or bushes. Test programs have been successful in a number of municipalities, some of which report a reduction in garbage removal costs of 50 percent.

Incinerate. Incineration (or combustion) provides yet another way to dispose of waste. Currently, 15 percent of all waste nationwide is disposed of in this manner. Some states, such as Florida and Maine, incinerate over 20 percent of their waste.[15] Unfortunately, combustion of waste creates environmental problems of its own and, as a result, is subject to a great deal of controversy. One principal concern is air pollution; however, it does appear that technical advances in scrubber systems and combustion control make it possible to overcome these problems in properly managed systems. As no management system is perfect, what this means is that, in practice, air pollution control may not be perfect. Because the air pollutants can include heavy metals, acid that leads to acid rain, and poisonous dioxin, this is no small issue.

A second problem is that 25 percent of the product remains as ash after combustion and must be placed in a landfill. Looked at another way, this means that combustion reduces waste by 75 percent (by weight). However, because the remaining ash contains toxic pollutants, the danger of eventual leaching into groundwater is a serious one. Specialized landfill sites with extra protection against leaching are needed.

A further concern put forward by environmentalists is the contribution that incineration can make to the greenhouse effect. Where the only alternative to incineration is dumping in a landfill, this concern is misplaced. Landfills generate methane, which traps heat radiation and, hence, contributes more to the greenhouse effect than would the gases given off by incineration. If, however, the alternative to incineration is recycling, recycling would be preferred both because of its environmental impact (air quality and elimination of ash) and because of its significantly lower cost to the community and to individual businesses.

Landfill. The least preferred, but most commonly used, method of disposal is the landfill. Fifty-seven percent of solid waste ends up in such sites.[16] They are costly to construct and maintain and are potentially long-term environmental hazards. They hide rather than dispose of the trash, which decays only very slowly and imperfectly under the landfill's conditions of lack of oxygen and moisture. As noted, they can contribute to a worsening of the greenhouse effect. It appears that the scarcity of landfills may eventually drive the cost of this method of disposal beyond what most operations can afford.

Fortunately for food service operators, residential recycling programs being set up by municipalities and other governmental agencies may eventually create the channels of collection, redistribution, and processing necessary to make large-scale recycling work. As our discussion makes clear, moving toward recycling is no simple matter, but at the same time, the amount of waste that is being recycled doubled over a 15-year period.[17] Managing the waste stream will almost certainly be a concern that touches your career, so it is good to have a broad understanding of it.

Technology

Back in the 1970s, a researcher looked into the future of food service, and this is what he saw:

The restaurant of the future will be automated. One individual will be capable of running a 10,000-meal-a-day commissary. Computer-controlled, automated equipment will run the food processing operation from storeroom to cleanup as well as take care of inventory control and the reordering process. In addition, the computer will handle all records, write all necessary business reports (including the annual report), forecast requirements, and perform all cost accounting duties.

Customers will dine in a computer-manipulated environment of aromatic and visual stimuli. They will stand before lighted menus picturing various entrées and punch out selections at order stations. Within 2½ minutes, they will be served the meal via conveyor belt running with the wall and stopping at the proper table. Dish busing commences upon the customer arising from the seat. Dirty dishes move onto a conveyor belt within an adjacent wall. The dishwashing process is completely automated. A 200-seat restaurant will require four employees and a manager.[18]

If technology can put an astronaut on the moon, it can surely bus tables. However, it's not what is technically possible that counts; it's what makes economic sense. In the foreseeable future, even in the face of steeply rising wages, the 10,000-meal-a-day commissaries that come into use will require a good many more employees, because it will make economic sense. Although a computer-operated food production, storage, and cleanup system is theoretically possible, it would be like using a computer just to add up a grocery bill. Less-expensive methods are available.

On the other hand, touch-screen ordering stations have become a common tool in restaurants, although they are more commonly used for servers to place orders than by guests. Even where they are available for use by guests, an alternative interpersonal ordering system is also available.

We have heard reports of "six-armed robots" being designed for use in food service for years, and it could be that they are finally coming to fruition. One of the most popular booths at the NRA show in 2000 belonged to "Flipper." A robot that previously had been employed by IBM for the purpose of assembling computers, it has now been redesigned to work in restaurant kitchens and is being marketed by AccuTemp Products, Inc. The estimated cost is $150,000 for a five-year lease.[19]

Although the computerized environment described previously or a fully automated food production system is unlikely to emerge in the foreseeable future, labor costs give mechanization and automation an appeal to operators. Much of the change in equipment is incremental, that is, small improvements that make the kind of equipment we

Technology is playing an increasingly important role in the management and operations of restaurants. (Courtesy Corbis Digital Stock.)

presently use even better. These applications of technology include better energy control and more mechanization of existing equipment to make control of the production process easier. Examples include timers on fryers and moving belts in ovens. In addition, in almost every area of food service, the potentially revolutionary elements of technological change loom larger than they did just a few years ago. On another note, a product that brings together new technology with the need for improved waste management systems, Double T Equipment Manufacturing Ltd. has partnered with two Japanese companies to sell an organic waste disposal system called the GOMIXER. The GOMIXER "uses water and heat to biodegrade food industry leftovers in four days. The only output of the system is nutrient-rich water that can be disposed or diluted and used on lawns and flowerbeds." Rey Rawlins, Vice President of Marketing for Advanced Biotechnology Inc, says that "the system is designed for restaurants, hospitals, hotels and other large facilities. By enabling these facilities to process food waste on site, the GOMIXER reduces or eliminates landfill use, landfill fees, and transportation costs." The system was designed specifically for hospitality organizations and is being used by several resort hotels.[20]

ENHANCING CUSTOMER SERVICE

Guest Ordering. Although we are not likely to see customers being waited on by anything resembling a robot (at least not in the near future), the ability to serve people is being enhanced by electronics and computerization. Handheld computer terminals are used by waitresses and waiters to take orders at tableside automatically and instantly convey the order to the kitchen. Computers give servers more time to spend with guests or permit servers to serve more guests. Computer terminals are especially helpful where the service area is remote from the kitchen. Whatever kind of ordering terminal is used, whether a handheld unit or a stationary touch screen used by several servers, they generate legible guest checks, avoid errors in addition, speed service, and improve productivity.

Another application of technology that affects the way customers use restaurants is a video-equipped drive-through order-taking system that permits a more personal interaction between order taker and guest. Evidence suggests that the system also improves transaction speed. Single-telephone-number systems in delivery firms use computerized guest histories to facilitate order taking. These computerized systems also enhance customer convenience for takeout and delivery and offer economies of scale as well as insight into customer ordering patterns through guest history computer files. Industry Practice Note 8.2 discusses one company that is leading the technology field in food service.

Guest Payment. Credit cards are convenient to the guest. Moreover, a study at one QSR chain showed that credit card customers spent well over 50 percent more than cash customers. Bank debit cards are also being used in more and more restaurants.

The credit card represents an important social technology supported in a number of ways by electronics. Credit cards are widely used in table service restaurants. Their increasing use in fast food is an important service improvement that offers greater convenience to the customer and improvements in sales and efficiency to the operator.

From order to payment, customer interaction is being facilitated by technology. We can turn our attention now to how the production process is being improved.

TECHNOLOGY IN THE BACK OF THE HOUSE

Food Production. Aside from Flipper the robot, described above, equipment is being improved by enhancing its energy efficiency both in terms of cooking and in terms of the effect on ventilation requirements. Safety improvements are also being made. The technologies that underlie these developments are impressive, but the impacts are in marginal improvements in cost and operation. Some (relatively) new equipment, such as the combination steamer/oven, adds flexibility to the kitchen because it can be used in more than one process. Another innovation, the two-sided griddle, reduces cooking times by one-third to one-half or more and also reduces shrinkage in the product. Newer still, ranges that use induction heating (which uses a magnet that creates current) result in cooking surfaces that never get hot. There are also portable units used for buffets.

ESP Systems

ESP Systems is a company devoted to improving service in casual dining restaurants through enhanced technology. Their business premise is that service represents the greatest opportunity for restaurants to improve the overall experience of customers.

CEO Devin Green suggests that restaurants have three components: (1) quality of service; (2) quality of food and beverage; and (3) quality of atmosphere. He feels that restaurants are becoming more and more similar with regard to atmosphere and that restaurants are already squeezed to get as much as they can out of food and beverage but that the greatest opportunity is in the area of service. This is why ESP's latest product was designed to help restaurants provide more attentive service to customers.

As their Web site states, "Simply put, ESP Systems' goal is to offer its restaurant clients a distinct, competitive advantage. Over the last several decades, with the casual-dining marketplace becoming more and more competitive, restaurants have continued to refine their food and atmosphere up to a point that—across concepts—these business components have become largely commoditized. Based on a number of demographic, competitive, and societal trends, the level of service a restaurant offers each guest remains today's greatest opportunity for differentiation, guest impact, and productivity gains. . . . and up until now, service has been an invisible and highly inconsistent component of a restaurant's business."

Their systems provide a "wireless bubble" in which customers and service employees are brought closer together. It is an enhanced table management system that identifies service problems such as neglected guests as well as any deviations from pre-established service standards. It also allows restaurants to collect performance data on individuals, service teams, and entire shifts.

As has been discussed extensively in this book, the demographics of the country are changing. This includes the demographic profiles of both employees and customers. It could be argued that at one time, both of these groups might have been resistant to technologies that involved the customer to such a great

Refrigeration. In the 1950s, frozen prepared foods were introduced into restaurants. Frozen entrées simplified delivery and inventory problems and reduced the level of skill needed while broadening the range of menu items that could be used in a kitchen lacking skilled cooks. The freezing process, however, has adverse effects on quality. Ice crystals that form at the time of freezing cut tissue in the product, which changes the consistency of some foods. Also, when products are reconstituted, they lose flavor-filled juices.

The next advance in the use of refrigeration was the development of chilled prepared foods. Foods are held in the latent temperature zone, from 28 to 30 degrees Fahrenheit. In this temperature range, holding characteristics, in terms of both flavor and microbiological quality, remain at the level of the fresh product's quality.

There are two methods of chilling a product: tumble chill (cooked food is packaged in plastic and chilled in cold circulating water) and blast chill (food held in pans extent (older readers will recall the challenges when ATMs were first introduced). ESP is taking advantage of the predisposition that younger employees and customers have toward technology. Employees are connected to the ESP System through watch-like devices on their wrists, which can show the status of a table or party at a glance. Guests are connected through monitors on their tables, which allow them to communicate with employees when the need arises.

The system allows restaurant management to capitalize on real-time information, management alerts when deviations occur, ongoing table status (where tables are labeled as Ready, Dining, Almost, and Busing), and performance reports. Because of its ability to help better manage service times, average table turns are reduced by approximately 10 percent. Finally, the system has applications for upselling. Restaurants using the system have experienced increases in their average guest check. Finally, the mere fact that restaurants are using the system creates a "buzz" where customers are likely to tell their friends, which, in turn, increases visitations.

ESP provides the system to restaurants for a monthly fee, provides training and support, and will visit restaurants to update or change desired specifications. At this time, three restaurant chains are using the product including Applebee's.

Devin Green indicates that their company is always working on a new generation of systems in an effort to be even more reactive to client needs. He further believes that point-of-sale systems are the "nucleus" of restaurant technology and that while much of the recent investment in technology has been in the back of the house, there is a shift occurring in which more attention is being paid to the front of the house. Finally, he sees additional possibilities and opportunities for guests to pay at different service points (such as at the table), guest loyalty programs, and co-marketing opportunities.

is chilled by exposure to high-velocity convected cold air). Foods chilled by cold water have a shelf life of up to 21 to 45 days, depending on the type of food product. Foods chilled by convected air have a shorter shelf life, up to 5 days, including the day of preparation and the day of use. Blast freezers are also being used with greater frequency.

A major advantage of this new storage technology is in the scheduling flexibility and productivity it gives the operation. Skilled cooks can be brought into a central facility to work from nine to five, Monday through Friday, preparing products to be held in inventory. Less-skilled employees can be used during all the hours of operation to reconstitute a varied menu of high-quality products that have not lost flavor through the freezing process. The applications of cook-and-chill range from health care facilities to cruise ships to correctional facilities.

Finally, there are new uses of older technology. A good example of this is the development of refrigerated drawers, which are placed under workstations. This allows the food product to be right at the workstation while also keeping it at the correct temperature. Refrigerated drawers have applications in both quick- service and table service restaurants. They are produced by companies such as Hobart.

There are many new developments being made in back of the house equipment. Looking to the future, perhaps the most anticipated development will be the "smart kitchen" as envisioned by the National Association of Equipment Manufacturers (NAFEM). According to a recent meeting of its members, "The smart kitchen will allow multiple pieces of equipment to communicate to a central intelligence area. Operators will be able to automatically manage everything from basic food safety to production and maintenance tasks. It will monitor equipment and enhance energy and labor efficiency of an operation, while improving food safety."[21]

TECHNOLOGY, THE INTERNET, AND FOOD SERVICE MARKETING

The Internet is an advertising medium of great power, and more and more restaurants are taking advantage of it. The most common approach to using the Internet is to use it for e-mail or to establish a Web site. In a survey by the National Restaurant Association, operators of restaurants with check averages of $15 or more indicated relatively high utilization of the Internet. Fifty percent of respondents indicated that their restaurant had a Web site, and 33 percent of full service restaurants indicated that they had an e-mail address.[22] The Web site can offer electronic couponing, the ability to make reservations, and an online review of menu offerings.

Although Internet commerce has only been around a relatively short time, there are clear indications that the Internet has capabilities that the restaurant industry has not even begun to utilize to its full extent. Restaurants offering home delivery service are appearing on the Net with increased frequency. Web sites typically use a shopping cart metaphor to allow surfers to browse product lines, select products for purchase, and complete payment.

Technology and Banquet Sales. Automatic sales and catering software makes it possible to combine management of an individual customer account with the overall management of group sales and catering. These systems are both accurate and more efficient in their use of people's time. A typical computerized sales and catering system would include a daily function summary showing space bookings for every day of the year, details on each function such as room setup and menu, and timing of meals and breaks. When the booking is complete, a contract reflecting the customer's requests is prepared automatically by the system. Where the restaurant is a part of a hotel or conference center, group rooms control is also provided.[23]

TECHNOLOGY AND MANAGEMENT

Computerized point-of-sale (POS) systems not only make the service process easier for employees but save managers work by preparing routine reports; tracking inventory, stock levels, and costs; and determining which items are producing a profit. Some companies are linked directly to their suppliers' computers, and ordering is done automatically as product is used. Red Lobster's management system prepares a daily food use forecast that is adjusted by unit managers and used as a basis to bring product from locked storage to the preparation area for the day. The same usage report is transmitted to the chain's Orlando headquarters, where it is translated into orders to suppliers. These are transmitted from Orlando to suppliers across the United States and Canada. Notice that this process not only increases control chainwide, but also saves a good deal of time for unit managers.

Clearly, the impact of the Internet, and technology in general, is growing but is not being felt in all quarters quite yet.

Summary

This chapter has covered a wide range of topics, each of which is having an impact on the food service industry. The first issue that we discussed was consumers' concern for nutrition in restaurant food. Although there is a concern about nutrition among consumers that cannot be overlooked, there is an even stronger preference for taste. Operators try for balance with menu offerings to suit both preferences. Consumerists criticize food service for not following what consumerists see as the path of virtue, but restaurants know that they cannot force consumers to behave in a certain way despite all their advertising. Marketing does best when it follows the lead of the guest.

The Nutrition Labeling and Education Act (NLEA) limits the health claims restaurants can make and requires them to provide information on any nutrient or health claim they make. Although enforcement of the NLEA is very uneven, most restaurants were in compliance with the act before it was passed.

Sanitation is a major concern for the restaurant industry, and the Educational Foundation of the NRA has certified several million workers and nearly a million managers in courses on that topic. The industry's interest is explained, in some part, by self-interest—bad publicity about sanitation can destroy a restaurant. The best approach to developing a sanitation program is to follow the principles and procedures of HACCP.

Environmental concerns about waste management can be acted on effectively at the unit level. The shrinking availability and mounting costs of sanitary landfills give a pragmatic basis for this concern, as do the sentiments of our customers who are concerned about the environment. We discussed six ways to deal with solid waste: reduce, reuse, recycle, compost, incinerate, and landfill. Choosing cost-effective solutions is complicated by program costs, availability of support channels, and unwanted side effects. Some of the costs and other issues were addressed.

Technology is playing a growing role in food service, but it is still subject to economics and customer acceptance. Technology is being used to enhance guest services as well as to control costs and increase efficiency. The chapter discussed the uses of technology in the following areas: guest ordering and payment, food production and refrigeration, marketing (specifically on the Internet), managing banquet and catering departments, and management control and communication.

Key Words and Concepts

Healthy eating	Health claim
Overweight	Food Safety
Dietary schizophrenia	Sanitation
Nutritious food and	Hazard analysis and critical control
consumer demand	points (HACCP)
Consumerism	Solid-waste disposal
Nutrition Labeling and	Sanitary landfill
Education Act (NLEA)	Waste stream
Food and Drug	Reduce, reuse, and recycle
Administration (FDA)	Composting
Nutrient claim	Incineration

Review Questions

1. What is meant by dietary schizophrenia? What do you think of the way the industry is responding to it?

2. Which of the consumerist issues discussed in this chapter have you encountered as a customer or employee of food service? What are your views on these issues?

3. What is the status of landfill availability and cost in your community? What is its outlook? What is the outlook for recycling and composting in your area?

4. What are some of the steps that you think a restaurant operator can take to help with some of the solid-waste problems?

5. Using as an example an operation with which you are familiar, describe the steps necessary to make recycling possible in that unit.

6. What problems hinder the use of technology? What technological innovations do you think operations should be seeking?

Internet Exercises

1. **Site name:** Center for Science in the Public Interest

   URL: www.cspinet.org

   Background information: The Center for Science in the Public Interest (CSPI) is a nonprofit education and advocacy organization that focuses on improving the safety and nutritional quality of our food supply. CSPI seeks to promote health through educating the public about nutrition and alcohol; it represents citizens' interests before legislative, regulatory, and judicial bodies; and it works to ensure that advances in science are used for the public's good. It has been very active in targeting the restaurant industry with their public interest issues.

   Exercises: Highlight the "Nutrition Action Newsletter," then click on "Archives." Choose and read a current or previous article that targets a segment of the restaurant industry.

   a. Discuss how the article you read might impact on the restaurant industry. Do you think this article will persuade the restaurant industry to change? Why or why not?

   b. Do you believe the issues raised by CSPI are justified? Should the restaurant industry change, or should CSPI just "mind its own business." Why or why not?

2. **Site name:** CSPI Booze News

   URL: www.cspinet.org/booze/index

   Background information: In 1981, the CSPI launched the Alcohol Policies Project to help focus public and policy-maker attention on policy reforms to reduce the health and social consequences of drinking. Since then, the project has worked with thousands of organizations and individuals to promote a comprehensive, prevention-oriented policy strategy to change the role of alcohol in society.

   Exercises:

   a. Go to the Booze News Web site and choose an alcohol policy project issue. Describe in detail how you feel the issue impacts the restaurant industry—both positive and negative. There is no right or wrong answer for this—purely your opinion.

   b. Do you believe the issues raised by CSPI are justified—are they right on target or they being too critical? Why or why not?

3. **Site name:** The Center for Consumer Freedom

   URL: www.consumerfreedom.com and www.cspiscam.com

   Background information: The Center for Consumer Freedom is a nonprofit coalition of restaurants, food companies, and consumers working together to promote personal responsibility and protect consumer choices. The growing cabal of "food cops," health care enforcers, militant activists, meddling bureaucrats, and violent radicals who think they know "what's best for you" are pushing against our basic freedoms.

Exercises:

a. Review the above site as well as both of the CSPI sites. Lead a class discussion on:

   i. The goals of The Center for Consumer Freedom

   ii. How do they differ from CSPI?

   iii. After reviewing this Web site and CSPI, which do you agree with most? Why?

4. **Site name:** Centers for Disease Control and Prevention

URL: www.cdc.gov/foodsafety/disease.htm

Background information: The Centers for Disease Control and Prevention (CDC) is one of the 13 major operating components of the Department of Health and Human Services (HHS). Its mission is to be at the forefront of public health efforts to prevent and control infectious and chronic diseases, injuries, workplace hazards, disabilities, and environmental health threats.

Site name: FDA's "Bad Bug Book"

URL: vm.cfsan.fda.gov/~mow/intro.html

Background information: This handbook provides basic facts regarding foodborne pathogenic microorganisms and natural toxins. It brings together in one place information from the Food & Drug Administration, the Centers for Disease Control & Prevention, the USDA Food Safety Inspection Service, and the National Institutes of Health.

Site name: Fight Bac

URL: www.fightbac.org/

Background information: Fightbac.org, is the Web site of the Partnership for Food Safety Education (PFSE). PFSE is a not-for-profit organization that unites industry associations, professional societies in food science, nutrition and health, consumer groups, and the U.S. government to educate the public about safe food handling.

Exercises:

a. Choose any three of the following pathogens that cause foodborne illnesses: E. Coli, Salmonella, Norovirus, Hepatitis A, Listeria, and Staphylococcal food poisoning. Collect the following information for each using the three Web sites above.

   i. Name of the pathogen

   ii. Foods typically associated with foodborne illness and this pathogen. Duration of time after the contaminated food is eaten and symptoms begin to appear

      iv. Symptoms typically caused by this pathogen

      v. Duration of the illness (include the likelihood of death resulting from the illness)

   b. What can a food service manager do to prevent a foodborne illness caused by the three pathogens you selected?

5. **Site name:** News Search Engines/Sources

   URL: Google—www.google.com

   AlltheWeb.com—www.alltheweb.com

   Yahoo—www.yahoo.com

   AltaVista—www.altavista.com

   Newspapers.com—www.newspapers.com

   Background information: All the major search engines have a "News" tab that can be selected to search thousands of news sources worldwide on any topic entered by the user. Newspapers.com is a directory of all the newspapers in the United States regardless of size. On Newspapers.com, you can search for a newspaper by title, state, or city.

   Exercises: Choose a topic such as food safety, food sanitation, alcohol abuse, alcohol and restaurants, happy hours, menu legislation, "Center for Science in the Public Interest," or a topic assigned by the instructor. Using a news search engine or a newspaper from your hometown, search for current news on a topic. If you use a news search engine, be careful to only select news from the country in which you are studying. Lead a class discussion on the news item to include the following:

   a. Describe the impact this news item has on the restaurant/food service industry.

   b. Indicate why this news is relevant to managers in the restaurant/food service industry.

   c. If you were a restaurant manager, how would your behavior change as a result of having this information? What would you do differently?

   d. Discuss what future changes you believe might occur in the restaurant/food service industry as a result of this news.

Notes

1. International Health, Racquet and Sportsclub Association. December 5, 2006. http://cms.ihrsa.org/IHRSA/viewPage.cfm?pageId=2.
2. American Dietetic Association, "Nutrition and You: Trends 2002."
3. International Health, Racquet and Sportsclub Association (www.ihrsa.org), December 5, 2006.
4. World Health Organization, www.who.int.
5. National Chicken Council (www.eatchicken.com), December, 2006.
6. World Health Organization, www.who.int.

7. Juliet Schor, *Do Americans Shop Too Much?* (Boston: Beacon Press, 2000).

8. Personal communication, Leila Leoncavallo, senior staff attorney, Center for Science in the Public Interest, November 2000. We are indebted to Ms. Leoncavallo and the CSPI for their helpfulness.

9. Quote from Dr. Margo Wootan, CSPI Web site (cspinet.org), December 14, 2006.

10. U.S. Food and Drug Administration Web site (http://www.cfsan.fda.gov/) December 9, 2007.

11. We are indebted to Pat Johnson, Director, Food Safety Programs Branch, Ontario Ministry of Agriculture, Food and Rural Affairs, for providing us with the information on food safety, sanitation, and HACCP.

12. Beverage Marketing Corporation, "Second Largest Category Leads Major Beverage Categories in Volume Growth." (www.beveragemarketing.com), December 2006.

13. Peter A. D'Souza and Leland L. Nicholls, "Waste Management: The Priority for the 1990's," Technical Paper, University of Wisconsin–Stout, n.d. Only the figure for institutions is given in the report. The quick-service food figure can readily be derived, using the check average given and a waste-per-1000-pounds figure. The table service figure, however, was estimated assuming an average of four chair turns per day for a seven-day week against an average of 25 pounds for family restaurants and 30 pounds for fine-dining operations.

14. The report uses the term "fine dining" where we have used "table service." The category found in the report for fine dining has a check average of $4 to $13. For the sake of consistency of usage in this text, we have changed this table. The authors note that the study was undertaken in a midwestern city and the findings may differ somewhat from those in other regions.

15. Environmental Protection Agency, "Municipal Solid Waste Management" (www.epa.gov/epaoswer/non-hw/muncpl/facts.htm). December 1, 2006.

16. Ibid.

17. Ibid.

18. *Institutions/Volume Feeding,* October 1975, p. 47.

19. Tim Jones, "Eateries May Flip Over Robo-Cook," *Chicago Tribune*, May 23, 2000, pp. 1, 6.

20. "GOMIXER: Turning food waste to water" Press release, *Advanced Biotechology, Inc.* March 23, 2003.

21. www.hobartcorp.com (December 22, 2006).

22. National Restaurant Association, "Technology Trends in Restaurant Operations," 2001.

23. We are indebted to Hodges Technology of St. Clair, Michigan, for providing us with the information on group bookings.

PART THREE

Lodging

The Hospitality Industry

The Hotel Crescent Court, Courtesy of Rosewood Hotels & Resorts.

CHAPTER NINE

Lodging: Meeting Guest Needs

The Purpose of this Chapter

In this chapter, we will look at lodging as a set of products and services that have evolved out of guest needs and preferences. We will begin with the evolution of lodging to fit **transportation and destination patterns** and individual guest preferences. We will then delineate different types of lodging properties, discussing the distinguishing characteristics of each. Different market segments will be explained in relation to their demographics and subsequently their needs and expectations when traveling. The tremendous impact of technology will be discussed from the perspective of changing guest expectations and from the standpoint of how technology has changed major facets of hotel operations. The most important aspect of the hotel industry, service, will be explored with a discussion of hotel rating criteria through organizations such as American Automobile Association (AAA) and directories such as the Mobil Travel Guides. The crucial role of employees as "internal customers" in providing service will be emphasized.

THIS CHAPTER SHOULD HELP YOU

1. Describe the evolution of lodging, and relate it to changing patterns of transportation, destinations, and guest needs.
2. Identify the five criteria for classifying hotels, and name the types of hotels in each classification.
3. Describe the principal customer types served by the hotel industry.
4. Name the two categories of business travelers.
5. Identify the needs and preferences of business travelers, and provide examples of how the lodging industry accommodates them.
6. Provide examples of the ways in which lodging is responding to the needs of growing market segments, including senior travelers, female travelers, and family travelers.

7. Explain why international travel is important to the industry, and describe what operators can do to develop this source of business.

8. Give examples of how technology has impacted lodging in the following areas: sales, marketing, guest amenities, and services.

9. Describe how AAA and the Mobil Travel Service evaluate lodging properties, and identify criteria used in determining these ratings, as well as describe how countries around the world approach the rating of hotels.

10. Define the term *internal customer*, and explain the importance of this concept in the delivery of quality service to guests.

The Evolution of Lodging

Today in the United States, there are 47,590 lodging properties containing over 4.4 million guest rooms. In 2005, this dynamic industry generated $122.7 billion in sales and directly supported over 7.5 million travel and tourism jobs.[1] The industry has surely come a long way since its origins.

THE HISTORY OF LODGING

The history of lodging, leading to this enormous growth, is rich in variety and encompasses thousands of years. The Code of Hammurabi dating back to about 1800 B.C., made a reference to "tavern keeping," another term used for innkeeping in that day. Later, the Romans built an extensive system of paved roads and included way stations and inns at regular intervals along the way. During the Middle Ages in Europe, religious pilgrimages were the primary reason for traveling, with charitable institutions and religious orders providing lodging facilities. In the fifteenth century, many European cities became centers of commerce and culture. Correspondingly, innkeeping for profit began. With the development of stagecoach routes connecting major cities, the first hotel boom occurred as inns were located along these routes. The development of inns along stagecoach routes was later followed by the location of lodging establishments convenient to the major travel modes of railroads, automobiles, and airplanes as the lodging industry responded to changes in destination patterns.[2]

In the American colonies of the seventeenth and eighteenth centuries, inns and taverns were important centers of activity. As meeting places for colonists planning to separate from England, the early inns were sometimes called "cradles of liberty." The inns of Colonial America, called "**ordinaries**," typically provided the midday meal or supper as part of the overnight stay. By the beginning of the nineteenth century, lodging establishments that were larger and more commercial than inns emerged, along with the term hotel. Early hotels in the United States included the six-story, 200-room City Hotel in Baltimore, built in 1826, and the Tremont House in Boston, built in 1829.[3]

Luxury hotels were still the exception in the United States during the nineteenth century, however. The grand hotels of the world were, for the most part, still in Europe, including such landmarks as the Grand Hotel in Rome, the Paris Ritz, and the Savoy of London. The Waldorf Hotel in New York City was one of the first properties in the States to provide many of the European amenities. Built in 1893 by William Waldorf Astor, the Waldorf was followed by larger and more elaborate hotels such as the Astoria Hotel, also in New York. A later combination of these two properties created the Waldorf-Astoria Hotel, which was the world's largest hotel of its day.[4]

Toward the end of the nineteenth century, North American hotels grew to serve the rail traveler. Often the hotel was physically connected to the railroad station. A few of these hotels still survive, and some, such as Toronto's Royal York, remain thriving centers. Of the hotels built during the first half of that century, those not physically connected to the railroad station were usually convenient to it and to the major destinations in the downtown sections of cities.[5]

By 1900, there were still fewer than 10,000 hotel properties of varying service levels throughout the United States. A typical luxury hotel might offer amenities such as steam heat, electric call bells, baths and clothes closets on all floors, barbershops, and liveries. The Hotel Statler chain, which started in Buffalo, New York, served as the model for construction of hotels for the next 40 years. With the opening of the Buffalo hotel in 1908, rooms had private baths, full-length mirrors, and telephones. The marketing slogan for the Statler Hotel in Buffalo was "A bed and a bath for a dollar and a half." Other Statler properties that followed were also known for the introduction of many firsts.[6] In 1927, the Hotel Statler in Boston became the first hotel with radio reception; individual headsets were provided in each guest room to receive broadcasts from a central control room.[7] The Hotel Statler in Detroit, which opened in 1934, was the first property to have central air-conditioning for every public room.

By 1910, there were 1 million total hotel guest rooms in the United States, with the industry employing some 300,000 people. The average property of that day had between 60 and 75 guest rooms.[8] The first two decades of the twentieth century saw the beginnings of several major hotel companies that are still prominent today. Conrad Hilton entered the hotel business in 1919 by acquiring the 40-unit Mobley Hotel in Cisco, Texas. Ernest Henderson, founder of Sheraton Hotels, acquired four hotels in the late years of the Depression, with the chain's name coming from one of these four hotels, the Sheraton Boston Hotel.[9] Around the same era, J. Willard Marriott Sr. entered the hospitality industry with the opening of his first root beer stand in 1927.

This modest beginning led to the Marriott name as a multi-billion-dollar giant in the lodging industry.[10]

THE EVOLUTION OF THE MOTEL

The Federal Road Aid Act of 1916 resulted in a new segment of the lodging industry, as thousands of rooms were added in properties along the new state and federal highways being constructed. The first roadside "**motel**" opened in San Luis Obispo, California, in 1925 with room rates of $2.50 a night. Sometimes referred to as "tourist courts," the first motels were small, simple affairs, commonly with under 20 units (or guest rooms). These properties lacked the complex facilities of a hotel and were generally managed by resident owners with a few paid employees. The big wave of motel construction followed World War II, accompanying the explosive growth in auto travel.

Motels tended to be built at the edge of town, where land costs were substantially lower than downtown. The single-story construction that typified motels until the late 1950s (and even the two-story pattern of later **motor hotels**) was significantly less expensive compared with the downtown high-rise properties that were built on prime real estate. Capital costs, such as land and building, represent the largest single cost in many lodging establishments, and so lower land and building costs and the lower capital costs that resulted gave motels significant advantages. These savings could be, and generally were, passed on to guests in the form of lower rates.

Probably more important was the fact that motels offered a location convenient to the highway. Because the typical guest traveled by car, he or she could drive to any local destination during the day, returning to the accommodations in the evening. Meanwhile, inexperienced travelers, who had always been put off by the formality of hotels, with their dressy room clerks, bell attendants who had to be tipped, and ornate lobbies, preferred the informal, come-as-you-are atmosphere of motels. In the motel, they might be greeted by the owner working the front desk. Motel operators were proud of their informality. The personal touch they offered guests and the motel's convenience and lower prices were their stock-in-trade.[11]

THE MOTOR HOTEL

For a few years, it appeared that hotels (in general, the relatively large downtown properties) and motels (usually, the small properties located at the edge of town) would battle for the new mobile tourist market. Unhappily for both the hotel and the mom-and-pop motel, the situation was not that simple.

In 1952, Kemmons Wilson, a Memphis home-building and real-estate developer, took his family on a vacation trip. He was depressed by the dearth of accommodations to meet his family's and the business traveler's needs. He returned to Memphis with a vision of a new kind of motel property that combined the advantage of a hotel's broad range of services with a motel's convenience to the auto traveler. That insight, which came to be known as the motor hotel, revolutionized the lodging industry.

Motels became larger and began to offer a wide range of services. Dining rooms or coffee shops, cocktail lounges, and meeting rooms appealed to the business traveler. Swimming pools became essential to the touring family. Room telephones, usually present in hotels but generally absent in motels, became the rule in motor hotels, thus requiring a switchboard and someone to operate it. Whereas hotels and motels had offered coin-operated radios and television, free television and then free color television became the rule.

Although there were experiments with smaller inns having 50 to 75 rooms, most lodging companies determined that generally a 100-unit facility was the smallest that made economic sense. That size permitted full utilization of the minimum operating staff and provided sufficient sales to amortize the investment in such supportive services as pools and restaurants. However, with the advent of the limited-service hotel, which does not include a restaurant, smaller properties in small cities are once again feasible.[12]

The basic distinction between hotels and motels has become more complex as different types of lodging properties have emerged since the advent of the motor hotel of the 1950s. Today's lodging properties fall into one of several categories, with some blurring of distinctions between lodging types. Many major hotel corporations, such as Marriott, have properties in each lodging category, addressing the varied needs of different market segments of travelers.

Many lodging properties are part of larger chain operations, typically with recognizable brand names, and corporately owned or franchised. Other properties, smaller in number, are known as independents; here the owner may be one or several individuals or a company but has no ties to a larger corporation or major brand name. Industry Practice Note 9.1 looks at the state of hotel chain affiliations in Europe (this topic is also explored further in Chapter 12 as it relates to U.S. properties).

Classifications of Hotel Properties

Lodging properties can be categorized according to varied criteria. Classification criteria can include price, function, location, particular market segment, and distinctiveness of style or offerings. It should be emphasized that many types of hotels can fall into more than one category.

Europe: A Continent of Lodging Distinctiveness

While some parts of the world such as Asia and the Middle East are experiencing rapid hotel growth, Europe remains the leader in hotel capacity. According to the World Tourism Organization (WTO), about 38 percent of the six worldwide tourism regions are located in Europe. European hotels are distinctive, compared to the other tourism regions, in that properties tend to be older and smaller in the number of rooms. European hotels also tend to be more fragmented, compared to other parts of the world, in that only 20 percent to 25 percent of room capacity is branded by an integrated chain. In North America, approximately 70 percent of hotels are chain-managed or franchised. Other regions of the world fall somewhere in between North America and Europe.

The degree of chain penetration in Europe varies by country. For example, France has the highest percentage of hotel rooms affiliated with a chain (not including consortia) at 38 percent. Spain follows (34 percent) along with Germany (24 percent) and Ireland (21 percent). Significant reduced affiliations exist in Italy (4.4 percent) and Switzerland (8 percent).

Paris-based Accor has the largest number of properties with 1,922 hotels (201,042 rooms) in Europe carrying their flag. In Europe, Accor manages the well-known brands of Ibis, Mercure, Novotel, Formula 1, and Etap. Accor also has the upscale brand of Sofitel and the extended stay brand of Suitehotels.

InterContinental Hotel Group also has a significant presence with 423 properties and 68,841 rooms in Europe and Societe du Louvre with 918 properties and 62,856 rooms. InterContinental's brands include Holiday Inn, Express by Holiday Inn, Crowne Plaza, InterContinental, and Staybridge Suites. Societe du Louvre is a publicly held company controlled by the Tattinger family (known for being Champagne producers). Their brands include the upscale Groupe Concorde hotels and budget Groupe Envergure. Hilton Group, a British-based chain with the rights to use the Hilton name outside the United States, also has a presence in Europe with 118 hotels containing 28,501 rooms.

The best affiliation solution for the average European hotel tends to be the voluntary chain or consortium option. These synonymous terms refer to a loosely structured hotel grouping which require less of the individual hotelier in terms of costs and prescribed standards. The affiliation with the voluntary chains is typically easier to cancel (usually within two years or less) whereas cancellations with the more structured hotels can stretch over several decades. While Switzerland, for example, has only 8 percent of its hotels affiliated with the "hard brand chains," an estimated 27 percent are affiliated with a consortium.

On the side of the chains, the usual European hotel is not as attractive as properties in other parts of the world. The smaller size and the location of many European hotels are not good fits with the larger worldwide chain model. Urban locations are preferred or close access to major transportation arteries by the large chains.

The major chains have recently lost capacity in Europe. One reason is linked to the tightening of standards by the consortia. Best Western, for example, added fourteen new operating standards. Best Western conducts yearly inspections of their properties as does Logis de France (with almost 4,000 hotels), the voluntary chain of Relais & Chateaux.

Source: M. Marvel, "Hotel Chain Penetration in Europe—Understanding the European Hotel Market," for EHLITE.com, January 8, 2004, http://ahlaradio.hsyndicate.com/news/4018166.html

Hotels come in many different sizes and offer room rates for all types of customers. (Courtesy of Las Vegas Convention and Visitors Authority.)

HOTELS CLASSIFIED BY PRICE

Categorized by price, lodging properties can range from limited-service hotels to full-service properties and up to luxury hotels.

Limited-Service Hotels. **Limited-service hotels** typically offer guest rooms only. There is little or no public space, no meeting or function space, and usually no or very limited food and beverage facilities. Room rates are correspondingly lowest for this type of lodging property. Terms previously used for this classification of properties included "budget" or "economy" hotels. The average daily rate per occupied room for limited-service hotels in 2005 was $71.35. The average size of this type of property in 2005 was 126 rooms. Business travelers make up 50.8 percent of the market mix for limited-service hotels followed by tourist or leisure travelers at 44.4 percent. Conference, convention, and other travelers account for 4.8 percent.[13]

Full-Service Hotels. **Full-service hotels** offer a wide range of facilities and amenities. Usually there will be, in comparison to budget/economy properties, more public space and meeting/function space, with at least one food and beverage facility. Room rates tend to be equal to or slightly above market-area average. In 2005, the average rate for full-service hotels was $127.20. These properties had, on average, 286 rooms and catered primarily to business travelers (41.5 percent), leisure travelers (27.3 percent), convention travelers (17.1 percent), conference attendees (7.4 percent) and other (6.7 percent).[14]

Luxury Hotels. At the top of the price category are the **luxury hotels**, which usually have from 150 to 400 guest rooms. Featuring upscale decor and furnishings that may be unique to the particular hotel, these properties offer a full array of services and amenities. Such hotels would typically have a concierge service and several food and beverage operations, including a gourmet or fine-dining restaurant, banquet facilities, and full room service (available 24 hours per day or close to this). Recreational facilities or access for guests to nearby facilities is also usually available. There is a high ratio of employees to guest rooms, and room rates are considerably above the market-area average. In the buying and selling of luxury properties in the United States, selling prices have reached $1 million per room for some hotels. In Milan, Italy, $2 million was paid per room for a luxury property in late 2006. One of the recent trends contributing to the climbing prices of these properties, has been high-end corporations such as Italian jeweler Bulgari and fashion designers Versace and Giorgio Armani entering the luxury hotel market.[15] The average daily rate for luxury chain hotels in the United States for the first part of 2006 was $273.66 according to Smith Travel Research. For that same time period, the average rate for the U.S. hotel industry as a whole was $96.42. Luxury hotels had an average occupancy rate of 71.6 percent compared to the overall hotel market with an average occupancy of 62 percent. As Joe McInerney, president and CEO of the American Hotel and Lodging stated: "The luxury hotel market is better than it has ever been. The economy is good. People are buying up. They feel good . . . (about their personal finances) and want to travel luxuriously while they can."[16]

HOTELS CLASSIFIED BY FUNCTION

Hotels categorized by function include convention hotels and commercial hotels.

Convention Hotels. Convention hotels are large, with 500 or more guest rooms. The average size of convention hotels in 2005 was 780 rooms. These properties offer extensive meeting and function space, typically including large ballrooms and even exhibition areas. Food and beverage operations tend to be extensive, with several restaurants and lounges, banquet facilities, and room service. Convention hotels are often in close proximity to convention centers and other convention hotels, providing facilities for citywide conventions and trade shows.[17]

Commercial Hotels. Commercial hotels, in comparison to convention hotels, are smaller, with 100 to 500 guest rooms. There is less public space, smaller meeting and function space, fewer food and beverage outlets, and limited recreational amenities. Many of these hotels tend to be located in downtown areas. Downtown properties (also

Luxury hotels cater to a guest's every need. (Courtesy of Rosewood Hotels & Resorts.)

mentioned in the next section) have many advantages. They are near the large office complexes and retail stores; by day, they are near business destinations; by night, they are close to many of a large city's entertainment centers. Many well-located older downtown properties have also been remodeled to include necessary facilities. Although on-premise parking has not always been feasible, reasonably convenient off-premise parking with valet service to pick up and deliver the car is common. Thus, nearly all first-class downtown properties are reasonably "auto friendly." One final note: Downtown hotels almost always command higher rates. The higher rate is needed to offset the higher land cost and to cover the cost of whatever public facilities they might have.[18]

Figure 9.1 illustrates some different operating characteristics of hotels in different property categories.

HOTELS CLASSIFIED BY LOCATION

Location can also be a criteria for categorizing lodging properties. Types of hotels under this categorization include **downtown hotels** (discussed above), **suburban hotels, highway/interstate hotels**, and **airport hotels**. Suburban hotels tend to be smaller (200 to 350 guest rooms) and involve low- to mid-rise structures. Highway/interstate hotels are even smaller, with 100 to 250 rooms, and are low-rise properties.

TYPE OF LODGING PROPERTY	OCCUPANCY PERCENTAGE	AVERAGE DAILY ROOM RATE
Full-Service Hotels	70.5%	$127.20
Limited-Service Hotels	69.4%	$71.35
Resorts	72.2%	$180.96
Suite Hotels	75.0%	$108.35
Convention Hotels	71.3%	$166.10
All Hotels	71.4%	$126.12

Source: Data from Hospitality Research Group, PKF Consulting, Trends 2006.

Figure 9.1

Average Occupancy and Average Room Rate for U.S. Hotels in 2005

The San Francisco Marriott is a prime example of a downtown high-rise hotel. (Courtesy of Marriott International.)

Suburban hotels would most likely have interior corridors and meeting and banquet facilities, whereas the highway/interstate properties most likely have exterior corridors leading to guest rooms, minimal banquet and meeting space, and some food and beverage facilities.

In the 1950s and 1960s, as air travel became more and more common, a new kind of property appeared, designed especially to accommodate air travelers. Airport hotels vary depending on location and size of the airport, with such properties offering a mix of facilities and amenities. Typically, airport hotels range from 250 to 550 rooms.[19] An important extra service provided by almost all airport hotels is the courtesy van, which offers guests transportation to and from the airport.

HOTELS CLASSIFIED BY MARKET SEGMENT

Particular markets served include executive conference centers, resorts, and health spas.

Executive Conference Centers. Executive conference centers are often in secluded or suburban settings and have fewer than 300 guest rooms. These facilities, which

Modern guest rooms can accommodate a variety of needs and types of guests. (Country Inns and Suites; Courtesy of Carlson Hotels Worldwide.)

Resort hotels provide ample opportunity for guests to relax in picturesque surroundings. (Courtesy of Rosewood Hotels & Resorts.)

offer well-designed learning environments, provide a variety of small meeting rooms and classrooms featuring full audiovisual and technological support. Meals and use of recreational facilities are often included in the quoted daily room rate. An example of an Executive Conference Center is the Georgia Tech Hotel & Conference Center in Atlanta, GA.

Resorts. Resorts are typically located in picturesque settings and have 200 to 500 guest rooms. An example of a well-known resort in the United States is The Breakers, West Palm Beach, FL. Resorts provide a comprehensive array of recreational amenities, depending on the geographic location. A variety of food and beverage outlets is available, ranging from informal to fine-dining restaurants. With many resorts located in remote locations, it is often not feasible for guests to have to leave the property for dining options. Resorts can be further characterized and defined in more explicit terms. Some resorts are "**destination resorts**"; these tend to be in dramatic, desirable locations such as Hawaii, Mexico, and the Caribbean. Hotel guests tend to have to travel at least several hundred miles to reach such a resort, and travel is typically by air. Visits to destination resorts tend to be infrequent, usually once a year or less. **Nondestination resorts** or regional resorts involve a two- to three-hour trip for visitors and are usually traveled to by car. The visits to such locations are more frequent but usually for shorter periods of time as compared to the destination resorts. It is very feasible for a resort to cater to both destination and nondestination visitors.[20] Resorts can also be classified on a seasonal basis, indicating the time of year when the resort is at a peak demand. Seasonal classifications include summer, cold winter (i.e., ski resorts), warm winter (such as south Florida or southern Arizona), and year-round. At one time, the majority of resorts operated seasonally. Today, most resorts operate year-round, with group business and lower-rate packages bringing in guests during the less desirable times of the year. Two cities that epitomize the year-round resort market are Las Vegas, Nevada, and Orlando, Florida. Orlando, with almost 113,000 hotel rooms,[21] and Las Vegas, with over 133,000 rooms (and 59 hotels with 48,292 more rooms in the pipeline)[22] lead the nation in hotel room inventory, surpassing even Los Angeles, Chicago, and New York City.

An interesting segment of resorts focuses on **ecotourism**. These typically remote lodging establishments are usually located in areas of significant natural beauty, and the design elements of the property blend with the surroundings and protect the ecosystem. Often incorporated with adventure travel, these lodging properties can be found from the Great Barrier Reef of Australia to the rugged highlands of Tasmania and the jungles of Costa Rica. As with P&O Australian Resorts, many of these hotels stress comfort, with luxurious rooms and gourmet food and beverage selections.[23]

Casino Hotels. Casino hotels and resorts[24] differ significantly in their operation compared to most hotels. In casino hotels and resorts, gaming operations are the

Casino hotels such as the Luxor in Las Vegas use architecture to convey the desired image of the property. (Courtesy of Luxor Casino Hotel, Las Vegas.)

major revenue centers. Most of these are in Las Vegas; a number of casino operations that include hotels are also located on Native American reservations throughout the United States. Casino operations are discussed more fully in Chapter 14. There are numerous examples of casino hotels discussed throughout the text. One well-known casino hotel in the United States is Wynn Las Vegas.

Health Spas. Health spas, often located in resort-type settings or as a part of a larger resort, provide additional amenities focusing on needs ranging from losing weight to reducing stress to pampering oneself. Resort/hotel spas are the second largest category next to day spas. Resort/hotel spas were also the fastest growing segment over the past five years, growing 290 percent between 1999 and 2004. Spas are increasingly being considered as a necessity to remain competitive in attracting both leisure and business travelers. In a sample of 88 U.S. properties, spa revenue for hotels averaged $2,076 per available room or 2.3 percent of total revenue. At resort properties, spa revenue was $3,117 per available room or 3.4 percent of total revenue. In comparison, golf revenue declined by 2.7 percent per occupied room.[25]

Spas have professional staffs that often include dietitians, therapists, masseurs, exercise physiologists, and in some cases, physicians. There are a number of categories of spas, including spas with natural mineral hot springs, beauty spas, fitness spas, international-style spas that emphasize health therapies, behavior modification spas, holistic spas, resort spas, and spa facilities within hotels.[26] Hotels providing spa and fitness facilities are now dedicating more space to comprehensive health facilities in order to remain competitive. With an aging population of 80 million baby boomers, more health-oriented services are expected as this segment focuses on improving the quality of life. Profits will also play a very big part in fitness centers and spas, as resorts and hotels realize the significant revenue potential. Industry Practice Note 9.2 describes several trends in spa services. A prominent health spa in the United States is The Boulders Resort and Golden Door Spa, Phoenix, AZ.

Vacation Ownership. Vacation ownership, also referred to as timeshares and vacation intervals, involves a "type of shared ownership in which the buyer purchases the right to use a residential dwelling unit for a portion of the year."[27] Major lodging companies such as Marriott, Ritz-Carlton, Four Seasons, Hyatt, Accor, Carlson, Starwood, and Disney are big holders of the vacation ownership market. In 2006, 4.1 million households owned one or more U.S. timeshare properties. There are 154,439 timeshare units at over 1,600 resorts throughout the United States. Each condominium or unit of a vacation ownership resort is divided into intervals, typically by the week, that are sold separately. The condominiums are priced according to a variety of factors including unit size, resort amenities, location, and season. Purchasers of vacation ownership properties can typically travel to other destinations through vacation exchange programs provided through the timeshare resort developers. The predominant type of timeshare property, according to the American Resort Development Association, is a seaside/ocean resort (31.9 percent) followed by regional resorts (13.7 percent) and golf resorts (10.2 percent). Florida has three times as many timeshare resorts as any other state with the number totaling close to 400.[28] Marriott Vacation Club Sunset Pointe, Hilton Head, SC is a good example of a Vacation Ownership facility.

OTHER HOTEL CLASSIFICATIONS

Types of hotels classified by distinctiveness of style or offerings include all-suite properties, extended-stay properties, historic conversions, and bed-and-breakfast inns. Boutique hotels can also be classified under this category.

INDUSTRY PRACTICE NOTE 9.2

Trends in Spa Operations

According to the International Spa Association, spas are the fourth-largest leisure industry in the United States. Not only are spas growing in number (13,757 in the United States) and locations (9 percent are in hotels or resorts), but they are growing in the types of services provided. Some of the latest trends include the following:

- Authenticity: Destination spas and resort hotel spas are differentiating themselves with the types of products and services of their region. For example, Cliff House Resort & Spa in Ogunquit, Maine, offers body wraps made from Maine blueberries and wild roses or juniper berries. Le Spa at the Radisson Plaza Resort in Papeeta, Tahiti, offers treatments featuring the traditional monoi oil used by locals.

- Wellness: Canyon Ranch Resorts, in Lenox, Massachusetts and Tucson, Arizona, are collaborating with the Cleveland Clinic in Ohio to offer programs in weight control, stress management, and cardiac care.

- Medical tourism: This controversial field is booming and is increasingly using new technology such as DNA analysis, antiaging treatments, BOTOX®, and laser surgery. Medical tourism agencies now exist to help arrange the traveler-patient's stay.

- Sleep therapy: Spas increasingly will be offering sleep techniques and treatments to a society that generally is sleep-deprived.

- Men: The International Spa Association states that 31 percent of spa-goers are men. The Lodge at Woodloch, in Hawley, PA, was designed with male-focus including lodge-style architecture, a golf course, full bar with tapas and a dinner menu that includes red meat.

- Labor Concerns: Because of the high cost of labor, particularly in the United States, spas are increasingly using "de-staffed" spa treatments including heat and water experiences. Pricing will also become more attuned to demand with treatments during busy timeframes (weekends, for example) costing more than lower-demand times (weekdays).

- Fusion: Fusion treatments and techniques are on the increase. Examples include Watsu (water and shiatsu), yogalates (yoga and Pilates), Neurobics (mind aerobics) and Kinesis (mind-exercise).

- Services for Children: The spa industry is responding to the growth in family travel with more spas adding children's activities. Children's activities are being offered in many locations while parents indulge in spa treatments. Spa services especially designed for children, such as chocolate manicures, are also creative additions.

Source: "2007 Spa Trends," Staff and Wire Services, January 7, 2007. North Jersey Media Group, Inc. Proquest Information and Learning, http://global.factiva.com/ha/default.aspx

All-Suite Hotels. All-suite hotels became known as a separate category in the 1970s. Guest rooms are larger than the normal hotel room, usually containing more than 500 square feet. A living area or parlor is typically separate from the bedroom, with some properties offering kitchen areas. All-suite hotels can be found in urban, suburban, and

281

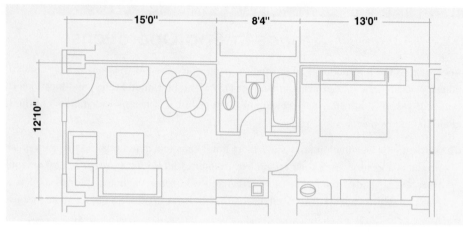

Figure 9.2
A typical guest unit at Embassy Suites. (Source: Embassy Suites.)

even residential locations. The amenities and services (availability of on-site restaurant operations, meeting space, and recreational facilities) can vary widely in this type of hotel. Figure 9.2 shows a typical guest unit at an Embassy Suites.

Extended-Stay Hotels. Extended-stay hotels provide many of the same features and amenities as the all-suite properties, such as a stove and/or microwave in the guest rooms, refrigerators, kitchenware or dishes, grocery shopping service, business services, and limited housekeeping service. As compared to all-suite hotels, however, the extended-stay room rates are often significantly less, with daily, weekly, and monthly rates quoted. Restaurants may be located nearby; typically there are no on-site food and beverage outlets in extended-stay hotels.[29]

Historic Conversions. Some hotel properties have historic significance and have been renovated to their original splendor. These classic hotels have great appeal for those wishing to experience some of the grandeur and elegance of earlier days with the comforts of modern-day features.

Bed-and-Breakfast Inns. A bed-and-breakfast inn (B&B) typically has five to ten rooms with the average size being eight rooms. Breakfast is served and included in the room rate for these properties. Most B&Bs are outside of urban areas with 29 percent being in rural locations and 52 percent being in suburbs/villages. The average length of ownership of a B&B is 13 years and most owners (88 percent) live on the

The Regent Wall Street is a good example of a beautifully restored boutique hotel. (Courtesy of Carlson Hotels Worldwide.)

premises. The number of B&Bs has increased from fewer than 1,000 in 1980 to about 20,000 properties today encompassing 148,000 rooms.[30]

Boutique Hotels. Boutique hotels span all price segments and are noticeably different in look and feel from traditional lodging properties. Interior-design styles in boutique hotels range from postmodern to homey. Soft attributes, such as image and

BY LOCATION	PROPERTY	ROOMS
Suburban	15,853	1,570,134
Highway	6,761	452,017
Urban	4,595	700,267
Airport	1,933	274,769
Resort	3,835	573,092

BY RATE	PROPERTY	ROOMS
Under $30	857	52,830
$30–$44.99	7,518	405,028
$45–$59.99	10,850	669,174
$60–$85	16,562	1,329,544
Over $85	11,803	1,945,890

BY SIZE	PROPERTY	ROOMS
Under 75 rooms	27,416	1,160,329
75–149 rooms	14,432	1,532,477
150–299 rooms	4,182	836,554
300–500 rooms	1,062	396,544
Over 500 rooms	498	476,562

Source: AH&LA, 2006 Lodging Industry Profile

Figure 9.3
2005 Property/Room Breakdown

atmosphere, typically distinguish these properties. Travelers' desires to be perceived as trendy, affluent, and artistic tie into boutique themes. Starwood Hotels & Resorts Worldwide has a version of the boutique concept with their W properties.[31]

Figure 9.3 displays types of hotels by location, rate, and size, along with the approximate percentage of U.S. properties that fall into these categories. Of the total number of lodging properties in the United States, it is interesting to note that 57.6 percent have fewer than 75 rooms, and 30.3 percent have 75 to 149 rooms. Although megahotels often garner much attention, the impact of small businesses on lodging is extremely significant. Slightly over three percent (3.2 percent) of the U.S. hotel inventory is comprised of properties with three or more rooms.[32]

Types of Travelers

According to the American Hotel and Lodging Association, the highest percentage of guests (52 percent) is leisure travelers. The number of leisure travelers has been steadily growing since 2000. The typical leisure room night is generated by two adults (54 percent), ages 35–54 (41 percent) who earn an average yearly household income of $75,400. The typical leisure traveler arrived by auto (74 percent), made reservations (85 percent), and paid an average of $94 per room night. Most leisure travelers spend one night (45 percent) followed by 28 percent spending two nights and 27 percent spending three or more nights.[33]

Business travelers accounted for 48 percent of hotel guests in 2005. The typical business traveler is male (68 percent) and in the age range of 35–54 (52 percent). The typical business traveler is employed in a professional or managerial position (48 percent) earning an average yearly household income of $82,000. These guests tend to remain in their rooms (73 percent), make reservations (85 percent), and pay an average of $99 per room night. Most business travelers (40 percent) spend one night, with 25 percent spending two nights and 35 percent spending three or more nights.[34]

BUSINESS TRAVELERS

Business travelers can be further characterized according to more specific profiles. The market segments of corporate travel and association travel offer a number of distinctions. The corporate market segment consists of for-profit companies and therefore may have more money to spend compared to nonprofit or other business segments. The **corporate market segment** tends to pay higher rates with the expectation of quality service and facilities.[35]

Association business may be more cost-conscious than the corporate segment. The **association market segment** consists of individuals or companies who have banded together in sharing common purposes or goals. Members in the association segment often pay for services themselves, which can intensify the cost-consciousness of these travelers. This segment can have very large numbers of attendees and may require large convention and exhibition facilities. Associations may be on the local, state, regional, national, and international levels.[36]

OTHER SEGMENTS

Another market segment for most lodging properties consists of **SMERF** business, so called because it originates from five primary sources: social, military, educational,

17%	Frequent travelers (10 + trips per year)
64%	Infrequent travelers (1–4 business trips per year)
	Average U.S. business traveler (7 business trips per year)*

Source: AH&LA's 2005 Lodging Industry Profile.
* Represents the number of trips per year that the "average" business traveler takes.

Figure 9.4
Comparison of Business Travelers

religious, and fraternal. Some of this business is leisure-based—the social category includes weddings, proms, and fund-raisers, for example, while the fraternal category includes fraternity- and sorority-related events. Other subsegments are more business-based, such as military, educational, and perhaps religious. A characteristic common to the five components is that SMERF customers tend to look for lower rates compared to corporate and association segments.[37]

Other market segments for lodging properties involving business and leisure travel include the tour/travel, cultural, sports, and governmental subsegments. Figure 9.4 shows the breakdown among business travelers based on number of trips taken per year.

INTERNATIONAL TRAVELERS

As the global economy expands, an increasing number of people travel internationally. In 2005, 49.4 million people traveled from abroad to the United States—a 7 per cent increase in travel over 2004. The United States receives a larger share of world international tourism receipts than any other country. The United States earned $82 billion in tourism receipts in 2005, leading the world's other top tourism earners—Spain, France, Italy, and China.[38]

Not surprisingly, North American hotel companies have been anxious to pursue the international travel market. American brands are expanding rapidly abroad. Much overseas travel takes place within the traveler's own region (i.e., most Asians travel within Asia, South Americans within South America, etc.). Overseas travelers, however, are more likely to visit the United States than other destinations when they travel outside their own area. To take part in the growth of international travel, companies have to have properties in those markets. Moreover, the best way to publicize a chain at the points of origin of international travel is to have a property in the country. This makes local people familiar with the brand.

Asia has been of particular interest to major hotel companies as they plan international growth. At the end of the third quarter of 2006, there were 656 projects in the Asian pipeline of hotel development. China has the largest development pipeline in the region and is second globally only to the United States. China has 316 projects and 107,725 guest rooms spread throughout the pipeline. The room count is a staggering 63 percent of the total rooms in the entire Asian pipeline. Many major cities in China are "under roomed" with the country having grown to the fourth-largest tourist destination by the end of 2006. The marked interest in China is linked to hotels projecting increased tourism in this part of the world, the entry of China into the World Trade Organization, and the 2008 Olympic Games, which will be held in Beijing.[39]

Anticipating Guest Needs in Providing Hospitality Service

Regardless of the category of lodging or the market segment, hotels are a service industry with the goal of meeting and exceeding guests' expectations. As consumers are consistently demanding more from their lodging experience, the challenge to hotel operators is to excel in consistently high-quality service that builds customer loyalty. This commitment to excellence may also involve product differentiation strategies involving imaginative amenities and experiences. For example, Sun International's Atlantis Paradise Island resort in the Bahamas has as a slogan "Blow away the customer," as in, exceed the customer's wildest expectations. Atlantis boasts the world's largest open-air aquarium and an encased water slide that takes riders safely through a shark-infested lagoon.[40] Industry Practice Note 9.3 illustrates the variety of lodging possibilities available for unique and adventurous travelers.

Meeting the needs and expectations of business travelers has resulted in major changes in guest room features and amenities, including **in-room technology**. Hotels have been challenged to keep up with the expectations and needs from this traveling segment. Whereas a few years ago, such travelers wanted to be "wired" during trips, now travelers expect wireless capabilities not only in the guest rooms but throughout the hotel, including meeting space. Major brands and independents have made great strides in wireless fidelity (WiFi) capabilities. The challenge to hotel companies is how to "future proof" for rapid technological changes. Hotels are finding that they need more robust systems, sound cable infrastructures, and bandwidth-shaping alternatives to meet these technological demands.[41]

The W Suites, part of Starwood Hotels, were conceived as properties for the "ultra connected business traveler." These hotels allow guests to remain in "virtual connect mode" from any location on the property. "Guests can print directly from their laptops

Creativity Is Evident in Hotel Properties

Responding to the growing market of savvy travelers who look for unique, and even at times bizarre, lodging choices, numerous hotels add an experiential factor beyond a comfortable bed and abundant in-room amenities.

One such lodging property is the Jules' Undersea Lodge in Key Largo, Florida. Located underwater, guests must first suit up in dive gear to get to this establishment. In Preston, Minnesota, the Jail House Inn Bed and Breakfast is a restored county jail built in 1869. For those guests preferring the authentic experience, there is a "cellblock" where they can sleep behind bars. The Library Hotel in Manhattan provides a different theme in each guest room. In addition, the Dewey Decimal System is followed for the numbering of guest rooms.

Historic.UK.com helps pair travelers to the United Kingdom with a variety of nontraditional lodging resources. The online service provides an inventory of castles, cottages, country estates, B&Bs, house hotels, and even boats. The Liberton Tower, for example, is one of the available options for travelers. Located in Edinburgh, Scotland, the Liberton is a magnificent fifteenth-century castle with acreage. Owned by a preservation trust, the Liberton Tower has won an international award for conservation, its grand interior combining tasteful period furnishings with modern comforts, elegantly laid out over three stories.

Internet Sites

Jules' Undersea Lodge: www.jul.com
Jailhouse Inn Bed and Breakfast: www.jailhouseinn.com
Library Hotel: www.libraryhotel.com
Historic United Kingdom: www.historic.uk.com

Sources: Emling, Shelley. "Hotels roll out deals, new twists to draw travelers." *Atlanta Journal-Constitution*, January 28, 2003, pp. E1, E5. www.historic.UK.com

to a secure and confidential laser printer," with the use of this printer possible whether the guests are working in their suites or outside by the pool. Another feature of W Suites is "broadband Internet access through a secure high-speed wireless Internet network." This technology allows guests to access e-mail, print documents, and surf the Net from anywhere on the property.[42] At the Ritz-Carlton Millennia Singapore, guests have access to a 24-hour "technology butler" who is on call to help with computer technology problems. With corporate guests as a focus, this hotel provides a full-service business center with secretaries, fax machines in suites, and private meeting rooms for rent.[43] Industry Practice Note 9.4 illustrates what the hotel of the future may offer in terms of technology amenities.

Lodging properties have also found ways to cater to other market sub-segments, such as senior travelers, females, and families. It is estimated that seniors comprise 47 percent

The Hotel of the "Not So Distant" Future

The "Hotel of Tomorrow Project" brought the brains of the hospitality industry together to debate the demographic and technological changes that will influence the guest room of 2025. A group of 41 participants were asked to consider six influential demographics that are and will increasingly impact the hospitality industry. These demographic trends included:

1. the aging population
2. environmentalists
3. leisure guests
4. the corporate/business traveler
5. wellness seekers
6. Generation Y

The hotel guest room that emerged was characterized by cutting-edge technology for work and play and extreme personalization. Features included:

- Guests being able to select digital artwork to meet personal preferences during their stay as well as carpet texture and television stations from his/her native country
- A multifunctional desk chair with a built-in microphone, speakers, and camera that is powered through a floor grid (power cords not needed)
- A retractable bed that can be raised and flipped to become a table or raised to the ceiling to become a light panel
- A bathroom floor pad that monitors vital signs
- Recycled gray water for use in toilets (for conservation)
- A robot that can carry luggage and remove trash

Source: P. Hayward, A. Taulane, and R. Little, "Lodging Innovators of 2006," *Lodging Magazine,* December 2006, http://www.lodging magazine.com/index.cfm?fm=Article,Detail&aid=126

of the leisure travel market or 144 million room nights per year. The Travel Industry Association of America states that retired individuals with an average age of 72 take about 32 million trips annually. The U.S. population of those 65 and older is expected to double in the next 25 years when 72 million people will be included in that age group. Hotels are already realizing the positive impact of the senior traveler and its growth potential. To capture this market segment, hotel companies are trying to understand the needs of the heterogeneous population that includes individuals in their 50s, 60s, 70s, 80s, and older. Marketing experts are sensitive to how to refer to this diverse group, spanning four or more decades, realizing that the younger baby boomers resist terms such as "mature," "senior" or "elderly." Industry experts do agree that there are interior design elements to better serve this market segment including better lighting, easy-to-read instructions (clearly printed materials in larger fonts), and nonskid flooring materials, as well as employee training to heighten awareness of the older travelers' needs.[44]

Women make 75 percent of all travel decisions. Female travelers account for almost 50 percent of all business travelers in the United States and the expectation is that they will outnumber male business travelers within the next ten years. In a survey of 13,000 female business travelers, the most important factors were close proximity to their clients (23 percent), followed by security of the lodging establishment (20 percent).[45] Hotels are responding to this increase with more emphasis on personal service, secure electronic door locks, express check-in and check-out, a selection of good restaurants on the property, and free airport shuttle service. Some chains offer special services and amenities for women. For instance, market research at Westin indicated that women wanted irons, hair dryers, full-length mirrors, and coffeemakers in the guest rooms. High-quality makeup mirrors are now standard at Crown Plaza properties. Guest rooms at Ritz-Carlton hotels feature both skirt and pants hangers, spray starch, scented sachets, bath salts, bath gels, makeup remover pads, and detergent for washing delicate clothing. The Loews Vanderbilt Plaza Hotel in Nashville has found gender-specific amenities to be very popular with guests. Whereas men might find cigars and a bottle of red wine in their room, women are more likely to find fresh flowers, fruit, candy, or white wine.[46]

Finally, families also represent a significant market. Although the percentage of U.S. households that are married with children is small (24 percent), new travel niches include travel with extended family members as well as travel by the nontraditional family. Multigenerational family travel, also referred to as grandtravel, has increased. About one-third of all leisure travelers are grandparents, and one-third of these took at least one vacation with their grandchildren last year. Hotels are correspondingly finding ways to compete for these young guests with features such as free-stay programs, children's menus in the restaurants and room service, pools, and in-room video games. Families are increasingly interested in emerging lodging alternatives such as condominium resorts and vacation ownership. There has also been a marked increase in families wanting participative programs for the entire family, allowing them to discover new things together, versus the more traditional "supervisory" programs for children only.[47]

Service, Service, Service

Whether a limited-service economy hotel property or one in the upper echelons of the luxury segment, each and every lodging establishment has the opportunity to deliver quality service. Quality service is service that "consistently meets and exceeds customer expectations."[48] Exceeding customer expectations results in a perception of

Service is an increasingly important dimension in all categories of hotels. (Courtesy of Las Vegas Convention and Visitors Authority.)

high-quality service. Failing to meet expectations results in the customer's perception of quality being relatively low. Since service is perception-based, the true measurement rests with the individual customer.

There are, however, a number of hotel ratings and measures that are based on a variety of perceptions, from guest surveys to rating-service inspectors. The ratings assigned by the **Mobil Travel Guides** and the **American Automobile Association (AAA)** are the best known in North America, but rating services also abound internationally. Hotels are rated on a multitude of criteria, including guest rooms, amenities, recreational facilities, decor and furnishings, public areas, housekeeping standards, restaurant operations including room service, and the maintenance of grounds and landscaping. The service-orientation and professionalism of hotel staff members, however, are foremost and include both the ability of employees to meet guests' needs through their knowledge and interpersonal skills and the employees' professional attire and grooming. Industry Practice Note 9.5 discusses the rating services further, both in the United States and abroad, providing a list of sample criteria used by one of the rating services and describing some of the world's most luxurious and exclusive hotels.

Hotel Rating Services

The Mobil Travel Guides offer a one-star to five-star rating system for hotels, motels, inns, resorts, and restaurants in more than 3,000 towns and cities in the United States and Canada. For 2006, five stars were awarded to an elite group of 34 lodging establishments. Stars can also be taken away from properties because of perceived lower quality in service and facilities. Based on on-site visits and inspections, some of which are unannounced until after the hotel stay, these ratings are considered extremely important in the hotel industry and are used extensively in advertising and other sales and marketing activities. Table 1 lists five-star hotels for 2006.[1] Table 2 presents several categories evaluated by Mobil in its expectations of a five-star lodging property.[2]

TABLE 1

2006 Mobil Travel Guide Five-Star Awards (by state)

CALIFORNIA

The Beverly Hills Hotel, Beverly Hills	The Peninsula, Beverly Hills
Raffles L'Ermitage Beverly Hills	Hotel Bel-Air, Los Angeles
St. Regis Resort, Monarch Beach	Chateau du Sureau, Oakhurst
Four Seasons Hotel, San Francisco	The Ritz-Carlton, San Francisco
St. Regis Hotel, San Francisco	

COLORADO

The Little Nell, Aspen	The Broadmoor Resort, Colorado Springs

CONNECTICUT

The Mayflower Inn, Washington

DISTRICT OF COLUMBIA

The Four Seasons Hotel, Washington, DC

FLORIDA

Four Seasons Resort, Palm Beach	The Ritz-Carlton, Naples

GEORGIA

Four Seasons Hotel, Atlanta	The Lodge at Sea Island Golf Club, Sea Island

HAWAII

Four Seasons Resort Maui at Wailea

ILLINOIS

Four Seasons Hotel, Chicago	The Peninsula, Chicago
The Ritz-Carlton Chicago, A Four Seasons Hotel	

MASSACHUSETTS

Blantyre, Lenox	Four Seasons Hotel, Boston

NEVADA

The Tower Suites at Wynn Las Vegas

NEW YORK

The Point, Saranac Lake

Four Seasons Hotel, Manhattan

The Ritz-Carlton New York, Central Park

Mandarin Oriental, New York

NORTH CAROLINA

The Fearrington House Country Inn, Pittsboro

SOUTH CAROLINA

Woodlands Resort & Inn, Summerville

TENNESSEE

The Hermitage Hotel, Nashville

TEXAS

The Mansion on Turtle Creek, Dallas

VIRGINIA

The Inn at Little Washington, Washington

The Jefferson, Richmond

TABLE 2

Sample Criteria for the Mobil Five-Star Designation

MOBIL TRAVEL GUIDE RATING CRITERIA	EXPECTATIONS OF A FIVE-STAR PROPERTY
Guest arrival phase:	Reservationist uses the guest's name throughout the conversation, thanks guest, and asks if there are any other needs. Background noise is limited. Guest name is used upon arrival at the hotel; guest key and credit card are placed in the guest's hand. Calls to desk ring no more than three times. A full explanation of the property is given at check-in or by bell staff. All guests are escorted to guest rooms. Guest rooms are prepped in advance.
Inspection of guest room:	Room has a sense of elegance, with quality products. The following amenities are available: fax, video, VCR, Internet connectivity, cell phones, in-room games. Telephones throughout the property should be answered within three rings.
	The guest's name is used, and wake-up calls arrive within five minutes of the requested time. Greetings should be friendly.
	Ice bucket is filled at turn-down, and a complimentary shoeshine is available. Housekeeping is impeccable. Staff is able to accommodate specific requests for time of service. Floors and counters are likely marble. Robes and towels are plush and large.
Food and beverage:	At least two full-service restaurants and cocktail lounges are available. One restaurant should achieve at least a four-star rating. Room service should be available 24 hours a day, with the ability to cater to almost any culinary request. Banquet and catering facilities are expected to be world-class.

Continues on next page

The American Automobile Association rates lodging properties based on a system of one to five diamonds. More than 57,000 properties are evaluated by AAA each year and less than one-half of 1 percent (0.26 percent) attain five-diamond status. Each property undergoes an unannounced evaluation, and properties receiving a five-diamond rating for the first time generally are reviewed at least twice. AAA also evaluates restaurants, campgrounds, attractions and events.

Zagat publishes ratings of U.S. hotels, resorts, and spas based on ratings and reviews from over 20,000 frequent travelers. Their categories of awards include "Top Hotel Chain," "Best Hotel," "Best Resort," "Best Small Property," and "Best Spa." Conde Nast Traveler publishes a Gold List based on a poll of approximately 37,000 readers. Hotels are rated based on rooms, service, restaurants, location, atmosphere, and activities. Added to the list of hotel ratings and awards are Travel + Leisure's World's Best Hotels, the Robb Report's Best Luxury Hotels, and Corporate Meetings & Incentives' Paragon Awards.

Hotel ratings in other parts of the world come from a variety of sources, if they exist at all. The government takes the role of hotel rater in some areas, whereas in others, it is tourism groups or the operators themselves. Examples of the variance in hotel rating systems abound within and among countries.[3] For instance:

- In the United Kingdom, the Automobile Association, Royal Auto Club, and English Tourism Council have adopted a standardized rating system for member properties. The criteria include cleanliness and housekeeping, service and hospitality, guest rooms, bathrooms, food quality and service, public rooms, safety and security, and exterior and interior appearance and upkeep. A one- to five-star rating system is used, with five-star hotels considered among the best in the industry.

- In France, hotels display the federal government-sanctioned star rating, ranging from one to four stars. Only four-star hotels are guaranteed to have adequate service and facilities for the typical meeting planner. A number of hotels, however, have opted to take lower ratings than four stars for tax reasons.

- In Germany and some Scandinavian countries, a one- to five-star system exists. By law, hotels can only promote these ratings for three years before the government requires a new inspection.

- Regarding overall hotel standardization in Europe, about 70 percent of hotels are independently operated. Internal criteria from chains may therefore be lacking in establishing standards for everything from room cleanliness to service basics.

- The respective country's ministry of tourism rates hotels across Latin America. Upon opening, hotels are inspected and granted from zero to five stars. Some hotels actually engage in rating themselves, thereby demeaning the star system and even, in some cases, going as high as seven stars. The other problem faced is that the governmental ratings are given for an indefinite period, even sticking for the life of the hotel, regardless of declining quality.

- In Asia, there tends to be no common rating system. Probably the most widely accepted rating system is the Institutional Investor system. This limited system only designates which hotels are world-class properties. In China, the government ranks hotels using the star system, with five stars being comparable to international luxury hotels. In Hong Kong, hotels are divided into three categories: high tariff, medium tariff, and hostels or guesthouses. In this country's rating system, price tends to be the most accurate indication of quality.[3]

What Are Some of the "Best of the Best" Hotels?

Although the list of the world's finest hotels varies depending on the source and time, there are a number of lodging properties that are well known for providing the ultimate in luxurious service and surroundings. As would be expected, these hotels attract some of the world's most exclusive guests, who readily pay top room rates for their pampered environment. Listed below are just a few examples of some of the "best of the best" in showcasing luxury suites in some of the world's best hotels:

Atlantis, The Bahamas

The Bridge Suite in Atlantis is one of the world's most expensive hotel suites. At $25,000 a night, guests enjoy a spectacular view from the suite, which is suspended between the two vast Atlantis Royal Towers. The master bedroom contains a spacious lounge area and a ten-foot four-poster bed. Hand-painted linens adorn the bed, and guests enjoy wardrobes the size of a garage. There is also the added comfort and convenience of round-the-clock butler and housekeeping service.

Burj Al Arab, Dubai, United Arab Emirates

At 1,053 feet, which is taller than the Eiffel Tower and only slightly shorter (60 meters) than the Empire State Building, the Burj is the tallest hotel in the world. The hotel is built on top of a man-made island, with only a bridge linking it to land. The toll for crossing the bridge is $50, which is just a mere fraction of the typical suite room rate of almost $7,000 per night. The hotel contains the world's fastest elevators and has been crafted from more than 96,000 square feet of gold leaf, marble, and crystal. The hotel has a dramatic view of the surrounding ocean. A submarine ride takes guests to an underwater restaurant containing a shark-infested aquarium. Other luxuries include a private screening room, rotating beds, private elevators, and a helipad. There are private butlers to give the ultimate in personal service. In addition, guests are provided with laptop computers to use during their stay.

The Fairmont, San Francisco

The Penthouse Suite, which spans the entire eighth floor of the Fairmont, typically rents in the range of $10,000 per night. The suite features three large bedrooms, a living room with a grand piano, an eat-in kitchen, a billiard room, and a view of San Francisco and the bay. The suite also contains a two-story circular library and a dining room that can seat 50 people. In addition to the customary personal services of private butlers and housekeepers, guests staying in the Penthouse Suite also have their choice of a Porsche 911, Cayenne, or Boxster to drive during their visit.

1. Mobil Rating Service, www.mobil.com
2. Auto Club South, "Club News: 2006 Five Diamond Awards," www.aaasouth.com/acs_news/5diamond03.asp
3. Megan Rowe, "Sorting Out Overseas Hotel Ratings," Religious Conference Manager, February 1, 2003, rcm.meetingsnet.com. Source: www.mobiltravelguide.com and Asian Hospitality (December 2002), "Checking out the world's finest," 1(4), pp. 9–11.

EMPLOYEES AS THE INTERNAL CUSTOMERS

The hotel industry employs approximately 1.4 million hotel property workers.[49] Each employee, directly or indirectly, impacts the service delivered in his or her respective hotel. The hotel industry is addressing the need to attract and retain the best of the best in the labor force. Many hotel companies are striving to become **employers of choice** through better wage and benefit packages, more career development opportunities, increased recognition, and mentoring.

For many hotel companies, a positive workplace is a fundamental aspect of the organizational culture. For example, the Marriott Corporation has, since its inception in the 1920s, had the philosophy of "Give to your employees and they will give back to you." J. Willard Marriott Jr., chairman of the Marriott Corporation, summarized the company's commitment to employees: "Motivate them, train them, care about them, and make winners out of them. If we treat our employees correctly, they'll treat the customers right. And if the customers are treated right, they'll come back."[50]

Whether it is offering English classes for international employees, providing child care assistance, including tuition reimbursement as well as flexible benefit plans to address different employee needs, or developing extensive employee recognition programs, hotels will increasingly have to address employees as their "internal customers."

The concept of the **internal customer** is a vital part of the quality goals and processes of the Ritz-Carlton Hotel Company. The lateral-service principle of this company reflects the internal customer role and states that an employee should always provide assistance if another employee asks for help in satisfying a guest's request or solving a guest problem. As a two-time winner of the Malcolm Baldrige National Quality Award, Ritz-Carlton was judged on seven quality categories including human-resources development and management. This category comprised human-resources planning and evaluation, high-performance work systems, employee education, training and development, and employee well-being and satisfaction.[51] The human-resources component will always be a crucial part of the hotel industry. Although technological advances have modernized an industry that began almost 4,000 years ago, the human factor in delivering service is more important than ever.

Summary

This chapter offered an introduction to a variety of aspects of the lodging industry, serving as a lead-in to the other chapters on lodging. It began with an overview of the history of the industry. Lodging follows the patterns of transportation and destinations of the times. Downtown hotels once served railroad passengers and still serve the needs of travelers who have business or entertainment interests in the center city. Motels and motor hotels serve people traveling by car, as airport hotels do air passengers.

Lodging properties can be classified according to various criteria such as price range, function, location, particular markets served, and distinctiveness of style. Types of lodging properties according to price range include limited-service hotels, full-service hotels, and luxury hotels. Commercial hotels and convention hotels are designated by function. The location category includes downtown properties as well as those in the suburbs, those along the highways and interstates, and those near airports.

The functional category includes executive conference centers, resorts, and health spas. Resorts can be quite diverse, ranging from mega-resorts such as those in Las Vegas to the remote resorts that incorporate ecotourism in blending with their natural surroundings. Health spas are increasingly found in resort hotels, and time-sharing is one of the fastest-growing travel and tourism segments. Additional types of hotels include those offering a particular, distinctive style, such as all-suite properties, extended-stay hotels, historic conversions, bed-and-breakfasts, and boutique hotels.

Hotel guests can be grouped according to the purpose of their travel. The highest percentage of travelers is leisure travelers (52 percent), with 48 percent traveling for business purposes. Business travelers can be further characterized as corporate or association guests.

Business travelers have a growing and distinct need for certain hotel services and guest room amenities. Increasingly, these are tied to technological needs, such as access to the Internet and data ports in guest rooms, as well as newer technological advances such as wireless access for laptop computers. Hotels are also adapting services and amenities for the growing percentage of international travelers, senior travelers, female travelers, and families traveling with children.

Quality-driven service—meeting and, whenever possible, exceeding guest expectations—is vital to the lodging industry. With diversified market segments, the ability to cater to the dynamic needs of guests is key to any lodging company's success. There are numerous hotel rating services that reflect the level of service and caliber of facilities of individual properties. Two of the best known are the Mobil Travel Guide star ratings and the American Automobile Association diamond ratings. Each year, a small group of elite hotels receives the highest ratings of five stars and five diamonds.

The delivery of consistent quality service hinges on versatile employees who are knowledgeable and skilled in their respective positions and who understand and gain satisfaction from their ability to positively impact each guest's hotel visit. The employees, as "internal customers," are truly the stars of the lodging industry.

Key Words and Concepts

Transportation and
destination patterns
Ordinaries
Motel
Motor hotels
Limited-service hotels
Full-service hotels
Luxury hotels
Convention hotels
Commercial hotels
Downtown hotels
Suburban hotels
Highway/interstate
hotels
Airport hotels
Executive conference
centers
Resorts
Destination resorts
Nondestination resorts

Ecotourism
Casino hotels and
resorts
Health spas
Vacation ownership
All-suite hotels
Extended-stay hotels
Bed-and-breakfast
inns (B&Bs)
Boutique hotels
Corporate market segment
Association market
segment
SMERF segment
In-room technology
Mobil Travel Guides
American Automobile
Association (AAA)
Employers of choice
Internal customers

Review Questions

1. How does transportation affect the hotel business?

2. What travel trends are favorable to lodging? Which are not? What do you think will be the best market segments for lodging in your community?

3. What are some means for hotel companies to increase sales to international travelers?

4. Of the hotels in your community, how would you characterize them in terms of type of lodging?

5. Identify hotels with which you are familiar. If you were a hotel rater, how would you rate these properties (1 to 5 stars and/or diamonds) and why? What criteria would you use in determining your rating?

6. If you were going to work in a hotel, what type of property would be of most interest to you as a potential employee? Why?

Internet Exercises

1. **Site name:** The American Hotel & Lodging Association (AH&LA)

    URL: www.ahla.com/

    Background information: Serving the hospitality industry for nearly a century, AH&LA is the sole national association representing all sectors and stakeholders in the lodging industry, including individual hotel property members, hotel companies, student and faculty members, and industry suppliers. AH&LA provides members with national advocacy on Capitol Hill, public relations and image management, education, research and information, and other services to provide bottom line savings and ensure a positive business climate for the lodging industry.

    Exercises:

    a. Review the history of lodging page on the Web site and analyze the industry performance statistics from 1980 to present (occupancy percentage, sales, number of properties, etc.). Has there been an increase or decrease in occupancy over the years? What are some possible reasons why this increase or decrease occurred?

    b. From the AH&LA Web site, describe the typical lodging customer for the most recent year that data is available.

    c. Who are the top five hotel companies worldwide? What hotel brands do they have in their portfolio?

2. **Site name:** Marriott

    URL: www.marriott.com

    Background information: Marriott International, Inc., is a leading worldwide hospitality company. Its heritage can be traced to a root beer stand opened in Washington, D.C., in 1927 by J. Willard and Alice S. Marriott. Today, Marriott International has more than 2,800 lodging properties located in the United States and 67 other countries and territories.

    Exercises: Under "Company News and Info." on the Marriott Web site, identify all the hotel brands in the Marriott portfolio. Based on the information on the Web site, determine which category each brand might fit into (limited service, full-service, luxury, resorts, suites, extended stay, etc.).

3. **Site name:** Mobil Travel Guide

    URL: mobiltravelguide.howstuffworks.com/ and www.howstuffworks.com/about-mtg1.htm and

    Background information: Since inventing the Five-Star rating system nearly a half-century ago, *Mobil Travel Guide* has provided travelers with an objective rating for hotels, restaurants, and spas in the United States and Canada. Their goal is to provide ratings and recommendations that you can trust to make the best possible travel decisions.

Exercises:

a. What criteria does Mobil Travel Guide use to rate hotels?

b. Do you feel that the criteria they use is valid or are they rigid and arbitrary? Why?

c. How difficult do you think it would be for a hotel manager to acquire each of the stars?

4. **Site name:** InterContinental Hotels Group

URL: www.ichotelsgroup.com

Background information: InterContinental Hotels Group PLC is the world's largest hotel group by number of rooms. InterContinental Hotels Group owns, manages, leases or franchises, through various subsidiaries, over 3,650 hotels and 540,000 guest rooms in nearly 100 countries and territories around the world.

Exercises:

a. List the seven hotel brand names in the InterContinental Hotels Group.

b. Explain what Priority Club Rewards entails through the InterContinental Hotels Group.

Notes

1. American Hotel & Lodging Association, "The 2006 Lodging Industry Profile."
2. PKF Consulting, "Hotel Development," 1996, Urban Land Institute, Washington, D.C.
3. Ibid.
4. Ibid.
5. Ibid.
6. American Hotel & Lodging Association, "History of the Lodging Industry," 2000 (webprod.ahma.com/ahma/media/hot_topics.asp).
7. PKF Consulting, "Hotel Development," 1996, Urban Land Institute, Washington, D.C.
8. American Hotel & Lodging Association, "History of the Lodging Industry," 2000 (webprod.ahma.com/ahma/media/hot_topics.asp).
9. PKF Consulting, "Hotel Development," 1996, Urban Land Institute, Washington, D.C.
10. J. W. Marriott and Kathi Ann Brown, The Spirit to Serve (Salt Lake City: Deseret Book Company, 1989).
11. American Hotel & Lodging Association, "History of the Lodging Industry," 2000.
12. PKF Consulting, "Hotel Development," 1996, Urban Land Institute, Washington, D.C.
13. Hospitality Research Group, PKF Consulting. "Trends in the Hotel Industry," USA edition, 2006.
14. Ibid.
15. R. Galbraith, "The luxury brand hotels," November 11, 2006. The Business, http://global.factiva.com/ha/default.aspx.
16. A. DaRosa, "People are packing their moneybags for luxury trips." July 23, 2006. The San Diego Union-Tribune, D-2.
17. Hospitality Research Group, PKF Consulting, 2006.
18. Ibid.
19. PKF Consulting, 1996.
20. Ibid.
21. Orlando/Orange County Convention Center & Visitors Bureau, 2006, www.orlandoinfo.com/cvb/research/occupancy.cfm.

22. R. Parets, "Large-scale projects in Las Vegas to promise to transform the skyline—again." Lodging archives, http://www.lodgingmagazine.com/index.cfm?fm=Article.Detail&aid=115.
23. James Ruggia, "Letting the Jungle in on Five-Star Luxury," Travel Agent, October 25, 1999.
24. Gerald W. Lattin, "The Lodging and Food Service Industry," Educational Institute of the American Hotel and Lodging Association, 1998.
25. A. Foster & R. Mandelbaum. "Hotel Spas—The New Recreational Vehicle for Hotel Profits," October 20, 2006, AH&LA Knowledge Base, http://ahlaradio.hsyndicate.com/news/4024991.html.
26. "2007 Spa Trends," January 7, 2007, *The Record,* http://global.factiva.com/ha/default.aspx.
27. American Resort Development Association, www.arda.org, January 2, 2007.
28. Ibid.
29. Ahmed Ismail, Hotel Sales and Operation (Albany: Delmar, 1999).
30. Information provided by the Professional Association of Innkeepers International.
31. Sean Hennessey, "Can Boutique Hotels Be Branded Without Losing Uniqueness?" *Hotel & Motel Management,* October 16, 2000.
32. American Hotel & Lodging Association, "The 2005 Lodging Industry Profile."
33. Ibid.
34. Ibid.
35. Ibid.
36. Ibid.
37. Ibid.
38. Ibid.
39. "First-ever Lodging Development Pipeline for Asia Reveals China," June 6, 2006, *Lodging Econometrics,* http://ahlaradio.hsyndicate.com/news/4027735.html.
40. www.atlantis.com
41. D. Fields "Coping with the advances in personal technologies in the guest room," Lodging archives, http://www.lodgingmagazine.com/index.cfm?fm=Article.Detail&aid=124.
42. R. Leigh Kessler, "21st Century Room Service," AAHOA Hospitality, February 2001, pp. 43–44.
43. Ibid.
44. S. Turkel, "The U.S. Population Age 65 and Over Is Expected to Double in the Next 25 Years: What does this mean for the hotel industry?" AH&LA Knowledge Base, http://ahlaradio.hsyndicate.com/news/4028342.html.
45. TIA, "Business and Convention Travelers' Habits Tracked in New TIA Survey," 2/12/2005, AH&LA-Knowledge Base, http://ahlaradio.hsyndicate.com/news/4022144.html.
46. Elaine Yetzer, "Upscale Hotels Tailor Amenities Specifically for Men, Women," *Hotel & Motel Management,* October 16, 2000.
47. J. Runice, "Resorts offer kids rousing activities, spa treatments." January 7, 2007, *Chicago Daily Herald,* page 4.
48. Robert H. Woods and Judy Z. King, *Quality Leadership and Management in the Hospitality Industry,* (East Lansing, MI: Educational Institute of the American Hotel and Motel Association, 2002).
49. American Hotel & Lodging Association, 2005.
50. Charles Bernstein and Ron Paul, *Winning the Chain Restaurant Game* (New York: John Wiley & Sons, Inc., 1996).
51. Woods and King, 2002.

The Hospitality Industry

(Courtesy of Courtyard Inn, Marriott International.)

CHAPTER TEN

Hotel and Lodging Operations

The Purpose of this Chapter

I t is impossible to teach someone how to run a hotel solely from a book. Only practical experience can teach a subject so complex. This chapter is intended, however, to help you learn more quickly from experience by familiarizing you with (1) the major operating and staff departments in a hotel, (2) the information flows that tie a hotel together and how they are handled, and (3) the patterns of income and cost that affect hotel operations. Finally, this chapter outlines the major hospitality career entry points and the paths available for advancement.

THIS CHAPTER SHOULD HELP YOU

1. Name the major functional departments in a hotel, and explain the relationships that exist among them.
2. Explain why the food and beverage department, although not the principal source of profit, can be very important to a hotel's success.
3. List the principal sources of income and expense by department according to the uniform system of accounts for hotels.
4. Define the term *yield management,* and explain why it is used in hotel industry pricing.
5. Describe the integral role of housekeeping to a hotel and the responsibilities of housekeeping staff.
6. Provide examples of hotel security issues and technical and managerial responses to preventing and minimizing security hotel problems.
7. Explain how accounting statements can be used to measure the performance of departments and executives.
8. Define the terms *occupancy percentage* and *average rate,* and provide the formula used to compute each; identify two other key operating ratios used by the hotel industry.
9. Explain the relationship of the financial structure of a hotel to its cost of operations.

Major Functional Departments

Hotel properties range in size from small to huge. Although large properties such as Chicago's Hilton and Towers or the Tower Suites at Wynn Las Vegas catch the public's imagination, the majority of properties in the United States have under 300 units. Because most students will gain their work experience in this kind of property, the examples in this chapter will assume a hotel in the 100- to 300-unit range.

Surprisingly enough, most properties perform basically the same functions, but the way in which they accomplish them varies with the property size. When there are significant variations in routine practices in larger properties, we will note them. Our emphasis, however, will be on the similarities found throughout the hotel business rather than on the variations.

Figure 10.1 shows the basic functional areas of a typical hotel. This figure includes elements not found in some operations, as some hotels lack food and beverage departments and many do not have a gift shop or garage. Our purpose, however, is not to draw a chart that represents all properties inclusively; that would be impossible. Rather, we have outlined the major activities usually present in most properties.

A large property may employ a general manager, under whom a hotel manager or resident manager assumes responsibility for day-to-day operations. There is often a rooms director who supervises the departments that make up the rooms division and a food and beverage director who oversees the departments in that division. Other key

Hotels perform essentially the same functions, no matter their size. However, size does influence how certain functions are carried out. (Courtesy of Cendant Corp.)

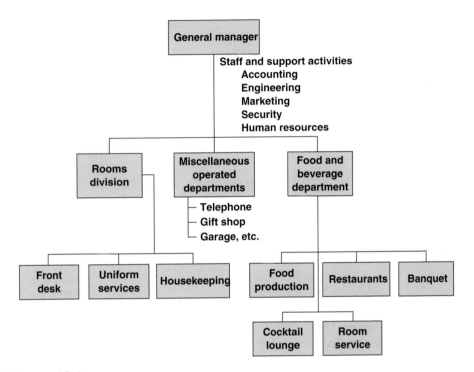

Figure 10.1
Major functional areas found in hotels.

members of the management team or executive committee of a large hotel include a director of sales and marketing, controller, director of human resources, and the chief engineer. Many hotels also include the executive chef, executive housekeeper, and director of catering as part of the management team.

On the other hand, in the 100-unit inn diagrammed in Figure 10.2, the general manager may be responsible—with an executive housekeeper and perhaps a front-office manager or supervisor—for running the **rooms departments** and for supervising an assistant manager responsible for food and beverage if the property contains a restaurant. At one extreme, in the small property, the executive staff may consist of two or three persons supported by a few department heads or supervisors and key employees. On the other hand, a large property requires a complex organization with several layers of authority.

It is important to note that a smaller property may have functional areas (food production, beverage department or bar, dining room, stewarding [dish room, pot washing, cleanup], and receiving, for instance, in the food and beverage area) but no true department heads. The restaurant in a small inn may be run by a restaurant manager who directly supervises all the employees with help from lead employees in each functional area on each shift. For instance, the hosts or hostesses for the day and evening shifts may

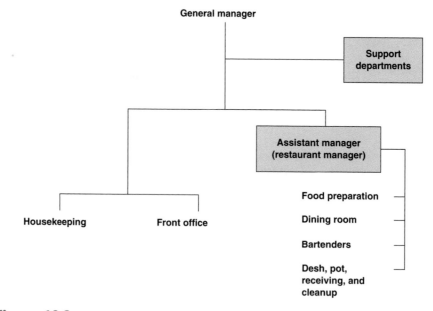

Figure 10.2
Functional operational chart for a small hotel.

provide leadership to the dining room staff during their shifts; a head cook on each shift does the same for the kitchen staff. The manager may be responsible for both shifts, usually along with someone designated as an assistant when the manager is off duty. This arrangement is economical and convenient in small properties as long as the restaurant manager delegates enough responsibility to avoid becoming overcommitted.

Lobbies are important in creating first impressions, as in this Microtel hotel. (Courtesy of U.S. Franchise Systems.)

The Rooms Side of the House

Room rental is a hotel's main business and its major source of profit. In larger hotels, the day-to-day operation of the typical rooms division yields departmental income (the revenue remaining after the direct operating costs of the departments in the division) of 70 percent or more, compared with 15 to 20 percent for the food and beverage department. Thus, the people on the rooms side of the house are crucial to the operation's financial success.

THE FRONT OFFICE

More than any other group, the front-desk employees represent the hotel to its guests. There are various position titles for the employees who check guests in and out of the hotel. Some hotels refer to these employees as front-desk receptionists, while others use front-desk agents or clerks. The front-desk receptionists have an integral role in determining guests' first impressions and last impressions of the hotel property. The attentive, warm greeting of a front-desk receptionist can have a tremendous impact in making the guest feel welcomed. If something goes wrong, most guests will complain first to the front desk. When the guests leave, the desk clerks check them out. If anything has gone wrong, this will be a good time to catch it ("I hope you enjoyed your stay"—and then listen to the answer). Although the duties of the desk differ somewhat by shift, they also, to an extent, overlap.

In the following discussion, a small hotel serves as a model. Our purpose is to describe the work of the **front office** and its functions. Your own observations will illustrate for you the variety of ways in which the work is organized.

The morning clerk typically works from 6:45 A.M. to 3:15 P.M. With a half-hour meal break, this is an eight-hour day. Because the evening crew comes in at 2:45 P.M. and the night auditor goes off duty at 7:15 A.M., all shifts overlap so as to ensure a smooth transition. Some properties maintain a logbook in which information or events with which later shifts should be familiar are noted. This logbook could also take the form of an automated database of information from shift to shift. The new shift's first task upon coming on duty is to check the logbook to make sure everyone is fully briefed.

The morning shift's work is concentrated in the early hours (from around 7:30 A.M. until midmorning) on checking out guests. At the same time, of course, the employees on this shift answer guests' questions and perform other routine tasks. Most hotel properties require check-out by a certain time, typically by 10 A.M. to 11 A.M., to facilitate cleaning and preparing the room for the next guest's arrival. A guest may request a later check-out time through the front office with approval typically depending on the number and estimated arrival of incoming guests.

When a guest is ready to leave, the clerk verifies the final amount of the bill, posts any recent charges, and assists the guest in settling with cash, check, or credit card, according to the house credit policy. This credit policy, which lays down guidelines for accepting checks and specifies the acceptable credit cards, is an important part of any clerk's training.

Although the technical aspects of the clerk's work are important, the courtesy a clerk accords a guest is of tremendous importance. A departing guest must have an opportunity to register complaints if he or she has had problems. The morning clerk's work thus includes a special responsibility for ensuring that guests leave with the intention of returning to the hotel on their next visit to town. Many hotel companies, in realizing the important role of front-desk employees in hearing guest comments and complaints, have empowered these employees to make necessary adjustments to guest charges or provide discounts to be used for future visits in order to maximize the number of return guests to any one property.

As guests check out and their rooms become vacant, housekeeping is notified. This permits housekeeping to make up the rooms promptly so that they will be ready when new guests check in later that day. As the rooms are made up, housekeeping notifies the desk so that early arrivals can be accommodated in rooms that are ready to rent. Alternatively, when the room is made up, the room status can be changed to "ready to rent" at housekeeping's computer terminal.

Most properties now have computerized reservation systems that keep track of the balance between rooms available and reservation requests. The morning clerk and her or his supervisor, the front-office manager (or guest services manager), monitor this process and block any special reservation requests. In a property that does not have a computerized reservation system, they will block the day's reservations.

The afternoon clerk's work is shaped by the fact that the heaviest arrival time begins, in most hotels, in late afternoon around 4:00 P.M. The afternoon clerk, therefore, takes over the reservation planning begun by the morning clerk and greets the guests as they arrive.

First impressions are crucial, and the desk clerk's warm welcome often sets the tone for the guest's entire stay. By remembering the names of repeat visitors, meeting special demands when possible (such as requests for certain floors or room types), and bearing in mind that the guest has probably had a hard, tiring day of work and travel, the desk clerk can convey the feeling that the guest is among friends at last. The clerk checks in the guest, which establishes the accounting and other records necessary for the stay.

The **night auditor** is a desk clerk with special accounting responsibilities. When things quiet down (usually by 1:00 A.M.), the auditor posts those charges not posted by the earlier shifts, including (most especially) the room charge. He or she then audits the day's guest transactions and verifies the total balance due the hotel from guests as of the close of the day's operations. The **auditing process** can be quite complicated, but simply stated, the auditor compares the balance owed to the hotel at the end of yesterday with today's balance. He or she verifies that the balance is the correct result of deducting all payments from yesterday's balance and adding all of today's charges. This process, summarized graphically in Figure 10.3, not only verifies today's closing balance of guest accounts owed to the hotel but also systematically reviews all transactions when an error in the balance is found. For this reason, the night auditor's job is important, requiring intelligence, training, and integrity. In most properties, even smaller ones, the night audit process is automated but still requires individuals to oversee the computerized processes and reports.

ADD:
Yesterday's closing balance of accounts owed by +
guests to the hotel

$64,217.91

Less:
Payments received today against accounts −
(say $4,340.97)

PLUS:
All charges made today to hotel or guest accounts +
(say $17,614.86)

EQUALS:
Today's closing balance of accounts owed by guests =
to the hotel

$77,491.80

Figure 10.3
A schematic view of the night audit process.

AUTOMATION OF THE FRONT OFFICE

Although the main elements of personal service—a smile, a friendly greeting, and courteous treatment of the guest—cannot readily be automated, much of the clerical work has been greatly simplified in most hotels by the installation of a **property management system (PMS)**. The PMS improves operational efficiency by eliminating repetitive tasks and improves service by providing information more quickly and accurately. At the same time, the PMS improves operational control. We need to understand the PMS in order to see how the front office functions.

The computer program (or programs) that make up the PMS prompt the clerk to follow an appropriate work sequence for every task. For instance, when a guest checks in to the hotel, the clerk begins by "telling" the computer whether the guest has a reservation or not. If the guest has a reservation, the clerk need only type in the name and the computer will retrieve the reservation and automatically print out the necessary records. In most cases, the guest is simply asked to sign his or her name. If the guest doesn't have a reservation, the clerk gets the necessary information, following the format on the front-desk computer screen (depicted in Figure 10.4), and types it in.

GUEST INFORMATION	ROOM DESIGNATION
NAME: Tom Farmer	ROOM TYPE: Dbl
PHONE: 612-999-1212	RACK RATE: 86.00
ADDRESS: 6199 Thorton Blvd	FOLIO RATE: 70.00
Minneapolis, MN	# NIGHTS: 2
SPECIAL REQUEST: Crib	EXTRAS: Crib-NC
MARKET: 12-15B	

CREDIT:

CREDIT CARD: Diners Club #99552211887712

Exp. 9/1/06

FOLIO LIMIT: $500

Guest Walk-In Display

(1) Room Info (2) Guest Info (3) Additional Info

(4) Post Charge or Credit (5) Change or Update

(6) Check In

02   27   15:07

Figure 10.4

The walk-in registration screen. Note the menu across the bottom of the screen that prompts the clerk as to the choices of activity appropriate to dealing with a walk-in.

When the guest checks out, the computer once again presents a screen with prompts (note the menu at the bottom of the screen in Figure 10.5) that will help the clerk to move through the appropriate sequence, verifying the balance with the guest, posting any late charges, and accepting payment by credit card or cash or by billing the account directly if prior arrangements have been made. Figure 10.5 shows the screen the clerk sees when checking out Mr. Farmer. An increasing number of hotels provide guests with the option of an automated check-out system utilizing the telephone or television in the guest room through which the guest can access their account and approve the ending balance. Hotels may also deliver a hard copy of the guest's folio during the night prior to check-out. The folio, which lists all guest charges and the predetermined method of payment indicated at check-in, is quietly slipped under the guest room door, typically in the early morning hours. If there are no changes, the guest can indicate so through the automated system and save time in leaving the hotel. It should also be mentioned that a number of hotel chains are testing the option of automated check-in for guests. Typically involving a lobby kiosk, the guest interfaces with a computerized system that prompts him or her through the registration process.

GUEST INFORMATION	ROOM DESIGNATION
NAME: Tom Farmer	ROOM TYPE: Dbl
PHONE: 612-999-1212	RACK RATE: 86.00
ADDRESS: 6199 Thorton Blvd	FOLIO RATE: 70.00
Minneapolis, MN	# NIGHTS: 2
SPECIAL REQUEST: Crib	EXTRAS: Crib-NC
MARKET: 12-15B	

CREDIT:

CREDIT CARD: Diners Club #99552211887712

   Exp. 9/1/06

FOLIO LIMIT: $500 BAL 270.13

Guest Check Out Display

(1) View Folio (2) Posting (3) Transfer (4) Payment

(5) Check Out (6) Print Folio

                         02   29   11:42

Figure 10.5
The check-out screen.

Even more advanced is the option for an incoming guest to preregister online. Issued with a hotel smart card, such as a loyalty card, and Internet access, once a guest has preregistered, the hotel can preprogram the allocated room lock with check-in and check-out time information. The system allows guests to use their cards to enter the hotel through special entranceways and gain elevator access to the specific guest floor. Although it is believed that there will always be a need for personal service for guests desiring the human interaction with a front-desk receptionist, the automated alterna-tive is similar to airlines now providing automated check-in for passengers who prefer to save time and forgo the pleasantries.

Where the front-desk computer is interfaced (i.e., electronically interconnected) to other systems, such as restaurant and bar point-of-sale (POS) terminals and a house-keeping department terminal, front-office clerical routines are further simplified. When guests settle a dinner or bar check by charging it to their room number, the cashier in the food or beverage outlet posts this entry on his or her POS terminal, and that post-ing is automatically entered on the guest's bill at the front-office terminal. This system ensures that all charges will be posted to the guest's bill immediately. Manual posting is required for any charges that are not automatically handled by the system. In prop-erties that do not have departments such as food and beverage interfaced to the front-office system, those charges are also posted manually. This is more time-consuming for both departments and is also likely to lead to more mistakes.

In much the same way, when housekeeping is interfaced, at the time the guest checks out, the room shows up as "vacant and dirty" on the housekeeping terminal,

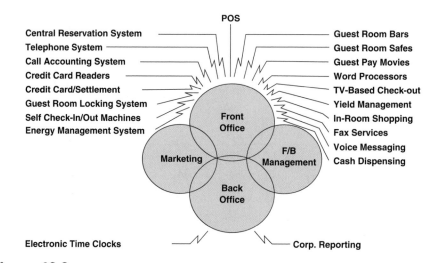

Figure 10.6

Hotel property management system interfaces. (Source: Chervenak, Keane and Company.)

indicating that the room needs to be cleaned. When housekeeping personnel have cleaned the room, they make the appropriate entry and the room is automatically added to the ready-to-rent total in the front-office terminal. Where housekeeping is not interfaced, lists of "on change" and "ready-to-rent" rooms are usually communicated back and forth by phone.

Most chain or franchised properties interface their front office not only with other departments but also with their group's central reservation system (CRS). This permits the CRS to determine room availability directly and automatically from the individual property. This is an important time-saver for front-office staff and helps maximize the usefulness of the CRS to the individual property. The PMS can also be used to automate and integrate a number of other functions in the hotel, as shown in Figure 10.6.

RESERVATIONS AND YIELD MANAGEMENT

Traditionally, the hotel industry has looked at occupancy as a measure of success. Another indicator of operational success that we have always consulted is the **average rate** per rented room (the average daily rate, or ADR). **Yield management** puts these two together and, using forecasting based on the history of past sales, sets out to get the best combination of occupancy and ADR.[1] Yield management, then, involves varying room rates according to the demand for rooms in any given time period. The argument is that when the hotel is going to be full, it makes no sense to sell any rooms at special discount rates. On the other hand, on a night when the hotel is definitely not going to fill, selling a room at a discounted price is better than not selling it at all.

Going beyond maximizing rates, hotels are using yield management to take more multiple-night (instead of single-night) reservations during busy periods on the theory that a multiple-night reservation offers less risk of having a vacant room following check-out and thus is worth more to the hotel. A potential guest, therefore, inquiring about room availability for a large event such as the Super Bowl may find that the hotel requires a minimum stay of two to three nights for this high-demand weekend. As with so much in hotel operations, careful employee training is essential to secure an effective yield management system that is operated in a way that will generate maximum revenue but not offend guests. Yield management is discussed further in Chapter 12.

Yield management has been used in a number of other industries, most widely in the airline industry. It can be used by any industry that experiences fluctuating demand, which includes most segments of the hospitality industry. As will be discussed in Chapter 12, the extraordinary growth of individuals using the Internet in booking hotel reservations, as has been the case with other travel arrangements such as airline reservations, has had a tremendous impact on the marketing and pricing of hotel rooms in all price and size ranges of properties.

HOUSEKEEPING

An essential requirement, for both business or leisure travelers staying in limited-service or luxury properties, is that the guest room be clean. The essential department of **housekeeping** is as much a production department of a hotel as the front desk and bell staff are service departments. It is clear that without clean rooms to rent, a hotel would have to close. Understanding how important a housekeeping department is to the proper functioning of a hotel, the management should always pay close attention to morale factors such as pay and worker recognition in that department. Because of the physical demands in cleaning between, on average, 16 to 18 rooms per day per housekeeper, safe and injury-free working conditions are also a priority in this department.

The housekeeping department is usually headed by an executive housekeeper. In a smaller property, this role may be held by a housekeeping supervisor. In larger properties, the executive housekeeper will have at least one assistant and several supervisors, generally known as inspectors, who supervise room attendants in designated areas. As hotels have flattened their organizational structures and empowered hourly employees, many properties have substantially reduced the number and role of inspectors, giving housekeepers the responsibility of inspecting their own rooms utilizing a checklist of cleanliness requirements.

The housekeeping department also plays a significant role in purchasing guest room supplies including linens, and guest room amenities. Guest room amenities may range from bars of soap to a full array of toiletries including shampoo, conditioner,

The housekeeping department plays a key role in keeping guest rooms looking clean and attractive. (Courtesy of Caesars Atlantic City.)

body lotion, sewing kits, and shoe-polishing cloths. Typically, the more extensive array of guest room amenities would be found in full-service and luxury properties. The housekeeping department also purchases equipment necessary to keep the hotel clean such as vacuum cleaners, carpet-care machines, and floor buffers. In addition, to be able to properly do their jobs, housekeeping employees require numerous chemicals, which must be inventoried. These cleaning products include everything from porcelain cleaners for the bathroom to glass cleaners, furniture polish, and carpet shampoos.

In most hotels, housepersons or main or maintenance workers take responsibility for cleaning the halls and public areas (lobby, elevator lobbies, ballrooms, meeting rooms). These employees also play a vital role in maintaining high cleanliness standards for a hotel.

Hotels with their own laundries often assign the supervision of that area to the housekeeping department. Generally, a working laundry supervisor or lead worker handles routine supervision under the executive housekeeper's general direction. In larger hotels, a laundry manager may well be warranted. Industry Practice Note 10.1 discusses what some hotels are doing to maximize hotel room cleanliness.

TELECOMMUNICATIONS AND CALL ACCOUNTING SYSTEMS

Because the system of accounting for hotels recognizes telephone activity as a separate department for revenue purposes, one often hears about the telephone department. Some hotels have broadened the title of this department to **"telecommunications"** to reflect not only revenue generated through guest room telephone use and public area phones, but also Internet connection services and faxes sent and/or received by guests. Only in the largest hotels, however, is there really a separate organizational unit to match this designation, whether called the telephone or telecommunications department, and in such hotels it is headed by a manager sometimes referred to as a communications manager or Private Branch Exchange (PBX) manager. The telephone service in smaller properties is handled by a person who also serves as a front-desk clerk. Many smaller properties, particularly those with 100 rooms or fewer and with automatic phone systems, often require the desk clerks to operate the phone system as part of their regular duties.

The increasing availability of voice mail and automated systems in hotels has expanded the services provided to guests—and, increasingly, expected by them. It is now common to provide voice mail in each guest room. In addition to improving the level of service available in the hotel, this has the effect of reducing staffing requirements to take and deliver guest messages. Automated voice-mail systems also minimize the translation needs seen with growing numbers of international travelers.

Housekeeping

Guest room cleanliness, regardless of the type or segment of hotel property, consistently rates of highest importance to guests. Hotel housekeeping departments are challenged with doing a thorough job of cleaning each guest room while also doing it efficiently—particularly in maximizing speed and productivity. Hyatt Hotels implemented a new approach in 79 hotels across the country aimed at more efficient and targeted housekeeping. The program, called the "Housekeeping Stay-Over Program," eliminated redundant cleaning tasks in stay-over rooms, which then allows housekeepers to focus on what matters most to those guests staying multiple nights at a Hyatt. The program was initiated from a survey of guests conducted by Hyatt. Guests stated that when first checking in to a hotel, they are most concerned about having a room that is thoroughly and properly prepared. After that, refreshing the room meets their expectations. Hyatt, as with most hotels, was having housekeepers go through the same cleaning process with each and every room, regardless of the room's status—check-in or stay over. Eliminating the redundant tasks reduced the cleaning time in a stay-over room from about 24 minutes (the average time of cleaning a room) to 15 minutes.

Other hotels have implemented similar changes. The Adam's Mark Hotel in St. Louis, Missouri, has a "Just Like Home" program. Bed sheets are changed every three days for stay-overs, unless the guest requests otherwise.

Another approach tried by some hotels is team-cleaning as compared to each housekeeper having his or her own rooms. Proponents of this approach claim that there is greater productivity in addition to reduced equipment costs. For example, instead of having a vacuum cleaner for each housekeeper, there can be one per team.

Source: Rob Heyman, "Cleaner Pastures—Shaping Up Hotel Housekeeping Programs," *Lodging Magazine*, http://www.lodgingmagazine.com/index.cfm?fm=Article.Detail@aid=113

The prevalent use of cellular telephones has certainly had a detrimental impact on hotel telephone revenue. Hotel telephone rates have typically been a source of guest complaints, and now most guests have a very accessible alternative in using their own cellular phones to bypass in-room telephone options. Facing revenue declines, many hotels have increased surcharges for telephone calls made from the hotel guest room. Some hotels allow local calls at no cost, while others charge anywhere from 50 cents to $1.00 or more for a local call. For long-distance calls, guests may pay a connection fee of about $1.50 and per-minute charges ranging from $1.00 upwards. Hotel operators justify such charges as necessary to cover the costs of the telephone departments, including salaries and equipment. According to PKF Consulting, sales in the telecommunications department dropped another 7.6 percent in 2005, which was the fifth consecutive year of revenue declines. While there are no regulations regarding what hotels can charge for direct-dialed calls, hotels are required to make information about telephone rates readily available to guests. Most hotels place rate cards next to the room telephones. The decline in telecommunications revenue is based on the increased use of cell phones, calling cards, and the growing number of hotels that offer free Internet access to guests. Combined with disgruntled guests who want to avoid hotel surcharges for telephone use, the revenue stream from telecommunications could continue to spiral downward.[2]

Not only do guests want to have an array of business services available through the hotel guest room; today's traveler expects in-room entertainment. The concept of in-room entertainment has expanded significantly in the last 15 years. Before the 1990s, a few television networks with decent reception met or exceeded the expectations of most hotel guests. Today, with individuals accustomed to satellite dishes or expanded cable networks at home, the traveler expects the same while away from home. In addition to wireless High Speed Internet Access (HSIA), technology has provided the capabilities to provide on-demand TV, video, and an assortment of in-room games. Perceived by guests as services provided by the hotel, these entertainment options may be the solution to increased guest room revenue opportunities to offset the decline in telecommunications.

UNIFORMED SERVICES STAFF

Uniformed staff who perform personal services for the guests are part of the rooms division. These include the **bell staff**, concierge, security, valet, and garage. Of course, the property classification, size, and location determine whether there is a need for these positions. We will discuss the bell staff next. Industry Practice Note 10.2 discusses the concierge.

The Bell Staff. Most limited-service hotels do not provide a bell staff because most of their guests prefer to room themselves. On the other hand, the bell staff plays an important role in the larger and more luxurious hotels. The process of rooming a guest includes more than just carrying luggage and showing a guest to a room. Rather, it begins when the front-desk receptionist assigns a room. At this point, a member of the bell staff takes charge, welcoming the guest in both word and manner. While escorting the guest to his or her room, the bell attendant has an excellent opportunity to acquaint the guest with the services and features of the hotel. Such information may include brief details about the food and beverage outlets in the hotel, as well as the available recreational amenities such as a swimming pool and fitness center and hours of operation. On entering the room, the bell attendant can provide a great service in demonstrating the room's operations and features. He or she can show the guest how to operate the air-conditioning and turn on room and bath lights. The bellperson will usually turn on the television and run through the channels and networks available.

The Concierge

In luxury hotels, the concierge offers the guests important services, including giving directions to local attractions, securing tickets to shows, and recommending local restaurants, tours, and other entertainment. The concierge knows about local transportation, tour schedules, and nearly any other information a tourist might want. The concierge, at one time more common in Europe, is increasingly being found in North American hotels as well as around the world. Conversations with a concierge at most any hotel will reveal stories of their most memorable requests, not all of which they were able to accommodate. Most requests are relatively common in nature, however, and restaurant reservations are among the most frequently encountered.

The professional organization for hotel concierges is known as Les Clefs d'Or. This is an international association of men and women concierges which first formed in 1929 when eleven concierges from the grand hotels of France realized that they could operate more effectively as a group than individually. Additional chapters of Les Clefs d'Or followed around the world. In April of 1952, delegates from nine countries gathered in Cannes to hold the first congress. The goal of Les Clefs d'Or is to help improve the quality of service provided by the concierges in their hotels and to ensure that the profession is given the recognition it deserves. The association encourages friendship and solidarity among its members and also teaches them to continually improve their professional skills. If you meet a hotel concierge wearing the association's "golden keys" pin on his or her lapel, you will know that this experienced concierge has achieved this recognition through Les Clefs d'Or.

For more information on Les Clefs d'Or, visit http://www.lcdusa.org. This Web site for Les Clefs d'Or USA provides interesting links such as "Concierge Characteristics," "Facts and Figures," and "Historical Perspective."

The Valet/Garage. As guests drive up to a hotel property, arriving in the motor lobby or porte-cochere (a covered entranceway), another important first impression is the valet who will be parking the guest's car. Many hotels outsource the valet parking operation to companies that specialize in the business of parking and retrieving guest cars. There are many liability issues associated with valet parking in any type of business. Cars are expensive commodities to be replaced or repaired. In addition, there are safety issues in employees driving the vehicles of others. For these reasons, it is not uncommon to find that the valet parkers are actually employees of a parking service that the hotel pays to run its valet operation. Many hotels offer valet parking in addition to the option of self-parking in the hotel's garage or parking area. If the hotel does not own a garage or parking lot, it may arrange with a nearby garage for guest parking. Comprehensive legal agreements with clearly specified indemnity arrangements in the event of car theft, loss, or damage are of utmost importance in working with valet operations. It is also important that the valet/garage operations adhere to the service standards of the hotel. Even if the valet/garage services are outsourced, for seamless service these operations must provide a quality experience for guests.

Gift Shop/Retail Operations. Hotels are increasingly finding a new revenue stream through retail store operations sometimes in conjunction with an online ordering option. Providing much more than the typical sundry or gift shop, hotels are finding consumers who want to buy everything from high-end bed linen and luxury mattresses to the best in bathrobes and spa products. The W Hotel in Union Square, Los Angeles, offers for sale almost anything in the hotel. The Charles Hotel in Cambridge, Massachusetts will sell artwork to guests—even pieces hanging in the hotel. A number of hotels have received added notoriety from celebrities who have publicized the hotels at which they prefer to shop.[3]

SECURITY

In a hotel of any size, **security** is a major concern. In a large hotel, security may be a department, but no matter what its organizational status, security has become the focus of top management attention.[4] Security came forcefully to the attention of hotel operators in 1976 when a well-known singer, Connie Francis, was raped at knifepoint in a Long Island motel. That such a terrible event could happen in a lodging property was enough to gain management's attention—but the $2.5 million awarded to the victim by the jury underlined that concern. The door in her room appeared to be locked but could be opened. In fact, security practices in many hotels had become lax. The jury found that the hotel had not exercised **reasonable care**. The question of reasonable care has been a continuing concern for operators since the Francis case. In recent years, bad publicity on television and in the newspapers has heightened hotel managers' attention to this problem.

In a survey of over 42,000 U.S. hotels conducted in 2006 by the American Hotel & Lodging Association and Smith Travel Research, it was found that hoteliers are increasingly improving critical aspects of hotel security. Many of these improvements were the result of a new generation of hotels now in operation as well as renovations that have incorporated security features. The survey found an increase in the use of closed-circuit cameras (CCTV), enhanced interior and exterior lighting, and greater access control through card readers including vehicle access to garages and parking areas.[5]

Many hotel chains have increased security with the elevated terror government-issued alerts. One example, Starwood Hotels & Resorts, parent of the Sheraton, Westin, and "W" chains, follows this system. Measures include increased security at entrances, loading docks, and in hotel garages and more scrutiny of unattended bags and cars. Armed guards are stationed at some properties. At the highest alert level, hotels in the company will typically not store luggage. In some areas of the world where terrorism is a more prevalent threat, such as the Middle East, hotels have installed metal detectors at entrances as standard equipment. In Israel, the government has made gas masks available free or for a discount to guests.[6]

Most hotel guests today do not get alarmed by security measures taken by hotels. In fact, most would perceive a strong positive relationship between good service and good security. As hotels strive to provide high-level, comprehensive security, there are technical components as well as management components that must be addressed. The matter of security can be approached as a technical problem as well as a management problem. Both approaches are probably necessary to reach a solution.

Technical Problems in Security. The largest technical commitment on the part of hotel operators has been the replacement of the metal key with electronic or card-based locks, a practice that is now being mandated by many franchise systems. A new combination is electronically or mechanically encoded on the key card with each guest registration. The card contains a magnetic strip that allows it to work (this is why these are commonly referred to as "**magstrip**" systems). The lock in the guest room door is reset electronically by the first entry of the electronic or card key. In the case of an online system, the door is reset from the front desk at the time of registration. Where installation of new key systems is not economically feasible, removal of room numbers from the keys, to be replaced by coded letter or number identification systems, is a minimum requirement. The guest room key and lock are an obvious and essential first line of defense for the guest's personal security. Hotels are beginning to move beyond the magstrip systems now, and many have introduced "smart card" technology, in which the same card that allows guests into their rooms also serves as a guest identification card and can be used for room charges. Contactless smart card technology, now available, does not even require that the key card be put into the lock. Instead, one can just approach the lock and the door opens.[7] The industry is also rapidly moving toward the use of biometric locking systems that can recognize an individual's fingerprint, whether it is for a guest to gain access to his or her room or to the in-room safe. A quick thumb scan avoids the use of any key or card.

Managerial Problems in Security. Management's problem is not just to protect the guest; the question of high damage settlements must be weighed, too. A minimal approach to ensuring that a hotel has exercised reasonable care for the guest's safety begins with a professional assessment, a broad overview of the hotel and the security of its guests and their property. With this overview in hand, the hotel management can take the steps necessary to exercise reasonable care. While increased technology as described above helps in offering more effective security option, the human element of having a sufficient number of well-trained security employees cannot be minimized. Just the presence of security equipment, whether electronic locks or CCTV systems, does not guarantee guests' safety. Only trained staff who know how to observe guest activities and respond appropriately should monitor the CCTV system. A written guide should, in addition, provide specific instructions for various emergencies with detailed response information also covered in training. There is no substitute for well-trained security staff, in sufficient numbers, to implement a comprehensive, well-thought-out security plan that ultimately involves all hotel employees.[8]

In essence, every employee of a hotel is part of the security team in staying constantly aware of what is happening in every area of the hotel property, being observant of suspicious occurrences, and following a standardized reporting system in a timely fashion.

Hotel Food and Beverage Operations

Originally, the hotel restaurant was designed to give a traveler in a strange city a place to eat where the food would be good, or at least palatable—and safe to eat. In recent years, however, the restaurant industry has grown in diversity of both concepts and menus. Moreover, that growth has meant the spread of restaurants into more and more locations, making restaurant food service readily available. Many successful chain restaurants carry well-known brand names to which travelers are accustomed. In the face of stiffening restaurant competition for the hotel guest's food and beverage patronage, some hoteliers have developed hotels, such as the economy and all-suite properties discussed in Chapter 9, that offer only very limited food service—usually a complimentary breakfast and, in all-suite operations, complimentary cocktails in the evening.

On the other hand, in full-service hotels, the food service operation continues to be not only a vital service but a key competitive weapon. Many full-service hotels have several quite different food outlets. For example, one urban full-service convention hotel offers a gourmet penthouse Russian restaurant, an authentic Polynesian restaurant, a more traditional three-meal restaurant, and a take-out service for guests needing food items on the go. All of these are in addition to the room service option. A 24-hour operating room service department is expected for five-star and five-diamond hotels.

Creative approaches in hotel food and beverage operations are not limited to varied theme restaurants within the hotel. For example, several Ritz-Carlton hotels feature a chef's table where four guests can eat in the kitchen and watch and interact with the chef during the preparation of a five-course meal.[9]

Hotel restaurants, such as the Bacchanal Restaurant in Caesars Atlantic City, often adopt themes that add to the overall experience. (Courtesy of Caesars Atlantic City.)

Offering several restaurant outlets extends the services available to the guest—and helps keep the guest's food business in the hotel. In a recent listing of Mobil Travel Guide's five-star restaurants in the United States, many are located in hotels. Renowned restaurants, located in hotels, have the added advantage of spotlighting the hotel's identity and bringing in out-of-town guests as well as local clientele who may, in turn, refer guests to the hotel.[10]

Many hotels in recent years have emphasized the **food and beverage department**'s role as a profit center, that is, a specifically identified, profitable part of the hotel's operation. The typical hotel food and beverage department in the United States creates about half as much in dollar sales as does the rooms department but generally provides only between 10 and 20 percent as much profit.

BANQUETS

Some large properties offer a catering department (or banquet department) headed by a catering manager who books and sells banquets. Smaller properties include this activity among the restaurant manager's duties. Larger properties have special full- and part-time banquet service staffs. Smaller properties draw banquet service personnel from their regular crew and often supplement them with part-time employees.

Banquets are often profitable, but once again, in many properties the banquet menus and banquet rooms are meant principally to serve the rooms department. Thus, a meeting may occupy one conference room all day. Perhaps the hotel supplies a coffee break and a luncheon in another room. Typically a hotel would waive charges for the meeting room if a sufficient number of guest rooms are being reserved or if the food and beverage revenue are high enough. If such a meeting accounts for 20 or 30 guest room rentals—or even only 10 or 15—the logic we have mentioned before clearly applies. The 70 percent profit on room sales makes this use of banquet space desirable.

Banquet space can be used to sell guest rooms by accommodating groups, associations, and organizations. (Courtesy of Caesars Atlantic City.)

FOOD PRODUCTION

In most properties, the person in charge of food production is called the executive chef. A chef is a person who has completed, either formally or informally, the training that qualifies him or her to be an excellent professional cook. The chef should also be an effective manager who can purchase food; hire, train, and discipline employees; and plan appetizing meals priced to yield a profit. A highly experienced, well-trained chef capable of large-scale food production is an investment for the typical hotel. Salaries of such chefs are very competitive. A skilled, talented chef, however, will usually help the success of the hotel's food and beverage operation, thereby offering a good return on the investment.

Food service is a critical component of full-service hotels. (Courtesy of Las Vegas Convention and Visitors Authority.)

An increasingly common title in American food service is food production manager. Although these managers are almost invariably accomplished cooks, they emphasize kitchen management and rely on strict adherence to written recipes, rather than on their craft skills, to ensure quality. The type of management chosen by a property generally reflects the dollar volume of food sales. More sales may permit the expense of a chef or food production manager. Smaller properties may have to content themselves with a head or lead cook. In this case, the restaurant manager generally works more closely with the kitchen.

With the greater availability of quality frozen prepared foods as well as the growing acceptance of limited menus, an approach to food service that requires limited culinary skills is becoming more and more common in hotels that don't try to reach the full-service or luxury standards.

Large convention properties may support a separate banquet sub-department of workers who prepare only banquet food. Some properties even use a separate banquet kitchen and have a designated banquet chef. The banquet culinary team of a hotel has tremendous opportunity in impacting the hotel's food and beverage reputation because of the volume of people served. A large convention hotel could serve several hundred or even several thousand individuals through banquet operations.

Hotels may also have additional specialized culinary sections of the main kitchen. These specialization areas include the garde manger area (where cold appetizers and salads are prepared), a butchering section, and a pastry shop (involving baking breads and preparing pastries and desserts). Typically, larger hotels or upscale, luxury hotels will have these specialized culinary sections.

SANITATION AND UTILITY

CAREERS IN HOSPITALITY

Sanitation is so important that many hospitality programs offer entire courses on the subject. Our purpose here is simply to repeat the point made in Chapter 4 regarding the importance of dishwashers, pot washers, and the cleanup crew often referred to in hotels as the stewarding department. In Chapter 3, we noted that many students find that the only summer jobs available are in these areas. They may not be the most interesting jobs, but as we said earlier, they provide an ideal observation point for learning about how a food service operation functions.

There is another reason for mastering these jobs while a student. The job of an assistant restaurant manager includes responsibility for this function in most hospitality operations—restaurants, hotels, and on-site food service. It is most commonly assigned to people just out of management training programs. Success in this job often launches a successful career, and a good working relationship with employees is helpful in this entry-level position. Few things will help you toward that goal more than the ability to roll up your sleeves and help out when one of your crew gets stuck. (Be careful, however, not to turn yourself permanently into a dishwasher just to win popularity contests.) You need not plan to spend your life in the dish room, but never be afraid to say you started there.

LEASED RESTAURANTS

The practice of leasing restaurants has become increasingly common. We can summarize the advantages and disadvantages of doing so. By leasing a restaurant, a full-service property permits hotel management to focus its attention on the more profitable rooms department instead of the time-consuming food service operation. In addition, that difficult operation is taken over by experts, often with a major franchised brand. Further, the hotel operator can count on a certain amount of guaranteed revenue as a result of the lease payment. On the other hand, one of the hotel's service departments is put in the hands of another company, which is concerned with its own objectives and profits. This topic is discussed again in Chapter 12. Industry Practice Note 10.3 discusses some of the issues to consider before outsourcing a food and beverage operation.

Staff and Support Departments

Some departments or activities in a hotel offer no direct guest services. Instead, they maintain systems for the property as a whole, such as sales, marketing, and engineering. Along with accounting and human resources, these departments are typically referred to as the **support areas** of a hotel. The departments support those departments that do provide direct guest services.

SALES AND MARKETING

With competition among lodging properties never more intense, the functions of marketing and sales are crucial to the success of a hotel. The main function of marketing

Pros and Cons of Outsourcing Food and Beverage Operations

One of the benefits of outsourcing food and beverage outlets is that, particularly when teaming up with a high-profile chef like Emeril or Wolfgang Puck, foot traffic and brand identity can surge. Casino hotels, such as the MGM Grand Hotel in Las Vegas, have certainly benefited. It contains both an Emeril restaurant as well as one of Wolfgang Puck's operations. Even with these types of limelight partnerships, most hotels do not outsource their food and beverage operations. According to the American Hotel & Lodging Association's 2006 survey, less than 10 percent of hotel companies had outsourced restaurants. In 2005, food and beverage sales at full-service hotels accounted for 30 percent of revenue, according to PKF Hospitality Research.

There are numerous ways to manage a restaurant partnership. A restaurant can lease space in a hotel, run the operation, and pay rent and utilities. A hotel can partner with a restaurant and operate the restaurant but pay a licensing fee for the right to use the restaurant's name. One complication that happens frequently is the determination of who will provide room service. One of the key recommendations, if outsourcing, is to pick the right partner (hotel or restaurant) to build on one another's brands.

Source: R. Little, "Five Issues to Consider Before Outsourcing Food and Beverage," Lodging Archive, http://www.lodgingmagazine.com/index.cfm.fm

is creating customers—guests that will visit a hotel and hopefully will become repeat visitors on a regular and frequent basis. Creating customers equates to having products or services that people want. For many potential guests, it may be the wide availability of meeting rooms, a business center within the hotel, and guest rooms with fast-speed Internet service. For others, the availability of spa services and recreational amenities may be key. A second marketing function, therefore, is encouraging the guests to choose your property by emphasizing all of the services and features that make the property pleasant or convenient or even, perhaps, particularly unique. Finally, marketing involves promoting the property among various potential guests and groups of guests. (This duty is often thought to be all there is to marketing, but it actually comes after the first two.)

Marketing is a general management function that involves all levels of the operation. One important day-to-day activity in this area is personal selling. In large properties, sales managers and sales associates are responsible for finding sales leads and following up on them with sales calls and booking functions. Larger properties typically divide the sales function into specific target markets to allow sales managers and associates a more defined focus. For example, a larger urban property would typically include national conventions as one target market. Other markets might be the local corporate segment or a target market including several components collectively known as SMERF business (social, military, education, religious, and fraternal groups). Determination of just which market to approach is a crucial top-management decision usually made by the general manager, the sales manager, and even the ownership. Corporate policy may dictate these decisions in chains, but most often the precise market for a particular property must be specifically designated by the local management. (Some properties hire outside sales firms, called hotel representatives, to undertake sales activities for them in key markets.)

In smaller hotels, the general manager is responsible for managing sales. He or she will commonly make the sales calls personally and entertain people from potential sales accounts in the hotel. In some properties, the general manager is assisted in this work by a full- or part-time sales representative.

Because marketing is essential, there is a major trade association, the Hospitality Sales Marketing Association International (HSMAI, formerly the Hotel Sales and Marketing Association). The association conducts educational and informational programs for both sales personnel and general management. This organization, which publishes excellent materials on sales and marketing, is a good one to join on graduation or as a student if there is a chapter on your campus.

ACCOUNTING

The role of accounting has changed over the years and no longer just involves bookkeeping and financial reporting. Hotels increasingly look to the controller, who heads up the accounting department, as a key member of the management team who can proactively advise and guide the hotel to increased profitability through better controls and asset management. In large hotels, in addition to the controller, the accounting department may contain several functional areas, including accounts payable (the area overseeing paying incoming bills incurred by the hotel), accounts receivable (the area receiving payments from various sources), and payroll (which oversees paying hotel employees). Additional accounting positions may include a credit manager who works with groups and individuals prior to arriving at the hotel to approve their billing arrangements based on their credit history. The hotel may also have a general cashier or cashier supervisor who works with the front-office manager and food and beverage managers in overseeing employees who handle cash as part of their job responsibilities. Preparing the monthly profit-and-loss statement, working with department managers in developing and implementing the hotel's budget, and overseeing the hotel's cost control systems are routine accounting responsibilities. Chains generally develop sophisticated corporate accounting departments that supervise work at the individual property. In a small property, on the other hand, the work is usually done by some combination of the innkeeper's secretary, a chief clerk, and an outside accountant.

When guests check out, they may pay their bills with cash, but they often charge this expense instead. The accounts receivable (bills owed by guests) in a hotel are divided into two parts. First, a **house ledger** (or tray ledger), kept at the front desk, is made up of bills owed by guests in the house. Charges by guests posted after they have checked out and charges by other persons, such as restaurant patrons not in the hotel, are kept in what is often called the **city ledger**. The name is derived from an earlier time when charging hotel bills was not common. Instead, guests paid cash when they checked out, and any charge not in the house ledger was a charge from some local customer, someone "in the city" who had a charge account at the hotel rather than someone "in the house." Incidentally, the word *ledger* originally referred to a book on whose pages these records were kept. Today, records of charges are usually maintained on a computer. The function, however, and even the terminology are the same.

HUMAN RESOURCES

Lodging is a labor-intensive industry with a relatively high employee turnover. As a result, issues related to human resources are an important consideration in any hotel and are commonly placed under the staff supervision of a human-resources department. This department may be responsible for any or all of the following functions: employee recruiting, developing and maintaining job descriptions, overseeing the employee selection process, providing employees with orientation to the company and the hotel, designing and reviewing compensation patterns and benefit packages, and complying with government labor regulations. Large hotels may actually have specialists in key human-resource areas such as employment, wage and benefit administration, labor relations (if the hotel is unionized), employee relations, and training. Most hotels, however, have human-resource generalists who are proficient in most or all of the specialization areas. Although the human-resources department, as noted previously, is closely involved with the employment process, the hiring decisions are usually made by the appropriate department head. While the human-resources department does not directly produce revenue, most hotels realize that a comprehensive, well-run human-resources function can definitely impact the bottom line. By better hiring and training, reduced turnover, fewer work-related accidents, and maximized employee satisfaction, which positively impacts productivity, the hotel's bottom line does benefit.

As we noted a moment ago, in large properties, a human-resources department manages most of the processes just listed. In smaller properties, this work is done by the manager and his or her secretary.

ENGINEERING

The engineering function is so important that many hospitality management programs have one or more courses devoted to the disciplines that support it. Once again, we will simply describe briefly the work of this area. Large- and medium-sized hotels usually employ a chief engineer, who supervises an engineering staff. Together, they are responsible for operating the hotel's heating and air-conditioning; for maintaining its refrigeration, lighting, and transportation (elevator) systems; and for overseeing all of the hotel's mechanical equipment. Breakdowns in these areas seriously inconvenience guests. And, of course, utility costs have always been significant and, in recent years, have been increasing at an alarming rate. Technological advances have been significant in the engineering area. Computerized energy management systems allow hotels to have enhanced control over energy usage whether it involves shutting down systems in unoccupied parts of the hotel during slow periods or regulating temperature control throughout the day in different hotel sections. The engineering department typically oversees a hotel's waste management program involving environmentally conscious programs such as recycling.

In small properties, the engineer is often more of a general repairperson who carries out routine maintenance and minor repairs. Outside service people supply the more specialized maintenance skills. In these properties, the innkeeper often supervises the engineering (or maintenance) function.

In any property, large or small, general management should at least do the following:

1. Determine what periodic maintenance of equipment is required (oiling, filter changing, making minor adjustments, and the like).

2. Establish a schedule for accomplishing that work.

3. Develop a reporting system and physical inspection system that assures management the work is carried out properly and on time.

Income and Expense Patterns and Control

As with so many subjects discussed in this chapter, whole courses are often devoted to the topic of this section. Our purpose here, therefore, is to provide you with an understanding of the control structure of a hotel and a limited introduction to the vocabulary of control in hotels and restaurants.

As will be described below, there are a number of key operating ratios that are used in analyzing the financial results of a hotel. Table 10.1 displays one type of financial analysis, ratios to total revenues. In this table, the figures are for full-service hotels.

To determine the property's overall efficiency, we deduct **undistributed operating expenses** from the total of the various departmental incomes. These costs—administrative and general expense; franchise fees including marketing fees, marketing, property operation, and maintenance; utility costs; and other unallocated operated departments—are judged to be costs that pertain to all departments in a way that cannot be perfectly assigned to any one department. For example, the salary of the general manager and his or her assistants would be located under administrative and general (A&G).

The amount remaining after deducting these four categories of expense from the total of departmental income is called total **income before fixed charges**. This figure is probably the best measure of the success not only of the total property but of the general manager as well. For this reason, many managers receive bonuses based on their performance as measured by this figure. The remaining costs, known as fixed charges or **capital costs**, include expenses such as the management fee, property taxes, and other municipal charges and insurance and are a direct function of the cost of the building and its furnishings and fixtures. The responsibility for these costs typically includes the owners, who made the decisions when the property was first built and furnished.

Key Operating Ratios and Terms. In Chapter 4, we introduced some key ratios and food service terms; these are used in hotel food service as well. In addition, the hotel industry has other indicators of an operation's results.

Occupancy is generally indicated as a percentage:

$$\text{Occupancy percentage} = \text{Rooms sold} \div \text{Total rooms available}$$

Average rate is an indication of the front desk's success in gaining the full rate on rooms sold rather than discounting:

$$\text{Average rate} = \text{Dollar sales} \div \text{Number of rooms sold}$$

The average rate is also a mix of the double-occupancy rooms sold (rooms with two or more guests). This is reflected by the following formula:

$$\text{Number of guests per occupied room} = \text{Number of guests} \div \text{Number of occupied rooms}$$

THE UNIFORM SYSTEM OF ACCOUNTS

Hotel accounting is generally guided by the **uniform system of accounts** for hotels, which identifies important profit centers in hotels as revenue departments. The uniform system first arranges the reporting of income and expenses so that the relative efficiency of each major department can be measured by the departmental income.

TABLE 10.1

Selected Revenue and Expense Items for 2005, Full Service Hotels: Ratios to Total Revenue

Revenue:	
Rooms	67.8%
Food, including Other Income	22.2
Beverage	4.6
Telecommunications	1.1
Other Operated Depts.	3.1
Rentals/Other Income	1.2
Total Revenues	100.0%
Departmental Costs and Expenses	
Rooms	17.9
Food	18.0
Beverage	2.3
Telecommunications	1.0
Other Operated Departments	1.9
Total Operated	
Departmental Income	59.0%
Undistributed Operating Expenses	
Administrative and General	9.0
Franchise Fees, including Marketing Fees	3.5
Marketing	5.1
Property Operations/Maintenance	4.8
Utility Costs	4.3
Total Undistributed Expenses	26.7%
Total Management Fees	
Property Taxes and Insurance	7.3%
Income before other fixed charges	25.1%

Source: PKF Hospitality ResearchTrends, 2006.

The **RevPAR**, or revenue per available room, is calculated as follows:

RevPAR = Rooms revenue ÷ Available rooms or

Paid Occupancy Percentage × ADR (Average Room Rate)

Because housekeeping is the largest and most controllable labor cost in the rooms department, many hotels compute the average number of rooms cleaned with the following formula:

Average rooms cleaned per room attendant day

= Number of rooms occupied ÷ Number of eight-hour room attendant shifts

All of these ratios are usually computed for the day, the month to date, and the year at year's end. Comparisons of these indicators with earlier operating results and with the budget provide important clues to an operation's problems or success.

Capital Structure. We will discuss some of the financial dimensions of the hotel business further in Chapter 11. At this point, however, we need to describe briefly the capital costs found on the hotel's income statement because they are a significant part of a hotel's cost structure. Capital costs include rent, depreciation, and interest. Related costs, such as property taxes and insurance, can be included here because these taxes or fees are dependent on the value of the land and the building.

Depreciation is a bookkeeping entry that reflects the assumption that the original costs of the hotel building, furniture, and fixtures should be gradually written off over these items' useful life. Interest, of course, is the charge paid to the lenders for the use of their funds.

The hotel industry is capital-intensive. That is, it uses a large part of its revenue to pay for capital costs, including real-estate taxes. Close to 20 cents of every sales dollar go to cover costs related to the hotel's capital structure.

Hotel development is attractive to some investors because it is highly leveraged. Leverage, as a financial term, refers to the fact that a small amount of an investor's capital can often call forth much larger amounts of money lent by banks or insurance companies on a mortgage. A fixed amount of interest is paid for this capital, and so if the hotel is profitable, the investor's earning power will be greatly magnified, but the investor's modest initial investment need not be increased. Earnings go up, but interest does not. Nor does investment—hence, the word leverage.

Leverage, as developers have discovered repeatedly, can be a double-edged sword. Operating profits boom in good times and cover fixed interest payments many times over. When times turn bad or the effects of overbuilding begin to be felt, revenues fall, but interest rates (and required repayments on the principal of the loan) do not. The result can be a wave of bankruptcies.

Entry Ports and Careers

A recent graduate with a hospitality degree may question what the best career path is if his or her long-term goal is to be a hotel general manager. There is no one path leading to the GM position. Most hotels promote based on performance, so work habits and accomplishments, regardless of the position, are key. Most typically, hotels look toward the two major operating divisions, rooms and food and beverage, to supply general managers. Some hotel chains have a specific development plan involving cross-training for promising division heads who aspire to become general managers. A rooms division head, with no food and beverage experience, would have an opportunity to work briefly in the food and beverage division, just as an aspiring food and beverage director would cross-train in the rooms division. General managers may also have a sales and marketing background or an accounting background. Although there are general managers that started in human resources, engineering, or culinary, these areas tend to be very specialized with fewer moves to general manager positions.

FRONT OFFICE

CAREERS IN
HOSPITALITY

Many people begin their career in the lodging industry in the front office, the nerve center of the hotel and the place where its most important sales occur. With the growing importance of the limited-service property, moreover, the front office increases in prominence because in those properties it is a critical area of technical knowledge. On the other hand, we should note that front-office techniques can be mastered fairly quickly. Moreover, this still leaves a good many of the hotel's important operating functions outside the front office yet to be learned. Although some executives have risen to general manager from the front office, most of them are found in small properties. If your ambitions include advancement to general manager, you will want to think carefully about building on a successful front-office experience by adding experience in another area. In a limited-service property, this should probably be marketing.

Many people find front-office work, with its constant change and frequent contact with guests, the most rewarding of careers. Moreover, improved pay scales in this area in recent years have upgraded the long-term attractiveness of this work, as has the increasingly sophisticated use of computers. Another advantage of this area is a more or less fixed work schedule, although the afternoon shift's hours (from 3:00 P.M. to 11:00 P.M.) and those of the night auditor (from 11:00 P.M. to 7:00 A.M.) are viewed by many as drawbacks to those specific jobs.

ACCOUNTING

It is certainly true that during the Great Depression of the 1930s, many successful managers were accountants. Today, however, accounting has become a specialized field, and successful training in this area can be so time-consuming that it may be difficult to master the other areas of the operation. Although accounting may not offer as easy a route to the general manager's slot as it once did, it does offer interesting and prestigious work for those who like to work with numbers. Moreover, the hours in this area tend to be reasonably regular, the pay is usually good, and the position is prestigious.

Although accounting per se is not as common a route to general manager as it once was, a new offshoot of accounting, operations analysis, is quite a different story. Operations analysts conduct special cost studies either under the direction of the auditor or comptroller or as a special assistant to the general manager. Some operations analysts work in corporate headquarters. The operations analyst's job is such a good training ground for young managers that a regular practice of rotation through this job for promising managers has become, in some companies, a feature of management development.

SALES AND MARKETING

The key to the success of any property involves having sales. Thus, it is not surprising that many successful hotel operators have a sales background. On the other hand, salespeople often find that a grounding in front-office procedures and in food and beverage operations (with special emphasis, respectively, on reservations and banquet operations) leads to success in sales. Successful sales personnel are much in demand, and a career in sales offers interesting and financially rewarding work to those interested in this aspect of hotel work.

The importance of sales and marketing tends to increase when there is an oversupply of rooms in a market. Increasingly, the marketing manager for a hotel is asked to conduct market research or to analyze market research done by others. Indeed, a common requirement for senior positions in marketing is the ability to prepare a marketing plan. Such a plan evaluates the local environment and the competition, sets goals for the plan period (usually one to three years), and presents the strategy and tactics to fulfill the plan. A solid educational background is a great help to the modern hotel marketing manager.

FOOD AND BEVERAGE

Food and beverage is one of the most demanding as well as exciting areas of the hotel operation. Success calls for the ability to deal effectively with two separate groups of skilled employees, cooks and serving personnel. Along with mastering both product cost control techniques (for both food and alcoholic beverages) and employee-scheduling techniques, the food and beverage manager must also work in sanitation and housekeeping and master the skills of menu writing. He or she must complete all these duties against at least three unyielding deadlines a day: breakfast, lunch, and dinner.

An advantage of careers in food and beverage is career progression flexibility. Accomplished management and supervisory people in the food and beverage field almost always enjoy the option of moving to work outside the hotel in restaurants, clubs, or on-site food service. Although food and beverage probably requires longer hours than does any other area in the business, it is typically a well-paid position and offers not only career flexibility but unusually solid job security. Finally, it forms a sound basis for advancement into general management.

Owning Your Own Hotel

Many students are attracted to the hospitality management field because they would like someday to own their own businesses. Whereas new hotels require large investments, existing operations can sometimes, under special circumstances of two different kinds, be purchased with little or no investment. First, after a wave of overbuilding and during economic recessions (and particularly when these two occur simultaneously), bankruptcies become common. In addition, when banks must take over a hotel, they need someone to handle operations. They are often willing to give an opportunity for an ownership interest to a person with the know-how to take the property off their hands.

Some older hotels in smaller cities offer another kind of opportunity. They may have lost their competitiveness as hotels while still occupying prime downtown real estate in a good food and beverage location. Because of this fact, together with an older hotel's extensive banquet facilities and liquor license, the property may be revitalized by a well-run and imaginatively promoted food operation. The profits of that food operation may then be plowed back into improving the hotel facilities. The improved facilities and the property's improved reputation, earned by its newly successful food and beverage operation, often result in a greatly improved rooms business. Examples of such operations can be found in many parts of the country. Where they are found, they always share these three characteristics: excellence in the food operation; unusually effective promotion, generally enhanced by the manager's community involvement; and very, very hard work by that manager, who seems to live and breathe the hotel and restaurant business.

In summary, the lodging business offers many rewarding careers in front office, accounting, marketing and sales, and food and beverage, and depending upon the individual and the circumstances, any one of them can lead to the top. For those whose ambition and temperament make them want to extend themselves, the top job is certainly within reach and ownership is in sight.

Summary

The first topic we discussed in this chapter was the major functional areas of a hotel and who runs them. Although big hotels have true departments and department managers, smaller hotels would designate these as areas, supervised by lead employees.

We next examined the rooms side of the hotel. The front office is particularly important, as it is the guests' first real contact with the hotel. The front office generally has a morning clerk, an afternoon clerk, and a night auditor, all with duties that both differ and overlap. All help in making reservations, generally through a computerized reservation system.

The property management system makes the operation of the front office more efficient and usually links it electronically to the hotel's other departments and, more often than not, to the hotel chain's central reservation service. Reservation systems often make use of yield management systems that are designed to get the best total dollar revenue possible through a mix of occupancy and average daily rate. Security is a concern that can be addressed technically through improved door-locking systems and other devices. Managerially, security involves ensuring that the hotel is exercising reasonable care for security of the guest's person and property by establishing an overall security system for the property. Other rooms-side departments are the telecommunications department, the housekeeping department, and the bell staff.

The food and beverage department is very important to the full-service hotel, as it may determine whether guests return to the hotel (or come in the first place). We described the kinds of restaurants that various types of hotels offer, banquet facilities (if any), food production, and sanitation and utility.

We next looked at hotels' staff and support departments: sales and marketing, engineering, and accounting. The accounting department is sometimes referred to as the back office. We explained hotel departmental income and expenses, operating ratios and terms, and finally, capital costs.

We finished the chapter with a look at the best routes to advancement in the hotel industry—front office, rooms division, food and beverage, sales and marketing, accounting—and the advantages and disadvantages of each. We also discussed the possibility of owning your own hotel.

Key Words and Concepts

Rooms department	Security: reasonable care
Front office	Magstrip
Night auditor	Food and beverage department
Auditing process	Support areas
Property management system (PMS)	House ledger
	City ledger
Average rate	Undistributed operating expenses
Yield management	Income before fixed charges
Housekeeping	Capital costs
Telecommunications	Uniform system of accounts
Bell staff	RevPAR

Review Questions

1. How does the organizational structure differ in large hotels and small ones?

2. Describe some of the duties of the morning clerk, the afternoon clerk, and the night auditor.

3. How is technology being utilized to provide greater hotel security for guests?

4. What are the benefits of a property management system? How does it make the front office run more smoothly?

5. What is the purpose of yield management? What problems does it pose?

6. Describe the different kinds of restaurants that a large hotel might have.

7. What are the advantages of the sanitation and stewarding area for a summer job?

8. What are typical departmental expenses for the rooms division and for the food and beverage division of a full-service hotel?

9. What are capital costs? How important are they in hotels?

Internet Exercises

1. **Site name:** *Lodging* Magazine

   URL: www.lodgingmagazine.com

   Background information: *Lodging* magazine profiles leaders driving hospitality to new heights, designers breaking the mold, and general managers applying new solutions to age-old problems in hospitality. The 30-year-old magazine reports on restaurant and food trends, best practices, and industry events.

Exercises:

a. Click on the "Operations" tab on the Web site. Read and scan several articles under this tab. Describe some of the challenges currently facing lodging managers in the operations area.

b. Click on the "Marketing" tab on the Web site. Read and scan several articles under this tab. Describe some of the challenges currently facing lodging managers in the marketing area.

c. What other operational categories are covered in the magazine?

2. **Site name:** *HOTELS* magazine

   URL: www.hotelsmag.com

   Background information: This publication serves the worldwide hotel market in 170 countries. *HOTELS* magazine covers the 100+-room hotels in the United States and the 50+-room hotels in the rest of the world that account for 76 percent of all worldwide hotel revenue. In addition, *HOTELS* magazine covers hotel management companies and major chain headquarters.

   Exercises:

   a. Read several articles under the "Editorial Archive" tab. Describe how hotels are changing to meet the challenges facing them in the lodging industry.

   b. Choose a challenge that is facing the hotel industry today. Scan several articles under the "Editorial Archive" tab and describe how the lodging industry is addressing that challenge.

   c. Describe how hotels are using different design techniques as a sales and marketing tool.

3. **Site name:** Hotel Property Management Systems

   URL: www.google.com

   AlltheWeb.com—www.alltheweb.com

   Yahoo—www.yahoo.com

   MSN Search—search.msn.com

   AltaVista—www.altavista.com

   Background information: Hotel property management systems improve operational efficiency by eliminating repetitive tasks and improve service by providing information more quickly and accurately, thereby improving operational control.

   Exercises:

   a. Using a search engine of your choice, enter the words "hotel property management system." From the results, choose two vendors of a property management system and identify the features and capabilities of both systems.

   b. Discuss the similarities and differences of the two systems.

   c. Based on features, which system would you choose if you were the general manager of a hotel? Why?

4. **Site name:** *Lodging* magazine

   URL: www.lodgingmagazine.com

   Background information: Link to Lodging Magazine through the AH&LA's Web site. Based on articles that can be downloaded in sections such as *Operations,* *Finance,* and *Technology,* answer the following questions:

   a. What are three current top priorities in the lodging industry?

   b. As a future manager in the industry, what would you consider to be the top priority in the lodging industry?

   c. If you were faced with implementing your top priority that you indicated in (b), how would you approach the challenge?

Notes

1. A good explanation of the concept of yield management can be found in Bill Quain, Michael Sansbury, and Dennis Quinn, "Revenue Enhancement," *Cornell Hotel and Restaurant Administration Quarterly*, April 1999, pp. 76–83. Yield management is also described more fully by one of its originators in lodging, Eric Orkin, in his article "Boosting Revenues Through Yield Management," *Cornell Hotel and Restaurant Administration Quarterly*, February 1988, pp. 52–58. More recent articles exploring yield management include J. Higley's "Discounting Isn't Bad When It's Done Correctly," *Hotel & Motel Management*, July 21, 2003, Vol. 218, Issue 13, p. 8; P. Yesawich's "The Trick to Discounting Is Using Good Judgment," *Hotel & Motel Management*, June 2, 2003, Vol. 218, Issue 10, p. 12; and S. Kimes' "Perceived Fairness of Yield Management," *Cornell Hotel and Restaurant Administration Quarterly*, February 2002, 43(1), p. 21.

2. Hospitality Research Group, PKF Consulting, Trends 2006.

3. P. Garfinkel, "Take the Hotel Room Home," December 13, 2006, *New York Times* online, http://www.nytimes.com/2006/12/12/business/12hotel.html?adxnnl=1&adxnnlx=116602.

4. Hotel security is such an important topic that entire textbooks have been written on the subject. A very good source of current information relating to this area is the *Hotel Security Report*, published by Robert Rusting. In addition to hotel security, this publication covers security related to casinos and resort properties. More details are available at http://www.rustingpubs.com/noname.html.

5. P. Hayward, "Designing for Security." *Lodging* archives, http://www.lodgingmagazine.com/index.cfm?fm=Article.Detail&aid=99.

6. Jayne Clark, "How Safe Is Your Hotel?" *USA Today*, March 28, 2003, p.1D.

7. Carlo Wolff, "Security Technology Business Brightening," *Lodging Hospitality*, March 1, 2003, p. 38.

8. Anthony Marshall, "Someone to Watch Over Me Should Be Camera Standard," *Hotel & Motel Management*, November 18, 2002, p. 10.

9. Kate Brennan, "How to Get Guests Hungry for the Hotel Restaurant," *Lodging Hospitality*, September 15, 2000, p. 561.

10. www.mobil.com/mobil_consumer/travel/winners/winners_content.html.

The Hospitality Industry

(The Lanesborough London, Courtesy of Rosewood Hotels & Resorts.)

CHAPTER ELEVEN

Forces Shaping the Hotel Business

The Purpose of this Chapter

Lodging is a capital-intensive business, and so capital plays a major role in shaping the hotel business. In just the recent past, lodging has seen a major inflow of funds from sources that were not formerly available to most hotels. Lodging is a unique industry in that it is cyclical and also characterized by long lead times on projects. As a result, supply and demand changes are not always as straightforward as they might appear.

The argument for understanding the economics of lodging and its capital structure are numerous. One day you may want to be an entrepreneur and consider becoming an owner, partner, or franchisee of a hotel operation. You could also one day work in a corporate office of a lodging company where you are directly involved in determining potential locations for new properties and subsequently working on the financing packages for the company's growth. Even as a manager in a hotel, it is advantageous to understand the economics of lodging and its capital structure. Your role in maximizing the profitability of your particular property for the owners or corporation can be facilitated with a thorough understanding of the economic variables involved.

THIS CHAPTER SHOULD HELP YOU

1. Explain the cyclical nature of the hotel industry.
2. Define the term *securitization*.
3. Explain the impact of the securitization of the hotel industry on capital availability.
4. Identify and describe the major means of raising debt and equity capital used for hotel development.
5. Define REIT and explain how a REIT functions.
6. Identify the drawbacks of being a publicly owned company.
7. List and define the dimensions of the hotel investment decision.
8. Define the terms *segmentation* and *encroachment*, and explain their relationship in hotel franchising.

The Economics of the Hotel Business

Hotel developers build long-term assets on the basis of relatively short-term cycles. Whereas a hotel's lifetime is usually 30 or 40 years (and sometimes 100 years or more), the cycle of hotel building is considerably shorter depending on the type of hotel. Figure 11.1 displays the hotel construction timeline by phase. This figure is based on an analysis completed for each of the chain-scale segments for hotels in the construction pipeline between 1994 and 2002.[1] Understanding the phase length of the preplanning, planning, final planning, and start-up to completion of construction is important in predicting the room-supply growth of hotel rooms. It is important to note that, between 1994 and 2002, only 25 percent of all projects in the preplanning stage

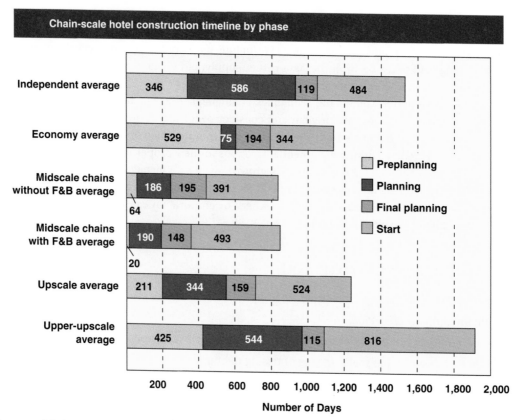

Figure 11.1

Chain-scale construction timeline by phase. (Source: STR/PPR/F.W. Dodge.)

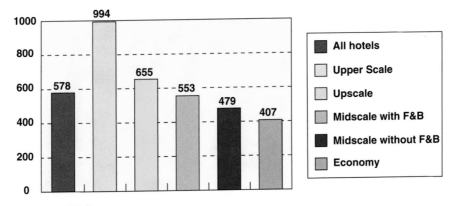

Figure 11.2

Hotel construction—average days from construction start to opening. (Source: STR/PPR/F.W. Dodge.)

actually were constructed. The percentage of completions increases for each subsequent stage to almost 95 percent of projects in the actual construction stage opening for business at some point in the future (see Figure 11.2). This pipeline ranging over several years results historically in periods of excess capacity followed by demand catching up with supply, followed in turn by periods of more or less frantic building.

Examples of the difficulty in forecasting the supply of hotel rooms can be seen in the more recent changes in estimated growth. *Lodging Econometrics* (LE) reduced its estimate of added room supply in 2006 resulting in 775 projects with 80,951 rooms. This was a decrease of 4,796 rooms as compared to earlier projections. Estimates were also reduced for 2007 with 1,087 projects having 115,956 rooms planned as supply additions. This represented a decrease of 3,470 rooms from an earlier forecast. Redesign and reengineering requirements were cited as the main reason for the supply reduction relating back to building supplies and construction crews. Although building costs including supplies and labor are easing somewhat, there are still challenges to completing projects on budget and on time. Analysts project that the growing pipeline totals may not have any meaningful impact on industry operations until 2008 when there will be a larger flow of luxury, upscale, and casino projects coming on line.[2]

The hotel business is cyclical. It is also highly **capital intensive**, with, depending on the economy, varying sources and levels of capital flowing into the industry. We will consider each of these points—cyclicality, capital intensity, and the impact of capital flows into the industry—in the following sections. In the next chapter, we will consider competition in lodging.

Hotels, large or small, require major investments in land, the physical plant, and equipment. As a result, expansion is very sensitive to economic conditions. (The Regent [Mumbai, India] Courtesy of Carlson Hotels Worldwide.)

A CYCLICAL BUSINESS

The fact that the hotel business is cyclical essentially means one thing: The demand for hotel rooms rises and falls with the business cycle. Generally, the demand for hotel rooms changes direction in direct relation to the economy but lags behind it by several months. This is not surprising, as both business and pleasure travel are easy expenditures to eliminate in a declining economy and to restore when it improves. In any local market, the hotel business is likely to have its own cycle, related to the supply of hotel rooms as well as the demand for them. However, the cycle generally starts with the demand for rooms, potential or actual. Perhaps the easiest way to see this cycle is to work through an imaginary, but quite realistic, example.

An Example of the Hotel Business Cycle. Oldtown, a quiet city of 100,000, has been a stable community with a balanced economy for many years. Not long ago, during a period of general economic expansion, a national company built a large factory complex in Oldtown. The ripple effect from this project spread to the suppliers for the factory complex, as well as to a number of other companies that, when they heard about the factory complex, learned what an attractive site Oldtown was. Employment soared; some people were transferred to Oldtown; others moved there seeking jobs.

Our study now shifts to Major Hotels' corporate offices, where, in a meeting with the vice presidents of operations and real estate, the vice president for development suggests that Major ought to look into building a hotel in Oldtown. There is immediate agreement to do a preliminary study. Three months later, the preliminary study shows encouraging results, and so several lines of activity are set in motion. A consulting firm is hired to do a formal feasibility study, an architect is hired to do preliminary design work, and informal conversations with Major's bankers begin. Six more months pass. The results of the consultant's feasibility study confirm Major's preliminary study, the preliminary design is a beauty, and everybody agrees this could be a great hotel. The bankers, having looked at the studies and the design, decide to process Major's loan application quickly. (They have had a surge in deposits and need to get that money into interest-earning loans. They need to lend, just as Major needs to borrow.) Best of all, the ideal location has been found, and negotiations to acquire a site are going well.

At a meeting of Major's executive committee, a formal proposal to go ahead is presented. The discussion touches briefly on the competition, but everyone quickly agrees that Oldtown's existing hotels are tired and will be no match for the proposed property. When somebody asks, "Is anybody else going in there?" the answer is, "A few people have been nosing around, but there's nothing firm as far as we can tell." Everyone agrees that it is time to purchase the site and sign a design contract with the architect. Because this is a meeting, everybody's commitment is a public matter.

The same series of events is taking place at Magnificent Hotels, LowCost Lodges, Supersuites, and a couple of other companies. However, because each company keeps things fairly quiet until everything is settled, there are only vague rumors that others are also interested in Oldtown.

Finally, 18 months after the first vice presidential meeting at Major, the company announces that a 300-room hotel will be built in Oldtown, and the groundbreaking is set two weeks hence. The story is front-page news. Over the next six months, similar announcements from Magnificent, LowCost, and Supersuites make the front page, too.

At Major, these other companies' announcements cause quite a stir. At a meeting of the executive committee, they all shake their heads and agree that those other companies are crazy; they have no sense at all in overbuilding like this. One very junior vice president who is sitting in raises the possibility that Major should abandon the project, but he is quickly shouted down. Thousands of dollars have already been spent on feasibility studies and architectural work, a site has been purchased, and contracts have been signed for construction. "Besides," says the financial vice president, "what would our banks say if we pulled out now? Do you think we'd get another loan commitment as easily next time?" Because everybody has agreed to the project publicly, for any to admit that he or she was wrong would also be publicly embarrassing.

Eighteen months later, Major's beautiful new property opens, and the general manager hands the following situation report to the vice president of operations:

> Within four blocks of my office, there are a thousand rooms under construction. Everyplace my sales staff goes, they trip over our competitors' people. Magnificent is slashing its convention rates for next year, LowCost has announced a salespersons'

discount when its hotel opens next month, and Supersuites is offering free cocktail parties every evening. I think we will do all right after the first couple of years because our operation is going to be stronger and of better quality, but don't expect much for our first two or three years until we are established. There are no further announcements of lodging construction in Oldtown.

We have spent quite a bit of time looking at this cycle of events to illustrate the significance of factors such as the complexity of the decision to build a hotel, the lead time required, the preliminary expenditures, and the public corporate and individual commitment to the decision. This cycle shows that an increase in demand can set off a series of events that usually cannot be stopped even when it becomes clear that the market is or will be overbuilt.

In other markets, it takes years for the demand to catch up with the overbuilding. In some, however, the demand keeps increasing, and in three to five years another round of building starts, this time fueled by all the old faces plus some new ones—for those who didn't get in the first time. All have a need to be represented in the growth market.

Our example was of a local market, but this is usually part of a larger, national market. Different local events related to a general national period of prosperity set off building booms in many local markets because demand for hotel rooms is closely related to general economic conditions. When the national economy turns down, so does the hotel business. Hotel building tends to come in waves or cycles that end, much to everybody's surprise, in an overbuilt industry.

HOTEL CYCLES AND FINANCIAL PERFORMANCE

In an ideal world for hotels, the demand for rooms would equal or exceed the supply of rooms. Pricing of rooms could therefore be maximized, resulting in higher average room rates. In reality, however, supply and demand cannot be precisely calculated or predicted. As discussed in Chapter 13 (Global Hospitality Note 13.1– Public Anxiety and the Travel Industry), unexpected catastrophic events have affected the hospitality industry as well as other segments of our lives. The tragedies of September 11 had a significant negative impact on the number of people traveling, subsequently greatly reducing the demand for hotel rooms. The operating profit for the average U.S. hotel dropped 19.4 percent in 2001. This was followed by a 9.6 percent drop in profits for 2002, marking the first two-year decline in hotel profitability since 1982 to 1983.[3] As evidence of the cyclical nature of the lodging industry, consider that 2000 was the most profitable year in the lodging industry, grossing $24.0 billion in pretax profits. This figure was 9 percent more than in 1999 and double the amount earned in 1996. Total industry revenue rose from $62.8 billion in 1990 to $112.1 billion in 2000. In 1990, the industry suffered a $5.7 billion loss during a recessionary period complicated by Desert Storm and the Persian Gulf War in the Middle East. Total industry revenue declined in 2002 to $102.6 billion from $103.5 billion in 2001.[4]

The domestic recovery following September 11 started in the third quarter of 2003. The year of 2005 showed profits in the hotel industry of 15.5 percent which was the greatest increase since 1996. Except for the Louisiana and Mississippi areas hit by Hurricane Katrina in the early fall of 2005, hotel occupancies for 2005 equaled or exceeded their long-term averages with strong gains in average room rates. For 2006 there was a 7.5 percent growth in total revenue with a 4.1 percent total revenue increase for 2007 with profit gains of 14.9 percent and 7.0 percent respectively. This equates to U.S. hotels achieving a profit of almost $14,800 per-available-room in 2006 and $15,800 in 2007. This figure slightly exceeds the $15,674 profit level of 2000 but, in real dollars, still puts the hotels about 20 percent behind where they were in that year.[5] Industry Practice Note 11.1 discusses the impact of Katrina on the lodging industry of the Gulf Coast of Louisiana and Mississippi.

One factor that is typically considered in analyzing the financial performance and predictions of the hotel industry is the inventory of available hotel rooms. During the hotel industry crisis of the late 1980s/early 1990s, clearly hotel development and financing communities contributed to the catastrophic impact with the illogical growth of the 1980s in which the hotel market was excessively overbuilt. Until 1986, the growth was driven, to some degree, by tax considerations, which developers seemed to think made profit a secondary consideration. Another factor explaining hotel growth in the face of losses in operations (between 1982 and 1993, the lodging industry lost a staggering total of $33 billion) was the increasing emphasis on segmented room products (the industry has never been segmented to the extent that it is now). Although the market as a whole in a city might have enough rooms to satisfy demand, if there was a shortage of one specific category—say, limited service or all-suites—then developers in that category saw an opportunity and new rooms were built to satisfy that specialized need. In some cases, rooms were built where there was no shortage of any kind but simply because of competitive pressure for major brands to be represented in an important market. In the late 1980s and early 1990s, property values fell far below replacement costs. Part of the meaning of a cyclical market is that there are good times as well as bad (expressed in terms of profit). The industry broke even in 1992 and had a profitable year in 1993, leading up to the best industry year in 2000. Overbuilding has not, however, been identified as a factor in the downturn starting in 2001. Depressed demand (resulting in lower occupancy rates) and collapsed rates (lower average room rates) were due to a combination of a depressed economy, terrorism, war, travel complications, and SARS.[6]

With better economic times becoming evident in 2003, one might expect a surge to follow in hotel development. Analysts, however, unlike the late 1980s and early 1990s, see factors limiting rapid hotel supply growth. These factors include escalating land and construction prices that are not expected to become more reasonable in the foreseeable future. Construction costs were even further impacted with Hurricane Katrina particularly with lumber and wood-related products.[7]

The hotel industry throughout the downward business cycle of 2001 through 2003 showed that good management can make a significant difference in maximizing profitability with reduced revenue. Only a couple of midsized companies sought protection of bankruptcy laws since 2001. PKF Hospitality Research indicated that more than 80 percent of hotels were profitable at the unit level in 2002. Although hotel revenues were down after the peak in 2000, expenses—particularly big ones such as labor and interest rates—were also down. With this equation, it was possible that hotel income increased as revenues declined.[8] So while profits fell for hotels, according to the Hospitality Research Group of PKF Consulting, the average 2002 profit for properties was 27.5 percent—almost two full percentage points greater than the 25.6 percent average margin earned by U.S. hotels from 1960 to 2001. Subsequently, in 2003, buyers were willing to pay competitively for good hotel properties.[9]

The hotel industry, during the leaner times following September 11, learned how to operate more efficiently and these lessons will have long-term benefits. For example, in 2005, PKF Hospitality Research found in their sample of hotels that an 8.8 percent increase in total revenue was turned into a 15.5 percent increase in profits. According to this source, that was one of the largest annual gains in unit-level profitability in the past 25 years. There was some variance based on the hotel categories but all hotel segments had gains in total revenue in 2005. Limited-service hotels achieved the greatest increase in revenue (10.3 percent) in 2005 while full-service hotels achieved the greatest increase in profitability (19.3 percent) for the same time period. Convention hotels, while not faring quite as well, still had a 7.8 percent gain in revenue and a 12.2 percent increase in profits.[10]

For U.S. hotel properties in 2005, there was a 6.5 percent increase in total operating costs. The 5.1 percent increase in labor and related costs contributed largely to this total. For the second consecutive year, the increase in employee benefits overshadowed the increase in wages and salaries. Employee benefits increased by 6.4 percent compared to a 4.6 percent increase in salaries and wages. Employee benefits include payroll taxes, payroll-related insurance, subsidized employee insurance (the amount the hotel pays for the particular benefit plan to offset the employee-paid premiums for coverage such as medical, dental and life insurance), retirement plans and employee meals (again that are typically subsidized to offer low-cost or even free meals to employees during their work shifts). Some of these benefits are mandated by government on the federal, state, and local levels. Another reason for the increase in this area is that benefit packages are an important employee recruiting and retention tool. Regarding other operating expenses, the rooms department experienced the single largest increase in 2005 as compared to any revenue-generating department. Part of the increase in the rooms division reflects the higher occupancy (more guests for whom to provide supplies, clean rooms and staff departments). Along with this is the presence of amenity creep—a trend that has been steadily growing in the hotel industry for several years. Guests increasingly expect more in a guest room from free WiFi to an assortment of bathroom products (no longer just shampoo and soap but conditioners, body lotions, shoe mitts, sewing kits, shower caps, etc.) and enhanced bedding.[11]

Additional increases in hotel expenses for 2005 are noteworthy of separate mention. In that year management fees increased by 8.9 percent and franchise fees increased by 9.8 percent. These fees are usually based on a percentage of revenue and reflect the sizable revenue increases for that year. Another big contributor to hotel overhead was utility costs. In 2005, hotel utility costs increased by 13.6 percent, which made these

TABLE 11.1

YEAR	PERCENTAGE OF OCCUPANCY	AVERAGE ROOM RATE
2001	65.4%	$115.51
2002	64.3%	$105.96
2003	65.2%	$107.28
2004	69.4%	$117.39
2005	71.4%	$126.12

expenses the single largest increase on the financial statement. The prediction is that utility expenses will continue to remain high or climb to even higher levels.[12]

While the controlling of overhead and expenses is vital in order to maximize profitability in any hotel operation, the key drivers in the profitability of a lodging property are occupancy and average room rate. A property with a high occupancy can still lose money with low room rates. High room rates, however, are not totally the answer if there is insufficient occupancy. Obviously, management skill in keeping overhead costs in line is consistently important to maximize the hotel's profitability.

The average U.S. occupancy rate was the lowest in 31 years in 2002 at 64.3 percent with an average room rate of $105.96. This represents a drop of $9.55 from the previous year. In comparison, for 2005, the overall percentage of occupancy was 71.4 percent with an average daily room rate of $126.12. Table 11.1 shows the average occupancies for hotels in the United States from 2001 to 2005 and average room rates during that same time period.[13]

REVPAR

A well-established measure over the years in evaluating hotel performance has been **revenue per available rooms (RevPAR)**. RevPAR, resulting from the rental of guest rooms, is the key source of revenue for the lodging industry. A logical question would be: What drives profitability greater in RevPAR growth—occupancy or room rate? According to PKF Hospitality Research, when RevPAR growth is dominated by occupancy increases there are also costs in servicing the extra rooms and guests. Therefore, the gains in profit are less. When RevPAR growth is driven by increases in the average daily rate (ADR), "economies of scale allow for a greater percentage of the rooms revenue gain to drop to the bottom line."[14] During times of intense competition (as when business drops and every hotel is truly fighting for survival), properties can create an extremely detrimental situation in lowering room rates to the point that occupancy cannot help pull out the needed profitability.

International Hotel Operations. In an analysis of 2006 European hotel operations, London achieved the highest revenue per available room (RevPAR) for that year. The RevPAR of EUR166.63 was up 18.49 percent from 2005. These results were driven by an average room rate (ARR) of €205.30 and a year-end occupancy of 81.7 percent. Moscow was second in the European market with RevPAR of €161.78, an average room rate of €222.53, which equates to an increase of 15.1 percent over 2005. Global figures for 2006 showed improvement worldwide with RevPAR growth in Europe up by 11.61 percent, the United States was up by 7.5 percent, and there was a 20.12 percent increase in Asia Pacific. When including the Middle East markets with Europe, the third in absolute RevPAR was Dubai (€156.03), followed by Paris (€152.36) and Amsterdam (€104.27).[15]

HOTELS AS REAL ESTATE

Hotels may be built because an area or community development needs the property; that is, the hotel may be necessary to a larger project. At times, hotels have been built in areas slated for mega-events, such as a winter or summer Olympics. A saying in the industry is, "You don't build a church just for Easter Sunday." Applied to the hotel industry, that is interpreted to mean that it may not be wise to build a hotel just for a three-week sell-out event. A longer-term concern would be whether the travel industry (leisure and business) is going to support the addition of another hotel property in that particular area. Another reason supporting investing in hotels could be that the underlying value of the real estate and its appreciation are a more important consideration to the investors than the profitability of the hotel. For example, a number of foreign investors in North America have apparently, from time to time, been willing to invest money in hotel properties for their longer-term appreciation and as a safe haven for their funds.

Hotel pricing can make hotel real estate more attractive than other real estate, particularly in inflationary times, because of the ability to increase rates literally overnight. The ability to increase revenues is not as flexible in other real-estate projects, in which rents are generally fixed by long-term leases. As a result, hotels, although they have a higher risk than other real estate, find favor with investors, especially during the optimistic growth phase of the hotel industry cycle.

Hotel companies are highly active not only as operators and franchisors of hotels but as real-estate developers. Marriott, for instance, sustains their growth in part by buying, developing, and then reselling land and hotel properties. Indeed, such companies have a real interest in continuing expansion of their brands to gain a greater share of the market and to ensure that their brands have a presence in the widest number of local markets. Naturally, they also want to gain the profits from development. These motives to expand, however sensible they may be from the individual company's vantage point, often lead to the "overbuilding" that has been such a bane to the hotel business

Bellagio Las Vegas cost $1.6 billion to build, opening in 1998. (Courtesy of Las Vegas Convention and Visitors Authority.)

generally. Industry Practice 11.2 discusses a growing concept in hotel real estate—mixed-use developments including a special section on condo-hotels. Hotel investments reached $21 billion in 2005, which was 63 percent higher than the previous year. At least $20 billion is predicted in hotel investments in 2006.[16] Industry Practice Note 11.3 describes the process of a real estate transaction.

INTERNATIONAL HOTEL DEVELOPMENT

Regarding international hotels, the focus for new hotel development is in Asia. According to Lodging Econometrics (LE), Wall Street considers the "growing offshore development to be a significant component of their analysis of U.S.-based hotel companies and real estate investment groups." As of mid-2006, there were 386 "actively pursued" construction projects planned for Asia with 111,285 rooms. China leads this movement with 188 hotels in the pipeline representing 48 percent of all developments in Asia. The majority of these projects (134 out of 188) are four- or five-star hotels. China is projected to be the largest tourist destination in the world by 2020. The 2008 Olympic Games in Beijing is adding momentum to the development trend along with Shanghai, a major world-class financial center. Macau, a major gaming destination, and the nearby resorts of Taipa and Coloane, are contributing to the pipeline numbers with the average size property exceeding 700 rooms in these locations. India is also a major location for new hotels with 44 percent of the new properties planned near outsourcing office centers in the cities of Bangalore, Chennai, Hyderabad, and Mumbai. Thailand is

Condo-Hotels as Mixed-Use Developments

With the aging of the baby boomers and the realization that many from this era prefer luxury vacation-living, comes the proliferation of the condo-hotel. While condo-hotels have been around for many years, these developments were traditionally found in the luxury-resort locations of Florida, Las Vegas, and the Caribbean. Now the condo-hotel concept can be found in numerous locations worldwide. Traditional hotels have started adding the condominium units to properties, thus serving both transient guests and condo owners. Buyers of the condo unit are not burdened with any upkeep issues including furnishings or amenities. The owner of the condo unit in the condo-hotel developments simply has to reserve his or her room and show up to enjoy the services the hotel has to offer.

Condo-hotels do present some operational challenges, however, particularly when it involves booking those rooms for nonowner use. Because condo owners are not using their rooms at the same time, coordinating with blocking section in advance for group or convention use to maximize revenue can sometimes be difficult. There are different ways to structure the condo owners' use of their unit, which is addressed in the contract with the owner. Remington Hotels manages a condo-hotel in Orlando, Florida. Owners who have elected to put their rooms into the hotel's rental pool for transient use are given a calendar asking them, in advance, to plan when they wish to use the room. The hotel's transient business is then planned around the owners' calendars.

Another area of potential conflict concerns condo furnishings. Most condo-hotels do not allow owners to change the in-room furnishings. Hotels need a consistent, uniform room because this helps keep the repair and replacement charges in check.

Despite the challenges, real estate experts say that the condo-hotel option will be attractive, particularly to the baby boom generation.

Source: Rob Heyman, "Home Sweet Home—Dealing with the operational side of today's mixed-use properties." *Lodging*, http://wwwlodgingmagazine.com/index/cfm?fm=CurrentIssue.operations

the third-largest area in Asian hotel development. Many of these projects are part of the redevelopment process following the tsunami of December 2004.[17]

PRIVATE EQUITY INVESTMENTS

Private equity firms accounted for 44 percent of hospitality transactions in 2005 and were the single largest group of investments. Publicly held companies made up the second largest portion of transactions. Private equity is a broad term that can include individuals or families (such as the Pritzker family, who have owned Hyatt Corporation for over 50 years) to pension funds or university/foundation endowments. Pension

The Elements of the Hotel Real-Estate Deal

A seven-year process was involved in the development of the $300-million, 950-room JW Marriott Desert Ridge Resort & Spa located in suburban Phoenix, Arizona. The hotel, which opened in November of 2002, had more than 450,000 room nights on the books from the start, with reservations booked into 2009. JW Marriott Desert Ridge Resort & Spa is the largest resort in Arizona.

The first step in the development of this resort took place in the mid-1990s. In analyzing the market, Marriott International saw that Arizona was lacking facilities for large-group business. According to JW Marriott, Jr., Marriott's chairman and CEO, "I'm a strong proponent of the big-box hotel. If you build them bigger and better than the competition, people will come."

The initial step was followed by a series of focus group meetings. The objectives of these meetings included testing the concept and creating a vision for the property. Information from these meetings helped determine that a hotel was needed with between 1,000 and 1,200 rooms. In addition, adequate meeting space was essential—in the area of 100,000 square feet. In keeping with the resort setting, multiple golf courses were essential, as was a major spa.

With these parameters defined, the development team went to work looking for the right city in Arizona as a location. The choice of Phoenix was facilitated by the fact that one of Phoenix's civic goals was to make the city a major convention destination. At this point, Marriott began discussions with Northeast Phoenix Partners, who controlled 6,000 acres of land. The master plan project was called Desert Ridge. Talks with the department of transportation were also initiated to clarify plans for expanding the freeway system serving that area of town. By 1999, Marriott acquired an existing golf course and a lease interest in the land for the hotel and a second golf course. Discussions continued over the next several months to determine the hotel's number of rooms, height, traffic flow, and other details.

By early 2000, almost 90 percent of the property design was complete. Marriott approached CNL Hospitality Corp. CNL became a capital partner through equity investments, including a real estate investment trust (REIT). Other financing included a private placement to high-net-worth investors (which raised $28.5 million), the addition to several major institutional investors, and a mezzanine loan provided by Marriott. Marriott maintained a minority equity interest.

Construction started in early 2001. The second golf course opened in February 2002, with the hotel opening the following November. Seven years had transpired since the project's conception. The resort contains 100,000 square feet of indoor meeting space and 100,000 square feet of dedicated outdoor meeting and gathering areas.

Source: From Ed Watkins, "Anatomy of a Big Deal," *Lodging Hospitality*, July 1, 2003, p. 26.

funds have made a sizable impact with their investments in hotel properties including California's teacher pension fund.

Private equity firms manage pooled money to acquire properties and oversee investments. Examples of large-scale private equity companies are the Blackstone Group,

RLJ Development and Colony Capital. The Blackstone Group had the second and third largest portfolio acquisitions in 2006 with the LaQuinta Corporation and MeriStar Hospitality. These transactions totaled $6 billion. Fueling the interest of private equity investments in hospitality has been the increase in travel by both leisure and business segments. Supply of hotel rooms remains limited because of higher construction costs and land prices. The underperformance of other investment options such as commercial, multifamily, and retail real estate has also attracted the private equity firms to the hotel industry. Private equity firms are motivated by high-yield returns and therefore tend to have shorter holding periods of typically two to four years. For example, the Blackstone Group bought Wyndam Hotels and sold the name, franchising, and management company to Cendant (which is now Wyndam Worldwide) in less than a year.[18]

THE SECURITIZATION OF THE HOTEL INDUSTRY

The "**securitization**" of the hotel industry refers to the influx of funds into the industry in return for equity and debt securities issued by publicly traded hospitality companies.[19] There have always been the Marriotts, the Sheratons, the Hiltons, companies that obtained most of their financing from public markets.[20] However, in the 1990s expansion of financing vehicles emerged that were relatively new to the hotel industry, such as **commercial mortgage-backed securities (CMBSs)** and **real-estate investment trusts (REITs)**. These forms of financing led to an unprecedented growth in the funds from public markets invested in lodging. To understand this development, we will briefly consider these forms of debt and equity capital. As a point of clarification, when speaking of debt, we will be referring to borrowed funds such as mortgages, bonds, debentures, and the like. We will use the term equity to refer to ownership, here in the form of stock sold to individual and institutional investors. In 2005, publicly held companies made up the second largest group of transactions. Of these, REITs were responsible for 20 percent of industry investments.[21]

Debt Investments and Commercial Mortgage-Backed Securities. For many years, the primary sources from which companies borrowed for purposes of hotel construction were limited to banks and insurance companies—except for a handful of public companies. There are now additional sources of debt for hotel construction. Hotel developers can access such funding through **conduit lenders** that we will discuss in a moment. This wider availability of loans, however, poses some real questions about the dangers of overbuilding. A commercial mortgage-backed security (CMBS) is "a security, often a bond rated by bond agencies, backed by a pool of commercial mortgages" and the future income those mortgages will generate from payments of interest and principal.[22]

Well-financed companies are especially well suited to carry out large complex hotel development. (Courtesy of Trump's Castle.)

CMBS debt is assembled by conduit lenders who use their own funds to lend initially to the borrower. When a sufficient dollar amount has been assembled, the mortgages are "packaged" and sold to the public and institutional investors. There are specialized firms that engage in this business. Banks, brokerage firms, and other financial institutions also have divisions that act as conduit lenders. The CMBS market was one of the best sources of financing for hotel owners post-September 11. With corporate-bond markets turning away from hotels and portfolio lenders reluctant to take concentrated risks in hotel assets, the CMBS market found that, if properly sized and priced, hotels can produce profits.

Other Sources of Debt Financing. Owners may find that they can obtain at most a 65 percent first mortgage on a property. To decrease the amount of their own funds required, they resort to what is called **mezzanine financing**.[23] Mezzanine financing, sometimes referred to as **gap financing**, "bridges the gap between the first mortgage and the amount of equity committed to a project."[24]

It is very much like a second mortgage. Mezzanine financing is not secured by a mortgage—or else is subordinated to a first mortgage. It carries a higher interest rate than mortgage financing because of its higher risk. In the previous example, however, if the owners could obtain 65 percent first-mortgage financing and another 20 percent mezzanine financing, the amount of their own capital required to build the property would be reduced from 35 percent to 15 percent of the cost, effectively increasing their power to expand. The primary advantage of mezzanine debt is that it provides additional capital while allowing current ownership to maintain control of the asset without having to take on additional equity partners. The cost of these funds can range from 15 to 20 percent interest with three- to seven-year terms. Mezzanine funding does add another debt obligation to the hotel. Overall leverage is thereby increased as well as downside risks are elevated. Even with these added risks considered, it can be advantageous, because long-term mezzanine funding is less expensive than having equity partners if a project is successful.[25]

Sources of Equity Investment. Principal sources of equity investment in lodging include real-estate investment trusts (REITs), **initial public offerings (IPOs)**, and secondary stock offerings.

Real-estate investment trusts. Real-estate investment trusts (REITs) are companies that own, and in most cases, operate income-producing real estate. Real estate may include residential properties, shopping centers, offices, lodging/resort properties and malls, for example. While some REITs finance real estate, others directly own and/or operate income-producing real estate. To be a REIT, a company must distribute at least 90 percent of its taxable income to its shareholders annually in the form of dividends. The growth of REITs has been so significant that Standard & Poors added REITs to its major indexes including the S&P 500.[26]

REITs do offer benefits over merely buying and selling real estate, including hotel properties, individually. One of the advantages of this type of investing is that it helps reduce the risks of doing this individually while reaping the benefit of income generated from multiple properties. If one property is doing poorly, it can be offset by others that could be more profitable. REITs, in general, returned 34 percent in 2006, on average. For the five years through December 2006, the annualized return was 23.2 percent. By contrast, the Standard & Poor's 500-stock index returned 15.8 percent in 2005 and 6.2 percent, annualized, over the 2002–2006 span. Industry experts predicted that many hotel companies, REITs and non-REITs, will do well in 2007 as demand for hotel rooms outpaces supply.[27]

An example of a lodging REIT is FelCor Lodging Trust (NYSE:FCH), which acquires, renovates, redevelops and rebrands hotels. FelCor owns approximately 115 consolidated hotels in 28 states and Canada with a market cap of $3.3 billion. This company has formed strategic alliances with three leading brand owners: Hilton Hotels Corporation, Starwood Hotels and Resorts, and InterContinental Hotels Group. Their portfolio includes Embassy Suites Hotels, Doubletree, Sheraton, Westin and Holiday Inn.[28]

Other publicly held companies. As we noted earlier, companies such as Hilton and Marriott have long been publicly held, that is, owned by stockholders whose shares are publicly traded. These and other publicly traded corporations are often referred to as **C corps** to distinguish them from REITs, which are also corporations.[29] (Note: Blackstone/Group purchased Hilton in the fourth quarter of 2007.)

Host Marriott was initially created in 1993 in the split of Marriott in which Host Marriott became owner of lodging real estate and operator of airport terminal concession businesses and Marriott International was the manager of lodging and contract-service businesses. Later, Marriott created two separate companies, with one focused on lodging real estate. In 1999, Host Marriott reorganized to qualify as a real-estate investment trust. Based in Bethesda, Maryland, Host Marriott typically buys conservative four- and five-star hotels in major urban areas and owns properties that carry the brands of Marriott, Ritz-Carlton, Renaissance, Four Seasons, and Hyatt. Starting in 2003 Host Marriott became very active in selling and buying properties. One purchase in 2003 was the Hyatt Regency Maui Resort and Spa in Hawaii, purchased for $321 million. By August of 2003, the REIT had already sold four hotels, with plans to see several more hotels bringing in proceeds of $100 million to $250 million. Proceeds were planned to repay debt, invest in their current portfolio, or acquire additional hotels.[30] Late in 2005, Host Marriott Corporation announced an agreement to purchase 38 hotels. The seller was Starwood Hotels & Resorts and the price tag was $4.1 billion for the properties located around the world. With the increased diversity, Host Marriott changed its name to Host Hotels & Resorts and became the world's largest lodging REIT and one of the largest owners of high-end hotels and resorts with 128 properties encompassing 67,000 rooms.[31]

Secondary offerings. When a company that is already publicly traded issues additional shares, they are referred to as a secondary offering. From 1991 to 1997, REITs and C corps raised $11.5 billion through secondary offerings. Including both debt and equity, that amount reached nearly $27 billion during the seven-year period, the vast majority of it in the last four years of that period.

Equity investment and joint ventures. More investors are turning to hotels and real estate as stocks and mutual funds have not provided meaningful returns. This has resulted in a great deal of capital seeking hotel investments often from nontraditional hotel investors. Instead of selling the asset outright, an option is to sell a portion of a hotel. This capital can then be used for expansion, renovations, or new projects. There are benefits for the new investors in enjoying the current yield while entering a new industry, as long as skilled operators are involved.[32]

Public funding. Public funding refers to public tax dollars. The use of public tax dollars particularly in the building of convention center hotels has been a contentious issue for some time. Typically supported by city leaders, investment bankers, convention bureaus, meeting planners, and some hotel management companies, many hotel owners feel that use of public funding to compete with their own hotels is unfair. These hotel owners contribute to the pool of public funding with the bed, corporate, and other taxes they pay to the city, county, and state. In essence, they are contributing to underwrite or subsidize a hotel to compete with their own. Advocates of such funding emphasize that such projects can infuse new vitality and revenue into a city's convention market, thereby benefiting more than the convention center hotel. With funding as the key, the average building price of $175,000 to $225,000 per room cannot be handled by the private sector without some type of assistance from the government. An example of such funding is with the 1,100-room Hyatt Regency Denver at the Convention Center. Tax-exempt revenue bonds totaling $350 million were secured for this project; otherwise, it was unlikely to become a reality.[33]

Securitization and Competition. Although we will defer most of our discussion of competition in the lodging business to the next chapter, this is a good point at which to consider the impact of the huge influx of capital on the hotel business and its competitive structure. When more funds flow into the industry, it becomes easier to build more rooms, increasing competition. When capital has been more readily available and, in a rising stock market, effectively less costly, mergers and acquisitions (M&A) activity has increased as well.

Real-estate investment trusts have been active players in the mergers and acquisitions field, too. The financial power of the REITs is substantial. Because of their ready access to the public capital markets, they can manage large acquisitions with new stock issues. The stock either can be used to raise cash toward the purchase price or can be given to the seller as part of the purchase price. In effect, they have the power to virtually coin money—as long as their stock market value holds up.

An interesting example of financial muscle is the purchase by Starwood Lodging of two leading upscale international chains within a two-month period. In early September of 1997, Starwood purchased Westin Hotels and Resorts for just under $1.6 billion. Then, in October, the company announced the purchase of ITT Sheraton for a price of $14.6 billion.[34]

Almost overnight, this company jumped from being a minor player in the industry to becoming a Fortune 500 company with more than 700 hotels worldwide. The company included the well-known brands of Sheraton, Westin, W Hotels, the Luxury Connection, Four Points by Sheraton, as well as the top brand of St. Regis.[35]

One prominent acquisition that took place post-September 11 was the acquisition of Candlewood Suites by InterContinental Hotels Group PLC. Candlewood Suites was the sixth brand in the InterContinental portfolio. Others, in addition to the InterContinental brand, include Holiday Inn, Holiday Inn Express, Crowne Plaza, and Staybridge Suites & Resorts. The acquisition positions InterContinental in two tiers of the extended-stay hotel market. Staybridge Suites would be in the upscale tier, with room rates that average about $30 more per night than rooms at Candlewood.[36]

Cendant Hotel Group acquired the Baymont Inn and Suites brand and 115 franchised properties in April 2006. Cendant, in July 2006, In July of 2006, Cendant Corporation completed a spin-off of Realogy Corporation and Wyndham Worldwide Corporation. Cendant sold its Travelport subsidiary to The Blackstone Group. With those sales, Cendant became comprised principally of its vehicle rental operations through the Avis and Budget Brands and became the Avis Budget Group. Wyndham Worldwide, one of the largest hotel companies in the world, was comprised of Wyndham Hotel Group, RCI Global Vacation Network Group and Wyndham Vacation Ownership. The hotel group includes ten brands including Amerihost Inn, Baymont Inn & Suites, Days Inn, Howard Johnson, Knights Inn, Ramada, Super 8, Travelodge, Wingate Hotels & Resorts and TripRewards.[37]

Although it may be appropriate to assume that the increase in the concentration of ownership of hotels is a result of the influx of capital and M&A activity, we need to realize that we are still left with a highly competitive industry. Over 80 percent of the industry is still held privately. It does seem clear, however, that ownership in some areas of the industry, particularly in the upscale segments, has become somewhat more concentrated. It is unlikely, on the other hand, that concentration is sufficient for any firm to exert market control (i.e., to control the price level).

THE HAZARDS OF PUBLIC OWNERSHIP

There are a number of factors that influence stock prices, but there is wide agreement that the most powerful influence is a company's earnings—or the prospect of earnings. For this reason, management in publicly held companies is under constant pressure not only to maintain but to increase earnings each quarter. In some cases, this pressure can encourage a short-term focus by managers. This relentless pressure has been characterized by an entrepreneur from the food service sector of the hospitality industry, Howard Schultz, founder and president of Starbucks:

> Alongside the exhilaration of being a public company is the humbling realization, every quarter, every month, and every day, that you're a servant of the stock market. That perception changes the way you live, and you can never go back to being

The flow of public funds into the lodging industry has been especially helpful to growth-oriented companies such as U.S. Franchise Systems and their Microtel brand, which is shown here. (Courtesy of U.S. Franchise Systems.)

a simple business again. We began to report our sales monthly including comps—"comparable" growth of sales at stores that have been open at least a year. When there are surprises, the stock reacts instantly. I think comps are not the best measure to analyze and judge the success of Starbucks. For example, when lines get too long at one store, we'll occasionally open a second store nearby. Our customers appreciate the convenience and the shorter lines. But, if, as often happens, the new store cannibalizes sales from the older store, it shows up as lower comps, and Wall Street punishes us.[38]

Case History 11.1 describes the experience of Sam Barshop, founder of La Quinta Inns, as that publicly held company became the target of a takeover. There is a possibility, too, that having a significant portion of the industry in public hands, particularly those of REITs, where shareholder expectations are often focused on dividend yields, may pose some long-term problems to the stability of the industry. As one knowledgeable observer put it:

Historically, the hotel business has been cyclical in nature and characterized by widely dispersed ownership operating with a long-term development outlook. Considering Wall Street's preoccupation with quarter-to-quarter growth and ever-increasing yields for shareholders, [the hotel business] would seem an unlikely choice [for public shareholders]. Whether these interesting times are ultimately viewed as a blessing or a curse will depend on how effectively our industry's leadership responds to Wall Street and its fickle ways. A heavily consolidated industry may, in the end, prove a curse if the industry overextends itself and falls out of favor with the investment community.[39]

Going Public: Some Good News and Some Bad

In 1968, the first two La Quinta Inns were built by Barshop Motel Enterprises in San Antonio, Texas, to serve visitors to the 1968 world's fair, HemisFair.[1] Although Sam Barshop had not intended to start a chain, the limited-service concept of La Quinta was so successful that he was approached by developers and investors, and soon his company began to expand. In 1973, in order to secure funds for expansion, the company went public. By 1978, ten years after the first inn opened, there were 56 inns in operation, with an occupancy of 90 percent. Another 19 inns were under construction. By the end of the 1980s, there were about 200 La Quinta Inns in operation.

In 1989, however, a Hong Kong firm, Industrial Equity, began to acquire shares of La Quinta, and by early 1990, it controlled 10 percent of the outstanding shares. Shortly thereafter, a second group of investors headed by two Texas financiers, the Bass brothers, began to acquire shares. In January of 1991, La Quinta hired Goldman Sachs, a New York investment banking firm, to explore ways to "increase shareholder value"—including the sale of the company.

However, at that time, mergers and acquisitions activity was depressed, as were La Quinta's shares, by a recessionary stock market. La Quinta stock, which had been as high as $26, was selling in the $11 to

A contemporary La Quinta Inn. (Courtesy of La Quinta Inns.)

$15 range, and a suitable buyer for the company could not be found. La Quinta's management spent an estimated $2 million in fees to attorneys, management consultants, advisors, and investment bankers in its fight to retain control of the company. The company's operations and expansion were seriously compromised as executives spent time fending off what they saw as a hostile takeover bid.

Finally, in June 1991, an accommodation between La Quinta's management and the dissident shareholders was reached. Five of La Quinta's 11-person board were asked to resign, and new directors representing the Bass-led group (which by then owned 14.9 percent of the company's shares) were elected in their place. Barshop's supporters on the board retained five seats, and the eleventh seat on the board went unfilled. Working with the new board, the consulting firm of McKinsey & Company conducted a three-month management study of La Quinta. As a result, the company was restructured, reducing its workforce by 72 people, 50 of whom were at the corporate offices. The company also took a $7.95 million restructuring charge, including $3.94 million for severances. At that time and shortly thereafter, several senior executives resigned. Then, in March 1992, Barshop turned over the presidency of the company to a former executive vice president of Motel 6, remaining as chairman of the board for another two years until he resigned in March 1994.

In June of 1991, at the time of the first compromise with the Bass-led group, Barshop had these comments on being a publicly held company:

There are a lot of advantages to not being a public company. You're not responsible to the Securities and Exchange Commission or a large number of shareholders. You run your own business. You can focus on cash flow rather than earnings per share. . . . It's been stressful. Business isn't as much fun as it used to be. I've never dealt with anything like this before. Things aren't done the way they used to be. I've learned more about proxies than I ever wanted to know. It's been an interesting experience. But I hope it's a one-time experience.[2]

Mr. Barshop ultimately lost control of his company, a company that by that time had 220 inns in 29 states. He sold 80 percent of his shares for $17.4 million and was paid something on the order of a million dollars during the last two years he served as chairman. Finally, we should note that he will go down in hospitality history as the man who invented the limited-service hotel.

1. This note is based, except as noted, on news stories reported in the *San Antonio Express News*, the *San Antonio Light*, and the *San Antonio Business Journal*, between January 1990 and March 1994; the June 1988 issue of Innput, an employee publication of La Quinta; and public statements by La Quinta Inns to its employees and the press. I would like to thank Mary Starling, secretary to Sam Barshop, for her assistance with the preparation of this note.

2. R. Michelle Brewer, "The Private Woes of Going Public," *San Antonio Light*, June 16, 1991, pp. A1–A2. A contemporary La Quinta Inn. (Courtesy of La Quinta Inns.)

Update on LaQuinta Inn:

LQ Management LLC is one of the largest operators of limited-service hotels in the United States. The company operates and provides franchise services to more than 500 hotels in 40 states and Canada under the La Quinta Inn® and La Quinta Inn & Suites® brands. Their corporate headquarters is in Irving, Texas near Dallas. For more information on this brand, visit http://www.lq.com

Dimensions of the Hotel Investment Decision

The decision to invest in a hotel has at least three dimensions, involving financing, real-estate values, and operations. Although all three are important, the weight each will receive varies with the particular merits of an individual decision and with economic conditions. In the first half of the 1980s, financial and tax considerations often led to building hotels whose profitability was uncertain. A depressed real-estate market played a very prominent role in the purchase of hotel properties in the early 1990s. The catastrophic events of 2001 certainly dealt the hospitality industry a severe blow with a recovery that continued for several years. Those of us whose chosen vocation is operations—running a hotel—need to be reminded that our own set of interests is only one leg of the hotel tripod.

FINANCIAL

As we have noted previously, hotels are capital-intensive. Because most of the capital used in building a hotel—or buying one—is borrowed, it is not surprising that interest rates, availability of capital, taxation, and, in the international environment, exchange rates are all important considerations.

Interest Rates, Inflation, and Leverage. One of the reasons given for the popularity of hotel investments in the latter half of the 1990s was unusually low interest rates. When there are fears of inflation, hotels have been seen as a good **inflation hedge**. Although the value of money decreases in inflationary periods, the value of hotel assets often increases enough to offset inflation and perhaps show a gain, even after deducting interest costs.

Leverage refers to the ability to invest some of your own capital and do most of the deal with borrowed capital. With $1,000 of debt attracting, say, $4,000 of mortgage money, the $1,000 of equity is able to earn the profits, after fixed interest payments, provided by the full $5,000. The debt is said to leverage earnings because all of the profit after interest charges goes to the owners. When times are good and profits high, leverage is looked on very favorably. When profits fall, however, interest charges do not—and so leverage cuts two ways.

Taxes. As noted earlier, the U.S. tax laws of the early 1980s encouraged the construction of hotels by offering special tax credits that meant investors could sometimes make money on the project even if the hotel was not profitable.

Although those artificial inducements to construction are gone, the deductibility of interest on loans still constitutes a tax advantage. Take, for example, one corporation that paid interest of 9.2 percent on its debt; after paying taxes of about 40 percent, the cost of the loan, after taxes, was only 5.6 percent.[40] The tax saving arises because although all of the interest must be paid, some 40 percent of it in this example is balanced by a reduction in income tax. In a capital-intensive business such as hotels, this can lend an advantage to borrowers.

AN OPERATING BUSINESS

The hotel's profitable operation is often the first dimension of a hotel deal that students of hotel management consider. As we have just noted, however, hotel companies—and other developers—have significant business interests outside of operations in both development and franchising of hotels. This does not mean they are uninterested in operations, however. In fact, Marriott requires the buyer to sign a **management contract** on hotels they develop so that Marriott retains the right to control the operation's quality and to profit from the management of the property while expanding their chain.

SEGMENTATION: FOR GUESTS OR DEVELOPERS?

Much of the development of varied **product segments**—economy, all-suites, executive floors, superluxury—can be related to specific market segments. For example, economy segments are aimed at rate-conscious consumer groups such as retirees. (Days Inn reports that a significant proportion of its guests are seniors.) Residence Inns has a clearly targeted segment in mind, as do other extended-stay properties, and full-service hotels' upscale range of products, from executive floors to superluxury, is for the expense-account market. Transient all-suite hotels target upper-level executives on weekdays and upper-middle-income families on weekends. Segmentation certainly meets guest needs.

On the other hand, we have noted that many hotel companies are real-estate developers, and a strategy of segmentation has also met their business needs as developers. Having several brands that appeal to different consumers permits hotel companies to put more than one hotel in a market. Thus, if Hilton had an Embassy Suites in a city, it could still quite legitimately develop its other brands for other segments—a Hampton Inn for the limited-service market and a Homewood Suites for extended-stay guests. This helps sell hotels and franchises to investors, as well as rooms to guests.

As a result, hotel companies may be developing more than one property in the same city—a Hampton Inn and an Embassy Suites or perhaps a Marriott Courtyard and a Fairfield Inn. Although the company's brands are not generally competitive with each other, there is, inevitably, a degree of overlap. It is not as clear, however, that all such development is noncompetitive.

From an ethical point of view, there is nothing even faintly questionable about a company's developing two hotels that will compete with each other. The franchisor is

Segmentation in the lodging industry seeks to develop a product for a specific customer segment but it also gives the hotel company another brand with which to expand. (TownePlace Suites, Courtesy of Marriott International.)

in the business of selling franchises, the franchisee wants to invest in a property, and a developer needs a property to round out a project. Each pursues his or her own interest in an informed way. The resulting increase in competition is a business risk that should surprise no one. Nevertheless, such practices have led to serious problems between franchisors and franchisees.

Encroachment. In the franchise business, the practice of loading additional franchisees into the same market with one or more existing franchisees is called **encroachment**. The new franchisee is seen as encroaching on the market area of the existing franchisee. (In the hotel business, encroachment is often referred to as impact. The sales and profits of the existing franchisee are said to be unfavorably impacted.) Encroachment has been a significant problem in the past for some companies. Specifically, the problem becomes very clear when the additional property has the same brand name and shares the same reservation service. The problem is only slightly less difficult where the brand name is different but the market segment and reservation service are the same. An example is Choice Hotels' Rodeway Inn and EconoLodge properties. What happens where impact is serious is that the property affected suffers a loss in occupancy and average rate. Although encroachment is difficult to prove in a court of law, it has been the frequent subject of negotiation for franchisees, who have often gained concessions in franchise fees to offset the impact of a new property.[41]

As a result of growing problems with encroachment, it is unlikely that any franchise would be written today without specific geographic protection. Michael Levin, when he was president of the Americas Division of Holiday Inn Worldwide, predicted that, in the future, arbitration will be used whenever a new franchise is granted in an area, even before any dispute arises.[42]

MANAGEMENT COMPANIES

The arrangement between the **management company** and the hotel owner, a management contract, is described by Professor James Eyester of the Cornell Hotel School:

> A management contract is a written agreement between a hotel owner and operator in which the owner employs the operator as an agent [employee] to assume full operational responsibility for the property and to manage the property in a professional manner. As an agent, the operator pays in the name of the owner, all property operating expenses from the cash flow generated from the operation; it retains its management fees, and remits the remaining cash flow, if any, to the owner. The owner provides the hotel property to include land, building, furniture and fixtures, equipment, and working capital and assumes full legal and financial responsibility for the project.[43]

The first management company may have been the Caesar Ritz Group. At the end of the nineteenth century, Ritz, with his famous chef, Escoffier, was "paid a retainer to appoint and oversee the managers of separately owned hotels. That arrangement allowed the hotel to advertise itself as a Ritz hotel."[44] The first U.S. hotel management company was the Treadway Hotel Company, which began operating small college inns in the 1920s.[45] During the 1930s, the American Hotel Corporation managed bankrupt hotels, but as late as 1970, there were only three or four management companies in operation in the United States.

In the 1970s and 1980s, as the number of hotels expanded rapidly, much of the development was undertaken by people whose abilities and experience lay in finance and real estate rather than in hotel operations. To manage the hotels developed by these nonoperator owners, the number of hotel management companies expanded rapidly.

There are two kinds of management companies. First, most chain organizations such as Hilton or Marriott serve as management companies for hotels under their franchises. Chains dominate the management contract field for properties with more than 300 rooms. Chains require a substantial minimum fee just to defray their central-office overhead. They have difficulty in working with smaller properties that don't generate enough revenue to cover the minimum fee. Accordingly, smaller management companies have an advantage in the under-300-room category. Independent management companies are able to operate smaller properties, often under different franchises. They offer owners more control over daily operations and more flexibility in contract terms.

Typically, a management contract fee is based on a modest percentage of sales and a larger percentage of gross operating profit. Management companies enjoyed their greatest growth following the boom in hotel construction in the 1980s when they assumed the management of distressed properties. Under those circumstances, contracts were short-term and involved little, if any, ownership interest in the hotel on the part of the management companies. In contrast, contracts being written today may require some form of equity or debt participation in the financing of the property by the management company.[46]

After the economic challenges starting in 2001, some hotel owners challenged contractual terms of management agreements. Contracts with management companies tend to be long-term, lasting as long as 20 years. One of the most publicized cases initiated in 2002 involved a legal battle between the owners of a Charleston, West Virginia, Marriott and the management company, Marriott International. The hotel owners charged that Marriott had defrauded the owners by hiding rebates received from vendors and wrongly allocated corporate overhead to the hotel. The settlement, coming a year later, included Marriott agreeing to lend the owners $1 million to upgrade guest rooms at the hotel and pledging $2 million toward the development of another of the owners' hotel projects. Parts of the contract were also renegotiated in exchange for the owners extending the contract an additional ten years.[47]

CAREERS IN HOSPITALITY

Independent management companies offer several advantages to those starting a career in the hotel business. The company with a successful track record will have experienced and knowledgeable people in its senior ranks. Working with such well-qualified and broadly experienced managers can be an education in itself. Moreover, a larger company will probably have properties of varying sizes and franchise affiliations and thus offer both opportunities for career progression from smaller to larger properties and a broad variety of experiences.

With any company you are considering, it is a good idea to inquire about the company's reputation before signing on in a responsible position. And again, as with any company, a good way to get to know a prospective long-term employer is through employment in the summer or part-time during the school year.

ASSET MANAGEMENT

Asset managers and management companies are two distinct entities, but both work together for the benefit of the hotel owner. The management company, as described in the previous section, handles the day-to-day operation of the hotel, from hiring and supervising staff to negotiating contracts with suppliers to planning menus and determining marketing strategies. The asset manager, on the other hand, acts as the "eyes and ears" of the owner. In bridging the gap between the owner and the management company, the asset manager delivers regular reports to the owner. Specifically, the asset manager would be involved with the management company regarding the budget, reviewing the franchise contract, inspecting the property and franchise requirements, and analyzing cash flow. The asset manager can also benefit the management company by helping with the communication process, helping evaluate the management company, and pointing out to the owner when the management company is doing a good job. It is estimated that more than half of upscale hotels and resorts in the United States currently use some form of asset management. This figure is double that of five years ago. Although the use of asset management companies has been stimulated by a challenging economy, it is thought that their use will continue to escalate even in better economic times.[48]

ENTREPRENEURIAL OPPORTUNITIES

We should pause here to note the significance of the management company's function for those who want to have ownership interest in a hotel. Management companies serve a need for mortgage holders and developers that can also be filled by individuals. Those individuals who, through education and experience, prepare themselves to manage a hotel can regard a time of economic reverses for the industry as a time of opportunity for themselves. In particular, with locally financed (i.e., mortgaged) properties that get into trouble, there is a real opportunity from time to time to secure an ownership position in return for assuming an existing mortgage. This kind of opportunity is more likely to occur with older properties, and so the importance of a good food background—in order to merchandise the property—is clear.

Summary

We have repeatedly made the point in this chapter that lodging is capital-intensive and cyclical. Because of long lead times, supply often continues to grow even after demand has stopped growing or begun to decrease. As a result, in the 11 years ending in 1993, the lodging industry lost $33 billion while construction continued throughout the period. In 1997, however, hotel profits were once again at a peak.

Securitization is selling an ownership or a debt instrument (such as a bond) in a property through the public security markets. Major developments have included the widening of lodging's access to debt through CMBSs, to equity through IPOs and secondary offerings, and to both equity and debt through REITs. An additional form of financing has involved the public funding through a special tax. The impact of securitization has been to enable a considerable boom in hotel building. Although securitization brings advantages in the availability of capital, it also has the inherent risks associated with a falling stock market.

The hotel investment decision has three dimensions: financial, real estate, and operating. The large amount of debt associated with hotel construction gives leverage, and in the international market, changing currency values can also provide financial advantages. Low interest rates are especially advantageous to leveraged deals. Hotel real estate can provide an inflation hedge, and the speed with which hotel rates can be raised provides flexibility in rentals rates few other forms of real estate offer. Real-estate development also offers profits to development companies, including hotel companies such as Marriott, which are active developers. A final means of profiting from a hotel is by operating it profitably, but this is not always the largest source of profit.

The tendency toward overbuilding in a cyclical industry is sometimes exaggerated by the segmentation strategies of major hotel companies. Segmentation can lead to a multibrand hotel company seeking to build one of each of its brands in a market. In some cases, the company may feel that being represented in a major market is more important than the short-run profit potential. Building multiple brands can also lead to problems of encroachment where the same reservation network is divided between two or more properties, and in many cases, multiple properties with the same brand in a market can reduce the advantage of a franchise. Management companies have grown up to serve nonoperator owners. In difficult economic times, these companies' services are especially in demand as lenders become "involuntary owners." These same difficult times, however, often offer those with operating know-how major entrepreneurial opportunities.

Key Words and Concepts

Capital intensive	**Gap financing**
Revenue per available rooms (RevPAR)	**Initial public offerings (IPOs)**
	C corps
Securitization	**Inflation hedge**
Commercial mortgage-backed security (CMBs)	**Leverage**
	Management contract
Real-estate investment trusts (REITs)	**Product segments**
	Encroachment
Conduit lenders	**Management company**
Mezzanine financing	**Asset managers**

Review Questions

1. How does the hotel business react to the business cycle? Explain why hotel building continues after demand turns down.

2. What does securitization mean? How is it affecting the hotel business?

3. What have been the major effects of securitization on competitive conditions in lodging?

4. What do the acronyms CMBS, REIT, C corp, and IPO stand for? To what does each of them refer?

5. What is mezzanine financing and what are some of its advantages?

6. What are the hazards of public ownership?

7. What is RevPAR and what can positively or negatively impact it?

8. What are the main elements of a hotel investment decision?

9. Has segmentation contributed to encroachment? What are the effects of encroachment?

10. Why did hotel management companies come into existence?

11. What is the importance of asset management to lodging owners?

Internet Exercises

1. **Site name:** Hotel Online
   URL: www.hotel-online.com
   Background information: Hotel Online is the hospitality industry's online meeting place, providing the latest and most relevant news, trends, discussion forums, employment opportunities, classified advertising, and product pricing available anywhere.
   Site name: Lodging Econometrics
   URL: lodging-econometrics.com
   Background information: Lodging Econometrics is a recognized authority on all hotel real estate including the Development Pipeline and the Sale and Transfer of Lodging Real Estate nationwide. They also compile and maintain the Industry's Census of Open and Operating Hotels including the Names of Owners and Management for more than 60,000 hotels in the United States and Canada.
   Exercises:
   a. Find and discuss at least two trends that are occurring in the hotel industry as defined by the consultants on this Web site.

b. Based on the news articles from Hotel Online, along with your current readings in the newspaper, textbooks, and so on, discuss a trend you believe is impacting on the hotel industry and indicate why you think it is important.

2. **Site name:** Starwood Hotels & Resorts Worldwide, Inc.

URL: www.starwood.com

Background information: Starwood Hotels & Resorts Worldwide, Inc. is one of the leading hotel and leisure companies in the world with approximately 850 properties in more than 95 countries and 145,000 employees at its owned and managed properties. Starwood Hotels is a fully integrated owner, operator, and franchisor of hotels and resorts.

Site name: Host Hotels and Resorts

URL: www.hosthotels.com

Background information: The vision of Host Hotels and Resorts is to be the premier lodging real estate company. Their focus is the acquisition of high quality lodging assets in prime urban and resort locations which have the potential for significant capital appreciation.

Site name: Felcor Lodging Trust

URL: www.felcor.com/

Background information: FelCor is one of the nation's largest hotel real estate investment trusts and the owner of the largest number of upscale, all-suite hotels in the nation. FelCor's consolidated portfolio is comprised of 92 hotels, located in 26 states and Canada.

Exercises:

a. Browse through the Web sites for the three REITs. What are the similarities and differences among them?

b. Who is the target market for each REIT?

c. What hotels and resorts are in the portfolio for each REIT?

d. Which of the above REITs is/are considered a "paper clip REIT"? How does it differ from a standard REIT?

3. **Site name:** American Hospitality Management

URL: www.american-hospitality.com

Background information: American Hospitality Management Company provides hotel, motel and resort management, consulting services, oversight and asset management, receivership services, and technical and preopening services in all areas of the hospitality industry.

Site name: American Property Management Corp. (APMC)

URL: www.americanpropertymanagementcorp.com

Background information: APMC is an opportunistic-focused lodging company, based in San Diego, California. Ranked by HotelBusiness magazine as the seventeenth largest hotel owner in the United States, APMC is a growing leader in the hospitality industry. The company's 36 hotels and resorts are located from coast to coast.

4. **Site name:** Kevin Regan's Testimony before the Committee on Homeland Security and Governmental Affairs

    URL: www.ahla.com/pdf/111605Regan.pdf

    Background information: Testimony of Kevin T. Regan, Regional Vice President of Operations, Southeastern United States and Caribbean, Starwood Hotels & Resorts Worldwide, Inc., before the Committee on Homeland Security and Governmental Affairs United States Senate Hearing November 16, 2005 "Hurricane Katrina: What Can Government Learn from the Private Sector's Response?"

    Exercises:

    Read the entire transcript of Mr. Regan's testimony. Mr. Regan emphasizes throughout his presentation that the keys to successful crisis management are planning, leadership, teamwork, and communication.

    a. Describe how these four components were evident throughout the description of how Starwood managed the crisis caused by the storm.

    b. What lessons can be learned by hotel managers from his testimony?

    c. Lead a class discussion on the importance of training staff for crisis situations whether they are the result of a severe storm, earthquake, terrorist activity, fire, and so forth.

Notes

1. The research on the hotel construction pipeline was conducted by Smith Travel Research and was reported in *Hotel & Motel Management* (Mark V. Lomanno, "Likelihood of Hotel Openings Related to Construction Cycle," August 2003, p. 18).
2. *Lodging Econometric*, "LE Revises Supply Side Downward for '06 and '07 and Identifies Seven Trend Setting Markets to Monitor for '08 and Beyond," October 20, 2006, http://www.lodgingintelligence.com/PR/3Q06IndPress.htm.
3. PKF Hospitality Research, "Trends in the Hotel Industry," 2003.
4. Smith Travel Research, "2002 HOST Study Findings," www.smithtravelresearch.com.
5. PKF Hospitality Research, "Trends in the Hotel Industry—Where is the risk?," 2006.
6. Ed Watkins, "Leaven Your Caution with Optimism," *Lodging Hospitality*, July 1, 2003, p. 2).
7. PKF Hospitality Research, Trends, 2006.
8. PKF Hospitality Research, Trends, 2003.
9. PKF Hospitality Research, Trends, 2006.
10. bid.
11. Ibid.
12. Ibid.
13. Ibid.
14. Ibid.

15. AH&LA Knowledge Base, "London tops European Hotel Revenue Survey/The Bench and KPMG Report," January 18, 2007, http://ahlaradio.hsyndicate.com/news/154000320/4029978.html.

16. Little, Rebecca, "Private Matters—Private equity firms have become big-time players in the lodging industry. How did they become a driving force in hospitality?" *Lodging* archives, http://www.lodgingmagazine.com/index.cfm?fm=Article.Detail&aid=116.

17. AH&LA Knowledge Base, "Lodging Econometrics Completes Development Pipelines and Three-Year Supply Growth Forecasts for 21 Asian Countries." October 12, 2006. http://alharadio.hsyndicate.com/news/4029159.html.

18. Little, Rebecca, "Private Matters."

19. The phrase "securitization of the hotel industry" is used by Patrick Ford in his article "Flood Tide," Lodging magazine, May 1997, pp. 56–61. This section draws extensively on his work.

20. Steven Shundich, "The Art of the Deal," *Hotels*, September 1997, p. 44.

21. Little, Rebecca, "Private Matters."

22. Steven Shundich, "The Art of the Deal."

23. The original use of the word mezzanine was to designate the floor between the lobby floor and the first floor in a building.

24. Mark Cahill, "Lending a Hand," *Hotels*, May 1997, p. 62.

25. Mark Cahill, "Buy, Sell, or Refinance?" *Lodging* magazine archives, March 2003, www.lodgingmagazine.com/articles_view.asp?id559.

26. Patel, Kison and Robin Trehan, "Real Estate Investment Trusts (REIT) within the Hospitailty Industry," *Lodging* magazine archives, http://ahlaradio.hysyndicate.com/news/4027198.html.

27. Ibid.

28. Ibid.

29. The term *C corp* is also derived from the classification of these corporations under Subchapter C of the IRS tax code. See *Hotels,* September 1997, p. 43.

30. Host Marriott Corp.: Several Hotels May Be Sold over Next Six to Nine Months," *The Wall Street Journal,* October 20, 2003, p. 1; "Marriott Eyes High-End Hotels," Real Estate Alert, August 20, 2003, p. 3.

31. Hayward, P., A. Taulane, and R. Little, "Lodging Innovators of 2006—Development, Chris Nassetta," Lodging archives, http://www.lodgingmagazine.com/index.cfm?fm=Article.Detail&aid1=26.

32. Mark Cahill, "Buy, Sell or Refinance?" *Lodging* magazine archives, March 2003.

33. Russell Shaw, "Public-Funding Issue Stirs Strong Emotions," *Hotel & Motel Management,* August 2003, p. 3.

34. The information is taken from "Timeline of Events—1997," which was issued by Starwood Hotels & Resorts and Starwood Trust (n.d.). The final purchase price for Sheraton is taken from the companies' press release of February 24, 1998. The months cited in the text are those of the announcement of the "definitive agreement" and not the closing date of the purchases.

35. *Westchester County Business Journal,* "Starwood Celebrates Fifth Anniversary of ITT and Westin Acquisitions," March 31, 2003, p. S2.

36. Ryan Chittum, "InterContinental to Buy Brand," *Atlanta Journal Constitution,* October 29, 2003, p. D2.

37. AH&LA Knowledge Base. "Cendant Corporation Completes Spin-offs of Realogy Corporation and Wyndham Worldwide Corporation." August 1, 2006, http://alharadio.hsyndicate.com/news/4028335.html.

38. "Starbucks: Making Values Pay," excerpt from Howard Schultz and Dori Jones Yang, *Pour Your Heart Into It* (New York: Hyperion, 1997); reprinted in Fortune, September 29, 1997, pp. 268–69.

39. Patrick Ford, "Flood Tide," *Lodging* magazine, May 1997, p. 56.

40. Avner Arbel and Robert H. Woods, "Debt Hitchhiking: How Hotels Found Low Cost Capital," *Cornell Hotel and Restaurant Administration Quarterly,* November 1990, pp. 98–104.

41. Peggy Berg, president, Highland Investment Advisors Group, remarks made during a workshop, "The Franchise Impact Issue: The Value of Flag Conversion," Hospitality Industry Investment Conference, New York, June 7, 1994.

42. Michael Levin, remarks made during a workshop, "The Value of Branding," Hospitality Industry Investment Conference, New York, June 7, 1994.

43. James J. Eyester, The Negotiation and Administration of Hotel Management Contracts, quoted in Robert M. James, "Management Companies," *Lodging* magazine, June 1985, p. 105.

44. Daniel R. Lee, *Lodging* (New York: Drexel Burnham Lambert, 1984), p. 23.

45. Robert M. James, "Management Companies," *Lodging* magazine, June 1985, p. 105.

46. Megan Rowe, "Inhospitable Hotel Management Contracts?" *National Real Estate Investor,* September 2003, p. 16.

47. Gordon Platt, "Hotel Outsourcing Helps Close the Financing Gap," *Global Finance,* June 2003, p. 37.

48. Patricia Alisau, "Third-Party Managers Work with Asset Managers to Achieve Profitable Goals," *Hotel & Motel Management,* June 16, 2003, p. 25.

The Hospitality Industry

(Courtesy of Caesars Atlantic City.)

CHAPTER TWELVE

Competition in the Lodging Business

The Purpose of this Chapter

In this chapter, we will be concerned with competition in lodging. As we did when we considered the food service business, we will use the marketing mix as a framework for the analysis of competition. First, however, we must consider the somewhat special conditions in lodging under which this competition takes place. Then it will be necessary to describe the way in which the marketing mix is applied to lodging. Finally, we will use this perspective to consider the competitive practices of the industry.

THIS CHAPTER SHOULD HELP YOU

1. Identify the five conditions of competition in lodging, and explain their effects on the hotel business.
2. Explain how the four Ps of the marketing mix are applied in lodging competition.
3. Describe the upstairs-downstairs segmentation in the lodging industry and how it meets the differing needs of customers.
4. Describe and provide examples of how hotels differentiate themselves through the variety and mix they provide in food service options and other services and amenities.
5. List the strengths and weaknesses of the use of yield management in the hotel business.
6. Describe the effects on lodging of travel intermediaries and distribution channels.
7. Describe the impact of the Internet on the hotel industry.
8. Explain how partnerships and frequent-guest programs operate and why they are important to marketing the lodging industry.

The Conditions of Competition

The beginning of the twenty-first century was characterized by extreme changes for the lodging industry and the North American lodging industry in particular. The losses experienced by the industry were related to a weakening economy, the tragedies of September 11, the war in Iraq, and the outbreak of SARS. Unlike the lodging industry crisis of the 1990s, the challenging times starting in 2001 were not directly related to overbuilding of hotels and a surplus of room inventory. Overbuilding, however, is always a concern in terms of how it can significantly and negatively impact the industry even in better economic times such as the turnaround that started in 2003. Indeed, the increasing role of public capital markets, which we discussed in the last chapter, increases the availability of capital for possible overbuilding. The low variable cost of the industry makes price cutting in the short run tempting—and price cutting is always tempting when overcapacity is a problem. Moreover, technological changes related to where, how, and when a hotel room is sold are changing the marketplace every day. The impact of the Internet on the hotel pricing structure has been a major factor—more than ever could be imagined when hotel-related Web sites first emerged. In the following sections, we will discuss each of these conditions of competition.

A FRAGMENTED MARKET

The facts of the marketplace are that the ownership of hotel properties is spread among a wide number of individuals and corporations. The presence of national and regional

A chain brand has come to be called a "flag." (Courtesy of Carlson Hotels Worldwide.)

hotel brands gives the appearance of a few dominant chains. Ownership in the hotel business, however, is not highly concentrated; rather, it is a highly **fragmented market**. A hotel brand or franchise has come to be called a "flag." Although it is not as easy for a hotel to drop a franchise as it is to take down a flag, the analogy is compelling. In converting from a chain affiliation to becoming an independent sometimes is a voluntary move on the part of the hotel's ownership. Sometimes, however, the chain drops their affiliation with the hotel for a number of possible reasons. It could be that the hotel's owners did not pay the required fees to the chain. It may have involved the hotel not maintaining the chain's standards of service or cleanliness. Franchise agreements between franchisors and franchisees stipulate in detail reasons for terminating the relationship on both the part of the chain as well as the ownership of the hotel.

The lodging industry is not static in terms of the types of hotels that may be competing against one another. The pipeline forecast included 847 new hotels opening in 2006 with 89,269 rooms and 1,084 hotels in 2007 with 119,665 rooms. The segment mainly driving the pipeline in 2006 and 2007 was the mid-market property without food and beverage. InterContinental's Holiday Inn Express and Hilton's Hampton Inn and Suites are front-runners of new hotels in this segment. Other strong developer favorites were Comfort Inns and Suites and LaQuinta Inns and Suites. The midscale segment with food and beverage was also up 120 percent with leaders being the Holiday Inn brand and Best Western. Of the hotels in the pipeline in 2006, 94 percent were less than 200 rooms. Of the luxury projects in the pipeline, another strong segment during that same period of time, 80 percent had some combination of private residences, condo hotel units, fractional vacation club or timeshare interests. An additional 20 percent of the luxury projects were part of major office or retail development projects.[1]

The supply and demand patterns are major causes of shifts in the hotel industry. Large firms have large stakes and are less likely to do something unpredictable. In a fragmented market, with many small firms seeking their own interests and survival, competition is much less predictable. When survival is at stake, as it often is in lodging, desperate measures taken by one or a few players can destabilize an entire market.

A CYCLICAL MARKET

A second condition that shapes competition in lodging, as noted in Chapter 11, is that lodging is a **cyclical industry**, one that has been characterized by periods of demand outpacing supply as well as supply surpassing demand. The immediate outlook for the industry depends, in large part, on where the industry is in the cycle. Generally, when overcapacity threatens an industry, pricing stability is undermined.

Cost Structure

A third critical competitive characteristic of the lodging business is that it has a **low variable cost** in relation to sales and a correspondingly high fixed cost. A low variable cost means that there is very little cost associated with the sale of one more room. The variable cost can be as low as $5 per rented room, ranging up to $15 or $20, while the corresponding room rate might range from $30 to $120. This large margin over costs makes it easy to cut prices and still show a profit—in the short run. The temptation to cut prices is particularly strong in periods where supply exceeds demand, occupancies and revenues fall, and the need to meet the burden of high fixed costs becomes more pressing.

Securitization

Another related condition, also discussed in Chapter 11, is the growth in **securitization** in the industry. Securitization, by making capital more readily available to developers, makes overbuilding more of a threat. New sources of financing clearly increase the total financing available for purchase of hotels and bring an increased number of firms with deep pockets (i.e., well-financed firms) to the hotel business in all of its segments.

Technological Revolution

A final factor is the **impact of technology** on the hotel business. Technology and the change it brings cuts across all areas of the hotel business: improving service, facilitating control of costs, heightening security, for example. As a condition of competition, however, we need to note that in the area of marketing, the technological revolution has fundamentally altered the way hotel rooms are offered for sale. The Internet has had a tremendous impact on the way hotels do business. Internet-based channels of distribution such as Travelocity and Expedia have put the hotel consumer in the driver's seat in terms of shopping for the most competitive room rates. Finally, computerization of guest and customer prospect information makes possible the use of individualized information in planning and executing promotional plans.

Collectively, these five factors of competition describe an industry that is, on a scale of competitive to monopolistic, highly competitive. Within the boundaries of these conditions of competition, we can use the marketing mix to analyze competitive

INDUSTRY CHARACTERISTIC	IMPACT
Fragmented ownership	Unpredictability, especially in down markets
Cyclical Periodic overbuilding	Overcapacity exerts downward pressure on
Low variable cost High fixed cost	Exerts downward pressure on prices
Increasing securitization	Makes capital more available for development
Technological revolution	Heightens role of travel intermediaries (travel agents, reservation services, airlines, etc.), adding to marketing costs and reducing control over price

Figure 12.1
The conditions of competition in lodging

practices in lodging. Figure 12.1 summarizes the five conditions of competition in the lodging industry.

The Marketing Mix in Lodging

The **marketing mix** is conventionally thought of as encompassing the four Ps: product, price, place, and promotion.[2] In most cases, the application of these four terms varies somewhat as one moves from industry to industry. In lodging, then, we can hardly be surprised that we need to modify the four Ps to make the concepts that underlie them in lodging clearer.

Product, for instance, includes both physical goods and services. It also involves characteristics that are present in the individual property, such as the guest rooms, the lobby, and the amenities package, and services offered by a hotel. However, product also refers to the lodging system's (chain's or franchise group's) services. Ultimately, the product the guest consumes is an experience—what happens to her or him, in its totality, during a visit.

Price refers not to some fixed rate but a price that varies with levels of demand and with customer groups served. Because there is no inventory of yesterday's rooms, there is pressure to sell rooms each day. Alternatively, what is for sale is a fixed capacity, and so price tends to rise in periods of high demand. The truth is that the rack rate (the listed price you might find in a directory) is paid by only a small percentage of guests,

The lodging product consists of the guest's entire experience. In Las Vegas, the Excalibur and other huge resort hotels seek to capture the guest's imagination. (Courtesy of Excalibur Hotel and Casino.)

probably less than one-fifth. It is more realistic, therefore, to speak of pricing policy rather than just price. As noted previously, the industry is cyclical, and fixed costs tend to exert downward pressure on prices in markets where there is overcapacity.

Place, referring to the location of an individual property, is a very important aspect of the lodging marketing mix, but the places where the hotel room is sold—for instance, travel agents and other travel intermediaries—are also extremely important. This latter aspect, we will find, is also a system characteristic in chains and other lodging groups.

Promotion refers to marketing communication, generally taken to include persuasive activities such as advertising, sales promotion, and public relations. We will also include here persuasive activities such as frequent-traveler programs and other individualized means to reward customers for brand loyalty.

Figure 12.2 summarizes the lodging marketing mix as it is discussed in this chapter. In the next section, we will explore these concepts in detail in terms of market tactics.

LEISURE TRAVELERS	BUSINESS TRAVELERS
Value for the price	Location of hotel
Location of hotel	Previous experience with hotel or chain
Room rate	Reputation of hotel or chain
Previous experience with hotel or chain	Value for the price
Reputation of hotel or chain	Room rate

Figure 12.2
Hotel/Resort Selection Factors—Extremely/Very Influential in Determining Selection in 2003

Source: Peter C. Yesawich, "Business and Leisure Travelers: Is There Really a Difference? *Hotel and Motel Management,* November 3, 2003, p. 10.

COMPETITIVE TACTICS

The competitive strategies and tactics used in the lodging marketplace are implemented by using the elements of the marketing mix to target guest segments and to differentiate one hotel offering from another. The notion that "if you build a better mousetrap, the world will beat a pathway to your door" may have an element of truth in it. The success of the hospitality transaction does begin with the product, but in a competitive market, it must be priced right and conveniently placed for the purchaser. Finally, the offer of the hotel must be persuasively communicated to the right target markets.

Product in a Segmented Market

Lodging products are made up of both goods and services. By the term goods, we mean the tangible aspects of lodging such as a lobby or a guest room. Services, on the other hand, involve guest interactions with staff or hotel facilities. Both goods and services are crafted to meet the needs and preferences of particular target markets. At a very basic level, the industry is divided into properties that serve the **"upstairs" guest** and those that serve the **"downstairs" guest**.[3]

Upstairs guests are interested in what you find upstairs in a hotel, that is, guest rooms. They want comfortable, clean accommodations. This market is willing to give up extra services—that is, services that they don't want—for a lower price. The success of the limited-service segment clearly indicates that there is a large upstairs market that focuses on just the basics in the guest room. Fairfield Inns, Comfort Inns, or Hampton Inns represent a midscale version of the upstairs market, while many all-suite properties represent a deluxe approach to the upstairs market, just as Motel 6 aims at the economy-minded. It is important to see how each focuses on guest preference in a different way.

The downstairs market, on the other hand, either needs the more extensive services of a full-service hotel or finds them desirable. Downstairs guests want the traditional lobby floor attractions of full-service hotels: dining rooms, cocktail lounges, meeting and banquet facilities, and the like. Downstairs guests are willing to pay for the additional services because they are necessary or because they can readily afford them. Generally, we would include not only full-service transient hotels but also convention hotels, conference centers, and resort properties in the service-intensive downstairs segment. One of the most basic service decisions involves food service. Another decision involves the level and kind of other services and amenities offered to the guest. We should note again that downstairs guests traveling on business during the week on an expense

Limited-service hotels offer a free continental breakfast in pleasant surroundings, such as Wingate Inns, shown here. (Courtesy of Cendant Corp.)

account may be upstairs guests seeking a lower price when traveling at their own expense on the weekend.

It is important to realize that the upstairs-downstairs segmentation represents basic strategies, active programs aimed at achieving customer patronage. The upstairs strategy reduces certain services to permit the property to operate profitably while offering the guest a superior guest room and a lower price. The downstairs strategy is more service-intensive and is aimed at a guest who is willing to pay for more service.

Another perspective regarding guest needs and expectations involves comparing leisure travelers to business travelers. The distinction between these two groups of guests is often stressed in the industry literature. Researchers regularly try to gauge what are the most important factors to each group as they travel and make hotel selections.

Food Service

Hotels serving the upstairs market have chosen to eliminate or reduce drastically the food service available in the property. It is important, however, to realize that they have not ignored food service. Off-premise food service is almost invariably available nearby, and basic guest needs—breakfast, for instance—are often met in the property. Some examples of what we mean are described below.

Limited Food and Beverage. The practice of giving away a continental breakfast is certainly not new. It has been common in small hotels and inns for years. However, the advertised, standardized availability of a free breakfast—that is, one covered by the price of the room—has a special appeal. In the economy market, for instance, a continental breakfast of juice, pastry, and coffee is generally all that is provided. In some all-suite properties as well, a continental breakfast is the standard, but a number offer a full, cooked-to-order breakfast.

Many all-suite properties also provide a scaled-down on-premise restaurant, but very few offer substantial meeting and banquet facilities. Residence Inns has a grocery shopping service available to its guests, and Homewood Suites provides an on-premise convenience store. Because long-stay suites provide a full kitchen, they do not offer any food service beyond a complimentary breakfast. Among all-suite properties, then, there is not the uniformity in curtailment of food service that is found among most budget properties. In general, however, elimination or at least simplification of food service is the rule. The purpose is to meet the preferences of the upstairs guest while maintaining a competitive rate.

While limited food and beverage options are appropriate for many hotel guests, there are visitors that look forward to fine-dining experiences during their hotel stays or want the availability of room service or banquet facilities. Full-service hotels are going to be more appropriate for these guests who are, in most cases, willing to pay a higher room rate.

Managing Food Service. For full-service hotels, the option of discontinuing food service—or limiting it to breakfast—just won't work. For lower-priced hotels, this has been effective but has driven down margins. On the other hand, managing a food service operation presents many problems. Although growth in lodging food service is keeping pace with the food service industry growth overall, over the long run most hotel restaurants make little, if any, profit. This is largely due to their capital costs and a fair share of undistributed operating expenses.

Operating a restaurant that is not very profitable or even losing money presents some real problems. The most obvious is a poor or negative return on investment, but this is really the least of the difficulties. More serious is the fact that an unsuccessful operation is always facing pressure to reduce costs, to cut the losses. There is a point, however, beyond which cost cutting impairs service and annoys or offends the guest, thus risking high-profit rooms revenue.

Even if the cost-cutting pressure is manageable, food service demands a great deal of attention from top management. When top managers in a hotel lack food service experience, it is difficult for them to supervise the skilled people they have hired to run the restaurant. Even where the general managers have the experience, they may feel their time and attention should be spent elsewhere.

Our discussion to this point makes a good case for turning the hotel's restaurant over to a company more expert in food service. The practice of **leasing** the restaurant to an outside food service operator has a long history in North America but is now being viewed in a new light. It is becoming particularly popular in small to midsized full-service operations and in all-suite hotels. Embassy Suites leases most of its restaurants, and because Embassy operates its own complimentary breakfast, basic services are assured for the rooms guests. Properties that have selected good operators generally have good results. Some hotels report having as much as doubled their food and beverage revenues after turning their restaurants over to a third party.

Unfortunately, although leasing can solve some restaurant problems, there are some real disadvantages to leasing a hotel's food service. The most fundamental problem is that there are now two companies running major parts of the hotel, and each company has its own business objectives and priorities. In good times, the clash of interests is often not apparent. When business turns down, however, because of the restaurant's higher variable cost structure, the restaurant company has to cut costs—and services—to survive. However, this is just the point where the hotel needs its restaurant to be a service department if it is to be competitive. Maintaining service levels may benefit rooms sales—but there is no way for the restaurant to derive much benefit from the sale of a few more rooms. With this situation, it is no wonder that leased operations work out reasonably well until business goes through a bad patch, at which point disputes multiply.

Reductions in Food Service. Another option that hotels have at their disposal is to simply limit the food service options for their customers. For example, Marriott Courtyard (a 500-unit brand) offers a very limited food service program. When the company determined that, although they had strong breakfast and lunch sales, their dinner business was minimal, they closed their restaurant at dinner and eventually for lunch, leaving the restaurant open for breakfast only. This once would have been an unthinkable reduction in service for a hotel, but with the great expansion in midpriced and upscale dinner houses, there are undoubtedly plenty of restaurants in the immediate area of these hotels to fill their guests' needs. Other hotels have since followed Marriott's lead.

Brand-Name Restaurants. At a minimum, the availability of some kind of food service in the immediate area is essential for most hotels that do not operate their own food service facilities. Probably the best-known company to rely on the **on-site franchised restaurant** is La Quinta Inns. This limited-service hotel chain offers restaurant operators a build-to-suit leased restaurant on the motel site. It has used this arrangement with several restaurant companies, including Denny's, Cracker Barrel, Bob Evans Farms, Shoney's, and Waffle House.[4]

Full-service hotels have begun to lease out their restaurants to franchisees of major food service chains. Alternatively, some hotel operators have become franchisees of these chains themselves. The names of chains now operating within a hotel, such as Denny's, Pizza Hut, Bennigan's, T.G.I. Friday's, and Steak and Ale, are well known to the traveling public and, as such, serve as a draw for the hotel. In addition, as franchisees, these operations receive field support and advice from the franchise organization that can help smooth out some of the rough spots.

Leased Specialty Restaurants. Upscale operators such as Hilton are generally not prepared to give up their basic food service operations. They have found, however, that leasing some space to a well-known brand-name operator not only will result in substantial revenue but will enhance the image of the hotel and act as a draw to rooms guests. One of the longest-standing examples of this tactic is Trader Vic's, a Polynesian restaurant, which, after an initial success in Hilton's Palmer House in Chicago, has gone on to lease and operate in other Hilton hotels. At the other end of the scale of complexity, Sheraton decided to improve its coffee sales and "jump on the bandwagon for recognizability" with its new long-term relationship with Starbucks Coffee. Sheraton is taking a two-tiered approach: Some hotels have run Starbucks outlets through licensing arrangements, while other locations have a leased Starbucks. Starbucks outlets can also be found in numerous Marriott hotels. Starbucks Coffee Company and Marriott International, Inc. have a long-term licensing agreement for coffeehouse locations in select Marriott Hotels, Resorts, and Suites; Marriott Conference Centers; and Renaissance Hotels, Resorts, and Suites properties.[5]

Conventional Hotel Restaurants. A single direction for hotels' food services is by no means clear. Some hotel operators are finding that they can't compete successfully with local top-quality food service restaurants in attracting local trade and so are building smaller restaurants and reducing the number of food service outlets in the hotel from two or three to one. Some luxury hotels are opting for casual outlets rather than formal dining rooms. A growing number of hotels are opening European-style bistros and brasseries that combine a casual atmosphere with an upscale feel.

Upscale hotel companies such as Marriott and Hyatt, as well as luxury properties such as Four Seasons, continue to meet guest expectations for full service with a variety of restaurants in their properties, and these almost always include a top-of-the-line, luxury restaurant. The editor of *Hotels* put the case for hotel restaurants as follows:

> Hotel companies such as Sheraton, Shangri-La, Kimpton Hotels, Disney, London's Savoy Group and many others run successful restaurants and, in some cases, enormously successful banquet and catering departments. The potential residual effect

Upscale full-service hotels provide a variety of food and beverage options. (Courtesy of Caesars Atlantic City.)

of a well-run F&B department is increased occupancy—in some cases by as much as 33 percent—and support for your company's quality image.[6]

It is true that food service has been greatly simplified in the economy segment that serves the upstairs market. It has frequently been de-emphasized or leased out in some midscale properties. Nevertheless, in the downstairs market of convention, resort, and big-city luxury hotels, a successful food service operation continues to be absolutely essential.

Restaurants as a Competitive Strategy. Hotel restaurants have historically not been profitable after all costs are considered. This difficulty arises because food service is one of a hotel's service departments. The argument for devoting significant time and effort to food service, however, is fairly straightforward: In many markets, food service adds points to occupancy rates and secures local referrals. The resulting higher occupancies more than offset the lower profit on food service.

On the other hand (and perhaps as a result of their financial history), hotel food and beverage departments have become much more profit-driven. After all of the restructuring, downsizing, reimaging, and outsourcing, there is evidence that suggests that food and beverage has begun to contribute to a hotel's profitability.

Properties serving the upstairs market have opted to offer limited services to guests—and, as a result, can offer attractive room rates. They know they can count on restaurants in their immediate area to supplement the complimentary services they offer in-house. In both cases—upstairs and downstairs—product, service, and resulting price are being crafted as a means to serve the guests' needs and preferences and, thus, gain patronage in a highly competitive market.

OTHER SERVICES AND AMENITIES

A wide range of services (other than food and beverage) is used by hotels to differentiate a property from its competitors. **Differentiation** can be achieved through distinctive physical plant features, upscale services, and other products as described below.

The Concierge and Superfloors. As we noted in Chapter 10, the basic function of the **concierge** is to provide guest service and information. The crossed-keys symbol of the concierge is intended to convey a degree of expertise and knowledge significantly above that of the bell staff. The concierge knows the right restaurants and the best shows, and can probably get reservations or tickets if they are required. In many ways, the concierge acts as a friend to the stranger, giving service and rendering that "extra" in service that makes a stay a distinctive experience in hospitality.

Many hotels have added a concierge to the lobby staff, whereas a number of companies associate the concierge closely or exclusively with their special areas, often restricted only to guests staying on floors such as executive floors and tower suites. On these floors, special lounges and other services are commonly provided. Luxury hotels, such as the Four Seasons or Dallas's Mansion at Turtle Creek, offer substantially the same services as those available on the executive floors, but to all their guests. At the other extreme, limited-service operators, particularly in the economy and budget segments, have pared extras to the bone. As one well-known economy chain's advertising put it, "We don't have it because you don't want it."

Fitness Facilities. Fitness has become a major concern for many North Americans. It is not surprising, therefore, that **fitness facilities** of some kind have become fairly standard in most hotels. Some provision for fitness is commonly found even in economy hotels. One of the latest trends in this area is hotels providing fitness equipment that can be actually used in the guest room. Some hotels, like Hilton Hotels, are investing in portable equipment such as StairMasters and treadmills that can be easily brought to the guest room for private and flexible workout regimes.

Spa Programs. Tremendous growth has occurred in **spa facilities**, which are no longer limited to just resort properties. Hyatt, Fairmont, Four Seasons, and Ritz-Carlton hotel companies have urban spas catering to the needs of business travelers. These companies have found that business guests, needing relief from travel-related

Fitness facilities, such as these at the Wingate Inn, are increasingly in demand by travelers. (Courtesy of Cendant Corp.)

stress, have little price resistance. Both men and women relate the spa visits to increased performance whether related to helping mitigate jet lag, getting better rest during the stay, relieving stress, or overall just being more productive. The hotels have found that when the spa services get results, the fees are typically not an issue. Hotels with urban spas have found scheduling important to meet the demands of busy travelers, with many facilities open from early morning to late evening hours.[7]

Business Centers. Even with guest rooms equipped in many properties like mini office suites, business travelers expect and use **business centers** particularly in full-service hotels. Although an increasing number of business travelers are equipped with their own laptop computers, some business and leisure travelers may need the computer access typically found in a hotel's business center. For other guests, the guest room Internet access and printer and/or fax machine may not be sufficient to handle larger projects. In such cases, a business center like the one found at the Marriott World Center in Orlando, Florida, is vital, with computers and copying equipment for large-scale jobs, faxes, secretarial support, and even a bindery for books. In Seoul, South Korea, the Radisson Hotel has a business center with two conference rooms, workstations, Internet hookups, audiovisual equipment, secretarial and translation services, courier and shipping services, and business card printing services. Even economy motels make business services available, but typically with limited, self-serve options. Business travelers are on the road frequently and are potential repeat guests. It makes sense to cater to their needs in order to gain their regular patronage.

Wingate Inns, and other chains, provide extensive business centers for their guests. (Courtesy of Cendant Corp.)

Service. Another differentiator that is very difficult to copy is excellence in service across the board, in all departments. In this connection, it is interesting to note that it was limited-service chains that led the way with the 100 percent satisfaction guarantee. The guarantee, in turn, is based on an operating strategy of empowerment, that is, of giving employees the discretion to take care of the guests' needs or problems right away. The result has been very high consumer satisfaction ratings and a more motivated workforce. Reportedly, the guarantee itself costs very little (0.3 percent of sales), and fulfilling it gains much more favorable public relations and word of mouth than could be purchased for such a modest cost.[8] The degree to which service guarantees have been widely adopted, however, suggests that at least the statement of a guarantee is not difficult to copy. The development of a company culture that is really capable of fulfilling the promise of the guarantee, however, is something that cannot be easily duplicated.

Assessing Services and Amenities. As a competitive tactic, what stands out is the ease with which many of the services and amenities we have been discussing can be copied. The first hotel in a city that put in a television set undoubtedly had an advantage—but not for long. In addition, shampoo—once rarely seen in a hotel room—has now become commonplace. Indeed, in regard to personal-care amenities, it is becoming necessary to have them just to avoid damaging the property's reputation, but it is difficult to see them as offering any lasting competitive advantage. Similarly, exercise facilities are an easily duplicated service. However, finding or training a good concierge is almost as difficult as providing memorable food service. Again, food service is very

Hotel Honored among World Business Hotels

In addition to hotel rating services such as Mobil and AAA, hotels can be recognized by professional associations and trade publications. One such publication is *Institutional Investor,* a trade publication that conducts an annual survey of chief executive officers regarding their travel experiences. The survey measures room quality, service, dining, location, and overall design. For the first time in the survey's 26-year history, a hotel in the District of Columbia won. The Mandarin Oriental Washington was selected in December 2006 as the top business hotel in the world. In 2006, the hotel hosted 453 events and conferences with 90 percent of the guests comprised of corporate or convention guests. In 2005, 49 percent, or 14.1 million, of the travelers to Washington, D.C. were there on business. The hotel, in distinguishing their service from other properties, has added several creative options for the business traveler. One is a service whereby meeting planners can book spa meeting breaks for convention-goers. The hotel's location was also indicated as a plus with proximity to Reagan National Airport, Union Station, and the Capitol.

Source: K. Wilmeth, "Mandarin Oriental Washington takes top honors among world business hotels." *The Examiner,* December 13, 2006.

difficult to do well, and its very complexity ensures that it will not be easy to copy. Although some property types may be able to dispense with food service and rely on restaurants in their neighborhood, it seems likely that they will have greater difficulty in differentiating themselves from their competitors, especially as the number of properties multiplies and properties age. Industry Practice Note 12.1 illustrates one of the many forms of recognition given to hotels in highlighting their services and amenities.

SYSTEMWIDE SERVICES

In franchise organizations, the franchisor is responsible for the design of the basic business system. A successful franchise will be designed to provide the services its target markets seek. Moreover, routine services such as those provided by property management systems will ensure error-free operation of functions including accounting, billing, and credit, which are important to the guest. Thus, the franchisor is responsible for establishing a mode of operations that is professional and leaves the guest feeling that he or she is in secure hands. This enhances the guest's experience.

Franchising provides a brand with a means to move relatively quickly into many geographic markets. Although franchising is well established in the United States, it is still a fairly new business practice overseas, where conditions for franchising vary from one region to another.

The maintenance of quality in operations is a property-level responsibility, but **quality assurance** through inspection systems is a vital function of the franchisor. You can maintain your property, but your reputation is really in the hands of all your fellow franchisees. Establishing an acceptable level of quality, ensuring that quality through frequent inspections, and providing assistance when a problem persists are all important activities of the franchisor, as is the encouragement of high operating standards. Some franchisors award ratings somewhat like the Mobil star rating system and publish those ratings in their directories. They also encourage franchisees to publicize their ratings in their advertising. Franchisors also arrange for mentoring staff of properties that are experiencing quality problems by teams from more successful franchise members. Another important service rendered by the franchise or chain organization is a national or, more commonly, international reservation service. This will be discussed in a later section.

Another aspect of product involves the brand name of the hotel. Brand is thought of as an aspect of product because it affects the consumer's perception of the product. When you see a sign that says Motel 6, Hampton Inn, or Hilton, you undoubtedly have different images before you set foot in the property. We will be concerned with brands again when we discuss advertising.

Brand names are not inexpensive. PKF Hospitality Research found franchising fees to average 3.7 percent of total revenues. There was variation, however, in franchising fees based on the type of hotel. Limited service hotel franchise fees averaged 5.8 percent, whereas resorts averaged 1.4 percent.[9] Figure 12.3 shows franchise fees as a percentage of total revenue for hotel companies based on category. Typical franchise fees include the initial fee, royalties, marketing contributions, reservations fees, loyalty-program expenses, and other applicable charges. Selecting a brand is a major decision of the property's owners. According to one source, a major determinant in the selection process should be the central reservation contribution. A reasonable expectation

PROPERTY TYPE	RATIOS BASED ON TOTAL REVENUES	PER AVAILABLE ROOM PER YEAR
All Hotels	3.7%	$1,712
Full Service	3.7%	1,766
Limited service	5.8%	1,066
Resort hotels	1.8%	1,602
Suite hotels	6.8%	2,272
Convention hotels	2.3%	1,583

Figure 12.3
Franchise Fees (Including Marketing Fees)

Franchisors–Franchisees: A Growing Team Approach

The relationship between the franchisor and franchisee has not always been harmonious in many industry segments, including hospitality. There are several examples in the hotel industry of how franchisors and franchisees are starting to work as a team for the mutual benefit of both parties.

For example, historically, franchise fees have been set in stone by the franchisors, with no flexible relief allowed for franchisees. Vagabond Franchise System offers royalty and marketing fees that start at 3 percent for the first year and increase to 3.5 percent by year two and 4 percent by the third year and following years. The graduated fee structure acknowledges that a franchised hotel typically is not an instant success. The new hotel starts a process of building clientele by becoming known by the traveling public. The money saved in a cheaper royalty fee can be utilized for local marketing efforts in helping to build the business.

WestCoast Hospitality Corporation may offer one of the industry's most flexible systems, with the royalty fee ranging from 2 percent to 4 percent of room revenue. WestCoast franchises the Red Lion brand. The sliding scale system for Red Lion franchisees is based on the amount of room revenue contributed by the company's central reservation system. If the central reservation system (CRS) contributes as much as 19.9 percent of the property's room revenue, there is a 2 percent royalty charge. If the revenue ranges from 20 percent to 24.9 percent, the royalty fee goes up to 3 percent and 4 percent if more than 25 percent of the room revenue is generated through the CRS. WestCoast also provides windows in which the franchisee can terminate their franchise agreement without paying any fees if the franchisor's contribution doesn't exceed 15 percent of the hotel's total revenue during the prior 12 months. According to executives with the franchisor WestCoast Hospitality, their approach focuses on the franchisor working for their money. One stated, "If we deliver reservations, franchisees will not want to leave. If we don't deliver, they have the right to leave."

WestCoast is not alone in their commitment to franchisor performance. Baymont Inns and Suites has performance benchmarks in the brand's franchise agreements. If the benchmarks are not met, there is a sliding scale for fees. If the franchisor is not producing over a period of time, the franchisee can leave for no charge.

Another growing trend is the areas of protection that are increasingly being written into franchise agreements. A typical concern among hotel operators is the competition with another hotel under the same flag or with hotels in the same family of brands within a company. Franchisors are starting to commit to observing established zones around franchised hotels in which they will not license other hotel properties.

Sources: Bruce Adams, "Fee Structures under Microscope: Reservations, Years in Franchise System Can Determine Royalty-Fee Percentage," *Hotel & Motel Management,* May 19, 2003, p. 1; Tony Dela Cruz, "Sliding Fee Scales, Areas of Protection Promote Fair Franchising," *Hotel & Motel Management,* May 19, 2003, p. 24.

is that central reservations will contribute from 15 percent to 20 percent of occupancy. Other items that an owner should analyze are how marketing dollars are spent, the availability of regional marketing support groups, stringency of quality standards, effectiveness of customer satisfaction scores, and frequency of property visits from sales and marketing staff and operations consultants. Industry Practice Note 12.2 discusses changes that are occurring between franchisors and franchisees.

Price and Pricing Tactics

Some would say that the goal of price is to maximize profit—and that may be the intention of many who set prices. However, in anything but the short term, the very competitive hotel market restrains price gouging. There is also a lower limit on rates, which is set by cost—the cost of the property (capital cost), the cost of operating the property, and a reasonable return for ownership. Otherwise, the hotel will go out of business. Thus, we can say that upper and lower boundaries for price are set by competition in the market and cost.

With a low **variable cost**—say, $10 to rent one more room—and plenty of margin between that variable cost and a selling price of, say, $75, the decision to discount is not difficult. Add to that the fact that there are **fixed costs** (payroll for a minimum crew size, fixed overhead costs, a mortgage and interest or rent) that must be met to keep the doors open. Pricing is also subject to the fact that unsold rooms have no value the next day; that is, there is no inventory. As a result, during slow periods, whether a recession or just an off-season, there is a tendency toward discounting when demand is slack.

Location is a critical factor in the success of a hotel, inn, or resort. (Courtesy of Four Seasons Hotels.)

On the other hand, in times of peak demand, prices tend to be at their maximum. Pricing is subject to the pressure of limited capacity—there are only so many rooms that can be sold on any given night, and so when demand is expected to be very high, there is very little give in rates. Limited capacity supports and raises price in good times.

Under these circumstances, there is a natural tendency for hotel prices to vary with demand: discounted during slow periods but at their upper limits when demand is strong. However, hotels can't afford to drift at the mercy of these short-run currents. Hotel pricing, in practice, is proactive; that is, pricing, like other elements of the marketing mix, should be used to attract customers' long-run patronage, not just to generate revenue for the short run. If a convention will bring in 1,000 room nights (three days for 330 people), it may make sense to rent rooms with a regular rate of $175 for $165 to convention attendees in order to get the convention, especially considering the food and beverage, meeting room rental, and other spending such a large group will bring to the property. If there is logic to reducing rates in order to attract a convention, a similar process of reasoning can be used to set a special corporate rate for companies that will use, say, 1,000 room nights a year. The principle is that of a discount for a large-volume sale.

The regular rates may be too high for some types of customers who can't afford full rates or who have a low level of reimbursement: clergy, government employees and military personnel, sports teams, and academics. These market segments might never consider the hotel if all that was available was the regular rate. Recall that a hotel has busy periods but also slow periods, and it becomes clear that these groups of people, even at reduced rates, can add significantly to profit as customers during a slow weekend or off-season period. The alternative is to have the rooms stand empty, yielding no revenue.

We could add to the list of special cases, but this should be enough to suggest why price is not some fixed figure but one that varies with conditions and with the customers being served. The question does arise, however, as to when special rates should be honored. Simple logic suggests that during very slow periods, a hotel might be glad to have all the special cases described previously, even at rates discounted 25 to 50 percent. On the other hand, a hotel is not interested in selling a $175 room for $95.50 during a period when the hotel is certain to be full. In between peaks and valleys in demand, there are times when the rates that should be charged are not quite so clear and may have to be decided on a day-by-day basis. To deal with this set of issues, the tool of yield management was adapted from a similar practice developed by the airlines.

YIELD MANAGEMENT

No discussion of pricing is complete without mentioning **yield management**, a concept that is often misunderstood even by those who practice it. One knowledgeable researcher defines yield management as follows:

Yield Management is a method that can help a firm sell the right unit to the right customer at the right time and for the right price. It guides the decision of how to allocate undifferentiated units of limited capacity to available demand in a way that maximizes profit or revenue. The question is, how much should one sell at what price and to which market segment.[10]

The process of developing a yield management system begins with a study of room demand in a property over a period of some years. Based on this history, regular patterns of slow and peak periods—and those in between—are identified, and, via a computer, the information is modeled so as to give a theoretical forecast of demand. Managers then begin to plan their pricing tactics based on history and a forecast of actual expected events. The following conversation might take place during a hotel's planning session:

> Week A is theoretically a busy week, but that's because that's when the Intergalactic Homebrewer's Association meeting is held. Since that piece of business has moved to another city, we'd better open up the special rate categories or we'll be in real trouble. On the other hand, week B has usually been slow, but this year we have the World's Best Bicycle Show and so we'll be full. Let's close out all special rates except to our best corporate accounts.

Yield management, then, is based on combining a history of room demand with a current forecast for demand. Normally, forecasts are made for a period of a year but reviewed quarterly, monthly, weekly, and, finally, daily. As demand shifts, apparent slow periods heat up, and forecasted busy days turn soft. Throughout this period, the rates are adjusted up and down to try to maximize revenue. Although a computer is not absolutely necessary for this activity, most hotels use a special computer program to manage yields, and indeed, many central reservation systems have a yield management function built into their programs for each property served.

The Problems of Yield Management. Although yield management helps solve recurrent problems regarding day-to-day rate variations, its implementation presents some serious problems. From the customer's point of view, pricing may appear arbitrary and unfair. Guest A visiting with Guest B in the lobby may discover that the two of them have identical rooms but quite different rates. The rate listed in a chain's directory (often called the rack rate) may be charged to only a few unknowing customers.

Rate differentials, during the same time period and for the same room type are due to a number of reasons as delineated below:

- The guest may have a group rate because of attending a conference, convention, or social event at or nearby the hotel.

■ The guest may have a corporate or governmental special rate.

■ The room was reserved at a different point in time—perhaps before room demand escalated (then the rate would likely be lower) or after the room demand escalated (resulting in a higher room rate).

■ The rate is part of a package perhaps with an airline ticket, rental car, or event tickets included.

■ The guest is staying for a longer period of time and subsequently received a lower rate.

■ Increasingly, the consumer (i.e., guest) shopped on the Internet between hotel distributors such as Travelocity.com or Expedia.com and the hotel's own Web site and found a discounted room rate.

There is no question that extensive discounting has taken place in the lodging industry. Discounting, as related to the impact of the Internet, will be explored more in the next section. Whatever public perception there may be of inconsistent discounts, the pressures on managers to maximize revenue based on yield management are here to stay. One researcher suggests four ground rules for practicing yield management in ways that are more acceptable to guests:

1. Disclosure of the rate structure and the concessions offered should be available to customers, "for example, a hotel can advertise the various rates available and the restrictions or benefits associated with each of these rates."

2. Cancellation restrictions can be offered along with a reduced rate so as to match the customer's benefit with one for the hotel, "for example, Marriott offers a substantially lower price for advance purchases."

3. Other reasonable restrictions such as a minimum length of stay may be offered in exchange for a favorable rate.

4. Different prices are offered for products that are perceived to be different. A room with a view or one on an "executive" floor may carry a higher price; lower prices are seen as fair where these guarantees are not required.[11]

Another area of problems for yield management lies in staff training. If a customer stayed in a hotel for $75 last time and asks for the same rate, a well-trained reservationist can explain that that category of rooms is sold out. An untrained (or disgruntled) reservationist might respond instead, "Sorry, we're almost full, so we're only selling at our maximum rate."

The reservationist's and desk clerk's jobs are to try to "sell up," to get the highest rate possible. Today's varying rate structures are complicated, however, and a poorly trained reservationist who does not know the twists and turns of special rates may end up having them explained to him or her by a regular guest. Once the guest is in control of the transaction, minimum rate and maximum upgrade are the most likely outcome.

Place—and Places

LOCATION

Location is a widely recognized factor in the success of a hotel. Ideal hotel locations have long been at the center of travel networks and near destinations. Airport hotels and roadside hotels come immediately to mind. Downtown hotels were once located downtown because they were near the railroad station, then the hub of the principal means of transportation. Today, downtown hotels' locations are advantageous because they are close to the business and cultural destinations their guests come to visit.

The decision to build a specific hotel in a particular location is generally based on a feasibility study. The contents of a feasibility study are outlined in Figure 12.4. The location of an individual hotel is of vital importance to that property for the present and future. A feasibility study, therefore, must incorporate confirmed, tentative, and speculative plans for an area or city that could impact a hotel's location.

Many American franchise operators have a presence overseas. (Radisson St. Thomas Mount [Chenai, India]; Courtesy of Carlson Hotels Worldwide.)

Site location	Relative to transportation systems and destinations
Demand analysis	Demand in immediate areas as well as in the wider (i.e., city- or areawide) community
Market characteristics	Trends in demographic and economic conditions; used to support demand projections
Analysis of the competition	1. Quality of competitive operators
	2. Number of competitive units relative to present and projected demand
	3. Outlook for new competition
Financial analysis	1. Projection of occupancy, average rate, total income, and expense
	2. Commentary on feasibility of the project

Figure 12.4

Contents of a feasibility study. (Source: Adapted from Stephen Rushmore, CRE, How to Perform an Economic Feasibility Study of a Proposed Hotel/Motel.)

DISTRIBUTION CHANNELS

There are a number of ways that connections are made between hotel rooms and perspective guests. Collectively, these "conduits" between potential guests and the hotel rooms awaiting their arrival are called **distribution channels**. The businesses and other entities that are active in the distribution channels are referred to as channel members. These include hotel chains, franchise systems, and referral (membership) services such as Best Western, as well as hotel sales and representation companies such as Utell and Unirez. It is rare that a hotel can fill its rooms from just one distribution channel. Each channel has a cost associated with it along with a rate structure that each channel delivers in selling the property's rooms.

The changing dynamics of distribution channels is described in Industry Practice Note 12.3. Travel agents are channel members, as are other agencies that make travel arrangements such as travel wholesalers and incentive houses. The latter put together packages to be used by companies to reward their employees and dealers for outstanding performance. Although individual hotels are channel members and can influence other channel members to gain sales, the franchisor (or chain headquarters) takes the heaviest responsibility for determining and maintaining the group's relationship with the other channel members.

Hotel chains and franchise organizations maintain national and regional sales offices and provide central reservation services to hotels that are part of their system. One

Travel Intermediaries: Utell Acquires Unirez

In November of 2003, Pegasus Solutions, Inc. bought its competitor, Unirez, for $38 million in cash. This purchase involved two of the largest travel intermediaries, Utell and Unirez, joining forces. The purchase by Pegasus was expected to expand the reach of its Utell division, particularly with a stronger presence in the United States. Utell is the industry's largest reservation service provider, with customers who are based mostly in Europe.

Both Utell and Unirez operate call centers and help hotels distribute property information such as price and availability, on central reservation systems used by travel agents and on the Internet. By acquiring Unirez, Pegasus can sell services to hotels that are more cost-conscious.

Unirez, although a young company, had an extremely fast and successful growth pattern. The company was formed in the late 1990s by Dwight Hendrickson, who had previously worked for competitor Lexington. Unirez made a profit after its first full year of business. The simple-to-use format and flexibility of Unirez contributed to its success. It was Internet-based and had the capability of hotels to make changes within minutes. Utell's system, on the other hand, was more sophisticated and was used by larger customers, but it did not have the capability for making immediate changes. With the merger, it was expected that the two companies can grow much more quickly than when, as Dwight Hendrickson was quoted, "they were trying to eat each other's young."

Source: Suzanne Marta, "Dallas-Based Hotel Reservation Firm Pegasus Solutions to Acquire Rival Unirez," *Knight Ridder Tribune Business News*, November 6, 2003, p. 1.

CHOICE HOTELS INTERNATIONAL:

Comfort Inn

Quality Inn

Sleep Inn

Clarion

Cambria Suites

Comfort Suites

Mainstay Suites

Suburban

Econolodge

Figure 12.5

Different Franchise Brands Owned by Choice Hotels

group of franchises, owned by Choice Hotels, manages the nine different franchise brands shown in Figure 12.5. Providing an international central reservation system for hotels is one of the most important services a franchisor can provide to its franchise properties.

Travel agents have long played an important role in selling hotel rooms. Travel agency business has been severely affected with the increased use of the Internet by individuals in making their own travel arrangements. Many travel agencies have therefore moved into specialization niches such as working with corporate travel (approximately 71 percent of their business), exotic travel, or particularly upscale or luxury trip planning. There has been a huge increase in the number of online travel agencies (OTA).[12]

Another group of channel members is the airline CRS. When making travel arrangements, an airline, via telephone, in person, or on the Internet, can offer to place the customers' room reservations for them as well. The large car rental companies and virtually all travel agents are also interfaced to one or more of the airline CRSs. A moment's reflection suggests how many "virtual front desks" have been added to the hotel industry, not only through airline reservation systems but through all the other agencies interfaced to the airline systems. A study conducted by J.D. Power and Associates found that twice as many people book reservations directly with the airline, hotel, or rental agency Web site rather than the independent online agencies such as Hotwire, Expedia, or Hotels.com. According to the study, the main reason these branded Web sites are preferred has to do with convenience. When hotel reservations are made through an airline or car rental site, this service to the hotel is not free. Commissions are required for hotel reservations made through airline and other travel companies in very much the same way that they are for travel agents.[13]

The growth in channels of distribution has the favorable effect for hotels of increasing distribution—the number of places their product is sold. Channels, however, usually add marketing costs for the hotel and also another dimension to competition, putting added pressure on hotel prices. One factor that makes the Internet appear so very attractive to hotel operators is that it offers the chance to minimize the payment of fees to travel intermediaries.

The Internet is being used by hotels and customers for much more than individual travel. For example, Passkey is a Web-based booking product that includes on-line capability to create multiple attendee types and room blocks—two features that are very attractive to meeting planners. Large hotels and resorts, such as the Wynn Las Vegas, use MeetingBroker to manage hundreds of leads they receive each week from various channels. MeetingBroker is an Internet-based exchange lead management solution capable of capturing and integrating leads for hotel business from a variety of sources.[14]

More follows on the impact of the Internet and the various forms of Internet-related distribution channels.

Internet Distribution Channels. There are several different types of electronic business-to-consumer distribution channels for hotel rooms. One form is a chain's own Web site. As described above, many chains have added the capability to market and book not only guest rooms but also banquets and other catered functions, meetings, and conferences. This distribution channel provides the hotel company an invaluable, multimedia marketing tool if the business wants to invest the time, money, and maintenance of the Web site. The Internet contributed 40 percent or 8,581,936 reservations of the total Central Reservation Office (CRO) reservations at major hotel brands as of the third quarter in 2006. This was a 24.8 percent increase compared to the same time period in 2005.

There are also channels that utilize data and the reservation engine from the **Global Distribution System (GDS)**. Examples of such companies are Expedia and Travelocity. An additional electronic channel is a company such as WorldRes, which is a Web-based channel with an inventory and reservation database maintained online. A company such as Travelweb is based on the database and reservation engine of a switch company. Travelweb.com is controlled by five hotel companies that formed a partnership to help compete with the online travel sites. The five, who are competitors, are Marriott, Starwood, Hyatt, Hilton, and Intercontinental. Lastly, there are the auction-style Web sites such as Priceline.com in which people try to get hotel rooms with the lowest bids. For the third quarter of 2006, the importance of GDS commerce was evident with 34.7 percent or 7,419,408 booking coming through those channels.[15]

The Impact of the Internet. The impact of the Internet on the hotel industry, as well as other facets of the broader travel industry, has been revolutionary. Half of all travelers buy travel online and even more go online to research travel plans. PhoCusWright projects that by 2008 online travel bookings will constitute 64 percent of all leisure gross bookings versus 45 percent in 2006. It is estimated that 48 percent of all corporate travel bookings will occur online as compared to 31 percent in 2006. It is projected that the industry will experience a one-third increase in the number of online bookings over the Internet between 2006 and 2008.[16]

One study found that competitive pricing was the key motivating factor that encouraged consumers to purchase travel online. The pricing advantage outweighed the additional benefits of saving time, getting bonus loyalty club points, having more control, or obtaining better information. In the third quarter of 2006, brand Web sites continued to grow and to gain share compared to third-party merchant and opaque Web sites. Third-party sites are increasingly used for hotel rate shopping prior to consumers booking directly on hotel Web sites. The response from hotel chains has been to withhold inventory from the online travel sites, as well as feature cheaper rates on their own Web sites. Independent hotels have benefited from the Internet as well. Customers can inspect the rooms and get information on the unfamiliar independent hotel's services through the property's Web site. These hotels subsequently can compete in ways that they could not prior to this technology.[17]

The Internet's impact on hotel pricing is even more widespread in impacting hotel group revenue and presenting challenges for meeting and convention planners. The traditional process has been for a hotel to "block" or reserve a number of guest rooms for a particular group. A specified rate is provided as the "group room rate." Oftentimes, room rates, along with the number of rooms to be reserved, are decided years in advance of the actual meeting, convention, or event. Before the Internet, a meeting attendee, for example, would routinely make a reservation at the specified hotel under the "special" group rate without checking nearby hotels for lower rates. With the Internet, researching competing room rates is now at a person's fingertips. It could even happen that the incoming attendee can find a cheaper rate at the same exact hotel that initially provided the "special" group rate. Because group rates are established in advance, they may not reflect the current supply and demand conditions that could possibly drive room rates lower than what was expected weeks, months, or years ahead of the needed dates. Because meeting planners are committed to book a certain percentage or rooms from the established block, attrition damages often result when attendees do not stay at the designated hotel or reserve rooms "outside of the block."

Hotel operators are challenged by possible solution strategies to the dilemmas presented by Internet shopping. One recommendation, in contrast to most current group contracts, is to adjust room rates according to industry or market conditions. This means that room rates could go either up or down, but hotels and meeting planners would then have the benefit of the flexibility utilized by Internet travel sites. Also important is for hotels to consider their competitive services and amenities. It is not feasible for many hotels to be able to compete solely on room rates. Exceptional service and additional amenities may provide an even stronger competitive advantage.

Although the Internet has certainly impacted hotel discounting, there have been benefits in transaction charges. The traditional reservation process is often cumbersome, time-consuming, and labor-intensive. Accor hotels, in analyzing how the Internet impacts transaction costs, found an 80 to 90 percent savings by selling directly to the consumer online. Additionally, many hotels, as do the airlines, sell last-minute package deals characterized by low prices and short lead times. This gives the hotels the opportunity to dispose rather quickly of unsold inventory.[18]

Online Shopping Patterns. Consumers take a very competitive approach in shopping for hotels. When shopping on the Web, most people will visit numerous sites in searching for a hotel room. One study found that just 10 percent of would-be guests visit only one site to book a hotel room. An additional 43 percent visit two to three sites, and 22 percent visit four or more sites.[19]

Consumers will see travel e-commerce with more products aimed at the buyer's need for quick "sound bytes" of information, pricing and travel options prior to, during, and post travel. Mobile devices, such as phones, PDAs and iPods, will become increasingly important for receiving hits of information, including that focused on travel-related items.

Promotion: Marketing Communication

Marketing communication is persuasive communication. It uses the tools of mass communication and individualized communication to encourage patronage of a hotel or a group of hotels such as a chain or franchise group. Advertising, sales promotion, and public relations are the principal mass-medium selling tools.

Until quite recently, individualized communication for hotels largely meant personal selling. Although personal selling is still a vital tool of hotel marketers, an increasingly important role is played by individualized communication based on information about customers (and people similar to them) captured in the databases of guest history systems and transaction records, which we will discuss in a moment.

ADVERTISING IN MASS MEDIA

Advertising is paid communication. It uses print media (a favorite among hotels) such as newspapers and magazines; electronic media such as television, radio, and the Internet; and outdoor media such as billboards. Another mass medium is direct mail, but the possibilities for individualizing direct-mail offers have been multiplied so greatly by the databases mentioned earlier that we need to qualify its classification as a mass medium.

Advertising carried out by the individual property may be aimed at the local community as well as directed at potential guests in cities that serve as a major point of origin for visitors. Brand advertising is carried out by chains and franchise and membership organizations. Hotels experienced significant declines in marketing budgets after September 11. These declines continued into 2002 and 2003. Some properties found creative approaches to maximize the limited marketing dollars. Sandestin Golf and Beach Resort, for example, entered into a number of partnerships, most notably with the local tourism commission to sell beach towns along the Gulf Coast in Florida as destinations. Other hotels have experienced similar benefits from partnering with state tourism commissions and convention center groups. E-mail blast advertising is also on the increase, costing less than one cent per blast compared to the seven cents per postcard. Marketing budgets started to increase in 2004 and 2005 saw 5.1 percent of revenue in full service hotels going to marketing as compared to 4.3 percent in 2004.[20]

Even with larger budgets, hotels have to be aware of the return on investment of marketing dollars. Many properties have decreased spending on television and radio ads because it is hard to track the impact of that type of advertising. Print, which is much more trackable, allows a hotel to have more certainty regarding its return on investment.

The online distribution channels have continued to have sizable marketing budgets. Hotels.com, one such online service, outspent all the major hotel chains, with an advertising budget for 2003 of $56 million. Hotels.com extended its target market beyond the price-sensitive traveler to those who might pay more to get what they want. Although the budget is big, the company does not spend indiscriminately. Production, media buying, and online ad serving are all done in-house in addition to monitoring and tracking. In May 2003, Hotels.com was the top online booking site with a 42 percent share of the 32 million online impressions received by the top ten sites.[21]

ADVERTISING ON THE INTERNET

Hotels are turning to Internet advertising with their more limited marketing budgets. This form of advertising is trackable and has been demonstrating noteworthy returns on investment. The advertising landscape has been shifting with customers who are using Web sites run by airlines and hotels over the big travel sites like Orbitz, Expedia and Travelocity. New rivals for online travel searches have also emerged. Meta-search sites like SideStep and Kayak scan the inventories of dozens of airline sites as well as online travel agencies like Orbitz. Internet giants such as Yahoo and AOL have also upgraded their travel sites.[22]

Internet advertising involving hotel Web pages typically feature photographs and information on the hotel and the surrounding area. Most Web sites have the capability for guests to make reservations. Many Web sites offer visitors the opportunity to take a virtual tour of the hotel, including guest rooms, restaurants, lobby, and pool, spa, or recreational areas.

At Marriott's Web site (www.marriott.com), visiting customers can use a mapping system to locate any Marriott, Courtyard, Residence Inn, or Fairfield Inn in the United States. Once the location is mapped, the visitor may zoom in or out for desired detail. Also, at the click of a button, the system can calculate estimated driving times and road-by-road directions to and from any location, including any of the 16 million businesses and attractions found in the database. Westin Hotels & Resorts is using the Internet to feature a program called, "Westin Sights and Sounds." Created by MSN, Web surfers can experience five-minute vacations with soothing music and different Westin properties.[23]

Boston's convention and visitor bureau has a site (www.meetingpath.com) where Boston-area hotels can post short-term guest room availability. New England hotels that participate in the site can display detailed text and graphics to describe their properties.[24]

Hilton is one hotel chain that offers a reward program for loyal customers. (Courtesy of Las Vegas Convention and Visitors Authority.)

SALES PROMOTION

Sales promotion is "a marketing communication activity which offers an incentive to immediate action."[25] At the property level, sales promotions are often special events or individualized rewards for frequent guests.

One of the most common forms of sales promotion has as its target customers who are already patronizing the system's hotels. These are the frequent-traveler programs. **Partnerships and Reward Programs**. Frequent-guest clubs offer regular guests a reward for brand loyalty. **Frequent-stay programs** may be a hotel chain's biggest marketing expense, yet the hope is that they instill loyalty that helps drive business. Such programs also provide opportunities to collect more and better information about customers.[26] With price being a major determinant in hotel selection, particularly among the leisure segment, the concept of "brand loyalty" among the buying public has been recently questioned, particularly with the competitive shopping advantages offered by the Internet.

The first hotel frequent-guest program was introduced in 1983 by Holiday Inns, followed quickly by Marriott. Early in the process, hotels learned that many guests preferred air miles to hotel points, which were exchangeable only for free hotel stays. As a result, hotels formed **partnerships** with airlines. Hotels purchased frequent-flyer miles at wholesale rates and offered their guests a choice between airline miles or points good for hotel stays. As airline partners, the hotels also receive favorable coverage in airline frequent-flyer publications. The partnership makes especially good sense for hotels, because the largest hotel programs have over 10 million members, while major airlines have more than 20 million members. Most hotel programs offer miles, points, or both. Points can be either converted into air miles, used to purchase merchandise, or used for hotel stays. The merchandise programs were begun when hotels discovered that the most frequent travelers had more frequent-flyer miles than they could use and were interested in some other form of reward. Hilton's HHonors program even provides vacation benefits for members when buying, selling, financing, or refinancing a home with their "Awards for Mortgage and Real Estate."[27]

Frequency Marketing and Databases. Frequent-traveler programs do more than reinforce customer loyalty. They provide a wealth of detailed information on customers. From membership information, hotels can learn about the demographics of their customer base, as well as where they come from. From transaction records, it is possible to build up a record of individual spending patterns and preferences. These databases permit hotels to learn who their best customers are. They also make it possible to custom-design offers to guests, which can be delivered by direct mail or phone. Does a guest come most frequently in the fall? Perhaps he or she would like to see the area in the spring. Had the guest been coming regularly but has not visited the property for some time? Is something wrong? What needs to be done to remedy the problem?

Moreover, once a profile of the hotel's best customers has been developed, it is possible to purchase other databases on people who have a similar profile:

> Many hotel companies overlay an online data base with information from credit card companies or transportation companies. Secondary overlays are available from geodemographic and psychographic information firms. In combination, the data from these external sources provide invaluable enhancement to a hotel's in-house records.[28]

Summary

Our discussion of competitive practices was structured by the model of the marketing mix. Competition should be proactive, not reactive. In each element of the marketing mix, there is a tool for reaching and attracting guests. With the development of data-based marketing, moreover, the appeal can be more carefully crafted to motivate our guests and people like them, and even to reach them individually with the appeal best suited to them.

Product is ultimately the guest's experience. Ways of improving that experience include food service, other services and amenities, and systemwide services. Limited-service properties do not offer restaurant service to their "upstairs" guests, but food service continues to be a major competitive tool in reaching the "downstairs" guests in full-service hotels. Food service is difficult to manage, and some properties have leased their food service operations. This solution has built-in problems related to giving up control of the "service department" of the hotel. Other hotels use franchised restaurants to gain a successful food service format, field supervision, and the power of an additional brand. Still others have sought to limit the problems of and skills required by food service by simplifying their food service operations. The problem with most services and amenities is that many are easily copied and so do not offer differentiation. Systemwide services provided by franchisors include quality assurance for the entire system, an international reservation service, and the establishment and maintenance of a brand name and image.

The low variable cost and consequent wide margin in room sales offer many opportunities for special rates. These are extended to volume customers and, during slow periods, to specially targeted customers such as sports teams. Rates can also vary according to demand as yield management dictates. The practice of yield management runs the risk of offending customers who are charged different rates for the same product at different times. Good practice in yield management dictates full disclosure of pricing to customers and restrictions on rooms sold at lower rates, such as advance purchase or minimum stay.

Place refers not only to the property's location but also to the channels of distribution. Promotion or marketing communication uses mass advertising in the electronic and print media. Brand advertising in large chains involves very large expenditures to establish and maintain a brand name and image. The Internet has become prominent in advertising, and interactive Web sites make the Internet an additional channel of distribution. Although such mass promotion remains important, hotels are moving toward tighter targeting in their marketing, based on databases made up of information on customers and their transactions.

Key Words and Concepts

Fragmented market	**Differentiation**
Cyclical industry	**Concierge**
Low variable cost	**Fitness facilities**
Securitization	**Spa facilities**
Impact of technology	**Business centers**
Marketing mix	**Quality assurance**
Upstairs guest	**Variable cost**
Downstairs guest	**Fixed costs**
Leasing	**Yield management**
On-site franchised	**Location**
restaurant	**Distribution channels**

Global distribution system (GDS)   **Sales promotion**
Marketing communication   **Frequent-stay programs**
Advertising   **Partnerships**

Review Questions

1. What are some of the conditions of competition in the hotel business? What is their impact?

2. What is the difference between the upstairs and downstairs markets?

3. What is the role of food service in lodging? Why have some segments chosen to reduce or eliminate their food services?

4. What means of differentiation other than food service were discussed in the text? What is your assessment of the effectiveness of each?

5. What is meant by low variable cost in the lodging industry?

6. Describe what yield management is. Discuss the pros and cons of yield management.

7. What is meant by channels of distribution? What are the established channels for hotels? What are the new channels? What is the outlook for travel intermediaries in lodging?

8. What is the impact of partnerships on hotel marketing?

9. What are several of the advantages that have been provided to hotels through the Internet? What are several of the disadvantages that hotels have experienced because of the Internet?

Internet Exercises

1. **Site name:** Choice Hotels

    URL: www.choicehotels.com

    Background information: Choice Hotels International is one of the largest and most successful lodging franchisors in the world with over 405,000 rooms in more than thirty-three countries. Built on the foundation of the venerable Quality Inn brand, a pioneer in consistent mid-priced lodging, Choice Hotels today is the worldwide franchisor of ten branded hotels.

    Site name: Wyndham Worldwide

    URL: www.wyndhamworldwide.com

    Background information: Wyndham Worldwide was previously part of the Cendant group. It is one of the world's largest hospitality companies spanning six continents and offering individual consumers and business customers a broad array of hospitality products, services and price ranges through a diverse portfolio of world-renowned brands.

Exercises:

a. Review both of the above sites. How do the Wyndham Hotel group and Choice Hotel Group position themselves to compete with one another?

b. Surf both sites and describe the franchise information that is provided by each company. Which company provides the most extensive information?

2. **Site name:** Site name: Four Seasons Hotels and Resorts

URL: www.fourseasons.com

Background information: As one of the world's leading operators of luxury hotels and resorts, Four Seasons currently manages over 70 properties worldwide. The company also offers a growing network of branded vacation ownership properties and private residences.

Site name: The Ritz Carlton

URL: www.ritzcarlton.com

Background information: Among the grand hotels of the world, the Ritz-Carlton hotels and resorts are renowned for indulgent luxury. Sumptuous surroundings and legendary service are their trademark. They currently manage 58 hotels worldwide (35 city hotels and 23 resorts).

Site name: Rosewood Hotels & Resorts

URL: www.rosewoodhotels.com

Background information: Rosewood Hotels & Resorts is a privately held ultra-luxury hotel management company. Rosewood is a collection of unique hotels that offers luxurious accommodations and personalized service. Each hotel features architectural details, elegant interiors, and innovative culinary concepts that are reflective of the local region where the hotel or resort is located.

Exercises:

a. All three of the above hotel companies compete for the same target population. What marketing strategies do they use to attract customers to their hotels? How do they differ?

b. In your opinion, which hotel company has the best marketing strategies on their Web site? Why?

c. What are the similarities and differences among these three companies regarding how they market their hotels versus how the Choice and Cendant hotel groups market their hotels?

Notes

1. Lodging Econometrics. "LE Revises Supply Side Forecast Downward of '06 and '07." http://www.lodgingintelligence.com/PR/3Q06IndPress.htm.

2. There are a number of other ways of viewing the marketing mix. See, for instance, Leo Renaghan, "A New Marketing Mix for the Hospitality Industry," *Cornell Hotel and*

Restaurant Administration Quarterly, August 1981, pp. 32–33. The present view is adopted less as an analytical device than as a means of exposition.

3. The upstairs-downstairs guest dichotomy originated, we believe, with the Marriott organization.

4. La Quinta Support Services, personal communication, February 2001.

5. Judy Liberson, "Strategic Alliances Create Profitable Blend," *Lodging,* January 1997, p. 63.

6. Jeff Weinstein. "Don't Turn F&B Space Into Guestrooms Just Yet," *Hotels,* May 1997, p. 17.

7. C. Valhouli, "Super Spas 2005," Forbes.com, http://www.forbes.com/lifestyle/travel/2005/01/20/cx_cv_0120feat.html.

8. David C. Sullivan, executive vice president, Promus, remarks during a panel discussion, "Suite Hotels and Limited Service Hotels." Hospitality Investment Conference, New York, June 4, 1994.

9. PKF Hospitality Research, Trends 2006.

10. Sheryl E. Kimes, "Perceived Fairness of Yield Management," *Cornell Hotel and Restaurant Administration Quarterly,* February 1994, pp. 22–29.

11. Ibid.

12. C. Green. "Are global distribution systems going away? Hardly." *Lodging* archives. http://www.lodgingmagazine.com/index.cfm? Fm=Article.Detail&aid=93.

13. "Brand names resonate when it comes to online bookings." Hotelmarketing.com, December 11, 2006.

14. R. Hill, "Does group booking software have all the answers?" *Lodging* archives. http://www.lodgingmagazine.com/index.cfm? fm=Article.Detail&aid=104.

15. "Hotel chains report double-digit Internet growth," December 5, 2006, Hotelmarketing.com

16. PKF Hospitality Research, Trends 2006.

17. Ibid.

18. Ruth A. Hill, "Electronic Partners," *Lodging* magazine, February 1998, p. 73.

19. C. Green, Lodging archives.

20. PKF Hospitality Research, Trends 2006.

21. Gary Boulard, "Tightening the Belt," *Hotel & Motel Management,* September 15, 2003, p. 44.

22. "Online travel—a big change in direction." Hotelmarketing.com, April 6, 2006.

23. "Westin, MSN Offer '5-Minute' Vacations." Hotelmarketing.com, December 5, 2006.

24. Mike Pusateri and Jeff Manno, "Growing with the Web," *Lodging* magazine, January 1997, p. 71.

25. Robert H. Marriott, "Promotions—A Key Piece in Your Marketing Puzzle." Proceedings of the Chain Operators Exchange Chicago International Foodservice Manufacturing Association, 1987).

26. Global Online Retailing," Ernst & Young, 2001, www.ey.com/global/gcr.nsf/International/Welcome-Retail.

27. Kathleen Cassidy, "Miles, Miles and More Miles," *Lodging* magazine, February 1997, pp. 48–52.

28. Paula A. Francese and Leo M. Renaghan. "Data-Base Marketing: Building Customer Profiles." *Cornell Hotel & Restaurant Administration Quarterly,* May 1990, p. 62.

PART FOUR

Travel and Tourism

The Hospitality Industry

(Courtesy of Southwest Airlines.)

CHAPTER THIRTEEN

Tourism: Front and Center

The Purpose of this Chapter

Travel and tourism at the local, state, national, and international levels are vital to the health of our economy as well as that of the hospitality industry. Indeed, tourism is big business and continues to grow in North America and worldwide. The economic and social impacts of tourism are significant, and this chapter discusses both of these dimensions.

THIS CHAPTER SHOULD HELP YOU

1. Describe the important impact of tourism on local and national economies.

2. List the factors contributing to the growth of travel and tourism, and explain their impact on the industry.

3. Identify current trends in mode of travel and trip duration.

4. Provide statistics supporting the importance of tourism in generating employment.

5. Explain why international visitors to the United States are an important means of improving the balance of payments and receipts, and how tourism affects international trade.

6. Identify major businesses outside the hospitality industry that service travelers, and explain the trends that are changing the way they do business.

7. List the noneconomic impacts of tourism, both positive and negative.

The Importance of Tourism

The importance of **tourism** to the hospitality industry is obvious. Some parts of the industry, such as hotels, derive almost all of their sales from travelers. Even food service attributes roughly 25 percent of its sales to travelers. Moreover, many **leisure**-oriented businesses with a major food service and hospitality component, such as theme parks, are also dependent on travelers.

The importance of tourism to the hospitality industry is increasing each year. As employment in smokestack industries—that is, manufacturing—continues to fall, the service industries, including those businesses serving travelers, must take up the slack by providing new jobs. Tourism, then, is central not only to the health of the hospitality industry but also to the economy as a whole.

The tourism industry is the collection of productive businesses and governmental organizations that serve the traveler away from home. These organizations include restaurants, hotels, motels, and resorts; all facets of transportation, including rental cars, travel agents, and gasoline service stations; national and state parks or recreation areas; and various private attractions. The industry also includes those organizations that support these firms' retail activities, including advertising companies, publications, transportation equipment manufacturers, and travel research and development agencies.

Tourism is made up of many varied businesses. (Courtesy of Las Vegas Convention and Visitors Authority.)

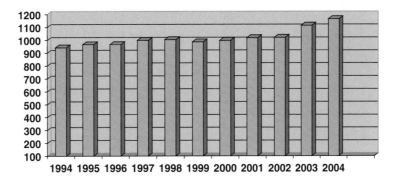

Figure 13.1
U.S. resident domestic travel volume, 1994–2004. (Source: 2005 Travel Market Report, Travel Industry Association of America.)

FACTORS AFFECTING TRAVEL AND TOURISM

Travel and tourism are as American as baseball, hot dogs, apple pie, and the interstate highway system. Figure 13.1 illustrates the growth in domestic travel from 1994 to 2004 to a level of over 1 billion person-trips. (A person-trip is defined as one person taking one trip. If two persons go on that trip, that equals two person-trips. A trip is any travel 100 miles or more away from home.) That is an increase of over 12 percent since 1994.[1] In addition, Americans took over 29 million trips overseas in 2005. With domestic travel, the main form of travel is by auto, truck, and RV, which, together, account for 75 percent of all trips. There are also numerous transportation industries—air, rail, and bus—that help move travelers and are allied with the hospitality industry in tourism.

Moreover, tourism growth continues to be fueled by more leisure time (among certain age groups), rising family incomes, and the favorable demographic trends we have discussed in earlier chapters. We will look briefly at each of these factors.

GROWING LEISURE TIME?

The debate about whether Americans have more or less leisure time than they had in the past rages on. Indeed, the trend seems to have been an increase in work for most people for most of the last two decades. Indications are that this is changing, though. In the annual Harris Poll Work and Leisure Poll, which asks respondents about work and leisure habits, it was found that the average number of hours worked per week in 2002 dropped from 50 hours to 47 hours, representing the first decrease since 1997/1998. Since then, it has risen again (back to 50). At the same time, the median number of hours spent on leisure activities has remained essentially unchanged since 1989, at 19 hours per week.[2]

Over the last several years, many companies' vacation policies have become more liberal, and the number of legal (and paid) holidays has increased. This latter point is significant in that more of these are timed so as to provide three-day weekends. At the very least, Americans take their leisure time as seriously as ever, and this impacts how they spend their time, where they go, and how much they spend.

INCOME TRENDS

The two-**income** family has become a major factor in travel. The majority of women today expect to work outside the home. A two-income family not only increases total family income but also adds to the family's security: If one spouse loses a job, that does not eliminate all of the family's income. One scenario suggests that a portion of women leave the workforce for a period of time at the birth of a child, and many women return to work only on a part-time basis while young children are still at home. For those committed to a career outside the home, however, the ultimate intention is to return to full-time work. A further element of stability to family incomes today is the fact that if a husband loses his job or otherwise suffers an economic reversal, young mothers can and will expand their working commitment outside the home earlier than they may have originally intended.

Two-income families are not all well-to-do "yuppies" (young urban professionals). Many families pool two modest incomes to support a comfortable lifestyle. Because they are working to maintain a comfortable life, it is not surprising that they are disposed to spend their money on the goods and services they want. They are good customers—and even in bad times, they can usually maintain at least one income, making the stability of family spending greater today than it was a generation ago.

Almost all two-income families have time pressures. When both parents work, the household chores still need to be done and children must be cared for. This means that many people may have to sacrifice leisure time for household and family maintenance chores. Therefore, when they do get away, time is at a premium, and they seek "quality time." Though sensitive to price/value comparisons, these travelers generally seek good value for their money rather than low-cost recreational experiences.

DEMOGRAPHICS AND TRAVEL

As has been suggested in previous chapters, **demographics** play a role in consumption and travel behaviors. As the population ages, much of it approaching middle age, there will be a tremendous impact on tourism. Middle age generally means higher income and a greater propensity to travel. The age group that travels most, whether for **business travel** or **pleasure travel**, are those age 35 to 44. This age

Families are an important demographic group for the travel and tourism industries. (Courtesy of National Park Service.)

group is most likely to use hotels and to take longer trips (1,000 miles and over). Close behind them are the 45-to-54-year-olds. It is also important to consider household behavior. According to the Travel Industry Association of America, "Traveling households are more likely than overall households to be headed by someone who is married and/or more highly educated."[3]

Another significant demographic development for tourism is the growth in the mature market, that is, people 55 and over. In 2010, this segment of the population will equal 75 million people or approximately 25.5 percent of the overall population. Growth in the same population segment from 2010 to 2020 will be 28 percent.[4] Although this group represents a smaller share of household income, people 55 and over control over half of household wealth. In fact, *American Demographics* states that average net worth is at its highest between 55 and 74, an average of $500,000.[5] In effect, their mortgages are paid and a large proportion of them have a nest egg of savings and retirement benefits on which to draw. This puts them in a position to be able to travel.

The pattern of growth in the mature market suggests two subsegments that will be especially important. The 55-to-64 year-old group will grow by almost 19 percent between 2010 and 2020 as the first baby boomers move into their mature years.[6] This segment will be a very active group of consumers seeking new experiences and learning to deal with extended leisure, that is, the ability to take longer vacations as seniority increases vacation entitlements and as retirement approaches or as early retirement permits. In addition, the 65-to-74-year-old age group will grow just over 13 percent during the same time period. Among other things, these two age groups have the discretionary

419

income as well as the time to take extended holidays. Households in this age group already spend about $17 billion a year on travel.[7]

Travel Trends

The most frequent reason for (domestic) travel is to visit family and friends. Other pleasure travel, for outdoor recreation and entertainment, is just behind that. All pleasure travel accounts for approximately 80 percent of the some billion domestic person-trips taken in 2005. Business and convention travel (and combination business and pleasure trips) accounted for another 19 percent.[8] As Figure 13.2 indicates, travel sales vary with the economy but have grown (historically) somewhat more rapidly than the economy. In the three years around 2001, however, business travel took the hardest hit. Pleasure travel, too, has been impacted but has come back. It has been impacted by the Iraq war, SARS, and the recession, but business travel has suffered tremendously from post-September 11 effects as well as the lingering recession. Travel growth, then, is likely to come from pleasure travel, which has grown at a steady rate in each of the recent years. The effects of various events are explored more in Global Hospitality Note 13.1.

MODE OF TRAVEL

According to the U.S. Department of Transportation, automobiles are the most utilized **mode of transportation**, being used for almost 90 percent of all long-distance trips. Airlines are the second most frequently used means of transportation, and they are far and away the dominant **common carrier**, despite the effect that recent

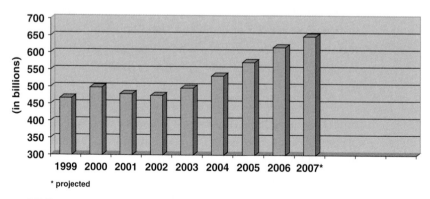

* projected

Figure 13.2

Domestic travel expenditures in the United States, 1999–2007. (Source: Travel Industry Association of America. Web site: www.tia.org [January 1, 2007].

Air travel is the preferred mode of transportation for longer trips (Courtesy of Southwest Airlines.)

events have had. In fact, airlines are used more than twice as often as all other forms of public transportation combined. Further, they are the most utilized mode of transportation for trips of 2,000 miles or more. Travel by private vehicle is still the dominant form of travel for Americans, however.

Air travel increased throughout the 1990s, as measured by revenue passenger miles (with the exception of a slight dip between 1990/1991 and again in 2001/2002). Air travel has also claimed an increasing percentage of overall passenger miles. When long-distance auto and air travel are compared, even though auto travel is the mode of transportation used for most trips, air travel accounts for 55.8 percent of all miles traveled (for long-distance trips) and auto accounts for 42.6 percent of total miles traveled.

TRIP DURATION

As two working spouses in a family have become more common, vacations have become shorter. The typical vacation of the 1950s and 1960s was an annual event lasting 10 to 14 days. During the 1970s and 1980s, vacations, on average, were shortened to five to seven days, and taken twice a year. In the 1990s, the two- to three-day "minivacation" has become increasingly popular. Now, most domestic trips that are taken are only one to two nights in duration.[9]

Public Anxiety and the Travel Industry

The first decade of the millennium has brought with it no shortage of significant events—each creating new challenges for the hospitality and tourism industries. September 11, 2001, was the most significant event and the one most still in Americans' collective minds. Before we discuss the impacts that this day had on our industry, though, we need to point out that its effects reached far beyond the hospitality and tourism industries. Attitudes and behaviors of Americans changed on that day. We continue to hear that people began to reassess their relationships, saw their families in a new light, were kinder to strangers, became more aware of (and concerned with) international events, and had improved feelings toward their fellow citizens. In addition, American Demographics reports that 80 percent of respondents indicated that their appreciation for their families increased as a result of that day, that safety and security of family have become more important and that people are seeking psychotherapy at a greater rate (as a way of dealing with the events).[1] That day affected families, businesses, educational institutions, nonprofit organizations, and governments. So, yes, the hospitality and tourism industries were affected, but it is important to see the larger picture.

With that being said, at this writing, the airline industry and the hotel industry have suffered the most and are still having serious problems. The terrorist attacks of September 11 had an immediate effect on travel, tourism, and the hospitality industry in general. It has been said, more than a few times, that this industry was the most affected by the events of September 11. Consumer (traveling) confidence was shaken, and there were feelings of uncertainty surrounding personal safety and security. This resulted in immediate reductions in personal travel, which affected hotels, restaurants, and the like. To complicate matters, the United States was on the cusp of a recession, which only exaggerated and prolonged the effects. The U.S. airlines shut down in the days following September 11—something that would be hard to recover from even under the best of circumstances. Some U.S. airlines still have not yet recovered. United Airlines and US Airways are both operating under bankruptcy protection, and most other major U.S. airlines lost a great deal of money between September 2001 and September 2003. Total travel expenditures by Americans dropped in the last quarter of 2001 and continued to drop in 2002 (compared to the previous year's statistics). Travel to and from most countries dropped. Even tourism in the Caribbean (considered to be a "safe" destination) dropped by 10 percent in the last quarter of 2001. It should also be noted that airlines elsewhere in the world experienced problems at or around this same time, including Ansett (Australia), Swissair (Switzerland), and Sabena (Belgium). Internationally, it is estimated that the airline industry lost $13 billion dollars in 2002.[2]

The results of the shutdown of airspace on September 11 were felt across the United States as well as globally. Some estimates suggest that global travel revenues dropped as much as 30 percent in the days and weeks to follow. Hotels saw decreases in all pertinent performance measures—occupancy rates, average daily rates, and RevPAR. These decreases occurred in most major destinations as well.

While September 11 has come and gone, concerns about safety and security remain. Further, the compounding effects of the lingering recession are all contributing to a very slow recovery. Tensions in the Middle East, war in Iraq, and new and misunderstood diseases are all being used as excuses not to travel. SARS is perhaps the most recent and best example of how an illness can create widespread concern. SARS (Severe Acute Respiratory Syndrome) originated in China, and the first case was identified in February 2003 (but believed to have been first contracted in November 2002). From there it spread to Canada, Singapore, Hong Kong, Vietnam, and 13 other countries. The syndrome, which causes flulike symptoms, resulted in almost 800 deaths worldwide. In reaction, the World Health Organization (WHO) issued a global alert on March 15, 2003, recommending limiting travel to affected countries. The virus continued to spread until about July of that year. Even though most (new) cases were contracted from patients in hospitals, the public reacted with some concern. Travel to the SARS infected places was affected, and the economies of Hong Kong, Toronto (and other parts of Canada), and other travel destinations were severely impacted. Cities such as Toronto appealed to the federal government for financial assistance in the wake of decreased tourist revenues. It wasn't until several things happened that the economic recovery began to occur. First, the WHO dropped its alert, then individual destinations began offering incentives, and finally, the simple passing of time helped matters tremendously. In the end, it is estimated that SARS cost Canada over $500 million, including lost hotel revenues, dining revenues, and actual health-related costs of dealing with the disease. Hong Kong, perhaps the hardest hit area, initiated a $1.5 billion plan to overcome the effects.[3] KPMG reported that at the height of the SARS episode (April 2003), visitor spending was down over 70 percent from the same period in the previous year.[4]

One result of recent security and safety issues has been the change in airport (and other transportation) procedures. One scholar has dubbed this the "hassle factor" of traveling. Indeed, given the lengthy waits in airports, the extra forms to fill out, the added cost of flying, and numerous personal searches during it all, some people are simply avoiding air travel altogether. Much will have to change to convince this segment of the population that flying is still worth the cost and aggravation.

In light of all of these developments, the Harris Poll conducted a survey to determine the level of fear with regard to American travel plans and behaviors. The poll was conducted in May of 2003 and revealed some interesting results. Some highlights include:

- Fifty-nine percent of respondents feel that the risk to American tourists traveling outside of the United States is much worse or somewhat worse than it was three years earlier.
- Specific actions to reduce risk include fewer Americans planning to travel to Europe as a direct result of safety and security issues.
- Frequent travelers are more likely to reduce their travel as a result of the risk factor.[5]

To sum this up, the business environment has changed for airlines, hotels, and all other services serving the traveler. Fear and concern, and altered travel patterns, are now an accepted part of the business landscape. Certainly, one result has been that Americans are taking shorter trips, closer to home, and often by automobile. Most operators have accepted the fact that it will be a long time before things return to "normal," if it happens at all. It remains to be seen whether travel will reach the same level as pre-2001 or if the fear and hesitation will remain.

1. Rebecca Gardyn, "The Home Front," *American Demographics,* December 2001.
2. Standard & Poor's Industry Surveys—Airlines, March 27, 2003.
3. Canadian Broadcasting Corporation, "The Ecomomic Impact of SARS" (www.cbc.ca), November 26, 2003.
4. KPMG, "Tourism Expenditures in Major Canadian Markets," October 2003.
5. Harris Interactive, Harris Poll # 29 (www.harrisinteractive.com), May 14, 2003.

The mode of travel has changed a great deal just over the last 100 years. (Courtesy of National Park Service.)

Weekend vacations and shorter trips combining pleasure and business are more prevalent among younger travelers. Affluent travelers, with an average age of 50 or over, on the other hand, prefer vacations of a week or more.

The Economic Significance of Tourism

In total business receipts, tourism has consistently ranked second or third among all retail businesses. Only grocery stores—and, in some years, automobile dealers—have greater sales. The travel industry (international and domestic) accounted for $702.5 billion in direct expenditures in 2006. Measuring the industry in terms of employment, as Figure 13.3 does, we see that tourism provides more jobs than any other industry except health care services. In 2005, tourism provided 7.2 million people with employment. Tourism also provided various levels of government with tax receipts of over $100 billion.[10]

Although tourism currently accounts for over $700 billion in receipts in the U.S. economy, that is only a superficial, first-order measurement of travel importance. A **travel multiplier** measures the effect of initial spending together with the chain of expenditures that results. (For example, when a traveler spends a dollar in a hotel, some portion of it goes to employees, suppliers, and owners, who, in turn, re-spend it—and so it goes.) Figure 13.4 illustrates how the multiplier works in practice. Although

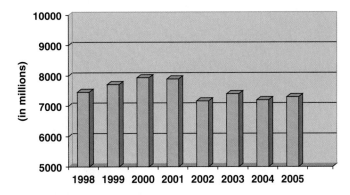

Figure 13.3
Travel employment in the United States, 1998–2005. (Source: Travel Industry Association of America, American Hotel and Lodging Association.)

TOURIST SPENDING FOR	TOURIST INDUSTRY EXPENSES	SECONDARY BUSINESS BENEFICIARIES
Hotels	Wages, salaries, and tips	Employees
Restaurants	Payroll taxes	Govt. agencies
Entertainment and recreation	Food, beverage, and housekeeping supplies	Food industry
		Beverage industry
Clothing	Construction and maintenance	Custodial industry
Personal care	Advertising	Architectural firms
Retail	Utilities	Repair firms
Gifts and crafts	Insurance	Advertising firms
Transportation	Interest and principal	News media
Tours	Legal and accounting	Water, gas, and electric
Museums and historical	Transportation	
	Taxes and licenses	Telephone companies
	Equipment and furniture	Insurance industry
		Banks and investors
		Legal and accounting firms
		Air, bus, auto, and fuel
		Taxi companies
		Government companies
		Wholesale suppliers
		Health care

Figure 13.4
The tourist dollar multiplier effect: tourist dollar flow into the economy. (Source: Michael Evans, *Tourism: Always a People Business*, Knoxville: University of Tennessee Press, 1984.)

The travel industry provides many jobs for many people. (Courtesy of National Park Service.)

the precise computation of the travel multiplier need not concern us, the final impact of the travel market for 2006 is estimated to be over $1.3 trillion.

TOURISM AND EMPLOYMENT

There is clearly a strong link between **tourism and employment**. Just over 1 in every 17 civilian employees is employed in an activity supported by travel expenditures. The travel industry contributes to job growth well in excess of its size. Employment in the last decade, as indicated in Figure 13.3, has consistently grown more rapidly than employment in the economy as a whole. Approximately one-quarter of food service employment can be traced to tourism, and a much larger proportion of hotel and motel employment serves travelers away from home.

PUBLICITY AS AN ECONOMIC BENEFIT

Communities often spend large sums of money to advertise their virtues to visitors and investors. They establish economic development bureaus to bring employers to town, and even offer tax incentives and low-cost financing. Aside from its direct economic impact, tourism also offers a chance to achieve many of these same benefits. That is, a tourist attraction brings visitors to a city or area, and they can then judge for themselves the community's suitability as a place to live and work. A major tourist event in a city or region attracts huge numbers of visitors, often for their first visit to the area. Assuming the region has natural charms and man-made attractions, some visitors are likely to become interested in relocating there—or at least in making a return visit.

The United States as an International Tourist Attraction

Tourism is the world's largest industry, accounting for over one-tenth of worldwide economic activity. In fact, according to the World Travel & Tourism Council (WTTC), tourism now accounts for 10.3 percent of total economic contribution.[11] In 2006, world tourism spending was $5 trillion.[12] By 2012, the WTTC estimates that spending will have reached $6 trillion. Such numbers perhaps boggle the mind as much as they enlighten it, but they are cited to help us grasp an important fact: The international tourism industry is, indeed, a huge set of businesses whose effects are worth taking the time to understand.

MEASURING THE VOLUME

There are two different ways to measure the volume of international tourism. **Arrivals and departures** measure the volume of people traveling; **receipts and payments** measure money spent. Dollar figures have the disadvantage of being distorted by fluctuating currency values, but to measure the economic impact, currency measures must be used. The best measure of activity, on the other hand, is the physical measure, arrivals and departures.

Arrivals and Departures in the United States. Figure 13.5 shows arrivals and departures to and from the United States. Total arrivals to the United States show some interesting fluctuations—they dropped between 2000 and 2003, and then rose

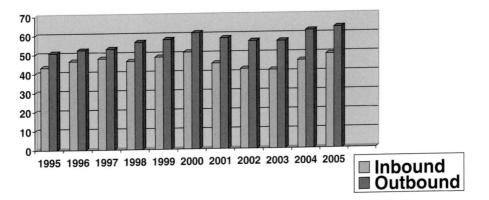

Figure 13.5
International arrivals to the United States versus U.S. travelers outside the United States. (Source: U.S. Department of Commerce, Office of Travel and Tourism Industries, 2006.)

again through 2005. The drop-off can be attributed to a variety of factors but can be boiled down to two things: the strength of the U.S. dollar against other currencies and certain events (including September 11)—keeping in mind that much of the travel reflected here represents other North Americans traveling to the United States. As a result, the amount of travel is largely dependent upon how well the Canadian and Mexican economies are doing at any given time. The value of the Canadian dollar (against the U.S. dollar) decreased between 2000 and 2002, and then increased through 2006. Generally, changes in exchange rates directly impact visitations, which is what has happened with Canadians travelling to the United States. Another example, involving Mexican tourists, is illustrated by the crash of the peso in 1995, which resulted in decreased travel from Mexico for several years. There was a slight stabilization in 1996, which saw inbound travel increase again. Then, the subsequent drop through 2002 was due to a variety of reasons, as discussed earlier in the chapter (and specifically in Global Hospitality Note 13.1). The Mexican peso has since stabilized as has the Canadian dollar. Just over half of total arrivals from year to year are from Canada and Mexico. A large portion of these are very short stays, many less than a day. In the end, over a near 20-year period, the number of overseas visitors has more than doubled (since 1988).

The Travel Trade Balance. From the end of World War II until the mid-1980s, there was considerable concern about what was then called the "travel gap," the much larger number of persons—and travel dollars—leaving the United States than arriving here from international destinations. Even as recently as 1985, the number of Americans traveling outside the country was more than the number of international visitors, creating an unfavorable **travel trade balance** of nearly $9 billion. The travel trade balance turned in favor of the United States by 1989 and increased for several years. Since 1996, it has decreased in size but still remains in favor of the United States (although it increased in size in 2004). Today, a favorable travel trade balance exists in the amount of over $7.4 billion, which is expected to increase over the next several years.[13]

REASONS FOR GROWTH OF THE UNITED STATES AS A DESTINATION

One of the principal reasons for growth in travel to the United States is the world's rising standard of living, particularly in Western Europe, Asia (particularly China), and Latin America. Moreover, the political changes in Eastern Europe led to a large percentage of growth in travel, although from a very low starting point. Another factor appears to be increasing competition among international air carriers, which has held fares down. In addition, as more people travel, more people want to travel. People hear about places from friends and want to go there. The United States also has the destinations, whether it be Disney World, natural attractions such as the Grand Canyon, or urban centers such as New York City and Washington, D.C. International travel is seen less as a venture into the unknown and more as something everybody's doing.

An important factor in international travel, and in the long-term growth of the United States as a destination, is currency fluctuation. Following World War II, the U.S. dollar was the strongest currency in the world. Other currencies were weak largely because those countries were recovering from war damage. By the 1970s, however, that recovery was complete, and other currencies gained against the dollar. In the 1980s, economic growth in many of these countries accelerated the trend. The cheaper dollar, then, made the United States a travel bargain, and travelers to the United States and travel spending increased dramatically. This factor is a double-edged sword. When Asian currencies crashed in 1996 and 1997, the visitor flow from those countries to the United States slowed appreciably. More recent fluctuations have had similar effects. Now the U.S. dollar has rebounded slightly after weakening aginst other major currencies.

In the hotel industry, some properties in large cities with large numbers of international tourists attribute one-third or more of their occupancy to visitors from outside the country. Twenty-five percent of international visitors' budgets goes for lodging. Many hotels, responding to the needs of this market, are anxious to hire multilingual managers, clerks, and service personnel. Some hotels have also begun actively to promote international business through representation at travel trade fairs abroad and through solicitation of international tour business from travel agents. The importance of international visitors to restaurants is suggested by the fact that their second most popular recreation activity (after shopping) was dining and food and beverage purchases. Nineteen percent of international visitors' expenditures is for food and beverage. Nearly half of international visitors' spending, then, is accounted for by the hospitality industry.

Businesses Serving the Traveler

PASSENGER TRANSPORTATION

Earlier, we looked at travel trends as a part of tourism. Here, our concern is to see travel as an allied industry that works with hospitality firms in serving travelers. You may recall that growth in travel by air has increased compared to travel by auto or other private vehicle. Bus travel has been increasing, while rail travel has declined. Bus and rail, in any case, account for only a small share of travel. The growth component in common-carrier travel, then, has been air. The growth of the airline industry during the last decade is detailed in Figure 13.6. The figure expresses growth in terms of

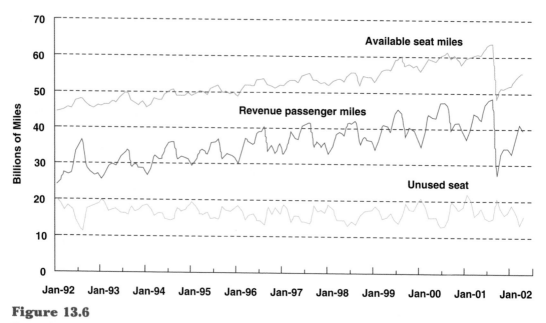

Figure 13.6

Domestic air seat passenger miles. (Source: U.S. Department of Transportation, Bureau of Transportation Statistics, *Transportation Indicators Report, 2005,* www.bts.gov/publications/transportation_indicators.)

(1) available seat miles, (2) revenue passenger miles, and (3) unused seat miles. Available seat miles is a measure of capacity, revenue passenger miles is a measure of volume, and unused seat miles is a measure of utilization. Keep in mind, however, that while revenues may be increasing overall, deep dips in airline sales volume can occur. Airlines, like most tourism industries, are very sensitive to the general economic climate.

Trends in Air Travel. The airlines have grown from an oddity in the transportation world of the 1920s, when only the daring flew, to the dominant common carrier worldwide. Following deregulation in 1978, the number of airlines increased dramatically and competition became fierce on most routes. In order to achieve greater economies of scale, large airlines developed the **hub-and-spoke system** in the early 1980s. In this system, passengers are assembled at a central point—a hub—such as Chicago, New York, or Detroit by smaller aircraft that form commuter airlines. There they board larger aircraft that fly to another hub, from which passengers are distributed to their final destinations by the same feeder system. If large aircraft fly with efficient load levels on high-volume routes, the hub-and-spoke system achieves the advantages of economies of scale.

On the other hand, there are some offsetting disadvantages to hub-and-spoke systems. Because of the complex schedules required to service such a system, traffic

Airlines represent a complex system of transportation, communication, coordination, and customer service.
(Courtesy of Southwest Airlines.)

control and weather delays can create serious problems. Delays multiply through the system, increasing costs because of idle aircraft and personnel time—to say nothing of passenger annoyance. Moreover, the large investment in people and equipment at hubs raises the fixed costs for operators using the centralized system.

An alternative to the hub-and-spoke system is the short-haul airline, specializing in **point-to-point service**. In the mid-1990s, these short-haul airlines became more aggressive in both price and service. Point-to-point carriers manage short aircraft turnarounds, minimize staff, and hold down investment. As a result, they can offer lower fares and more frequent service, generally of the no-frills variety. As the point-to-point system has proved to have real competitive advantages, many of the larger carriers began launching no-frills, short-haul carrier subsidiaries that duplicated the shorter routes, limited service, and lower fares offered by short-haul carriers. One of the first and still most successful airlines using the point-to-point strategy is Southwest Airlines.

Southwest is a notable company for many reasons. Southwest is the sixth largest airline company in the country (by revenues) and the first in terms of "passenger miles." Its average fare in 2006 was $104.75. It is able to keep fares low because of its focus on short-haul and high-frequency flights. In addition to using the point-to-point strategy (which has since been adopted by other companies), it is the only major airline company to have made a profit in recent years and, in fact, just recorded its thirty-fourth consecutive year of making a profit. This is quite remarkable given that the airline industry lost $10 billion in 2005. It is particularly notable given the high costs associated with running an airline, which include high capital costs, high labor costs, and the fluctuation (and high expense) of fuel. Finally, another differentiating factor is its booking model—the majority of fares are booked directly though the company and 73 percent of the company's revenue is booked through their Web site.

The Airline Industry. Several factors have affected the way in which business is conducted in the airline industry. One of the most significant was deregulation of the industry, which took place in 1978. It had the effect of lowering costs and allowing more carriers into the market. Deregulation also had the effect of encouraging greater price competition. There are literally hundreds of thousands of special fares—many available only for a short period of time, ranging from a few minutes to a few days. (Special fares generally appear on the computer network used by airlines and travel agents and can be discontinued at will by the carrier.) Almost all of these special fares are discounted fares, and the impact of discounting has been to hold down the cost of travel for cost-sensitive travelers. Most special fares, however, are structured so that they will not be attractive to the business traveler. Many, for instance, require travelers to stay over a Saturday night, a night when most business travelers would rather be home with their families. The effect of discounted fares has been to keep personal travel costs down while business travel costs rise. As a result, the volume of personal travel has been more buoyant than business travel.

Another significant development in air travel has been the growth of partnerships between airlines, generally airlines with noncompetitive route structures. These partnerships offer advantages to both customer and airline through the practice known as code sharing, whereby airlines share marketing and operating expenses over a route structure that is larger than either of their individual routes. As an example, consider the alliances that exist between international carriers. One such arrangement is the Star Alliance, which includes a partnership between Air Canada, United, and Singapore Airlines, among others. Through code sharing, the airlines can sell tickets on the same aircraft, whether it is operated by United, Air Canada, or any one of the other partners. Each airline will have a flight number designating that flight, say, United Flight 1 and Air Canada Flight 001. When the passenger goes to the terminal, he or she will be directed to the same aircraft by both airlines—with a simple explanation if the passenger has any questions. This permits the airlines to achieve a higher load factor. The term "load factor" refers to the percentage of seats sold and is analogous to occupancy in the hotel business. Like the hotel business, airlines are a low-variable-cost, high-fixed-cost industry. As a result, efforts that raise the efficiency of their use of resources have a pronounced favorable effect on profits. Overall, with regular rises and falls, airline load factors have been increasing. The biggest factor in this improvement, however, has been the reduction of overcapacity that existed in the early 1990s.

Another aspect of partnerships is that, by means of code sharing, airlines can quote through fares, which are substantially less expensive than two separate tickets would be. Thus, Northwest can quote a fare from Minneapolis to Antwerp, Belgium, working with its partner KLM. In all probability, passengers will travel on both Northwest and KLM but use the same ticket. This makes each airline more attractive in its own origination markets while adding passengers to each other's aircraft to achieve higher load factors. Notice, too, that because they can both advertise this "better deal" of a through fare, they share marketing expenses as well as aircraft. The increased efficiency is passed on, in part, to the customer with the lower through fare mentioned a moment ago. Another feature that is attractive to passengers is that frequent-flyer miles earned on both airlines can apply to the frequent-flyer program of the passenger's choice. Code sharing is under active consideration between airlines whose principal routes are in the United States, but questions of antitrust regulation and acceptance by the unions must be resolved.

The Infrastructure Crisis. What is likely to interfere with the growth in air travel and ultimately retard or even halt it is the **infrastructure crisis**. Air transport congestion is one potential problem. Airports all over the world are trying to address this issue through expansion, upgrading, and redesign. This overload is even worse in Europe and approaching critical proportions in much of Asia. New airports are being built in large metropolitan areas. It is not unusual now for a major city to have two, or even three, major airports.

CHANNELS OF DISTRIBUTION

In lodging, the emergence of **channels of distribution** as a significant factor is a relatively new development (see Chapter 12). On the other hand, in other industries, distribution channels have long been a fact of business. Those who manufacture consumer goods have several layers of businesses between the manufacturer and the final customer. Some of these intermediary businesses and agents are wholesalers, manufacturer's representatives, and brokers. Typically, these intermediaries move the product from the manufacturer to the retailer, who then sells to the final user, the retail customer. Although much of the hospitality industry is made up of retailers who provide goods and services directly to the customer, the travel agent and tour operators represent an important channel for many hotels, as well as for other tourism operators.

Travel agents have played a large part in the growth of the cruise industry. (Source: Radisson Seven Seas Cruises; Courtesy of Carlson Cruises Worldwide.)

Travel Agencies. The Office of Travel and Tourism Industries defines **travel agencies** as follows: "Travel agencies make travel reservations for the public and sell transportation, lodging, and other travel services on behalf of the producers of the services. They are retailers: they sell travel services provided by others directly to the final customer." As we speak, the role of travel agencies is changing. Commissions are dropping (or being eliminated entirely), consumers are doing more of their own travel planning, and travel agencies are becoming more specialized, focusing on niche markets. Some of the basic services offered by travel agencies, as well as some more current issues, are discussed below.

Although the large travel agencies are the most visible, the smaller agencies with gross billings (i.e., ticket and travel package sales) under $2 million annually still constitute the largest majority of agencies. In total, there are an estimated 20,000 agencies in the United States (as associated with the Airlines Reporting Corporation).[14] This doesn't begin to reflect how many businesses there are that offer travel-related services, though. American Express, Carlson Wagonlit Travel, and Navigant International are the three largest "traditional" travel agencies.

Expedia, Travelocity, and Orbitz (all "online" travel agencies) are also in the top ten in terms of sales. Online travel agencies now account for just over 10 percent of travel agent revenues but continue to grow at the expense of traditional travel agencies. The lines between traditional agencies and online agencies are becoming blurred, though, with more and more traditional agencies offering online services as part of their overall services. With the decrease in potential commissions from the sale of airline tickets, (as well as the increasing use of the Internet) travel agents are booking fewer airline tickets. A study by the Travel Industry Association of America found that 43 percent of travelers booked some travel plans online and 36 percent of them booked airline tickets online, by far the most common type of travel product or service that was booked online. In addition, they found that more consumers booked their airline tickets online than any other type of travel-related product or service (such as hotel rooms or tickets for attractions).[15]

Smaller agencies have been hit especially hard by the airlines' cutback in the commissions they pay travel agencies, from 10 percent to 8 percent to none at all in some cases. Many of the larger U.S. airlines stopped paying commissions in March of 2002. Agents continue to collect commissions for sales of other types of sales, however, and earn income from either incentives from airlines (for selling a certain volume of tickets) or from charging service fees to customers (an average of about $25 per ticket). Although airline commissions have been reduced, hotel, tour package, and cruise line commissions, which range from 10 to 15 percent, encourage travel agencies to devote more of their efforts to selling those products to travelers. Many agencies earn more overall through the sale of these activities than they do from the sale of airline tickets. Travel agents not only make reservations and sell tickets but also sell packaged tours. About one-fifth of their sales of leisure travel are packaged tours. It's clear that travel agents have considerable influence on the consumer and, thus, on the sales of other firms serving travelers. A majority of pleasure travelers, for instance, seek the advice of their travel agent on hotel selection, package tour choice, and car rental. Roughly 60 percent of business travelers still use travel agents to make their travel arrangements. Travel agencies have had to adjust to the decreased margins in the travel industry by offering solutions to their customers. Some have repositioned themselves as "travel consultants," essentially charging for offering travel advice rather than selling tangible products. One example of how a travel agency "reinvented" itself is the Rex Travel Organization in Chicago. Rex Fritschi, the owner of the company, is a well-traveled veteran of the industry. When he began to notice the changes taking place in the travel planning industry, he began to change what he offered customers. Instead of just offering his customers tickets and brochures of destinations, he now allows customers to tap into his personal knowledge base of some 144 countries that he has visited. He now runs something closer to a travel consultancy—charging customers for inside knowledge of an area, travel tips, and even providing local contacts. Similar agencies offer the same services but to niche markets. One company in New York only offers its services to professional tennis players. The business of providing travel consultation is a growing field—travel counselors can even earn a professional designation now.[16]

Travel wholesalers and tour brokers represent another segment of the industry. Brokers and wholesalers arrange to purchase space and services from all of the firms that serve travelers—carriers, hotels, restaurants, and attractions. Then they sell the services of these firms to the consumer, generally through retail travel agents in return for a commission on those sales. Travel wholesalers such as American Express often retail their own tours, but they also work with the retail travel agencies that sell the tour packages to customers in their local markets. Carriers (such as airlines and bus and rail operators) also have their own tour operations and act as wholesalers of package tours. Tour wholesalers purchase services at deep discounts. They make their package attractive by offering a retail price that is still significantly less than the cost of all the package elements if the traveler purchased them separately. Even after this discount, both the tour broker and the retail travel agent have a margin for their operating costs and profit.

Hotels (especially resort hotels) often profit handsomely from their associations with travel agencies. In return for the commissions they pay these agencies, the hotels have their properties represented in many communities. The travel wholesaler, too, can be important to hotels, because a listing in a wholesale package guarantees a listing with all of the wholesaler's retail affiliates. Some hotels, however, avoid travel agent representation and the accompanying commissions if it produces, on balance, relatively little income.

RESERVATION NETWORKS

In the past, airline companies made airline reservations, and hotels and car companies made their own reservations. Travel agents called the appropriate reservation system to inquire about or reserve a seat, room, or automobile. The revolutionary development in the area of **reservation networks** has been the linkup of these systems. All of these reservation systems can communicate with one another on virtually a worldwide basis. Because nearly all travel agents have computer terminals linked to one or more of the airline systems, the emerging system has literally thousands of instantaneous selling points. More and more of these companies are offering online booking systems to Internet users. As a result, what is emerging is an even more competitive travel marketplace. Offering to book tickets is no longer enough for survival. Travel agents, increasingly, must use the tools of their information-rich environment and their expertise to provide services to consumers they cannot readily provide for themselves. Although the information revolution is making a great deal possible, it is not necessarily making it easy—and the information environment of travel is becoming increasingly complex. Ultimately, travel agencies and other intermediaries who make it possible for the consumer to choose intelligently from the many options now available will survive. Those who simply book tickets may not.

Noneconomic Effects of Tourism

So far, we have stressed the economic structure and impact of tourism. As we will see, however, tourism has other impacts, both unfavorable and favorable and certain **noneconomic effects**.

CROWDING

A successful tourist attraction may, in effect, self-destruct from its own success. One of the major potential problems of tourism is **crowding**: So many people want to see the attraction that its own success destroys its charm. Many students can probably think of one of their own personal experiences that could support this.

At successful theme parks, this problem is addressed by designing places where guests will be waiting in line as "staging areas," with interesting views and even live or mechanized entertainment to distract the visitors. Another theme park tactic is to have lots of cleanup help, so that paper, cigarette butts, and other trash never accumulate, thus reducing or eliminating some of the evidence of crowding.

Another example can be found in areas of scenic beauty such as popular national parks, where trails often become more and more difficult as they progress. Most people turn around and return to the parking lot once the pavement ends, and even fewer continue once the unpaved trail actually becomes difficult to follow. In effect, reducing the amenities is a subtle form of rationing; the ultimate example of this is the

Theme parks have been particularly effective at mitigating the effects of crowding through creative strategies. (Courtesy of Busch Gardens Tampa Bay; © 2004Busch Entertainment Corporation.)

wilderness area, where entrance is only on foot or by horse. Difficulty of access can thus reduce crowding. Another reaction to mass tourism and its impact is ecotourism, which is discussed further in the next chapter.

Along with crowding, tourism can result in noise, odors, and pollution. A special form of crowding is the traffic jam. In many areas, tourist traffic has increased but the local infrastructure—roads, bridges, and airports, for instance—has not kept up. The result is traffic overload, causing delays and, in some cases, accidents and injuries as well. The traffic jam is equally annoying to visitors and local inhabitants. This is an especially serious problem in the developing world, where infrastructure was not highly developed in the first place. In the face of exploding traffic, the situation often becomes critical. Not surprisingly, people who live in a tourist attraction area may have mixed or hostile feelings about further development because of their concern for privacy, the environment, or just their ability to get safely to and from home on crowded highways. This can contribute to the love-hate relationship that often exists between tourists and locals.

Another possible impact of crowding is "crowding out." For example, a beach or other scenic area formerly used by local people may be bought and its use restricted to paying visitors. This has happened on several Caribbean islands and, in some cases, has resulted in the local populace's becoming unfriendly or even hostile as they found themselves deprived of access to their beaches. This has led, in a number of instances, to sharp clashes between local people and visitors, an unfriendly

Golf is becoming an increasingly popular vacation activity. (Courtesy of ClubCorp.)

environment, and a subsequent drop in the number of visitors. Another example, albeit an extreme one, is Mount Everest, where few people travel to (and climb) but that is experiencing the effects of the garbage left behind by trekkers. Because of the extreme weather, garbage can remain intact for decades. There are now policies in place for the removal of garbage.

These potentially unfavorable developments related to tourism give rise to the notion of "carrying capacity," that is, the idea that an area can accept only a certain

Volunteer Tourism[1]

Education and social status have long been motivations for travel, as have pleasure and sightseeing. Since the latter part of the twentieth century, tourists have begun to search for new and different forms of travel other than mass travel. Along with backpacking, adventure tourism, and eco-tourism, volunteer tourism has emerged as a popular type of alternative tourism. Volunteer tourism is often identified with international volunteering, social work, and conservation corps work.

Volunteer tourism generally covers these four major themes: Nature Based, Community Involvement, Learning Experience, and Interaction/Exchange. Volunteer tourism offers an opportunity to participate in various activities, such as scientific research, conservation projects, medical assistance, economic and social development, and cultural restoration. Actual activities can include translating, cooking, cutting wood, curriculum planning, and organic farming. In addition to these activities, the volunteer has an opportunity to take part in local activities and interact further with the community.

Volunteer opportunities cover all regions of the world with Africa, Asia, and Central and South America as some of the more popular locations. The tourism experience can take place in varied locations such as rainforests, conversation areas, developing communities, hospitals, and high schools.

Project duration can range from 1 to 2 weeks, to several months, to 2 years and beyond. According to McGehee and Santos[2], although the interactions between volunteers and the locals may not be particularly lengthy, the intensity often makes up for the duration. The fact that volunteers often need to share meals, sleeping areas, training time, and even travel to and from sites suggests that there are many opportunities to exchange information and develop meaningful connections.

The volunteer activities are indeed mutually beneficial, benefiting locals and visitors. While providing much needed community development, tourists themselves experience a direct interaction that creates changes in their values, consciousness, and lifestyle. It has a substantial impact on the personal development of the participants. They often feel empowered, feel that they have made a difference, and often become more confident in their ideas and beliefs. Thus, volunteer tourism can be viewed as a development strategy leading to sustainable development and centering the convergence of natural resource qualities.

Volunteer tourists are usually required to have free time and money to spend on sustainable development efforts. Volunteer tourists usually pay an amount that is more than an average tourist would

number of visitors without being made less desirable as a destination. That carrying capacity can be seen in terms of the physical infrastructure we discussed in an earlier section of this chapter, but the notion extends to social institutions as well.

FAVORABLE NONECONOMIC EFFECTS

Not all noneconomic effects, however, are necessarily unfavorable. Successful tourist destinations can often fuel local pride: Some tourist events, such as festivals expect to pay on a regular holiday to a similar location. Some organizations such as Earthwatch, Community Aids Abroad, and Youth Challenge International (YCI) often provide some international support or sponsorship programs. Information regarding volunteer travel opportunities is relatively easy to locate through student travel agents on the Internet. GoAbroad.com,[3] for example, is a leading international education and experiential travel resource. Its directories contain over 25,000 opportunities abroad, including volunteer opportunities.

The volunteer tourism market segment includes tourists from all demographic groups and individual characteristics. High school students and early university students are the major part of the market. This explains why more and more youth development programs are integrated into volunteer programs. The nonprofit YCI, for example, provides the opportunity for over 4,000 17- to 25-year-olds from all over the world to work on different projects in over 30 countries. The representatives of its SERR Project were generally college students with an average age of 21 to 22 years old.

A well-designed volunteer program requires collaboration from different tourism sectors (governments, private enterprise, local communities and organizations, conservation, nongovernmental organizations, and international institutions). To enhance the future of volunteer tourism, there is a need for tourism infrastructure, supply-led marketing, and the establishment and monitoring of the carrying capacities (environmental and cultural). Volunteer tourism introduces new business structures, new travel motivations, new experiences, and undeniably a new emerging type of tourist. It requires a people-oriented approach. In the future, it is believed that volunteer tourism practices can move the industry toward more ethical practices, helping to embed these tourists more richly in the local cultures so that they may gain a more thorough understanding of host values and traditions.

1. The information in this note was gathered from: Wearing, S. (2001). Volunteer Tourism: Experiences that make a difference. U.K.: CAB International. This Note was prepared by Novie Johan, Graduate Research Assistant.
2. McGehee, N. G. and Santos, C.A. (2005). "Social Change, Discourse and Volunteer Tourism," *Annals of Tourism Research*, 32 (3), 760–79.
3. GoAbroad.com (www.goabroad.com).

and fairs, may even be staged to celebrate some aspect of the local culture. Agricultural fairs, for instance, which draw thousands—and sometimes hundreds of thousands—of visitors, celebrate a region's agricultural heritage and its favored crops, as well as provide important educational activities such as 4-H meetings and contests.

In other cases, a local tradition may be observed. In a Portuguese community, it may be a blessing of the fishing fleet; in an area where many of German descent live, it could be Oktoberfest. In these cases, adults are reminded of their background, and the young see their heritage dramatized as visitors come to admire it.

Another positive noneconomic effect occurs through volunteer tourism, a concept discussed in Global Hospitlity Note 13.2.

Because of its importance to the hospitality industry, tourism is significant to students of hospitality management. However, even if this weren't your field of study, it would be important for you to know about it. This is because whatever problems tourism raises, its positive economic, cultural, and social impacts make it an important phenomenon of contemporary mass society.

Summary

This chapter opened with a discussion of the reasons that tourism is important to the hospitality industry. We then explained why people are traveling more: changing use of leisure time, rising family incomes, and more middle-aged people who have the time and money to travel.

The most common reason for traveling is pleasure, followed by business. More people travel by car than by any other means. Travel by air increased over the last ten years but is somewhat subject to price sensitivity when fares increase.

The economic significance of tourism is clear: Tourism ranks in the top three industries for total business receipts. Moreover, about 1 in 17 people is employed in an activity supported by travel expenditures. Indeed, communities seeking potential employers may profitably use tourism as an attraction.

The United States is a popular international tourist attraction; its popularity is often based on the value of the U.S. dollar versus that of other currencies, as well as a number of other factors. International visitors to this country are an important means of improving the U.S. balance of payments and receipts, as well as the U.S. employment outlook.

We have also examined other businesses serving the traveler, such as passenger transportation companies and travel agents. In looking at air travel, we considered the competition between hub-and-spoke and point-to-point airline systems and the strengths and weaknesses of both. While discussing channels of distribution, we noted the impact that technological change is having on this industry, made up predominantly of small businesses. Finally, we closed the chapter by touching on the noneconomic effects of tourism, both unfavorable (such as crowding) and favorable (such as festivals, fairs, and the celebration of local traditions).

Key Words and Concepts

Tourism	**Receipts and payments**
Leisure	**Travel trade balance**
Income	**Hub-and-spoke system**
Demographics	**Point-to-point service**
Business travel	**Infrastructure crisis**
Pleasure travel	**Channels of distribution**
Mode of transportation	**Travel agencies**
Common carrier	**Travel wholesalers**
Travel multiplier	**Reservation networks**
Tourism and employment	**Noneconomic effects**
Arrivals and departures	**Crowding**

Review Questions

1. What is tourism, and which organizations does it include?

2. What are some of the factors that have caused the increase in tourism?

3. What are the main reasons that people travel?

4. Which age groups travel most, and what kinds of trips does each group take?

5. What are the recent trends in automobile and airline travel, and what are their causes?

6. Is tourism important economically to the United States? Explain.

7. What factors account for the improvement in the U.S. travel trade balance? What could threaten the favorable balance?

8. What are the relative advantages of hub-and-spoke and point-to-point airline systems? How does each work? Give examples of airlines that rely on each type of system.

9. Describe some of the favorable and unfavorable noneconomic effects of tourism.

Internet Exercises

1. **Site name:** eTurboNews

    URL: www.eturbonews.com

    Background information: Since the launching of eTurboNews in April 2001, their readership has increased from 26,000 of mostly U.S. subscribers to more than 209,000 international subscribers in 230 countries and territories. This achievement places them at the forefront of the industry, making them the largest international newsletter for the travel trade. Their database of readers is composed mostly of travel agents, tour operators, airline employees, cruise operators, resorts, and hotels. Both national and international government personnel, private tourism marketing organizations and associations, and more than 3,500 media companies and journalists subscribe to eTurboNews.

    Exercises:

    a. Browse the eTurboNews Web site. List and describe five reasons why a tourism professional could benefit from the information on this Web site.

    b. Choose a recent travel and tourism news item and lead a class discussion on the importance of that news item to the tourism industry.

2. **Site name:** Orbitz

    URL: www.orbitz.com/

    Background information: Orbitz is an online travel company offering leisure and business travelers a wide selection of low airfares, as well as deals on lodging, car rentals, cruises, vacation packages, and other travel. The site was created to address consumers' need for an unbiased, comprehensive display of fares and rates in a single location.

    Site name: CheapTickets.com

    URL: www.cheaptickets.com

    Background information: CheapTickets is a leading seller of discounted leisure travel products online through its Web site. CheapTickets provides consumers access to its collection of airfares, and discounted travel products to include hotel accommodations, cruises, rental cars, vacation packages, condo rentals, and Last Minute Trips.

    Site name: Travelocity

    URL: www.travelocity.com/

    Background information: Travelocity is an online travel company featuring deals on flights, hotels, cars/rail, cruises, last minute packages, and a variety of vacation activities.

    Site name: Expedia

URL: www.expedia.com/

Background information:

Exercises: Expedia delivers consumers everything they need for researching, planning, and purchasing a whole trip. The company provides direct access to one of the broadest selections of travel products and services to include airline tickets, hotel reservations, car rental, cruises, and many other in-destination services from a broad selection of partners worldwide.

Exercises:

a. Describe the services these Web sites provide as compared with the services of a travel agency.

b. What are the benefits and drawbacks of using these Web sites versus using a travel agency to plan a trip?

c. What role do these Web sites play in the overall travel/tourism distribution system?

3. **Site name:** Site name: Priceline.com

URL: www.priceline.com/

Background information: Priceline.com is a travel service where you can choose your exact flights and times or name your own price and save even more.

Site name: Hotwire.com

URL: www.hotwire.com/

Background information: Hotwire's mission is to offer low prices on travel and lodging.

Exercises:

a. What are the similarities and differences between these two Web sites from the standpoint of the services they provide?

b. How do these two Web sites differ from Orbitz, CheapTickets.com, Expedia, and Travelocity?

c. What role do these Web sites play in the overall travel/tourism distribution system?

4. **Site name:** U.S. Department of State

URL: www.state.gov/

Background information: The Department of State leads the United States in its relationships with foreign governments, international organizations, and the people of other countries. It aims to provide a more free, prosperous, and secure world.

Exercises:

a. What international travel services/information does the U.S. Department of State provide on its Web site?

b. The Department of State issues "Consular Information Sheets" for every country of the world. What information is contained on these information sheets and why is it valuable for an international traveler?

c. What travel tips does the Department of State issue for the following groups of Americans when they travel abroad:
   i.   Older Americans
   ii. Students
   iii. Women traveling alone
   iv. Travelers with disabilities

d. What travel tips are provided for our neighboring countries of Canada and Mexico?

5. **Site name:** Site name: World Tourism Organization (WTO)

   URL: www.world-tourism.org

   Background information: The World Tourism Organization is a specialized agency of the United Nations and is the leading international organization in the field of tourism. It serves as a global forum for tourism policy issues and practical source of tourism know-how.

   Exercises:

   a. One of the programs of the WTO is "market intelligence and tourism promotion." What are the objectives for this program?

   b. What is the "Global Code of Ethics for Tourism" and what are the ten principles included in the code?

   c. What services does the WTO provide for its members?

Notes

1. "2005 Travel Market Report," Travel Industry Association of America, www.tia.org.
2. Annual Work and Leisure Poll, The Harris Poll, December 8, 2004.
3. Travel Industry Association of America, 2005, *Domestic Travel Market Report*, page 28.
4. U.S. Census Bureau, "Projections of the Population by Age, Sex, Race and Hispanic Origin: 1999–2100" (January 23, 2006).
5. Peter Francese, "Older and Wealthier," *American Demographics*, November 2002.
6. U.S. Census Bureau, "Projections of the Population by Age, Sex, Race and Hispanic Origin: 1999–2100" (January 23, 2006).
7. Peter Francese, "The Exotic Travel Boom," *American Demographics*, June 2002.
8. "2005 Travel Market Report," Travel Industry Association of America, www.tia.org.
9. Ibid.
10. Ibid.
11. World Travel & Tourism Council, http://www.wttc.org/framesetsitemap.htm, January 17, 2007.

12. Ibid.
13. The Office of Travel and Tourism Industries (www.tinet.ita.doc.gov).
14. Standard and Poor's Net Advantage, *Survey of Airline Industry,* November 2006.
15. Traveler's Use of the Internet, Travel Industry Association of America, 2005.
16. Susan Carey, "Travel Agents Morph as Industry Evolves," *The Wall Street Journal,* College Journal, May 30, 2002.

The Hospitality Industry

(Courtesy of Busch Gardens Tampa Bay; © 2004 Busch Entertainment Corp.)

CHAPTER FOURTEEN

Destinations: Tourism Generators

The Purpose of this Chapter

T ravel destinations (whether natural or created) are the magnets that set the whole process of tourism in motion. In this chapter, we look at the motivations of travelers, as well as the nature of mass-market travel destinations. Many of these are, to all intents and purposes, a part of the hospitality industry and offer attractive career prospects for students. You will need to be familiar with the economic and operating characteristics of destinations to round out your understanding of tourism.

THIS CHAPTER SHOULD HELP YOU

1. Equate travelers' motives with their destinations by listing five common reasons people travel and a corresponding site they might select to visit.

2. Explain the difference between primary and secondary attractions, and provide an example of each.

3. Identify and describe four categories of planned play environments created specifically for tourism, and list elements they have in common.

4. Describe the activities offered by theme parks to attract travelers, and explain the difference between regional and national theme parks.

5. Name the three primary forces currently driving the growth in casino gambling.

6. Describe the significance of large- and small-scale urban entertainment centers as a part of a community's tourism industry, and provide an example of each type of facility.

7. Describe the important contributions that fairs and festivals make to their host communities.

8. Explain the role of natural attractions in tourism, and describe the overall contribution they make to the industry.

Motives and Destinations

If people had no place they wanted to go, tourism would be in jeopardy. However, people travel, and they travel for many reasons—for instance, work and **recreation**. In this chapter, we will be concerned almost exclusively with travel for purposes of recreation. Even when people travel for this reason, however, their motives are varied, primarily because recreation is more than just play. Building upon Webster's definition of the word, recreation can also involve revivification, new vigor, refreshment, and reanimation, as well as amusement, diversion, or gratification.

Recreation has a function. It is not just the opposite of work; it is its counterweight. Recreation relates to relaxation but also to stimulation and gaining renewed energy as well as to playing. In short, it contributes to the attainment of balance in our lives. It is a necessary and vital part of life, and, not surprisingly, different things attract different people. For instance, perhaps the earliest motive for travel was religion and the sense of renewal of commitment that was and is experienced by the pilgrim. Today's pilgrimage attractions include Lourdes in France, Santiago de Compostela in Spain, Guadalupe in Mexico, and Ste. Anne de Beaupré in Quebec. In fact, such religious destinations exist all over the world.

Like religion, good health has always been a major concern, and health interests have long been a major travel motive. In ancient times, the Romans were drawn to springs thought to have health-giving properties, which became fashionable again in the eighteenth century. There are many hot springs in the United States, including Hot Springs, Arkansas, and Ojo Caliente in New Mexico, which saw their heyday between the 1880s and the 1940s. Springs exist all over the world, including Germany, where people still travel to such places as Bad Hamburg for the healing waters. While the healing power of natural springs is enough to attract some travelers, others seek to manage their health by different means—the Mayo Clinic, for instance, attracts so many people that its home city of Rochester, Minnesota, has one of the highest ratios of hotel rooms per resident of any city in the United States.

Another reason that people travel is to be able to experience scenic beauty, especially the mountains and the seashore. Scenic beauty is often coupled with health-building activities—hiking, skiing, and cycling, for example—so that both body and mind are refreshed. A good example of this is the current popularity of state and national park systems across North America, which are the most extensive response in history to these touring motives (discussed more fully at the end of this chapter).

Sporting events are big business but have long been popular—from the first Olympics in 776 B.C. to today's NCAA Final Four basketball tournament, the Kentucky Derby, and the Super Bowl. Events such as these attract thousands of serious sports

The Addi Galleries in Las Vegas offer a different type of diversion in that city. (Courtesy of Las Vegas Convention and Visitors Authority.)

enthusiasts as well as untutored onlookers. Indeed, sports arenas have become such big business that some on-site food service companies have created special divisions just to manage sports food service (as discussed in Chapter 7).

Culture, including history and art appreciation, is judged by some as not very interesting stuff, yet every year, yesterday's battlefields throng with thousands of visitors

A vintage locomotive (1882) at the National Railway Museum in York, England. (Photo by Robert Alan Creedy.)

Theme parks such as Busch Gardens Tampa Bay offer high-quality performances for their visitors. (Courtesy of Busch Gardens Tampa Bay; © 2004 Busch Entertainment Corp.)

on guided tours. The popularity of the Vicksburg National Military Park in Mississippi and the Gettysburg National Military Park in Pennsylvania are but two examples, each drawing over 1 million visitors each year. In the area of art appreciation, the Louvre is one of France's major cultural treasures. Closer to home, the Smithsonian museum complex in Washington, DC, is one of the biggest draws in that city. There are museums for almost everything—even museums that celebrate work and industry, such as the Museum of Science and Industry in Chicago. (Imagine people on vacation visiting a museum that focuses on work!) The various Halls of Fame (for baseball, hockey, rock and roll, etc.) could also be considered museums of sorts. Other cultural events that attract tourists include the many music and theater festivals all across Europe and North America, many focusing on classical music (Tanglewood in Massachusetts) and Shakespeare (Stratford Theatre in Ontario). Such events are often used by cities to celebrate and enhance the cultural life of the area, as well as to attract visitors' spending to strengthen the local economy.

Theater and spectacle, whether Broadway's *The Producers* or Walt Disney's theme parks, are currently among the most significant tourist attractions. In addition, there are literally thousands of lesser-known theaters and amusement parks that stimulate the local culture and economy by catering to the interests of people close to their homes.

Although we have been discussing the reasons that people travel, it should be noted that what these motives for travel also have in common is their focus on a destination. Destinations can be of different types, such as **primary (touring) destinations** and **secondary (stopover) destinations**. Primary destinations have a wide

The Grand Canyon is a popular tourist destination. Visitors to the Grand Canyon enjoy the vistas; the more adventurous can hike to the canyon floor. (Courtesy of National Park Service.)

market and draw travelers from a great distance. These kinds of destinations, such as some of the religious and health-related destinations discussed previously (as well as more current examples such as Walt Disney World and Las Vegas), attract visitors from the entire North American continent and all over the world. Because such a high proportion of their visitors are away from home, these primary destinations can create a heavy lodging demand. Orlando, Florida, for instance, like Rochester, Minnesota (home to the Mayo Clinic), has a disproportionately high number of hotel rooms per capita.

Secondary destinations, on the other hand, draw people from nearby areas or induce people to stop on their way by. Some secondary destinations may, in fact, have a higher number of visitors than many primary destinations. As a primary attraction, the Grand Canyon attracts about 4 million visitors a year, although they come from all over the world. In contrast, many regional theme parks (as examples of secondary destinations) draw at least that many visitors. Atlantic City, for example, which is mainly a regional casino gambling center, attracts about ten times that many. In general, we can say that a primary attraction requires more services per visitor, but this does not detract from the importance of successful secondary attractions. Indeed, even smaller secondary attractions make important contributions to their locale.

The balance of this chapter will examine those destinations and attractions to which hospitality services are important enough that the attraction can usefully be thought of as part of the hospitality industry. We will consider primary destinations such as theme parks and casinos as well as significant secondary destinations in urban centers such as sports centers, zoos and aquariums, and museums. We will then consider temporary destinations such as festivals and fairs. Finally, we will also look briefly at attractions in the natural environment, such as national parks, seashores, and monuments. Our main interest will be in the impact of these kinds of destinations on opportunities in the hospitality industry, their significance for hospitality managers, and possible careers in such complexes.

Mass-Market Tourism

It was not so long ago that travel was the privileged pastime of the wealthy. The poor might migrate, moving their homes from one place to another in order to live better or just to survive, but only the affluent could afford travel for sightseeing, amusement, and business. That condition has not really changed; some affluence is still required for recreational travel, and certainly one's level of affluence directly affects the number and types of vacations one can take. What has changed is the degree of affluence in our society. We have become what economists refer to as an affluent society.

When travel was reserved for the higher social classes, its model was the aristocracy. In hotels, for example, dress rules required a coat and tie in the dining room. As travel came within the reach of the majority of Americans, however, the facilities serving travelers adapted and loosened their emphasis on class. Many of the new establishments have, in fact, become mass institutions. Any discussion of these types of facilities would have to include Las Vegas and Walt Disney World in Orlando.

In Las Vegas casinos, mink-coated matrons play blackjack next to denim-clad cowboys. These are not social clubs that inquire who your parents are or which side of the tracks you live on. The color of your money is the only concern. Likewise, anybody with the money can buy a reserved seat in any of the new domed sports centers (such as Minute Maid Park in Houston with its retractable roof) or stroll through one of the new megamalls, which will be discussed later in the chapter. What we see developing (and continuing to evolve on larger and larger scales) are new "planned play environments," places, institutions, and even cities designed almost exclusively for play—that is, pure entertainment for the masses. Again, social class is meaningless in such places—Disney World has virtually no dress code for its guests. People come as they are. All comers are served and enjoy themselves as they see fit within the limits of reasonable decorum.

These essentially democratic institutions supply a comfortable place for travelers from all kinds of social backgrounds. Accordingly, as the popularity of these facilities increases, we see a new, more egalitarian kind of lodging and food service (and other hospitality-related) institutions flourishing.

Planned Play Environments

R ecreation is as old as society itself. However, a society that can afford to play on the scale that North Americans do now is new. Some anthropologists and sociologists argue that "who you are" was once determined by your work, what you did for a living, but that these questions of personal identity are now answered by how we entertain ourselves. Some years ago, futurist Alvin Toffler spoke of the emerging importance of "sub cults" whose lifestyles are built around nonwork activities. For these people, work exists as a secondary matter, as only a means to an end. Although there is some debate regarding the balance of work and play, play is destined to serve an increasingly important role in our civilization. We are already seeing the pleasure principle being elevated to a higher level in our society.

To talk about a society in which leisure is the most important thing flies in the face of the work ethic and religious codes that have dominated the United States and Canada, Japan, and many countries in northern Europe for generations. It is becoming clear, however, that the new century will see a society in which leisure plays an increasingly dominant role.

Planned play environments have actually been around longer than one might believe. **Fairs and festivals** at which work (or trade) and play were mixed date back to the mid-1800s in the United States and to medieval times, or even earlier, in Europe. Amusement parks are anything but a twentieth-century American phenomenon—according to the International Association of Amusement Parks and Attractions, early amusement parks in Europe included Bakken in Denmark (established in the 1500s) and Vauxhall Gardens in England, built in the 1600s. In

Golf courses represent an early form of planned play environments. The golf industry is booming, causing incredible growth in the number of golf courses, both public and private. (Mission Hills Country Club; Courtesy of ClubCorp.)

contrast, the oldest continually operating U.S. amusement park, Lake Compounce (in Connecticut), dates back to the early 1800s. Others date from the 1940s and 1950s. What is new, however, is the sophistication that a television-educated public demands in its amusement centers today, and the scale on which these demands have been met since the first modern **theme park** opened at Disneyland. Disneyland, in effect, showed the commercial world that there was a way to entice a television generation out of the house and into a clean carnival offering live fantasy and entertainment. That television generation has now grown up and is busy raising a newer, younger television generation or watching their children raise subsequent generations. Together, these generations are shaping the scope and nature of today's tourism destinations.

There is a variety of leisure environments that have been artificially created for the enjoyment of tourists. These include theme parks, **casinos**, urban entertainment centers, and fairs and festivals. We will discuss each of these in the following sections.

THEME PARKS

In the early 1970s, a number of old-style amusement parks closed their doors because they offered little more than thrill rides and cotton candy, even as modern Americans began to demand more from their entertainment venues. Many of the old amusement parks fell in the face of more sophisticated competition from theme parks that catered more effectively to people's need for fun and fantasy.

Many of the new themes at theme parks focus on the natural environment, such as Rhino Rally at Busch Gardens Tampa Bay. (Courtesy of Busch Gardens Tampa Bay; © 2004 Busch Entertainment Corp.)

LEGOLAND®CALIFORNIA attracts over 1 million visitors each year. (Courtesy of LEGOLAND®CALIFORNIA.)

According to industry sources, the United States has about 600 major themed attractions and other, more traditional amusement parks. The number of visitors to theme and amusement parks in 2005 was estimated at 335 million (the equivalent of more than one visit for every person in the United States), and revenues earned were just less than $10 billion.[1] Worldwide, the industry is estimated to total $19 billion.[2] Outside of the United States, there are about 300 amusement parks in Europe and it is a growing industry in Asia. In fact, according to the International Association of Amusement Parks and Attractions, four of the top ten grossing parks in the world are in Asia. Tokyo Disneyland, which will celebrate its twenty-fifth anniversary in 2008, draws more visitors than any other park in the world (17 million) and is successful despite the difficulty that theme parks in Japan have had over the last few years. Hong Kong Disneyland is Disney's most recent venture in Asia.

Although fewer in number, it is the theme parks that account for the lion's share of park receipts. These parks have clearly become an important part of both the national tourist market and the local entertainment market. In practice, though, about half the guests visit at least twice a year.

THEMES

Just as restaurants are expected more and more to offer entertainment as well as food (note the popularity of the Hard Rock Cafe and Hooters), today's television-oriented traveler expects a park environment that stimulates and entertains in addition to offering rides and other amusements. One way to meet this demand is to build the park around one or more themes. An excellent example of this is Walt Disney World in Orlando,

A boat ride takes visitors by sculptures built of LEGO® blocks. (Courtesy of LEGOLAND®CALIFORNIA.)

Florida, where there are themed areas within themed areas. Most people are familiar with the different theme parks at Disney World, which include the Magic Kingdom, Epcot Center, Disney-MGM Studios, and the newest park, Disney's Animal Kingdom. Within these different parks, however, are additional themed areas. For instance, the themed areas within the Magic Kingdom include Main Street USA, Adventureland, and Frontierland, among others.

Some parks are built around one general theme. LEGOLAND, for instance, is built around the LEGO toy that originated in Denmark. LEGOLAND California is one of four LEGOLAND theme parks around the world (Denmark, England, Germany and California); it is the only one in North America. The park has some 5,000 models built from LEGO blocks, including entire replica cities (such as New Orleans and San Francisco). The park attracts over 1 million visitors each year, mostly from southern California.

Whatever the theme, parks are known for their rides, among other things. One of the most popular types is water rides. In fact, Busch has developed a separate theme park, adjacent to its Busch Gardens in Tampa, Florida, built around water and water rides. Adventure Island, as it is called, offers 25 acres of tropically themed lagoons and beaches featuring water slides and diving platforms, water games, a wave pool, a cable drop, and much more.

Although some parks cater to nostalgia (a romantic longing for the past), others re-create the past in a more realistic way. The Towne of Smithville, in New Jersey, for instance, is a restored mid-1800s crossroads community. It offers a Civil War museum and a theater as well.

Some parks take their themes from animal life. Busch Gardens in Florida offers a 335-acre African-themed park that includes the Serengeti Plain, home of one of the largest collections of African big-game animals. It also serves as a breeding and survival center for many rare species. The animals roam freely on a veldtlike plain where visitors can see them by taking a monorail, steam locomotive, or skyride safari.

The sea offers enticing themes as well. Mystic Seaport, in Mystic, Connecticut, is designed around a nineteenth-century seaport town complete with educational and recreational activities. A quite different type of experience (also based on the sea) can be found at Sea World (also owned by Busch Entertainment), which has been successful with parks in Florida, Ohio, Texas, and California. Sea World of Florida (in Orlando) features many different live shows, including Cirque de la Mer, which is labeled as a "nontraditional circus"; the Shamu Adventure, featuring numerous killer whales; and shows focusing on other sea life such as sea lions and otters. Like many theme parks, Sea World offers organized educational tours featuring the work of Sea World's research organization. A liberal amount of education-as-fun is found in its regular, entertainment-oriented shows. An official of the Disney organization summed up the theme parks' approach to education this way: "Before you can educate, you must entertain." Theme parks do, indeed, constitute a rich educational medium.

SCALE

Theme parks are different from traditional amusement parks not only because they are based on a theme, or several themes, but also because of their huge operating scale. As in nearly everything else, Disney leads the way here. The entire Walt Disney World (WDW) complex in Florida comprises an amazing 47 square miles and offers four distinctly different theme parks, each with its own activities, food service operations, and retail stores. The original Magic Kingdom offers seven different lands or distinctively themed areas. The Epcot Center offers Future World, featuring high-tech pavilions, and the World Showcase, which boasts representative displays from nations around the world. Disney-MGM Studios gives visitors a firsthand look at the backstage workings of a major film and video production facility. Disney's Animal Kingdom is the latest addition. The Animal Kingdom alone, which opened in early 1998, is five times the size of Disneyland (in Anaheim, California). It includes five themed areas and celebrates animal life—quite a different venue from the other three parks in the Disney complex.

Walt Disney World also includes several smaller themed areas such as Disney's six-acre Pleasure Island, billed as being for "young adults." This area includes several nightclubs such as the Adventurers Club, Rock 'n' Roll Beach Club, Pleasure Island Jazz Company, and Comedy Warehouse. Downtown Disney, located nearby, offers shopping and dining for visitors. Also located here is the theater that houses a branch of Cirque du Soleil, with over 1,600 seats. Finally, one of the newer additions to WDW is the Wide World of Sports Complex. This area includes venues for various professional sporting events, such as a 7,500-seat stadium where the Atlanta Braves play during baseball's spring training. The area also boasts a 34,000-square-foot field house and multipurpose sports fields.

Disney is also a major provider of overnight accommodations. In total, it operates 23 different lodging facilities, including campgrounds and villas, on or adjacent to the parks that are operated by, or affiliated with, WDW.

With 55,000 employees, the career significance of WDW and similar enterprises is obvious. In fact, WDW is the nation's largest single-site employer. We should also note here that Disney's Orlando complex represents just one portion of its operations. In recent years the company has opened theme parks in France and Japan and has plans to expand further in the Asia/Pacific area, most notably in Hong Kong in 2005.

REGIONAL THEME PARKS

Theme parks catering to a regional rather than a national market have been growing at a rapid pace in recent years. At least some of this development is attributable to the increasing cost of transportation and the pressure of economic insecurity and inflation on many incomes. The convenience, however, of nearby attractions and the fact that a visit can be included in a weekend jaunt or a three- or four-day trip is probably an equally strong force. Not everyone can take the family on an extended trip to Disney World. Regional theme parks offer an alternative to many travelers.

Roller coasters continue to be a popular attraction at theme parks both large and small. (Courtesy of Busch Gardens Tampa Bay; © 2004 Busch Entertainment Corp.)

Regional parks, aside from serving a smaller geographic area than parks such as Disney World, often target particular groups in their marketing. For instance, Six Flags Over Georgia offers special parties for high-school graduating classes, and its annual Gospel Jubilee features top Christian talent that might not be as popular in other regions of North America. In Pigeon Forge, Tennessee, near Knoxville, Dollywood re-creates the Great Smoky Mountains of the late 1800s through crafts and country music as well as atmosphere, old-time home-style food, and rides. Dollywood has a host of special events in addition to its atractions. These include National Gospel & Harvest Celebration as well as holiday celebrations, craft competitions, and performances. There is even a church on site with nondenominational services held every Sunday. Regional parks such as Dollywood are clearly major sources of tourism: Dollywood attracts over 2 million visitors each year and is the most popular attraction in Tennessee (besides the Smoky Mountains).

Regional parks, though not as large as Walt Disney World, are not small, either. Six Flags Over Georgia, for instance, offers over 100 rides, shows, and attractions. Rides in these parks are of impressive scale. Six Flags recently added its tenth themed area, called Gotham City. One ride in this area, Batman: The Ride, is a fast-paced roller coaster that takes passengers through parts of Gotham City. This single ride's carrying capacity is close to 1,300 passengers per hour. Another ride, Splashwater Falls, is equally as spectacular and cost nearly $2 million to build. Although not on the same scale as Disney, Six Flags Over Georgia (and the 27 other Six Flags parks) are on a scale that is large and impressive enough to draw very effectively from their respective regions. A further look at LEGOLAND, a regional theme park mentioned earlier, is provided in Industry Practice Note 14.1.

THEMES AND CITIES

By definition, theme parks are focused on a central theme or themes. Similarly, entire cities sometimes evoke a singular theme. Examples include Hershey, Pennsylvania; Cooperstown, New York; and Plymouth, Massachusetts.

When one thinks of music, Nashville, Tennessee quickly comes to mind. Nashville is hardly a one-theme town, but it is closely associated with country-and-western music. Since 1925, it has been the site of the Grand Ole Opry, the wellspring from which have poured thousands of country songs and where many of the major country music stars have gotten their start.

The rise in country music's popularity in recent years is undisputed. The country music audience continued to increase throughout the 1990s, and even though it seems to have plateaued, country music is estimated to hold a 10 percent market share nationally (making country music the number one music format on the radio today). The

A Different Kind of Theme Park

LEGOLAND California, located in Carlsbad (in northern San Diego County) is a good example of a regional theme park. Organized around a single theme—LEGO blocks—LEGOLAND is referred to as "the less frenetic park." The LEGO company was founded in 1932, and the LEGO block was invented in 1949. The company branched out into theme parks in the 1960s. The first LEGOLAND opened in Denmark in 1968, and LEGOLAND California opened in 1999. According to Courtney Simmons, manager of media relations and government affairs, the park attracts its guests primarily from within the confines of the state. Out of the 1.3 million visitors each year, approximately 70 percent come from southern California and an additional 10 percent from northern California, meaning that 80 percent of guests are from within the state. The remainder come from outside the state and country. Interestingly, many of the remaining 20 percent of visitors (coming from outside of California) come from the Chicago area. Ms. Simmons attributes this to the popularity of LEGO toys and the fact that there is a LEGO store in downtown Chicago that has proven to be very popular. Many of the international visitors come from Australia.

The park consists of 128 acres of entertainment, shopping, rides, and shows. Some of the LEGO models consist of as many as 30 million bricks. There is even a model shop where visitors can watch models being built. The attractions, rides, and models are complemented by the Big Shop (which has the largest collection of LEGO toys in the United States) and extensive food service operations. There are also numerous celebrations throughout the year, including Halloween, Christmas, New Year's Eve, and U.S. Independence Day. Their New Year's celebration, which starts at 6:00 P.M., includes music and dancing and the LEGO "brick drop."

LEGOLAND California has won numerous awards as being one of the best family-oriented theme parks in the United States and has become an important part of the LEGO corporate portfolio. A new park, the fourth, recently opened in Germany. It is estimated that theme parks contribute approximately 15 to 20 percent of the company revenues.

popularity of country-and-western music (some of which is becoming closer to rock) is probably a function of many factors, including the aging of the baby boomers. As the boomers, with babies of their own, turned off hard rock and heavy metal, they began to explore country music's more traditional themes. Country music saw a large increase in listeners with the emergence of Garth Brooks in the early 1990s, and entertainers such as Faith Hill and Carrie Underwood help to maintain its popularity.

Music fans not only listen to country music on their stereos but also enjoy hearing it live. Although the Grand Ole Opry is the best-known aspect of the country music scene centered in Nashville, it is only one part of the larger Opry Mills complex, formally Opryland USA. The area encompasses 1.2 million square feet of entertainment and shopping. The complex is operated by Gaylord Entertainment.

On one side of the complex is the Cumberland River, where the General Jackson, a giant four-deck paddle-wheel showboat, docks. The General Jackson operates lunch and dinner cruises and "tailgate" parties on days on which the Tennessee Titans play. On the other side is one of America's most successful convention hotel properties, the 2,884-room Opryland Hotel. The hotel includes 600,000 square feet of meeting and convention space. The famous Grand Ole Opry is also part of the complex and is housed in a 4,400-seat auditorium, complete with its own radio station, which broadcasts to 30 different states. Rounding out the attractions at Opry Mills are 200 retail outlets and restaurants.

The Opryland Hotel, on the other hand, draws from a quite different market than does the rest of the complex. Its business is driven primarily by conventions—80 percent of the hotel's customers, an upscale market, are there to attend conventions, meetings, and trade shows. Although country-and-western music, and the fun that goes with it, is an important plus to this market, it is not the main draw. Rather, the key is the hotel's extensive facilities; the hotel claims more meeting, exhibit, and public space than any other hotel in the United States. The Opryland Hotel's size means that it can accommodate 95 percent of U.S. trade shows and exhibitions, and the property's luxurious public facilities, guest rooms, and excellent service are another draw. The Opryland Hotel itself resembles a theme park at times, complete with a conservatory, a water-oriented interior courtyard called the Cascades, and lots of indoor greenery. Within these areas, which are covered with acres of skylights, and elsewhere in the hotel are situated numerous restaurants and lounges, 30 retail shops, 600,000 square feet of meeting space, and various fitness facilities including swimming pools, a fitness center, and tennis courts.

Opry Mills is a clear case of synergy between attractions, entertainment, retail shopping, and communications media that has created a major international tourist attraction. At the same time, it is a vital part of the local economy. Although Nashville and the Opry Mills complex are clearly leading the way, other cities that have made country music a major tourist attraction are Branson, Missouri, and Myrtle Beach, South Carolina.

EMPLOYMENT AND TRAINING OPPORTUNITIES

CAREERS IN
HOSPITALITY

The growth of theme parks (and themed entertainment destinations) is a favorable development for hospitality students because of the opportunities they offer for employment and management experience. Theme parks often operate year round, but on a reduced scale from their seasonal peak. Others close for several months of the year, particularly those in the northeastern United States and Canada. For others, business fluctuations can be extreme, as is the case at Paramount Canada's Wonderland (in Ontario), which has

3,500 seasonal employees but only 150 permanent employees. Few parks experience such employment swings, however. During the months when school is out or when outside weather conditions favor park visitation, attendance soars. As it does, food service volume (and demand for other support services) expands with it. Sometimes demand for these support services is quite large in proportion—Disney earns over 10 percent of its revenues from food service. In order to meet these peaks, the crew expands each summer. To supervise this expanded workforce, college-age people are chosen, usually from last year's crew, as supervisors, assistant managers, and unit managers. These positions are often quite well paid, but more significantly, they offer a chance to assume responsible roles beyond those that most organizations offer to people early in their careers. Generally, these opportunities are accompanied by training and management development programs. Many of the supervisors and managers at LEGOLAND California, for instance, began their careers in summer jobs there and in entry-level positions such as ride operators.

The authors have graded more summer field-experience papers than we care to recall, and consistently some of the best opportunities and training experiences we have encountered have been in regional theme parks. Take a close look at the regional and local theme parks in your area as possible summer employers. They offer a type of hospitality experience different from what students might normally expect.

In conclusion, theme parks, both regional and national, represent one type of manmade environment available to travelers. They are increasingly popular, and the market is becoming increasingly competitive. This is only one type of such environments, however. Some very different types of tourist destinations are discussed next.

Casinos and Gaming

To move from the innocence of theme parks and country music to casinos and gaming may seem like a giant step, but they do have a good deal in common as tourism attractions—and they are becoming more similar all the time. Just note the many similarities that are now drawn between two tourist destinations: Las Vegas and Orlando. In fact, many aging baby boomers, who once brought their children to theme parks such as Disney World, are being lured to **casinos** and gaming destinations (in some cases, they continue to go to both). We will begin by looking at two quite different **gaming markets**: Las Vegas and Atlantic City. Also, a relatively newer gaming area, the Gulf Coast of Mississippi, will be presented. First, however, some discussion of gambling in the United States is in order.

Gambling of all kinds has grown radically in the past decade. By 2007, 47 states and the District of Columbia had state- or city-operated lotteries, commercial casinos, or allowed charitable gaming. When all gaming opportunities are considered, it becomes clear that few jurisdictions are unable to offer their residents the possibility of a legal wager. According to the American Gaming Association, 25 percent of the adults visted a casino in 2005, allowing the industry to grow by 5 percent between 2004 and 2005 and gross $30 billion. This growth occurred despite the loss temporary loss of casino operations on the Mississippi Gulf Coast as a result of Hurricane Katrina.

The casino gambling environment is unique in that it combines the games usually associated with such operations with entertainment, food, and drink, lodging, and, increasingly, shopping. This makes it more of a total recreational experience, rather than a single, discrete activity conducted in isolation.

Casino gaming has exploded, driven by two developments in particular. The first of these was the Indian Gaming Regulatory Act of 1988, requiring that any kind of gambling that was permitted anywhere, at any time, in a U.S. state be per-

Las Vegas is still the most popular gaming destination in the United States. (Courtesy of Las Vegas Convention and Visitors Authority.)

mitted on reservations in that state once a compact between the state and the Native American tribe had been concluded. In 2005, 224 federally recognized tribes offered some sort of gaming on their land. This represents a significant increase, up from 184 in 1998 and 81 in 1993. The facility that is generally believed to be the largest, as well as the most profitable, is the Mohegan Sun, the Mohegan Nation–owned facility in Uncasville, Connecticut (along with Foxwoods which is number two). In total, this segment of the gaming industry generated just under $23 billion in 2005. Sixty different Native American–run casinos had gaming revenues in excess of $100 million in the same year.[3]

The other relatively recent gaming development, modern riverboat gambling, did not come into being until 1991, when Iowa legalized the first gaming riverboat. There were 40 boats operating in 1994. In 2006, there were 83 boats in operation (some riverboats are really just casinos at the water's edge) with total gaming revenues of over $10 billion. Riverboat gaming is most common in the Midwest and deep South. Analysts expect the riverboat gaming market to continue to grow, albeit at a slower rate with fewer new casinos opening.

Harrah's operates this riverboat casino on the Missouri River in North Kansas City. (Courtesy of Harrah's Casinos.)

Three primary forces appear to be driving the current growth in gaming. The first is a change in consumer tastes in which people have come to see gaming as a legitimate form of entertainment, rather than something that is done only by people of questionable background.

A second force that seems to be driving the industry is convenience. It is clear that the consumer's propensity to gamble is influenced by proximity to a gaming facility. Couple this with the estimate that there is a gaming facility within a short distance from every urban area in the country. In short, most of the U.S. population is already within an easy day's drive of a casino, and there are still many sites available for gaming, either on reservations or on riverboats.

A third force that explains why gambling is now so widely permitted is the intense need state and local governments have for funds. New gambling establishments are usually subject to a relatively high level of taxation because of the potential for profit. Gaming, in effect, is a voluntary tax. A high proportion of the drop (the total amount wagered) becomes win (winnings by the house), and a high proportion of the win is taxed by the state. Even in states that may not tax gaming facilities as much as others, "gifts" to the state may be made—and these "gifts" may often be in the tens of millions of dollars. It is important to recognize that as the many taxation and employment benefits to gaming are recognized by civic and business leaders in areas that have not as yet legalized gambling, there is a strong inducement to legalize it in new jurisdictions. Most recently, the state of Pennsylvania approved slot gaming in designated areas (and will issue 14 licenses). Figure 14.1 summarizes current gaming jurisdictions.

	CASINOS AND GAMING		
	LAND-BASED	RIVERBOAT/DOCKSIDE	INDIAN[1] GAMING
Arizona			X
California			X
Colorado	X[2]		X
Connecticut			X
Idaho			X
Illinois		X	
Indiana		X	
Iowa		X	X
Kansas			X
Louisiana	X	X	X
Michigan	X		X
Minnesota			X
Mississippi		X	X
Missouri		X	
Montana			X
Nebraska			X
Nevada	X		X
New Jersey	X		
New Mexico			X
New York			X
N. Carolina			X
N. Dakota			X
Oklahoma			X
Oregon			X
S. Dakota	X[2]		X
Washington			X
Wisconsin			X
Totals	6	6	23

[1]Indicates only Class III Indian casinos
[2]Indicates limited stakes casinos
(Source: American Gaming Association, 2007.)

Figure 14.1
Current gaming jurisdictions with gaming operations.

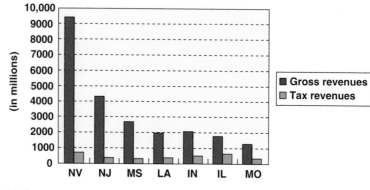

Figure 14.2
Gaming revenue of top seven states, 2002. (Source: American Gaming Association, State of the States, 2003.)

An additional note needs to be made regarding the gaming jurisdictions as indicated in Figure 14.1. The figure would suggest that only 27 states offer casino gaming. In reality, many other states offer some form of legalized gambling aside from or in addition to lotteries. Horse races, video poker machines at truck stops, card houses, bingo halls, and offshore gambling are all available throughout the United States. The figure only includes land-based casinos, riverboats, and Class III Indian casinos. Figure 14.2 provides revenue figures for the different gaming jurisdictions.

LAS VEGAS

The first settlement in Las Vegas can be traced back to 1829, but the town's formation dates from 1905, when it was a small desert railroad town. Casino gambling was legalized in 1931. Following World War II, Las Vegas grew more rapidly as large hotels were built, and by the 1950s, Las Vegas had become an established tourist destination combining casinos, superstar entertainment, and lavish hotel accommodations. Today, the Las Vegas metropolitan area has over 1.8 million residents and over 133,000 hotel and motel rooms—roughly one room for every 12 inhabitants. There were 50,000 new hotel rooms built in the decade between 1992 and 2002! There are another 55,000 new hotel rooms planned, although some of these represent replacement rooms where older hotels are being torn down and replaced with larger hotels. The greater metropolitan area's annual occupancy rate averages well over 80 percent, with estimates of closer to 90 percent by some accounts. It remains to be seen how the new hotel projects scheduled to be built will affect citywide occupancy. As of this writing, nine of the ten largest hotels in the world are located in this city.

Interior of the casino in New York, New York Hotel in Las Vegas. Courtesy of New York, New York Hotel.

Las Vegas has a good deal more to offer than just casinos and hotel rooms. The city is also known for its incredible stage shows, such as Cirque du Soleil, which is currently running five different performances at five different casinos. Mystère is the longest running of their shows. It began in 1993 and is performed at Treasure Island. It is described as a show "where dreams become reality and reality is only a dream." It has drawn over 8 million spectators since it opened. They have also started performing their newest show, LOVE, based on the music of the Beatles and performed at The Mirage. At the nearby Excalibur, King Arthur's Tournament features medieval knights mounted on horseback, charging one another in the fashion of a joust. Down the street is the Tropicana's Folies Bergère, which brings a bit of Paris to Vegas, complete with showgirls and dancing. At the Luxor, which mimics an Egyptian pyramid, guests are transported by boat down the river Nile to the elevator that takes them to their rooms. The Luxor also has the King Tut Museum for visitors. The Venetian hosts the Blue Man Group, whose performances have been popular in Chicago, Boston, and New York. In a very different vein, one of the newer attractions in Las Vegas is Star Trek: The Experience, located at the Las Vegas Hilton. A $70 million attraction, it is complete with theme restaurants, rides, and movie and television sets. Many attractions are free including the Sirens of TI battle at Treasure Island (which replaced the pirate battle), the fountains at Bellagio (complete with music and lights), the volcano explosions outside the Mirage, and the circus acts at Circus

Circus. One other attraction that is quite different bears mentioning. At the MGM Grand, one is able to partake in the prescreening of television shows and television movies at Television City. Participation is free. Participants enter a screening room, watch a screening of a show that is either in production (or partial production), and then rate it at the end. Respondents' feedback is then considered as a factor in the decision whether to finish production and eventually televise the show on national television. In addition, there are many other free attractions that one encounters walking down the Strip. Finally, downtown is the Fremont Experience (an incredible light show billed as the world's biggest).

Hotel room rates in Las Vegas are among the most affordable in the resort industry, and eating inexpensively is no problem. Hotels still advertise rates for as little as $29.00. While the 99-cent breakfast is becoming harder to find, travelers can select from packages that include meals. Las Vegas also sports over 30 golf courses, many of them of championship caliber. In addition, there are numerous tennis and racquetball courts, as well as other recreational facilities. Entertainment and sports facilities, as well as lodging and food service bargains, are used to attract visitors to the city and to play in the casinos.

Las Vegas literally is able to offer the tourist the "entire package." In addition to the activities and attractions available within the city limits, there are also natural attractions that enhance the city's image as a destination. The famous Hoover Dam and Lake Mead, with its 500 miles of shoreline, are less than a half hour away. Death Valley is a half day's drive away, and the Grand Canyon is an easy day's drive from Las Vegas. Less well-known attractions within an hour's drive include the Valley of Fire, Red Rock Canyon, and a clutch of ghost towns.

Las Vegas is a fully developed tourist mecca, served by 60 major airlines—McCarron International Airport averages over 900 flights daily. The city drew over 39 million visitors in the year 2006. Almost 5 million of these were from international origins. Most international travelers to the city come from elsewhere in North America, Japan, Germany, and the United Kingdom.

In addition to its recreational features, Las Vegas has a highly developed convention business, including a 3.2-million-square-foot convention center with another 7 million square feet available at major hotels in the area. Las Vegas regularly hosts some 4,000 conventions per year, drawing over 4 million conventioneers.

There is not a lot in Las Vegas except tourism, the businesses that serve the tourist, and the businesses that serve those businesses and their employees. Las Vegas is the ultimate in destinations—the city that tourism built.

Although gambling continues to be Las Vegas's biggest business, the city has been repositioned as a place to go for entertainment, including gambling but certainly not limited to it. As more people across the country are exposed to gambling and consumers' perceptions of it evolve to a much wider acceptance, the kinds of people coming to Las Vegas are changing. There are many more first-time visitors, and more families are making it a family destination. In addition, the city is now drawing a great many more international visitors than ever before.

Even with its entry into family entertainment, however, it is important to remember that gambling is the mainstay of the Las Vegas (and greater Clark County) economy. Casinos take in roughly $11 billion in Nevada (2005 figures), with most of that being generated in Clark County.[4] Tourists spend over $400 each per visit on nongaming expenditures, while conventioneers and trade show attendees consistently spend more in addition to the sums spent on gaming. In 2005, visitors contributed over $36.7 billion to the local economy.[5]

Those newly acquainted with gambling, it seems, want to visit the big one. Las Vegas is a national, and increasingly international, center that probably stands to gain from the spread of gaming without suffering unduly from the proliferation of riverboat and Native American gaming competitors. On the other hand, it is likely that local and regional gaming centers will, in time, feel the effects of intensifying competition. It's even possible that some markets are now approaching saturation.

LAUGHLIN (CLARK COUNTY)

Laughlin is also a part of greater Clark County and is another gambling center, albeit of a different type. Its location, about 90 miles south of Las Vegas, may be part of its appeal. Casino gambling began there in a modest way in 1969. In 1984, Laughlin's population was only 95 people. Ten years later, it had risen to 8,500, but more significantly, the town had grown from one small casino and restaurant to a city sporting ten major hotels along the Colorado River with over 10,000 rooms, most of them having been built over a five-year period in the 1990s.

Where Las Vegas's casinos are shut off from the outer world, in Laughlin picture windows are all the rage, everything is brightly lighted and open, and most casino employees wear Western dress, even the pit bosses. Much of the volume of traffic comes from nearby prosperous cities in Arizona such as Phoenix, while most of the rest are from southern California. In the winter, however, there is a significant number of snowbird customers who fill parking lots with recreational vehicles. A more laid-back, family-friendly atmosphere seems to account for the success of Laughlin. However, the area has been losing market share to other Nevada gaming areas. Although it bills itself as the "fastest-growing entertainment area in the world," it experienced several years of increasing declines.

ATLANTIC CITY

Atlantic City has a lot to teach us about tourism, both good and bad. Atlantic City has always been a tourist city since its founding in the mid-1850s. It was once the premier resort city on the East Coast of the United States, famous for its boardwalk and its resort hotels, catering principally to prosperous upper-middle-class Americans. With the coming of automobiles, motels, cheaper travel, and changing tastes in leisure, however, Atlantic City began to deteriorate. From 1960 to 1975, the city's population declined by 15,000, the number of visitors fell to 2 million, the number of hotel rooms decreased by 40 percent, and Atlantic City became a case study in the difficulty of reviving a tourist center once it has gone downhill.

As one observer put it, Atlantic City was a tourist resort without any tourists.[6] From a peak tourist center for earlier generations, Atlantic City became virtually an abandoned hulk, rusting away at its moorings. Like many older, worn-out tourism centers, its plant was outmoded and in bad repair. Perhaps more serious, it no longer had any appeal in the market, and the revenue wasn't there to rebuild. Then, in 1976, gambling was approved, and in 1978 the first casino hotel opened.

The city's turnaround has been remarkable. Atlantic City is now drawing about 35 million visitors each year, making it one of America's largest tourist attractions.

Caesars Atlantic City has over 120,000 square feet of floor space devoted to gaming, including a variety of slot machines and 139 table games. (Courtesy of Caesars Atlantic City.)

Planning has also played a large role in its success. Atlantic City casinos are required to reinvest 1.25 percent of their gaming revenues in the community and state through the state-run Casino Reinvestment Development Authority. Literally billions of dollars have been invested in the city's infrastructure and housing stock. Atlantic City now boasts a new convention center and thousands of new hotel rooms, with more in various stages of planning.

Atlantic City is quite different from Las Vegas, aside from being a much younger gaming destination. Although there are two major cities within a day's drive of Las Vegas, Los Angeles and San Diego, Atlantic City has one-quarter of the U.S. population within a 300-mile range. New York City, Philadelphia, and Washington, DC, are all within 150 miles. Over two-thirds of Atlantic City's visitors arrive by car, and just one-fourth arrive by motorcoach. Few, in comparison, arrive by rail or air.

In contrast with Las Vegas's hotel and motel rooms, Atlantic City has far fewer (less than 30,000) rooms, although this number is expected to increase in the next couple of years. With the large number of day-trippers, Atlantic City has never needed, and probably will never need, as many overnight accommodations as does Las Vegas. On the other hand, Atlantic City hotel operators and tourism officials have recognized that overnight guests have a potentially greater impact on the economy. As a result, the agencies responsible for marketing Atlantic City and southern New Jersey have launched a collaborative effort to encourage longer-stay guests. Visitors are encouraged by this new regional program to see the historic and scenic attractions that abound in the area. New Jersey is, after all, one of the original 13 colonies, rich in history. Moreover, its beaches, which border the Atlantic Ocean, have long been famous as vacation spots.

Atlantic City's skyline was once a study in contrasts. Its new or renewed casino hotels are the latest word in casino glitter, but between them, for a long time, were either run-down buildings where speculators had purchased property or open spaces where old buildings had been razed. Outside the boardwalk's immediate vicinity, much of the city was filled with dilapidated slum housing—an element that many often focused on when discussing Atlantic City. In recent years, however, the face of the city has begun to show the impact of the Casino Reinvestment Development Authority, as well as other private and public investment. Today, the city is benefiting from a $1 billion face-lift. At its core is a new $250 million convention center, part of a corridor that was designed to create a spectacular entrance to the city. The corridor is a multiblock complex of enclosed shops, as well as an urban entertainment center that includes the new transportation center and connects the convention center to the famous boardwalk and several of Atlantic City's casino hotels. Further, new hotels are being built—some of the noncasino variety. Finally, much of the empty space on the other side of the main street has been filled with public parking garages to accommodate the many cars that visitors drive to Atlantic City.

The economic impact of Atlantic City is also being felt outside this city of 40,000 people, in the 125,000-person Atlantic County and in the wider southern New Jersey area. Much of the tax revenue is dedicated to funding programs for the disabled, the disadvantaged, and senior citizens. Further, casinos in Atlantic City (still the only municipality in the state where casinos are allowed) employ about 47,000 employees (the vast majority are state residents). Finally, regulatory savings are being used to develop new facilities—recent additions include a professional baseball park (where the Atlantic City Surf play) and an aquarium, the Ocean Life Center. A summary of some of the changes that are taking place in Atlantic City are described in Case History 14.1.

MISSISSIPPI GULF COAST

The growth of the Mississippi Gulf Coast is perhaps the most significant development in the gaming industry in recent years. Over the course of a mere decade, the Mississippi Gulf Coast (including the towns of Biloxi, Gulfport, and Bay St. Louis) has become a major player in the hospitality/gaming industry. Mississippi has 29 state-licensed casinos (plus two Indian casinos), 12 of which are located on the Gulf Coast. These casinos generated about $1.2 billion in gross gaming revenues in 2004. In August of 2005, the area was struck by the devastating Hurricane Katrina, after which all activity came to a halt. The casinos were closed for several months and only began to reopen in December, with limited activity. They began to come back in early 2006 and by the end of the year, ten casinos were open generating almost as much revenue as 12 did in earlier years. At the time of this writing, ten are open, one is under construction and there are eight more planned to open. This is all the result of a focus on redeveloping the area, the state issuing new licenses, and a change in the law, which now allows land-based casinos.

An area that used to attract mainly regional tourists for their annual beach vacations now attracts travelers in the millions—upward of 12 million per year (calculated as person-trips). The number of hotel rooms has increased by 400 percent, convention space has doubled, and the airport continues to expand. The area is also interesting given that, prior to Katrina, the state of Mississippi allowed gambling only on riverboats, so all of the casinos are at the water's edge, and most are situated on large barges, giving the appearance of more permanent buildings.

One of the more recent additions to the landscape is MGM Mirage Resorts' Beau Rivage, in Biloxi. The complex originally opened in 1999 with an investment of $800 million. It also changed Biloxi into a resort destination as well as a gaming hot spot. It reopened in August, 2006 after a $550 million renovation. With the area's 20 golf courses and its own course, a 1,550-seat theater, extensive meeting space, and a 20,000-square-foot spa, Beau Rivage offers plenty of entertainment choices besides its 85,000-square-foot casino.

Changes Come to Atlantic City

This chapter has outlined some of the key differences that exist, and have existed, between Las Vegas and Atlantic City (AC) as gaming destinations. Consider the comparisons of the two cities in terms of scale: Las Vegas has over 130,000 hotel rooms; Atlantic City has fewer than 30,000. The state of Nevada has well over 200 casinos (the majority in Las Vegas); Atlantic City has 12 casinos. Las Vegas has been a gaming capital since 1931; Atlantic City has only offered it since 1978. Still, Atlantic City remains the second largest gaming market in the United States (about 20 percent less in gaming revenues than Las Vegas) and draws almost as many visitors. Historically, though, these visitors have come from shorter distances, stayed for shorter periods, and spent less than the visitors to Las Vegas. However, changes are ocurring that could help Atlantic City to become more like Las Vegas and become more of a direct competitor.

Unlike Las Vegas, Atlantic City does not "reinvent" itself every few years. In fact, the city went 13 years without a new casino until the Borgata opened in 2003 in the marina district. The Borgata was a billion dollar project, the likes of which Atlantic City had not previously seen. Besides bringing a new emphasis to AC (including shopping and fine dining) the development also prompted further growth and development in the way of other new casinos, hotels, shopping, and nightclubs. Borgata, already with 2,000 hotel guest rooms, has a planned expansion underway. Other casinos are also renovating and expanding including Tropicana (with 500 new guest rooms). Atlantic City already has the famed boardwalk, but has also added other entertainment districts including The Pier at Caesars and The Quarter, which boasts fine dining, shopping, and nightclubs. The city itself is also redeveloping parts of town away from the boardwalk, including an area called The Walk which offers many shops and

The Gulf Coast area continues to expand, with several new projects scheduled to open over the next few years. Interestingly, the area of Mississippi known as the North River region, in the northwest part of the state, generates even more gaming revenue than does the Gulf Coast (although the gap is lessening). Whereas most of the visitors to the Gulf Coast come from other gulf coast states (Florida, Alabama, and Louisiana), most of the out-of-state visitors to the North River region come from the greater Memphis area and the midwestern United States.[7]

OTHER MARKETS

Certainly, Las Vegas, Atlantic City, the Mississippi Gulf Coast, and the native-run casinos in Connecticut represent some of the major markets in the United States. There are some other gaming markets in the world that merit discussion though, including: Britain (almost 100 new casinos in two years), France, Australia (where much of the parking. There is a new convention center, new retail space, and numerous non-casino hotels and restaurants.

In making these changes, the city is attempting to market to a younger, more affluent crowd as well as becoming more family oriented, as did Las Vegas several years earlier. So far, it seems to be working. Gaming revenues increased between 2004 and 2005 and the city has increased the average length of stay for visitors from 8 hours to 1.3 days. Also, the city is attracting a more diverse crowd.

The city learned (as did Las Vegas a decade earlier) that the longer tourists stay in town, the more they will spend on hotels, gambling, shopping, and the like. As a result, AC has made a concerted effort to move beyond its reputation for attracting "day trippers" to a destination that can provide more things to do beside gambling, and thus encourage people to spend additional time there.

It is unlikely that the city will ever rival Las Vegas in terms of scale. After all, Las Vegas still has almost 10 times the number of hotel rooms and the state of Nevada has over 200 casinos while AC has 12. However, Atlantic City has changed tremendously in just the last few years, with additional changes to come—including additional teardowns, expansions, new casino licenses, and an expected increase to 35,000 hotel rooms in just a few years.

Information for this Note was gathered from the following sources:
Personal communication with Jim Wortman, Director of the Gaming Education and Research Institute, University of Houston.
Personal communication with Cliff Whithem, Director, Hospitality and Tourism Management, The Richard Stockton College of New Jersey.
Standard and Poor's Net Advantage, *Lodging and Gaming Survey*, August 2006.
The AC, Washington Post.com, March 13, 2005. www.Washingtonpost.com

gaming takes place in private clubs), Mexico, Singapore, and other parts of Asia (including South Korea). Perhaps the market with the most potential is Macau. According to Standard and Poor's, Macau is already the second largest gaming market in the world (after Las Vegas) and is positioned to grow even more. Macau is a Special Administrative Region of China—the only such area of China where gambling is legal. Several U.S.-based companies are partnering with local operators to open large casinos between 2005 and 2010. One of the reasons that Macau is expected to continue to grow is because of its location and its proximity to China and other populous Asian countries. Two factors have contributed to Macau having become an international gaming destination—the area being given back to China (by Portugal) in 1999 and a 2002 law allowing foreign companies to invest and operate there. Its popularity is also rising because more and more Chinese are traveling each year.

CASINO MARKETS AND THE BUSINESS OF CASINOS

The business of casinos is gambling, with table games such as roulette, blackjack, and dice. In addition, a major and growing gambling pastime is the slot machine. From the casino's point of view, what matters in evaluating a customer is his or her volume of play, because the odds in every game clearly favor the house. Big winners are good news for the casino because of the publicity they bring. In the long run, however, the casino wins.

Casino markets can be divided into four general groups: tourists, **high rollers** at the tables, high rollers at the slot machines, and the **bus trade**. Tourists are those who visit the city to take in the sights, see a show, and try their hand at the games, but with modest limits in mind as to how much they are prepared to wager and lose, usually up to $100 but often as much as $250 or $500.

The high roller, as one Atlantic City casino executive put it, is a person who plays with black chips, that is, $100 chips. In Las Vegas, industry experts indicate that a high roller's average bet would be in the $150 to $225 range and that he or she would be expected to have a line of credit of $15,000 during a typical three-day visit to Las Vegas.

For high rollers, gambling is the major attraction, but they also thrive on the personal attention given to them by the casino and hotel staff. They benefit as well from **comps**, complimentary (no-charge) services and gifts provided by the casino. Some high rollers wager more than the average, and a few bet much more. In general, the level of comps is based on the volume of play, with some casinos prepared to provide free transportation, luxurious hotel suites, meals, and show tickets, for instance. More modest but still significant is the high-roller slot player. In Atlantic City, a $500 gambling budget qualifies someone as a slot high roller, but $2,000 is a closer figure in cash or line of credit for Las Vegas. Comps and special recognition are extended to these players, too, according to their level of play. Casinos issue cards with an electronic identification embedded in them. These cards are inserted into the machine to record the player's level of play, and comps are based on the volume of play (not losses). In fact, a $1 slot player is worth more to the house than a player who bets $100 in a table game.

Because there is very little labor associated with slot machines, the house earns an 80 percent operating profit compared to 20 to 25 percent on table games. Some areas depend greatly on such machines. The increasing proportion of casino space taken up by slot machines is explained, in good part, by a changing consumer base that includes a much wider spectrum of society than it did 20 or even 10 years ago. As you can see, however, the superior profit margins of slot machines probably enter into the calculation, too. On Las Vegas's Strip, slot revenue is 49 percent of the market, while table games account for 51 percent. In the newer gambling areas, however, such as riverboat and Indian-owned casinos, slots can account for as much as 75 percent of the wagering. In Atlantic City, slot machines represent 70 percent of gaming revenues—across the country they account for about 60 percent of revenues. Standard & Poor's survey of the gaming industry estimates that there are some 700,000 legal machines in the United States.[8] A final category of players is the bus trade, effectively, the "low rollers." These are often retirees and, surprisingly, people on unemployment compensation. They, too, come for the gambling but usually have a budget of only $35 to $70. They are often attracted by a bargain price.

In Atlantic City, this bus trade still provides a substantial portion of the year-round volume of business, but as we have already noted, the city's casinos are deliberately reducing the significance of this segment while trying to build volume among more well-heeled players. Like their high-roller neighbors, the bus trade, too, is attracted by relatively generous comps. A bus deal, costing $10 to $12, might include round-trip bus transportation, a $5 meal discount coupon, and a $10 roll of quarters ("coin," as it's called in Atlantic City) to get them started.

CASINO STAFFING

CAREERS IN HOSPITALITY

The casino gaming staff is made up of dealers (and croupiers), casino hosts (who play a very important role), a floor person who supervises several dealers, and a pit boss. (In craps, a box-man assists the dealer, handling the bank.) In the pit, a group of similar games, the pit boss is assisted by a pit clerk who handles record keeping.

The pit boss is really a technician, expert from years of experience in the practice of the game. He or she generally supervises the play, approves "markers"—that is, the extension of credit (within house limits)—approves in-house food and beverage comps for known players, and generally provides personal attention to high rollers.

Casino hosts serve a very important function at many casinos around the world. They help customers in a variety of ways, from handling special requests to helping to interpret for

Casinos employ large numbers of well-trained employees. (Courtesy of Las Vegas Convention and Visitors Authority.)

international visitors. They also handle problems that may arise at the tables. Finally, high rollers are assigned their own hosts when they are in the casino.

The floor person supervises between two and five dealers, depending on the game, and never more than four games. He or she is also responsible for closely watching repeat customers to estimate their average bet, a figure that is crucial to the casino's marketing intelligence.

Slot machine areas are staffed by change people working under a supervisor. Change people and supervisors also offer recognition and personal contact for frequent visitors and slot high rollers.

Comps above a certain dollar level are generally approved by the casino's senior management. Comp services for a junket group are approved by the casino's marketing staff. Junkets are similar to tours that might be sold by a travel agent, except that the sights are generally the casino and its hotel environment, and there may be no charge for any of the services because of the expectation of casino play by the visitor. Junkets are put together by the casino or, more commonly, by junket brokers in distant cities.

Dealers need to be alert to players' attempts at cheating, and they themselves are constantly scrutinized by supervisors and security personnel because of the temptation of dishonesty where so much cash is changing hands. The security systems in casinos are incredibly sophisticated and unlike anything in other segments of the hospitality industry. After tours of casinos, students inevitably comment on the security before anything else.

Working in casinos is very challenging. It requires a quick mind and an ability to work with people who are under considerable pressure. Players sometimes become abusive and unreasonable, and whenever possible, staff are expected to avoid a difficult scene, which may permanently alienate a player and his or her friends. Not surprisingly, the higher the roller, the greater the patience that may be expected of the staff. As is true with other segments of the hospitality industry, the casino industry is not for everyone. However, for those who like the excitement and the challenge, the segment provides great opportunities.

Urban Entertainment Centers

When traveling for recreational purposes, people do not just limit their visits to theme parks and casinos. There are many other types of environments that people are drawn to when vacationing. The term "**urban entertainment centers**" means just that—destinations located in cities (or even the cities themselves) that offer a variety of tourist-related activities. Urban entertainment centers vary widely. Some are designed on a smaller scale as a draw for local traffic and an enhancement to the local environment. Others are on a scale nearly as grand as those we considered in regard to theme parks, and there are many that fall between these two extremes.

Sports stadiums, one type of urban entertainment center, have been with us since the time of Rome's Colosseum, but a relatively recent variety of such centers is the covered superdome (and increasingly with retractable roofs), such as those in Houston and Toronto. These types of stadiums have only been around since the 1960s. Domed stadiums tend to be multipurpose (or used for more than just one sport). These facilities (particularly the covered stadiums) host not only sports events but various types of entertainers, rock concerts, and circuses, and may also double as a convention center of sorts, such as the Superdome in New Orleans.

Turning our attention to baseball, a more recent development in stadium design has been to re-create the stadiums of old, as has been done at U.S. Cellular Field, formerly Comisky Park (Chicago), Jacobs Field (Cleveland), the Ballpark at Arlington (Texas), and Camden Yards (Baltimore). Further, after decades of relocating sports teams to the suburbs, teams are returning to the cities they once left. These stadiums (along with their teams, of course) have been given credit for drawing baseball fans back to the games as well as building all-important foot traffic in downtown areas. Sporting events do not just attract locals, however. They can be a major tourist attraction. Some fans/tourists take this to the extreme and go on extended trips during which they attend as many games as time will allow. Such travels have been chronicled in a number of recent books, such as Bruce Adams and Margaret Engel's Baseball Vacations (Fodor's, 2002). Spring training is also a major tourist attraction. Major League baseball teams train in February and March of each year in Arizona (referred to as the "Cactus League") and Florida (referred to as the "Grapefruit League"). The *Wall Street Journal* estimates that the visitor spending on attending spring training games contribute $600 million to local communities in Arizona and Florida. Stadiums used for spring training games tend to be much smaller, and as a result, fans are able to be much closer to the action.

A close relative to "sports centers" are downtown convention centers, which allow for a mixture of business and pleasure. The visitors to a convention or trade show are on business. However, many of these gatherings are more social than professional, and even the most business-oriented meetings are, in large part, devoted to having a good time. Conventions bring major influxes of people and spending. Chicago, for instance, attracted over 7 million delegates who were attending various conventions, trade shows, and corporate meetings in 2006. Case History 14.2 examines one of the better-known hospitality industry trade shows.

The National Restaurant Association Restaurant Show

The annual National Restaurant Association (www.restaurant.org) Restaurant Show, held in Chicago, celebrated its eighty-seventh anniversary in 2006. It is the food service industry's largest gathering of people, exhibitors, and products/supplies. In order to appreciate the sheer magnitude of the show, consider the following:

- Attracts over 75,000 attendees
- Offers almost 2000 exhibits, which include anything and everything having to do with the restaurant/food service industry
- Shows the latest products and services available to the industry
- Covers 1.3 million square feet of exhibit space
- Offers culinary competitions, speakers, and activities for attendees, including the "Salute to Excellence," to which select hospitality students are invited[1]

The show should be of interest to hospitality students for a variety of reasons: It represents a "destination" for people either in or affiliated with the restaurant industry; it is a good example of an enormous convention/trade show, as discussed in this chapter; and it is a major industry event that every hospitality student should attend at least once. About 60 hospitality programs were represented at the 2006 show. Each of these programs managed a booth on the show floor, where they were able to promote their schools. In most cases, the booths were staffed by both faculty and students of the program. Those who go each year already know what a valuable learning experience the show provides. Additional information about the show is available from the NRA office.

1. NRA Exhibit Guide and Program, 2006.

Convention, trade show, and sports centers were once largely the preserve of great metropolitan centers such as New York, with its Jacob Javits Convention Center, and Chicago, with McCormick Place. Increasingly, however, cities such as Seattle and San Jose, California, large but of second rank in size, have developed urban entertainment centers as a means of challenging established travel patterns and increasing the travel business in their markets. It should be noted that many cities are currently in the midst of expansion projects that will allow them to compete more effectively with New York, Las Vegas, and Chicago.

Although medium-sized cities cannot bid in the national convention market for the very largest conventions, they often can attract smaller national meetings and regional conferences. Many cities successfully sell bond issues to build civic meeting centers that improve a community's ability to compete for its share of the travel market. That travel market, more and more city leaders are learning, means higher sales for local businesses, increased employment, and greater tax revenues.

Whether the results of these civic efforts always justify such an investment is subject to debate. In any case, though, somebody must operate these centers, and the skills involved (dealing with various travelers, providing food service, and managing housekeeping and building operations, to name only a few) clearly fall within the hospitality management graduate's domain. The significance of this new area of hospitality management may be measured by the fact that ARAMARK has a special division to manage conference centers.

Increasingly, urban planners are including in their developments plazas designed to accommodate amusements, dining, and other leisure activities. One is also likely to find fine arts, gardens, and other visually appealing items adorning the area. The prototype of this kind of plaza is Rockefeller Center, in the heart of New York City. Rockefeller Center takes up all of 11 acres of prime real estate, which represents a combination of leisure/tourist and business activities. Among other things, it has fine shops, restaurants (including the world-famous Rainbow Room), and tourist attractions, such as tours of NBC studios. The 6,000-seat Radio City Music Hall is also located in the complex. It even has an ice-skating rink in winter, and it hosts horse shows, karate demonstrations, and model airplane contests in milder seasons.

Chicago is another city known for its architecture and public spaces. Some of the developments in that city include the First National Plaza, in front of the First Chicago Building, which is a model for plazas to come. A computer controls the fountain, so that visitors won't get splashed on windy days. From May to October, the plaza features free noontime entertainment, late-afternoon concerts, and an outdoor café. It also has, year round, a restaurant, a bar, a legitimate theater, and retail shops.

City waterfront redevelopment projects, too, have become centers that attract visitors and enrich the lives of local people. Both Boston's and Baltimore's efforts have received a lot of attention over the last couple of decades; they literally changed the image and demeanor of those cities. Other cities, albeit with different types of waterfronts, include New Orleans and San Antonio. These cities have done an effective job of using waterways as a central focus of their cities.

Restoration and revitalization of aging sections of a city require the involvement of hospitality industry operations. Dallas Alley (in Dallas, Texas) was built in what was a half-forgotten place that housed freight cars, warehouses, and factories. In an old Sunshine Biscuit factory and an adjoining building that was once a Coca-Cola bottling plant, a group of private investors built Dallas Alley, an aggregation of nine nightclubs. The center is located near a $25 million festival marketplace housed in a former cracker and candy factory. Dallas Alley alone attracts over a million visitors annually. Similarly, the old Jax Brewery in New Orleans was converted and now houses retail shops and restaurants.

SHOPPING CENTERS

Shopping centers are usually thought of as catering principally to local shoppers. Even so, such centers can be more than a little ambitious. The St. Louis Centre suggests the scale of a large, locally centered mall and the often close relationship of such centers to the hospitality industry. The Centre was begun as an urban renewal project in 1972 and was completed 13 years later at a total cost of $17.5 million. Comprising a two-block stretch of downtown St. Louis, the Centre serves about 10 million people each year, comprising a mix of locals, conventioneers, and tourists. The Centre has a mix of retail shops, sit-down restaurants, and a food court. Despite the fact that it has had financial problems in recent years and has subpar retail occupancy, it is still considered a key project in enhancing the downtown area. Another landmark is Water Tower Place, prominently located on North Michigan Avenue in Chicago. The mall is a marvel to look at and a shopper's destination—it has over 100 stores, many food service operations, and visual spectacles. The mall draws over 20 million shoppers each year. It recently underwent a $17 million renovation. Other cities that have established similar retail attractions include New Orleans and Boston, among many others. As shopping continues to grow in popularity (some have labeled it as the new religion), malls such as the ones described above will only proliferate and will continue to anchor both urban and suburban development. The fact that shopping has become the most favored tourist activity will only fuel this growth (40 percent of shoppers at Water Tower Place are tourists). Retail shopping centers only continue to get larger, as well, as illustrated in the examples given below.

Finally, let's look briefly at four exceptionally large shopping centers, one in western Canada, one in Minnesota, and two in China. In the case of the West Edmonton Mall (in Canada), the aim from the very beginning was to attract tourists, as well as local residents to the center. This was necessary because Edmonton, Alberta, a city of less than 1 million, could not support a mall of this scale by itself. Such facilities have been termed **megamalls**.

The scale quite literally boggles the mind. Consider its total indoor area of 5.3 million square feet, equivalent to 28 city blocks. It is a combination megamall/amusement park/food court/hotel/recreation center/museum/casino. In fact, it combines all of the elements already discussed in this chapter. Malls are also supposed to have stores, and it has 800 of them, along with over 100 restaurants, miniature golf, an aquarium, movie

Many of the 40 million travelers who visit the Mall of America each year choose to extend their stay in one of the many hotels available. (Courtesy of Carlson Hotels Worldwide.)

theaters, and several major attractions unto themselves. The ceiling peaks at 16 stories with a mile-long, two-level main concourse. The interior plantings include $3 million worth of tropical plants, which includes a grove of 50-foot palm trees. The mall houses an amusement park and a water park with a 5-acre pool where you can surf on 6-foot waves, water-ski, ride the rapids, and get a suntan, even when the outside temperature is well below zero. The sights include a dolphin show, a Spanish galleon, an 18-hole miniature golf course, a 50,000-gallon aquarium, and four submarines. The 33-foot-long computer-controlled subs will seat 24 people. The mall is dedicated to the idea that shopping is more than just a utilitarian chore and can be an opportunity for fun.

About a third of the visitors to the mall are from Edmonton and its trading area. Nearly a fifth are from Alberta outside the 60-mile trading area. The other half comes from the rest of Canada and the United States. Half of these Canadian visitors and 75 percent of the Americans come specifically to visit the West Edmonton Mall. Visitors from the United States average a four-day stay. Visitors, interestingly enough, spend as much or more money outside the mall as they do inside.

In Bloomington, Minnesota, just outside Minneapolis, is another megamall only slightly smaller than the West Edmonton Mall. The Mall of America covers 4.2 million square feet (about 78 acres). An indoor 7-acre theme park, Camp Snoopy, at the heart of the mall, offers 50 rides, shows, and other attractions. The mall also includes over 500 retail outlets as well as an 18-hole miniature golf course and over 50 restaurants, nightclubs and bars, movie theaters, and live entertainment. To top it off, there is a university, a health care clinic, and the "Chapel of Love" for those maritally inclined.

Thirteen thousand people are employed at the Mall of America. The mall drew 35 million visitors during its first year, and it continues to draw between 35 and 40 million people each year. The mall even has its own newspaper to keep its faithful properly informed of current and upcoming events.[9] Although a description of the mall cannot begin to do it justice, readers might want to visit its Web site and take the virtual tour (www.mallofamerica.com).

For a long time, the two malls just discussed claimed supremacy in terms of size and traffic. This has changed, though, as China and other Asian countries have begun to build malls on a grand scale. It is estimated that eight of the ten largest malls in the world are now located in Asia, and most of these are located in China. The South China Mall (in Dongguan) and the Golden Resources Mall (in Beijing) are two of the largest. At a size that is 50 percent larger than the Mall of America, Golden Recources is advertised as "the mall that will change your life." The growing economy of China is driving the building (and patronage) of such malls. The malls in China have more diversity of offerings than typical North American malls. More malls are currently under development, including some that are on an even larger scale.[10]

Zoos, Sanctuaries, and Aquariums

Zoos and aquariums can be major tourism generators. For instance, each year roughly 5 million people visit the San Diego Zoo. The zoo also operates an 1,800-acre wildlife preserve 30 miles north of San Diego. The zoo and preserve, like so many other tourist destinations, have a substantial educational mission. The preserve, for instance, is visited by 40,000 elementary- and secondary-school children each year. Other well-known zoos in the United States include the Bronx Zoo and the Washington Zoo. Aquariums, too, are becoming ever more popular. Fine aquariums exist in Baltimore, Boston, New Orleans, Chicago, and Vancouver, as well as some smaller cities throughout North America. Well-known international zoos include the London Zoo and the Antwerp Zoo in Belgium. Unique sanctuaries exist all over the world as well. In Central America, the Community Baboon Sanctuary in Belize helps to protect the locally known baboons (or Black Howler Monkeys). The Sanctuary has received funding from the World Wildlife Fund and is a major attraction for visitors to that country. In Australia, the Currumbin Wildlife Sanctuary (outside of Brisbane) allows visitors to interact with kangaroos, wallabies, and koalas. Revenues help support the local wildlife hospital.

As with other attractions discussed earlier in the chapter, zoos, sanctuaries, and aquariums must provide food service to their visitors. Also, like other attractions, the number of visitors to these destinations expands when school is out. As a result, these operations can offer summer employment opportunities to students, with a decent chance at getting into a supervisory position.

Aquariums are helping to attract tourists to downtown areas. (Courtesy of Las Vegas Convention and Visitors Authority.)

Temporary Attractions: Fairs and Festivals

Here we change our orientation somewhat, from the new megamalls to a very different, and longer-lived, type of attraction: fairs and festivals. Fairs date from the Middle Ages, when they served as important centers for economic and cultural revival. Festivals also have their roots in history and were originally religious events. Towns both large and small have long hosted such events.

World expositions (world's fairs or expos) are yearlong attractions, but even a local event such as the agricultural fair in DuQuoin, Illinois, which annually attracts a quarter of a million people to this town of 7,000, can have a major impact on a city. Some fairs celebrate local industry, whereas others have cultural, religious, and historical roots, as is the case with Mardi Gras in New Orleans (Mardi Gras could perhaps be best characterized as a citywide celebration rather than a festival per se). Tradition is not enough, however. A successful event must attract tourists, whether local, regional, national, or international.[11] Indeed, a festival or fair is a quasi-business activity. Its success is measured by its ability to attract visitors, cover its costs, and maintain sufficient local support to keep it staffed, usually almost entirely with unpaid volunteers. World's fairs, perhaps the most renowned of fairs to most North Americans, continue to prosper and dazzle.

Festivals may be seasonal in nature. For instance, winter festivals reposition the season of slush and rust as a community asset. The growing popularity of winter sports fits well with ice carnivals. The one in St. Paul, Minnesota, which dates all the way back to 1886, includes events such as concerts, skiing, sleigh rides, ice sculptures, hot-air balloon rides, parades, a royal coronation, car racing, and a softball tournament on ice. Carnaval de Québec, a winter celebration, began in 1954 to energize a stagnant economy and is now the city's third largest industry. It attracts over 1 million visitors each year and generates $36 million annually. Summer festivals in warmer climates may accomplish similar objectives.

Events such as these clearly affect the economy of the cities and regions that sponsor them. Local patrons spend money from their family entertainment budget that might otherwise have left the community. Visitors spend on food, lodging, souvenirs, gasoline, public transportation, and the like. In most cases, the event itself makes purchases that contribute to the local economy.

The economic effects of fairs and festivals can have a major impact on the community and especially on its hospitality industry. For this reason, hospitality industry managers are often prominent sponsors and backers of such events. In some instances, festivals and events may actually be organized by the local industry. This was the case with the French Quarter Festival in New Orleans, which was established in an effort to draw locals back into the downtown area.

We ought not lose sight of the fact, however, that like so many other aspects of tourism, fairs and festivals also bring important social and cultural benefits to their communities: They celebrate the local heritage and bring members from all parts of the community together to work as volunteers. A good example of this comes, again, from New Orleans. The New Orleans Jazz and Heritage Festival, known worldwide for its music, actually brings together several elements of local and international cultures into one big festival. It has grown from a small local event that drew several hundred people to one that attracts about 500,000 people each year (see Case History 14.3). Money from the event also goes to support the local community radio station, fund grants, and provide numerous other community benefits.

Festivals may also celebrate a particular food or beverage product, be it local or otherwise. Festivals have been organized around shrimp, garlic, mirliton (a type of squash), wine, and beer. It seems that with the increasing popularity of microbrews, more and more festivals focusing on beer appear on the scene. Examples include the Great American Beer Festival held in Denver each year, the Great British Beer Festival (which will celebrate its 30th year), and the International Beer Festival held in Qingdao, China. Qingdao is a city in the eastern part of China and is famous for its beer (the name was formerly translated as Tsing Tao). In June 1991, the city successfully organized its first International Beer Festival. Since then, the Beer Festival has been held annually, getting larger and larger each year. The number of attendees has increased from about 300,000 in 1991 to over 1.6 million. The Qingdao International Beer

CASE HISTORY 14.3

The New Orleans Jazz Fest

Many festivals have music as their primary focus: the Newport Jazz Festival, the Chicago Blues Festival, and (once upon a time) Woodstock. Internationally, there are such renowned annual musical events as the Montreux Jazz Festival (Switzerland) and Sunsplash (Jamaica). One festival that stands out in the United States, however, is the New Orleans Jazz and Heritage Festival (or Jazz Fest, to locals). New Orleans itself is a melting pot of cultures, which is one of the reasons it is so unique, and Jazz Fest is uniquely New Orleans.

Jazz Fest celebrates all that is New Orleans, as well as cultures that have a direct connection to New Orleans. Over 4,000 artists (musicians as well as crafts and culinary practitioners) participate in the festival each year. Imagine a festival with eight major music stages and several smaller ones; three crafts areas, each representing a different genre of crafts; over 70 food booths offering the best food that New Orleans (and the rest of the world) has to offer; plus interviews, cooking demonstrations, exhibits, activities for the kids, and much more. It's a music festival, culinary event, and crafts fair all rolled into one. Every year, in addition to the usual offerings, one particular country is highlighted (such as South Africa in 2004) with exhibits, performances, and dances from that country.

The Jazz Festival, along with the rest of New Orleans, suffered tremendously from the effects of Hurricane Katrina in 2005. But the festival was held in 2006, in the spring following the hurricane. As Quint Davis, the executive producer said,

The true heart and soul of the New Orleans Jazz & Heritage Festival, as with New Orleans itself, is music. It is the force that drives and defines us. Not merely for entertainment, but to feed our souls. It is overwhelming how our musical family has rallied to our cause, especially the New Orleans musical mainstays, many scattered throughout the country, all committed to returning to be a part of the renewal of our spirit. Jazz Fest 2006, the great New Orleans homecoming. Anybody who comes to this year's Festival will bear witness to the healing power of music.[1]

Jazz Fest grew from a small gathering, where there were actually more performers than attendees, to a major event, with close to 500,000 people attending in recent years. In a city that is known for its Mardi Gras, Jazz Fest has become the preferred event for a lot of people and a good example of a festival that truly has a positive impact on its host city.

1. New Orleans Jazz and Heritage Festival (www.nojazzfest.com).

Festival not only focuses on beer but also explores the integral aspects of local tourism, culture, economy, and technology. The Qingdao International Beer Festival has truly grown into an internationally recognized special event.

Large or small, then, festivals of all kinds can be a vital part of the life of a community, city, or region. In some cases, they may help to define or reinforce a community. They clearly serve a variety of functions and, like other entities discussed earlier, offer opportunities for graduates of hospitality programs.

Natural Environments

Urban entertainment centers may be the epitome of man-made tourism attractions. Not everything that contributes to tourism, however, is man-made. In the public sector, national and state parks, forests, and waters (all part of the **natural environment**) should interest hospitality students just as much. These uniquely American recreation areas have been copied the world over. As far as hospitality innovation goes, they are, in fact, relatively new. The first park created by Congress, Yosemite, was established toward the end of the Civil War in 1864.[12] The National Park Service itself was not established until 1916.

The number of visits to national parks grew rapidly in the 1950s and 1960s, expanding roughly to four times the 1950 total by 1965 and doubling again by 1980. The early 1980s saw both a serious recession and an energy crisis. As Figure 14.3

The National park Service oversees many parks, some lesser known, such as Big Bend National Park in Texas. (Courtesy of National Park Service.)

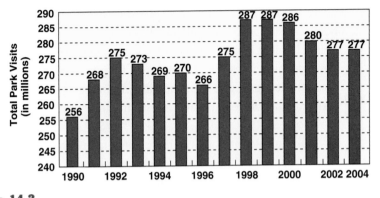

Figure 14.3

National Park Service recreation visits. (Source: National Park Service; www.nps.gov.)

indicates, growth began to decrease up to 1990 but has since leveled off and begun increasing again. Because the largest number of parks and other reserved areas under National Park Service (NPS) administration are located in areas distant from population centers in the midwestern and eastern United States, national park visits are sensitive to economic conditions and to the price and availability of gasoline. Total park visits (for recreation purposes) exceeded 273 million in 2005, about the same as It was In 2004. Nonrecreation visits added another 150 million visits.[13] Interest in nature and environmental experiences continues to grow beyond visits to national parks. Americans seem to have rediscovered the great outdoors, and this trend appears to be cutting across demographic lines, with a mix of individuals getting involved.[14]

In 2005, there were over 14 million overnight stays in national parks. Lodging in park concession hotels and tent camping accounted for most of those stays; recreational vehicles and backcountry camping accounted for much of the rest. The balance is largely accounted for by organizational group camping and overnight boating trips.[15]

The National Park Service Organic Act of 1916 established the national park system with the clear intention of providing recreation and, at the same time, preserving the parks for the enjoyment of future generations. The increased crowding of existing facilities has led those interested in preservation as well as recreation, including the National Park Service itself, to propose drastic limitations on the use of private automobiles within the parks. The National Parks and Conservation Association (NPCA), a private group that supports a conservationist view of natural parks, has suggested that such accommodations as hotels, cabins, and campgrounds be restricted or even reduced within these parks.

The NPCA does not argue that hospitality facilities and services should be unavailable. Instead, it proposes that staging areas with lodging and other services be established in nearby communities and that these staging areas be connected to the parks by low-cost transportation. Proposals such as this would reduce private auto use and help preserve parks' natural beauty, which is their principal attraction and reason for being. It might also create major new commercial recreation areas and opportunities for hospitality firms and graduates of hospitality management programs. Moreover, given the leadership of the national parks in the field of recreation, this pattern might well extend to state parks and forests in future years if it is accepted by Congress and the people.

This huge tourism activity has created many opportunities for tourism enterprises serving the areas that surround natural recreation sites. Although park management is a specialized field, addressed in professional parks and recreation management programs at colleges and universities, the management of the auxiliary services in and around parks—particularly food services, hotels, and motels—lies within the hospitality management career area. Park lodging and food service concessions hire large numbers of students and, in fact, are staffed largely by students during peak periods. People who work for the same concessionaires for several summers have a good opportunity of gaining supervisory experience and of seeing some beautiful country.

On a Lighter Note. . .

We will end this chapter on a somewhat more "qualitative" rather than "quantitative" note. Behind all of the facts and figures surrounding travel and tourism, destinations, and tourist behaviors lies an undying interest to explore new things, to be surprised, and to see something strange. This is the only way to explain some of the out-of-the-ordinary tourist attractions that have gained some press over the last few years. And not to think that North Americans have a monopoly on zany tourist attractions, they are to be found all over the world. Here is a short list of some of the "destinations" that have captured tourists' imaginations in recent years:

- *The Spy Trail.* Capitalizing on the popularity of James Bond and other British spies, this walking tour of London includes many historic "spy" landmarks.
- *Cemetery Tours.* Tours are given of New Orleans cemeteries, one of the most fascinating features that the city has to offer.
- *The International UFO Museum.* The museum is located in Roswell, New Mexico, believed to be the site of a UFO crash in 1947.
- *The Ice Hotel.* First built in Sweden, and later in Quebec, guests are able to spend the night in a room lit by candles on a bed made of ice. The hotel is rebuilt every winter.

The cemeteries in New Orleans are a very popular tourist destination. (Courtesy of Save Our Cemeteries, Inc., www.saveourcemeteries.org)

- ■ *Cadillac Ranch.* Vintage Cadillacs are buried headfirst in the ground.
- ■ *Tornado Chases.* These tour companies offer close-up looks at tornadoes during tornado season in the "Twister Alley" region of the United States.
- ■ *Space Tourism.* Independent companies have been rushing to become the first to be able to offer private flights into space. This may be the next big industry in the years to come.

Summary

In this chapter, we discussed recreation, its motives, and different types of destinations. After explaining why people travel, we divided destinations into primary (touring) and secondary (stopover). Then we talked about planned play environments such as national and regional theme parks, casinos (as exemplified by Las Vegas, Atlantic City, and the Mississippi Gulf Coast), urban entertainment centers such as sports stadiums and megamalls, temporary attractions, and the natural environment, especially national parks. Finally, we looked at some of the more offbeat attractions/activities that have been attracting tourists in recent years.

Along the way, we pointed out the possible employment opportunities for both temporary jobs and permanent careers. Destination attractions are often big hospitality businesses in themselves and act as magnets that keep the flow of tourism not only going but also growing.

Key Words and Concepts

Recreation	Casinos
Primary (touring) destinations	Gaming markets
	High rollers
Secondary (stopover) destinations	Bus trade
	Comps
Planned play environments	Urban entertainment centers
Fairs and festivals	Megamalls
Theme parks	Natural environment

Review Questions

1. What are some of the reasons that people travel?

2. What is the difference between primary and secondary destinations?

3. What do country music, theme parks, and casinos have in common as tourist attractions? How are they different?

4. Briefly describe a theme park that you have visited, and explain why you think it is popular.

5. How do national theme parks, such as Walt Disney World, differ from regional theme parks, such as Six Flags?

6. Besides gambling, what else does Las Vegas offer?

7. What are comps and why are they important to casinos?

8. Describe how megamalls combine different tourism elements.

9. Describe the role of the national park system and why it is important to tourism in the United States.

10. Which of the destinations and attractions identified in the last section are primary destinations? Which are secondary?

Internet Exercises

1. **Site name:** Vegas.com

   URL: www.vegas.com/

   Background information: Vegas.com features more Las Vegas travel choices than any other Web site, from hotels to shows to tours to front-of-the-line nightclub passes and beyond.

   Site name: LasVegas.com

URL: www.lasvegas.com/

Background information: LasVegas.com is a destination for hotels, air-hotel packages, shows, golf, spas, weddings, dining reservations, and more. You'll find extensive information to help you plan your trip. And when you're ready, we have everything you need, all in one place.

Site name: Atlantic City

URL: www.atlanticcitynj.com/

Background information: A complete guide to Atlantic City including nonstop gaming action, top-name entertainment, world-class golf and fishing, luxurious casino hotels and resorts, and beautiful white sandy beaches. You'll also find information on Atlantic City, NJ dining and shopping, attractions, outdoor recreation, and so much more.

Site name: Visit Nj.org

URL: www.state.nj.us/travel/wheretogo_casinos.html

Background information: This is the official New Jersey Web site with a special page for the Jersey Shore and the casinos.

Site name: Mississippi Gulf Coast

URL: www.gulfcoast.org/

Background information: This is the official Web site for the Mississippi Gulf Coast.

Exercises:

a. After reviewing the Web sites above, which Web site is the most attractive to you and why?

b. Which Web site(s) provide the most information for the prospective traveler to these cities?

c. There are two Web sites for Las Vegas and two for Atlantic City. Of the two for each city, which one do you like the best and why? Which one provides more information?

2. **Site name:** National Park Service

URL: www.nps.gov

Background information: Most people know that the National Park Service (NPS) cares for national parks, a network of nearly 400 natural, cultural, and recreational sites across the nation. The treasures in this system—the first of its kind in the world—have been set aside by the American people to preserve, protect, and share the legacies of this land.

Exercises:

a. Choose a state that would be of interest to you. Indicate the state you chose and the national parks that are in that state.

b. Describe the educational opportunities that are available through the NPS.

c. Go to the employment page on the NPS Web site and select a state of interest to you. Next, choose a job series where you think you would qualify after graduation and search for job openings. Indicate the openings that would be of interest to you.

d. Go to the employment page for the NPS and select a job series that would be of interest to you and search for all jobs nationwide that are available in that job series. What positions did you find most interesting and where were they?

e. It is important that tourism planners consider how tourism will impact on the environment. Surf the NPS Web site and describe how they strive to make their parks environmentally friendly.

3. **Site name:** Theme Park City

   URL: www.themeparkcity.com

   Background information: Theme Park City provides a comprehensive listing of theme parks, amusement parks, water parks, and zoos in the United States (by state), Canada, and Europe. It also provides directories for circuses and carnivals.

   Site name: Theme Park Insider

   URL: www.themeparkinsider.com

   Background information: Theme Park Insider provides a listing of theme parks in the United States (by state), Canada, Europe, Japan, and Australia. It also provides directories for circuses and carnivals.

   Exercises:

   a. Describe the similarities and differences between these two Web sites. Which Web site provides the most comprehensive information to potential theme park enthusiasts?

   b. Choose a theme park in the United States and one overseas. In a class discussion, describe the overall theme, rides/attractions/shows, prices, job opportunities, and so on for each theme park.

4. **Site name:** World Casino Directory

   URL: www.worldcasinodirectory.com

   Background information: World Casino Directory is a complete and current directory of casinos worldwide that is arranged by geographical region, then by alphabetical order. They also provide news and a newsletter for those interested in casinos.

   Site name: Casino Seekers

   URL: www.casinoseekers.com/casino/land_based_casinos

   Background information: This Web site provides a listing of land-based casinos in the United States.

   Exercises:

   a. Discuss the similarities and differences between these two Web sites. Which one provides the most information? Which one is the most user-friendly?

b. Choose a casino in any state (for example, the Trump Taj Mahal in Atlantic City, New Jersey). Which Web site provides the most complete information on the casino you have chosen?

5. **Site name:** The American Gaming Association

URL: www.americangaming.org/

Background information: The American Gaming Association (AGA) represents the commercial casino entertainment industry by addressing federal legislative and regulatory issues affecting its members and their employees and customers, such as federal taxation, regulatory issues, and travel and tourism matters.

Exercises:

a. Browse the Web site and find the page with gaming fact sheets. Review the variety of fact sheets available and choose at least three categories to review.
   i. What information is contained on these fact sheets? Is the information backed up by research or is it opinions presented by the association?
   ii. What statistical information is included on these fact sheets? How would this information be helpful to groups who would like their state legislature to approve gaming in their state?

b. What is the code of conduct for responsible gaming and what are the major elements of this code?

c. Review "The AGA Survey of Casino Entertainment" for the most recent year. What information is contained in this document? How would this information be helpful to managers in the gaming industry?

Notes

1. International Association of Amusement Parks and Attractions Web site, www.iaapa.org/media/f-stats.htm.
2. Christina Valhouli, "The World's Best Amusement Parks," *Forbes*, March 21, 2002.
3. National Indian Gaming commission (http://www.nigc.gov) January 20, 2007.
4. American Gaming Association, www.americangaming.org/.
5. Las Vegas Visitors and Convention Authority, Vegas FAQ, March, 2006.
6. David Gardner, executive vice president, Atlantic City Casino Association, personal communication. Gardner was employed as a city planner in Atlantic City during the 1960s.
7. "Economic Impact for Tourism and Recreation in Mississippi, 2004" annual report prepared by the Mississippi Development Authority, January 2005.
8. Lodging and Gaming Industry Survey, Standard & Poor's, February 2, 2006.
9. Mall of America Web site, www.mallofamerica.com.
10. China's Supersized Mall, *Christian Science Monitor*, November 24, 2004.

11. Donald Getz, Festivals, *Special Events and Tourism* (New York: Van Nostrand Reinhold, 1991).

12. The first national park was Yellowstone, established in 1872. Yosemite was originally a California state park created by the U.S. Congress. It became a national park in 1890.

13. Public Use Statistics Office, National Park Service, www2.nature.nps.gov/stats/.

14. Joan Raymond, "Happy Trails: America's Affinity for the Great Outdoors," *American Demographics,* August 2000.

15. Public Use Statistics Office, National Park Service, http://www2.nature.nps.gov/stats/.

PART FIVE

Management in the Hospitality Industry

Stephen Jack, C.E.C.

The Hospitality Industry

(Courtesy of Sodexho.)

CHAPTER FIFTEEN

Management: A New Way of Thinking

The Purpose of this Chapter

North Americans, especially management students, are so management-conscious that we often forget how new a field of thought and kind of work management actually is. Like any growing idea, management is still moving toward maturity. As a student, therefore, you would be wise to be skeptical about any "eternal truths" or unchanging principles you may hear associated with the field of management. One useful way to develop a sense of management as a growing and changing field is to review its brief history. This chapter conducts that tour.

Management practices and innovations have had a profound impact on the hospitality industry. In this chapter, we examine closely organizations that pioneered the development and application of modern management in the hospitality industry.

THIS CHAPTER SHOULD HELP YOU

1. Describe the contributions of early-twentieth-century management thinkers Frederick Taylor and Henri Fayol, and explain how their ideas influenced later management developments.
2. Describe the significance of the contributions E. M. Statler, Vernon and Gordon Stouffer, Howard Johnson, Harland Sanders, Ray Kroc, Kemmons Wilson, and Sam Barshop made to the development of hospitality industry management.
3. Explain how modern franchised systems have energized the hospitality industry.
4. Describe how the customer, not the operator, ultimately defines a business.

Management and Supervision

Students considering a career in hospitality **management** naturally want to understand the hospitality profession in general and the various kinds of opportunities it offers. It is equally important for them to understand the work that supervisors and managers do. We have devoted a major portion of this text to discussions of this work. Let's turn our attention first to **supervision**.

The word *supervision* is derived from two Latin words that, taken together, mean "to oversee." As such, supervision involves principally the direction and leadership functions of management. (These two functions will receive special attention in Chapter 20.) Supervisors are also involved in the other functions of management that we will soon be discussing. They must plan, and they must understand the plans made by senior management that they will follow in their operations. They must understand and come to function effectively within a complex organization. One particularly important responsibility, staffing (discussed in Chapter 18), is at the heart of a hospitality supervisor's work. Additionally, the control function cannot be carried out without supervisors becoming sources of information and of the corrective action indicated by control systems.

There are some slight differences between supervision and management. The supervisor's work occurs at the operating level; that is, he or she works directly with the employees as they do their work. Management, on the other hand, is concerned with the totality of the organization's problems. Managers engaged in long-range planning may well discover a need, for example, to redesign the organization structure or the control system. Very often, especially in large organizations, managers direct the work of supervisors, who, in turn, direct the employees' actual tasks.

From a student's perspective, it is important to remember that in the hospitality industry, nearly all managers begin as supervisors, and able supervisors usually advance through the ranks to senior positions. Even there, however, a manager's work may have a supervisory component—the actual direction of employees in productive tasks. As a practical matter, then, management and supervision are so closely intertwined as to make distinguishing between them a theoretical exercise with little practical value for us. To be sure, we will often refer to supervision and management, but by itself, the term management usually includes supervision and is the preferred term when speaking in generalizations. The next six chapters will explore the work of managers and supervisors. In this chapter, we will define management and address its development as a body of knowledge.

Although managing—both the designing and organizing of work and the overseeing of it—is as old as civilization, management as an organized body of thought is only about 100 years old. Indeed, until recent times, the way that society was orga-nized made it unlikely (useless, really) to consider management as a field of study and thought.

In this and the following chapters, we will also use the term business. In fact, mod-ern management has been mainly a development of the private sector, or the business community. However, students whose interests lie in nonbusiness areas such as administrative dietetics or community food service programs should not feel at all left out, because nonprofit and government-funded food service programs now widely use these same techniques. In fact, minor adjustments make modern business management relevant to almost any managerial task.

The Economizing Society

The economist Robert Heilbroner identified three means of organizing a society and dealing with its economic problems: **tradition**, **command**, and the **market system**.[1] The two means with the longest history are tradition and command, whereas the market system, by contrast, emerged from medieval Europe along with our mod-ern age.

Tradition embodies the wisdom of experience, gained through trial and error, in a set of social customs regarded as nearly unchangeable. Primitive societies are tradi-tional societies. Primitives regard the idea of change with fear, and so their whole society is based on the absence of change. For this reason, tradition offers only mea-ger guidance in the modern world.

Command—imposed authority—is a solution to society's problems often associ-ated with traditional society. Command was the mode of social control of such ancient empires as the ones the Egyptians and Romans built, and it is the means by which modern dictatorships rule.

The market system (as defined by economists) emphasizes the free choice of individuals. In theory, consumer decisions govern the allocation of resources, and com-petition sets the prices in the marketplace. In practice, critics point out, there are many imperfections in the market system, but we must recognize it as a system that offers consumers—and workers—more choice than does any other system the world has ever seen.

One central idea of the market economy completely foreign to most other cultures (including that of medieval Europe, out of which our society developed) is the idea of individual gain or profit seeking not just as a legitimate activity but also as a cornerstone of our civilization. Traditional societies are based principally on community interests, but the market system encourages, indeed exalts, individual interest.

Management focuses on the problems of large organizations, though it is used in all sizes of organizations. In premodern times, such management thought served the church and the military. As royal power and ancient tradition were displaced by an economizing society and the market system, the creative energies of businesspeople began to occupy a more central place in Western civilization, particularly in the United States. In the nineteenth century, large business organizations came into being, and with them came a need to develop theories to deal with the complex problems associated with those organizations. The field of management was born.

Management is struggling to deal with a greater consciousness of community values regarding matters such as the environment as well as individual gain as joint determinants of economic action. Because management's values derive from the changing values of the society in which it works, we can expect that a change in society's consensus on the importance of individual choice in the marketplace will have a major impact on management now and in the future. Management, still barely 100 years old, has already passed through a number of changes. Given the changing society out of which management arises, there is bound to be further development in the field.

Management is a very modern institution; indeed, it is a new way of viewing the problems of work in an expanding and increasingly wealthy society. This new way of viewing problems has become one of the strongest forces in the last 100 years of our civilization's development. Because this development has been so rapid, our view of management problems has changed dramatically during that period. Management continues to change along with the dynamic society in which it operates, and so those entering a career in management must prepare themselves for constant change. It is useful, therefore, for us to examine briefly the contributions of the early management theorists to see the power of their ideas and how this young field of ours grew.

The Managerial Revolution

The problems that management deals with weren't really problems at all in the traditional and command economies. People worked at what their parents had worked at; they did what they were told to do. The problem of motivation was largely solved by the fact that the worker's alternative to following orders was starvation. Even in early modern times, when democracy was still growing in the political realm and had little to do with our economic way of life, people worked for low wages. More applicants were always standing at the door if any employee wanted to leave.

The two thinkers generally credited with laying the foundation of modern management are Frederick Taylor and Henri Fayol. As we will learn, they were concerned with quite different problems. Taylor formulated industrial engineering principles and

Managers must understand all aspects of the operation. (Courtesy of Sodexho.)

a wholly new way of organizing tasks. Fayol voiced the first ideas underlying what has come to be called organizational theory.

TAYLOR: THE WORK PROCESS FOCUS

Frederick Taylor founded the scientific management movement. He believed that "the most prominent single element in modern scientific management is the task idea." Taylor argued that instead of "herding men in large groups" and relying on brute strength of numbers, a careful study of the work to be done and the worker would result in greatly increased productivity, that is, in more units of output per unit of labor input. Although the Industrial Revolution achieved a revolution in productivity through the use of machines, Taylor offered a further revolution through improved work planning and a **work process focus**. Here is Taylor's own summation:

> Scientific management consists of a certain philosophy which results in a combination of four underlying principles of management: first, the development of a true science; second, the scientific selection of the workman; third, his scientific education and development; and fourth, intimate, friendly cooperation between management and men.[2]

Let us briefly consider each of Taylor's points. His "true science," based on time-and-motion studies, eventually became the new field of industrial engineering. His idea was to make management's study and planning of the work, rather than numbers and strength (or traditional skill), the controlling factor in work. It was a revolutionary proposal. His method of studying and planning the work meant analyzing each task and developing the "one best way" to do it. Moreover, his approach replaced the artisan shop, based on traditional skills, with the controlled shop, a productive process in which management planning rather than worker skill or strength directs the enterprise.

This idea of management planning reappears in Taylor's second notion—the scientific (we might say "studied") selection of the worker. Rather than relying on the low wages of the time to offset low productivity, Taylor wanted employers to choose the right person for the job. Such an obvious idea hardly seems revolutionary to us, but most of the managers of his time resisted this approach.

The "scientific education" of the workers is a third factor in the controlled-shop notion. Having planned the work and hired someone qualified to do it, Taylor advocated training the worker in the one best way to accomplish each task. He also advocated supervising workers closely so that no other method inadvertently entered the process. Management and the methods it prescribed, rather than the worker's skill or brawn, controlled the productive process.

Finally, Taylor wanted to achieve "friendly cooperation between management and men," principally through giving workers "what they most want, namely high wages." Taylor proposed using some of the increased profitability of the now more productive business to improve the workers' wages.

Taylor's ideal worker was "Schmidt," a laborer whom he introduced to his foreman in this way: "When this man tells you to walk, you walk—and don't talk back to him." Taylor called Schmidt a "**high-priced man**" because Schmidt would receive much more than the going wage if, by obedience to Taylor's methods, he achieved greater productivity.

It is easy to criticize Taylor for his extreme emphasis on pay as "what they most want" and for expecting unfailing obedience. What critics forget is the dramatic social change that has taken place in the world of work in the short time since the days of Schmidt, the "high-priced man."

In Taylor's time, the workforce was ill-educated, largely immigrant, and in a poor bargaining position compared to its powerful employers. Today, legislated social programs such as unemployment insurance have removed the fear of starvation from the employer–employee equation. Most employers eagerly seek employees, and these employees are far better educated and more conscious of their own worth. Primarily as a result of hugely improved productivity, the American employee works shorter hours for enormously improved pay. However, at least two key ideas of Taylor's remain as centerpieces in the American work scene: the **task idea** and the **controlled shop**.

The Task Idea. We learned, through Frederick Taylor, that there is one best way to do work. Thus, the study of layout and design in a hospitality curriculum usually involves finding the most efficient means of laying out the workplace. Using outside experts to lay out work and design workplaces in a way that fails to take account of human social needs, however, is coming increasingly under challenge. Nevertheless, no one is ready to give up the idea of work design through the close study of the task idea to achieve maximum productivity, for such a move would be costly to employer and employee alike.

The Controlled Shop. Taylor brought a shift away from achieving productivity through the skill of the artisan or unskilled brawn "herded in groups." The shift has been toward achieving productivity through work methods designed by management and work performance tightly controlled by supervision. As we will see shortly, Vernon and Gordon Stouffer, in developing the recipe kitchen, brought the controlled shop to food service. (McDonald's and other quick-service operators, through systems design and planning, have extended it even further.)

The notion of the controlled shop, too, is under challenge. Workers in some places now demand (and often receive) greater participation in the control of the workplace. Our discussion of this issue in Chapter 21 will reveal that no one challenges the notion that some agreed-upon system should be developed and followed. The discussion, rather, seems to focus on how the system should be designed and the amount of worker involvement in that design. Neither labor nor management wants to give up the high wages and profits that come from the high productivity bequeathed to us by Taylor and his successors.

Other Contributors. Our brief discussion may encourage you to explore further the development of management thought. Among other things, you would learn of the many contributions made to scientific management by Taylor's colleagues and those who came after. We note in passing three other pioneers. Frank and Lillian Gilbreth advanced the study of the task by developing the therblig (Gilbreth spelled backward), defined as the smallest unit of human movement that can be measured. Developing standardized therbligs for all work motions speeds and simplifies the task of the industrial engineer.

H. L. Gantt, like Frederick Taylor, insisted on close supervision of the work and the worker. He developed a system of charting work operations that relies on the now-familiar Gantt charts. These charts have been adapted for use in hospitality employee scheduling. The discussion of staff planning in Chapter 18 includes a brief description of their use.

Although a changing world has challenged and altered the early work of the scientific management movement, in many ways the movement's contributions continue to have a lasting impact on our lives.

FAYOL: ADMINISTRATIVE MANAGEMENT

Whereas Taylor and his colleagues focused on the task and the shop, Henri Fayol focused on the organizational problems of departmental division, work coordination, and **administrative management**. The discussion in the next five chapters of this book is organized around management functions. This frame of analysis was originally advanced by Fayol in 1916, albeit in a somewhat different form. However, his conceptual scheme for viewing the work of managers has had a profound, shaping effect on the development of management thought. Fayol was French and his work, written in French, had limited circulation in English-speaking countries until 1929. It did not reach print in the United States until 1949. For this reason, it is difficult to trace Fayol's influence precisely. Doubtless, however, some scholars, students, and managers heard his work discussed. In any case, his ideas gained wide acceptance, which they still enjoy today.

Beyond describing management as a common set of activities—now called management functions—Fayol was among the first civilians to rationalize the staff role. He contrasted it with the role of line management and offered a clear statement of staff limitations. Line workers are defined as those whose work directly affects customers. Staff workers are functional specialists who act in a support role. Our discussion of these topics in Chapter 17 owes a great debt to his early formulations of these issues. Fayol first suggested two bases for dividing work into departments: functional and geographic. (An Englishman, L. H. Gulick, expanded his notion into four bases for departmentalization: function, process, clientele, and location.)

Fayol was concerned, too, with the number of people a manager could efficiently supervise, and his ideas on this subject were expanded by V. A. Graicunas into the notion of **span of control**. Departmentalization and span of control are discussed in Chapter 17.

HUMAN RELATIONS: WORK AS A SOCIAL PROCESS

In the late 1920s, the Western Electric Company conducted a series of tests to study the effect of light levels on worker productivity. Each time the researchers raised the level of light in the factory, productivity rose. Then, to test their results, they lowered the level of light, but productivity increased again. They lowered it still further, and again, productivity rose! Here was a puzzle. What was going on?

The researchers gradually formed a hypothesis that the way the workers felt about their work was significant. The experimental process, the attention that the researchers paid to the workers, seemed to stimulate their productivity. The research was thus expanded to include a close study of the human interaction in the work groups being observed. The researchers discovered that social pressures in the work group were at least as important as pay in determining level of effort and output of workers.

This work was begun under the direction of Elton Mayo and carried out largely by Fritz Roethlisberger and W. J. Dickson, all famous names in management thought. It set in motion a process of research and controversy that continues to be a lively area of debate among management theorists as well as managers and supervisors. Although there is wide disagreement over exactly how to interpret and put into practice these findings about human relations (or, as it has more recently been termed, organizational behavior), few would argue today that pay is all that counts. Most managers are much more sensitive to the human and social needs of workers than they were just a few years ago.

IMPLICATIONS FOR THE MODERN HOSPITALITY MANAGER

We have noted the influence of the early theorists Taylor, Fayol, and Mayo, and the practical uses to which their theories are put to this day. By way of a summary, we should note that the basic issues in hospitality management for the foreseeable future are embodied in the work of these three men and those who followed them. From Taylor, we get a concern with efficient production methods. Fayol set us to thinking about the design of the working organization. And Mayo and his followers alerted us to a concern for the worker as an individual and as a social being. Students of the hospitality industry should be able to observe the effect of each of these researchers' work on how today's hospitality organizations are managed.

Management: A Dynamic Force in a Changing Industry

The hospitality industry, too, has had its managerial pioneers. Although we cannot, in the space allotted here, discuss them all, we will offer a brief description of the work of **E. M. Statler** and **Vernon and Gordon Stouffer**, and describe the development of modern hospitality franchise systems as exemplified in the work of **Howard Johnson**, **Harland Sanders**, **Ray Kroc**, and **Kemmons Wilson**. The contribution of another conceptual pioneer, **Sam Barshop**, founder of La Quinta and inventor of the limited-service hotel, is detailed in Case History 15.1. These sketches will help demonstrate the impact of management ideas on the evolution of the hospitality industry.

STATLER: THE FIRST "NATIONAL" HOSPITALITY SYSTEM

Ideas, especially as textbooks present them, often appear neat and tidy. However, they are usually the result of complicated development. The central perception of Ellsworth M. Statler—that a national market existed for quality accommodations for the growing American middle class—probably evolved from his experience in serving that market as his hotel holdings grew from the original Buffalo Statler to a chain serving many of the nation's major cities. After developing and operating two "temporary" hotels for the Pan American Exposition in Buffalo in 1901 and the world's fair in St. Louis in 1904, Statler opened his first permanent hotel in Buffalo in 1908, where he had already made a name for himself with a successful, popular-priced restaurant. His hotel featured all the amenities of a luxury hotel, but both its plant and organization were designed for maximum efficiency. His slogan— "A room with a bath for a dollar and a half"—shook an industry that associated the luxury of a bath with high prices. Statler's became the first popular-priced, full-service hotel. In the hotel business of that day, a substantial portion of the hotel rooms were plain rooms, that is, rooms without a bath. All of the popular-priced rooms were of this variety. Thus, "A room with a bath for a dollar and a half" represented a major social innovation.

As the size of the Statler organization grew, the company developed central staff services in control, architectural design, and personnel. Statler produced the first centralized corporate staff (as opposed to line management, a concept we will discuss in Chapter 17) in the hospitality industry. The enforcement of uniform standards in all Statler hotels provided a guest with the assurance of a familiar quality level wherever he or she went. Moreover, Statler was the first hotelier to perceive the power of the American middle-class market, and his was probably the first true hospitality chain, with common operating standards for all properties.

It would take a much longer discussion of Statler's many contributions—including his important role as the first influential backer of hospitality education—to give full credit to this pioneer. Fortunately, such a discussion is available in a full-length book published by the Statler Foundation.[3]

STOUFFER'S MODERN MANAGEMENT TECHNIQUES

Vernon and Gordon Stouffer were sons of the owners of a successful family restaurant. In the early 1920s, they attended the Wharton School of Finance, where they studied the ideas of Frederick Taylor and the other management pioneers. As a result of that experience, the Stouffers introduced ideas that transformed the artisan- and craft-based field of restaurateuring into the modern American restaurant industry. In short, the Stouffers adapted the thinking of Taylor and Fayol to the restaurant.

The Recipe Kitchen: A Controlled Shop. Their mother oversaw the original kitchen, but the Stouffer brothers could not build a chain on the skills of one person approaching retirement age. On the other hand, they did not want a chef, because (they argued) when you lose the chef and replace him or her, your food could change and your organization might fall apart. With this insight into the weaknesses of the craft-based kitchen, the Stouffers sought to achieve management control over the kitchen by developing a set of recipes that would produce a standard product. For many years, the Stouffers hired only women for work in the kitchen or pantry because (they argued) women were accustomed to following recipes, whereas men were inclined "to become chefs," making things their own way and destroying the uniformity of product for which Stouffer's ultimately became famous.

The food production supervisor and her assistants were called managers: They planned the work; organized that work around stations; staffed the kitchens with the right people, properly trained for the right job; and controlled food costs through yield checks and portion control devices. Finally, the food production manager, while leading and directing her crew, placed great emphasis on following the recipes and methods specified by management.

The introduction of the management-controlled **recipe kitchen** greatly improved productivity over the traditional kitchens of the day. Closer management control also ensured remarkably low food costs. The result was a highly competitive price. As Statler had done with hotels, the Stouffers brought the amenities of fine dining within reach of the American middle-class mass market.

Before the Stouffers, restaurant organization centered on the roles associated with traditional workstations; the relations among workers and between work groups reflected the old chef–maître d'–steward pecking order. The Stouffers, however, adopted a modern system of departmentalization. Reporting to the general manager were the executive assistant manager and his or her assistants, a director of service, and the dietitian (or food production manager). Although these formally prescribed relationships changed somewhat from time to time, Figure 15.1 is a reasonably accurate description of the way the typical Stouffer's unit was arranged.

An organizational hierarchy, with the rigidity and symbolic trappings of an almost military organization, was developed—complete with titles of address (Mr., Miss, or Mrs. for supervisors and managers, first names for workers) and uniforms that clearly differentiated management from worker.

The Stouffers were in the area of personnel management as well. They offered fringe benefits such as paid vacations, paid holidays, and group insurance long before these practices became widespread. The Stouffers were among those who supported the pioneering work of William Foote Whyte, which finally took the form of his study Human Relations in the Restaurant Industry. Whyte looked specifically at

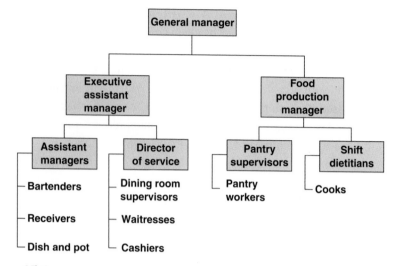

Figure 15.1
The Stouffer restaurant organization (circa 1960).

individual behavior and how employees related to one another in the restaurant environment.

Thus, the three kinds of ideas that constituted then—and still do now—the agenda of management thought had a profound effect in shaping the Stouffer organization: The controlled shop focused on the task, a rational organization design, and concern for the worker as an individual human being.

THE BUILDING OF COMPLEX HOSPITALITY SYSTEMS

Any discussion of management must also include the concept of how systems are organized. No one person can take credit for the development of hospitality systems, as these multiunit organizations evolved over a number of years. One of the key foundations on which these organizations are based, however, is franchising, and the pioneer in hospitality franchising was Howard Johnson. He began to build a franchise organization around a standard restaurant format in the 1920s. A generation or so later, Harland Sanders and Ray Kroc were the entrepreneurs most clearly associated with the development of franchised fast food. Kemmons Wilson made unique contributions to the development of modern lodging **franchise systems**.

Each of these people had an idea that solved a consumer problem. To make those ideas widely available, they needed to develop an operating system and an organization that could finance its own expansion; this meant giving up the owner-hired management pattern on which hospitality organizations had been previously based. It meant developing a whole new basis for organization based on shared interests and acceptance of authority on a voluntary basis. That acceptance, in turn, was motivated by a desire to share in a unique idea, that is, to share in the knowledge of the central organization. Moreover, the franchisee shared in the power of a large organization in marketing, purchasing, and operating system design. Much of that power related to the collective knowledge of the franchising organization. Finally, each of these men created a powerful consumer acceptance for his product and service that outlived its initial corporate organization and its founder.[4]

Howard Johnson. In the 1920s, as automobile ownership became more common and people began to travel more, travelers confronted the problem of finding a safe, reliable place to eat. Howard Johnson, whose initial success was in manufacturing ice cream, hit upon the idea of a restaurant with a standard appearance and menu and quality standards that would be immediately recognizable to travelers. Anyone who has ever driven into a strange town and wondered where to eat without risking food poisoning will know how critical Johnson's idea was to travelers of that day. Although his idea was excellent, Johnson did not have the funds to expand his operation. He decided to franchise his operating system to others, following the method of expansion first pioneered by Singer Sewing Machines and used very successfully in Johnson's time by soft-drink companies and automobile manufacturers to achieve rapid expansion in a growing national marketplace.

At one point, Howard Johnson's was the largest restaurant "chain" in the United States. We put "chain" in quotes here because until that time, as in Statler's day, the word implied common ownership. Johnson's restaurants were owned by many local operators (and investors), all of whom followed the same pattern in menu, decor, and operating procedure, not because of the legal force of common ownership but because of their compelling common interest.

Harland Sanders: Kentucky Fried Chicken. Harland Sanders operated a very successful restaurant that was bypassed by a new highway. He needed a new idea to regain his customers' patronage, so he developed a method of frying chicken quickly under pressure. This method permitted frequent small-batch cooking to ensure freshness and flavor. He also developed a batter that was flavored by a "secret recipe of herbs and spices." (This recipe, although changed a number of times since, is still secret.) Finally, he coined the phrase "finger lickin' good" to describe his Kentucky Fried Chicken. His slogan caught people's fancy. Customers came flocking back to his store, but he could make only limited use of his combination of operating idea, equipment innovation, and sloganeering in one town in Kentucky. Rather than try to build an organization based on ownership, he took to the road, presenting his business system to other restaurateurs and offering them a chance to share in it in return for a royalty. Those who were interested were licensed to use his system—and many of them became millionaires several times over. Once again, a "chain" emerged based on shared interests and mutual agreement rather than on the force of property rights.

Ray Kroc: McDonald's. Ray Kroc was a manufacturer's representative who sold milk shake machines very successfully. One restaurant that he sold to, which was owned by the McDonald brothers, bought an unusually large number of machines, and Kroc went to see what made that restaurant so successful. What he saw so impressed him that he acquired the rights to license the operating system to others and eventually bought the McDonald brothers out.

What the McDonald's system offered was the solution to two problems. The first was a customer need, and the second was an operating problem. The customer problem involved the needs of the parents of the baby boomers. When the boomers were still little children and families were larger than they are today, these young parents needed a place to feed the whole family without spending a lot of money they didn't have. The McDonald's restaurant offered the most popular foods in America—hamburgers, french fries, and milk shakes—and promised change from a dollar for a whole meal. Moreover, there was no problem with serving little children. Even after McDonald's evolved out of its early drive-in and take-out format, McDonald's restaurants were places where everybody could come dressed for play or work and where kids could run around and not have to "be good." Not just the children loved it—McDonald's was a place for the whole family.

The operating problem that fast foods solved—and this is nearly as true for Sanders as for Kroc—was that of delivering food service at a price that made it an attractive buy. The first key to achieving this goal was the limited menu. Menu limitation meant economies of scale in both purchasing and preparation. The second key was to take the idea of the controlled shop to its extreme. Every procedure was spelled out in detail, and work methods were designed that removed virtually all need for skill. Because quality was based on procedure rather than skill, it could be ensured with minimum-wage workers—and uniformity could be ensured in many outlets, eventually worldwide.

Kroc brought all the talents of the modern corporation to bear on developing and redeveloping his products and services. His redevelopment of the company's french fried potato product, for instance, has been compared to the systems engineering that the National Aeronautics and Space Administration first made famous in the space program. More than anyone before him, Kroc was able to tap the talents that were drawn into his growing organization of franchisees. Most of the newer products, such as the Egg McMuffin and the Big Mac, were ideas initially developed by franchisees. Moreover, Kroc built an organization that was at once uniform and yet flexible enough to change with its markets and respond to competitive pressure.

McDonald's did not build its early success on advertising, but as fast food became more competitive in the 1970s, Kroc oversaw the development of the awesome advertising muscle that has made McDonald's a household word around the world. The campuslike headquarters in Oak Park, Illinois, resembles nothing so much as the Versailles of Louis XIV. There, not only does the job of governance of this vast, largely voluntary (i.e., franchise) organization get accomplished, but visitors are awed by the massiveness of the resources and the restrained splendor of the setting. One of the authors, during a visit to McDonald's headquarters, watched two new franchisees, one from Southeast Asia and the other from Germany, arriving at these headquarters. They were so visibly impressed that any idea they might have had that this "hamburger stand" company was anything other than all-competent was quickly banished. Hamburger University, a training school, is one of the major tools that the organization Kroc built uses to secure uniformity in product, commitment in operation, and enthusiasm in management. Detailed training rather than strict discipline is the cement of the McDonald's organization. It is, ultimately, knowledge rather than discipline that holds the organization together.

Kemmons Wilson: Holiday Inns. Kemmons Wilson, with his close associate Wallace Johnson, applied the idea of franchising to the lodging industry in the early 1950s in a way that swiftly built a national organization that set the pace for change in the lodging industry for 20 years. Seeing a need based on his own travels on business and with his family, Wilson developed a motor hotel, Holiday Inn, that met the needs of both businesspeople and vacationing families. The organizational needs for a reservation system, a well-known brand name, and standardized services were successfully surmounted, and his Holiday Inns became a popular favorite. It was this consumer preference that made Holiday Inns first a major and then the dominant force in the lodging industry of the 1950s, 1960s, and 1970s. The rapid expansion of his idea was possible because of Wilson's success in enlisting ownership financing through many local investors in local projects—and these local people were usually able to find local mortgage money to complete the capital needs of the new Holiday Inns. Once again, a successful idea that solved consumer problems was expanded through the power of mutual self-interest, through a network of franchisees who conformed to the system because of their own self-interest. (The development of another lodging innovation, the limited-service midscale hotel, is discussed in Case History 15.1.)

Where Does a Concept Come From?

One of the most significant innovations in the lodging business in the last half of the twentieth century has been the development of the midscale limited-service hotel, a concept that includes first-class guest rooms but very few of the other services of the full-service hotel. The man who first developed this concept is Sam Barshop, the founder of La Quinta Inns (www.laquinta.com).

The interesting thing about the development of this concept is that it is a good example of learning from experience. The successful development of La Quinta was certainly no accident—but it was also not a blinding flash of inspiration.

Sam Barshop and his brother Philip began building and leasing Ramada Inns in the early 1960s and then switched to a new franchisor, Rodeway Inns.[1] As Barshcp Enterprises, they obtained the exclusive franchise from Rodeway for the states of Texas, Oklahoma, Kansas, and Arkansas. Between 1961 and 1968, they built 20 Rodeway Inns.

The 1968 world's fair, HemisFair '68, was sited in San Antonio, and Sam and Philip decided to build two properties there to accommodate visitors to the fair.[2] With their experience with Ramada and Rodeway under their belts, they tried to buy out their franchisor. That proved not to be possible, and so La Quinta was born. They chose the name La Quinta—which means "country place"—to match the Spanish motif of the buildings. No one had any notion of building a chain of La Quintas. To quote Sam Barshop, "We were going to build two motels in San Antonio and that would be that."[3] Early success, however, was an important learning experience, and the chain began to take form.

One of the basics of the La Quinta concept—and the limited-service concept in general—was to avoid the operational headaches and costs of a restaurant operation. But the first five La Quintas did have restaurants, which Sam and Phil later characterized as "the biggest mistake we ever made." They learned from that mistake, however, and the La Quinta operating concept soon included a freestanding leased restaurant operated by a successful franchise company such as Denny's, Cracker Barrel, or Shoney's.

The common elements that these pioneers share form the basis not only of the organizations that still bear their names but also of the many other organizations that have learned the lessons their success taught. One significant cornerstone is the largely voluntary nature of these organizations. While not all hospitality chains today are franchised, the power of multiunit systems was first demonstrated by franchise organizations, and the dominant forces in mass-market hospitality today generally involve a significant proportion of franchised units.

Franchise organizations multiply the center of authority rather than concentrating it. Because the owner is generally closely involved with the unit, a number of advantages are secured. First, the owner's capital and credit are used to secure financing. Each franchised operation is a manageable small-business investment; however, in the

Another important element of the concept was value. A critical aspect of that value was price, which was set at 20 to 25 percent below that of the competition. Eliminating the capital and operating costs of a restaurant made that room rate possible. The other aspect of the La Quinta value was quality. La Quinta provided a room that had all the features, quality, and cleanliness of the industry standard of the time, Holiday Inns. La Quinta targeted the business traveler, and one measure of its success was that 65 percent of its customers were businesspeople, a large proportion of them repeat customers. Inns were located so that they had easy access to the interstate highway system, airports, and business destinations such as office complexes, industrial parks, medical centers, and universities, yet were outside the downtown core, where real-estate prices were too costly for their rate structure.

Barshop described the La Quinta concept in this way: "Try not to make things too complicated. You can't be everything to everybody. We've got a simple concept, and we're going to cookie cut, and cookie cut, and cookie cut, until there aren't any more cookies left to cut."[4]

As we all know now, the cookie-cutter formula was one others could copy, but for about 15 years, La Quinta had its concept to itself. Then, along came Hampton Inns, Fairfield Inns, and a number of other similar concepts. In time, too, came other investors, proxy fights, and Barshop's eventual retirement.[5] The fact of Barshop's innovation, however, is that it changed the face of lodging.

1. The following discussion is based, except as noted, on articles from the June 1988 anniversary issue of *Innput*, a monthly publication for the employees of La Quinta Motor Inns. We would like to acknowledge our indebtedness to Mary Starling, secretary to Sam Barshop, in preparing this case history.
2. Philip Barshop left La Quinta in 1977 to run the family real-estate business.
3. Christopher H. Lovelock, "La Quinta Motor Inns," Management Case Study, Harvard Business School, 1980, p. 1.
4. Ibid., p. 6.
5. For a discussion of the takeover of La Quinta, see Case History 11.1.

aggregate, they create a huge capital plant that spreads into every attractive location across the continent and eventually around the world. The national organization they build is one with local roots, tying local needs to a national program and vice versa.

The management within a franchised unit is not much different from that in any other hospitality unit. Above the unit level, however, the functioning of the organization is quite different. It is the owner's self-interest and the franchising corporation's knowledge that are the cement of the organization, rather than the legal force of central ownership. Franchise systems are really a means for the dissemination of ideas. The voluntary joining together of these organizations also secures for each of the participants economies of scale in research, development, purchasing, and, most significantly, marketing.

As we said at the outset, no one person can take credit for this development, but we can certainly recognize the seminal contributions of Howard Johnson, Harland Sanders, Ray Kroc, and Kemmons Wilson and try to learn from them.

What Is Management?

In order to better understand the management function, one must understand the nature of work and the organization. Let us look at the basic work of a business (or any other organization, be it a hospital, nursing home, or school cafeteria). Peter Drucker, the economist and management consultant, stated that the basic purpose of business is to "create a customer," that is, to determine unfulfilled consumer needs and find a way to fill them. Drucker argued that the customer determines what a business is and that the central functions of a business are innovation and marketing.

Before discussing Drucker's theory and applying it to our industry, we should pause for a moment to consider whether his line of reasoning applies to all of us in management and supervision. Some, for instance, would argue that marketing is an activity of the sales department. However, marketing is, basically, determining what the customer wants and then providing it in a way that makes it reasonably easy for the customer to obtain, while pricing it to recover the cost and make a profit. The specific work of marketing is usually handled by a separate department. Marketing, however, also includes a way of thinking about problems that is often the hallmark of the successful manager. Drucker put it this way:

> Marketing is so basic that it cannot be considered a separate function (i.e., a separate skill or work) within the business, on a par with others such as manufacturing or personnel. Marketing requires separate work and a distinct group of activities. But it is first a central dimension of the entire business. It is the whole business seen from its final result, that is, from the customer's point of view. Concern and responsibility for marketing must, therefore, permeate all areas of the enterprise.[5]

This marketing viewpoint can actually guide us not only in dealing with guests but in dealing with employees as well. Employees are, after all, "customers" who "buy" jobs from employers with their time and effort.

We might also hear the argument that innovation is really a function of top management only. Surely opportunities for innovation exist, however, on a smaller scale and at all levels of the organization. Indeed, it is almost un-American to attribute all the opportunity for creative work to some "top group." The supervisor or junior manager who does not try to develop his or her own solutions to problems will be less useful to an organization than if he or she sees innovation as part of the work. Our earlier discussion of franchising underlines the importance of bringing ideas up through the organization.

The marketing and innovation work of junior managers must take place on a smaller scale and lower level, and it will be subject to the policy of the organization. Nevertheless, thinking your work through in terms of the needs and wants of those you deal with—employees and guests—and trying to find a new solution when old ways seem ineffective will make your work more fulfilling for you and more valuable to your operation. Finally, an understanding of the significance of marketing and innovation should make you more ready to support the efforts of others in these areas.

Indeed, Drucker pointed to what he called "the fallacy of the unterneymer." *Unterneymer* is German for "top man." He noted that the definition of business purpose is most often thought of as the concern of the owner or, at most, a few people at the top of the organization. In the German tradition of the unterneymer, Drucker said, the top man (and especially the owner-manager) alone knows what the business is all about and alone makes all the entrepreneurial decisions. Drucker further suggests that everybody else is a virtual technician who carries out prescribed tasks.

> [T]his may have been adequate in the nineteenth century business in which a few men at the top who alone made decisions, with all the rest manual workers or low level clerks. It is a dangerous misconception of today's business enterprise.
>
> In sharp contrast to the organization of the past, today's business enterprise [also today's hospital or government agency] brings together a great many men of high knowledge and skill, at practically every level of the organization. But high knowledge and skill also means decisions impact on how the work is to be done and on what work is actually tackled. They make, by necessity, risk-taking decisions, that is, business decisions, whatever the official form of the organization.[6]

The continuing definition of what a business is remains important to managers at all levels of an organization.

WHAT IS OUR BUSINESS?

To answer this question, Drucker posed a series of additional questions:

- Who is the customer?
- What is value to the customer?
- What will our business be?
- What should our business be?

We have seen how Statler and the Stouffer brothers, in different areas, thought through the needs of the emerging American middle-class market—a market that really constituted a "new" customer. The developers of franchise systems, such as Johnson, Sanders, Kroc, and Wilson, established organizations that harnessed the interests of ownership to serve a common organizational purpose. Each of these pioneers then used the field of management to serve that market efficiently.

Let's illustrate Drucker's frame of analysis with some examples from the hospitality industry: community nutrition programs, the community hotel, and franchised hospitality chains.

Who Is the Customer? The answer to this question is complicated by the fact that there are usually at least two customers, and generally more. Recall that the school lunch program got its start as a national program not only to fill the needs of hungry students but also to use up surplus farm commodities and help solve the nation's unemployment problem during the Great Depression.

Although we can't trace the process exactly, we know that the great expansion in the school lunch program was a response to the growing participation of women in the workforce. Indeed, the development of preschool feeding and the school breakfast program are more recent innovative responses to the twin problems of working mothers and poor families. Although the customer is the child who eats and the parents who need no longer remain home to prepare a meal, the buying decision is made by Congress and other state and local funding agencies, and the ultimate customer is the American people. Much the same can be said for congregate feeding programs for the aging.

It is hardly possible to identify the single "entrepreneur" responsible for the growth of community nutrition programs. They have resulted from the work of many people, both within and outside the school lunch program and other food service programs. This revolution in the way social obligations are arranged to provide nutrition is still going on—a dramatic example of identifying customer needs and innovating to fill those needs, with people at all levels of many operations involved in the work. Neither community nutrition programs nor any of their elements—school lunch, preschool feeding, congregate meals—is the work of an unterneymer.

On a smaller scale, community hotel promoters discover every generation or so that town leaders in smaller communities can benefit from a small first-class hotel. The guest is also an important customer, but as the discussion in Chapter 9 suggested, many community hotels would never have been built were it not for the positive influence (expected or real) of these hotels on real-estate values, employment, and community growth in a small town. Thus, community leaders are important customers for community hotel developers, in many ways as important as the guests the hotel is built to serve.

The franchise systems we discussed earlier illustrate the notion of multiple levels of customers. The guest who buys the product or service is an important customer, but so is the potential franchisee. The franchise organization must not only satisfy the guest but also develop a system that fills the needs of local investors and entrepreneurs who want to run a successful business in their community.

What Is Value to the Customer? Each customer has different values to be fulfilled. The guest at a Holiday Inn values a standard level of product and service that is conveniently located and priced within his or her means. (These means are defined by the American middle class, to which the guest almost invariably belongs.) The franchise holder, on the other hand, buys a familiar hospitality brand name, national advertising, and a referral system.

Value to the guest in a community hotel is clean, comfortable accommodations. Value to the local investors, however, results from factors such as improved property values and a community that can more readily attract other employers with new local job opportunities.

The value of community nutrition programs to students, young children, and senior citizens is adequate nutrition and a palatable meal. Government supports such programs for these reasons. However, we can speculate that perhaps even more significant is the fact that these programs solve other problems. They fill the needs of families in which the mother works and can no longer serve a midday meal (or sometimes even breakfast). Congregate feeding for the elderly also supplies services that families no longer provide for their aging members. The flip side of this is also true: Congregate feeding often frees the elderly from dependence on their children.

What Will Our Business Be? This question recognizes the simple fact that the only constant is change—that for organizations to survive in a changing environment, they must change with it. Holiday Inn was originally and for many years a company of roadside inns located on the outer edges of cities, along expressways, or near airports. As urban renewal began to revitalize downtowns, and as many downtown hotels continued to deteriorate or even closed their doors, a large new market began to emerge. Accordingly, the company developed prototype properties to serve urban centers and changed from strictly a motel company to a hotel-motel company.

In the mid-1980s, as segmentation became more widespread, Holiday Corporation—its name changed to recognize the company's broadened commitments—evolved into a multibrand company represented in nearly every significant area of lodging: Hampton Inns in the economy market, Holiday Inns in the conventional motor hotel market, and the Crowne Plaza properties and Embassy Suites in upscale markets. Holiday recognized, as well, the significance of its destination activities and high profits in the casino business and expanded its commitment to its Harrah's division. Then, in 1990, Holiday sold off what had once been its flagship brand, Holiday Inns, to another company. This reflected management's judgment that the casino business and the newer, more segmented lodging concepts, Hampton, Embassy, and Homewood, offered the company's stockholders the best return. The successor company to Holiday Corporation's non–Holiday Inn assets, Promus, in time split Harrah's gambling business from its hotel operations and, even more recently, Promus Hotel Corporation merged with Doubletree to form one of the most powerful hotel corporations in North America (and was subsequently purchased by Hilton).

What Should Our Business Be? Drucker began his discussion of the question in this way:

> "What will our business be?" aims at adaptation to anticipated changes. It aims at modifying, extending, developing the existing, ongoing business.
>
> But there is a need also to ask "What should our business be?" What opportunities are opening up or can be created to fulfill the purpose and mission of the business by making it a different business?[7]

The school lunch program began by serving children in public schools. As public food service programs expanded to include preschool children, however, many officials of the school lunch program started to wonder whether their organization could be expanded to embrace other community food service programs such as congregate meals for the elderly. The school lunch program in every community already has a production plant. Moreover, it maintains central service facilities in lunchrooms unused except during the noon recess (and, perhaps, the early morning). It also has skilled workers and managerial and nutritional savvy, and it is genuinely community-based. Thus, the question "What should our business be?" is properly raised by school lunch leaders. It will be interesting to watch how food service answers these four questions in the next generation.

McDonald's began as a drive-in restaurant on the outskirts of a city, serving hamburgers, french fries, and shakes, principally at lunch and dinner. Because of its great success, McDonald's might have been content. Instead, management constantly asked what its business should be, and today's McDonald's features attractively decorated dining facilities where guests can sit and eat their meals rather than carrying them to the car. McDonald's has also moved aggressively and successfully into the breakfast market and, more recently, became a major factor in downtown food service. Instead of resting on its laurels as the country's most successful drive-in chain, McDonald's management continually looks for new opportunities. "What should our business be?" asks McDonald's. The answers account for McDonald's steady expansion and its place as the world's largest restaurant system, serving all three meals and available in most market areas in North America and throughout the world.

IN BUSINESS FOR YOURSELF?

CAREERS IN HOSPITALITY

Some students certainly plan to enter business for themselves. Those who succeed will remember the key questions we have just reviewed. Students whose careers involve working as supervisors and managers for others must realize that they are also, in a sense, in business for themselves—selling their services and making a career based on their reputation for effectiveness. If this is your choice, the analysis we have just offered serves you, too—you must answer the questions of who your customers are and what value means to them. The patrons of your operation are obviously customers, and their needs and wants must be satisfied. The employer is your customer, and in an important way, especially for junior managers and supervisors, the employees you direct are also your customers. If they were not there, there would be no need for a supervisor. The balancing of the needs of all these "customers," properly done, will require creative marketing and innovation on your part.

What will your business be? And what should it be? Career change is so common in North America that we all should consider the possibilities together. Is there an area of the industry that might offer greater opportunities? Or shorter hours? Or higher pay? At some point you may want to change the nature of your business—for instance, from supervisor in a large operation to unit manager. As these changes arise, you should ask yourself questions about your ability to "change your business." Perhaps additional work in accounting, a human-relations training program, or some other specialized work or study would help you supply value to your proposed new customers.

Success—defined as income, advancement, or more work satisfaction—will come from taking a creative approach to the work of management. In the next five chapters, we will consider just what kind of work supervisors and managers do. We emphasize here, though, that even during that time when you prepare for managerial duties by working as a server or a dishwasher, you can use an understanding of management functions. Servers, cooks, and bartenders are "in business for themselves," building knowledge through experience, building a reputation for effectiveness, and deriving personal satisfaction and self-confidence from work well done. This "business" is worth managing, and more success will come from having managed it well.

Summary

This chapter began our discussion of management. First, we defined management and supervision. Second, we outlined the history of coping with economic problems: tradition, command, and the market system.

We turned then to three pioneers in management theory: Taylor and his work process focus, the task idea, and the controlled shop; Fayol and administrative management; and Mayo and his concern with the worker.

We moved to a discussion of pioneers in the hospitality industry. Statler introduced the idea of a popular-priced, full-service hotel, as well as uniform standards in all his hotels. He was perhaps the first to recognize the power of the middle-class market in regard to the hospitality industry.

The Stouffers adapted Taylor's and Fayol's ideas to their restaurants. They used a recipe kitchen—a controlled shop—which standardized the management and organization of their restaurants. Johnson, Sanders, Kroc, and Wilson all played key roles in developing franchise organizations based on voluntary adherence, mutual interest, and shared knowledge. They offer a national organization a local focus in every market they serve.

The last section of this chapter was devoted to a study of Drucker's theories of management and how they apply to the hospitality industry. We considered several questions: What is management? Who is the customer? What is value to the customer? What will our business be? What should our business be?

Key Words and Concepts

Management	Span of control
Supervision	E. M. Statler
Tradition	Vernon and Gordon Stouffer
Command	Howard Johnson
Market system	Harland Sanders
Work process focus	Ray Kroc
High-priced man	Kemmons Wilson
Task idea	Sam Barshop
Controlled shop	Recipe kitchen
Administrative management	Franchise systems

Review Questions

1. How do management and supervision differ?

2. Describe Taylor's principal contributions to management theory.

3. What were Statler's main contributions to hospitality management? What were the Stouffers' main contributions?

4. What are the forces that bind modern franchise organizations together?

5. According to Drucker, what should our business—the hospitality industry—be?

Internet Exercises

1. **Site name:** Search Engines

   URL: Google—www.google.com

   AlltheWeb.com—www.alltheweb.com

   Yahoo—www.yahoo.com

   MSN Search—search.msn.com

   AltaVista—www.altavista.com

   Background information: Many current management philosophers differentiate management from leadership skills. As a manager in the hospitality industry, you will be using both management and leadership skills throughout your career. The key is to determine how they differ and when to use them appropriately.

   Use your favorite search engine or one listed above and search for articles/information on management versus leadership.

   Exercises:

   a. Determine what characteristics differentiate a manager from a leader.

   b. Lead a class discussion on which is more important—managers or leaders.

   c. When is it most appropriate to use management skills and/or leadership skills?

   d. Choose an article that addresses the issue of management versus leadership and discuss the author's perspective on the differences and similarities. Do you agree with the author? Why or why not?

2. **Site name:** Search Engines

   URL: Google—www.google.com

   AlltheWeb.com—www.alltheweb.com

   Yahoo—www.yahoo.com

   MSN Search—search.msn.com

   AltaVista—www.altavista.com

Background information: There have been many leaders in the hospitality industry such as Ray Kroc, Howard Johnson, Harland Sanders, Kemmons Wilson, Vernon and Gordon Stouffer, Sam Barshop, John Q. Hammons, Horst Schultze, and so on. Choose a current or past leader and search for information on that individual using your favorite search engine or one of the search engines listed above.

Exercises:

a. Discuss the contributions this individual has made to the hospitality industry and how the industry has changed as a result of his or her actions.

b. Where do you see your chosen individual using management skills and/or leadership skills most effectively?

3. **Site name:** The Art and Science of Leadership

    URL: www.nwlink.com/~donclark/leader/leader.html

    Background information: This leadership guide is for supervisors, managers, lead employees, and anyone wishing to move up through the ranks as a leader.

    Site name: The Free Management Library: Introduction to Management

    URL: www.managementhelp.org/mng_thry/mng_thry.htm

    Background information: The Free Management Library provides easy-to-access, clutter-free, comprehensive resources regarding the leadership and management of yourself, other individuals, groups, and organizations. The content is relevant to the vast majority of people, whether they are in large or small for-profit or nonprofit organizations. Over the past ten years, the Library has grown to be one of the world's largest well-organized collections of these types of resources.

    Exercises:

    a. Choose one of the "chapters" on the Web site that is of interest to you. Lead a class discussion on the management and leadership concept you chose and describe why this information would be important to a hospitality manager.

    b. Read the section on leadership styles. Which style do you think is the most appropriate for a hospitality manager? Why?

Notes

1. Robert L. Heilbroner, *The Making of Economic Society*, 4th ed. (Englewood Cliffs, NJ: Prentice-Hall, 1972).

2. Frederick W. Taylor, *The Principles of Scientific Management* (New York: Norton, 1967).

3. Floyd Miller, Statler: *America's Extraordinary Hotelman* (Buffalo: The Statler Foundation, 1968).

4. Nothing said here should be interpreted to imply that franchise organizations are more perfect, necessarily more humane, or freer of error, politics, and the arbitrary exercise of power than are independently owned operations. In fact, no human organization achieves

perfection, and neither do franchise organizations. They do, however, have the substantial advantages set forth here.

5. Peter Drucker, *Management: Tasks, Responsibilities, Practices* (New York: Harper & Row, 1974), p. 63. The discussion in this section takes many of its ideas from Chapters 6 and 7 of Drucker's book. This is a classic text with which all hospitality students should be familiar.

6. Ibid., p. 76.

7. Ibid., p. 92.

The Hospitality Industry

TOTAL QUALITY
MANAGEMENT

T.Q.M

WINNING

(Courtesy of Sodexho.)

CHAPTER SIXTEEN

Planning in Hospitality Management

The Purpose of this Chapter

Planning is a necessary everyday activity both in life and in managing. Planning should go on at every level of the organization, from dishwasher to the chairman of the board. Unfortunately, it often gets overlooked at all these levels. Planning for your life's work is as essential as planning today's menu. Accordingly, this chapter presents planning as an active process related to both long-range organizational goals and day-to-day work. Although the concepts we present are most clearly related to planning in organizations, they need only be adapted to be useful to students considering their career goals.

THIS CHAPTER SHOULD HELP YOU

1. Provide an example illustrating the necessity of planning at all levels.
2. Explain why it is important that the supervisor/manager's role involve both planning and acting on the plans of others.
3. Define and describe the following key planning concepts: policies, plans, rules, methods, procedures, standards, budgets, strategies, and tactics.
4. Provide an example illustrating how the needs and wants of a guest/client drive the goal-setting and planning process.
5. Describe planning as a general management function (strategic planning), as an operation management function (tactical planning), and as work done by individuals for the organization and for themselves.
6. Explain why policy development and long-range planning are important, and describe the following tools related to these activities: return on investment and cost-benefit analysis.

Why Study Planning?

Planning is something that everybody agrees is important—from students to stay-at-home parents to entrepreneurs. Planning, however, is often neglected, probably because it requires hard thinking and involves the uncomfortable work of dealing with uncertainty.

An absence of conscious planning in the workplace leads to two potential types of problems. First, because employees must know what their employers expect of them, an absence of management planning leads to confusion at work. Second, to settle that confusion, employees often plan for themselves. Their plans may be aimed at goals completely unrelated to the organization's goals. For example, if management fails to develop a seating chart for the dining room, the servers will almost certainly work out their own system. Such a system may or may not be good for guest service, but you can bet it will suit the convenience of the servers.

Failure to plan invites trouble. Three different examples illustrate why planning is necessary at all levels of the organization. Consider, first of all, the server who does not plan his or her next trip to the dining room in light of the needs of the entire station. He or she will probably have to run back and forth to get one or two items that could have been brought all at once. In this way, two precious resources are wasted: time and energy. By the end of the day, the server has worked harder than his or her co-workers and probably has earned less in tips from those customers who had to wait.

If you have ever been in a restaurant that ran out of eggs at breakfast or bread during a rush on the sandwich station, you have seen our second example—the results of poor operational planning. And you know its costs: dissatisfied guests, upset employees, and the loss of some of those inconvenienced customers and perhaps some of the people they talk to. In general, the operation's reputation suffers.

For our final example, you are asked to recall the discussion in Chapter 11 regarding the difficulties that the hotel industry has had over the years—illustrating the importance of planning on a larger scale. The higher the level of decision making, the more widespread the effects of poor planning. The decision-making process (of building new hotels) is one that leads to periodic overcapacity even while building continues. As noted in Chapter 11, the hotel industry lost $33 billion in the 11-year period, but for most of that time, building continued at a brisk pace.

The failure to plan entails serious risks at any level. Your own plans are most important to you. Just as the server wasted time and the restaurant that ran out of eggs lost profit opportunities, you may waste a good deal of effort and miss opportunities if you fail to plan in both your personal and professional life.

First, you need to plan for yourself at several levels:

1. Whatever work you do (desk clerking, college homework, or motel housekeeping), your work will be easier and quicker if you can plan it.

2. As a supervisor or manager, you must learn to plan the work of others. (Moreover, senior-level managers must not only plan work—how to do—but must also plan on the grander scale of organizational goals—what to do.)

3. In addition to planning the work you do for others, you must think of your own career as a business, as we suggested in the last chapter. Thus, your career development means planning for the kinds of services you want to be selling at some future point—banquet manager, sales representative, food production supervisor, general manager, and so forth—and then planning how to achieve that position within a reasonable period.

Second, you will probably have to accept that, as a member of an organization, you are part of somebody else's plans. The point is that understanding the planning process helps you understand the need of a well-managed company for carefully developed plans. As an understanding participant in planning, you should be a more effective employee and find greater meaning in your work.

The following discussion should help you work effectively by improving your readiness to plan your work and the work of others. Moreover, the basic approach to business can be applied to your own career planning. Case History 16.1 gives an example, from ARAMARK's experience, of operations planning in action.

Planning in Organizations

Planning is the work that managers (and workers) do to visualize the future in a concrete way and to determine courses of action that will achieve the organization's goals over a definite period.

As we have noted, planning at the different levels of the management hierarchy has different characteristics. The pyramid in Figure 16.1 provides a convenient way of symbolizing some of these characteristics (although we acknowledge the newer, preferred "inverted pyramid," this traditional one serves our purposes here). The higher in the organization the planning activity takes place, the fewer persons will be involved in the planning and the more general the nature of the plan and commitment will be. At lower levels, the planning involves more people and more detail. For example, the server's work plans might cover a period of one meal or, perhaps, just a turn on her station (the time it takes to serve a party—to "turn" the table). Purchasing at the operating level

Planning on an Olympic Scale at ARAMARK

In the ancient Greek Olympics, athletes confined themselves to vegetables, figs, nuts, barley, and porridge—and after the games, in celebration, they ate roasted oxen. No such simplicity is possible, however, in planning for the feeding of modern Olympians.

ARAMARK had provided food service at 12 Olympic Games since 1968 (in Mexico City), including recent games in Atlanta and Sydney. The company also served the 2004 Olympics in Athens. When you know how, though, such a complex undertaking calls for a lot of planning. In fact, ARAMARK estimates its managers spend 100,000 hours in planning before the first meal is served.

Consider the nature of the challenge. In Sydney, ARAMARK fed 28,000 people each day, including some 10,000 athletes and various coaches, staff, officials, and visitors from 197 countries. In total, 1,500 menu items were planned for the athletes (from a standard of about 550 recipes). The main service area was the athletes' cafeteria, with close to 5,000 seats. The facility included over 20 food stations plus a McDonald's. Round-the-clock dining had to be provided in the Olympic Village (as always), in two separate dining facilities.

The planning process starts, of course, with the needs of the customer. Meals have to provide for the nutritional needs of athletes and, at the same time, offer diners a taste of home and choices that suit their religious, cultural, and ethnic preferences. The ARAMARK Culinary Center in Philadelphia, the company's research and development arm, plays a huge role in the massive project of planning for the Olympics. ARAMARK's managers compile data on Olympic meals served since 1968, their popularity, and potential production problems; moreover, they take into account nutrition, flavor, texture, color, and variety. From this planning process comes a ten-day rotating selection of recipes that suits people from all corners of the globe—from Russian borscht to Japanese miso soup and Korean kim chee, Moroccan fish tagine, and kangaroo prosciutto. As was the case in Atlanta (in 1996) where southern-style fried chicken was a staple, Australian BBQ was made available every day to suit the Sydney location. Extensive recipe testing and "preview dinners" take place to give ARAMARK opportunities to train members of the Olympic staff in diverse locations. In total, ARAMARK estimates that it trains about 6,500 people to plan, prepare, and serve Olympic meals. In total, staffing needs for the most recent Olympics in Sydney were as follows:

seldom covers a period of more than a week, and usually just a day or two. These are good examples of short-range planning.

Although short-range planning is absolutely essential, it differs from long-range planning, in which resources are committed on a much larger scale. Not surprisingly, specialized tools for long-range planning have been developed to assist managers at that level. We will examine these long-range planning tools at the end of this chapter.

17 senior chefs

30 supervising chefs

236 qualified chefs

95 production cooks

270 kitchen hands

410 kitchen assistants

210 kitchen runners

Preparation can involve erecting off-site production facilities, complete modular kitchens, and the necessary energy supplies. In Atlanta (in 1996) an aboveground dining tent was installed to provide air-conditioned dining in the Georgia summer weather, as well as space to install the additional electrical, plumbing, and gas lines a food service operation requires. In total, the plant erected by ARAMARK provided a 150,000-square-foot food service operation, including a tented seating and serving area of 75,000 square feet, a modular kitchen measuring 25,000 square feet, and an additional 50,000 square feet for food storage, employee services, and office space.

In planning for the 2004 Olympics in Athens, ARAMARK worked with a local partner for what was the largest Olympic Village at the time. In addition to ARAMARK staff from around the world, they also had close to 100 students helping out from the hospitality management program at the University of Delaware.

To manage this complex process from a standing start is a challenge for ARAMARK. Of course, its experience in managing food service at previous Olympic events stands them in good stead, but in the end, the task would be next to impossible without detailed, meticulous planning. Indeed, the company's broad experience in all kinds of food service had long ago convinced its management of the vital importance of planning.

Sources: The information in this note was compiled from a variety of sources including ARAMARK's Public Information Office, the *University of Delaware Daily, Nation's Restaurant News*, and ARAMARK.com.

Formalized business planning is increasingly common in multiunit chains. A survey of chain food service executives revealed that nearly three-quarters of their companies made annual strategic plans with five-year future projections.[1]

A full-fledged plan is complex. A marketing plan, for instance, will contain a research summary, a statement of marketing goals, a statement of both **strategy** and **tactics** for achieving the plan's goals, and provision for measuring progress toward the plan's goals and for revising the plan if conditions change. It is important to

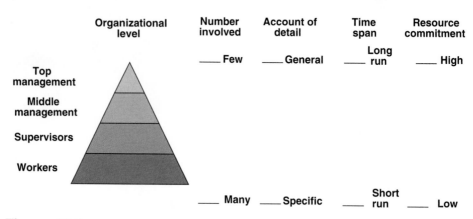

Figure 16.1
Dimensions of planning in organizations.

remember, though, that the banquet manager's plan of how to serve tomorrow's banquet is no less a plan, even if it is more straightforward.

SOME PLANNING CONCEPTS

The term planning denotes anticipating several different sets of circumstances for different purposes. Several other key concepts will help you fill out the idea of the planning process.

Policies are general guidelines for dealing with the future. They don't tell what to do; they indicate how to reach a decision. Policies leave much to the discretion of the decision maker. However, they provide a predetermined, agreed-upon basis for decisions.

Consider this example: The unit manager of a large chain of restaurants is approached every week for small contributions to local charities. The company's policy does not say what to give or whom to give to. Policy does say what general kinds of organizations can be considered, what the limits on the manager's discretion are, and what the maximum amount is that can be given each year. (The manager may be able to give, for instance, as much as $100 to a single organization without approval—but only if the total budget has not already been spent.) It is still up to the unit manager to gauge the situation and decide whether to make any particular donation and how much to give up to the maximum set by the guidelines of policy.

A plan is a reasoned means of moving toward some selected goal. A plan reflects policy and may include **rules**, **methods and procedures**, **standards**, and **budgets**. A plan may have both strategic and tactical elements.

The most comprehensive of plans may not be written down in one place. On the other hand, the operations manual of a well-run company is a useful example of a group of plans. Some companies, particularly larger ones, develop strategic plans over a long period; these plans express management's vision of the organization's future and elaborate goals, methods, budgets, and the like. Both these examples suggest that a full-fledged plan is complex. But your plan for tackling the week's work is no less a plan just because it is less complex. Complex or simple, a plan attempts to describe future events of whatever complexity in a way that shows how they will be ordered to achieve the organization's goals. Rules state what must be done (or must not be done) in a given situation. Rules leave no discretion in their execution. For example, the rule "Food production employees must wear hairnets in the kitchen" answers a question about one aspect of an employee's future behavior. Most companies have a rule that certain paperwork must be done before a new employee can go to work, receive a paycheck, or take a vacation.

Methods and procedures resemble rules. Methods indicate how a standard job is to be done. The method for performing a repetitive task may be determined by a food service operator with the help of industrial engineers. As a result of these studies, waste motions are minimized, and the time required is reduced to a minimum and standardized. Procedures are really a sequential set of rules. Most hotels have a procedure that specifies the process that a guest's records should go through during his or her stay—just as most health care institutions have a similar procedure for patient records.

Standards may specify both procedures and outcomes. For instance, a standard may dictate how a food product is to be purchased, such as calling for three quotes. Or a standard may dictate a predetermined figure such as a restaurant's food cost (as a percentage of food sales).

A budget is a numerical plan, generally expressed in dollars, although sometimes units of weight or time may be used as well. The budget specifies the dollar results expected from a plan of operation.

Most well-run operations prepare budgets that express in dollars the results they expect. Those budgets may be supported (in their estimates for housekeeping payroll, for instance) with a statement about hours budgeted at various levels of occupancy as a base for departmental payroll projections.

Strategy and tactics are concepts borrowed from the military to denote level of importance and time dimensions in plans. Strategy implies large-scale, high-level, and long-term commitment. In Figure 16.1, strategy would lie at the upper end of the pyramid. Tactics are often of great importance, but they are intended to implement the strategy. To give one set of examples of the difference between strategy and tactics, Taco Bell embarked on a diversification strategy. A further strategic decision Taco Bell took was that diversification would be accomplished by acquiring successful companies whose concepts were already a proven success rather than develop new concepts themselves. Finally, they determined that, once acquired, the companies (such as the drive-through chain Hot n' Now or Chevys, a Tex-Mex chain) would be expanded aggressively. [2] These were strategic decisions and, as such, concerned with overall goals (diversification and expansion) and the general means of achieving them (buy companies and grow them). Tactics, on the other hand, are specific, relating methods to individual circumstances. In this example, the question of where to expand a new concept or when and where to open a new store would be tactical decisions.

Goal Setting

Planning also includes **goal setting**. But how does one go about setting goals in organizations? Some traditionalists insist that we should already know what our goals are. For example, in answer to "A great hotel is . . . ," generally they fill in the blanks with a description of the way things have always been done. If we press them, however, we find they really don't intend to offer the same level of service as the "great hotel" offered a generation or two ago. In most operations, anyway, this goal is just not possible. Costs, particularly labor costs, have risen astronomically, and the supply of labor for some jobs has decreased to the vanishing point. So it turns out that what the traditionalist really proposes is for us to come as close as we can to "what we've always done."

The traditionalist's eyes, you see, are set firmly in the past. He or she defines what's to be done in terms of the standards derived from past experience. We, of course, do not argue that we can't learn from experience; we can and we must. The past, however, is not where one begins goal setting in a consumer-oriented society.

The logical place to begin goal setting is with the person who indirectly sets the goals: the guest. Accordingly, we should take a marketing approach to our operations.[3] If the needs and wants of the guests aren't met, they will take their business elsewhere. (If guests in a congregate meals program, on the other hand, don't like what they are served, they will complain to the agency, to their representative in Congress, or to the newspaper.)

Examine these examples of goals and see how they relate to the guests' needs and wants: Elaborate service requires highly skilled servers, an attentive maître d', and a large backup staff. This is great service, most restaurateurs would agree. However, we would never put it in a truck stop. The reasons are obvious but revealing.

Our guest at the truck stop wants a hearty meal of the kind of food he or she is used to. Correct classical service would seem "snooty." This guest wants friendly and fast service, simple food, and modest prices. Traditional forms of formal service may still be effective in some operations, but we can no longer assume uncritically that the traditional way is the only way. Moreover, we certainly cannot uncritically accept traditional forms of service as goals to strive for.

A field with close ties to hospitality, health care, presents an unusually interesting example of shaping products and services to guests' needs and wishes. For example, most hospitals now realize that the meals they serve their patients can, to an extraordinary degree, raise or lower the morale of those patients. For some, the meal may be nearly the only pleasant thing that happens to them all day. For this reason, many hospitals have begun to spend more effort and money on food service than would ordinarily be necessary. Providing special diets is, of course, an even more obvious example of how guests' needs determine service.

Guests' needs may, however, be only one of the goals to be met. Our society has made school systems largely responsible for feeding children their noon meal. In specifying the approved plan lunch requirements, the U.S. Food and Nutrition Service amplifies the young guest's goal (a good lunch) to include the need for the lunch to contain an adequate and balanced diet. The agency has yet a further goal mandated by Congress: nutrition education. A school must use the approved plan lunch to help teach young people what a balanced diet is. However, the school lunch manager must still design a menu that will appeal to the students, or else he or she will face complaints from the students and their parents.

CHARACTERISTICS OF WELL-THOUGHT-OUT GOALS

"Our goal is better service." That is the kind of statement to be wary of. Specifically, what does it mean? In the process of setting goals, we might better ask ourselves, "How will I know when I achieve the goal?"

Some people suggest a checklist nicknamed the "Five Ws and an H" to help a manager make sure that the issues have been examined from every angle:

Who

What

Where

When

Why

How

Perhaps most important, though, is to set objective and measurable goals: "How will I know when I get there?"

The front-desk staff of a motor hotel in the middle of a large city were criticized for being cold and impersonal. A number of unsuccessful "courtesy campaigns" were tried but had little effect—this front desk was very busy, and the clerks felt themselves under pressure during periods when customers were waiting in lines and the like. Finally, a clerk suggested that everybody adopt a rule: Always smile at the guest during your first words. Then a "police officer" was appointed to remind those who forgot. Within a week, the smile had become habit, and—just as that clerk thought—many of the guests responded with a smile, too. Overall, the interchange became much friendlier.

Goal: Be friendlier

Objective behavior: Smile

Measure: Informal inspection

A hotel that served mainly a business clientele felt that a fast breakfast service would attract guests. The guests at this hotel generally had appointments to keep and planes to catch. When management began to talk about fast service, though, it specified that "fast enough" was:

■ The guest gets a menu when he or she takes a seat.

■ The guest gets water and is offered coffee within two minutes.

■ The order is taken within three minutes (of seating) if he or she is in a hurry.

■ A "jiffy breakfast" will be served within six minutes (of seating) if a guest orders it.

From this list of specific goals, the hotel established seating procedures that tried to ensure that a server would arrive on the station or one of the two adjoining stations at the time of seating. (If there was no server, the host would detail a busperson to get water or coffee, or get it him- or herself.) Servers were prepared to take orders on the station next to theirs and turn over those orders to the appropriate person later. A special serving point (and procedure) was established in the kitchen for the jiffy breakfast.

Goal: Fast service

Objective behavior: Follow schedule

Measure: Management could (and did) time the service

Neither of these useful approaches would fit in every operation. In a small-town motor hotel with a fairly slow pace, the extreme effort on the part of employees to get a smile out of themselves wouldn't be needed. It might even make a nice friendly person look like a windup doll. In a resort hotel where guests come to relax, attentive service may be appropriate, but the hurry-up breakfast pattern would make them feel rushed. Our examples do not represent solutions; they represent goal-setting procedures that solve problems in such a way that we can tell when we have, in fact, reached a solution.

GOAL CONGRUENCE

In setting its goals, an organization should be realistic. If a service goal requires a server to lose tip income, we can expect the server, one way or another, to resist the goal. For example, restaurants sometimes promote their wine sales. Management reasons that the increased beverage check will increase tips. It urges the servers, "You really ought to want to sell wine." However, their procedure makes it difficult for a waitress to obtain a bottle of wine quickly for the guest because of inadequate stocking (and staffing) of the bar where the wine is kept. The server finds that he or she loses more in slow turnover and guest dissatisfaction because of delays in getting the wine that has been sold. Management cannot understand why the servers don't try to sell wine— "they really ought to." When people don't do what they "ought to," though, management should look at the system design to see what went wrong, rather than urge compliance because "you ought to want to."[4]

Management scholars often use the term "**goal congruence**." This term refers to the need to design and present an organization's goals in such a way that organizational goals and individual employee goals mesh rather than clash. Goals of different people in an organization should also fit the goals of the organization if maximum harmony and efficiency are to be achieved.

GOALS AND POLICIES

Once an organization has established its goals, it is ready to develop policies to implement them. Policies, you may recall, are general guidelines for dealing with the future. They leave much to the decision maker's discretion while providing a basis for reaching decisions.

There are goals at all levels of the organization, of course, but policies address goals that affect the entire organization; they have, in short, a significantly broad effect. In the hospitality industry, one major policy issue centers on guest self-service, an idea that arises largely from the goal of holding down costs and menu prices as much as possible in spite of rising wages, food costs, and utility bills. Eliminating or reducing the bell staff in motor hotels is one example of a policy decision; so is the increasing use of buffets and self-service salad bars. Once a company has established its policy on self-service, decisions on individual issues become clearer.

Companies often regard policies on unionization as especially important. Some companies set a goal of avoiding unionization and resist it by every legal means available, whereas others are indifferent to an organizing drive. A few companies actually encourage union representation. We take no position here on the pros and cons of a union. We merely point out that this illustrates how policy serves as a guide for action. In the three instances just cited, an incipient union-organizing drive would trigger three quite different reactions: a hurried and worried call to the home office, a yawn, or a friendly greeting.

As policies evolve, they call forth programs of action, strategies, and tactics to implement policy and achieve goals through action.

Planning in Operations

When management establishes goals and determines policies, its planning work has only begun. It needs a plan of action to specify how the policy will be implemented. Those two concepts borrowed from the military, strategy and tactics, distinguish between levels of plans. Strategy tells you where you want to go and why you want to get there. Tactics deal with how to get there.

Operational planning is critical no matter what the setting. (Courtesy of Sodexho.)

Strategic Issues

Strategy concerns long-range basic plans. Our discussion will focus on examples in three strategic areas out of many that could be chosen: product and service strategy, human-resources strategy, and community relations. These three areas conveniently illustrate how policy guides decisions and is implemented by both planning and action.

Product and Service Strategies. In food service, a menu is a plan; the general pattern of an operation's menus represents a strategy; and the customer you intend to reach dictates the strategy you will develop. Consider a steakhouse such as Steak and Ale. The menu reflects a policy of limited selection. This limited selection simplifies production and service. A strategy of self-service for salads represents a decision to give up portion control in return for the advantage of having the guests serve themselves. The advantages of the self-service are (1) the server has one less course to serve and (2) the guests can eat salad while their steaks are being cooked. A server can carry a larger station, and so fewer servers are needed. Moreover, the guest begins to eat sooner, the wait between courses is shorter, and table turns are more rapid. With faster turns, a restaurant can serve more guests during peak meal periods. The trade-off for portion control on salads is more than worth the advantages gained.

In a similar vein, McDonald's and other quick-service operators have chosen a menu strategy (developed a particular menu) that dictates most everything that takes place in their operation, from staff selection to layout and design. Similarly, the economy motel's product and service strategy defines the market it will aim for, the kind of building it will construct, and the size of its staff.

Human-Resource Strategies. We will briefly examine two important personnel-related issues to suggest the policies and strategies they dictate. Many companies wishing to avoid unionization use a compensation strategy that offers pay and fringe benefits well above union scale. In other cases, an aggressive compensation strategy may be adopted by a company not because of unionization but simply to help it hire the cream of the crop in its labor market.

Such a strategy dictates the rule that whenever the wage level in the local labor market rises, the company raises its wages. To follow this strategy, the company must initiate a procedure of regular wage surveys in the area.

Community Relations Strategies. Not surprisingly, different sectors of the hospitality industry court community favor in different ways. Let us look briefly at policy—and resulting strategy—in the commercial restaurant, hotel, health care, and school food service sectors.

The traditional way to offer the goods and services of a fast-food chain is to buy advertising in various media. Although a hotel or a local independent, high-quality restaurant may also purchase advertising, many of these kinds of operations rely more on public-relations activities. Thus, a local innkeeper may devote a great deal of time to public-service activities in order to build a favorable public image for the inn. This active public-relations strategy may differ from that of a nearby quick-service food operation that depends on advertising to bring the public through the door. The quick-service manager must spend his or her working time closely supervising operations; public relations may well be a minor part of the job.

In health care, it is usually just proprietary facilities that advertise, and even then, that advertising tends to be low-key. On the other hand, community hospitals actively involve themselves in public relations. Although they do not generally seek sales per se, hospitals do rely on periodic fund drives to raise capital for expansion or improvements. Thus, a favorable image in the community is helpful to them, too.

In recent years, the school lunch program has discovered that an active, interested group of supporters in the community can help them obtain the financial and moral support of the school board and school administrators. Consequently, a strategy of community involvement for school lunch managers dictates their being active with parent groups and other influential groups, especially those interested in nutrition in the community.

Each of these institutions—fast food, restaurant, hotel, hospital, and school lunch—needs financial support from the community in the form of sales, donations, or appropriations. Each has a policy of seeking community support, but their strategies differ according to the operational circumstances of each and the guests or clients they serve.

From Strategy to Tactics

Tactical issues are generally concerned more with short-range and localized actions. Like strategies, however, tactics are plans, the means of implementing policy.

In one high-occupancy chain hotel in a busy city, the property's marketing strategy was dictated by its franchise affiliation. This affiliation attracted the middle-income traveler who wanted comfortable accommodations but could not afford a luxury hotel. The property's downtown location gave it a special appeal to businesspeople. The manager realized, however, that a very large number of hotel rooms were being built in this market area. It became apparent that when all the properties under construction opened, the area would have an oversupply of rooms for several years to come. To prepare for this future marketing problem, the manager developed what was dubbed "FIRM Service."

A list of the largest firms in the area was compiled, and the hotel's sales representatives' work concentrated almost exclusively on these firms. At each of these firms, contact was established with one or more individuals who placed rooms business, and they were given a special number to call for reservations.

Furthermore, the manager instructed the front-office staff to hold a small number of rooms each day for FIRM Service accounts and to release them only as the house was filled. Only in exceptional circumstances was a FIRM Service request refused, and FIRM Service reservations were never "pulled" (canceled in the evening on the assumption the guest would not arrive).

The manager was too shrewd to assume that the property could keep business simply out of loyalty or gratitude; customers can be pretty fickle. What the manager did think—and rightly so—was that when the market became more competitive, the hotel's sales personnel would be in a good position to reach key people at important accounts in the community. This tactic cost practically nothing, and it dealt with the problem of heavy future competition by gaining an advantage in that local market, which seemed most promising.

The Individual Worker as Planner

If an operation is to be successful, individual workers must begin to consider themselves as planners. Notice the planning that a server automatically engages in when moving from kitchen to dining room and back. As the server steps out of the kitchen, the server quickly sums up the situation in the station: One of the three tables (Table A) has just been seated. A second party has finished its main course (Table B). A third party (Table C) is waiting for the dessert (which the server is carrying). The server's priorities might be as follows:

1. Serve dessert (Table C).
2. Greet and assure return while serving water (Table A).
3. Take dessert order (Table B).
4. Take appetizer and main course orders (Table A).
5. Return to kitchen.

As the server carries out this plan and heads back to the kitchen, she realizes that she also must plan her movements in the pantry to minimize wasted time and effort. On the way out of the dining room, she asks the busperson if he can clear Table B. With his assurance on that, she plans her moves in the kitchen:

1. Call dinner orders (for Table A).

2. Pick up appetizer (for Table A).

3. Pick up dessert (for Table B).

4. Return to dining room.

Her pattern is not necessarily the right way to handle a three-table station, and an actual situation would certainly not be this neat. The point is that a server relies heavily on planning, whether or not she is conscious of it.

When the head cook arrives at work at 8:00 A.M., she realizes that three meals confront her with immediate problems: Breakfast is now in progress and unusually busy. The short-order cook is in trouble because he's running out of his setup (raw food stored in a nearby refrigerator). The turkey on the menu for dinner needs to come out of the freezer right away. A round roast has to go in the oven immediately to be ready for an early banquet.

A great many different steps, the cook realizes, must be taken later in the day, but these immediate matters are of pressing concern. She takes these steps in order of priority and with a view to saving time and effort:

She enters the walk-in with a cart, steps into the adjacent freezer (which can be reached only from the walk-in), and places the turkeys on the cart. Back in the walk-in, she places the round on her cart. These actions delay her only a minute. Now she loads the bacon, sausage, and eggs the short-order cook needs and proceeds to the kitchen, giving the supplies to the short-order cook.

Her solution here may not be absolutely correct, but the incident should illustrate how essential planning is for that cook: Grab a cart so she can carry everything. Take one minute while she's in the walk-in to get the two other things she needs from there. While she is there, solve the breakfast cook's problem. It's going to be a busy day, so she shouldn't make three trips when one will do.

Not surprisingly, the hospitality industry rejects those management "experts" who assert that planning is exclusively a management function. Planning obviously pervades the well-run hospitality operation at all levels, from the housekeeper who checks the stock on his or her cart to the general manager who orchestrates all the planners he or she works with.

PLANNING AS A PERSONAL PROCESS

In Chapter 1, we discussed the notion of knowledge as retained earnings. We suggested that someone interested in a hospitality career can begin to accumulate useful learning experiences in the earliest, least-skilled jobs. Now it is time to reinforce that concept with the conviction that personal career goals need to be identified as early as possible (without an artificial forcing).

These goals may well dictate a policy of putting skill learning first and income second in choosing jobs while in college and perhaps for those first years out of college as well. This learn-first-earn-second strategy ensures practice. If income is more important (or essential), however, you may have to alter your strategy. Planning, policy, and strategy are not something somebody else does. No plan is more important to you than your own plan for yourself.

Long-Range Planning Tools

You can often plan for today and tomorrow "in your head." The situation may be simple enough for you to grasp intuitively. However, when you make decisions that will have an effect for months or years, you need more sophisticated planning tools. These tools are usually considered at some length in courses on management accounting and finance. Moreover, we might properly include them in a later chapter on control. We will discuss them here, however, in order to emphasize the quantitative side of planning.

Planning is carried out at every level of the organization. (Courtesy of Sodexho.)

RETURN ON INVESTMENT

When an organization makes an investment, it generally expects to earn that investment back within some definite period. Take the following simple situation: A new vacuum sweeper for use in public areas costs $2,000. The larger machine is more efficient, and it reduces the number of hours required to vacuum the area from 100 a month to 90. If the operator's time costs $8 per hour, we can calculate two crude measures of value, and these measurements are common, simple decision aids. They are called the **payback period** and the **return on investment**. A useful formula is

$$P = \text{Payback period}$$
$$OS = \text{Operating savings}$$
$$NI = \text{Net investment}$$
$$P = \frac{NI}{OS}$$

For our problem

$$OS = 10 \text{ hours} \times \$8 = \$80 \text{ per month}$$

and

$$P = \frac{\$2000}{\$80 \text{ month}}$$
$$P = 25 \text{ months}$$

Notice that we have specified the monthly savings, so the payback period is also expressed in months. These calculations tell us whether we can plan on this investment paying for itself in a reasonable period of time.

Another way of analyzing this problem is to determine the return on investment (ROI). Here, we just invert our formula, but the results are usually expressed in annual terms, and so the monthly savings in the previous problem are multiplied by 12.

$$ROI = \frac{OS}{NI} = \frac{\$960.00}{\$2,000}$$
$$= 0.48 \text{ or } 48\%$$

In a business in which money to invest is at a premium and many departments require funds for new equipment, these techniques give us the means to establish investment priorities. Most organizations have specific rules for investments that relate to return on investment. Thus, these calculations help to consider the purchase in the context of those rules, sometimes called hurdle rates. (The word hurdle is adopted from the track-and-field sports scene. The hurdle is something you have to be able to reach or surpass, much as a runner must clear the hurdle in a race.)

In more complex cases, a time-adjusted **rate of return** may be used as the hurdle. This tool recognizes that a dollar today is worth more than a dollar will be a year from now because of the interest today's dollar can earn in a bank. The interest rate (called in these problems the discount rate) can be changed to reflect varying costs of capital and risk assumptions.

Another common quantitative planning tool is the **break-even point** computation. This technique is similar to the payback period method. Suppose a new banquet room is proposed. Management expects the banquet check average to be $9 and the banquet check food costs to be 33 percent. All other costs of the proposed banquet department are fixed. If the fixed costs (the monthly payroll; heat, light, and power; depreciation; and so forth) for this room amount to $15,000, how many banquet covers must be sold per month to cover the cost of the banquet room (in other words, to break even)? Our new formula follows:

$$
\begin{aligned}
\text{BEP} &= \text{Break-even point} \\
\text{MR} &= \text{Marginal revenue (revenue less variable cost)} \\
\text{FC} &= \text{Fixed costs (the costs that will occur regardless of} \\
&\qquad \text{volume of sales if the decision is made to go ahead)} \\
\text{S} &= \text{Sales} \\
\text{VC} &= \text{Variable cost} \\
\text{MR} &= \text{S} - \text{VC} = \$9 - \$3 = \$6 \\
\text{BEP} &= \frac{\text{FC}}{\text{MR}} = \frac{\$15,000}{\$6.00} \\
&= 2,500 \text{ meals}
\end{aligned}
$$

Thus, 2,500 meals per month will cover all costs for this room. Management can now plan whether or not to build this room on the basis of its judgment about the number of meals it will probably serve.

COST-BENEFIT ANALYSIS

In business, the measure of dollar profit earned is not just useful—it is the principal decision-making guide. In school lunch or congregate feeding, however, such a measure is not enough. To begin with, revenue from guests is not always a significant factor, because the cost of the program is covered by government funds. The program's goal is not to earn a profit. Moreover, the decisions cannot always be measured in dollars. (In school lunch, how much is a hungry child worth?)

Although the variables cannot all be measured in dollars, a first step in **cost-benefit analysis** (or **cost-effectiveness analysis**) is to make explicit those costs and savings that can be identified.

Suppose a congregate meals program is trying to decide whether to use 20 small feeding sites distributed throughout the county or to transport all its clients to a central point. The costs and savings to be specified would include the savings in food production and service staff in the central location and the reduction in food distribution expense (trucking food to 20 sites), in contrast with the cost of transporting clients to a central site.

Once this calculation is done, however, it is still necessary to weigh the possibility that some aged clients might not feel up to the long trip and that others might feel uncomfortable in a strange neighborhood. For these reasons, participation might decline. These problems would actually reduce costs and subsidies, but that is hardly what the staff wants! Planning in the public sector is sometimes more complicated than in private business, because not all costs and benefits have dollar values. Public programs, however, must still do their homework so they can report what cost effects result from changes in plans.

Goals and policies provide the basis for developing plans, both strategic and tactical. As the goals addressed relate to longer periods, however, those responsible for planning cannot rely on intuition. They must use more formal and often complex means of analysis.

To conclude, planning, strategy, and tactics are important at every level of the organization. At the top levels of the organization, leaders must plan for action—taking into consideration various expectations and the possibility of unforeseen events. As one final example, a recent report by the Conference Board asked several industry leaders about their top challenges and priorities in the upcoming years. Not surprisingly, many of them were directly related to planning and corporate strategy including: (1) sustained and steady top-line growth; (2) profit growth; (3) consistent execution of strategy by top management; (4) speed, flexibility, and adaptability to change and; (5) and customer loyatly and retention.[5]

Summary

Planning in organizations was the principal topic of this chapter. We first explained the reasons for planning and its different levels.

We defined and described several planning concepts: policies, plans, rules, methods, procedures, standards, budgets, strategies, and tactics.

Next, we discussed goal setting, and after defining and illustrating it, we turned to some of the subsets of goals. These included the characteristics of well-thought-out goals, goal congruence, and goals and policies.

Planning in operations requires strategy and tactics. We considered product and service strategies, human-resources strategies, and community relations strategies. We then gave an example of successful tactics.

The last section covered the individual worker as a planner, which we illustrated with examples of a server and a cook. We ended with a short discussion of planning as part of career preparation.

The long-term planning tools we explored were return on capital and cost-benefit analysis.

Key Words and Concepts

Planning	Goal congruence
Strategy	Payback period
Tactics	Return on investment (ROI)
Policies	Rate of return
Rules	Break-even point
Methods and procedures	Cost-benefit analysis
Standards	Cost-effectiveness analysis
Budgets	
Goal setting	

Review Questions

1. Outline some of the reasons why you should study planning.
2. Define policies, plans, rules, methods, procedures, standards, budgets, strategies, and tactics.
3. What are the five questions that might be asked when setting goals?
4. What does goal congruence mean? What is the importance of this concept?
5. Is planning part of your study habits? Explain.

Internet Exercises

1. **Site name:** Starwood Hotels & Resorts Worldwide, Inc.
   URL: www.starwood.com/corporate/company_info.html
   Background information: Starwood is one of the world's largest hotel and leisure companies. The company's brand names include St. Regis, The Luxury Collection,

Sheraton, Westin, W, and Four Points by Sheraton. Through these brands, Starwood is well represented in most major markets around the world. The company's operations are grouped into two business segments, hotels and vacation ownership operations.

Exercises:

a. What are the goals and objectives (business strategy) of Starwood?

b. What are their competitive strengths?

c. Is there goal congruence (organizational goals and individual employee goals mesh rather than clash) at Starwood?

2. **Site name:** Accor

   URL: www.accor.com/gb/groupe/accueil.asp

   Background information: With 158,000 associates in 140 countries, Accor is the European leader and one of the world's largest groups in travel, tourism, and corporate services, with two major international activities: Hotels and Services.

   Exercises: Compare the Accor and Starwood Web sites

   a. Which company provides more information on its goals and objectives?

   b. Which company identifies their role in employee and community relations as part of their business strategy?

   c. Since environmental issues are very important, what plans do these companies have to sustain the environment?

3. **Site name:** Alliance for Nonprofit Management

   URL: www.allianceonline.org/FAQ/strategic_planning

   Background information: The Alliance for Nonprofit Management is the professional association of individuals and organizations devoted to improving the management and governance capacity of nonprofits. The alliance is dedicated to assisting nonprofits in fulfilling their missions.

   Note: Nonprofit organizations are private organizations whose primary objective is to benefit their members or people within society by supporting an issue of private interest or other endeavor for the public good. Even though their mission is not to generate a profit, all the functions of management still apply because nonprofits must still generate income to meet their expenses. Among the many nonprofit organizations related to hospitality are the following: Chefs for Humanity (www.chefsforhumanity.org), Share Our Strength (www.strength.org), Meals on Wheels (www.mowaa.org), and City Harvest (www.cityharvest.org).

   Site name: The Free Management Library: Planning in Organizations

   URL: www.managementhelp.org/plan_dec/plan_dec.htm

   Background information: The Free Management Library provides easy-to-access, clutter-free, comprehensive resources regarding the leadership and management of yourself, other individuals, groups, and organizations. The content is relevant to the vast majority of people, whether they are in large or small for-profit or non-profit organizations. Over the past ten years, the library has grown to be one of the world's largest and best-organized collections of these types of resources.

Site name: QuickMBA

URL: www.quickmba.com/strategy/strategic-planning/

Background information: QuickMBA is an online knowledge resource for business administration. The goal is to help you to quickly find the business knowledge you need, when you need it, wherever you may be. Topics are presented as frameworks and summaries in the various subjects of business administration, as taught in the world's top MBA programs.

Exercise:

a. Choose one of the "chapters" on any of the three Web sites above that is of interest to you. Lead a class discussion on the management function of "planning" in an organization and describe why this information would be important to a hospitality manager.

Notes

1. Bryan G. Herron, "Strategic Planners or Restaurateurs...One and the Same?" Proceedings of the 12th Annual Chain Operators Exchange (Chicago: International Foodservice Manufacturers Association, 1985).
2. Wall Street Journal, May 14, 1993, p. B4. and May 19, 1994, p. B6.
3. For the best statement of this point of view, please see Peter Drucker's work, particularly *Management: Tasks, Responsibilities, Practices* (New York, Harper & Row, 1974).
4. For an excellent and witty discussion on this point, see Robert Mager and Peter Pipe, *Analyzing Performance Problems or You Really Oughta Wanna* ((Belmont, CA: Fearon Publishers, 1970).
5. CEO Challenge 2006, Conference Board of Canada, June 2006.

The Hospitality Industry

(Courtesy of Honeywell, Inc.)

CHAPTER SEVENTEEN

Organizing in Hospitality Management

The Purpose of this Chapter

This chapter discusses the way people come together to work, an enjoyable and interesting subject. In a "society of institutions," to use Peter Drucker's words, knowing how institutions get put together can also help guide both work and life. Working relationships are rarely arbitrary. Moreover, an understanding of the limits of authority—and the limits on accepting authority—is essential to someone building a career in managing and supervising others. We are all on the receiving end of organizational decisions and the exercise of authority from time to time. So the basic argument is that understanding how management organizes will help you polish your hospitality management skills.

THIS CHAPTER SHOULD HELP YOU

1. Explain how a manager should respond to the leadership of informal work organizations within a formal work group.

2. Name two sources of authority within the workplace, explain them, and state their limits.

3. List five common bases for dividing work into organizational units/departments, and name a specific segment of the hospitality industry likely to use each basis.

4. Describe line management and staff assistance functions, and explain the differences in authority that each exercises.

5. Explain the advantages and disadvantages of the following elements of organization theory and practice: the roles of committees, bureaucracy, and the one-boss theory.

Authority: The Cement of Organizations

What is a real emergency? Except in organizations set up specifically to deal with them (fire companies and ambulance crews, for example), emergencies are nonroutine, serious situations in which nobody knows for certain what to do. Some people shout orders, others run toward the door, and still others do whatever seems best to deal with the problem. To try to achieve results without organization is to invite a permanent emergency.

Organization is necessary to any operation. A small restaurant or motel needs only the simplest of organizations (and, in fact, it may seem that small operations have established no real organization at all). You will recall from Chapter 5, however, that small restaurants have been declining in significance in the market, and the same is true of small motels. Your future, therefore, will probably involve work in an organization of some complexity, such as a hotel, convention center, restaurant chain, or hospital. Although we will discuss organizing principally from the perspective of the larger organizations in our industry, our discussion applies in a general way to the smallest organizations as well. When we feel special solutions to organizing problems are useful, we will identify and discuss these solutions.

Before we begin, here is a definition of the organizing function in management: Organizing is the work managers do to bring order to the relations between people and work as well as among the various people at work.

Organization charts sometimes give the impression that the company just fits together in that way. In fact, for any group to function, it must have authority at several levels to make it come together and stay together.

THE BASIS OF AUTHORITY

Formal **authority** has its basis in law, but there are limits placed on that authority by the way that people in the work group perceive the organization and their relation to it.

The Legal Basis for Authority. Laws and the **legal system** imply a community's potential use of force to maintain order. In our society, private property is a central social institution; in the business firm, the basic rationalization for management has been ownership. In the small firm, in effect, authority is often based on this notion: "I own this company and have the right to control my property. If you want to work here, you'll have to do as I say."

In the large corporation, the line of reasoning is more complex (stockholders elect a board, the board hires a top manager, the top manager delegates authority to subordinates). However, the essence of it is simply "I represent ownership" instead of "I own."

Franchise organizations present a more complicated case. The franchisor undoubtedly has a legal right to enforce agreed-upon procedures and quality standards with its franchisees. Franchise organizations, however, rely more on persuasion, advice, and peer pressure (from other franchisees) to maintain standards. In fact, only a very small proportion of franchisees have their franchises terminated for unsatisfactory operations. Moreover, introducing change in a franchise organization, except in matters clearly spelled out in the franchise agreement, is possible only through negotiation and persuasion. Often, the persuasion is based on the fact that the franchisee would be better off with whatever change is desired. As you can see, the mutual interest of all franchisees is a strong force that parallels the legal rights inherent in the franchisor's authority.

In governmental activities such as school lunch programs and congregate feeding, the basis of authority is legislative activity exercised by the duly elected representatives of the people. The enabling legislation authorizes the activity, together with periodic appropriation legislation that specifies the amount of money available and how it can be spent.

In either the company or a public agency, there lies behind the manager's order the ultimate force of authority of the law. When the boss says, "You're fired," he or she can call on public authority to back up this position. The same is ultimately true for a franchisor's regulation: Failure to comply will result in termination of the franchise. Although the law is the ultimate basis of formal authority (and some such fundamental basis is undoubtedly necessary to give stability to social institutions), constant resort to the law is not an effective tool for getting people to do things on an everyday basis. A sure sign of a weak, inadequate manager is the repeated use of social force ("You do it or I'll fire you").

Acceptance as a Basis for Authority. Subordinates can undermine a manager's authority in all kinds of subtle ways. In a rich society, the simplest way is to quit and get another job. Of course, an employee can stay and simply ignore orders whenever the manager's back is turned. These two approaches are by no means rare in the hospitality industry. Thus, to gain the employees' support, a supervisor or manager must win their acceptance of his or her authority and the employees' recognition that he or she is a person qualified for responsibility. In the hospitality industry, this acceptance generally means, first of all, credibility as a person qualified in the work the employees themselves do. An illustration from the personal experience of one of the authors may help:

> Unfortunately, I can't cook. This hasn't usually been a problem, as I've generally had a qualified food production supervisor to work with. I was once hired, however, as general manager to replace a man who had been promoted. On arriving at work, I learned that

1. The restaurant manager had just been fired.

2. The general manager was staying on "for a while."

3. I was the new restaurant manager.

4. I could take over as general manager as soon as the restaurant, which had been losing $16,000 on average each month since it opened, became profitable.

All of this came as a surprise, but I wasn't too concerned, as much of my experience had been in food service management. The problem I did have, however, was that there was no kitchen organization—just some cooks, with no one in particular in charge! I knew there was no way I could supervise those cooks because I didn't know enough about their work to be credible to them. I'd have been laughed out of the kitchen.

Fortunately, I was able to find a retired chef willing to help me out for a few weeks. I could explain to him what results I wanted—hours of service, menus, price ranges, and so forth—and he could interpret this need into specific directions for the cooks. Without the necessary credibility, in short, I needed an intermediary.

Aside from being another good argument for wide professional experience, this story illustrates the need, in a complex organization, for supervisors whose authority is acceptable to the work group. It would be equally difficult to supervise a front-office staff's work without any understanding of the technical aspects of what clerks do. Supervisors don't have to be experts, but they do require a sufficient familiarity with the work to "speak the language" and understand what is happening.

This principle does not apply just to the skilled workstations. Anyone who has ever seen an executive housekeeper whom the room attendants thought of as "too good to get his or her hands dirty" or a restaurant manager who couldn't, in an emergency, help out in the dish room or bus a few dishes knows how difficult this detachment makes their work with their subordinates.

Informal Organizations. Sociologists who study work groups note that right alongside the formal organization established by management is an informal social organization that grows up within the work groups. This **informal organization** usually has a leader who is consciously or unconsciously recognized by the group. The group develops its own expectations (norms) on what constitutes a fair day's work. And it develops an informal way of ranking its members (a status system). An insecure manager can feel threatened by an informal work group like this. The experienced manager or supervisor comes to accept the work group as a part of the natural order

Authority that is based on competence and the acceptance of others is the strongest kind of authority. (Courtesy of Sodexho.)

of things, like sunrise and sunset. He or she should establish working relations with this informal structure to ensure that the work at hand gets done. Most of all, the experienced manager realizes that the informal group constitutes a real limitation on his or her formal authority.

AUTHORITY AND RESPONSIBILITY

It is an axiom of organizational theory that the manager can be rightly held responsible for results only as far as his or her effective authority extends. For instance, you may recall from Chapter 10 that the uniform system of accounts for hotels records income and costs, so each manager is held responsible for results in the area that he or she controls. The innkeeper, for instance, is not responsible for capital costs because these costs reflect decisions made by the owners at the time of the construction or purchase of the property.

AUTHORITY: A SUMMARY

The effective manager seeks to establish authority on the basis of competence acknowledged by the people he or she works with. The experienced manager accepts the social nature of a work group and learns to work effectively with its informal leaders. The ultimate basis of authority, however, lies in the legal reality of ownership or legislative authorization. The effective manager, though, has little need to rely on these fundamental sources of authority.

Departmentalization

For work to be done in complex organizations, these organizations must divide authority according to some logical basis. One manager cannot, after all, do everything. This division of authority is called *delegation*. Sometimes, as can be seen in Case History 17.1, it becomes necessary to rearrange authority relationships to meet new circumstances.

We turn now to a discussion of **delegation**, which is necessary before we can properly understand **departmentalization**.

THE DELEGATION OF AUTHORITY

In formal organizations, authority must be shared. Management scholars assert that authority must extend in an uninterrupted scale, or series of steps, from the top to the bottom of an organization—a concept known as the scalar principle. Responsibility is accepted at each level, and in turn, some authority is delegated to the next lower level. Although authority certainly can be delegated, most management scholars agree that responsibility cannot. That is, if something goes wrong because of a subordinate's error, the boss still must take responsibility along with the subordinate.

The scalar principle has been defined in one authoritative text as follows:

> The more clear the line of authority from the ultimate authority for management in an enterprise to every subordinate position, the more effective will be responsible decision making and organized communication.[1]

The delegation of authority may not be particularly important in small organizations in which management works closely with workers and can exercise control through actual participation. However, in larger, more complex organizations such as a hotel or hospital, a large restaurant, or a school district made up of many lunch programs, delegation becomes necessary just to get the work done. For instance, a hotel manager cannot simultaneously direct housekeeping, the front office, and the kitchen. Thus, senior managers must delegate authority to subordinate managers, that is, managers below them in the scale.

Delegation is necessary to get the work done. A second, less obvious reason for delegating authority is to develop management talent in the organization. As people leave for other jobs or enter retirement, the organization must keep up with the turnover. New positions are created, too, because organizations seek to expand. Most companies like to draw on their own employees to fill these openings. A third, related benefit that comes from having junior management and supervisory jobs in an organization is to

Reorganization in a Multibrand Company

When Jon Luther was appointed the new CEO of Allied Domecq Quick Service Restaurants (ADQSR), one of the first things that he did was to change the way that the company was organized to better suit corporate objectives. Allied Domecq QSR is a division of Allied Domecq PLC, a global food and beverage company based in the United Kingdom. ADQSR has three concepts for which Luther oversees—Dunkin' Donuts, Baskin-Robbins, and Togo's. One of the strengths of the company is considered to be the synergies that the different concepts have with one another, since they each command a separate "day part." Luther was attracted to the new position, after years with Popeyes, largely because of the portfolio of concepts and the potential to make them work together as larger units. This has resulted in "combos" or even "trombos," where the different brands are situated together.

The organizational changes Luther made were at both the corporate level as well as among the concepts. At the corporate level, Luther created a "leadership team" of 15 executives whose responsibilities it is to oversee ADQSR's business strategy, operational excellence, and concept and menu development.[1] Among other things, the team is charged with reenergizing the concepts and growing the company, focusing on new markets. Changes were also made with the way that the different concepts were managed—from a market-based organization to a brand-based organization. The company is now divided into domestic and international divisions, and within each of those there are "concept officers" for each of the three brands.

This latest reorganization reminds us that a company's form of organization is, in many ways, a management tool, and as such, it is open to change in order to achieve a particular result. In this case, each brand needs its own development, and so a centralized organization is less appropriate than one that gives the people responsible for each brand more opportunity to innovate.

1. Source: "Allied Domecq Quick Service Restaurants Names Executive Team to Lead Newly Restructured Organization," Press Release, September 17, 2003.

keep bright, eager employees engaged and excited about their work by assigning them increased responsibility.

Unfortunately, many people have trouble delegating authority. This is especially true of people such as chefs or dining room supervisors, who may have begun their working life as skilled workers, in this case as a cook or server. They are used to doing the job themselves, and they find it difficult to turn the work over to somebody else.

The fact is, when a manager delegates a task, it is sometimes done incorrectly. The newly promoted supervisor who is skilled in the work at hand becomes very frustrated. He or she may feel "it's easier to do it myself." In the very short run—dealing with just one task—the supervisor is correct in that feeling. The reason for delegation, though, is the multiplicity of tasks that confront the work group for which the supervisor is responsible. Although any one task may be easier to do oneself, it's literally impossible for one person to do all of them. To get all the work done (with high average standards but probably some tolerance for error), the supervisor must delegate and concentrate his or her efforts on developing the competence of the work group.

SPAN OF CONTROL

An early management scholar, V. A. Graicunas, attempted to develop a mathematical approach to determine how many people a manager can supervise directly. This span of control, Graicunas thought, was stretched taut by the increasing number of relationships between manager and subordinate, between subordinate and subordinate, and between manager and various combinations of subordinates. The number of relationships rises rapidly, as Table 17.1 shows.

Although the number of subordinates reporting to a manager cannot really be stated precisely, some management scholars assert that the ideal lies between three and eight subordinates. The exact number that a manager may supervise depends on the complexity of the work itself, the ability and training level of the subordinates, and the ability of the manager.

This concept of **span of managerial responsibility** is related to Graicunas' **span of control**, which refers to the number of people the manager supervises directly. The span of managerial responsibility, on the other hand, refers to the number of persons with whom the manager routinely interacts, that is, the number who have direct and unhindered access to the manager. For instance, a hotel manager may have a food and beverage manager, a rooms department manager, a sales manager, a chief engineer, and a comptroller, all of whom report directly to him or her. In addition to these five, the manager may routinely consult with supervisors one or two levels below. He or she might discuss problems with a hostess, or the banquet chef, or one of the housekeeping inspectors. These people may feel quite free to consult with the general manager personally if a problem arises. Even at the top of a very large organization, consultation and interaction extend beyond the span of control. Examples abound in our industry regarding executives who visit their units from corporate headquarters, to connect with employees, managers, franchisees, and customers.

For most hospitality organizations, span of managerial responsibility is as important a concept as span

TABLE 17.1

Increase in Relationships

NUMBER OF SUBORDINATES	NUMBER OF RELATIONSHIPS
1	1
2	6
3	18
4	44
5	100
6	222
7	490
8	1,080
9	2,376

of control. Span of control refers to formal reporting relationships, but hospitality organizations tend to develop important informal supervisor-subordinate relationships that don't fit the narrow span-of-control concept.

The principle of unity of command dictates that everyone has just one boss. This notion is generally sound, but as the discussion in the preceding paragraph indicates, reality is a good deal more complicated. In the hospitality industry, unity of command generally means that a manager does not routinely interfere in the workings of a subordinate's department. Rather, he or she discusses problems with the department head and lets that person take any remedial action necessary. When a serious problem of guest satisfaction or some other emergency arises, however, rules often are put aside, and the manager may intervene directly. It should be noted at this point that the "span of control" as it applies to the hospitality industry is being reevaluated. Many companies are increasing the number of subordinates that a manager oversees—the increased number of units supervised by area managers of certain restaurant chains is perhaps the best example of this.

BASES FOR DEPARTMENTALIZATION

There are five common bases for dividing the work (and the authority over the work) into departments: function, product or service, geography, customers, and process. The hospitality industry uses each of these departmental divisions. Function and product are the most common bases of departmentalization at the operating level, whereas territory and customer are the most common at the corporate level. A short discussion of each basis follows.

- *Function.* The clearest example of functional departmentalization is found in food service, in which each functional department performs a different kind of work. Thus, the restaurant may be divided into service, food preparation, and sanitation. The kitchen may be further divided into such stations as meats, salads, and desserts. The organization of a restaurant, which we discussed earlier, is a good example of functional organization at the unit level.

- *Product or service.* Hotels are divided into quite different product-service units, each with its own expertise. The most obvious divisions are between rooms, food and beverage, telephone, and other departments (for instance, garage). Below that level, however, functional division is the rule.

- *Geography.* In restaurant and hotel chains, it is common to assign supervisory responsibility for the operations in a particular region to a single manager. For example, Shoney's area supervisors have a geographic area of responsibility. In school lunch, in which each lunch program is located in a separate school, geographic divisions make one manager responsible for each unit.

- *Customers.* Some companies that operate in several different hospitality business areas divide their operations by customer type. For instance, ARAMARK groups much of its food service by customer. The Business Services division serves B&I dining, vending, and coffee services accounts. The Campus Services division services college and university food service, while the School Support Services provides services to schools. Other divisions are devoted to health care, stadiums, arenas, convention centers, conference centers, parks and resorts, and correctional facilities.

- *Process.* Many large hotels divide their food and beverage activities into a restaurant department, a bar department, and a banquet department because the preparation and service in these three areas can involve such different processes.

No one set of these departments represents the "best" means of division. What is important is that authority and responsibility be divided in a way that suits the particular needs of the market being served and the organization doing the work. We should note, too, that smaller organizations may not identify formal departments at all. In a small motor hotel, for example, the manager may serve as sales manager and personnel manager and take operational responsibility in the rooms or food and beverage department as well. Nevertheless, as different functions are performed, the manager—and other "double-duty" management people—realizes the need to shift gears and call different skills and styles into play. Organizational people who serve in multiple roles sometimes lament their unpredictable existences. However, they also tend to enjoy the recognition that attends their ability to get several different jobs done.

Line and Staff

LINE MANAGEMENT

Line authority is closely related to the ideas inherent in the scalar principle. Line authority passes from one operations person to another in a direct line from the top of the organization to the bottom. The rooms manager reports to the general manager. The hostess, food production manager, and banquet manager report to the food and beverage manager and, in turn, oversee subordinate supervisors and workers, as shown in Figure 17.1. A direct, unbroken line of authority runs from, say, a banquet server to the general manager. The work of line people directly affects guest service at all levels. Moreover, **line management** is the preponderant managerial role in the hospitality industry.

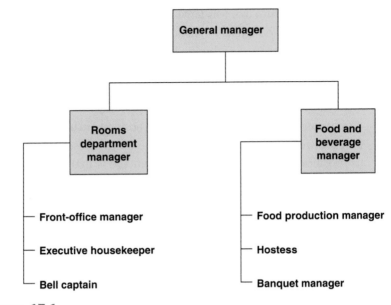

Figure 17.1
Line organization in a hotel.

STAFF SUPPORT

Staff roles were originally limited to providing specialized assistance to line managers. Staff people, in effect, service the people who serve the guest. The staff person's special expertise is important, but a number of related kinds of staff activities have also become common.

The Advisor. The human-resources manager and comptroller are two good examples of advisory staff positions in the hospitality industry. They have specialized knowledge about their area of work—wage-and-hour laws or accounting procedures, for instance—that the line manager they report to can and should call upon. Each of these persons also acts for the manager in his or her area of specialty; that is, these staff people not only give a manager their expert advice, but they also act for him or her and for other line people by interviewing and screening applicants or maintaining accounting records. In these acts, however, they function as representatives of the manager, and they amplify the manager's ability in a specialized field.

Staff Service. The purchasing manager, like other staff people, renders a service to the line departments rather than directly to the guests. Similarly, the engineering department assists the line departments in maintaining the physical systems necessary to the guests' comfort.

The "Assistants to." In large properties or at the corporate level, senior executives commonly designate a person as, for instance, the assistant to the manager. This person has no specific authority, but he or she assists the manager with any project requiring special attention. Persons in such jobs are not mere errand runners. The "assistant to" slot is often used to train rising young managers, and they are commonly given fairly wide-ranging (if temporary) authority for completing any project to which they are assigned. Because people in this position are usually junior to those with whom they are working, while at the same time they represent high authority, the "assistant to" position requires great tact. Its advantage is that it expands the capacity of the senior executive because it equips him or her with a trusted, able assistant who can pursue details closely and report back. Moreover, as we just suggested, it can be a valuable training slot.

The Staff as Boss. A staff person exercises authority in two kinds of situations. When the comptroller or chief engineer directs his or her subordinates in tasks, the authority exercised is clearly identical with line authority. Beyond that, as we shall see shortly, staff people are sometimes given "functional authority" over line people. Thus, the comptroller may direct the dining room cashiers (who regularly report to the hostess) in how to complete a new form. Similarly, the human-resources manager may issue a directive to all departments laying out the procedures for handling grievances. This functional authority amplifies the competence of the line, but it sometimes creates confusion.

The Staff in the Small Organization. In a small organization, the staff work may consist of part-time jobs assigned to regular employees, or it may be handled by outside specialists who provide services as needed. For instance, a 100-room motor hotel probably cannot afford a comptroller, chief engineer, or personnel manager. That property will, however, probably retain a firm of auditors to inspect its books regularly and develop an internal controls manual. Maintenance may consist of routine work done by a handyman, with the expert service of plumbers, refrigeration specialists, heating contractors, and so forth called in as needed. Finally, the general manager, his or her secretary, or some other key person probably handles the personnel work.

Issues in Organizing

Lest the student consider organization a cut-and-dried matter, we should examine some of the areas of organization theory that are, more than most, unsettled. Because each of these areas also sheds light on special problems in hospitality organizations, this section will serve the dual purpose of explaining theory and increasing your understanding of practice.

FUNCTIONAL STAFF AUTHORITY

We mentioned that organizations sometimes authorize staff people to give orders across the entire organization within their special field of expertise. To illustrate the value— and some of the difficulties—of this practice, consider the problems of a chain hotel organization.

Figure 17.2 illustrates the organization of this chain at the corporate level and the organization of a typical unit within the chain at the operating level. As the figure shows, one vice president is "in the line." The vice president for operations is charged with overseeing all properties, and the general manager of each hotel reports to him or her directly.

There are five other vice presidents. These officers are specialists in the field of marketing, engineering, food and beverage, finance, and human resources; each is responsible for developing programs in his or her respective area.

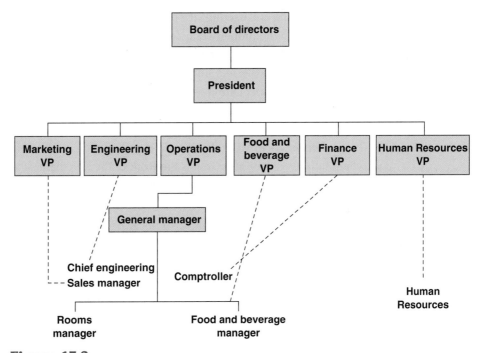

Figure 17.2
A hotel chain organization chart.

The work of the corporate marketing vice president, for instance, includes developing the company's advertising program and directing its national sales office. The engineering vice president develops energy conservation measures and commands a small, highly technical staff. The vice president for food and beverage is an expert in that area of operations. He or she serves as a combination inspector, troubleshooter, and consultant in matters pertaining to food and beverage. The financial vice president oversees the company's accounting. The human-resources officer is concerned with companywide compensation and fringe-benefit policies and monitors changes in legislation affecting employment and work practices.

Notice that each of these staff vice presidents is connected by a dotted line to a function of management at the unit level. This line indicates that each exercises staff supervision or functional staff authority over his or her special fields of work at the unit level. Now, who does the hotel's accountant work for? Does he or she have two bosses? The answer to this question for each of these dotted-line relationships, as they are sometimes called, depends on a number of factors.

First, the relationship is essentially technical. A new financial reporting procedure may be developed, and directions for implementing it may come from the vice president. Notice, however, that it is a fairly narrow, specialized exercise of authority.

Second, the staff supervisory activity varies in intensity with both the function and the circumstance. The engineering vice president, for instance, probably interacts with the chief engineer at the property only infrequently, as, for example, when some new piece of equipment is installed or a new energy control procedure is developed. Most of the chief engineer's work in a hotel is routine, although the work of the vice president is almost entirely specialized and technical. On the other hand, if a major renovation of the hotel is undertaken, the engineering vice president would work much more closely with the property.

The human-resources vice president does not tell the local human resources manager whom to interview or hire. That is the work of the line managers at the property. On the other hand, the vice president will take an interest in the hiring process as it relates to complying with law, as in fair-employment practices.

The possibilities of mixed loyalties on the general manager's staff and of clashes between general manager and staff vice presidents are remote, but clearly these relationships call for tact. The disadvantages that accompany these blurred lines of authority are more than offset by the top-quality expertise made available. The hospitality industry is becoming too complex a business to do without such an expert staff.

One area in which staff supervision has proved uncommonly difficult is food and beverage. This area really involves a line function; therefore, a number of companies have eliminated staff supervision in this area, leaving it entirely in the hands of the general manager.

Independent operators avail themselves of various kinds of expert advice. We noted some of them earlier: an accountant, an attorney, specialized engineering people. The manager of the operation must often achieve the necessary expertise to act as a staff specialist in some areas, particularly marketing. Many a general manager has been heard to remark, "I'm wearing my sales manager's hat today." In fact, hotel general managers often join the Hospitality Sales and Marketing Association International specifically for this reason.

INCREASING THE SPAN OF CONTROL: EMPOWERING MANAGERS

Only a generation ago, a leading French management writer, Jean Jacques Servan-Schreiber, pointed out that one of the major factors in the success of American companies was their more fully developed organization structure.[2] Companies in the United States had more supervisors and more levels of supervision, and as a result, they had better control over quality. Now this pattern is reversing itself and the "flat organization" (i.e., one without a hierarchical, many-tiered management structure) is becoming the norm. Many multiunit companies are reducing dramatically the number of levels of field supervision, with the result that the remaining supervisors oversee more units.

Taco Bell and Pizza Hut have been prominently associated with restructuring their organization to eliminate intermediate layers of management. This increases the responsibilities of the remaining managers. The span of control for field supervisors, such as area managers at Taco Bell, went from one area manager for every "five-plus stores to one for every 20-plus stores."[3] Pizza Hut did away with one whole level of management, the district managers. District managers used to supervise five to seven stores. Now, area managers supervise 11 or more stores.[4] The difference between the span of control at these two Yum! Brands subsidiaries is probably accounted for, in large part, by the greater complexity of the Pizza Hut operation.

The reduction in middle managers and the increase in span of control has more than one effect. It cuts out an expensive layer of managers, complete with salaries, fringe benefits, expenses, clerical support, and office space. More important, perhaps, the role of the multiunit manager changes.

The remaining area managers now have about twice as many stores to oversee. They obviously can't spend as much time with each store. That means the individual store manager has more responsibility for her or his own operation. The kind of supervision, moreover, that an area manager can give 20 or 12 stores is different from that which one district manager used to give 5 or 6 stores. There is much less time for detail and personal involvement in the operation. We might expect the role to be more that of a consultant than of a boss, and the nature of the interaction to be more that of one who gives expert advice than of one who gives detailed orders. This makes the store manager much more responsible for the success or failure of his or her own unit. No doubt, that sometimes feels like sink-or-swim.

The evidence to date suggests that increasing the span of control works. We see it being done by more and more companies. Domino's eliminated a number of middle-management positions by consolidating eight regional offices into five. The lodging company Promus (since broken up) put it this way:

> As we reduce layers of management, we improve communications and allow each employee to expand his or her responsibilities. This is our commitment to empowerment—allowing our employees to grow and assume more responsibility to provide excellent service to every customer every time. . . .
>
> Empowerment requires an environment of teamwork and cooperation with minimal layers of supervision and maximum individual responsibility.[5]

COMMITTEES

Complex organizations that make decisions involving several departments, or disciplines, need methods for communicating and involving different kinds of specialized expertise. Although "management by committee" is really a contradiction in terms, committees often serve as management devices in health care, education, and all kinds of governmental activities, such as congregate feeding and school lunch programs. Although the role of **committees** is not so prominent at the unit operating level in the private sector, many properties find committees useful in a number of areas, particularly in energy conservation and environmental management and recycling programs. Most companies make extensive use of committees at the headquarters level.

Committees allow a number of different interests to gain representation. In health care, the dietary department often prepares food that is delivered to the nursing-care staff, which, in turn, delivers the food to the patients. The food may be purchased for the dietary department by a separate purchasing office, which may also receive the deliveries and handle bulk product storage. The staff cafeteria is sometimes intended as a fringe benefit to employees, providing subsidized meals to the staff below cost. This makes the dietary department important to the personnel officer, just as the need for cafeteria and other accounting procedures makes the dietary department important to the accounting office. The nature of the dietary department's work might well require an advisory committee, to help it react to proposed operating or policy changes.

Such a committee offers all the advantages usually advanced for committees: It helps coordinate plans and transfer information. Committee membership by junior management provides an opportunity for management development as the junior members come to learn how the organization functions. Occasionally, the committee also builds morale: When everyone is consulted, no one is offended, or so the argument goes.

The disadvantages of committees can offset their advantages to some degree. Committees tend to consume a great deal of time. A one-hour meeting of six people consumes six labor hours. Moreover, committees often avoid action rather than take it, and they can be used to avoid or shift responsibility for unpopular or risky decisions. In addition, because committees are supposed to give a hearing to many views, they often encourage compromise.

The case for consultation in the hospital dietary department does not necessarily call for a committee. A committee will regularize consultation, but the same consultation could take place informally among the interested parties. This approach might take a little more time for the person seeking the consultation, but it would almost certainly take less time for all the participants.

Committees are unquestionably useful where the purpose served warrants their use. For example, in energy and recycling management, many hospitality organizations find the committee approach unusually effective in communicating technical information across the organization and in funneling practical suggestions to management. In these cases, committees also serve as a motivational tool by allowing all participants to be involved.

BUREAUCRACY

Bureaucracy is a bad word to most Americans. It is curious, therefore, to realize that Max Weber, the German sociologist who invented the term, developed his theory of bureaucracy as an ideal type of large organization and an ideal way of how it should be run. The following characteristics are those that Weber identified as part of a large hierarchical organization:

1. The organization's work is embodied in statements of fixed official duties.
2. Decisions are governed by abstract, rational rules that are the only proper basis for decision.
3. The bureaucratic official avoids emotionalism and is impersonal.
4. Technical qualification in the appropriate field is the basis for entry and advancement in a bureaucracy.

Weber's model of bureaucracy seeks the most efficient solution to problems on strictly impersonal, rational grounds. Bureaucracy is a means of avoiding the arbitrary exercise of power as in an absolute monarchy, in which people exercise power because of their relationship to the monarch or some other person in power. It also seeks to avoid the problem of political organizations in which the "in" clique holds sway over everyone. In sum, then, it seeks to replace personal relationships—with their possibility for favor and lack of fairness—with an impersonal, rational, efficient organization.

As large organizations have come to play a more and more important role in our society, we have discovered that bureaucratic politics (a notion that Weber would have abhorred) has become a problem and that bureaucrats can, in fact, be arbitrary and unfair, bending rules to their own purposes. Bureaucracies, moreover, can seek "efficient" solutions in ways that are wildly wasteful.[6]

Weber's contribution, however, remains. He asserted (and subsequent management scholars have confirmed) that large organizations have special problems. The special organizational rules along the lines that Weber suggested, although far from perfect, clearly constitute a useful starting point for solutions to organizational design problems in an increasingly complicated society.

AD HOCRACY

In his book Future Shock, Alvin Toffler pointed to a significant development in organizations that began in the aerospace industry and other science- and engineering-related activities. Toffler dubbed this new approach to management "**ad hocracy**." The term is derived from the Latin phrase ad hoc, meaning "to this." The idea is that of an organization responding forcefully to particular situations in an environment that constantly changes. In these situations, the work to be done, rather than a traditional organizational structure, dictates who is in charge. The structure can best be described as a team with changeable captains. If the problem to be solved involves engineering, the team leader will be an engineer with the skills appropriate to the current need. If the problem lies in another area, the person with the necessary abilities will take the reins.

Although most hospitality organizations follow the traditional line or line-and-staff organization, operations whose problems resemble those of the aerospace industry are emerging, especially among the new, large resort and casino operations.

Casino Resort Hotels. A large casino resort hotel is actually involved in five different businesses in a big way (and a few other businesses less closely connected to its operating format and organizational structure). First, casino resort hotels are among the world's largest hotels. Second, they are among the world's largest gambling centers. Third, many are a major factor in the convention business in North America, with numerous meeting and banquet rooms ranging in capacity from under 100 to thousands. Fourth, they are large centers for entertaining and dining, boasting numerous restaurants, each with a distinctive menu and atmosphere. Finally, they usually feature large and extravagant stage shows.

Operating these businesses for one common clientele would be challenge enough. The hotel's situation is complicated, however, by the fact that it caters to three different markets: the casual visitor, who comes alone or with family for a Las Vegas vacation; the convention guest; and the junketeer.

These hotels serve the first market, the traditional class of guest, with the traditional departments that operate according to an organization structure similar to that of any other hotel. The other two kinds of guests, however, present special cases, because each has been attracted by a specific marketing activity in a highly competitive area.

The national convention market receives the attention of literally hundreds of top hotel sales organizations. As a result, when a convention is sold, the hotel's marketing department must follow up on the service. If, for instance, the sales department has promised a special registration procedure on arrival or has agreed to some special service for a banquet, sales must have the means of seeing to it that the special agreement is met. Moreover, if a problem develops for the convention group, the group's contact person will probably want to turn for help to the sales representative with whom he or she first dealt. That sales representative needs the organizational means to solve problems.

Junket guests are gamblers (with good credit ratings) who visit Las Vegas as guests of the hotel with all expenses paid, often including transportation both ways. Although some of these visitors win at the gambling tables, the perfectly legitimate casino percentages favor the house more than enough to cover the cost of visits over the long run. Many of Las Vegas's major hotels solicit junket business. This solicitation is principally directed by the marketing department. Once again, when junket guests get to the hotel, these high rollers must receive excellent treatment so that the marketing department's efforts to secure return visits remain fruitful.

To solve the problem of these special markets, many Las Vegas hotels have evolved an unusual organization structure. In the typical hotel, a simple (oversimplified) organization structure might look like the one in Figure 17.3. The marketing department sells, and the operating departments service the sale. The convention guest might have some contact with the sales representative, but this contact is probably just either a quick, friendly visit or some limited liaison with the operating department.

Many casino hotels, however, have built a somewhat different structure, as illustrated in Figure 17.4. When an individual guest arrives, the organization functions much as it does in traditional hotels. When a convention arrives, however, the marketing department stations a representative at the front desk during registration. This representative has the authority to intervene and settle any problems related to servicing the sale. Similarly, a representative of the marketing department is present at convention banquets, working right along with the food and beverage department's supervisors again to guarantee the service sold by the marketing department. A similar, though less formalized, system operates for junket guests.

Large casino hotels resorts have developed flexible organizational structures to respond to a complex mix of customers. (Courtesy of New York, New York Hotel, Las Vegas.)

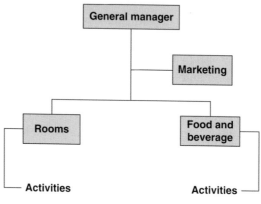

Figure 17.3

Traditional hotel organization.

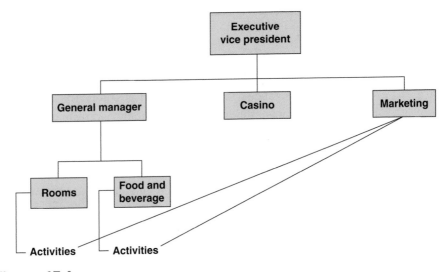

Figure 17.4
Ad hocracy in a casino resort.

For this reason, we have to draw solid lines in Figure 17.4, indicating authority between the marketing department and the operating department activities.

Although confusion undoubtedly arises from time to time, this organization functions smoothly. People who work in complex organizations learn to live with relationships that are more complex. Casino hotels must determine authority by the task at hand.[7]

Walt Disney World. Walt Disney World (WDW) is another highly complex resort organization comprising several distinct businesses, including a theme park, food service, hotel operations, entertainment districts, outdoor camping, and sports. The problems at WDW are twofold. First, the park is constantly changing and growing, and will be for many years to come. This problem of growth and change is complicated by dramatic swings in volume that see the workforce at WDW more than double during the summer's peak season.

During a visit to WDW, we were impressed by one small but interesting fact: The food service organization chart was drawn on a large metallic blackboard. Departments and organizational units were connected by chalk lines, and all the names on the board were on small magnetized plaques that could easily be moved around on the board. Conversation confirmed the impression suggested by the board: The organization structure changed so fast at WDW that the only way management could keep up with it was to use a medium on which changes could be made often and easily.

We do not intend to imply that blackboards are better than paper for organization charts; rather, the point is that dynamic organization forms are increasingly required in growing, changing, complex hospitality firms.

Summary

Our description of organization began with a discussion of authority, its legal basis, and its acceptance by those supervised as a basis. The last of these led us to touch on the informal organization and then authority and responsibility.

We then turned to departmentalization and the delegation of authority. Span of control is an approach used to determine the number of people that a manager can supervise directly, and span of managerial responsibility refers to the number of people with whom a manager routinely interacts. The five bases for dividing work (and authority over it) are function, product or service, geography, customer, and process. Authority also refers to line management and staff assistance, which we also described. We considered some of the issues in organization theory: functional staff authority, committees, bureaucracy (as defined by Weber), and ad hocracy (as defined by Toffler). We finished with two examples of flexible organizations, those of the large casino resort hotels in Las Vegas and of Walt Disney World in Orlando, Florida.

Key Words and Concepts

Authority	Span of control
Legal system	Line authority
Informal organization	Line management
Delegation	Staff
Departmentalization	Committees
Span of managerial	Bureaucracy
responsibility	Ad hocracy

Review Questions

1. Does an effective manager often use his or her legal basis for authority? Explain.
2. Describe how informal organizations in work groups operate.
3. What is the scalar principle?
4. Differentiate between span of control and span of managerial responsibility.
5. What are the five common bases for dividing work? Briefly describe each in regard to the hospitality industry.
6. What are some of the advantages and disadvantages of committees?
7. Outline Weber's definition of bureaucracy.
8. What is meant by ad hocracy?

Internet Exercises

1. **Site name:** Hotel, Restaurant and Tourism Online Professional Trade Journals

   URL: www.wku.edu/,hrtm/journal.htm

   Background information: This Web page provides links to hospitality professional journals online and serves as a launch pad to retrieve information from these journals.

   Exercises: Choose several of the online journals and search for recent articles on authority, informal organizations, departmentalization, delegation, span of control, reorganization, line-and-staff relationships, or any topic deemed appropriate by the instructor. Read the articles and lead a class discussion on the topic you have chosen. Describe how the articles supplement the information contained in the textbook. Be sure to provide the other students with the names of the journals where the information was found.

2. **Site name:** Free Management Library: Management Function of Organizing: Overview of Methods

   URL: http://www.managementhelp.org/orgnzing/orgnzing.htm

   Background information: The Free Management Library provides easy-to-access, clutter-free, comprehensive resources regarding the leadership and management of yourself, other individuals, groups, and organizations. Content is relevant to the vast majority of people, whether they are in large or small for-profit or nonprofit organizations. Over the past ten years, the library has grown to be one of the world's largest, best organized collections of these types of resources.

   Exercises: Choose one of the "chapters" from the above Web site that is of interest to you. Lead a class discussion on the management function of "organizing" in an organization and describe why this information would be important to a hospitality manager.

Notes

1. Harold Koontz and Cyril O'Donnel, *Management: A Systems and Contingency Analysis of Managerial Functions*, 6th ed. (New York: McGraw-Hill, 1976), p. 379.
2. Jean Jacques Servan-Schreiber, *The American Challenge* (New York: Atheneum, 1968).
3. Leonard A. Schlesinger and James L. Heskett, "The Service Driven Company," *Harvard Business Review*, September–October 1991, p. 77.
4. *Cornell Hotel and Restaurant Administration Quarterly*, May 1991, p. 94.
5. Michael G. Muller, *Restaurant Industry Review* (San Francisco: Montgomery Securities, January 1994), p. 48.
6. For a witty but telling analysis of the problems of "dysfunction" of bureaucracies, see C. Northcoat Parkinson's book, *Parkinson's Law* (Boston: Houghton Mifflin, 1957).
7. This example was originally based on a 1976 interview at what was then the MGM Grand. More recent interviews in 1989, 1991, 1994, and 1997, however, indicate that what was true at the Grand back then has now become a widely observed practice in casino resort hotels.

The Hospitality Industry

(Courtesy of Sodexho.)

CHAPTER EIGHTEEN

Staffing: Human-Resources Management in Hospitality Management

The Purpose of this Chapter

O ne of the major contributions made by Taylor and scientific management theory was the principle of fitting the right person to the job rather than hiring just whoever came along. Accordingly, modern hospitality management has developed effective procedures for selecting its employees. This trend has been helpful because personal service—and personal interaction with a guest—are crucial to our field. Since a hospitality firm spends somewhere between 20 and 40 percent of its revenue on direct and indirect wage costs, an understanding of the management function concerned with managing human resources has become essential to the education of managers in our industry.

THIS CHAPTER SHOULD HELP YOU

1. Explain why job descriptions are important, and describe how they are developed.

2. Name the major internal and external sources for identifying prospective employees, and list the advantages of each source.

3. Describe the selection and employment process and its major component activities of information gathering, induction, and training.

4. Outline the general procedure of staff planning, and identify and describe the major tools used in that process.

Issues in Human-Resources Management

Human-resources management at all levels is one of the major concerns of hospitality managers. Staffing hotels and restaurants with willing and qualified employees has been a challenge for some time now. During the 1970s, when the hospitality industry's growth was fastest, there was also a continuing influx of young people into the workforce as the baby boomers entered their teenage and college-age years. By the beginning of the 1980s, however, the number of young workers began to decline, a decline that has continued steadily and will persist into the near future. Because the industry has continued to expand, a growing shortage of workers has developed in more markets, reaching crisis proportions for some operators. The current shortage is frequently mentioned by managers as one of their more serious challenges.

As early as 1985, more than 80 percent of quick-service managers surveyed by *Nation's Restaurant News* reported their operation to be understaffed, and even when we have faced recession, most labor markets have continued to report periodic scarcity. We have noted, too, in earlier chapters, that competition for workers from sectors such as health care and retail is fierce now and likely to become more so. Quick service has felt the shortage of young workers more severely than have some other hospitality businesses, but virtually all segments are significant employers of young people, and all draw from roughly the same total labor pool. When the pool is in short supply, it doesn't take long for all segments to be affected.

Operators have found that where labor shortages have been severe, it meant that managers often had to work stations to cover for absent crew members. Moreover, when not working to cover missing employees, they had to spend an excessive amount of time on recruiting. Later in the chapter, we'll look at what they and others have done to address the labor shortage. Even if there weren't periodic labor shortages, though, human-resources management would be a major concern for two good reasons.

First and most important is that in a field whose stock in trade is **personal service**, the success of the whole enterprise often rests on the kind of employee and how he or she performs a certain job. In particular, the public-contact employee—the waiter or waitress, counterperson, or desk clerk—must be chosen with special care. The back-of-the-house employee must also have definite qualifications. If the cook that the waitress must deal with in the back of the house is a temperamental plate thrower or a foul-mouthed grouch, it will be hard for her, regardless of how pleasant she may be, to show her good side in the dining room.

A second reason for the importance of staffing is the significance of its cost. Few hospitality firms spend less than 25 percent of their sales on **payroll costs**, and some hotel food service departments spend as much as 40 percent of food and beverage sales on payroll and related costs. Moreover, wages had been increasing rapidly in the hospitality industry even before there was a labor shortage. With wages rising at all levels of operation, you can be sure that wage cost will be a major concern for the rest of your career.

Aside from wage rates, one of the major contributors to the high cost of labor is high turnover. There are definite costs associated with hiring and training an employee. If that employee leaves just when he or she is about to become productive, the turnover will be both expensive and wasteful. Reducing turnover, then, is a primary goal of the human-resources function. This reduction involves some key ideas: matching the person to the job, giving the new employee a favorable first impression of the company, stressing the importance of the job, and providing enough training to make the new employee feel able to do the work required.

Actually, human-resources management involves, at one time or another, all the other components of the management process. As you will see in the last section of this chapter, staff planning is crucial, and staffing reflects management's organizing efforts at controlling labor costs. The process of induction and training is closely tied to the function of directing and leading. Because of the importance of people in our industry, however, we must isolate the staffing work of managers for the purposes of study. We can define staffing—or human-resources management—in this way: Staffing is the work that managers and supervisors do to determine the specific personnel needs of their operations—to attract qualified applicants and to choose the best-suited of these for employment and training. The manager accomplishes the human-resources management function by using specialized staff planning tools.

Fitting People to Jobs

Although most managers have always tried to choose the right person for the job, particularly in responsible positions, there was no general awareness of the importance of this practice until Frederick Taylor's time. In some places, tradition determined who would take a job. Labor was often so poorly paid that people were chosen for the jobs on the basis of how little payment they would accept. Thus, although it may seem obvious to us, the modern practice of matching person to job has been the general practice for only about a hundred years.

We should note that some people in hospitality management still don't have an organized notion of the human-resources function, and an even larger group sometimes appears not to understand it. Some managers are constantly surprised when work does not get done, even though they have not staffed their positions so that it will get done. Such people hire whoever comes in the door and put him or her to work with little or no training. Either hospitality managers who proceed in this way fail or they succeed in spite of their staffing weaknesses because of some other special strengths. Just because some operators do not understand the principle of wise staffing, however, is no reason to follow their lead and ignore these principles.

Many successful independent operators appear to follow no formal staffing procedures but achieve effective staffing results anyway. Although they may ignore formal procedures, these operators generally follow informal procedures picked up through experience, in talking with competitors, at trade shows and industry meetings, and so forth. In practice, these informal procedures may come close to more formalized programs. These operators, by and large, are the "old pros." Although their results are good, beginners would probably do better to start with proven fundamentals. Figure 18.1 spells out those fundamentals as a set of steps managers should follow in the selection process.

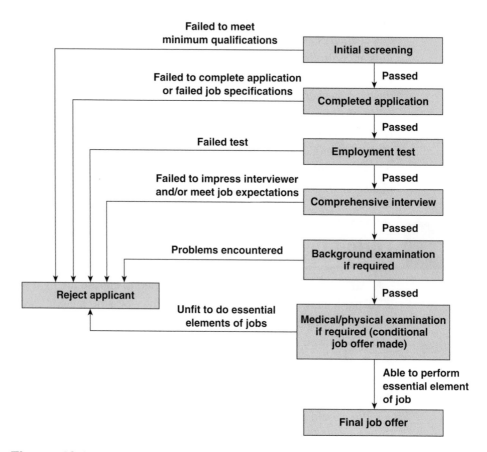

Figure 18.1

Steps in the job selection process. (Source: David A. DeCenzo and Stephen P. Robbins, *Human Resource Management,* 5th ed., New York: John Wiley & Sons, 1996, p. 171. Reprinted with permission.)

Job Descriptions

If a company has no formal staffing procedure, the first step in adopting one will be to identify each job being done. For each job identified, the company prepares a **job description**. (Job descriptions for workers are often based on formal task analyses prepared by someone with industrial engineering training.) Figures 18.2 and 18.3 illustrate sample management job descriptions. **Job specifications**, on the other hand, specify the exact requirements that a person must bring to a job.

The logic of the job description should be obvious. We can hardly hire the right person for the job until we have a good idea of what the job is. Once a job is analyzed carefully, some minimum standards for an applicant should emerge. Sometimes these standards are broken down into physical requirements, mental ability, and emotional or attitudinal characteristics.

Physical Requirements. The person hired must be able to do the job. If a server must reach across a booth, the applicant may have to conform to some minimum height requirement (5 feet is used by some companies). A receiver's job may require someone able to lift 100 pounds and generally able to do heavy physical work. A company must be cautious when establishing any physical requirements for a job and be confident that they are indeed necessary qualifications. Federal regulations such as the Americans with Disabilities Act (in the United States) have complicated this process. An employer, however, still has the need to fit the person to the job to a certain degree.

Mental or Intellectual Abilities. Some jobs require specific intellectual abilities. Desk clerks and other public-contact employees must speak reasonably clear English. (In Quebec, they will need English and also are required to be fluent in French. In some parts of the United States, Spanish is helpful and/or necessary.) Waitresses and waiters must have sufficient arithmetic ability to total a check. Cooks and bartenders must be able to convert recipes from one yield quantity to another. Testing is one method that employers use to determine if a job candidate has the necessary abilities.

Emotional or Attitudinal Characteristics. Once again, public-contact employees should express by their manner a reasonably pleasant disposition. Those who are hired to work under pressure, such as servers and bartenders, should not project a nervous or irritable disposition. An increasing number of companies are concerned as well with an employee's ability to get along with fellow workers and to work in a team.

Employees with Disabilities. In some jobs, physical or mental disabilities are not a drawback. Food service is a major employer of handicapped workers. Among operators who employ disabled workers, 90 percent reported that disabled workers'

NAME: _____   DATE: _____ /_____ /_____   Page_____ of_____

POSITION TITLE: Food Service Manager	JOB CODE:	EFFECTIVE DATE:	
REPORTS TO: Food Service Director	LOCATION: East		
DIVISION: Educational	AREA GROUP	REGION/DEPT	DIST/SEC/UNIT

Basic Function:

Handle all assigned responsibilities in a professional manner.

Scope:

1. Responsible for all phases of unit as designated by FSD.
2. Responsible for all phases of the cafeteria.
3. Responsible for all catered events.
4. Responsible for expanding business volume in the above-listed areas.

Principal Duties (by Key Result Area):

1. Training and developing staff to full potential.
2. Ordering, using competitive bids and approved suppliers.
3. Manning/pricing.
4. Developing two specials per month as per schedule forwarded to FSD and DM: that is, "monotony breakers."
5. Determining pre- and postcost to attain a financial success.
6. Maintaining records for following year reference.
7. Attaining financial goals.
8. Maintaining a high level of satisfaction.

Position Specifications:

1. Must be able to work as an integral part of a management team.
2. Must be able to maintain a rapport with superiors and subordinates.
3. Must be able to cope with work pressures.
4. Must be innovative and willing to take the initiative.
5. Must maintain a professional appearance as deemed necessary to satisfy the client.
6. Must have the ability to plan and organize.

Where/How to Obtain Training:

1. Second-phase management development program.
2. On-the-job training.
3. Company-initiated programs and films.
4. Management meetings.

Figure 18.2

Job description—manager.

POSITION TITLE:	JOB CODE:	EFFECTIVE DATE:		
Chief Dietitian	FO 6			
REPORTS TO:	LOCATION:			
Food Service Director	East			
DIVISION:	AREA GROUP	REGION/DEPT	DIST/SEC/UNIT	
Health Care				

NAME: _____ DATE: _____ /_____ /Page_____ of_____

Basic Function:

To obtain or improve nutritional status of patients.

Scope:

To be responsible for high-quality nutritional patient care and instruction.

To be responsible for overseeing the activities of one other dietitian.

Principal Duties (by Key Result Area):

1. Visiting and instructing patients and recording in medical charts.

2. Supervising diet aides and ensuring that all patients are visited within 24 hours of admission.

3. Working closely with in-service department orienting new hires and students to procedures of dietary department.

4. Operating an outpatient diet instruction clinic.

5. Supervising proper preparation and distribution of tube feedings and nourishments.

Position Specifications:

BS degree in foods and nutrition.

1 year ADA-accredited internship.

ADA membership.

ADA registration.

Where/How to Obtain Training:

Local monthly dietitian's journal club.

State and national dietetic association meetings.

Local and state diabetes association meetings.

Figure 18.3
Job description—dietitian.

performance was excellent or good when compared to nondisabled workers. Since the passing of the ADA in 1993, many businesses within the restaurant sector have been extremely proactive at hiring and training disabled workers. Certain restaurants have worked hard at hiring from this group and received tremendous recognition for their efforts. Of the 27 employees at the Wilson Street Grill in Madison, Wisconsin, over one-third have some sort of disability. The owners indicate that they haven't changed their high standards and continue to require tests and a probationary period for all employees. The organization has simply been successful matching employees with the right job in the restaurant.[1]

Recruiting

Once we know what kind of people we want for each job we've identified, we must try to attract a pool of applicants that permits us to select the best-qualified. This activity is known as **recruiting**. Indeed, we will shortly argue that, in the face of labor shortages, it has become as necessary to segment the labor market as it has been to target the appropriate customer group. The major sources of prospective employees are the operation itself (the internal source) and various outside sources. Each has its special strengths and problems.

It is interesting to see what steps are taken in the search process when there is a severe labor shortage such as the one we mentioned earlier. What one company did was to appoint a special task force of human resources and operations people to lead a crash recruiting program in the area. The task force compared the company's operating, pay, and human-resource practices with those of its competitors. As a result, wages and benefits were adjusted as appropriate, an incentive program was introduced for suggestive selling, and the employee food discount and vacation programs were improved. Moreover, the task force used mobile recruiting vans and developed a reward program for referrals of new employees by those already on staff.

As you can see, recruiting involved thinking through the job the company had to offer in much the same way it might have looked at a product for sale. Increasingly, employers are seeing themselves as having, in effect, "jobs for sale," with their prospective employees as their customers. Day in and day out, crisis or not, recruiting follows the same general pattern.

INTERNAL SOURCES

Recruiting via **internal sources** can be accomplished in a variety of ways. Employees often recommend their friends and relatives for work. Many hotel and food service employers pay a bonus to employees who refer applicants who take a job and stay in it for a specified period of time. Hiring people who come with the recommendation of reliable employees increases the chances that the new employee will fit in with the existing organization. Because the person recommending the new employee has to go on record not only with the boss but also with fellow employees, he or she is likely to make recommendations cautiously. Besides, the current employee will have to work with the new hire, too.

A second internal source is the pool of former employees. Some may have left to raise children or pursue further schooling; others may have changed employers for what looked like a better opportunity. Because former employees are a known quantity—and because they know the company and its practices—they have an advantage over a new applicant. Many firms make a practice of using former employees, particularly servers, on a **part-time** basis for parties and banquets or for an extra-busy day such as Mother's Day or a football weekend.

Of course, when trying to fill higher-level positions (supervisory and above), there is always the third source, which consists of current employees themselves. Some companies pride themselves on taking care of employees first by promoting from within. This practice will necessarily leave a vacant position at some level below the newly filled position, however, requiring the company to eventually search externally.

Although internal sources offer the advantages of a known quantity, these sources may not supply enough people in a tight labor market. If an operation requires a major addition to its workforce—for example, after expansion—these sources are often inadequate, and so the operation must look outside.

EXTERNAL SOURCES

The three major means of contacting employees via **external sources** are through traditional advertisements (such as in the newspaper), on-line recruiting (such as on Monster.com) and **employment agencies**. Also, some applicants walk in. Finally, operations that are organized by a union can call the hiring hall and ask that members be referred for employment.

Advertising. The strengths and weaknesses of **advertising** lie in the number of applicants it generally yields. In help-wanted ads, posted either online or in traditional print media, you direct your request to a large readership. People who read help-wanted ads are usually searching for a job or thinking of changing jobs. From this large number of readers, a good number of people are likely to apply. Thus, the employer can choose those who appear to have the best qualifications from among a large pool of applicants. When several positions must be filled or when a new operation is being started, the large number of applicants offers obvious advantages.

On the other hand, those large numbers can be a disadvantage. Dealing with a great number of applicants is time-consuming. Each applicant submits an **application** (and in some cases, must be told how to complete it), and then each application must be processed. These clerical duties are compounded by management's commitment to interview the applicants, which also takes a great deal of time. Because applicants are members of the public—that is, members of the community from which the customers come—each applicant must receive courteous attention, or management risks losing their patronage and that of their relatives and acquaintances. Because of the time commitment necessary, many employers advertise jobs only if they have a number of positions to fill or if the labor market is especially tight.

Some firms have found job fairs and open houses an effective approach to mass recruiting. Job fairs provide a neutral atmosphere where job seekers and employers can meet informally. The setting lends itself to brief, informational exchanges that also offer the employer an opportunity to screen applicants and call back those who seem interesting. An open house functions in much the same way but gives the company an opportunity to acquaint applicants with its operation.

Online Recruiting. This medium is becoming the preferred method for many hospitality companies as it allows for prescreening and is an efficient means of sorting through large numbers of applications. Furthermore, it enables efficient matching of applicants and companies. Companies typically use two means of online recruiting—job boards or their own employment Web sites. Popular job board sites include Monster.com (and MonsterTRAK which is specific for colleges and universities), CareerBuilder.com, Hotjobs.com, Flipdog.com, Idealist.org (for nonprofits), Simplyhired.com, and Hotelscareers.com. From a company perspective, the advantage of a job board is that it provides a greater reach than what other media advertising might provide. Similarly, for students, it allows them to research companies (and jobs) outside of their local areas.

A more targeted type of job board includes sites such as MonsterTRAK which, in addition to offering specialized service to students at individual colleges and universities, has special features that allow students to connect with alumni.

More and more companies are developing their own sites, including many of the larger hospitality companies such as Marriott, Hyatt, and McDonald's.

Both recruiters and campus representatives continue to remind students that as efficient as online sites can be, students still have to be proactive in their job searches. It is not enough to simply post a résumé and sit back and wait for a company to contact you.

Employment Agencies. Each state maintains employment offices in or accessible to all communities in the state. The agencies are operated with tax revenue; thus, they require no placement fee from either the employer or the employee. Because people must register with the employment service when they are out of work in order to qualify for unemployment compensation, this office remains constantly in touch with job seekers.

Many employers make it a point to become personally acquainted with the state employment office's manager and counselors. If the employment office staff knows an employer's applicant standards, the office can save a great deal of time by screening applicants for the employer. Then, too, these staff people are often contacted by people they have helped before who are considering a change of employer. The experienced counselor often helps employers make hiring choices, and the counselor's recommendation can also influence a capable employee's choice of employer.

Private employment agencies charge a fee, which is sometimes paid by the employer. Although some private agencies handle hourly personnel in the hospitality industry, the authors' experience suggests that the greatest users of private employment agencies in our field are supervisory and executive personnel.

SEGMENTING THE EMPLOYEE MARKET

Each segment—teens, working mothers, or older workers—has special needs. For teens, part-time and weekend work is important. Many mothers are interested in working while their children are in school. Older workers have quite different perceptions of the hiring process and do not necessarily respond well to the same advertising media as others. Rather, they are more likely to respond to specialized employment organizations and state, city, and local agencies. They, too, prefer part-time employment and flexible scheduling.

In today's workforce, an educated and often discriminating employee decides where to work. Under the circumstances, recognizing recruiting as more like selling just makes sense.

Selection and Employment

Until this point, we have explored ways to determine what kinds of employees we need and ways to contact potential employees. We turn our attention now to the process of selecting and "breaking in" new workers. The first step, employee **selection**, is followed by orientation and then by training. Each step is crucial to developing productive workers.

SELECTION

Rich Melman's Lettuce Entertain You Enterprises (LEYE) has one of the hospitality industry's lowest turnover rates (47 percent). Suzie Southgate-Fox, the company's senior vice president for human resources, sums up the secret of Lettuce's success: "We hire carefully. We look for people with things we can't teach." She uses words such as "aware, caring, sweet, giving, team player" to describe the traits they want.[2]

The selection process involves gathering, classifying, and analyzing information available from several sources. An application often tells more than an applicant realizes. For instance, if an applicant cannot follow the simple directions on the form, a manager is entitled to wonder if he or she will be able to learn the job. If an applicant does not bother to fill it out completely, he or she may be unwilling to do assigned work. If the open position—say, that of a desk clerk—involves writing, an application filled out in an illegible scrawl may disqualify the applicant.

A properly completed application should account for the applicant's work over the period specified on the application. Any blanks or "extended vacations" should be carefully checked. (The cashier you're about to hire may have spent some time in jail for embezzlement.)

The application form usually helps screen out applicants, allowing management to pinpoint the ones it is interested in inviting for an **interview**. The application can even help start the interview. During the first part of the interview, an interviewer should clarify any ambiguous information on the application. The interviewer will also want to give the applicant information about the company and the job. This interchange helps most interviewers begin the process of sizing up the applicant, determining what kind of a person he or she is and how he or she would get along with the present employees. Interviewing should also focus on the applicant's background and indicate whether he or she is, in fact, qualified (or what is sometimes a bigger problem, overqualified) for the job and whether he or she would actually like the job and be likely to continue in it. Two forms that suggest one company's approach to summarizing an interview and an applicant evaluation are shown in Figures 18.4 and 18.5.

Applicants should list their references and former employers on the application blanks, and these entries should be checked. Most references are selected because the applicant thinks he or she will receive a good review, and so it is important to check with the employers to verify the employment history and, where possible, to learn how the applicant performed. At the end of the interview, the applicant should be told when he or she will be contacted regarding employment or a follow-up interview (depending upon company policy). If several people are being considered, an applicant should be told when a decision is to be made. Those applicants who are not hired should be notified promptly so they can continue their search for employment. Most employers

TO: _____

FROM: _____

INTERVIEW REPORT

DATE OF THIS

NAME OF APPLICANT: _____ INTERVIEW: _____

ADDRESS _____ PHONE _____

CANDIDATE FOR: _____

(Job Title)

INTERVIEWER: _____

PLEASE REPORT YOUR INTERVIEW IMPRESSIONS BY CHECKING THE ONE MOST APPROPRIATE BOX IN EACH AREA.

1. APPEARANCE

| ☐ Very untidy; poor taste in dress. | ☐ Somewhat careless about personal appearance. | ☐ Satisfactory personal appearance. | ☐ Good taste in dress; better-than-average appearance. | ☐ Unusually well groomed; very neat; excellent taste in dress. |

2. FRIENDLINESS

| ☐ Appears very distant and aloof. | ☐ Approachable; fairly friendly. | ☐ Warm; friendly, sociable. | ☐ Very sociable and outgoing. | ☐ Extremely friendly and sociable. |

3. POISE, STABILITY

| ☐ Ill at ease; is jumpy and appears nervous. | ☐ Somewhat tense; is easily irritated. | ☐ About as poised as the average applicant. | ☐ Sure of himself; appears to like crises more than average person. | ☐ Extremely well composed; apparently thrives under pressure. |

4. PERSONALITY

| ☐ Unsatisfactory for this job. | ☐ Questionable for this job. | ☐ Satisfactory for this job. | ☐ Very desirable for this job. | ☐ Outstanding for this job. |

5. CONVERSATIONAL ABILITY

| ☐ Talks very little; expresses himself poorly. | ☐ Tries to express himself but does fair job at best. | ☐ Average fluency and expression. | ☐ Talks well and to the point. | ☐ Excellent expression; extremely fluent; forceful. |

6. ALERTNESS

| ☐ Slow to catch on. | ☐ Rather slow; requires more than average explanation. | ☐ Grasps ideas with average ability. | ☐ Quick to understand; perceives very well. | ☐ Exceptionally keen and alert. |

(Continued)

Figure 18.4

Analysis of requirements for a food service director.

7. INFORMATION ABOUT GENERAL WORK FIELD				
☐ Poor knowledge of field.	☐ Fair knowledge of field.	☐ Is as informed as the average applicant	☐ Fairly well in-formed; knows more than aver-age applicant.	☐ Has excellent knowledge of the field.
8. EXPERIENCE				
☐ No relationship between appli-cant's back-ground and job requirements.	☐ Fair relation-ship between applicant's background and job requirements.	☐ Average amount of meaningful background and experience.	☐ Background very good; consider-able experience.	☐ Excellent back-ground and experience.
9. DRIVE				
☐ Has poorly defined goals and appears to act without purpose.	☐ Appears to set goals too low and to put forth little effort to achieve these.	☐ Appears to have average goals; puts forth aver-age effort to reach these.	☐ Appears to strive hard; has high desire to achieve.	☐ Appears to set high goals and to strive incessantly to achieve these.
10. OVERALL				
☐ Definitely unsatisfactory.	☐ Substandard.	☐ Average.	☐ Definitely above average.	☐ Outstanding.
THIS IS:	1st INTERVIEW ☐ 2nd INTERVIEW ☐ 3rd INTERVIEW ☐			

Figure 18.4
Continued.

maintain a file of applications from people who were not hired. Thus, a person not chosen at one time may be contacted later. (Incidentally, a file like this helps estab-lish that management has followed fair-employment practices.)

Although the object of the selection process is to find the right people, in part that means avoiding the wrong people. One group most employers want to avoid is peo-ple who use drugs. Estimates of the proportion of drug users range as high as 30 per-cent of the workforce—and 75 percent of drug users use drugs on the job, so this is not a small problem. Experience indicates that drug users have five times as many workers' compensation cases and draw three times as much in health claims, thus im-pacting insurance premiums unfavorably. Absenteeism among drug users is two and a half times that of employees who do not use drugs, and people with this problem are 25 percent less productive than the rest of the workforce. Accordingly, many employers have begun to use preemployment drug testing as a means of excluding

Applicant _____

Job considered for _____ Grade _____

Evaluated by: _____ Date _____

| Rating Overall: | ☐ Matches Requirements | ☐ Exceeds Requirements | ☐ Below Requirements | ☐ Recommend Hire |

Major Strong Characteristics

_____

_____

_____

Major Weak Characteristics

_____

_____

_____

FACTOR EVALUATIONS FOR THIS POSITION

See Management Employment Program for definitions.

SKILLS, KNOWLEDGE, ABILITIES

Appearance and presentation
Education
Mental ability
Mobility
Experience
Physical condition
Special skills and knowledge
Relationships background

HABITS, AMBITIONS, DRIVES

Leadership
Perseverance
Stability
Self-reliance
Energy
Maturity
Ability to get along with others
Need for income
Need for status and power
Need to serve

✓Check	The Applicant in Relation to This Position		
Matches	Almost Matches	Exceeds	Fails to Meet

Matches	Almost Matches	Exceeds	Fails to Meet

SFS 0121-0567

Figure 18.5
Applicant evaluation form.

these undesirable prospects.[3] Marriott, Houston's, and Disney are just a few of the hospitality companies that have earned strong reputations for their selection processes.

ORIENTATION

It's an old saying—and a true one—that first impressions are lasting impressions. It is surprising, then, how often new employees are told to sign some papers, given directions to the locker room, and then promptly forgotten. Such casual procedures destroy the golden opportunity to start a new employee off on the right foot. Common sense should suggest that the new employee be enthusiastically and cheerfully introduced to the operation, to fellow workers, and to the new job. **Orientation** presents companies with that very opportunity.

Ritz-Carlton puts heavy emphasis on orientation of new employees because it is the company's experience that the first three or four days are crucial in determining the outlook an employee will have in his or her work. It is not a coincidence that many successful hospitality companies have adopted this same attitude toward orientation.

The Operation. Your restaurant, hotel, or dietary department is old ground to established employees. However, it is unmapped territory to a newcomer. For this reason, a guided tour by a member of management helps make an employee's first day comfortable. Basic information, such as where the employees enter the building, where and when smoking is permitted, and where personal belongings are kept, should be provided. Some employees report spending a very uncomfortable first day because they were too embarrassed to ask strangers directions to the restrooms.

Are you proud of your operation? Are there certain dining rooms that are especially nice, certain views especially attractive? Let the newcomer share in these high points, too.

Certainly, a part of this orientation should be a statement of the standards of the operation with regard to both quality of product and service and personal conduct and hygiene. Such a statement should be made in a friendly way by a member of management, and it may also be presented to the new employee in the form of an orientation handbook. Such a postinterview conversation also gives management an opportunity to restate its policies on wages, fringe benefits, working conditions, days off, and so forth, as well as to make sure any questions the new employee may have are answered.

Fellow Workers. Don't assume a new worker is a gregarious person who quickly strikes up friendships. Introduce the new employee to the individuals in the work group and to others with whom he or she will come into contact. Thus, for instance, the host or hostess should introduce a new server not only to the other servers but to cooks, pantry workers, and dishwashers as well.

The Job. Finally, the new employee (1) should be shown exactly where he or she will work, (2) should receive a full description of the job, and, if possible, (3) should get an opportunity to observe the work in action. Such an experience can be brief, but it gives the employee an overview of the work and lays a good foundation for training.

Training

Some operations—especially independent operations that do not feel they can afford a continuing **training** program—prefer to hire trained employees. Even when experienced workers take a new job, they must still receive enough training to orient them to the operation's special procedures. Many companies prefer to hire people with no experience at all. These companies argue that it is easier to train from scratch than to hire someone who has to unlearn what the employer, at least, views as a satchel of bad habits. An employee who knows only one way to do the work is unlikely to stray from approved practice.

Training is unquestionably costly. Employees must be paid for the time during which they are learning but not yet productive, and trainees also consume a good deal

Training is a critical function with which most managers are involved. (Courtesy of Sodexho.)

of the trainer's valuable time. This is why the selection process we discussed earlier is so important. There is no point in spending time, money, and effort on somebody who turns out to be unqualified for or uninterested in the job.

The alternative to training—not training—may be even more expensive. Training does cost a lot; but the cost of not training is poor service and lost customers, and a lost customer may never return. Thus, the lost revenue from poor service far exceeds the cost of training a worker properly.

Not only does management lose customers by not training, but it is liable to lose the employee as well at just about the time he or she becomes productive. An employee who is thrown into a job that he or she does not know is bound to feel inadequate, to say the least, and is likely to begin looking for other work. In fact, many studies have shown a strong relationship between the training an employee receives and employee turnover.

Training and retraining can be the key to maintaining quality in products and, at the same time, reducing turnover. At Ritz-Carlton, for instance, training leads to certification for quality performance—and then to periodic retraining for recertification.

Global Hospitality Note 18.1 reports on training problems presented by other cultures.

MANAGEMENT TRAINING

Companies, particularly those planning to expand, often develop large entry-level training programs for new or promotable management employees. Companies may accelerate their management training activity in advance of a major expansion drive so as to have a pool of assistant managers to draw from as new unit managers are needed. Some chains cooperate with local educational institutions, using both their facilities and staff to handle a surge in training needs. Some companies, too, are finding that management training helps reduce turnover. Such courses include content relating to both people skills and new technical skills needed on the job. Managers are often encouraged, too, to continue their training by means of company correspondence courses, local continuing education courses, as well as through professional reading.

Because managers are responsible for the productivity of all their employees, it makes good sense for companies to concentrate their efforts on preparing productive managers. For the future hospitality manager, management training programs may offer a shortcut to acquiring practical management know-how. Looking into your prospective employer's training program is just enlightened self-interest.

A note of caution about what to expect, however, may be in order. William Lombardi, former vice president of Olive Garden, said of his company's management training program:

Training in a Global Hospitality Industry

Some examples from an international trainer's notebook suggest that training in different cultures requires a trained sensitivity to the culture and to local secular and even religious norms of conduct.

■ When a trainer in Indonesia asked training class participants to critique each other's presentations orally, "one man burst into tears and ran out of the room sobbing uncontrollably," according to Carol Sage-Robin, a trainer for Westin. In Indonesian culture, she discovered, criticizing someone else's work publicly was unacceptable. Thereafter, participants used written critiques.

■ Training schedules in Muslim countries need to build in regular prayer breaks.

■ In China and Bahrain, unmarried men and women would be embarrassed to work together without supervision.

■ In some countries, the accustomed pace is slower than in North America. During a training class for restaurant servers in Sumatra, Ms. Sage-Robin indicates, "I was having a hard time getting the employees to move as fast as I needed them to. I tried playing fast rock music, but that did not work." Then she noticed the outdoor swimming pool. She took the class outside, where it was hot as blazes, and asked everyone to follow her—and to keep up with her as she walked at a fast pace around the pool. Those who didn't keep up were not allowed to return to the air-conditioned restaurant until they did keep up. In this way, she communicated to the class the speed at which food servers had to move to give satisfactory service.

■ Another trainer had great success in the Caribbean with an exercise in which employees rewrote the company song and then sang their version. In Bahrain, however, the exercise was repeatedly a flop, and the trainer realized what the problem was when she discovered that to the Shiite Muslims in her class, singing in this way was forbidden.

Source: Elizabeth Johnson, "Training in an International Setting," *Hotels*, May 1997, p. 32.

We lose a lot of people, sometimes in the first few weeks of our management training program, because they want a rule book and they want 50 policies or 500 policies. They want to know what they are supposed to do in every situation. And we say, "Do the right thing. Do the thing that's going to get you a happy guest. Do the thing that's going to keep your employee motivated." And a lot of people struggle with that!

ON-THE-JOB TRAINING

The most common method of training in the hospitality industry is pairing the new employee with an experienced worker (also called "shadowing"). Unfortunately, this pairing is often done haphazardly: A new worker is assigned to whichever experienced worker may be handy. A "market research" study of restaurant employees' views on training found that many felt their training had not been formal enough and that it lacked manager involvement. Employees prefer to train with a training specialist or a manager instead of "just another employee."[4]

Although the details of developing an actual training program extend beyond our concern here, we can note that the basic elements involve developing trainers who know—and will show—the approved way of doing the task, and are trained in training as well as in the job. Both the National Restaurant Association and the American Hotel & Lodging Association Educational Institute offer excellent train-the-trainer courses.

Task analyses that spell out in writing the steps necessary in each job greatly facilitate training. The learner can be given them to study, and the trainer can use them to be ready to give instruction.

At the beginning of World War II, a huge number of war plant workers had to be trained for new jobs in a hurry. At that time, management experts identified a four-step procedure as the best way to go about this rapid training:

1. *Tell me.* Explain the task to the worker. Include why it needs to be done and why it must be done in just this way.

2. *Show me.* Demonstrate the job, explaining as you go along. Continue demonstrating until the worker is ready to try it.

3. *Let me do it.* Let the worker perform the task slowly, asking questions as needed. Not until trainer and trainee are comfortable with the trainee's independent performance should he or she be allowed to do it alone.

4. *Follow up.* Once the new employee achieves enough proficiency to be able to perform independently, he or she should receive close supervision to be sure that shortcuts or bad habits don't grow gradually to mar performance.

Many hospitality companies, particularly quick-service restaurants, follow this exact method of training.

Notice that an employee is not generally trained in a job but in tasks. Thus, training for a new dishwasher might involve the following:

1. Scraping—removing garbage from plates

2. Racking—putting dirty dishes in racks

3. Feeding—feeding dirty dish racks into the dishwasher

4. Catching—receiving dish racks from the "clean end" of the machine

5. Stacking—removing clean dishes from the rack and stacking them in a temporary storage place

6. Transporting—moving clean dishes back to where they are used, often in special carts

Each of these (and the list could be extended a great deal further) is a separate task, and for each, "one best way" will permit the greatest possible speed and the least breakage and injury. Teaching tasks separately, one at a time, may seem slow, but it is really the best way to prepare a new employee for the complete dishwasher job.

EVERYBODY GETS TRAINED

A final point is worth noting here: Training never stops. When a new employee comes to work, management can take charge of that learning process or leave it to whatever influences come along. Either way, the employee will be trained. Clearly, however, common sense sides with a planned, management-controlled training effort.

Retaining Employees

Because so much effort goes into recruiting qualified people, and so much time and trouble goes into training them, there is a clear need to hold on to good people once they come on board. We can hardly solve so complex a problem here, but this may be a good place to review some key provisions that some companies are finding helpful. Several factors are crucial to **retaining employees**. As we've already indicated, taking the effort to get the right people is an important first step.

Second, the way people are treated makes a great difference. Praise in public for a good job, but reprimand in private when things don't go right. Efforts to improve the two-way flow of information are important, too. In smaller units, face-to-face conversation may be enough. In larger companies, company newspapers can recognize employees' accomplishments. At some companies, employees fill out an "employee comment slip" reporting what customers say, evaluating the food they served, and commenting on what was good or bad on their shift. Managers read these carefully. Even more companies use periodic employee surveys to assess employee morale and managers' effectiveness in dealing with people.

Offering opportunities for advancement is important. Companies that promote from within find most of their management trainees from their own hourly ranks. They offer an opportunity for advancement that is an added inducement to performance.

Bonus and incentive programs are another method that companies use to retain employees. For example, several years ago, Buffets Inc. introduced a new incentive program designed to help them retain restaurant managers. If the unit manager signs a commitment letter and agrees to remain at his or her assigned restaurant for three years, he or she will receive a $20,000 bonus, which is in addition to the manager's base salary and annual bonus. The unit managers then receive an additional

$30,000 bonus for every three-year period they remain at their assigned restaurants. Buffets, Inc. feels that the new program saves them money. The company estimates that it loses more than $20,000 in sales after a good unit manager leaves a restaurant.[5]

Many companies pride themselves on offering competitive pay and good benefits. A growing fringe benefit intended to reduce both turnover and absenteeism is a company-sponsored day-care program. Some employers subsidize day care. A spokesman for a 300-unit Hardee's franchisee, for instance, noted that his company did this because it employed a lot of single parents. One Burger King franchisee found that when it started to subsidize its hourly employees' day-care costs, its turnover rate fell to one-third the industry average.

Companies are approaching their employees' child care problems in several different ways. Some offer subsidies to the employees' child care costs, while others provide flexible hours and make information on local day-care services available to employees. Still others make special arrangements with a national day-care provider. For instance, one company negotiated a 10 percent discount for its employees and then offered them another 10 percent subsidy. Finally, some employees pool their resources with neighboring businesses to establish a joint child care effort or establish a center themselves on site.

Staff Planning

Hospitality managers concentrate on **staff planning** not only because of the high proportion of income they spend on salaries and wages but also because of the great importance they attach to adequate coverage—that is, always having sufficient staff in the appropriate jobs to meet the operation's needs. Anyone who has seen a hotel coffee shop flounder when the key breakfast cook failed to show up, or a kitchen where the pot washer walked out in the middle of a meal, knows the chaos caused by the absence of just one key person. On the other hand, you may have noticed some food service operations that open at 7:00 A.M. and bring in a full dish room crew at the same time. The crew then sits around with nothing to do until the dirty dishes gradually start to collect a half hour or 45 minutes later. Proper staff planning ensures coverage, but it would avoid superfluous, wasteful coverage like this.

Because staff planning is so important, most hospitality curricula devote at least a large part of one course, and sometimes more than that, to it. In our brief discussion, we can only introduce this form of planning and some of its key tools.

JOB AND WORK NEEDS

Staff planning begins by identifying each workstation in the operation. Next, a **schedule** showing the number of persons needed at these stations in the course of each day,

Staffing and scheduling is as important for employees as it is for managers. (Courtesy of Sodexho.)

by time period, is prepared. This analysis usually follows the graphic pattern shown in Figure 18.6. This kind of chart shows at a glance where there is double coverage for a job and what, if any, rest periods are provided.

Because the volume of business may vary from one day to another, many operations prepare a separate schedule for each day of the week and sometimes separate sets for different seasons. Comparing actual coverage needs with staffing schedules results in constant revision of these schedules. A dollar of unneeded labor cost at one station can, at a moment's notice, be moved to reinforce the coverage someplace else.

Once management prepares schedules of its operating needs for each day, thereby ensuring adequate coverage for each job, it can draw up a weekly schedule providing for day-off relief. The schedule for the dish, pot, and receiving crew shown in Figure 18.7 is primarily a management tool (1) to analyze seven-day schedule needs (the problem is simpler but similar in six- or five-day operations), (2) to ensure adequate coverage for each job each day, and (3) at the same time, to be sure that each employee receives the appropriate time off.

A schedule like the one shown in Figure 18.7 is also a communication tool. When posted, this schedule shows employees which person works what job for which hours each day of the week. Managers who keep their schedules in their heads and rely on simply telling people when they are to work are almost bound occasionally to have two people showing up for the same job at times and no people on other days! The result is increased cost, inadequate coverage, poor service, and low morale.

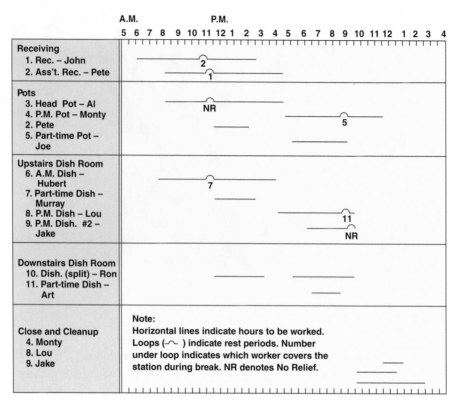

Figure 18.6
Typical daily schedule.

PART–TIME EMPLOYEES

To complete our discussion of staff planning, we should offer a word about part-time employees. An operation often needs a position covered for only part of a shift, and it sometimes needs extra people on a job only on busy days. To hire a full-time person would obviously be an expensive solution; instead, the hospitality industry is using more part-time employees to avoid overstaffing.

Some added costs and problems result from relying on part-time people. First, an operation that uses part-time help extensively carries more people on its payroll. The same (and often a lesser) number of labor days can be worked, but more people will fill the jobs. This means more payroll records and more recruiting, interviewing, hiring, and training. Moreover, a part-time employee usually works part time because he or she has a main commitment elsewhere. (Part-timers are usually housewives, students, or "moonlighters" taking a part-time job in addition to their main employment.) Scheduling people with responsibilities outside your establishment creates special

	MON.	TUES.	WED.	THURS.	FRI.	SAT.	SUN.
Receiver 6–2:30 John						off / N.R.	off / N.R.
Ass't. Receiver 8–4:30 Pete						off / N.R.	off / N.R.
Head Pot Washer 8–4:30 Al	off / Hal	off / Hal					
P.M. Pot Washer 4:30–1:00 Monty						off / N.R.	off / N.R.
Part-time Pot Washer 5–9:00 Joe					off / Hal		
A.M. Dishwasher 7:30–4:00 Hubert	off / Mac	off / Mac					
Part-time Dishwasher 11:30–2:30 Murray						off / N.R.	off / N.R.
P.M. Dishwasher 4:00–12:30 Lou			off / Mac	off / Mac			
P.M. Dishwasher #2 5:30–2:00 Jake					off / Mac	off / Mac	
Dish (split) Ron 11:30–3:30 & 5:30–9:30			off / Hal	off / Hal			
Part-time Dish–P.M. 6:30–9:00 Art						off / N.R.	off / N.R.
Dish, Relief Mac	A.M. Dish 8–4:30	A.M. Dish 8–4:30	P.M. Dish 4–12:30	P.M. Dish 4–12:30	P.M. Dish #2 5:30–2:00	off / N.R.	off / N.R.
Pot. Dish. Relief Hal	Head Pot 8–4:30	Head Pot 8–4:30 & 5:30–9:30	Dish Split 11:30–3:30 & 5:30–9:30	Dish Split 11:30–3:30 4:30–1:00	Part-time Pot	off / N.R.	off / N.R.
Pot. Relief/ Part-time Noah						P.M. Pot 4:30–1:00	P.M. Pot 4:30–1:00
Dish. Relief Part-time Norm				P.M. Dish 4:00–12:30			

Figure 18.7
Weekly posted schedule.

problems—a spouse's vacation; exams, semester breaks, or graduation; and fatigue, to name only a few.

One significant cost advantage of part-timers is that they receive fewer fringe benefits (in many companies, virtually none). This advantage, however, is under political attack and may well disappear as future wage-and-hour legislation is enacted at the state or national level.

Although part-time employees present some problems, greater flexibility and lower payroll costs often make them economically attractive. You can expect that the work of hospitality managers in future years, as the industry's labor shortage continues, will be even more involved with supervising and motivating part-time employees than it is today.

COMPUTERIZED SCHEDULING

Computer programs to schedule employees are increasingly common. However, people can schedule at least as well as computers can, and so scheduling programs don't generally seem to reduce payroll hours. Rather, their great advantage is their speed. By using a computer, managers can complete their scheduling work in roughly one-third the time that doing it by hand takes. Computerized scheduling is especially helpful when there is a change in managers in a unit. Much of the experience of the manager who has been there awhile is programmed into the computer: workstations, staffing requirements, employee availability and work preferences, and peak-and-valley days and time periods. When the new manager comes in, he or she doesn't have to learn who everyone is and what their job is. Thus, the computer offers a real convenience to managers and is a time-saver for them.

This chapter, more than the other management function chapters, has focused on the nuts and bolts of hospitality management. Staffing in the hospitality industry is obviously a nuts-and-bolts function, but one that is vital to the success of an operation.

Our approach in this chapter illustrates another fact about hospitality management: the importance of attention to detail. It is essential for management to develop sources of good employees, to look at the details found on an application, to check references carefully, to pay special attention to a new employee's introduction to work, to base that employee's training on individual task analysis, and to undertake painstaking staff planning. As one of the earliest hospitality educators, Bernard R. Proulx, the first head of the School of Hotel, Restaurant and Institutional Management at Michigan State University, used to tell his students, "The secret to success in the service industry is attention to detail."

Summary

In a service-oriented field such as the hospitality industry, human-resources management is especially important. Also, because the hospitality industry usually spends so much of its income on wages, selecting the right employees is essential.

First, the employer must define the right type of person for a particular job, in terms of both physical and mental abilities. Second, that kind of person must be recruited for the job, using internal and external sources to find suitable candidates. When a pool of applicants has been gathered, some must be selected, by means of the application, an interview, and a reference check. Then comes the employee's induction, or orientation to the job and to fellow employees. Training is necessary and generally involves on-the-job training.

Retaining people and planning staffing needs are also important. In regard to the latter, we talked about using part-time employees and computerized scheduling.

Key Words and Concepts

Personal service	Advertising
Payroll cost	Application
Job description	Selection
Job specifications	Interview
Recruiting	Orientation
Internal sources	Training
Part-time	Retaining employees
External sources	Staff planning
Employment agencies	Schedule

Review Questions

1. What has given rise to the current labor shortage?

2. What kinds of qualifications should be considered when recruiting an employee for the dish room? As a server? As a supervisor?

3. Describe some of the internal and external sources that employers use to find employees.

4. What does orientation to a job involve, and why is it important?

5. Why do some companies prefer to hire people with no experience?

6. Explain why management training is especially important before opening a new operation.

7. What are the advantages of hiring part-time employees? The disadvantages?

Internet Exercises

1. **Site name:** Directory of Hotel and Restaurant Homepages
URL: www.wku.edu/,hrtm/hotlrest.htm—Hotels, restaurants, and food management companies
www.ehotelier.com/browse/chains.php—Hotel chains
www.unlv.edu/Tourism/dining—Restaurants
Background information: These directories list the Web addresses for numerous hotel and restaurant chains.
Exercises: Select a hotel and a restaurant from the list and browse their Web sites. Determine whether they offer employment opportunity information on their Web pages.
   a. What job opportunities are listed on their Web pages?
   b. What training do they offer for entry-level managers?
   c. Do they list job requirements so one would know what the job entails?
   d. Do you consider this an effective method for recruiting employees? Why or why not?
   e. What is the difference between the recruiting efforts of the hotel versus the recruiting efforts of the restaurant?

2. **Site name:** Newspapers.com
URL: www.newspapers.com
Background information: Newspapers.com is a directory of all the newspapers in the United States regardless of size. You can search for a newspaper by title, state, or city. The directory provides the name of the newspaper plus a hot link to the newspaper's Web site.
Exercises: Choose a newspaper, perhaps a newspaper from your hometown or state. Search the classified advertisements for hotel and/or restaurant management jobs.
   a. Did you find the advertisements informative?
   b. What were the strengths and weaknesses of the advertisements you looked at?
   c. Print out the best and worst advertisements you found, and discuss them in class.
   d. Based on what you have seen, what information would you have included in a classified advertisement to attract potential candidates for management positions?

3. **Site name:** Free Management Library: Online Guide to Staffing

   URL: http://www.managementhelp.org/staffing/staffing.htm

   Background information: The Free Management Library provides easy-to-access, clutter-free, comprehensive resources regarding the leadership and management of yourself, other individuals, groups, and organizations. The content is relevant to the vast majority of people, whether they are in large or small for-profit or nonprofit organizations. Over the past ten years, this library has grown to be one of the world's largest, best organized collections of these types of resources.

   Exercises:

   a. Choose one of the "chapters" on the above Web site that is of interest to you. Lead a class discussion on the management function of staffing in an organization and describe why this information would be important to a hospitality manager.

Notes

1. *Restaurants USA*, September 2000, pp. 14–19.
2. Margaret Sheriden, "Head Count," *Restaurants & Institutions*, January 1, 1998, p. 62.
3. *Restaurants & Institutions*, March 15, 1993, p. 121.
4. Joan Viewager, "Research Summary: Exploring the Effectiveness of Hourly Employee Training," Proceedings of the Twenty-First Annual Chain Operators Exchange, (Chicago: International Foodservice Manufacturers Association, 1994).
5. Amy Zuber, "Buffets, Inc. Aims to Keep Managers with $20K Incentive Program," *Nation's Restaurant News*, October 27, 1997.

The Hospitality Industry

(Courtesy of Marriott International.)

CHAPTER NINETEEN

Control in Hospitality Management

The Purpose of this Chapter

I f you've ever found yourself working on too many projects at once and suddenly felt the need to sit down and figure out just what you're getting done, you will understand how important it is to control projects before they begin to control you. A hospitality system has so many varied activities that the control function is absolutely essential to its efficiency and success. In this chapter, therefore, we will explore the ways in which organizations measure their results against goals—how they appraise exactly what they are getting done.

Control is too often thought of as exclusively something for the accountants to worry about. However, nothing could be further from the truth. The information from control systems exists, first and foremost, to guide management action. In fact, in hospitality operations, control information often does not even enter the accounting stream; it may not even be numerical. Although whole courses—indeed, entire curricula, such as accounting—are devoted to a detailed study of control, our purpose here is more basic: We want you to see control as the heart of hospitality management.

THIS CHAPTER SHOULD HELP YOU

1. Explain how control relates to other functions of hospitality management.
2. Provide an example of how control functions as a future-oriented process and as a basis for management action.
3. Identify and describe four common characteristics of an effective control system.
4. Identify the two principal financial accounting statements used to report results of business operations, and explain their managerial purpose.
5. Identify the principal concerns of managerial accounting in the hospitality industry, and describe the tools used to address them.
6. Define decision accounting, and explain how it differs from financial and managerial accounting.

The Importance of Control

Because specialized courses are taught in the area of **control**, hospitality students sometimes get the impression that control is separate, something located "over there" in the accounting office. However, as we will see in this chapter, control is an integral part of every manager's and supervisor's work: Control is the work that managers and supervisors do to measure performance against standards, detect and analyze variances from target performance, and initiate corrective action.

Control affects and is affected by all the other functions. For instance, the standards that result from planning are meaningless without some way of measuring performance, just as a set of numbers measuring performance is meaningless without some idea of the results desired (i.e., some standard).

Similarly, a major function of organizing is to fix responsibility for results. Once again, if we have a measure that can tell us something is wrong but no means of saying who takes responsibility for corrective action, the purpose of control will be stymied.

In Chapter 18, we saw that proper staffing is necessary to achieve the productivity that allows us to meet payroll cost targets and that staff planning is the basis for that control. As you read Chapter 20, on the directing and leading function, you will want to remember that information is an important basis for management action. A **control system** is part of a larger plan to measure performance and make improvements. If control systems yield nothing but numbers, they will be useless. Perhaps an illustration from the personal experience of one of the authors can demonstrate this point best:

> I once was hired to relieve a man—let's call him Mr. Brower—who was the food and beverage manager in a hotel whose food operation was losing money badly. Mr. Brower had received his early training in a well-established hotel company with several operations.
>
> When I was introduced to Mr. Brower, he took me into his office and pulled out a set of ledger books. As he opened the first, he said, "We've got a terrific control system. All our food is issued from the storeroom only on requisitions, and the storeroom man sends the requisition slips up to me and I post them. As you can see, we have a daily food cost in 18 categories!"
>
> As I talked further with Mr. Brower, I learned that most of his early experience had been as a food controller—someone responsible for maintaining the food cost accounting system for the hotel where he worked. What he had done

was to come as close to duplicating the elaborate control system at the hotel where he used to work, and then he labored long and hard to maintain the system.

Unfortunately, he had produced a system that told him in great detail that his operation was going broke. He didn't know what to do about it, so he sat in his office and kept his records straight! The process of untangling the mess involved getting rid of the storeroom man, who really wasn't needed in an operation of that size (and who had been regularly stealing the food), establishing food and payroll cost standards, and then correcting performance on specific work stations and food products.

Control and the "Cybernetic Loop"

The word *cybernetic* is derived from the ancient Greek word for the steersman on a ship. In early times, the steersman would aim the ship toward some point on the horizon. If the ship's course veered to the left, he'd move the tiller to steer a bit to the right and vice versa.

In modern management, control systems fill a similar function. As an operation progresses, various information about the progress is collected and presented to management in a usable form. If the report indicates that the food cost is on target, management can turn its attention elsewhere. If the food cost is off, however, it's up to the manager to "move the tiller" and to take corrective action on the basis of the information, just as the steersman reacted when he saw the bow of the ship moving off the point to which he was steering. The term loop is used in conjunction with *cybernetic* because the process is continuous. Action constantly takes place, and information about that action must constantly pass through the loop to indicate either that the process is on course or that corrective action is required. This constant vigilance results in more information being sent through the loop, and so on.

A simple example of the **cybernetic loop** in action—a cashier's report—is shown in Figure 19.1. A simple diagram of the cybernetic loop appears in Figure 19.2.

Mary, a cashier, starts her shift with a $100 bank. Throughout her eight-hour shift she accepts cash from customers

Cashier's Report

Shift: A.M.
Cashier: Mary

Sales	319.72
Cash Deposit	319.87
Over (Short)	.15

Figure 19.1
Cashier's report.

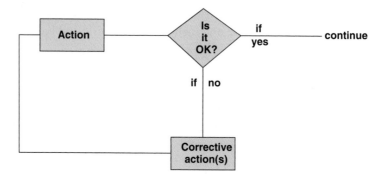

Figure 19.2
The cybernetic loop.

who are paying for their meals or making change. As necessary, Mary rings up each sale on a cash register. At the end of her shift, she prepares a report that shows:

1. The amount of sales rung up on the register
2. The amount of money she is depositing (which is always the amount of money in her cash drawer, less her $100 bank)
3. The difference between the sales she has collected and her deposit, or the amount she is over or short

Most cashiers make small errors, and so they may be over or short a few cents. However, if the error is greater than 50 cents (or some other prescribed amount), management approval of the report may be required.

Notice what this procedure accomplishes. If Mary's report indicates she's on course, no management action will be needed. If she makes an error over the prescribed amount, management must be informed. Depending on the circumstances, management can accept the error or initiate corrective action. The corrective action is not intended so much to correct an error that has already occurred as it is to find the cause of the error and take steps to avoid it in the future. Once management locates the error that Mary has been making, it can help her avoid it. Thus, control is forward-looking. Control, in effect, records and studies what has happened, not principally to place the blame on someone, but to discover what went wrong so that the error can be avoided in the future. We study the past not for itself but for what it can teach us for the future.

This example also provides a good illustration of an **information system**, a concept that we've encountered repeatedly. An information system collects, transcribes, and summarizes information about transactions or other events and provides management with a summary for analysis and action. Figure 19.2 shows a simple version of an information system as a cybernetic loop. An action is followed by some test against standards. If the performance is acceptable, the process will continue; if it is not, some corrective action or actions will be taken, and then we will try again.

Information systems are concerned with more than just financial data. For instance, some information systems involve personnel and marketing. Many states have developed nutritional audits for the custodial and health care institutions they operate. These nutritional audits measure not so much the cost of food as the nutritional adequacy of the diets being served.

The key to designing an information system is to determine just what information is needed—or, to use the language of the systems analyst, just what information output is required of the system. An information system, then, is any means of collecting information (cash register tapes, meat yields, guest counts) and translating the raw information into an intelligible, usable summary form. Examples shown in Figure 19.3 are a cashier's report, a meat yield report, and a summary of guest arrivals per ten-minute time segment.

The final element is that the report must go to the right management person to be useful. Figure 19.3 illustrates this simplified concept of a control system using the three examples cited.

Lest the term "information system" discourage a student with its apparent complexity, let us look at some examples of control through management action based on exceedingly simple information systems.

CONTROL THROUGH MANAGEMENT ACTION

Many food service operators have found that the recipe itself can be one key to controlling food quality and reducing waste. At some food service operations, the food production director and other members of the management taste samples of all the food that has been prepared to be sure that it has been prepared correctly. Because these managers are trained to taste (and have tasted the same recipe many times before), what better way to be sure that quality standards have been met?

Recipes also specify portion sizes, but it takes skill to portion correctly when carving a roast, for example, and errors are common. To aid a carver, many operations use the over-and-under portion scale. This scale is actually a simple information system that permits a carver to correct over- or underportioning and to know when his or her carving hand has grown a little heavy or a little light. If the person portioning the meat keeps a simple record of how many portions are served from a cut of meat, at the end of the meal a supervisor can prepare a yield report and compare the results (portions served) with the standard that has been established for that product.

The control function
includes maintaining
proper levels of in-
ventory. (Courtesy of
Southwest Airlines.)

Indeed, some food production managers actually study the garbage can. By periodically raking through the garbage, they can see what kind of food and how much of
it is being left on plates. If one item consistently becomes waste, it can indicate either
poor quality or overportioning. Further study of the information serves as the basis for
management action. In short, regular garbage inspection can be part of an information
system.

In large- and medium-sized hotels, housekeeping supervisors below the executive
housekeeper level are often called inspectors. Their supervisory duties include not only
assigning work and issuing supplies but also physically inspecting each room as it is
finished to be sure it has been made up to the hotel's standards and reporting the results to the housekeeper and front desk.

Many hospitals (and other hospitality institutions as well) collect patient comments
and tally them. If the dietary department complaint rate suddenly goes up, the dietitian knows there is a problem and can begin the necessary study to correct it. These
complaints can become the focus, again, of an information system.

CHARACTERISTICS OF CONTROL SYSTEMS

We can conclude our discussion of control systems by identifying four of their common characteristics:

1. *Control systems are continuous.* Data are collected and stored on a continuing basis so that if something goes wrong, the data can be carefully analyzed to direct management's corrective action.

2. *Reports must be timely.* Data must be collected and reported so that management can act to correct a problem before there is too great a loss. Thus, many food service operators compute their food costs weekly or every ten days, rather than monthly, in order to catch and correct promptly any unfavorable food cost patterns that develop.

3. *Control is aimed at some key point, and no action is called for unless a problem is detected.* This approach is sometimes called management by exception. Thus, a food cost is computed periodically because it is a key cost in a food service operation. If the food cost is out of line, further study and action will be initiated. If no problem is detected in the routine report, no action will be taken.

4. *Control is action-oriented.* At the risk of belaboring this point, we repeat that nothing really is controlled until somebody does something about the problem. Thus, control systems and information systems are similar, but a control system not only includes the information but also provides for corrective action if it is required.

With profit margins as slim as they can be in the hospitality industry, particularly in food service, it is imperative to develop and maintain a workable control system. It is no coincidence that the companies that are leaders in hospitality do a particularly effective job of control. One company, Essex Partners, was highlighted in a recent issue of the Cornell Quarterly focusing on best practices. Essex follows three simple steps to achieve their control objectives: (1) they hire managers who are aware of the importance of control, they tie rewards to performance, and they provide adequate support in this area; (2) they prepare a carefully developed budget with input from various sources; and (3) they hold weekly meetings to review progress, focusing on controlling costs that include costs not typically considered a direct management responsibility.[1]

Tools for Control

Managers use two somewhat different kinds of tools to achieve control: **financial accounting** and **managerial accounting**. Although each form of accounting has significant similarities, each is designed to meet particular needs.

FINANCIAL ACCOUNTING

Students will recognize financial accounting as the subject routinely taught in their first college accounting course. Financial accounting is based on a series of conventions adopted by the accounting profession to ensure a common basis of reporting the results of business operations. Financial accounting is principally designed for outsiders: for bankers who may be asked to lend money or for stockholders or potential investors who want to evaluate the firm's performance in comparison with other investments.

The principal financial reports used in financial accounting are the **balance sheet** and the **statement of income and expense**. The balance sheet is simply a statement of the firm's value and ownership. On one side, it lists the firm's assets, and on the other, the claims against those assets by those to whom the firm owes money and by the owners. Table 19.1 provides an example of a hospitality industry balance sheet. The balance sheet offers a great deal of information to financial analysts, but its use in day-to-day operations is limited.

The statement of income and expenses, on the other hand, is used by operations people both to evaluate performance on a month-to-month basis and, as we shall see, to prepare budgets for future periods.

Each segment of the hospitality industry has a uniform system of accounts that tells accountants how to classify the various kinds of income and expenses. The uniform systems of accounts serve two purposes. First, they present income and cost information so that results in one operation can be compared to those in other operations or with industry averages. Second, uniform systems of accounts collect information in a way that pinpoints performance against responsibility. In a restaurant, the chef or food production manager is responsible for the food cost; the people responsible for certain groups of workers (cooks, wait staff, dishwashers) are responsible for their component of payroll cost; and the restaurant manager is responsible for the restaurant's overall operating performance. The accounting profession has developed the term **responsibility accounting** to describe this means of classifying and reporting financial information. This form of accounting is not, however, new to the hospitality industry. The hotel industry (with its own uniform system of accounts) has long pioneered responsibility accounting.

Income and expenses are divided among departments—in hotels, these departments include rooms, food and beverage, and telephone—and a departmental net income is derived by subtracting the departments' expenses from the revenue it generates. Each departmental net income represents an accurate reflection of the department head's performance. The general manager's performance is assessed by total income before fixed charges, which is the total of all departments' net operating incomes less certain unallocated expense items.

Just as the American Hotel & Lodging Association periodically updates and publishes a uniform system of accounts for hotels, the National Restaurant Association publishes a uniform system of accounts for restaurants. The American Hospital Association supplies similar guidance in health care, and the Food and Nutrition Service publishes guidelines for school lunch accounting.

One major purpose served by following the appropriate industry accounting system is that it permits your operation to compare its results with industry averages. For the hotel-motel industry, the accounting firm of PKF publishes an extensive study of hotel industry performance based on the uniform system of accounts. The National Restaurant Association publishes a statistical study for restaurants called *Restaurant Industry Operations Report.* Other organizations and associations publish similar reports for other segments of the hospitality industry.

MANAGERIAL ACCOUNTING

Financial accounting is prepared according to accounting conventions that enable outsiders to evaluate performance. Financial accounting statements, particularly the statement of income and expenses, are useful to managers as

TABLE 19.1

Travel-On Motel Balance Sheet as of December 31, 200X

Assets	
Current assets	
Cash	$10,000
Accounts receivable	15,000
Inventories	12,000
	$37,000
Fixed assets	
Building	$1,000,000
Less depreciation	250,000
	750,000
Furniture and fixtures	$110,000
Less depreciation	55,000
	55,000
TOTAL ASSETS	
Liabilities and Capital	
Current liabilities	
Accounts payable	$15,000
Accrued expenses	7,000
Mortgage payable (within one year)	10,000
Long-term liabilities	$32,000
Mortgage	600,000
Capital	
Common stock	$100,000
Retained earnings	110,000
	210,000
TOTAL LIABILITIES AND CAPITAL	$842,000

well as to outsiders, we should note, but they must always follow the conventional form prescribed by the accounting profession. Managerial accounting, on the other hand, is prepared by and for insiders, that is, management. For that reason, it can take any form that is helpful to managers. The principal concerns of managerial accounting in the hospitality industry are **food and beverage cost control** and **payroll control**. Some operators pay fairly close attention to such miscellaneous direct operating costs as cleaning and guest supplies as well as utilities, but much less time and effort are generally spent on these. The information these control systems yield, in turn, is used in the budgeting process.

Food and Beverage Cost Control. Food and beverage cost control can be divided, in turn, into two general areas: **precost control** and **postcost control**. Precosting refers to the process of determining in advance the cost of a portion of food or drink (or of a whole meal). This represents the "standard" cost. The best way to do this is to work from standard recipes and determine the cost of the recipe ingredients. Then, if standard portions are used, the recipe cost can be divided by the yield to determine the cost per portion. The cost developed in this process becomes an important selling price determinant. Once (1) the cost, (2) the selling price, and (3) the quantity of each item sold are known, an operator can predict food or beverage cost with reasonable accuracy—if nothing goes wrong.

Postcost control, sometimes called historical control, focuses on what has happened so that if something does go wrong, management will know about it at the earliest possible moment and will have the information necessary to find out specifically what did go wrong. The purpose of postcost control, then, is not so much to remedy errors that have already taken place but, as we noted earlier, to provide a basis for steps to prevent the same mistake from being repeated.

Payroll Control. Our discussion in Chapter 18 showed that the principal technique for controlling payroll costs is staff planning that includes a tight, analytical scheduling process to ensure adequate coverage for each station and to avoid wasted coverage. Scheduling may be likened to precost control. For each payroll period, the payroll cost (i.e., the ratio of payroll cost to sales) is computed and compared with the target that management has established for that cost. When costs are out of line, management can institute special reporting systems for overtime hours (hours in excess of 40, for which time and a half must generally be paid) and for "extra" hours (hours in excess of those budgeted for the period).

Specialized Controls. Some operations develop **specialized controls**, or special reporting procedures, to control other direct operating costs such as cleaning supplies.

These procedures generally take the form of issuing systems that permit management to monitor closely the use of supplies such as soap, cleanser, and paper towels.

Some restaurants control china, glass, and silver breakage costs by taking a periodic inventory to determine the number of pieces broken or lost. This figure is then related to sales in a ratio called "the number of guests per broken piece." This kind of information can be tabulated simply by noting breakage as it happens. If management notes who broke each piece (usually by sorting the broken pieces into bins for each worker group), it becomes possible to categorize daily breakage by worker group. Management can then focus attention on those who are most responsible for the breakage.

Budgeting. The process of operating the controls described here yields a great deal of information about the business patterns that can be expected in the future. A **budget** is basically a plan of action spelled out in dollars, and it is usually based on information provided by the management accounting systems. Sales for some future period are estimated; then, applying the percentage for each expected cost (food cost, payroll cost, supplies cost, and the like), management can prepare an expense budget. Because cost patterns change, expense budgets may be based in part on past experience and in part on expected future cost trends.

The procedure for preparing budgets in many hospitality operations, especially at the unit level, need not be especially complicated. On a copy of a current or recent statement of income and expenses, write the estimate for the budget period alongside the figures for the past period. Base the new figures on experience and expected future trends (as shown in Table 19.2). These estimates may then be formalized after discussion with key department heads.

In multiunit companies, budgets are sometimes drawn up at the company's headquarters using computerized records of past performance and are then "rolled down" to the district and unit levels. At that point, the process reverses itself, with the units forwarding the revised unit budgets to the district level. Once approved at that level, the district totals its unit budgets and sends them to the control office as the district budget. As you can imagine, this process often involves a good deal of negotiation among the different levels of a multiunit firm.

Whereas business firms base their budgets on sales, public-sector food service operators (such as school lunch programs) must use appropriations as a basis for starting the budget process. Thus, for school lunch, the local school board may supply some operating funds; the state is another source of funding; and the federal government supplies a certain amount for each lunch served, and an additional amount for each free and reduced-price lunch. Finally, most students pay a certain amount for each meal. The income portion of the budget is basically a reflection of the number of meals served (student payments and the federal subsidy) and, thus, is similar to the

TABLE 19.2

Mid-Town Restaurant Statement of Income and Expense, Year Ending December 31, 200X

	$	$	
Sales			
Food	747,251	77.0	848,000
Beverage	226,507	23.0	252,700
Total	983,758	100.0	1,100,700
Cost of Sales			
Food	326,375	43.1	356,100
Beverage	61,116	27.0	66,000
Total	387,491	39.4	422,100
Gross Profit	596,267	60.6	678,600
Other Income	14,759	1.5	66,000
Total Income	611,023	62.1	744,600
Controllable Expenses			
Payroll	252,286	25.6	290,600
Employee Benefits	46,237	4.7	53,900
Direct Operating Expenses	54,107	5.5	60,500
Music and Entertainment	5,902	.6	6,600
Advertising and Promotion	15,740	1.6	17,600
Utilities	20,659	2.1	23,100
Administrative and General	59,025	6.0	66,000
Repairs and Maintenance	16,724	1.7	18,700
Total	470,680	47.8	537,000
Income Before Occupation Costs	140,343	14.3	207,600
Occupation Costs			
Rent, Property Taxes, and Insurance	45,253	4.6	48,000
Interest	5,998	.6	5,000
Depreciation	19,651	2.0	19,600
Total	70,902	7.2	72,600
Net Income Before Other Deductions	69,441	7.1	135,000
Other Deductions	4,918	.5	5,000
Net Income Before Taxes	64,523	6.6	130,000

sales item in a commercial operation. In some cases, additional sources of revenue may also be identified.

In health care, sales (except in the pay cafeteria) are not the determining figure for budgeting. That figure is, rather, some budgeted amount based on (1) the number of patient days expected and (2) the budgeted cost per patient day for food service.

Although sales, as such, are not the key, the starting point in the budget is the number of physical units (i.e., meals) that management expects will be consumed—a concept fundamentally quite similar to the sales estimate of a commercial operation.

Expense items in nonprofits' budgets are prepared in much the same way as in the commercial sector—that is, they are based on past experience and adjusted for expected change. In some cases, the expenses themselves are different. For instance, public institutions may receive commodities donated by the federal government. These donations change the cost of some items, but the budgeting procedure remains basically the same.

A budget should be the basis for management's cybernetic action: Actual results are compared with budgeted results, variances from budget target are analyzed to determine causes, and corrective action is initiated.

DECISION ACCOUNTING

Both financial accounting and management accounting are basically cyclical and repetitive. Budgets, for instance, can be prepared monthly, quarterly, and annually. As a month elapses, statements of results are reflected on accounting statements and compared with the budget. Then the whole cycle begins again the next month.

Financial accounting statements, moreover, embody the conventions accepted by the accounting profession. For instance, when an asset is acquired, a useful life for that kind of an asset is assumed, and the cost of the item is written off by means of an accounting entry reflecting its depreciation. Thus, a motor hotel valued at $1 million with a 20-year useful life will charge $50,000 a year to depreciation on its accounting statements. At the end of five years, following accounting conventions, the motor hotel will be valued at $750,000. Quite clearly, these conventions are convenient and permit standard treatment (or one of several standard treatments) to be applied in a way that helps make the resulting accounting statement understandable to insiders and outsiders alike. However, although accounting conventions are necessary, they often distort what is really happening. For instance, if the motel just described has been bypassed by an expressway, its value may have dropped far more than the depreciation entry indicates; by contrast, if a new office park has been built across the street, the motel's value may have doubled instead of depreciated.

Decision accounting, which is often related to strategic planning, differs from financial and management accounting in that it is not cyclical. The information for a decision is assembled in numerical form on a one-time basis.

Also, the conventions of accounting play no part in decision accounting. The assumptions made are those deemed appropriate to the analysis of the particular decision at hand. For instance, decision accounting tends to focus on direct variable costs such as food cost and payroll. It tends to ignore bookkeeping entries such as depreciation. Some examples of decision accounting tools—the payback period, rate of return, and break-even point computation—were presented in Chapter 16.

Summary

Control is the means by which management measures performance, detects and analyzes variances, and initiates corrective action. In this context, we defined a cybernetic loop and gave an example of it, a cashier's report.

Most control is carried out through an information system of some sort, and we also illustrated this with some examples: food portion sizes, inspections of cleaned rooms, and patients' comments on hospital service.

We then enumerated the characteristics of control systems and examined the principal tools to achieve control: financial accounting and managerial accounting. In regard to managerial accounting, we discussed food and beverage cost control, payroll control, specialized controls, and budgeting. Finally, we considered decision accounting.

Key Words and Concepts

Control
Control system
Cybernetic loop
Information system
Financial accounting
Managerial accounting
Balance sheet
Statement of income and expense

Responsibility accounting
Food and beverage cost control
Payroll control
Precost control
Postcost control
Specialized controls
Budget
Decision accounting

Review Questions

1. What is a cybernetic loop? How is it used in connection with cash control?
2. Give some examples of information systems in the hospitality industry.
3. What are the four characteristics of a control system?
4. How is managerial accounting used in food and beverage costs?
5. Describe decision accounting.

Internet Exercises

1. **Site name:** The Hilton Family of Hotels
   URL: http://phx.corporateir.net/phoenix.zhtml?c=88577&p=irol-irhome
   Background information: Hilton Hotels Corporation is one of the leading global hospitality companies with more than 2,800 hotels and 495,000 rooms in over 80 countries, including 105,000 team members worldwide.

Exercises:

    a. Describe Hilton Hotels Corporation's performance in terms of occupancy percentage, daily rate, and revenue per available room (RevPAR).

    b. Did the Hilton Corporation perform better or worse than in the previous quarter/year? What are the reasons it did better or worse?

    c. What are Hilton's financial goals for the future?

2. **Site name:** Brinker International

    URL: www.brinker.com

    Background information: Brinker International, Inc. is the parent company of a diverse portfolio of casual-dining restaurant concepts. They are principally engaged in the ownership, operation, development, and franchising of Chili's Grill & Bar, Romano's Macaroni Grill, On The Border Mexican Grill & Cantina, and Maggiano's Little Italy. Brinker controls 1,600 restaurants located in 49 states and 22 countries.

    Exercises: Go to the Brinker International Web site and browse the "Company Information" and "Investor Relations" Web pages. Compare the most current year's reports with those of the previous year.

    a. Identify and describe the financial indicators used in these reports.

    b. Did Brinker International perform better or worse? What are the reasons for it doing better or worse?

    c. What are Brinker's financial goals for the future?

3. **Site name:** The Free Management Library: Management Function of Coordinating/Controlling: Overview of Basic Methods

    URL: http://www.managementhelp.org/cntrllng/cntrllng.htm

    Background information: The Free Management Library provides easy-to-access, clutter-free, comprehensive resources regarding the leadership and management of yourself, other individuals, groups, and organizations. The content is relevant to the vast majority of people, whether they are in large or small for-profit or non-profit organizations. Over the past ten years, this library has grown to be one of the worlds largest, best organized collections of these types of resources.

    Exercises:

    a. Choose one of the "chapters" on the above Web site that is of interest to you. Lead a class discussion on the management function of Controlling in an organization and describe why this information would be important to a hospitality manager.

Note

1.   Judy Siguaw and Cathy Enz, "Best Practices in Hotel Operations," *Cornell Hotel and Restaurant Administration Quarterly*, December 1999.

The Hospitality Industry

(Courtesy of Sodexho.)

CHAPTER TWENTY

Leadership and Directing in Hospitality Management

The Purpose of this Chapter

The most visible work the manager does is to function as the leader of the work group: giving orders and instructions to employees, checking employee performance, and commending or correcting that performance. This chapter describes this work first as a function of worker needs and then as a function of the manager and his or her abilities. We intend for this chapter to help you develop a style of leadership that suits you personally.

THIS CHAPTER SHOULD HELP YOU

1. Describe how leadership and directing relate to three other functional responsibilities of management.

2. List and describe seven incentives that motivate people to accept direction on the job.

3. Explain and contrast two theories of leadership based on perceptions of employee attitudes toward work as identified by Douglas MacGregor.

4. List the factors that inhibit and support communication in the workplace.

5. Describe five key activities in which managers engage when directing.

6. List factors to consider when developing a flexible leadership style designed to achieve desired results.

Leadership as Viewed by Social Scientists

Management scholars and other social scientists have devoted a great deal of attention to the study of **leadership**. This attention is appropriate because leadership is clearly an important activity in what Peter Drucker calls "a society of institutions." Unfortunately, these scholars have raised more questions than they have been able to answer to everyone's satisfaction. Indeed, one sometimes gets the impression that those in the knowledge industry who concern themselves with management earn a living by disproving one another's theories.

Social science research models itself on the kinds of definitive, quantitative proofs found in the physical sciences, but it may never reach definitive conclusions about such subjective concepts as leadership. Fortunately, our purpose is less ambitious than that of scholars. To be sure, we want a theory that will guide practice, but we can accept some ambiguity in both our analysis of this subject and the conclusions we draw from it. Because leadership remains an open subject, we all have a great deal more to learn about it.

Some management scholars differentiate between **directing**—a management function—and leadership. Leadership is seen as a kind of influence, a way of bringing people to work willingly toward the company's goals, or technically, to "show the way" to employees. In this view, employees will respond to the boss's authority alone, but this response will likely be just enough to get by. As one source puts it, "being in charge doesn't automatically make anyone a leader."[1] Leadership is seen as an art, that of involving people's full voluntary cooperation. We have no quarrel with this description of leadership and, indeed, will have more to say on the subject later in the chapter.

The distinction between authoritative directing and leadership may be theoretically valid, but it does little to guide practice. Implicitly, managers lead when they simply direct. If the leadership is effective, the results will be raised above the minimum; if it is ineffective, the results will remain at some minimal norm or may even be pushed below that norm by personal antagonism.

As a practical matter, however, a manager's act of directing can never be separated from his or her leadership. Thus, we will use the terms interchangeably: When we use the word direction, we imply leadership, because, for better or worse, it is always present and in action.

Social science research has given us numerous insights into the process of leading and directing, and it has identified the key factors that managers must take into account as they go about building their leadership style. A brief review of some of these conclusions is useful in itself; moreover, it will help round out your understanding of the other management functions.

RELATIONSHIP TO OTHER MANAGEMENT FUNCTIONS

Perhaps the clearest way to show how closely the management functions are interrelated is to try to imagine leading without fulfilling the other functions. The results would be at once chaotic, dictatorial, and apathetic.

Without planning, work becomes chaotic. The order in which things are to be done, the quality of work deemed acceptable, and how much work must be done all would be determined by individual judgment and on the spur of the moment. The manager would be reduced to direction based on guess, and only the simplest or most stable operations would survive. Consider, as an example, the problems of staffing and staff planning: Without a clear plan of the work to be done and a plan that provides the right people to do it, an operation would be paralyzed.

Without organization—without some reasonable and coherent means of structuring authority relationships so that the work gets done—the authority of the strongest (power) becomes the only basis for directing. This is never the best approach to directing in any society, and it simply will not work in our affluent, educated society. In any case, only small and simple enterprises can operate on this authoritarian basis. We occasionally see operations in which direction is based solely on the authority of the owner ("Do it or I'll fire you"), but the employees rarely stay there for long.

Without control, employees begin to believe that nobody cares because nobody detects and corrects deviations from standards. Employees become apathetic about standards. Without feedback, no organism (let alone human employees) can learn. Once again, we are reduced to a chaos in which nobody really knows what to do or who is in charge.

Your leadership must be informed by understanding the plans of your organization, as well as the plans you make for yourself. Moreover, leadership must be exercised within the bounds of authority, implicit or explicit, in an organization. Finally, you must base your continuing acts of leadership both on measures of your own performance and on the performance of the units and the people under your direction.

Why People Follow

People enter an organization and perform their work, as directed by a manager with definite plans, for several good reasons, all of them selfish. Understanding in a general way what people expect from their work will permit you to base your directing activities on their needs and wants. This understanding is the essence of leadership. Our subject in this section, then, is really **motivation**. You will come to understand employees' motives first through study and observation and later, as a new manager, through practice. This growing understanding will permit you to shape your management activities to reflect the motives of the people working with you.

NECESSITY AS WORK MOTIVATION

The time-honored and most basic reason that people work is to provide themselves and their dependents with food, shelter, and clothing. When human labor was in excess supply and society's attitude was less protective of the disadvantaged, this motive was indeed powerful. When the alternative was between work and starvation, the threat of a job loss was terrifying, and this fear maintained a society based on wages.

Economic and social policy in our society today has greatly eroded the power of an employer. To be fired or laid off is certainly an inconvenience and may involve severe hardship. Economic policy in most Western countries, however, is committed to maintaining high employment levels. Moreover, unemployment compensation provides sufficient income to stave off disaster, and government employment services facilitate placement in another job. Besides, the majority of families today have two incomes. If one working partner is laid off, the other family member's income, along with unemployment compensation, will help most households cope. Thus, the manager's threat to fire (which would, in any case, be a last resort) has much greater limitations as a motivator than it did in earlier times.

ADVANTAGE AS WORK MOTIVATION

In a positive way, people seek not just enough money to live but also an income to satisfy the many aspirations now taken for granted in an affluent society. Thus, people work not only for money but also for more money. Many employees are motivated to work harder to keep a good job, to gain a raise, or to earn a bonus.

As ambitious people repeatedly demonstrate, workers will often put forth extra effort to secure promotion in rank. They do this not only for the increased income but often for the increased social status as well. We are social animals, and once we have taken care of our basic needs, we begin to pursue socially recognized rewards other than money. Not everyone, however, chooses to pursue such goals at work. Rather, recognition in their other reference groups—family, religious organization, neighborhood, fraternal organizations—may be more important to them. Thus, personal ambition often, but not universally, spurs increased effort at work.

PERSONAL SATISFACTION AS WORK MOTIVATION

We all know people who love their work, and work hard because they enjoy what they do. Such people may include the chef whose whole life is centered on preparing delicious food, the hostess or waitress who enjoys her contacts with people so much she seems to bubble, or (significantly) the mentally challenged dishwasher who is devoted to his or her work. In some cases, the work itself may not be so interesting, but the job may provide other rewards of a social nature. For example, many people enjoy coming to work because that is where their friends are.

INDEPENDENCE AS WORK MOTIVATION

Many people are motivated toward self-direction and independence. The idea of "being your own boss" as a unit manager entices many managers and employees. Servers and cooks often find that an important part of their work satisfaction is that they are good enough at what they do to require almost no direct supervision. However, this is by no means a universal motivation. Hardly anyone wants a work situation in which he or she is hassled, but not everyone seeks independence. Some prefer or need clear company (or work group) norms and frequent encouragement to achieve them. Indeed, for many employees, encouragement, praise, and personal recognition outweigh independence as motivation.

ENCOURAGEMENT, PRAISE, AND RECOGNITION AS WORK MOTIVATION

We have to recognize that many unskilled jobs in our industry are filled by people who find the work itself dull and unrewarding. We can do a great deal to reduce that dullness by fostering a friendly climate at work, praising good performance, and recognizing the worker as a person who makes an important contribution. We set unrealistic goals, however, if we expect everyone to respond warmly to these managerial efforts. In the final analysis, people are hired to do a job, not to be cheerful. (Being—or at least appearing—cheerful should, however, be part of the job of public-contact employees.) It is much more pleasant for everyone if workers are happy in their work, but the essential need is to have the work done according to the approved standards.

MONEY AS WORK MOTIVATION

Social science research has focused largely on the significance of nonmonetary rewards. That research, however, also provides ample evidence that pay is important. Money is, of course, an economic reward, but workers and managers often see it as a form of social recognition as well. For some people, a fancy title is important, whether a young manager is called "assistant vice president" or the dishwashers are renamed "sanitation specialists." Most people, however, expect and want utilitarian rewards for superior effort.

COMPANY POLICY AS WORK MOTIVATION

Company policy regarding such important matters as fringe benefits and working conditions can be an extremely important motivator. Some social scientists maintain that these conditions are taken for granted by workers. They argue that their absence would cause dissatisfaction but that their presence is not positively motivating. In the hospitality companies the authors have studied, however, it seems clear that these factors are important positive forces for employees who stay with a company over the long term. Because these loyal employees are especially valuable, we should view company policies as important motivators in our industry.

Fringe benefits include, among other things, vacation; sick leave; paid holidays; free or reduced-price employee meals; uniforms; group health, accident, and life insurance; educational benefits; child care assistance; and pension plans. Some fringe benefits, such as social security and unemployment insurance, are required by law. Fringe benefits took their name originally from the fact that they were a minor part—only the "fringes"—of an employee's compensation. Today, however, fringe benefits account for up to one-third or more of some employers' wage bills. As they become a more significant part of compensation, employees consider them in choosing which jobs to take and, especially, in deciding whether to stay with an employer or to change jobs.

Working conditions include both the physical and the social aspects of the workplace. One employer may offer an air-conditioned, clean, well-lighted kitchen, employee lockers and restrooms, and an acceptable employee dining area. The employee who can choose will prefer this place (other things being equal) to a hot, dingy workplace where the employee's personal belongings are unprotected and where he or she must take meal breaks in a remote corner or eat standing up.

Similarly, people prefer to work in a friendlier environment in which they feel accepted and respected by their co-workers and by management. People generally like to work with other people similar to themselves. This means that the employee selection process should take into account whether or not a prospective employee is likely to fit in and to accept the kind of work and interpersonal norms management and the work group expect.

Our discussion to this point suggests many different motives for working. An operation that recognizes that the motives for working vary from one worker to another will train its managers to respond to each worker as an individual. This means not only respecting the individuality of each worker but also shaping a manager's directing activities as much as possible to call forth the best effort from each worker.

DOES HAPPINESS LEAD TO PRODUCTIVITY?

Morale is the attitude a worker or work group feels or expresses toward the work. However, inexperienced managers often assume, incorrectly, that if morale is high, the work will automatically go well. In fact, research results find little direct correlation between high morale in the workplace and productivity. People may be happy at work and spend a good deal of their effort visiting with one another and in other ways expressing their happiness instead of working. Certainly, then, a manager's efforts to improve morale must include a clear expression of quality and quantity work standards. Just as we cannot expect every worker to be cheerful, we cannot settle for cheerfulness in place of adequate work.

In service organizations, however, employee morale (attitude and outlook) may be more important than it is in most other work. An employee with guest contact can hardly separate his or her attitude from the work, because work effectiveness depends on his or her manner toward the guests. The guests, in turn, do not recognize the physical service (a server brings the food) as separate from the way that service is performed (with a smile and a friendly word or with a frown and a snarl).

Moreover, employees in service systems are highly interdependent. Therefore, at least one criterion for acceptable employee performance has to be an ability to work with others. An irritable, unpleasant employee in a key position—whether or not the position deals with customers—can upset other employees. If employees are irritated with one another, then that irritation is often sensed by the guest. So employee morale is especially important in service organizations.

Leadership Theories

There have been numerous **leadership styles** and theories put forth over the years, but Douglas MacGregor's continues to be discussed in contemporary management thinking. Douglas MacGregor suggested that there are two different ways in which we can look at workers' attitudes toward work.[2] Each of these views, which MacGregor labeled *Theory X* and *Theory Y,* has implications for management.

According to **Theory X**, people do not really like to work, so they must be "coerced, controlled, directed, threatened with punishment" to get them to work. The average worker, this theory argues, avoids responsibility, is unambitious, and wants security more than anything else. Management based on Theory X is paternalistic at best and, at the very least, authoritarian. Rewards and punishment, the "carrot and stick," are assumed in this theory to be the key to employee productivity.

In contrast with Theory X, **Theory Y** is a more generous view of human nature. It sees "physical and mental effort in work to be as natural as play or rest," and it recognizes self-direction instead of external control as the principal means of securing effort. According to Theory Y, under the proper conditions people will, indeed, accept and even seek responsibility. Employees have (says Theory Y) a much greater capability for problem solving than most organizations realize. Management based on Theory Y relies on a worker's achievement-oriented motives and his or her desire for self-fulfillment rather than on sheer managerial authority. Theory Y calls for developing organizations in which employees can best fulfill their goals by working toward the success of the organization.

Which one of these theories is most correct? The best answers to the question of who's right are "Both of them" and "It depends." The question addresses but does not answer the central problem of management in a democratic society. Although we don't have any absolute and final answers, we can identify and consider the issues better in the light of the two theories just discussed.

THREE IMPORTANT ELEMENTS OF MODERN LEADERSHIP

To exercise leadership in our modern society, you must understand the nature of authority, both formal and informal, and the realistic limits on managers' use of authority. One of the most important limits on authority is the psychology of the individual worker, and an equally strong factor is that of informal group pressures. Leadership, then, is a result of the interaction of authority with the limits placed on management action by the psychology of the individual worker and the **work group**.

Authority. Authority in organizations is based on legal rights derived from business ownership and, in governmental organizations, from legislative acts. In franchise organizations, the leadership style franchisors use in their relationships with their franchisees is generally based on developing a consensus, but the underlying basis of authority is still the legal fact of the franchise agreement, which spells out the authority of the franchisor.

A somewhat different kind of authority may be conferred on a leader by a group. The term "informal group," a topic we discuss in more detail later in the chapter, refers to the social organization of the workplace that happens as a social process, in each work group. This distinction between formal and informal organization sets the ground for us to make the crucial distinction between a formal leader and an informal leader. The **formal leader** is in charge because of legal rights. Nevertheless, the formal leader can and should seek to supplement this legal authority with recognition by the group of his or her professional competence. A formal leader may also win acceptance as the group's informal leader or, more commonly, establish a productive relationship with the informal group structure.

An **informal leader** exercises a more subtle but very real kind of influence. Effective managers strive to work whenever possible with the person or persons whom a group chooses (more or less unconsciously) as leader.

Authority is accompanied by the right and ability to reward or punish. Although MacGregor and others see modern business relying less and less on formal authority, nobody expects it to disappear. To get results, however, authority must be tempered, in a relatively affluent society, in both substance and style. Your directing must be as fair as you can make it, and you should issue your directions in a manner that does not offend. Workers are entitled to their opinions, and employee turnover is too expensive to permit indulgence in arbitrary or offensive directing behavior. Theory X may not be altogether wrong, but certainly it is no longer enough.

The Psychology of the Worker—and the Work. The strength of Theory Y is in recognizing that many workers attempt to achieve personal goals and to find self-fulfillment in their work. For these workers, a clear communication of the organization's standards and goals during their training period is the most welcome form of direction. Workers who perfectly fit this pattern are not as common in our industry as we could wish, but persons who come close and require a minimum of supervision are not hard to find. The manager who is secure in his or her own competence will avoid unnecessary supervision and the appearance of harassment without losing sight of the need to assert the organization's standards when necessary.

A word about praise may be in order here. Most people thrive on encouragement, but praise is difficult to bestow graciously and may be subject to inflation. If an employee is competent and hardworking, a pat on the back from the manager may look like condescension. When you say, "You're doing a good job, Jane," she may say (to herself), "I know that. Who asked you?" Moreover, just as too much money in an economic system can lead to inflation and devalued currency, praise given too often and too easily loses its value.

The best kind of praise is your respect for the worker and your appreciation of work well done. This respect and appreciation usually come through in consulting with workers and in attending to their advice, solicited or unsolicited. This attention makes what they do, not what you say, important.

The work that people do may not really be important to them. For instance, a part-time waitress who sees herself principally as a wife, a mother, and a member of the PTA and her church group is unlikely to see her work as her principal means of self-fulfillment, even though she may take considerable pride in that work. Motivating her will thus require a different approach from, for instance, your boss's approach to motivating you, an ambitious, rising manager.

People in many unskilled jobs, such as dishwashers, simply do not find the satisfaction that Theory Y suggests they should be receiving. For that to happen, we need to redesign our organizations—and society itself, for that matter. Although such a grand redesigning is an interesting subject, it goes beyond the scope of this chapter and, to be frank, the realistic limits of hospitality managers today.

The Work Group as a Social Unit. Leadership and directing must use the authority that a manager derives from the formal organization, and it must take into account the various individual motivations—from pay to praise to self-fulfillment—normally found within a work group made up of individual employees. A third significant force is the work group itself as a social unit. When people come together to work,

It is important for leaders to understand the dynamics of work groups within the organization. (Courtesy of Sodexho.)

they develop a social organization with its own leadership, its own norms of work and social conduct, and, very often, a cliquish structure.

In a server work group, for instance, managers find strong feelings about how work should be distributed (including the number of guests that should be seated on a station). Some restaurants actually use a turn system in which each server serves a party seated at his or her station in rotation. The object is to be sure each server gets a fair share of the business. Variations from the order of turns can create a great deal of trouble for a supervisor.

In practice, however, some waiters or waitresses can handle more parties than others can. Following the turn system can, therefore, hold back the more able and place some guests at stations in which a slower server is actually overloaded. The result is that the fast service person may seek another employer and the guest who gets stuck with an overloaded, slow server may seek another restaurant. The turn system of seating, however, is most significant as an example of the power of a work group over weak or indifferent management.

In responding to the norms that workers develop among themselves, no manager should surrender the formal authority inherent in his or her position. Neither can a manager, however, afford to ignore a force as strong as social pressure. One way to deal with this force is exemplified by an incident from one of the authors' experience as a manager dealing with an informal work group leader:

When they encounter the person whom a work group has chosen (very informally, sometimes subconsciously) as their leader, many managers regard that person as a threat to their authority. But an alternative way to approach the situation is to view the informal group leader as a communication link to the work group. When I was a young manager, I met a waitress, Ethel, who was an unusually competent person and had the respect of all the other waitresses. She was also a very strong-willed person who often opposed steps I wanted to take in managing the restaurant. At one point, I wanted to fire her. But the man I worked for just laughed and said I could fire her "when you've learned what she knows." It took me a good deal of time to find out that if I consulted Ethel instead of ordering her to do things a certain way, I could get not only her cooperation but often some good advice. Building on this realization, I found that instead of announcing "policy," I could discuss a problem or goal with Ethel, indicating what I thought but remaining open to her reactions. Generally, the results of our discussions would make the rounds and, in a few days, become adopted as policy both by the house and by the waitresses—without any fuss. Moreover, the new policy carried force because it had been accepted voluntarily. Also, my own role as the formal leader was reinforced by my acceptance of the work group's social values.

Within larger work groups, subgroups or **cliques** often form. Sometimes relations between these cliques are friendly or neutral; sometimes they become unfriendly or downright hostile. Management cannot do away with clique formation, but knowledgeable managers can arrange their directing activities so that they take these strong forces into consideration.

We do not present these few words on the informal group as a full discussion of this complex subject. Rather, we intend to offer only a few examples to illustrate the meaning of this third force bearing on the manager's directing and leading activities.[3] This discussion sets a useful background, too, for the subject of worker participation in management.

PARTICIPATION

In a democratic society composed of educated and relatively affluent workers, the influence of the worker and the work group is increasing. However, this increase in power need not be seen as a threat to management. A manager secure enough to invite and accept participation in decision making can harness strong forces for obtaining results. The level of worker participation, however, may vary with the circumstances.

Information. Keeping employees informed about matters that affect their work represents only the minimum level of consideration for a prudent manager. Employees whose assignments must be changed deserve an adequate explanation of what changes are to be made and why they must be made. When changes affect an entire group, the group should receive enough information to understand what is going on. Many managers use regular staff and department meetings to accomplish this function.

Consultation. Before a decision must be made, a manager can prevent hard feelings by consulting the workers who will be affected by that decision, as well as others who are knowledgeable in the area. Because of their familiarity with the activity in question, workers often see problems that managers may miss. Technical issues aside, this consultation often eases tensions associated with change and increases its chances of acceptance. As the previous section suggests, it is particularly important to consult workers who have the respect of their fellow workers and whose support may be crucial in gaining acceptance. Consultation should not be viewed as relinquishing management's responsibility and authority for decisions based on the prerogatives of ownership or some other legally constituted authority.

Involvement. Managers often see a problem, develop a variety of solutions with the workers, and then present these alternatives to the employees themselves for their decision. If the first solution they choose does not work, further discussion and change are obviously in order. Often, however, the best way to gain acceptance of change is to involve those affected in the decision. Moreover, the solution to some problems probably belongs to and should be undertaken by the work group.

Thus, for instance, a group of servers may be asked to help management develop the best means for assigning sidework (housekeeping chores in the dining room such as stocking side stands or filling salt and pepper shakers). Management cannot really ask whether or not this work should be done; it must be done. The issue is how. Implicitly, if the solution offered does not work in practice, management must confer again with the affected workers and arrive at another solution.

Communication

For directions to be followed, they must be understood. The best-thought-out plan will fail if it is not communicated in a way that can be comprehended.

BARRIERS TO COMMUNICATION

Factors that inhibit clear communication pertain to the language we use, the differing backgrounds of the sender and the receiver, and the circumstances in which the communication takes place.

Semantic Barriers. Different people attach different meanings to words. The phrase "my work" may have quite a different meaning to a manager and to a busperson. To one, it refers to a life's work; to the other, a part-time job after school. The word

Much of leadership involves effective communication skills. (Courtesy of Sodexho.)

management also conjures up different images for the manager and the person responsible for busing the dishes. To the manager, it may mean responsible execution of carefully studied company policy. By contrast, the busperson may think of the fact that "the boss docked my pay because I was late." A communicator must, therefore, choose words that convey the meaning of the sender in such a way that the receiver understands that meaning. Loaded words with strong emotional meanings—"free enterprise," "the system," "right to work"—may do more to confuse the discussion than to clarify it.

Social Background. Social background is closely related to the problem just considered. The values of the middle-class American, the background typical among managers, carry certain assumptions that may not strike the expected response among some employees. A good example is the idea of ambition.

People brought up in middle-class families that encourage striving for success take ambition for granted. By contrast, people raised in poverty, who have acquired only limited schooling and who see themselves as never having had a chance, may look at ambition quite differently. When the middle-class manager assumes in his or her communication that the pot washer shares this enthusiasm for achievement, the manager may be in for some unpleasant surprises. It is important to consider exactly what point of view the other person is coming from.

Immediate Environment. The place where communication occurs can have an important effect on what gets understood. If a worker has been late, calling that person into the office to discuss the tardiness may be taken as a signal of a serious offense.

If that signal is appropriate, fine, but if the tardiness is a first offense, it may be better to mention the matter to the worker privately in the immediate work area at a time when he or she is not busy.

On the other hand, a reprimand in front of other workers has quite a powerful negative impact. (There's an old and good rule to remember: Praise in public, reprimand in private.) Similarly, discussion of complicated matters at the wrong time results in confusion. Let's suppose the broiler operator asked you about a problem on his or her withholding tax form at a time when you couldn't answer and you said, "I'll get back to you later." To try to answer that question in the middle of the rush hour when he or she is under considerable pressure will probably inhibit understanding and increase annoyance.

GATEWAYS TO COMMUNICATION

Listening. One of the most important acts in telling somebody something is—paradoxically—for you to listen. Communication is not a one-way street; it is an interchange. When you speak to people, they reply either in words or with body language—the way they hold themselves, the look on their face, a shrug. Listening and observing these body language cues will tell you a great deal about how your message has been received.

Empathy. Your ability to put yourself in the other person's shoes in a conversation can be crucial to understanding and dealing with his or her reaction.

The Elements of Leading and Directing

Leading and directing are really continuous processes, but we can break them down into some key activities in which managers typically engage. In fact, the actions (or elements) we discuss here portray the diversity of leading and directing and demonstrate how they can vary from situation to situation. They include (1) telling someone what to do, (2) providing information on how to do it, (3) seeing that he or she has learned how to do it, (4) making the performance of the work as appealing and comfortable as possible, and (5) conferring specific rewards or punishments for performance. Now, we will examine these elements of leading and directing in more detail.

1. Orders obviously tell someone to do something. They are acts of authority—authoritative directions.

2. Instruction provides information about some hospitality work-related activity.

3. Training involves guiding employees toward the mastery of often complex activities. Thus, a manager may give new employees a week's training to qualify her or

him to begin work as a server. Properly executed, training involves not only telling and showing the trainees how to do the work but also evaluating later—for the benefit of both the trainees and the trainer—the quality of that learning. Trainees are permitted to do the work under supervision and to repeat the process until they achieve adequate mastery.

4. Motivating moves beyond ensuring that the worker knows how to do something; motivating makes the employee eager, or at least willing, to do the work. A manager who motivates employees tailors the whole array of inducements—pay, recognition and status, self-fulfillment—in a way appropriate to the needs and wants of each worker (within, of course, the limits of what is possible).

5. Sanctions may be either positive or negative, rewards or punishments.

Although motivation generally may be thought of as continuous and positive, individual acts of sanction can be either a raise or promotion, on one hand, or a fine or reprimand, on the other.

If a manager has done his or her job correctly, the employees will know what to do and how to do it, and they will have sufficient mastery of the work to accomplish it properly. Managers must continually respond to the individual needs and wants of workers to gain their willing commitment to work. Finally, managers are expected to recognize outstanding performance and, when necessary, to penalize those who do not perform adequately.

LEADERSHIP AND CHANGE

To this point, we have been discussing leadership and directing as two aspects of the same management function. Moreover, we have been discussing that function as a part of everyday ongoing activity in an operation. In an organizational crisis such as in a company that is losing money, however, the leadership needs of that organization emerge as critical.

Current research in the area of leadership suggests that managing change is one of the leading competencies that a leader must possess.[4] In an organization that needs to make fundamental changes, the work of the leader has three basic elements:[5]

1. *Establishing direction.* Seeing where an organization needs to go and expressing that vision in a way that people can understand is vital. Moreover, the strategies for producing the necessary changes must be spelled out. Thus, the vision must be one that can be acted on effectively.

2. *Aligning people.* Getting the appropriate people in the organization not just involved but committed to achieving the new goals is a necessity. This involves lining

up coalitions in the informal organization who will support the program of change. Some might call this "selling" the vision.

3. *Motivating and inspiring.* In effect, this involves keeping people sold and keeping them moving in the right direction—often against obstacles that come from inside the organization, from people who are threatened by the needed changes.

We might consider the case of a new hotel manager who takes over an operation that has been completely demoralized.[6] The hotel is at a very busy airport in a booming city. For its first few years, the hotel had both high occupancy and profits, but management neglected both the physical plant and the organization's morale, that is, its people. Management turnover was high and employee turnover disastrously so. As new hotels were added in the area, the market became overbuilt at about the same time the city's boom ended. Occupancy in the hotel dropped from over 85 percent to below 65 percent, then to less than 60 percent, and profit turned to loss. Bill Wayle was hired as food and beverage director, but the general manager (GM) quit two days after he arrived. The company asked Bill to take the GM's job. He took over the operation but found almost immediately that the man he reported to was not prepared to make some key expenditures. Bill's response was to decline the GM's job unless he had the necessary support. He was given the modest financial support he requested, and so the turnaround could begin.

The first thing Bill did was to make some cosmetic changes in the lobby, replacing soiled and damaged furniture and light fixtures. The next thing he did was to announce a long-range improvement plan. He met regularly and frequently with department heads, attended department meetings, and spent a lot of his time moving around the hotel, talking with employees. Everywhere his message was the same: "We can't fix everything at once, but we can improve our service now. Will you help?"

Bill reexamined operating procedures, pruned unnecessary payroll from politically powerful departments, and spent that money where it really affected service. He spent a lot of time on the phone selling his boss on the need to replace items such as worn-out bedspreads and lampshades and to begin the long-term improvement plan he had already promised the employees.

Almost at once, employee turnover dropped, and people bought into Bill's program to improve service now. As service improved and the property began to look less shabby, occupancy improved. In less than a year, the hotel was profitable again. With these results, it became easier to sell his company on the need for major investment.

We can look at Bill Wayle's activities in the context of our description of leadership for change.

Establishing Direction. "Better service—now" was a vision everybody could be a part of. The few very visible changes Bill made helped employees feel that things were getting better and enabled them to respond to comments about worn facilities positively. "We're working on it. It's going to get better" is a more effective response—to both employee and guest—than "Gee, I'm sorry it's such a mess."

Aligning People. Bill's frequent attendance at department meetings and his almost daily meetings with department heads in the early days established a new attitude—that somebody cared about the property. The consistent, realizable vision of improving service was repeated in every conversation and sold people on the idea that the hotel could be turned around. People either left the organization or began to take responsibility for their actions with the guests. Significantly, Bill had to sell his boss and the corporate headquarters on every investment in the property. From the beginning, he took a serious career risk in refusing to continue without support. In the longer run, he used effective operating results to line up support both above and below for his vision of returning the hotel to first-class status.

Motivating and Inspiring. Effective employees were recognized. Virtually all supervisory positions were filled by promotions from within. Effective performance was rewarded with public and highly visible praise, and effective people found their salaries raised as much as company policy permitted. These actions supported the growing enthusiasm for the turnaround program.

In a time of crisis, when change is needed, leadership becomes especially crucial. Good solid management needs to accompany leadership, but leadership has to tell managers where they are going (direction), line up support for new direction (alignment), and keep everybody sold and enthusiastic (motivating and inspiring). All of these are important in everyday leadership, too, but especially so in a time when an organization needs dramatic change.

Industry Practice Note 20.1 looks more specifically at real-life leaders in the hospitality industry.

Developing Your Own Leadership Style

As we have argued earlier, a manager's leadership role in directing the work ultimately stems from his or her formal authority. To direct work effectively, managers must take into account at least three factors. The first is the work that needs to be done. The second is the person or persons who are to do the work—and their individual characteristics. The third is the informal socializing group structure of the work group in question.

In fact, then, leadership is not an inflexible behavior pattern. Leadership styles will vary from situation to situation and place to place. If you are a junior manager just out

Leadership in the Hospitality Industry

As we have discussed in this chapter, leadership has received a lot of attention over the years and continues to capture the attention of researchers and industry practitioners. Universities, which have taught the subject for years, have developed leadership courses, leadership programs, and even degrees in leadership. However leadership is defined, one thing is clear: It is an important characteristic of those who are in influential positions in a variety of fields, including the public sector, politics, the military, the private sector, religion, and the hospitality industry.

When the term "leader" is used, several names should immediately come to the minds of hospitality students: Bill Marriott, Norman Brinker, Herb Kelleher, Jan Carlzon, and Walt Disney, among others. These individuals have all led multimillion-dollar hospitality organizations, overseeing tens of thousands of employees, and most, if not all, have written books about their experiences. Further, it should come as no surprise that each of their respective organizations is associated with a strong culture—something that leaders help to form and maintain. To quote one scholar on the relationship between leadership and culture, "Leaders who appreciate the importance of culture spend more time communicating values than they do anything else. . . . They put values into action by treating employees as they want employees to treat their customers."[1] Culture, vision, and change all figure prominently in current discussions of effective leaders.[2]

So, leaders appreciate the importance of corporate culture, encourage specific workplace values, and are highly visible, both within the organization and without. But what else do they stand for and what are the other characteristics that make them what they are? Various authors and researchers have suggested that leaders have a vision; share that vision with the entire organization; are committed to organizational learning; are able to recognize, capture, and reward competence; and have the power of influence. They are described by both their personality traits and their behaviors. They are risk takers. They have led their companies through difficult times. They have been successful. They deal effectively with change. They inspire people within the organization. They accomplish goals. In short, while the definitions of leadership, and how to characterize leaders, will continue to be debated over time, most agree that one knows a leader when one sees one. The hospitality industry has been fortunate to have the leaders that it has had, as they serve as good role models for future leaders in the industry.

1. Robert Ford and Cherrill Heaton, "Lessons from Hospitality that Can Serve Anyone," *Organizational Dynamics,* Summer, 2002, p. 39.
2. Kenneth Greger and John Peterson, "Leadership Profiles for a New Millennium," *The Cornell Hotel and Restaurant Administration Quarterly,* February 2000.

of training and working with a group of senior workers, you will conduct yourself more tentatively than you might later as a general manager dealing with a similar group. If your employees' work is exciting and highly profitable, as might be the case for a server group in a topflight restaurant yielding generous tips, your leadership conduct might be different from what it would be toward the night cleanup crew that arrives as the restaurant is closing.

CAREERS IN HOSPITALITY

The dictionary provides several meanings for the word style. One of the meanings is a synonym for fashion—the way "everybody" is doing something. When we speak of management style, however, we certainly do not mean the current fashion. The definition that suits our needs better is "the manner or tone assumed in a discussion." The way leadership is carried out reflects the person who does the leading. Some leaders are flamboyant and confident; others, more reserved and (at least at first) unsure. The important point is that leadership in our industry is not some mysterious thing one is born with or without. Rather, it is a set of learned abilities. Just as people's personalities differ, so each person is likely to behave differently in directing the work of others. The difference, however, is usually in style, in manner and tone, not in substance. The basic goal of directing, as in all management functions, is achieving the desired results.

It will be up to you, finally, to determine how you best achieve results. Your success, however, will depend not only on the strength of your formal position, on the workers and work you direct, and on the work group, but also on who you are and what manner and tone, what style, works best for you in the situations you face.

You can begin to form your leadership style now, and you should. In field experiences, summer jobs, and part-time employment, you can observe the management style of others, even though you may not at first be given managerial responsibility. You can analyze the situations that managers confront and the people in those situations. Then you can decide for yourself how well you think the situations were handled, how they might have been handled better, and how you might feel most comfortable in handling similar situations.

In preparing for your future as a leader, keep in mind some of the research findings from recent studies:

- Leadership capacity of companies is on the decline.
- Companies do not seem to be doing what is necessary to develop replacements for current leaders.
- The emphasis in organizations is likely to become more focused on leadership rather than technical skills.
- Leaders of the next decade will need to be master strategists, change managers, relationship builders, and talent developers.[7]

You should certainly consider the process of learning to act as a leader and directing the work of others as continuous and lifelong. The most accomplished artists, after years of practice, will still speak of how much they have left to learn. Management, as it is implemented by individual managers, is definitely an art based on understanding and practice. It is a fascinating art one can learn through both study and practice. The fascination can last a lifetime, and the process has already begun for you.

Summary

First, we defined leadership, differentiated it from direction, and explained the reasons that it is important.

Our second subject was people's motivations for working: necessity; advantage; personal satisfaction; independence; encouragement, praise, and recognition; money; and company policy. This led us to consider whether happiness, or high morale, results in high productivity.

We discussed MacGregor's Theory X and Theory Y, plus three elements of modern leadership: authority, psychology of the worker, and the work group. Worker participation was also described as important.

Good communication between managers and workers is important as well, and so we talked about possible barriers (semantic, social background, and immediate environment) and possible gateways (listening and empathy) to effective communication.

The last topics were an enumeration and description of the elements of leading and directing, the special requirements of leadership in times of crisis, and ways to develop your own leadership style.

Key Words and Concepts

Leadership	**Theory X**
Directing	**Theory Y**
Motivation	**Work group**
Fringe benefits	**Formal leader**
Working conditions	**Informal leader**
Morale	**Cliques**
Leadership styles	

Review Questions

1. What is the difference between leadership and direction?

2. Describe what might happen in a quick-service restaurant without leadership.

3. List and briefly discuss the motivations for working.

4. How do Theory X and Theory Y fit with your management style—or intended style? Would you lean toward X, Y, or some other position?

5. Using the three basic elements of leadership discussed in this chapter, analyze a critical situation you have encountered, either at work or as a student. How did the leaders involved respond? How should they have responded? What would you have done?

6. Describe the informal structure of a work group to which you have belonged.

7. Describe a manager or boss you have admired, and explain why.

8. Do you think you would be a good leader? Why or why not?

Internet Exercises

1. **Site name:** Hotel, Restaurant and Tourism Online Professional and Trade Journals
   URL: www.wku.edu/,hrtm/journal.htm
   Background information: This Web page provides links to hospitality professional and trade journals online and serves as a launch pad to retrieve information from these journals. Some journal sites require a free registration in order to access their materials.
   Exercises: Choose several of the online journals and search for recent articles on employee motivation, work motivation, productivity, leadership, facilitating change, or any topic deemed appropriate by the instructor. Read the articles and lead a class discussion on the topic you have chosen. How do the articles supplement the information in the textbook? Be sure to provide the other students with the names and Web address of the journals where the information was found.

2. **Site name:** The Center for Public Leadership
   URL: www.ksg.harvard.edu/leadership
   Background information: The center is dedicated to excellence in leadership education and research. It is equally committed to bridging the gap between leadership theory and practice. It provides a forum for students, scholars, and practitioners committed to the idea that effective public leadership is essential to the common good.
   Site name: The Leader to Leader Institute
   URL: www.pfdf.org
   Background information: The Leader to Leader Institute has its roots in the social sector and its predecessor, the Peter F. Drucker Foundation for Nonprofit Management. Its mission is "to strengthen the leadership of the social sector" by providing educational opportunities and resources to leaders.
   Site name: CIO (Chief Information Officer)
   URL: www.cio.com/research/leadership

Background information: CIO and CIO.com are published by CXO Media Inc. to meet the needs of CIOs (chief information officers) and other information executives. *CIO* is read by more than 140,000 CIOs and senior executives who oversee annual IT budgets in excess of $175 million.

Exercises: Choose an article or research study from one of the Web sites above and discuss how the concepts in the article might help you fulfill a leadership role in the hospitality industry. Your discussion should include the following, as applicable:

a. What behaviors does this article suggest will help you to become a more effective leader?

b. Does this article suggest ways for managers to make decisions differently? If so, how?

c. Does this article influence the way you will communicate with people in the future? If so, how?

d. Does this article address the three elements of modern leadership as described in the textbook? If so, which elements and how does it address these elements?

e. Does this article address ways in which a leader can facilitate change in an organization? If so, how?

f. Does this article help you to develop your own leadership style? Why or why not?

Notes

1. Kenneth Greger and John Peterson, "Leadership Profiles for a New Millennium," *The Cornell Hotel and Restaurant Administration Quarterly*, February 2000.
2. Douglas MacGregor, *The Human Side of Enterprise* (New York: McGraw-Hill, 1960).
3. An excellent discussion of this subject is found in George C. Homans, *The Human Group* (New York: Harcourt Brace and World, 1950).
4. Conference Board of Canada, June 2006.
5. John P. Kotter, *A Force for Change* (New York: The Free Press, 1990).
6. This incident is adapted from a case provided by the executive described and is chronicled in more detail there. See Thomas F. Powers, *The Royal Hotel* (Guelph, Ontario: School of Hospitality and Tourism Management).
7. *Developing Business Leaders for 2010*, Conference Board of Canada, April, 2002, p. 6.

PART SIX

Hospitality as a Service Industry

The Hospitality Industry

(Courtesy of Four Seasons Hotels.)

CHAPTER TWENTY-ONE

The Role of Service in the Hospitality Industry

The Purpose of this Chapter

While details differ, the tangible side of the hospitality industry, within segments, is surprisingly similar. Quick-service operations resemble one another within food categories, one budget motel offers pretty much the same as another, and so forth. Whether it's Big Mac versus the Whopper or Hampton Inns versus Fairfield Inns, company offerings look a lot alike. Increasingly, companies are realizing that service is the best way to achieve differentiation and is what can give an operation a competitive edge. This chapter examines service as a process, considers the work of rendering service as a personal experience, and, finally, considers how companies manage service.

THIS CHAPTER SHOULD HELP YOU

1. Define service in terms of both guest experience and the operation's performance.
2. Describe the principal characteristics of service, and contrast it to delivery of a physical product.
3. Describe what is necessary to successfully fulfill both the task and the interpersonal requirements of service.
4. Identify and describe the two basic approaches to managing the service process.
5. Explain how market segmentation forms the basis for a service strategy, and identify the requirements for establishing a strong service culture.
6. Describe the importance of service as a basis for successful competition in the hospitality industry.

A Study of Service

"**D**ear Mr. Wilson," the letter from Mortimer Andrews to the company president began, "Yesterday I arrived at your hotel in Chicago with a confirmed reservation guaranteed by my credit card only to be told that no room was available. I was furious and let the desk clerk know how I felt in no uncertain terms. The clerk, John Boyles, handled the situation so well that I wanted to write and tell you about it.

"John responded to my very angry tirade about my reservation by admitting the mistake was the hotel's. He said that he had made reservations for me at a nearby Sheraton and that your hotel would take care of the difference in the room rate. When I reluctantly agreed, he called a cab—after letting me know your hotel would pay the cab fare, too.

"What struck me was John's real concern for my situation, his professional manner, and the fact that he didn't give me any excuses: 'It was our mistake and we're anxious to do everything we can to make it right.' John carried my bags out and put me in the cab, convincing me that somebody really cared about this weary traveler.

"I travel a lot and it's hard work without the extra hassles and foul-ups. On the other hand, everybody makes mistakes. John's concern and assistance make a big difference in the way it feels when one of them happens to you. I thought you should know about this young man's superior performance. He is a real asset to your company. He restored my faith in your hotel, and I'll be back."

This incident may not seem like a major event, but consider for a moment just what the stakes are. Mr. Andrews is a frequent traveler. If we assume that he is on the road an average of two days a week, at the end of the year his business would be the equivalent of a meeting for 100 people. If we assume an average rate (in all cities he visits, large and small) of $75 per night, the room revenue involved is $7,500. Using industry averages, he is likely to spend an additional $3,250 on food and beverage. In other words, the receipts from this one guest amount to a $10,000 piece of business—and there is no shortage of other hotels he could stay at if he doesn't like yours. Extend this over several years and one begins to understand the long-term importance of keeping guests happy (in fact, some hospitality companies conduct this very exercise to determine the long-term value that a customer has to a company).

The rule of thumb, moreover, is that a dissatisfied customer will tell the story of his or her problem to ten others. The possibility for bad word of mouth and potential loss of other sales makes the problem of the dissatisfied guest even more serious.

In fact, a study of 2,600 business units in all kinds of industries, conducted by the Strategic Planning Institute, has been summarized in this way: "In all industries, when competitors are roughly matched, those that stress customer service will win."[1] If this is true in manufacturing and distribution, how much truer it must be for those of us whose business is **service**.

The population group that has dominated the hospitality industry (and most of the rest of the economy) is the baby boomers. Over the next ten years, this group will continue to move into the relatively well-off middle years. They are the best-educated consumers in history. These relatively affluent, sophisticated consumers (as we have noted elsewhere in this text) can afford and will pay for good service. Moreover, competitive options give them plenty of other places to go if they don't receive the kind of service they seek. It is not too much to say that excellence in service will be a matter of survival into the foreseeable future.

The role that John Boyles played in keeping Mr. Andrews' business illustrates how important the service employee is in hospitality. That incident invites us to consider just what service is, how it is rendered in hospitality companies, and how companies can organize for and manage service. These are the subjects of this chapter.

WHAT IS SERVICE?

"Service," according to one authority, "is all actions and reactions that customers perceive they have purchased."[2] In hospitality, service is performed for the guest by people or (less frequently) by systems such as the remote guest check-out operated through a hotel's television screen. The emphasis in our definition is on the guest's total experience, which is made up of all of these so-called **moments of truth**. Indeed,

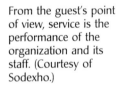

From the guest's point of view, service is the performance of the organization and its staff. (Courtesy of Sodexho.)

from the guest's point of view, service is the performance of the organization and its staff.

In most segments of the hospitality industry, the guest and the employee are both personally involved in the service transaction. If a customer purchases a pair of shoes or a car, he or she takes the finished product away without much, if any, concern about who made it or how. On the other hand, in hospitality, to give one example, a lunch is served. The service is produced and consumed at the same time. The service experience is an essential element in the transaction. If the server is grumpy and heavy-handed, it is likely that the guest will be unhappy. A cheerful and efficient server enhances the guest experience.

Notice we say "enhances." The tangible side of the transaction (the "product") must be acceptable, too. All the cheerfulness in the world will not make up for a bad meal or a dirty guest room. At the same time, it is also true that a good meal can be ruined by a surly server, just as a chaotic front office or poor service from the bell staff can ruin a stay in a hotel that is physically in excellent shape. The hospitality product, then, includes both tangible goods (meals, rooms) and less tangible services. Both are essential to success.

The server's behavior is, in effect, a part of the product (and of the total guest experience). Because servers are not the same every day—or for every guest—there is a necessary variability in this "product" that would not be encountered in a manufactured product. The guest is also a part of the service transaction. A guest who is not feeling well or who takes a dislike to a member of the staff may have a bad experience in spite of all efforts to please.

Because service "happens" to somebody, there can be no recall of a "defective product." It is now a guest's experience (and, in a sense, history). For this reason, there is general agreement that the only acceptable performance standard for a service organization is **zero defects**. Defects, however, should be defined in terms of the type of operation and the guest's expectations. At a McDonald's, waiting lines can be expected during the rush hour and will be accepted as long as they move with reasonable speed. However, a dirty or cluttered McDonald's, even in a rush period, represents a "defect," an emergency that needs to be remedied right away. On the other hand, a waiting line at a restaurant in a Four Seasons Hotel is, by Four Seasons' own definition, a defect. It is an emergency that needs to be remedied by a hostess or manager offering coffee or soft drinks and apologizing for the delay. Zero defects is the goal for which both organizations design their systems, but what counts as a defect varies according to company goals and **customer expectations**. This is the reason that hospitality companies establish standards—to help create consistency and to eliminate the margin for error. While neither McDonald's or Four Seasons is perfect, both have standards and dictate emergency action, such as management stepping in to help out, when a defect occurs. The notion of zero defects has also been approached in a more

Six Sigma Comes to the Hospitality Industry[1]

The concept known as Six Sigma has been around for almost 20 years now and originated, as many theories and techniques do, in the manufacturing segment. It was first used by Motorola and later embraced by General Electric, among others. It has only recently been introduced to the hospitality industry, though, when Starwood Hotels adopted it into their hotels in 2001.

Six Sigma is a statistically based business strategy that companies attempt to apply to help in reducing (and virtually eliminating) defects in products and services. In the case of the hospitality industry, in theory, it could be used to improve services from hotel check-in to waiting times for tables in restaurants. The name comes from the term sigma, which is the Latin word used for the standard deviation. In essence, it shrinks the acceptable range of performance. Six is the number from the mean (average) that is nearer to zero defects. In short, the technique attempts to quantify acceptable limits as they relate to customer satisfaction. In theory, the rate of errors (or defects) is reduced to less than one-thousandth of a percent. It is estimated that many firms operate within the three-sigma range.

While the technique/program has been in use relatively widely in manufacturing firms (approximately 15 percent of Fortune 1000 companies use it in one form or another), Starwood was the first hospitality company to introduce it. They have implemented a fully developed program that starts at the corporate level and identifies key people at the unit level to champion it.

The six steps of achieving Six Sigma are as follows:

Creating and identifying strategic business objectives
Creating core and subprocesses
Identifying process owners
Creating and validating performance measures
Collecting data on performance measures
Determining and prioritizing projects for improvement[2]

The prime objectives are to improve systems and delivery, increase customer satisfaction, and reduce costs. One scholar suggests that, in the hospitality industry, it may be more readily applicable to back-of-the-house functions than to the front of the house. Nonetheless, it is another example of how hospitality operators are attempting to improve their service and service quality.

1. Much of this note was based upon a paper presented by Harsha Chacko at the 2003 Council on Hotel, Restaurant and Institutional Education conference, "Six Sigma: Here to Stay or Just Another Fad?"
2. George Eckes, *The Six Sigma Revolution* (New York: John Wiley & Sons, 2001).

statistical manner focusing on the business method known as Six Sigma—the subject of Industry Practice Note 21.1.

Because the consumption of the service and its production occur simultaneously, there is no inventory. An unused room, as the old saw goes, can never be sold again.

A dining room provides not only meals but the capacity of a certain number of seats. While unused food remains in inventory at the end of the day, unused capacity—an unused table today—has no use tomorrow. This puts pressure on hospitality businesses to operate at as high a level of capacity as possible, offering special rates to quantity purchasers. A hotel's corporate rate structure is one example of such quantity pricing.

Let us summarize the **characteristics of service** that we have identified to this point. Service is experience for the guest, performance for the server. In either case, it is intangible, and the guest and server are both a part of the transaction. This personal element makes service quality control difficult—and quite different from manufactured products. Because there is no possibility of undoing the guest's experience, the standard for service operations must be zero defects. Finally, production and consumption are simultaneous. Thus, there is no inventory.

Face-to-face service transactions have the most power to make an impression on the guest. (Courtesy of Sodexho.)

TYPES OF SERVICE

There are three general types of service transactions: electronic-mechanical, indirect personal, and face-to-face transactions.[3]

Electronic-mechanical transactions in hospitality range from vending machines to such services as automated check-in and check-out. Other examples are the well-stocked in-room refrigerator that takes over much of the room service department's work in a hotel and a hotel's automatic-dial telephone system. Electronic-mechanical transactions are generally acceptable and sometimes even preferred by the guest where they eliminate inconvenience, such as waiting in lines. On the other hand, as frequently vandalized vending machines eloquently testify, electronic and mechanical failures often infuriate people. There is a premium on correct stocking, maintenance, proper programming, and adequate capacity so that breakdowns in service will not occur when no person is there to speak personally for the operation.

Indirect personal transactions include telephone (or e-mail) contacts such as hotel reservation services, the reservation desk at a restaurant, or the work of a room service order-taker. Some indirect transactions such as those just mentioned are generally repetitious in nature and, thus, subject to careful scripting. That is, because most of these interactions follow a few, very similar patterns, the employee can be trained in considerable detail as to what to say and when to say it. Some indirect contacts, however, are nonstandard. For instance, a guest calls the maintenance or housekeeping department directly from his or her room with a problem. An individual response to the particular guest problem is necessary, but the general procedure in such cases can be clearly specified in advance. Training in telephone manners—and careful attention to just who answers the phone in departments that don't specialize in guest contact work—is essential to maintaining the guest's perception of the property.

Face-to-face transactions have the most power to make an impression on the guest. Here, the guest can take a fuller measure of people—their appearance and manner. People whose work involves frequent personal contact with guests must be both selected and trained to be conscious, effective representatives of the organization. Because an increasing part of the services in modern organizations are automated, the personal contact that does take place must be of a superior quality. It is also important that public-contact employees be prepared to deal sympathetically with complaints about automated services. As John Naisbitt (a futurist and author of Megatrends) has pointed out, the more people have to cope with high technology, the more they require a sympathetic human response from the people in organizations. Naisbitt calls it "high touch."[4]

We must continue to be interested in all kinds of service transactions, whether personal or not. The work of designing computerized systems or scripting standardized indirect transactions, however, is generally specialized and done by experts. Virtually all of us, on the other hand, will have to deal with guests face-to-face. Accordingly, much of our attention in the balance of this chapter will focus on personal service. Figure 21.1 summarizes the characteristics, while Table 21.1 shows the three types of service interactions.

- An experience that happens to the guest. No recall of defects is preferred.
- Performance for the organization. Zero defects is the service systems design goal.
- A process whose production and consumption are simultaneous. Unsold "inventory" has no value.
- Because the employee is so much a part of the guest's experience, the employee is part of the product.

Figure 21.1
Characteristics of service.

TABLE 21.1

Three Types of Service Transactions

TYPE OF INTERACTION	EXAMPLE	KEY POINTS
Mechanical-electronic	TV check-out	Acceptable, if it eliminates inconvenience. Failure is unacceptable to guest, so plan should be error-free.
Indirect	Telephone contacts	Detailed scripting desirable so that each customer receives the same level of service.
	Housekeeping	General procedure must be specified and replicated in each and every room.
Face-to-face	Guest registration at the front desk	Person assisting the guest represents the organization.

Rendering Personal Service

S ervice involves "helpful, beneficial, or friendly action or conduct."[5] As we have just noted, some of these actions are provided by electronic, mechanical, or computerized devices or involve only indirect personal contact, usually by e-mail or phone. The most challenging service area involves helping that is performed person to person.

There are two basic aspects to the personal service act: that of the task, which calls for technical competence, and that of the **personal interaction** between guest and server, which requires what we can sum up for now as a helpful or friendly attitude (Figure 21.2).

TASK

As recently as the late 1980s, the hospitality industry's ideas on personal service as expressed in training programs and server manuals focused principally on procedure. Such training procedures tended to focus on how to carry trays, how to hold plates, the correct side of the guest from which to serve, and so on. Functional (or procedural) **task** competence is still an essential element in any service action. Guests don't want a thumb in their soup any more than they want a bellperson to get lost rooming them—or a front desk that can't find their reservation. The emphasis has changed, or is changing, however.

In modern service organizations, the task side of service is controlled by management through carefully developed systems that are supported by written procedures.

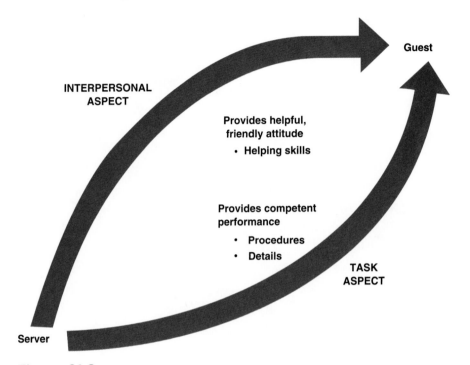

Figure 21.2
Two aspects of service.

Procedures of this kind control work in very much the same way that a carefully designed assembly line controls the way goods are manufactured.

As one authority on the study of services put it, "In real estate, the three components of successful investing have always been location, location, and location. In service encounter management, the components for success might be stated as details, details, details."[6] If a service organization is failing, blaming the employee is a cop-out. Getting the procedures right and a proper system functioning is the task of management.

Although there is no substitute for accomplishing the task of service competently, that alone is seldom enough to secure repeat business in a highly competitive marketplace.

INTERPERSONAL SKILLS

The other aspect of personal service involves the way in which the server (or desk clerk, etc.) approaches and deals with the guest. Perhaps the best model for thinking about the kind of behavior that secures a favorable response from the guest is that of "helping skills." These were originally derived from studying the working techniques of psychotherapists. The helping skills have now been simplified into a technique for

Both technical competence and good interpersonal skills are important to personal service. (Courtesy of LEGOLAND® CALIFORNIA.)

anyone whose work involves interacting with people. In fact, methods for its use have been developed for a wide variety of "people workers," ranging from police to college residence hall proctors and nurse's aides. All have in common that they are "people helpers" and provide services to people.

The core conditions of a friendly and helpful attitude can be spelled out more fully. Servers need to be able to put themselves in the other person's shoes; in a word, they need empathy. They need to present a friendly face to the guest and to do so in a way that is not going to be seen as just an act; they need to be (or at least appear) sincere.

Professionals who understand the skills that underlie successful interpersonal behavior assume that things such as eye contact, facial expression, hand movements, and body language generally are learned skills and, hence, readily teachable. For instance, such tactics as making eye contact with the guest send the message that the server is interested in communication and assisting.

Thus, employees must learn not just to have an attitude that is helpful and friendly to the guest but to convey that attitude to the guest by their behavior. Excellent interpersonal behavior is characterized by warmth and friendliness and a manner that imparts to the guest a sense of being in control—or the sense of being in the charge of someone who knows very well what he or she is doing.

Managing the Service Transaction

Most work done in the hospitality industry has the focused activity of a single process and can be supervised by someone who can keep track of what is going on. For instance, food preparation in a kitchen is organized around the process of cooking, usually following written recipes. If the food is acceptable, the process is being managed correctly. Hospitality service, on the other hand, is made up of transactions that are numerous, diverse, and often private. In a dining room each interaction between a server and a guest is really something just between the two of them—or, at most, between the server and the guest's party at that table. A multitude of these transactions are taking place in the dining room over the period of a single meal. The problems of managing this process are made more complex by the fact that the product is the guest's experience. The problem of producing a favorable feeling about an operation in numerous guests is too complex for any management to control in any detail.

Two somewhat different basic approaches to this challenge of managing service have developed.[7] The most common, which we can call the **product view** of service, focuses on controlling the tasks that make up the service. An increasingly important alternative is the **process view** of service, which concentrates on the guest-server interaction. The two views are not necessarily mutually exclusive. In practice, some of the elements of control that underlie the product view are found in any well-run service unit. In addition, attention to the way we treat people—that is, a process orientation—is necessary in any operation.

THE PRODUCT VIEW OF SERVICE

The product view looks at service as basically just another product that businesses sell to customers. The product view concentrates on rationalizing the service process to make it efficient and cost-effective as well as acceptable to the guest. The focus is on controlling the

Hospitality service is made up of numerous transactions including some that occur out of the sight of the guest. (Courtesy of Four Seasons Hotels.)

accomplishment of the tasks that make up the service. Employee behaviors that are part of that task are prescribed, often in considerable detail.

Perhaps the best example of the product view of service is McDonald's and quick-service food generally.[8] Theodore Leavitt has described old-style, European service as a process anchored in the past, "embracing ancient, preindustrial modes of thinking," involving a servant's mentality and, often, excessive ritual. Leavitt contrasts this with the rationale of manufacturing, where the orientation is toward efficiency and results—and where relationships are strictly businesslike. Leavitt sees the key to McDonald's success as "the systematic substitution of equipment for people, combined with the carefully planned use and positioning of technology." In fact, this formula is used by many companies besides McDonald's.

The quick-service formula for success is a simplified menu matched with a productive plant and operating system designed to produce just one specific product line. Leavitt suggests that giving employees choices in their tasks "is the enemy of order, standardization, and quality." The classic example of this simplification and automation is the McDonald's french fry scoop, which permits speed of service and accurate portioning with no judgment or discretion on the part of the employee. A McDonald's unit, Leavitt says, "is a machine that produces, with the help of totally unskilled machine tenders, a highly polished product."[9]

The product view faces obstacles on two different fronts. First, the pool of employees that hospitality service firms draw from shrinks and expands from time to time. In light of the occasional shortage of employees, employers often look for means to make service jobs more attractive. Because many employees prefer to be able to use their own judgment rather than just follow the rules, the close control of behavior required by the product view is increasingly called into question. Perhaps even more significant are guest reactions, particularly in upscale markets.

Widespread application of the product view of service has led guests to "ask where the service has gone from the service industries." As one writer put it:

> Recently, it has been proposed that offering goods and services is not enough, that customers must be provided with an experience. One common theme from the research . . . is the importance of the actual customer-employee encounter, with the focus on the service provider. An often-overlooked element, however, is the role a customer's perception has in a service exchange, which can have a major effect on the outcomes of the exchange.[10]

THE PROCESS VIEW: EMPOWERMENT

The product view of service, as we have just noted, sees service as a product that can be controlled efficiently in a production process that is typical of manufacturing. The process view, on the other hand, focuses on the interaction between the service organization and the guest.[11] The key contrast between the two approaches, as we will view them, is between control and **empowerment**. The process view of service calls for satisfying the guest's desires as the first priority. Service employees increasingly are being given the discretion—that is, empowered—to solve problems for the guest by making immediate decisions on their own initiative and discussing these later with management. Examples from the experience of Four Seasons, a premier hotel chain, illustrate the kind and degree of impact this approach is having on hospitality companies.[12]

■ A guest ordered a dinner of linguini and clams. When the order came, the dish was divided into white and black (squid ink) linguini. The guest ate the white linguini but left the black half untouched on the plate. The server inquired if the dinner was all right, and the guest responded, "I just don't like squid ink linguini." The incident came to light because the guest was a "spotter" employed by a firm retained by Four Seasons to "shop" its hotels and report on the quality of service.

In reviewing the incident, management learned that the description "squid ink linguini" was not indicated on the menu. As the guest had no way of knowing that something she didn't like was going to be served, the waiter should have removed the charge for this item from the guest's bill even though she didn't complain. The waiter did not do so, however, because the property's accounting procedure would have required a

Empowerment is especially important in situations where the employee is expected to exercise judgment and discretion. (Courtesy of Marriott International.)

lengthy process and management authorization for taking the charge off the guest check.

As a result of this incident, the property's accounting rules were changed to make it possible for a server to void an item on a bill immediately and account for that action later. (The menus were also reprinted to identify the squid ink linguini specifically.)

■ A guest called the desk and asked to have a fax machine installed in his room. The property did not have a fax machine available for this purpose, but the clerk undertook to rent one from an equipment supply house. Because the supply house required a sizable cash deposit, the clerk asked the guest for the cash.

When the front-office manager learned of this, she told the clerk to pay the deposit out of hotel funds and charge the guest's account for the "paid out." She then used this incident to teach not only this clerk but the whole front office as part of the hotel's constant retraining process to heighten everyone's sensitivity to the need to solve the guest's problem with a minimum of inconvenience to the guest and clean up the paperwork later. (The property also added fax machines to the equipment available for guest use.)

■ A guest's reservation had identified a preference for a club floor room with a king-sized bed and an ocean view. When the guest arrived, he found the room had all the requested features but was too small for his working needs. He called the concierge and told him of his problem. Looking at room availability, the concierge indicated he could meet all of the guest's requirements only with a room that was not on a club floor. That would mean the guest would not have concierge services available. The guest decided to stay where he was. A few minutes later, however, the concierge called the guest back. After studying his reservations, the concierge had been able to juggle some arrivals so as to make a room on the club floor available, one that had the ocean view and adequate space. The concierge offered the guest the room at the same rate although it was an executive suite, which normally carried a higher rate. The concierge was able to do this because of a recent change in procedure giving him the authority to make decisions to satisfy guests—and account for them later. The guest accepted the concierge's offer and, not surprisingly, later wrote to compliment the hotel's management on its superb service.

In these examples, we have seen how one luxury hotel group is trying to make its employees more concerned for the guest. It is changing operating and accounting rules and procedures to help employees do what they have to do to satisfy guests. This is precisely what is meant by the term *empowerment.*

Another example is a training program developed at the Cincinnati Marriott Northeast in which a 12-point service program was established for the purpose of "encouraging staff members to treat each guest as though she or he was part of the family and on a visit to your home." The program entailed employees carrying pledge cards to uphold the principles, energetic staff meetings in which guest service was celebrated, and staff recognition programs.[13]

PRODUCTION OR PROCESS VIEW?

Some kinds of operations are ideally suited to the production-line approach to service. Quick-service restaurants, amusement parks, and budget motels come to mind as having the need for the cost efficiency of the production approach. Patrons of upscale operations, however, demand the personal attention and individualized service that is facilitated by the process view of service, and midmarket operations are increasingly interested in empowering employees to achieve the competitive advantage that comes from committed service people.

As we noted at the outset of this discussion, some attention must be paid to the quality of personal interchanges in the most bare-bones economy operation. Similarly, basic tasks must be accomplished with competence and dispatch in the most luxurious of operations. It is not a matter of choosing between two different approaches but of adapting each approach to the needs of particular operations. The reliance on rule setting and the product approach is associated with mass-market operations, but we should note that several limited-service hotel chains have built "satisfaction guaranteed" programs for guests around employee empowerment with excellent results. Figure 21.3 summarizes key characteristics of the two views of service discussed.

PRODUCT VIEW OF SERVICE	PROCESS VIEW OF SERVICE
Emphasizes service as a task	Emphasizes interaction with the guest
Controls employee behavior	Empowers employee to satisfy guest's needs and desires to solve guest's problem
Cost of transaction process	
Objective, measurable standards	
Concentrates on what we do	Concentrates on what the guest wants

Figure 21.3
Managing the service transaction: two approaches.

How Companies Organize for Service

E arly in this chapter, we defined what service was. In the section we just finished, we were concerned with two approaches to managing numerous and diverse service transactions. These approaches were based on either control of the tasks or empowerment of individual servers to solve problems for guests. In this final section, we will consider the steps necessary on a companywide basis to achieve excellence in service.[14] To do this, we will consider what underlies a **service strategy**, the development of a service culture, the importance of people to service organizations, and the development of a service system as a competitive advantage.

SERVICE STRATEGY

The basis of a service strategy is market segmentation. **Market segmentation** identifies groups of customers and prospects who share sufficient characteristics in common that a product and service can be designed and brought to market for their needs.[15] A wide variety of service levels and types are available in hospitality. In food service, these range from quick service to coffee shop to dinner house to haute cuisine. Each of these levels of service denotes a different style—counter service; fast, simple table service; informal, unhurried table service with multiple courses; and, with haute cuisine, most probably formal European-style service. Each level denotes a particular price level and likely a distinctive ambience as well.

We said earlier that zero defects is the standard that service organizations must set. This very high standard, however, is set in the context of customer expectations for a particular segment and operation type. The level of service is an intrinsic part of the service segmentation strategy. A leading management book on customer service points out, "Segmenting by customer service, rather than by customer, often reveals that it is possible to give great service to a wide range of people who share a narrowly defined set of expectations."[16]

A rising young executive may take clients to an haute cuisine restaurant, his or her spouse to a casual dinner house, and the kids to a quick-service restaurant. When alone, the executive may lunch at a nearby family restaurant because it is convenient, serves the food quickly, and offers a suitable selection. The needs of the same person and that person's expectations of the operation vary according to occasions.

In some cases, customers are willing to participate in the service delivery. (Courtesy of Southwest Airlines.)

Similarly, different people in each of these situations will have different needs. The primary business of a restaurant is serving food. Second only to that, however, restaurants are in the business of providing guests with experiences that meet their expectations. Rather than targeting guests solely by demographic and lifestyle factors—though these are important, too—restaurants can target guests by the kind of dining occasion a guest is seeking. Quick-service restaurants fit relatively few kinds of dining occasions, though they fit a whole variety of demographic or lifestyle segments—depending, of course, on the occasion. Thus, restaurants are designed with particular occasions and dining experiences in mind as much as they are with particular groups of people in mind.

A point to consider is that there is no intrinsically "better" kind of service, only service that fits the setting and is designed to meet guest needs and expectations. With service level, of course, go other factors such as price, atmosphere, and location. Indeed, these are crucial to the zero-defect goal of a service operation. A Four Seasons room rate is roughly ten times that charged by Motel 6—and that rate differential is necessary to fulfill the luxury guest's expectations. On the other hand, Motel 6 customers are not disappointed by the service level they encounter. It is what the budget guest expects.

Earlier, in the lodging chapters, we segmented the market broadly into two groups, "upstairs" and "downstairs" customers. The upstairs customer is seeking a guest room (i.e., upstairs) for the night and minimal supporting service. For this customer, Marriott offers the Courtyard concept, with limited food and beverage facilities in the property, and Fairfield Inns, which have no food and beverage facilities but are located near other restaurants. Courtyard and Fairfield both offer topflight guest rooms and highly competitive rates for their segment. These properties have eliminated some services but, because of that, are able to provide attractive rates. Most significantly, the service level they do offer fits the guest's expectation for that kind of property.

On the other hand, some guests want the "downstairs" services of a full-service hotel. These include the luxurious lobby and a range of restaurants and bars as well as shops. Meeting and banquet facilities are important to the downstairs guest, too. Marriott targets the downstairs guest with its Resorts and Hotels Division—and a quite different price range. For each price and service range, operating standards are set to meet the target segment's expectations.

Strategy in service, then, involves picking a distinct segment and crafting facilities and services specifically to fit the expectations of those guests. Care must be taken not to overpromise, because anything less than the service your guest expects will result in disappointment, lost sales, and unfavorable word-of-mouth reputation. Figure 21.4 gives an overview of setting a service strategy.

- Choose market segment or segments.
- Determine appropriate service level.
- Don't overpromise.
- Fulfill expectations.

Figure 21.4
Setting a service strategy.

SERVICE CULTURE

A company's culture can be defined

. . . as a system of shared meaning held by members that distinguishes the organization from other organizations. This system is, on closer examination, a set of key characteristics that the organization values.[17]

To establish a strong **service culture**, an absolute prerequisite is commitment by top management.

"There's a sign on my desk that reads 'What have you done for your customer today?'" says Hervey Feldman, former president of Embassy Suites. "I worship at my sign every day, and all my hotel managers worship at theirs."

Other examples of commitment include the fact that such hotel luminaries as Bill Marriott write thank-you letters to their hotels' best guests, volunteering to fix anything they're unhappy with, as do the managers of Marriott Hotels.

The visible commitment of top management to the service culture sets the tone for the rest of the organization. The following conversation between a young trainee and the restaurant manager, overheard in a restaurant's dining room just after the breakfast rush, illustrates the logic of management commitment to service. During the rush, the restaurant manager had been on the floor almost continuously, generally pouring coffee and water refills for guests and occasionally even busing dirty dishes.

TRAINEE (jokingly): Hey! I thought you said managers weren't supposed to work stations. You looked like one of the busboys out there this morning.

MANAGER (smiling): Well, I know what you mean, but you have to understand another truth. We want our customers to be happy with our service so they'll come back—and send their friends here, too. So when there's a big rush like that, I like to pitch in and please a few customers. When the rest of the service staff sees me hustling, they know what I think is important, and they tend to reach a little harder to please people, too.

Say It and Mean It. Research on company culture in the hospitality industry suggests that where there is a wide divergence between what company officials say and what they do, employees will be cynical and indifferent to the quality of service. On the other hand, where there is a close relationship between what the company publicly claims its service policies are and the way things actually happen within the organization, employees' ratings of managerial competence tend to be high.

Communication. Top management must not only take a position but communicate it to employees. Department meetings and general employee meetings are important.

A popular tool in companies that have many low-wage employees in constant contact with customers is the employee council. Employees from each department elect a representative, and the representatives meet weekly with the general manager. The GM updates them on everything he or she is doing; they ask questions, offer suggestions, voice opinions, and then go back to their departments to explain what's going on.[18]

Other media such as employee newsletters, posters, or even the annual report to employees that ARAMARK publishes help create and maintain a climate of enthusiasm for service.

Manager as Helper. Service America! made famous the motto "If you're not serving the customer, you'd better be serving someone who is."[19] This approach sees employees as internal customers whose needs must be met. In effect, managers treat the employees as they'd like to have the employees treat the guests. The intention is that employees follow management's example. The philosophy underpinning this view is that "a manager's main responsibility is to remove obstacles that keep people from doing their jobs."[20] To quote an often-restated position of J. Willard Marriott, the Marriott Corporation's founder, "You can't make happy guests with unhappy employees."

Restraining Bureaucracy. Bureaucracy is a bad word for most North Americans, but it is actually a name for the kind of structure necessary to serve any large organization. In other words, in large companies, a certain amount of bureaucratic structure is needed. Nevertheless, a consistent effort needs to be made to resist bureaucracy's tendency to achieve internal efficiencies by making rules that, in their total effect, can strangle the service out of a service organization. With too much bureaucracy, employees quote the rules of the operation rather than satisfy the customers' requests.

It is useful to recall here the experiences cited earlier at Four Seasons. That company decided to reformulate a lot of its rules to make it possible for servers to make exceptions to the rules to satisfy guests based on their own judgment—and account for their decisions later.

Figure 21.5 summarizes the development of a service culture.

- Developing a service culture in a company requires commitment of top management in word, policy, and action
- Policy and practice to be the same
- High profitability is achieved when what should happen does happen
- Constant, clear communication, up as well as down the organization
- Employees to be treated as customers

  Manager's job: service to employees

- Restraining bureaucratic tendencies
- Customer is more important than rules

Figure 21.5
Developing a service culture.

THE EMPLOYEE AS PRODUCT: THE IMPORTANCE OF PEOPLE

Because the service employee (and often the back-of-the-house employee, too) is involved personally in transactions with the guest, the employee usually comes to represent the operation to the guest. Managing, it has been said, is getting results through people, and that is doubly true of managing service. The tools that are being used to undertake this job at the company level are employee selection, training, motivation, and employee award and reward programs. Each will be discussed briefly.

Selection. Employee recruiting has become, for many firms, a marketing activity. In spite of vigorous recruiting to fill positions, operations have to choose their hires with care, especially in public-contact service jobs. At Four Seasons, all employees hired must first be interviewed by the general manager or the executive assistant manager, as well as division and department heads. Ramada Franchise Systems is another lodging company that has very strict hiring procedures that pay off in hiring the right people and putting them in appropriate jobs.

Training. Companies that lead their industries in service tend to share two unusual characteristics. First, most such companies emphasize cross training. Embassy Suites, for instance, encourages employees to master several jobs. The wider training not only gives the property a more flexible employee but also heightens the employee's understanding of the total operation. Moreover, the increased training can add to the interest and excitement of the work.

A second characteristic is that all employees share certain core training experiences. McDonald's Hamburger University has a special four-day program through which staff, head office, and other nonoperations employees gain an understanding of the company's operations, products, and policies. Thus, all responsible employees pass through some Hamburger University orientation to the company. Virtually all senior executives at McDonald's, too, have store-operating experience.

Employee Awards. Awards programs "are formal expressions of encouragement and praise that effective frontline supervisors mete out continually. By creating service heroes and service legends, the programs charge up all employees, not just the winners." To succeed, programs must have "credibility, frequency and psychic significance" to the

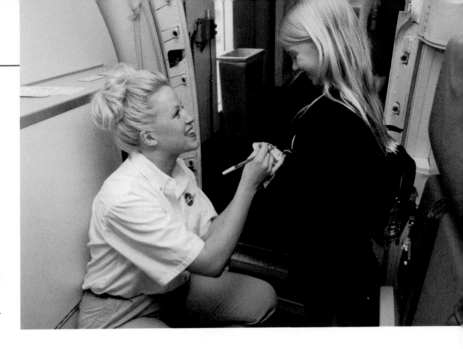

Service employees represent an organization to the guest. They are a critical component of the overall guest experience. (Courtesy of Southwest Airlines.)

employee. The process of selecting winners, if it is to have that credibility and significance to employees, must be "careful, obviously meritocratic and tightly linked to customer perceptions of service quality." Awards need to be made soon after the performance they are intended to recognize so that the linkage is clear; they must have tangible value, like a day off; and they have to involve active recognition and applause, "not just a name on a plaque." Otherwise, nobody will care.[21]

Participation in Planning. Workers must have a sense of ownership of service standards and procedures if the standards and procedures are to be accepted in the workplace. The necessary step to secure acceptance is to involve employees in planning, either by consulting them fully in the planning process or by asking them to actually do the planning themselves.

Both hotel and restaurant companies have found success with the formation of employee work groups designed to improve productivity. In fact, productivity targets as established by the employees often exceed those that are targeted by management. The process of making the employee a key part of the product is summarized in Figure 21.6.

REQUIREMENTS

Employees selected who fit the team

Training Emphasizes

- Cross-training
- Basic shared experience

Motivation offers

- Reward for desired performance
- Frequent feedback for team building

Awards provide

- Formal public recognition based on guest service

Participation in standard setting creates "ownership" of standards.

Figure 21.6
Making the employee the product

SERVICE AS A SUSTAINABLE COMPETITIVE ADVANTAGE

It has often been said that service is increasingly becoming the differentiating factor between companies. The products sold in hospitality are strikingly similar. One hotel room is very much like another. Although there are important differences among food service segments, within each segment there is considerable similarity—often, almost uniformity. Service offers the most important opportunity to differentiate one product from another. When a service system is established at the chain level, the ability to operate multiple units across a wide territory successfully gives the company an advantage over newcomers to the field. The company's reputation for a dining experience or night's (or week's) stay is an invaluable resource. Almost certainly, it is based on personal interaction with company employees. That is, the company's reputation, its sustainable competitive advantage, is most likely based on its service—and that means its service employees.

Summary

Service is an intangible experience of performance that the guest receives along with the tangible side of the product purchased. Both server and guest are a part of the transaction, which complicates quality control. Service quality has two sides: the task and the interpersonal interaction. Different planning and control problems arise for mechanical, indirect, and personal service transactions, with personal service the most difficult to manage.

The service transaction is the heart of service in hospitality. Controlling the details of task performance fits well with a product view of service, while a process view focuses more on the personal interaction between guest and server. In the process approach, servers are empowered to solve problems for the guest.

The basis of service strategy is market segmentation, largely based on consumer service expectations. Successful service companies develop a service culture based on commitment by top management, consistency between policy and practice, and well-developed channels of communication. Because service people are a part of the product, a good service team is essential. Service teams are based on careful selection and training and built on motivational programs that include rewards and involvement in service planning. Because most hospitality products are strikingly similar, service is the most significant sustainable competitive advantage.

Key Words and Concepts

Service	**Product view**
Moments of truth	**Process view**
Zero defects	**Empowerment**
Customer expectations	**Service strategy**
Characteristics of service	**Market segmentation**
Personal interaction	**Service culture**
Task	

Review Questions

1. What does zero defects mean in service? Does it mean perfection?

2. Discuss the three types of service transactions. What are the considerations managers need to take into account in planning for them?

3. What are the two aspects of service? Which is more important in your opinion?

4. What are the two views of managing the service transaction? Can you think of examples from your own experience where each was appropriate?

5. How is a service strategy designed? What is its basic determinant? What other considerations are important?

6. What do companies need to do to develop a service culture?

Internet Exercises

1. **Site name:** Baldrige National Quality Program, National Institute of Standards and Technology (NIST)

   URL: www.quality.nist.gov

   Background information: The Malcolm Baldrige National Quality Award is given by the President of the United States to businesses—manufacturing and service, small and large—and to education and health care organizations that apply and are judged to be outstanding in seven areas: leadership, strategic planning, customer and market focus, information and analysis, human-resource focus, process management, and business results. NIST's goal is to assist U.S. businesses and nonprofit organizations in delivering ever-improving value to customers, resulting in marketplace success, and improving overall company performance.

   Exercises:

   a. Browse the NIST Web site and determine which hospitality organizations have won the Malcolm Baldrige National Quality Award.

    b. Do you think the award has any impact on the hospitality industry? Why or why not?

    c. Describe the core values and concepts upon which the seven criteria for excellence are built.

    d. Choose one of the seven criteria for excellence and discuss in detail the information the judging panel looks for to determine excellence on that criteria.

2. **Site name:** Express Hospitality

    URL: http://www.expresshospitality.com/20051130/hospitalitylife01.shtml

    Background information: Express Hospitality is a hospitality Web site based in India and has valuable information that can be applied in the North American hospitality properties.

    Exercises:

    a. According to this article, what are the three basic commandments for the Six Sigma philosophy in the service sector?

    b. On the rooms side of a hotel, what areas might benefit from the implementation of the Six Sigma philosophy?

    c. In the food and beverage area of a hotel or a restaurant, what areas might benefit from the implementation of the Six Sigma philosophy?

    d. Lead a class discussion on the strengths and drawbacks to implementing the Six Sigma philosophy.

3. **Site name:** Search Engines

    URL: Google—www.google.com

    URL: Yahoo—www.yahoo.com

    URL: Ask.com—www.ask.com

    URL: AlltheWeb.com—www.alltheweb.com

    Background information: Many managers believe that to successfully deliver quality service, a "service culture" must be present in an organization. This "service culture" needs to be internalized by all employees in the organization and a major part of establishing a service culture is empowerment.

    Exercises: Using your favorite search engine or one of the top-rated search engines above, search for "service culture" and/or "employee/worker empowerment."

    a. Read at least two articles and discuss how the concepts in those articles could be implemented in a hospitality organization.

    b. Lead a class discussion on how a "service culture" can be implemented in a hospitality operation. What are some of the hurdles that might be encountered during the implementation process?

    c. Discuss why you think a service culture is not always a significant part of all hospitality operations.

Notes

1. William H. Davidow and Bro Uttal, *Total Customer Service: The Ultimate Weapon* (New York: Harper & Row, 1989), p. 40.
2. Christopher H. Lovelock, *Services Marketing* (Englewood Cliffs, NJ: Prentice-Hall, 2001).
3. This discussion draws on G. Lynn Shostock, "Planning the Service Encounter," in John A. Czepiel, Michael R. Solomon, and Carol F. Surprenant, eds., *The Service Encounter* (Lexington, MA: Lexington Books, 1985), p. 248. Shostock's terminology ("remote," "indirect," and "direct") is slightly different.
4. John Naisbitt, Megatrends: *Ten New Directions Transforming Our Lives* (New York: Warner Books, 1982).
5. *Webster's Unabridged Dictionary,* 2nd ed. (New York: Random House, 1999).
6. Shostock, "Planning the Service Encounter," p. 253.
7. Peter G. Klaus, "Quality Epiphenomenon: The Conceptual Understanding of Quality in Face-to-Face Service Encounters," in Czepiel, Solomon, and Surprenant, eds., *The Service Encounter.*
8. Theodore Leavitt, "Production Line Approach to Service," Harvard Business Review, September–October 1972, reprinted in *Service Management* (Cambridge, MA: Harvard University, n.d.), pp. 20–31.
9. Ibid., pp. 22–25.
10. Karthik Namasivayam and Timothy Hinkin, "The Customer's Role in the Service Encounter," *Cornell Hotel and Restaurant Administration Quarterly,* June 2003, p. 26.
11. Klaus, "Quality Epiphenomenon," p. 21.
12. Interview with James Brown, former senior vice president, Four Seasons Hotels.
13. Cathy Enz and Judy Siguaw, "Best Practices in Service Quality," *Cornell Hotel and Restaurant Administration Quarterly,* October 2000, p. 24.
14. This section draws extensively on Davidow and Uttal, *Total Customer Service.*
15. For an extended discussion of market segmentation for the hospitality industry, see Cathy Hsu and Thomas F. Powers, *Marketing Hospitality,* 3rd ed. (New York: John Wiley & Sons, 2001), especially Chapter 3.
16. Davidow and Uttal, *Total Customer Service,* p. 70. Emphasis added.
17. Stephen Robbins and Nancy Langton, "Organizational Behaviour," Prentice-Hall Canada, 1999, p. 615.
18. Davidow and Uttal, *Total Customer Service.*
19. Karl Albrecht and Ron Zemke, *Service America!* (Homewood, IL: Dow Jones–Irwin, 1985), p. 96.
20. Davidow and Uttal, *Total Customer Service,* p. 106.
21. Ibid.

INDEX